S0-ACB-264

Supplement & Price Trends

for

COLORED GLASSWARE OF THE DEPRESSION ERA

Book 2

Policy

This publication is not a price list. It is a price guide. It does not establish fixed prices but records price trends. It does not tell the collector what he should pay, but what he might expect to pay to stay within certain popular price ranges.

The price trends suggested in these pages are representative of price averages in the United States from coast to coast, allowing, of course, for price fluctuation due to regional scarcities of, or demands for, a particular piece, color or pattern.

As always, use PRICE TRENDS as a guide, but more importantly use your own judgment based on your knowledge of your particular area and circumstances. Remember that the price you pay must ultimately be your own.

A good portion of the new information included in PRICE TRENDS comes from you wonderful readers. I've said it before but I'll say it again: You are the life of this publication as well as its reason for living, and I can only hope that you know in your hearts of the gratitude I cannot express to you individually here.

International Standard Book Number 0-913074-17-9
Printed in the United States of America 1982

PRICE TRENDS 2
is the pricing supplement
to Colored Glassware
of the Depression Era
Book 2
published in 1974.
Book 2 identifies
1000 patterns
in colored glass not
already presented
in Book 1.

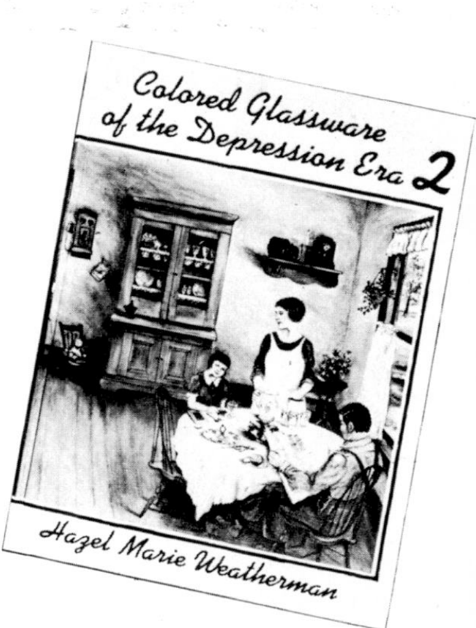

ABOUT BOOK 1

Book 1 to COLORED GLASSWARE OF THE DEPRESSION ERA first appeared in 1969, the first book to be published on Depression Glass.

Book 1 is still the best basic guide available, introducing you to the 80 most popular patterns of the era and identifying 321 others. PRICE TRENDS I accompanies it, offering much supplemental information.

Book 2 does not cover the same patterns as Book 1. For the whole story, you'll want both editions.

To order these and other Hazel Marie Weatherman GLASSBOOKS, see last page.

ACKNOWLEDGEMENTS

This year, we'd like to especially thank the following people for assisting in price research: Fern and Bill Smith, Mansfield MO; Mary Wetzel, South Bend IN; Mark Nye, Miami FL; Betty Bell, Verona MS; Nadine Pankow, Willow Springs IL; Michael Krumme, W. Los Angeles CA; Rosarita Zeigler, New Britain CT; J. W. Courter, Simpson IL; Paula Vassey, Gautier MS; Joyce Speed, Gautier MS; George and Roni Sionakides, Dewitt MI; Kevin Kelly, W. Orange NJ; Gail Krause, Washington PA; Zeta and Charles Todd, Aurora CO; Debbie Pugliese, Erie PA; Mr. and Mrs. William Medsger, Indiana PA; Jerry and Connie Monarch, Toledo OH; Ruby and Curtis Edwards, Modesto CA.

Others, too, have written in to share data and photographs: Bill Newhall, Baltimore MD; John Davis, GA; Cheryl Marotte, Toronto Canada; Nell Edwards, Birch Tree MO; Lucille Gaskin, Oxnard CA; Jane Robin, Raleigh NC; Doug Miller, Plover WI; Kay Shell, Las Vegas NV; Joe Strakaluse, Cranston RI; Danielle Deik, Morrisville PA; Joy Vavra, Irving TX; Doris Schwondt, St. Leonard MD; Ruth Lombardo, Clinton PA; Hazel Hazen, Rockville CT; John Maccagnon, Wyckoff NJ; Jan Kirkwood, Garland TX; Mrs. Walter Scott, Stillwater OK; Laurie Cruise, E. Schodack NY; Demetra Ferguson, Sonora KY; Landrum and Jody Cox, Detroit MI; Betty and Bill Newbound, Union Lake MI; Lorrie Kitchen and Dan Tucker, Toledo OH; Audrey Yerger, Wayne PA; Marion Richardson, Olympia WA.

To them we express our deep appreciation.

About Book 2

The big Book 2 -- further adventures in COLORED GLASSWARE OF THE DEPRESSION ERA -- was published in 1974. Never before had there been a glassbook like it and there may never be again, either in scope or in the effect it has had on the glass collecting public.

Here in one giant edition are the complete known wares of some 40 different glasshouses -- at least 15 books in one. And almost all of the 1000 plus patterns shown are being identified for the first time.

The effect on the collecting world is dramatic. Where before there had only been a vast sea of mysterious un-named wares, now there is clearly marked territory to explore. And those collectors who hadn't cared or dared plumb the uncharted regions take to the new fields like wildfire. Glass wallflowers become princesses and wildflowers are tamed, until the jumbled jungle is transformed into a collector's paradise.

The original Book 1, published in 1969, introduced the 80 most widely collected patterns in colored glass 1929-1940. So warmly did people respond to the new topic that "Depression Glass" became the hottest glass collectible in the world. If Book 1 created the field, Book 2 changed its landscape, planting new seeds and widening the boundaries of activity. Now kitchen and utility items, novelty lamps and figurines, and strange obscure patterns by strange obscure glass companies are sought after as avidly as jewel-finished handmade wares by Tiffin, New Martinsville, and Old Morgantown, to mention just a few. All of them are in Book 2.

Book 2 has another effect which pleases me immensely. Many of us advanced collectors are so challenged by Book 2 patterns that we ease up on Book 1 patterns a little bit, which leaves room for new fans. And every time one set is let go so that another new one can be started, the shake-up helps keep the whole field in motion. Newcomers give the hobby so much of its fresh life and reason for being.

Depression Glass continues to grow by leaps and bounds. It always was a phenomenon, but here looking into the 80s it's still an amazing race. Person after person meets D.G., falls in love, and starts zapping that glass. D.G. is sprung out of bushes, rescued from nooks, saved from crannies, ransomed from relatives, bidded up at auctions, divvied up at swap meets, angled after at garage sales, procured from procurers, shined up, shown off and spread out and bought-and-sold via glass shows and that very popular expressway, the Depression Glass DAZE. And everywhere it goes, Depression Glass takes the cake.

Inevitably, prices are driven up too, but luckily much Book 2 glass continues to be within the financial range of most of us. Your investment is going to be a good one, you can be sure, but let's face it, the best part of Depression Glass is its life-giving radiance, its propensity for giving light and color and joy and interest and these properties are real no matter what the market is.

About PRICE TRENDS 2

You should have no trouble using or understanding this book. A few matters only need quick mention.

FORMAT

PRICE TRENDS 2 is keyed, line for line and page by page, to the big Book 2, with the exception of the "Book 1 Update" portions of that book. Naturally, you will find those Update pieces listed in PRICE TRENDS 1.

CHAPTER HEADS

The chapter headings are updates, written to further the information line already presented in Book 2 and not to stand alone. In other words, they do not give nearly the whole story, and should be read in conjunction with the company histories in the big book.

SUGGESTED PRICES

Due to lack of space, it's almost impossible to categorize each color separately. You'll need to keep in mind that crystal is almost always lower than the suggested price shown, and the super colors like ruby, amethyst, cobalt, and canary, to mention a few, will often draw higher prices out of the old hat.

The middle ground defined here will almost always serve for pink, green, amber, yellow, and blue, the primary Depression Era colors.

CATALOG REPRINTS

We are lucky to have quite a bit of 'new' material to introduce to you in this PRICE TRENDS, in the form of old company catalogs and original advertisements you'll find reprinted throughout the book. Most were uncovered by me in my most recent research trip to 'glass country', and some were contributed by readers. Most have never been printed before.

ABOUT CLUBS

Over 100 active, thriving Depression Glass Clubs are now in existence, based in cities all over the United States and Canada. Approaches, programs, fun-and fund-raising events differ from one club to another but the collector is always offered an educational good time when meeting and trading with other enthusiasts. For an up-to-date list of D.G. clubs with current membership information, see the back pages of the DEPRESSION GLASS DAZE.***

ABOUT SHOWS

Almost every club gives a show, or even two shows a year, and many individual promotors sponsor them too. All-Depression Glass Shows are marvelous experiences, extravaganzas sporting table after sparkling table of beautiful glass for sale. Shows are attended by 800--2,500 excited fans, many of whom travel long distances to attend.

You won't want to miss the ones near your area. For an up-to-date listing of all D.G. shows and attendance information, see the pages of the DEPRESSION GLASS DAZE.***

***OKAY, SO WHAT ALREADY IS THE DEPRESSION GLASS DAZE?

Quite simply, the DAZE is just about the most wonderful help a D.G. collector could possibly have. There is nothing like the DAZE! Sixty or more pages of fun each month, with thousands of pieces of glass for sale every issue, via mail order, from every part of the country. Besides a multitude of ads and many feature articles about glassware, there is an activity calendar that lists upcoming shows. Know your fellow collectors and dealers! Have fun collecting! Give the DAZE a buzz through, and you'll never be quite the same. Editor Nora Koch, a rare individual you'll appreciate getting to know, will send you a sample copy on request. Or just subscribe now! $14.00 per year (12 issues), Box 57H, Otisville MI 48463-0008.

Happy Collecting!

1
2
3
4
5
6
SALT
7
8
9
10
11
12

13
14
15
16
17
18
19
20
21
22
23
24
25
26
HILLYARD CHEMICAL COMPANY, ST. JOSEPH, MO.
SEPTEMBER 1931 OCTOBER 1931 NOVEMBER 1931 DECEMBER
27
28
29
30
31
32

33
34
35
36
37
38
39
40
41
42
43
44
45
46
47

SUGAR
FLOUR
48
49
50
51
52
53
54
55
56
57
58
59
60
61
6
63
64
65
66
67
68
69

COLOR SECTION

Page 9

1. BELFAST TURTLE w/flower holder 35.00--45.00
2. U.S. Glass' FROG candlesticks, pr. 85.00--100.00
3. McKee's WREN HOUSE 75.00--85.00
4. McKee's NUDE Vase 65.00--75.00
5. Jeannette's HAT ashtray 12.00--15.00
6. U.S. Glass' SALT BOX w/wooden cover 90.00-100.00
7. U.S. Glass' SANTA CLAUS lamp 150.00-175.00
8. McKee's ELECTROLIER lamp (Innovation Cutting) 200.00-250.00
9. U.S. Glass' OWL lamp 110.00-135.00
10. Fenton's "LIL' FISH" 20.00--25.00
11. BIG RED APPLE cookie jar 25.00--35.00
12. McKee's LIFE SAVER decanter 40.00--50.00

Page 10

13. Jenkin's "HOB" bon bon and cover 15.00--18.00
14. Jeannette's Shell Pink (made for NAPCO) flower container 4.00-- 5.00
15. Jeannette's Shell Pink (made for NAPCO) grape flower container 4.00-- 5.00
16. Jeannette's Shell Pink PETALWARE wall vases 30.00--35.00
17. TULIP BY DELL candleholder, toothpick and relish dish, ea. 6.00-- 9.00
18. Colony's (made in Italy) 6" plate w/label 2.00-- 4.00
19. Jeannette's NATIONAL candydish 4.00-- 6.00
20. Cambridge's WEATHERFORD candy dish 18.00--22.00
21. Central's FRANCES bowl 12.00--15.00
22. Imperial's FANCY COLONIAL salt 12.00--15.00
23. Paden City's #221 S.S. DREAMSHIP bowl 10.00--14.00
24. Jeannette's RINGED wine decanter 25.00--30.00
25. New Martinsville's HOSTMASTER vase 15.00--18.00
26. Fenton's SHEFFIELD vase 15.00--18.00
27. Consolidated's MARTELE dessert set 20.00--24.00
28. DESK SET 1931 calendar 50.00--60.00
29. Central's FRANCES candlestick 12.00--15.00
30. L.E. Smith's ROMANESQUE candlestick 10.00--12.00
31. Westmoreland's ENGLISH HOBNAIL toilet bottle 30.00--35.00
32. Liberty's AMERICAN PIONEER
    Candy Jar and Cover 50.00--60.00
    Goblet 6" 20.00--25.00
    Covered Urn 7" 150.00-175.00
    Covered Urn 5" 120.00--140.00

Page 11

33. U.S. Glass' FLOWERGARDEN AND BUTTERFLIES heart candy dish 200.00-300.00
34. U.S. Glass' BABY CAT 85.00-100.00
35. "DUMBO" elephant 30.00--35.00
36. U.S. Glass' TORCHIERE vase 50.00--60.00
37. Westmoreland's PICKLE jar vase 40.00--50.00
38. Co-Operative's DOG and cover 45.00--55.00
39. ANGEL FISH ash tray 8.00--10.00
40. Co-Operative's FROG and cover 45.00--55.00
41. Fenton's TURTLE aquarium 85.00-100.00
42. U.S. Glass' PARROT lamp 13" 150.00-175.00
43. U.S. Glass' PARROT lamp 14" 200.00-250.00
44. Hazel Atlas' POLO tray set 50.00--60.00
45. CYPRUS jug and tumbler set 35.00--45.00
46. Imperial's JUNK center bowl 25.00--35.00
47. Co-Operative's ELEPHANT flower holder 35.00--40.00

Page 12

48. Hazel Atlas' SUGAR and FLOUR canisters 16.00--20.00
49. Hocking's Jade-ite FIREKING mug 6.00-- 8.00
50. Hocking's DIAMOND CRYSTAL salt 6.00-- 8.00
51. Jeannette's MEASURING CUP w/spout 12.00--15.00
52. Owen's Illinois WATER BOTTLE and shaker 4.00-- 6.00
53. Hazel Atlas' BATTER BOWL 30.00--35.00
54. MYSTERY SHAKER 2¾" green glass w/metal insert 12.00--15.00
55. Hazel Atlas' ONION chopper 5.00-- 7.00
56. RADNT reamer 30.00--40.00
57. Owens Illinois' WATER BOTTLE and shaker 4.00-- 6.00
58. U.S. Glass CRICKET cream and sugar 10.00--12.00
59. Hazel Atlas' CRISSCROSS crystal cream, sugar and cover 20.00--24.00
60. Hazel Atlas' CRISSCROSS
    Reamer 120.00-130.00
    Butter 1 lb. 50.00--55.00
61. MAYONNAISE MAKER (Wesson Oil) 12.00--15.00
62. McKee's SNOWFLAKE punch set 90.00--100.00
63. Hocking's SWEDISH MODERN mixing bowl 7.00-- 9.00
64. Indiana's #16 ORANGE reamer 10.00--12.00
65. Westmoreland's "JAUNTY" rooster 12.00--15.00
66. Hazel Atlas' MUG, 5¾" 9.00--12.00
67. Hocking's BATTER BOWL w/stick handle 10.00--12.00
68. Hocking's BATTER BOWL 7.00-- 9.00
69. MEASURING JUG 1 qt. 18.00--22.00

Book 2 Color Section

The color section in Book 2 has been a bit confusing. Several pieces there are not shown elsewhere in the book, and there are even some Book 1 pieces mixed in. The best plan, I think, is to make a special Color Section listing of suggested prices for your convenient reference.

1ST ROW — page 13

"TOP PRIZE" punch set 12 cups, bowl and ladle	135.00--150.00

2ND ROW

"RING OF RINGS" decanter and 4 tumblers	25.00--30.00
Cambridge's ice bucket	20.00--30.00
McKee's Seville (yellow) reamer	35.00--45.00
New Martinsville's cigarette holder	15.00--20.00
"STANDING RIB" cocktail set	20.00--25.00

3RD ROW

Paden City's "PARTY LINE" cocktail shaker	35.00--40.00
Paden City's "PARTY LINE" tumbler	5.00-- 7.00
L.E. Smith's "WIG-WAM" console bowl	20.00--25.00
L.E. Smith's "WIG-WAM" pink candleholder	8.00--12.00
Westmoreland's "WOOLWORTH" nappies	10.00--12.00
Imperial's pink nappy	8.00--10.00
Houze lamp	30.00--35.00
Burgundy "PRIME RIB"bowl	12.00--15.00
Hocking's ruby SANDWICH nappy	10.00--12.00
Westmoreland's cobalt "JUANTY ROOSTER" cup	12.00--15.00
Hocking's HOBNAIL wine set	30.00--35.00
L.E. Smith's jardiniere	9.00--12.00
"MR. BLUE" jug	20.00--30.00

4TH ROW

Jeannette's FLORAL ice tub	400.00-500.00
"COPE" cake stand	25.00--30.00
CLARK'S TEABERRY stand	30.00--35.00
L.E. Smith's pink satin bowl	9.00--12.00
Hocking's ruby SANDWICH bowl	20.00--25.00
L.E. Smith's cobalt "MT. PLEASANT" bowl	25.00--30.00
Duncan and Miller's SWAN	40.00--50.00
McKee's pink BROCADE bowl	12.00--15.00
U.S. Glass' "PEEP HOLE" bowl	10.00--15.00
Green "FAVE" vase	12.00--15.00
"AUNT POLLY" nappy	7.00--10.00
"AUNT POLLY" sherbet plate	4.00-- 6.00
New Martinsville's ruby "MOONDROPS" bowl	22.00--28.00
L.E. Smith's pink "DRIPPLE" console set	12.00--16.00
Hocking's HOBNAIL water set	25.00--35.00
Hocking's HOBNAIL jug	15.00--20.00
Hocking's tumbler	4.00-- 5.00
Jeannette's Ultra-marine DORIC and PANSY 7" plate	20.00--25.00
U.S. Glass' green "FLOWER GARDEN with BUTTERFLIES" plate	15.00--18.00
"BIRCH TREE" cream and sugar	25.00--35.00
Duncan and Miller's ruby 6" plate	4.00-- 6.00

TOP — page 14

Westmoreland's satin DOLPHIN lamp	75.00--90.00
Heisey's amber CHERUB candleholder	150.00-200.00

1ST ROW

Paden City's "LELA BIRD" jug	50.00--60.00
Co-Operative's ELEPHANT	30.00--50.00

Item	Price
U.S. Glass' "FLOWER GARDEN with BUTTERFLIES" vase	70.00--75.00
Westmoreland's basket	25.00--35.00
New Martinsville's "GENEVA" dresser set	50.00--60.00
New Martinsville's "JUDY" dresser set	60.00--70.00
New Martinsville's "WISE OWL" jug	60.00--80.00
Paden City's "LELA BIRD" vase	35.00--40.00
Heisey goblet	25.00--30.00

2ND ROW

Item	Price
Cambridge's ROSE LADY flower holder	150.00-200.00
Cambridge's dolphin candlestick	35.00--45.00
Cambridge's swan	65.00--75.00
Federal's SYLVAN jug	600.00-650.00
Federal's SYLVAN thin sherbet	100.00-125.00
Federal's SYLVAN ftd. tumbler	90.00--95.00
Federal's SYLVAN butterdish	200.00-250.00
Lotus's REVERE tall sherbet	15.00--20.00
Fostoria's VESPER candy dish	30.00--40.00
Westmoreland's No. 185 lamp	25.00--35.00

3RD ROW

Item	Price
Imperial's EARLY AMERICAN HOBNAIL toilet set	60.00--70.00
U.S. Glass' STIPPLE candy dish	30.00--40.00
U.S. Glass' "FLOWER GARDEN with BUTTERFLIES" console set	150.00--200.00
Westmoreland's ENGLISH HOBNAIL toilet bottle	30.00--35.00
Westmoreland's ENGLISH HOBNAIL egg cup	25.00--35.00
Westmoreland's DOLPHIN console set	125.00--150.00

1ST ROW page 15

Item	Price
Jeannette's ultra-marine "JENNYWARE" shakers	20.00--25.00
Jeannette's ultra-marine "JENNYWARE" reamer	60.00--65.00
Jeannette's ultra-marine "JENNYWARE" refrigerator bowl	14.00--16.00
SWIRL butterdish	175.00-200.00
SWIRL candy dish	60.00--65.00
DORIC AND PANSY cream	125.00-150.00
DORIC AND PANSY sugar	125.00-150.00
DORIC AND PANSY shaker	200.00-225.00
Westmoreland's ENGLISH HOBNAIL jug	90.00-100.00
Jeannette's DORIC cream soup	150.00-200.00
Federal's "INDIAN" tumbler	5.00-- 8.00
Westmoreland's ENGLISH HOBNAIL demitasse	12.00--15.00
Westmoreland's ENGLISH HOBNAIL cocktail	12.00--14.00

2ND ROW

Item	Price
Westmoreland's ENGLISH HOBNAIL lamps	75.00--80.00
Macbeth's fat "DOGWOOD" jug	500.00-550.00
Jeannette's CHANTILLY jug	18.00--22.00
Jeannette's CHANTILLY tumbler	4.00-- 5.00
Cambridge's WEATHERFORD bowl	12.00--15.00
Cambridge's WEATHERFORD serving plate	10.00--14.00
Imperial's EARLY AMERICAN HOBNAIL cupped vase	25.00--30.00
Dunbar's RAMBLER ROSE cream and sugar	18.00--24.00
Imperial's pressed glass bowl	22.00--26.00
U.S. Glass' "FLOWER GARDEN with BUTTERFLIES" dresser set	200.00- 300.00

3RD ROW

Item	Price
"AUNT POLLY" collection	350.00-375.00
Hazel Atlas' CLOVERLEAF shaker	25.00--30.00
Hazel Atlas' CLOVERLEAF ash tray	65.00--75.00
Hazel Atlas' CLOVERLEAF sherbet	12.00--15.00
U.S. Glass/Tiffin's black satin "MEFFORD" comport	35.00--40.00
Fostoria's No. 2395½ black candlestick	10.00--14.00
L.E. Smith's "MT. PLEASANT" sugar/cream, salt/pepper on a tray	50.00--65.00
McKee's Jade green "SARAH" vase	22.00--25.00
McKee's Jade green 3 foot jardiniere	12.00--15.00
McKee's Chaline blue reamer	100.00-125.00
McKee's Jade green and Old Rose (tan) BOTTOMS UP	40.00--50.00

Jeannette's Delfite match holder	15.00--20.00

4TH ROW

L.E. Smith's No. 433 vase	15.00--18.00
Fry's pearl-glass reamer	35.00--45.00
Ruby cocktails w/metal bases	9.00--12.00
Ruby "STORMY" ice bucket	20.00--25.00
Punch set w/Macbeth's ruby ROLY POLY tumblers	50.00--60.00
New Martinsville's ruby "MOONDROPS" butter and cover	350.00-400.00
New Martinsville's ruby miniature cream and sugar	20.00--25.00
New Martinsville's amethyst decanter	35.00--40.00
Macbeth's green satin 10¼" "DOGWOOD" light shade,	25.00--35.00
Cambridge's keg set	125.00-165.00

TOP OF PAGE — page 16

Jeannette's FLORAL jug	550.00-600.00
Jeannette's FLORAL footed comport	300.00-350.00
Macbeth's "AMERICAN SWEETHEART" lamp	1000.00-1200.00
Hocking's CAMEO sandwich server	600.00-800.00
McKee's ruby ROCK CRYSTAL FLOWER lamp	200.00-250.00
Hocking's PACHYDERMS	40.00--60.00
Fostoria's Azure ORLEANS pieces (ea.)	20.00--30.00

FRONT ROW

Jeannette's FLORAL vase	400.00-500.00
Liberty Works' AMERICAN PIONEER jugs and covers,ea.	140.00-175.00
Liberty Works' AMERICAN PIONEER dresser set	70.00--80.00
Liberty Works' AMERICAN PIONEER lamps, pink, green	55.00--75.00
Liberty Works' AMERICAN PIONEER ice bucket	30.00--40.00
U.S. Glass' "GALLEON" ash tray	8.00--11.00
"OLLIE MAY" dresser set	45.00--50.00
Indiana's No. 612 candy dish	90.00-100.00
Imperial's FANCY COLONIAL handled salt dip	10.00--15.00
Akro Agate's LEMONADE and OXBLOOD child's pieces, ea.	10.00--25.00
Federal's MADRID gravy boat and tray	700.00-800.00
Hazel Atlas' FLORENTINE candy dish	100.00-125.00
Federal's TRUMP BRIDGE SET pieces, ea.	6.00-- 9.00
Indiana's No. 612 jug	250.00-275.00

BACK ROW

Aladdin's Alacite CUPID lamp	135.00-150.00
Aladdin's G-22 lamp	45.00--50.00
Jeannette's "DAISY J" candy dish	20.00--25.00
McKee's AZTEC punch bowl	250.00-300.00
Westmoreland's DELLA ROBBIA candleholder	12.00--14.00
Lancaster's oil lamp	55.00--60.00
McKee's TAMBOUR ART clock	300.00-350.00
Indiana's TEA ROOM lamp	35.00--40.00
McKee's INNOVATION vase	25.00--35.00
Duncan and Miller's CARIBBEAN punch set	125.00-165.00

Akro Agate

Akro Agate glass is included in these pages because the popular childs' dishes came in transparent 'Depression' colors -- amber, blue, green, cobalt -- as well as the conspicuous 'Akro' opaque and marbleized ones.

Then too, we include Akro because it is so very lively an area!

We want to thank certain people for their help in the Akro field. It was Lela Koch of Creighton MO who organized the Akro data in the form presented here. It's one of the simplest ways to understand Akro, drawing attention to the various Akro twists and turns. Lela, of course, is well known as one of the pioneer enthusiasts of this ware.

Nadine Pankow of Willow Springs IL is another who has bought and sold much Akro through the years, as is evidenced by her large ads in the DAZE. Nadine has once again reviewed the Akro price picture and assisted in suggesting this year's prices, for which we thank her very much.

To date, we have found only 14 patterns in the children's line. They are:

1. CONCENTRIC RIB (A)
2. CONCENTRIC RING (A-2)
3. STACKED DISC (B)
4. STACKED DISC & PANEL (C)
5. STIPPLED BAND (D)
6. STIPPLED INTERIOR PANEL (D2)
7. INTERIOR PANEL (E)
8. DAISY (F)
9. MISS AMERICA DECAL (G)
10. OCTAGONAL (H)
11. OCTAGONAL "O" (H2)
12. CHIQUITA
13. PLAIN JANE
14. PANELED PLAIN JANE

However, most patterns were made in two sizes, and in transparent and a multitude of opaque colors as well. Thus it would be possible to have a hundred or more sets without duplication.

IN GENERAL, remember these points when collecting Akro child's pieces:

1. There are four different, basic types of glass:
   A. **Opaque.** This is a solid glass which one cannot see through. In some cases, however, Akro's opaques can be somewhat translucent.

B. **Marbleized.** This is an opaque of two completely different colors swirled together.

C. **Transparents.** This is glass that one can see through.

D. **Baked on color.** This is a color fired on over clear glass.

2. When two sizes were made, the large size often has matching bowls, and sugars with lids. In the small size, there are water pitchers and tumblers to match, but no sugar lids.
3. Some Akro is marked and some is not. The little crow flying through the A is the most common to us. But some of the sets are marked "J.P." Still others have only numbers. Some pieces have no mark at all.
4. Sets were boxed in many sizes. As few as 6 pieces or as many as 29 might make up a boxed set.
5. Most opaque sets were boxed in various colors. If you try to complete sets all of the same color you'll just come up with headaches. Green saucers are very hard to come by, for example. A quite common combination is: green plates, yellow saucers, and orange cups; with blue teapot, cream and sugar.
6. Boxes are worth $5.00-10.00 depending on condition and size.

PATTERNS

What holds true in one pattern will not always hold true in another, so let's get down to some hair splitting, one pattern at a time.

CONCENTRIC RIB (Con. Rib) (A)

This set is found in small size only. Should you find pieces which appear to be the large size, close examination will show them to be Concentric Ring.

To date, CONCENTRIC RIB has been found only in the opaques, issued two or more colors in a box. If the Akro opaques have found the way to your heart, then you'll have a ball with Con. Rib -- there's no end to the possible color combinations here. Sets with green plates and cups, white saucers with either green or white teapot and cream/sugar, are quite common.

The challenge is in the other colors: purple, yellow, caramel, clam, pink, bright aqua, pale aqua, orange and several shades of blue.

The CONCENTRIC RIB plate, cup, and saucer have a series of grooves around the outside edge. The cream/sugar and teapot have well-spaced horizontal bands from top to bottom and are decorated with five vertical darts at the top. The inside of these pieces are smooth. The most common piece to this set is the plate. The cream/sugar will be a slight bit harder to come by.

	Green	Blue	Pink	White	*Other Colors
Plate	1.50	2.75	4.00	3.00	6.00
Saucer	2.50	2.75	3.00	2.00	3.00
Cup	1.50	4.00	5.00	4.00	6.00
Teapot	3.50	4.00	4.50	3.00	7.00
Lid	3.00	3.00	3.00	2.50	4.00
Creamer	4.00	4.00	5.00	3.50	5.00
Sugar	4.00	4.00	5.00	3.50	5.00

**Triple the price for purple.*

CONCENTRIC RING (Con. Ring) (A-2)

This set is found in both large and small sizes. The small size is sometimes confused with Con. Rib but look closer and you'll see that the plate and saucer have distinct ridges rather than grooves around the outer rim. Also, the saucers have definite cup rings where the Con. Rib ones do not. The teapot and lid, cream and sugar look the same as Con. Rib on the outside, except that the bands extend around the handles. On the inside, these pieces are paneled while the Con. Rib ones are smooth.

In the large size, bands extend around the handles of the cups as well as the teapot, cream and sugar. The saucers in this large size do not have cup rings. Once you've discovered and studied these little things you should have no trouble with the opaque or marble sets. The transparents may fool you at first as the teapot, cream and sugar become Stacked Disc and Panel once the panels on the inside show through. For this reason, these pieces are interchangeable between the two sets. You'll have no trouble with the plates, saucers and cups as they look the same as the opaque -- except that you can now see the 3 bands on the underside of the plates and saucers.

The only transparent color found to date is cobalt; in the marble, only blue. Opaque sets most often have green plates, yellow saucers, orange cups, blue teapot, cream/sugar and white lids. Aqua bowls come in large size only.

Remember, the large size has a bowl and a lid for the sugar. The easy pieces to find will be the plates. The hardest will be the bowls and the lids. Remember the lids must have rings on the tops and panels on the underside to belong to this set.

Opaques	Small size	Large size	Transparent	Small size	Large size
Plate	5.00	6.00	Plate	9.00	10.00
Saucer	3.50	6.00	Saucer	6.00	10.00
Cup	6.00	18.00	Cup	15.00	18.00
Teapot	4.00	12.00	Teapot	8.00	15.00
Lid	10.00	12.00	Lid	12.00	18.00
Cream	8.00	12.00	Cream	16.50	15.00
Sugar	8.00	12.00	Sugar	16.50	15.00
		Lid 15.00		Sugar Lid	12.00
		Bowl 15.00		Bowl	18.00

STACKED DISC (B)

Stacked Disc seems to come only in the small size opaque, and it has a matching water set. It is most closely related to Con. Rib, the only difference being the cup. The cups and tumblers will be the hard pieces to find. The most readily found will be the plate. Again, a multitude of colors exist here.

	Green	Pink, Blue, Yellow	Cobalt, Pumpkin
Plate	1.50-- 2.00	2.50--3.00	5.00-- 6.00
Saucer	4.00-- 5.00	2.50--3.50	4.00-- 5.00
Cup	3.00-- 4.00	5.00--7.00	8.00--10.00
Cream	4.00-- 5.00	5.00--6.00	8.00--10.00
Sugar	4.00-- 5.00	5.00--6.00	8.00--10.00
Teapot & Lid	6.00-- 7.00	7.00--8.00	10.00--12.00
Water Pitcher	7.00-- 8.00	6.00--9.00	
Tumbler	8.00--10.00	5.00--7.00	

STACKED DISC AND PANEL (C)

This set comes in both large and small sizes, as well as in opaques, transparents and marbleizes. The large solid opaque set is very rare, but the demand seems to run more for the transparents and, of course, the marbleizes.

In the opaques, double the price for the large size. Also double the price for the pumpkin and cobalt in both the large and small size.

	Opaques	Transparents	Marbleized
Plate	3.00-- 5.00	5.00-- 7.50	7.50--10.00
Saucer	3.00-- 4.50	4.50-- 6.00	6.00-- 8.00
Cup	6.00-- 8.00	9.00--11.00	14.00--18.00
Cream	7.50-- 8.00	8.00--10.00	12.00--14.00
Sugar	7.50-- 8.00	8.00--10.00	12.00--14.00
Teapot & Lid	12.50--15.00	16.00--18.00	25.00--30.00
Water Pitcher	25.00--30.00	10.00--15.00	
Tumbler	10.00--12.00	5.00-- 8.00	
Bowl (large)	10.00--12.00	10.00--12.00	

STIPPLED BAND (D)

This set comes both small and large. You find only the transparents, however. The colors for the small sets are green and amber, while the large set was also issued in a very pretty azure blue.

	Green	Amber	Azure
Plate	2.00-- 3.00	3.00-- 4.00	10.00--12.00
Saucer	2.00-- 3.00	2.00-- 3.50	7.50--10.00
Cup	5.00-- 7.00	6.50-- 7.50	15.00--20.00
Cream	8.00--10.00	8.00--10.00	20.00--25.00
Sugar	8.00--10.00	8.00--10.00	20.00--25.00
Teapot & Lid	10.00--12.00	12.00--15.00	30.00--35.00
Water Pitcher	7.50--10.00	10.00--15.00	
Tumbler	5.00-- 6.00	6.00-- 8.00	

STIPPLED INTERIOR PANEL (D2)

A few opaque pieces have turned up but most often you find this set in the green and amber transparents, small size only.

	Green	Amber
Plate	4.00-- 5.00	5.00-- 6.00
Saucer	4.00-- 5.00	5.00-- 6.00
Cup	5.00-- 7.50	6.00-- 7.50
Cream	7.50-- 8.00	7.50--10.00
Sugar	7.50-- 8.00	7.50--10.00
Teapot & Lid	10.00--12.00	10.00--12.50
Water Pitcher	10.00--12.00	12.00--15.00
Tumbler	5.00-- 7.50	7.50--10.00

INTERIOR PANEL (E)

This pattern alone can become a sizeable collection, if one gathers both sizes in all colors and types. Marbleized sets will be the most difficult to obtain. The transparents in the small size will prove a problem when it comes to finding cream and sugars. And even the opaque pink, cobalt and orange are not exactly easy to come by.

All sets have the basic pieces, while only the small-size transparent sets have water pitchers and tumblers. Again, the large size in all sets come with sugar lids and bowls.

Some of the teapots, creams and sugars in this pattern are decorated with darts while others are not.

Opaque Small Size

	Green	*Yellow/Aqua*	*Orange Cobalt/Pink*
Plate	3.00	7.00	6.00
Saucer	2.50	5.00	4.00
Cup	6.00	14.00	18.00
Teapot	4.00	8.00	7.50
Lid	3.50	15.00	10.00
Cream	5.00	15.00	15.00
Sugar	5.00	15.00	15.00

Opaque Large Size

	Green	*Yellow/Aqua*	*Orange Cobalt/Pink*
Plate	4.00	10.00	7.50
Saucer	3.00	8.00	6.00
Cup	5.50	16.00	18.00
Teapot	5.00	7.50	10.00
Lid	12.00	15.00	18.00
Cream	6.00	15.00	15.00
Sugar	6.00	15.00	15.00
Lid	5.00	12.00	14.00
Bowl	6.00	15.00	15.00

Transparent Small Size

	Green	*Amber*
Plate	4.00	5.50
Saucer	4.00	4.50
Cup	6.00	8.00
Teapot	6.00	7.50
Lid	9.00	7.00
Cream	8.00	10.00
Sugar	6.00	10.00
Lid	5.00	6.00
Bowl	7.50	10.00

Transparent Large Size

	Green	*Amber*
Plate	4.00	5.00
Saucer	3.50	4.00
Cup	7.00	9.00
Teapot	4.00	5.00
Lid	6.00	7.50
Cream	15.00	17.50
Sugar	15.00	17.50
Water Pitcher	8.00	12.50
Tumbler	5.00	7.50

Marble Small Size

	Green	*Blue*	*Red*
Plate	8.00	12.00	12.00
Saucer	6.00	10.00	10.00
Cup	20.00	30.00	25.00
Teapot	10.00	12.50	10.00
Lid	8.00	16.00	20.00
Cream	20.00	25.00	25.00
Sugar	20.00	25.00	25.00

Marble Large Size

	Green	Blue	Red	Oxblood and Lemonade
Plate	12.00	15.00	15.00	12.50
Saucer	12.00	12.50	12.50	10.00
Cup	20.00	25.00	25.00	27.50
Teapot	12.50	20.00	20.00	25.00
Lid	25.00	25.00	25.00	15.00
Cream	25.00	30.00	30.00	22.50
Sugar	25.00	30.00	30.00	30.00
Lid	10.00	12.00	12.00	15.00
Bowl	12.50	17.50	17.50	20.00

DAISY (F)

This heart-warming little set comes only in the small size and only in opaques. The teapot has no lid and it doubles as the pitcher in the boxed water sets. And the tricky little teapot/water pitcher comes with or without the embossed daisy!

The teapot and cups turn up in both blue and green. The tumblers, cream, sugar and saucers come in yellow and caramel. So far the plate has only shown up in several shades of blue.

Plate	10.00--12.00
Saucer	7.50--10.00
Cup	20.00--22.50
Teapot	25.00--30.00
Cream	25.00--30.00
Sugar	25.00--30.00
Tumbler	20.00--25.00

MISS AMERICA (DECAL) (G)

This pattern comes in opaques, with or without the little roses decalled on. It also comes in a transparent deep green and orange and white marble. It was made in one size only, with open handles.

	White	Orange Marble	Green
Plate	8.00--10.00	10.00--12.00	10.00--12.00
Saucer	8.00--10.00	10.00--12.00	10.00--12.00
Cup	20.00--25.00	25.00--30.00	25.00--30.00
Cream	25.00--35.00	25.00--30.00	25.00--30.00
Sugar & Lid	30.00--40.00	30.00--40.00	30.00--40.00
Teapot & Lid	40.00--50.00	40.00--50.00	40.00--50.00

OCTAGONAL (H)

This pattern is quite common in the large size. the small size, however, is one of the rarest sets to be had. In the small size, we find only the opaque pieces. In the large size we find the marbleized oxblood/lemonade as well as the opaques -- all in all, a wide range of colors are possible. There are at least three or four shades of green and blue, plus yellow, caramel, pink, orange, white, ivory, aqua and more.

The teapot, cream and sugar, and the water pitcher in the small size will prove the most difficult to obtain. They may not even exist. Nobody I know has ever found them. The easiest will be the plates in the large size.

Prices on the rare small size are not feasible at this time. Just remember they're high!

Large Size

	White/Green	Blue/Yellow	Other	Oxblood and Lemonade
Plate	1.50	2.50	3.00	9.00
Saucer	2.00	2.50	3.00	5.00
Cup	1.50	3.00	5.00	30.00
Teapot	5.00	6.00	7.50	10.00
Lid	3.50	4.00	5.00	25.00
Cream	4.00	5.00	7.50	25.00
Sugar	4.00	5.00	7.50	25.00
Lid	2.50	3.00	3.50	
Bowl	4.00	5.00	10.00	15.00

OCTAGONAL "O" (H2)

This pattern was made in both small and large sizes. It comes in the opaques only. Here again, the sets seem to be most common with green plates, yellow saucers, orange cups with blue teapot, cream and sugar. With the wide selection of colors offered in this pattern, other combinations are readily possible.

A water set goes with the small size and a sugar lid and bowls for the large size. Here again, the plates will be easy to find while the sugars and creamers are the tuffies.

Small Size

	White/Green	Blue/Yellow	Other
Plate	2.00	5.00	4.00
Saucer	3.00	4.50	4.00
Cup	8.00	8.50	9.00
Teapot	5.00	5.00	7.50
Lids, white	4.00		
Cream	8.00	14.00	17.00
Sugar	8.00	14.00	17.00
Water Pitcher	8.00	10.00	10.00
Tumbler	4.00	6.00	12.50

Large Size

	White/Green	Blue/Yellow	Other
Plate	1.50	2.50	3.00
Saucer	2.50	3.00	4.00
Cup	6.00	6.00	8.00
Teapot	7.50	6.00	7.50
Lid	4.00	4.50	5.00
Cream	7.50	12.50	12.50
Sugar	7.50	12.50	12.50
Lid	3.50	4.00	5.00
Bowl	5.00	7.50	10.00

CHIQUITA

(Hazel's Note: The Akro Agate Company contracted to make this line of ware for the J. Pressman Company, with specifications that 1.) the Chiquita brand line would

not utilize any of the Akro molds proper and 2.) the Chiquita would not be made of a glass of equal quality to the Akro products.)

If you find this line marked at all, most likely it will be marked JP or with a number. You will find a "C" in one size only.

Chiquita was made in three types of glass: Opaques, transparents, and baked-on color. The baked-on sets found to date are colored in this way: Plates, green; saucers, yellow; cups, orange; and teapot, cream and sugar dark blue. The bowls are orange.

The only color in transparent Chiquita found so far is cobalt. Some will run toward gray and other pieces toward green, but basically they are all intended to be cobalt. I suppose it's like making fudge, some batches just turn out better than others.

The most common Chiquita found is the opaque green. At the same time, opaque pieces in any other color are very difficult to obtain. Full sets of green were issued while other opaque colors came in multi-colored sets. I've one set which has green-gray-black mottled plates, bright yellow saucers, deep purple cups, deep aqua teapot, cream and sugar.

Other colors found are medium blue, lavendar, caramel, white, and pale blue -- but who knows what we'll find next?

Transparent and opaque Chiquita pieces consist of the Plate, Saucer, Cup, Teapot, Lid, Open Sugar, and Creamer. The baked-on colors came in the same 7 pieces plus a bowl. There is no water set to this pattern.

The hardest piece to find will prove to be the plate. There's a reason for this: Two types of sets were boxed without plates. One was comprised of a teapot with lid and two cups and saucers. Another boxed the teapot and cover, 4 cups and saucers, and a cream and sugar. No wonder the plates are in short supply! The saucer will be the easiest to locate.

Baked-on Colors

Item	Price
Plate	5.00
Saucer	5.00
Cup	5.00
Teapot	6.00
Lid	6.00
Cream	7.50
Sugar	7.50
Bowl	7.50

Transparent Cobalt

Item	Price
Plate	6.00
Saucer	2.00
Cup	7.50
Teapot	6.00
Lid	8.00
Cream	6.00
Sugar	6.00

Opaque Green

Item	Price
Plate	3.50
Saucer	1.50
Cup	2.25
Teapot	3.00
Lid	3.00
Cream	4.00
Sugar	4.00

Other Opaques

Item	Price
Plate	6.00
Saucer	4.00
Cup	15.00
Teapot	10.00
Lid	8.00
Cream	15.00
Sugar	15.00

PLAIN JANE

Like the Chiquita, this pattern was made for J. Pressman and Company. It is marked JP. It comes in the same baked-on colors as the Chiquita. We also find it in three transparent colors; deep amber, green, and blue. there are two sizes of plates, for some reason not yet known. Also, the baked-on color set has bowls to match.

Prices for the baked-on are the same as for Chiquita.

	Baked-On	Transparent Green, Blue, Amber
Plate	3.00	10.00--12.50
Cup	6.50	18.00--20.00
Saucer	4.00	10.00--12.50
Teapot	6.00	20.00--25.00
Lid	6.00	15.00--20.00
Sugar	7.50	15.00--20.00
Lid	*none*	10.00--12.00
Cream	7.50	15.00--20.00
Bowl	7.50	

Plate, cup and saucer are shown in lower left corner of photo

PANEL PLAIN JANE

To date this pattern has only been found in transparent, very deep cobalt blue. I have a plate and cups and saucers; I do hope that teapot and creamer and sugar will turn up in the future! As far as I know, none of it is marked.

Plate	5.00-- 6.00
Cup	6.00-- 8.00
Saucer	4.00-- 5.00
Creamer	*haven't seen*
Sugar	*haven't seen*
Teapot & Lid	*haven't seen*

PLAIN JANE *plate, cup and saucer*
CHIQUITA *toy dishes* **TEA FOR SIX** *toy dishes*

Aladdin

At your first glimmer of interest in the special breed of lamp, send for J. W. Courter's newsletter "The Mystic Light of Aladdin Knights" (Box 125, Simpson IL 62985), as it is very useful.

Since 1974, two of the lamps, the Short and Tall Lincoln Drapes, were reproduced in crystal, amber, ruby, cobalt and one in moonstone. Some of these are marked, and some not. The differences are in the raised metal collar which holds the burner (the metal threads were embedded in the glass of the original lamps) and the fact that the new font and foot have been made separately and glued together.

Mr. Courter's annual price guide, keyed to his book ALADDIN --THE MAGIC NAME IN LAMPS, includes a chapter on repros and fakes.

Since color is the chief determining factor in valuing lamps, price ranges for the many lamp styles shown in Book 2 can be summarized as follows.

LAMPS

page 20, 21

	Crystal	*Amber, Green*	*Ruby, Cobalt*	*Opaques Other*
VENETIAN	150.00--200.00	60.00-- 80.00		
"COLONIAL"	70.00-- 80.00	100.00--110.00		
"CATHEDRAL"	50.00-- 60.00	60.00-- 70.00		100.00--125.00
"CORINTHIAN"	30.00-- 40.00	50.00-- 60.00		70.00-- 90.00
"MAJESTIC"				100.00--120.00
"ORIENTALE"			(Metal)	60.00--150.00
"BEEHIVE"	40.00-- 50.00	50.00-- 80.00	200.00--250.00	
"DIAMOND QUILT"				90.00--110.00
QUEEN				100.00--125.00
"TREASURE"			(Metal)	85.00--200.00
"VERTIQUE"				120.00--300.00
"SOLITAIRE"				800.00-1000.00
"WASHINGTON DRAPE"	25.00-- 30.00	60.00-- 70.00		
*"SHORT LINCOLN DRAPE"		1000.00-1200.00	275.00--325.00	250.00--300.00
*"TALL LINCOLN DRAPE"	1000.00-1200.00		325.00--425.00	70.00-- 80.00
"WASHINGTON DRAPE" (B-Style)	40.00-- 50.00	60.00-- 70.00		

**New 1974, 1976, 1977*

	Crystal	Amber, Green	Ruby, Cobalt	Opaques Other
"WASHINGTON DRAPE" (Bell Shaped pedestal)	70.00-- 85.00	125.00--150.00		
"WASHINGTON DRAPE" (Plain)	25.00-- 35.00	40.00-- 50.00		
VICTORIA			(China)	200.00--300.00
"SIMPLICITY"				75.00--250.00

MISCELLANEOUS ALACITE

page 21

Wall Vase, pr.	60.00-- 80.00	Bookends	80.00-- 90.00
Hndld Bowl, 11½" x 1½" deep	125.00--150.00	Egg Plate	125.00--150.00
Coaster Ashtray	35.00-- 45.00	Cigarette Box w/tray	200.00--275.00
Ash Tray, small	15.00-- 20.00	Cigarette Jar & Cover	80.00-- 90.00
Ash Tray, large	30.00-- 40.00	Nut Dish	70.00-- 80.00
Wall Switch	30.00-- 40.00	Powder Dish	60.00-- 70.00
Candle Holders (pr.)	125.00--175.00	Tissue Box Cover	300.00--350.00
Bell	90.00--100.00	Serving Dishes, part.	70.00-- 80.00

Photo courtesy Betty Bell

ALACITE
ashtray (inscribed Alacite by Aladdin), cigarette box w/tray
switch plate, pocket vase, egg plate, coasters/ashtrays
nut dish, vase/bookends, cigarette jar, and base to powder dish

B-C

Bartlett–Collins

Update: This past year Bartlett-Collins was sold to the Lancaster Colony Corp.

Zeta and Charley Todd, Denver CO, are collectors of "LOVEBIRD AND GRAPE", and helped update this pattern this year. Usually found in green on crystal, it's been found in red on crystal, green on green, and pink on pink. The GRAPE design, too, has been found in these combinations.

Bartlett-Collins has never ceased making lamps in crystal. From 1938 to 1942 a fired-on Scottie Dog motif and a Floral motif were popular; these can be seen in color in THE DECORATED TUMBLER book page 10.

In the 70s they made amber and avocado colored lamps as well. Now these are discontinued and only fired-on colors are available.

The point to remember is that only those lamps made in the DG colors are sure to be old.

Two additional styles of the original line which you might find in Nu-Rose or Nu-Green are reprinted here.

No. 236—A Lamp

No. 260—D Lamp

1927 catalog reprint

The following prices are listed in order as they appear in Book II and some appear more than once. The suggested prices are for Crystal, Nu-Rose and Nu-Green.

THE LAMPS	**page 22, 23**
No. 300 Library Lamp Complete	110.00--125.00
No. 246B capacity, 20 oz. *(Center lamp page 22)*	45.00--55.00
No. 260 capacity, 31 oz. (No. 39 in Book 1)	45.00--55.00
No. 261 D capacity, 31 oz.	45.00--55.00
No. 2 Phoenix Engraved Chimney *(Crystal)*	15.00--20.00
No. 236 A capacity, 15 oz.	40.00--50.00
No. 260 D capacity; 31 oz.	40.00--50.00

WATER AND ICE TEA SETS Decorated

No. 416 9 oz., Dec. 26	3.00-- 4.00
No. 416 13 oz., Dec. 26	3.00-- 4.00
No. 821 Jug, 72 oz., Dec. 36	12.00--15.00
No. 416 9 oz., Dec. 36	3.00-- 4.00
No. 415 13 oz., Dec. 36	2.00-- 4.00
No. 810 Jug, Dec. 36	12.00--15.00

SPECIAL ASSORTMENT Decoration No. 26

No. 87 Console Set 3 piece	20.00--25.00
Pr. candlestick holders	10.00--13.00
Rolled edge bowl	10.00--12.00
No. 88 Sandwich tray	8.00--10.00
No. 87 Sandwich tray	8.00--10.00
No. 87 Fruit bowl	8.00--10.00
No. 88 Fruit (sic) bowl	9.00--12.00
No. 90 Mayonnaise bowl (3 pieces)	12.00--15.00
No. 416 9 oz., tumbler	3.00-- 4.00
No. 423 Jug, 42 oz.	12.00--15.00

ASSORTMENT Decoration No. 40

You may find these pieces with other decorations.

Pink, green

No. 88 Sandwich Tray, 11"	8.00--10.00
No. 88 Cupped Bowl, 10"	9.00--12.00
No. 90 Salver, 11"	9.00--12.00
No. 87 Cupped Bowl, 10"	10.00--12.00
No. 90 Comport, 9"	9.00--12.00
No. 7820 Ice Bucket, 5½" tall	15.00--20.00

SHERATON page 24

Crystal, pink, green

Sugar and Cover	8.00--10.00
Nappy, 9"	8.00--12.00
Butter and Cover	35.00--40.00
Cream	4.00-- 6.00
Nappy, 4½"	3.00-- 4.00
Spoon	9.00--11.00
Punch Bowl, 12"	20.00--30.00
Custard, handled	2.50-- 4.00
Sherbet	3.00-- 4.00

MISCELLANEOUS

No. 500 Sugar and Cover	8.00--10.00
No. 500 Butter and Cover	15.00--20.00
No. 500 Sherbet, ftd.	2.00-- 3.00
No. 510 Nappy, 4"	2.00-- 3.00
No. 511 Nappy, 4"	2.00-- 3.00
No. 500 Nappy, 4"	2.00-- 3.00
No. 510 Nappy, 7"	7.00-- 9.00
No. 511 Nappy, 7"	8.00--10.00
No. 500 Nappy, 7"	8.00--10.00

NO. 450 LINE

A crystal pattern

Cream	4.00-- 6.00
Sugar and Cover	9.00--12.00
Spoon	6.00-- 9.00
Nappy, 8"	8.00--12.00
Butter and Cover	20.00--25.00
Nappy, 4"	3.00-- 4.00

WATER AND ICE TEA SETS

Crystal, pink, green

No. 800 Jug, Optic, 58 oz.	9.00--12.00
No. 851 Jug, Spiral Optic, 58 oz.	17.00--22.00
No. 417 Ice Tea Tumbler, 13 oz.	4.00-- 6.00
No. 416 Water Tumbler, 9 oz.	3.00-- 4.00
No. 807 Cracked Jug and Cover	16.00--20.00

BLOWN STEMWARE Cut No. 52 page 25

No. 820 Goblet	6.00-- 9.00
No. 820 Hi-ftd. Sherbet	5.00-- 7.00
No. 820 Low ftd. Sherbet	4.00-- 5.00
No. 820 Cocktail	7.00--10.00
No. 820 Wine	7.00--10.00
No. 91 Plate, 8"	3.00-- 5.00
No. 87 Sugar	6.00-- 8.00
No. 87 Cream	6.00-- 8.00

BLOWN STEMWARE

No. 1931 Goblet	5.00-- 8.00
No. 1931 Hi-ftd. Sherbet	4.00-- 6.00
No. 1931 Low ftd. Sherbet	3.00-- 5.00
No. 1931 Wine	7.00-- 9.00
No. 1931 Ftd. Ice Tea	7.00-- 9.00
No. 1931 High Ball	5.00-- 8.00
No. 1931 Sherbet, Cut No. 50	4.00-- 6.00
No. 201 Sham Tumbler, 1¼ oz., Cut 185	4.00-- 6.00
No. 531 Sham Tumbler 1½ oz., Cut 54	4.00-- 6.00

BLOWN BUD VASES

No. 385 10", Cut 210	6.00-- 9.00
No. 252 Cut 238	7.00--10.00
No. 375 10", Cut 260	7.00--10.00
No. 380 Cut 9	6.00-- 9.00

NU-GREEN AND NU-ROSE page 26

All these were made with decoration
Crystal, pink, green

No. 826 Jug, 66 oz.	12.00--18.00
No. 426 Ice Tea, 13 oz.	4.00-- 5.00
No. 426 Tumbler, 9 oz.	3.00-- 4.00
No. 828 Jug and Cover	20.00--25.00
No. 820 Ice Bucket	15.00--20.00
No. 820 Cookie Jar	15.00--25.00

CRYSTAL AND NU-ROSE GLASSWARE

Crystal, pink, green

No. 25 Goblet	5.00-- 8.00
No. 25 Champagne	4.00-- 6.00
No. 25 Sherbet	4.00-- 5.00
No. 25 Cocktail	6.00-- 9.00
No. 25 Wine	6.00-- 9.00
No. 26 Goblet	5.00-- 8.00
No. 26 Champagne	4.00-- 6.00
No. 26 Sherbet	4.00-- 5.00
No. 26 Cocktail	6.00-- 9.00
No. 26 Wine	6.00-- 9.00
No. 26 Ftd. Tumbler	5.00-- 7.00
No. 25 Oyster Cocktail	5.00-- 7.00
No. 25 Ftd. Tumbler	5.00-- 8.00

WATER AND ICE TEA SETS

No. 824 Jug and Cover, 72 oz.	18.00--22.00
No. 415 13 oz.	4.00-- 5.00
No. 415 9 oz.	3.00-- 4.00
No. 415 5 oz.	3.00-- 4.00
No. 823 Jug, 72 oz.	12.00--16.00
No. 416 Spiral Optic, 13 oz.	4.00-- 5.00
No. 416 Spiral Optic, 9 oz.	3.00-- 4.00
No. 416 Spiral Optic, 5 oz.	3.00-- 4.00

BLOWN WATER AND ICE TEA SETS

No. 820 Jug with Ice Lip, 72 oz.	14.00--18.00
No. 820 Ice Tea, 13 oz.	4.00-- 6.00
No. 820 Water Tumbler, 9 oz.	3.00-- 5.00
No. 820 Jug, 72 oz.	12.00--16.00
No. 416 Spiral Optic, 13 oz.	4.00-- 6.00
No. 416 Spiral Optic, 9 oz.	3.00-- 4.00
No. 416 Spiral Optic, 5 oz.	3.00-- 4.00

ENAMEL NO. 66 Assortment page 27

No. 90 Deep Nappy, 2 hdld., 8"	10.00--12.00
No. 90 Large Deep ftd. Comport, 9"	11.00--14.00
No. 90 2 hdld. Cake Plate or Plaque, 11"	10.00--12.00
No. 88 hdld. Sandwich Tray, 11"	10.00--12.00
No. 90 Ftd. Salver, 11"	11.00--14.00
No. 820 Cookie Jar and Cover, 76 oz.	15.00--25.00

SPECIAL 210 ASSORTMENT

No. 90 Hdld. Cake Plate, 11"	10.00--12.00
No. 90 Hdld. Deep Bowl, 8"	10.00--12.00
No. 90 Ftd. Salver or Cake Stand, 11"	12.00--15.00
No. 88 Hdld. Fruit Bowl, 10"	10.00--12.00
No. 88 Hdld. Sandwich Tray, 11"	10.00--12.00
No. 90 Ftd. Bowl or Comport, 9"	11.00--14.00

MISCELLANEOUS

No. 90 Mayonnaise Dish Plate and Ladle	14.00--18.00
No. 89 Cupped Fruit Bowl, 10"	11.00--12.00
No. 90 Salver, 10"	11.00--14.00
No. 90 Nappy, 8"	9.00--11.00
No. 90 Plaque, 10"	8.00--10.00
No. 90 Comport	8.00--10.00
No. 88 Cupped Fruit, 10"	10.00--12.00
No. 821 Cookie Jar, 2/3 gallon	15.00--25.00
No. 521 Cookie Jar, 1 gallon	18.00--26.00
No. 16 Beverage Tumbler, 1 oz. Sham	2.00-- 3.00
No. 531 Beverage Tumbler, 1½ oz.	4.00-- 6.00
No. 201 Beverage Sham, 1¼ oz.	4.00-- 6.00

NO. 820 BLOWN STEMWARE page 28

Goblet	6.00-- 9.00
Champagne	5.00-- 7.00
Sherbet	4.00-- 6.00
Ftd. Ice Tea	6.00-- 8.00
Wine	7.00--10.00
Cocktail	7.00--10.00
Parfait	7.00--10.00
No. 201 Beverage Sham, 1¼ oz.	4.00-- 6.00
No. 531 Beverage Tumbler, 1½ oz.	2.00-- 3.00

MISCELLANEOUS

No. 600 Ftd. Sherbet, 3½"	1.00-- 2.00
No. 610 Ftd. Sherbet, 3¾"	1.00-- 2.00
No. 300 Molasses Can, 12 oz.	15.00--20.00
No. 91 Plate, 8"	2.00-- 4.00
No. 632 19 oz. Tumbler	4.00-- 6.00
No. 260 Lamp, capacity 31 oz. (*page 22 Book II and in Book I*)	45.00--55.00
No. 820 Ice Bucket	15.00--20.00
No. 91 Card Case and Cover	15.00--20.00
No. 90 Coaster and Tray (*also in Cobalt blue*)	7.00--10.00
No. 16 Sham, 1 oz.	1.50-- 2.00
No. 91 Plate, 8"	2.00-- 4.00
No. 820 Cookie Jar and Cover, 76 oz., Dec. 66	15.00--25.00

No. 87 Candle Holder	4.00-- 6.00
No. 87 Flower Bowl, 11"	10.00--12.00
No. 87 Cupped Fruit Bowl, 10"	9.00--11.00
No. 87 Sugar	4.00-- 6.00
No. 87 Cream	4.00-- 6.00
No. 87 Sandwich Tray, 11"	8.00--10.00
No. 820 Candy Box	14.00--18.00

MISCELLANEOUS page 29

Percolator Top, 2-1/8"	2.00-- 3.00
Puritan, High ftd. Bowl, 5"	4.00-- 6.00
Oklahoma Ice Tub, 6½'	7.00--10.00
Colonial Percolator Top, 2-1/8"	2.00-- 3.00
No. 65 Nappy, 5"	2.00-- 3.00
No. 65 Berry Cream	4.00-- 6.00
No. 65 Berry Sugar	4.00-- 6.00
No. 60 Basket	15.00--25.00
Awning Rings; small, medium, large	2.00-- 4.00
Puritan Nappy, 8"	8.00--10.00

TWITCH

No. 92 Line
Green; Decorated all over enamel, green, blue, red or yellow

Tumbler, 5 oz.	3.00-- 5.00
Tumbler, 9 oz.	3.00-- 5.00
Ice Tea, 12 oz.	4.00-- 6.00
Jugs, 25 oz.	18.00--24.00
Sugar	4.00-- 6.00
Cream	4.00-- 6.00
Sherbet	2.00-- 4.00
Cup	3.00-- 5.00
Saucer	2.00-- 3.00
Plate, 8½"	3.00-- 5.00

BLOWN TUMBLERS, JUGS AND SETS

No. 422 Tumbler, 5 oz.	3.00-- 5.00
No. 422 Water Tumbler, 9 oz.	3.00-- 5.00
No. 842 Jug, 76 oz.	15.00--18.00
No. 422 Ice Tea Tumbler, 13 oz.	4.00-- 6.00
No. 842 Ice Lip Jug, 76 oz.	18.00--22.00

PURITAN LINE

Sugar and Cover	8.00--10.00
Cream	4.00-- 6.00
Nappy, 4½"	2.00-- 3.00
Oil Bottle	20.00--25.00
Nappy, 9"	8.00--10.00
Butter and Cover	20.00--25.00

LOVEBIRD AND GRAPE

Green Ice on crystal; Red Ice on crystal
Green Ice on green; Pink Ice on pink

Sugar	7.00-- 9.00
Creamer	7.00-- 9.00
Goblet	14.00--17.00
Tall Sherbet	10.00--14.00
Cake Plate, hdld., 10"	14.00--18.00
Bowl, hdld., 8"	14.00--18.00
Tumbler, 9 oz.	6.00-- 9.00
Tumbler, (820) 13 oz.	8.00--11.00
Ice Tea, 10 oz., ftd.	12.00--15.00
Cookie Jar & Cover	45.00--55.00
Jug, (810)	30.00--40.00

"LOVEBIRD AND GRAPE"

COVERED REFRIGERATOR JARS page 30

Green; Decorated all over enamel, green, blue, red & yellow

Jar and Cover, 6"	12.00--15.00
Jar and Cover, 7"	14.00--20.00
Jar and Cover, 8"	20.00--30.00

ROLLED EDGE BOWLS

Green; Decorated all over enamel, green, blue, red & yellow

Rolled Edge Bowl, 6"	6.00-- 9.00
Rolled Edge Bowl, 8"	8.00--12.00
Rolled Edge Bowl, 10"	10.00--14.00

MISCELLANEOUS

Green

No. 500 Footed Sherbet	2.00-- 3.00
No. 1 Lemon Reamer	8.00--10.00
No. 15 Salt and Pepper	10.00--15.00
No. 2 Orange Reamer	10.00--14.00
No. 3 Measuring Cup	12.00--16.00
Small Coaster Cup	2.00-- 4.00
Colonial Percolator Top, 2-1/8" Filter	2.00-- 3.00
Medium Coaster Cup	2.00-- 4.00
No. 20 Ice Tea Coaster	3.00-- 5.00
Large Coaster Cup	2.00-- 4.00
No. 63 Ash Tray	5.00-- 8.00

Belmont

On page 214 of Book I we show the #164 CHECKERBOARD AND WINDMILL plates and other Checkerboard items. We had, until that time, assumed that Hazel Atlas made the whole line, since the ashtray with checkerboard border is marked HA in the bottom and is shown in HA sales catalogs. None of the other pieces were marked, however, or ever appeared in catalogs.

But with the 1974 discovery that Belmont Tumbler Company made the CHECKERBOARD AND SHIP plate, it now seems likely that Belmont was the company that made CHECKERBOARD AND WINDMILL.

Former employees of the long-defunct factory feel they "definitely" remember the windmill. And Belmont did make iridescent, we know; now, two pieces in CHECKERBOARD iridescent are known to exist, providing further evidence. The candy dish, 4½" by 4½" high, is one and the butterdish and cover is the other.

Now that we have a special book to deal with tumblers, I sure wish we could turn up an old Belmont Tumbler catalog full of surprises. Advertisements from 1930 and 1931 indicate that the company was decorating tumblers with enamel at that time. Interesting!

"ABC-STORK" page 31

Child's Plate	25.00--35.00

BELMONT SHIP PLATE

Crackled, 8"	8.00--12.00
Checkerboard, 8"	8.00--12.00
Checkerboard Candy Dish	15.00--18.00
Checkerboard Butterdish	30.00--40.00

Bryce

Although we've found and attributed many colored stems to Bryce this past year we feel the chapter is in no way complete. We do know that most every company used their blanks over and over through the years, and we do see many unidentified stem characteristics, both in color and shape, that we think are Bryce.

Don't miss the Bryce stemware in ruby and crystal on page 271 in the McKee chapter.

Until I can find some clear cut lines belonging to Bryce, made in definite colors, it's impossible to suggest prices. The colored stems we do see offered for sale range from $10 to $18 each.

Reprinted below are some 1961 items of Bryce that I thought you might be interested in. They were also made in late colors redish orange and greenish blues.

page 32, 33

Examples of Bryce stems from Book 2

EL RANCHO

Mixed colors and milk crystal

Item	Price
Ice Tea, 15 oz., ftd.	8.00--12.00
Ice Tea, ftd., 12 oz.	7.00--10.00
Sherbet, 6 oz.	6.00-- 9.00
Tumbler, ftd., 6 oz.	6.00-- 9.00
Dessert, large	5.00-- 8.00
Tumbler, 16 oz.	8.00--12.00
Tumbler, 12 oz. water	7.00--10.00
Tumbler, 8 oz. old fashioned	7.00--10.00
Tumbler, 5½ oz. juice	6.00-- 9.00
Vase	20.00--25.00
Jug, 5 pt.	50.00--65.00
Vase, Toddy	20.00--25.00
Bowl, berry	25.00--35.00
Vase, ftd., Ivy	25.00--35.00
Vase, crimped, (3 sizes)	20.00--40.00
Dessert	5.00-- 8.00

See reprint next page

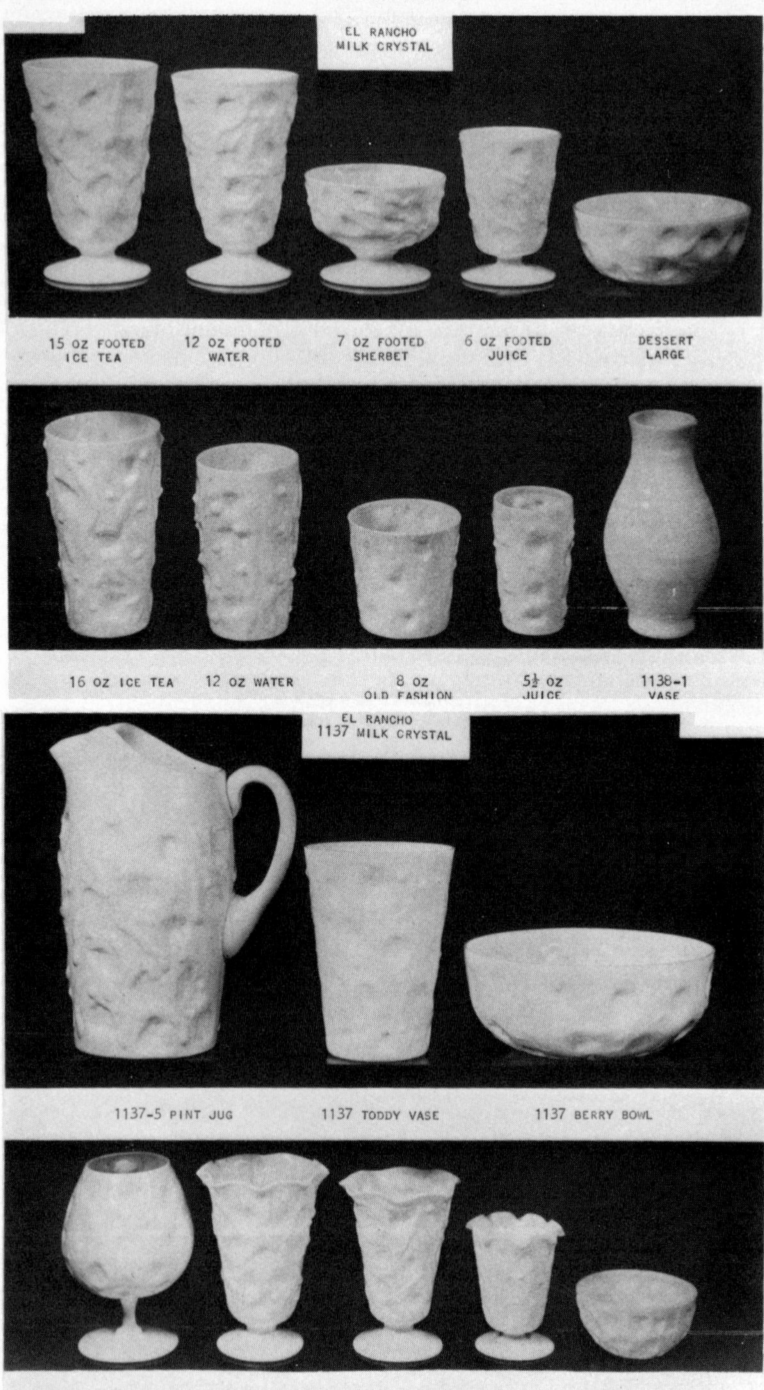
EL RANCHO
MILK CRYSTAL
15 OZ FOOTED ICE TEA
12 OZ FOOTED WATER
7 OZ FOOTED SHERBET
6 OZ FOOTED JUICE
DESSERT LARGE
16 OZ ICE TEA
12 OZ WATER
8 OZ OLD FASHION
5½ OZ JUICE
1138-1 VASE
EL RANCHO
1137 MILK CRYSTAL
1137-5 PINT JUG
1137 TODDY VASE
1137 BERRY BOWL
1137 FOOTED IVY
1137-15 CRIMPED VASE
1137-12 CRIMPED VASE
1137-6 CRIMPED VASE
1137 DESSERT

Cambridge

As you know, the Cambridge chapter in Book 2 is not comprehensive. It is only a sampling of hundreds of glass patterns made by this company. But it is a presentation of a chronology not presented in many other books available, showing good pictures, the dates of manufacture and years the various colors were introduced, and many of the important patterns of the Depression Era. For a wider survey of Cambridge Glass, you will want to consult other publications on the market, as one does with Heisey and Fostoria.

Because of many requests for the list of pieces and suggested prices, we've added to our Cambridge chapter ROSE POINT, a crystal pattern introduced to the trade November 1934. It was made for so many years it's the most often collected pattern in the Cambridge line.

If you've not already made friends with the National Cambridge Club (P.O. Box 416, Cambridge OH 43725), I suggest you do so. The organization has published two books on Cambridge glass, with value guides, and a newsletter, the "Cambridge Crystal Ball".

JUICE EXTRACTOR — page 34

1922 Vintage	20.00--25.00

SWANS — page 35

(Most, but not all will be marked with c-in-triangle)

	Crystal	Pink *Green	Ebony
3"	22.00	38.00	45.00
4½"	35.00	45.00	65.00
6½"	38.00	65.00	95.00
8½"	48.00	85.00	125.00
10"	75.00	125.00	175.00
13"	100.00	150.00	275.00

50% higher for amber, mandarin gold, blue & red. 25% higher for Crown Tuscan and white milk glass.

COMPORT—NUDE STEM — page 34

Transparent colors	50.00--75.00
Opaque colors	75.00-100.00

ANIMALS — page 35

BEWARE: The following items have all been reproduced.

Frog	20.00--30.00
Dog	20.00--30.00
Squirrel	20.00--30.00
Butterflies - 3 sizes	
No. 1 (Sometimes called Moth)	20.00--30.00
No. 2 (medium size)	25.00--32.00
No. 3 (largest size)	25.00--35.00
Birds, No. 1, 2, 3	15.00--25.00

TURKEY

Watch out for imitations. Cambridge lid is at angle to the ground. Others are parallel to the ground.

Crystal 8" high	250.00- 300.00
Pink	400.00- 500.00
Ritz Blue	800.00-1000.00

MISCELLANEOUS page 36

ETTA, Goblet	11.00--14.00
BORDEAUX, Goblet	12.00--15.00
DECANTER SET, 6 Glasses, one pint Decanter, and Tray	65.00--75.00
BLOCK OPTIC, Jug and Tumblers	60.00--75.00
VANITY SET, 3 piece	35.00--50.00
UNIQUE, Wine Set, Decanter w/6 Glasses on Tray	50.00--65.00
1924 ART GLASS	
Comport, Ebony stripped w/Silver or Gold	45.00--60.00
Candlestick, Ebony stripped w/Silver or Gold	35.00--40.00
Vase, ftd., Jade Green w/Gold encrustations	50.00--60.00
Vase Basket, Ivory w/enameled decoration	60.00--75.00
FLOWER POT and SAUCER, No. 705	20.00--25.00

MISCELLANEOUS page 37

FLOWER BLOCK*, small,	50.00-125.00
Large	110.00-200.00
CONSOLE SET	200.00-250.00
DANCING GIRL, Jar	125.00-150.00
DOLPHIN, Candlesticks, pr.	75.00-100.00
GEISHA GIRL*, Flower Holder, 12"	150.00-250.00
MARJORIE, Goblet	12.00--15.00
CLEO, Goblet	12.00--15.00
ROSE BUD, Candy Box	40.00--45.00
WEATHERFORD DESIGN *See Photo*	
Plate, 11½"	10.00--14.00
Bowl, 4½", cupped	8.00--10.00
Bowl, 8½"	12.00--15.00
Cream	7.00-- 9.00
Sugar w/lid	10.00--14.00
Comport, 7"	10.00--14.00
Candy w/Cover, low	18.00--22.00
Candy w/Cover, tall	20.00--30.00
Dresser Set	40.00--55.00
SALAD PLATE No. 596, 8"	6.00-- 8.00
SUGAR and CREAM SET, No. 620	15.00--25.00
ASHTRAY, No. 618	25.00--30.00
COMPACT, No. 680	12.00--16.00

****Color and style affect price here***

MISCELLANEOUS page 38

NIGHT SET, Jug w/Cover, Tumbler and Tray	35.00--45.00
BOOKENDS	35.00--45.00
DESK SET	40.00--60.00
CHEESE DISH and Cover	25.00--35.00
BOWL and CANDLESTICKS, 4-foot (*Note the error in the ad*))	40.00--45.00
SQUARE DISHES	8.00--12.00
BOWL and COVER	20.00--30.00
RELISH, 5 compartment (*Note the error in the ad*)	15.00--20.00
BLOWN STEMWARE, GOBLET, Tumbler, Sundae	9.00--14.00
SALTEERS AND PEPPERETTES, ea.	7.00--10.00
AQUARIA, 11"x7"x6"	16.00--20.00
AQUARIA OR FTD. VASE, 8"	16.00--20.00

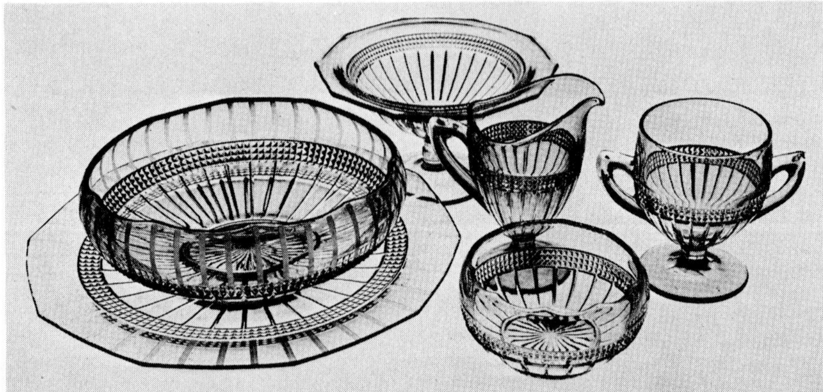

WEATHERFORD DESIGN

AREO OPTIC — page 39

Ice Tea Set	45.00--60.00

HANDY CONDIMENT SERVICE

Cream, Sugar, Shakers, Tray	30.00--40.00

CANDY BOX W/COVER

No. 864, etched	25.00--35.00

STEMWARE

Tumbler, 9 oz.	6.00-- 9.00
Goblet, 8 oz.	9.00--12.00
Goblet, soda, 10 oz.	9.00--12.00
Sherbet, tall	7.00--10.00

SALAD SET

No. 971, 972, 698, 8 pieces	75.00--85.00

CLEO ETCHED DECAGON DINNERWARE

Plate, salad, 7½"	6.00-- 8.00
Cup	5.00-- 8.00
Saucer	3.00-- 4.00
Cream	10.00--13.00
Sugar	10.00--13.00
Cake or Sandwich Tray w/handle	18.00--24.00
Cream Soup w/Saucer	12.00--16.00
Pickle, 9"	9.00--12.00
Cereal, 6"	6.00-- 8.00
Bowl, vegetable, oval, 9½"	16.00--22.00
Platter, 11½"	15.00--20.00
Bowl, serving w/handles, 8½"	14.00--18.00
Mayonnaise Set, 3 piece	25.00--30.00

RELISH SET — page 40

5 Pieces, serving Dish, 4 individual Dishes	25.00--30.00

LORNA ETCHING

Plate, salad, 8½"	7.00-- 9.00
Cup and Saucer	10.00--12.00
Cream	10.00--14.00
Sugar	10.00--14.00
Cream Soup w/Saucer	10.00--14.00
Bon-Bon, 2 hdld., 6¼"	10.00--12.00
Fruit, 5½"	5.00-- 7.00
Bowl, vegetable, oval, 9½"	20.00--25.00
Relish, 2 part, 11"	12.00--16.00
Goblet, 9 oz.	20.00--24.00
Wine, 2½ oz.	22.00--26.00
Sherbet, low, 6 oz.	10.00--14.00
Sherbet, tall, 6 oz.	16.00--20.00
Tumbler, ftd., 12 oz.	14.00--18.00
Tumbler, ftd., 10 oz.	12.00--16.00
Tumbler, ftd., 5 oz.	11.00--14.00
Cocktail, 3 oz.	22.00--24.00
Claret, 4½ oz.	22.00--26.00

AQUARIUM

No. 736 Bird etching	55.00--75.00

CIGARETTE CASE

Etched w/Hunting Dog	35.00--45.00

PINCH DECANTER SET

Jug w/6 Tumblers	65.00--85.00

PLATES

The CLEO and No. 732 Etchings are somewhat less desirable than the floral types and the DECAGON and round shapes are also less desirable. They were made in the same range of pieces.

The shape shown for the APPLE BLOSSOM and GLORIA etchings is the No. 3400 line, making these pieces a little more desirable. There is probably less than $1 difference per piece.

CLEO, etched	7.00--10.00
APPLE BLOSSOM, etched (see LORNA)	8.00--11.00
No. 732, etched (see CLEO)	7.00--10.00
GLORIA, etched (see LORNA)	7.00--10.00

SWEET POTATO — page 41

Vase	15.00--20.00

MARTHA WASHINGTON Glassware

Plate, salad, 8¼"	8.00--14.00
Plate, bread and butter, 6¼"	5.00-- 9.00
Cup and Saucer	10.00--16.00
Sugar and Cream	15.00--30.00
Fruit, 5¼"	5.00-- 8.00
Comport, 6"	10.00--20.00
Bowl, hdld., ftd., 9½"	25.00--45.00
Bowl, 9"	20.00--30.00

Plate, sandwich, 11½"	22.00--30.00
Tumbler, ftd., 5 oz.	8.00--16.00
Tumbler, ftd., 8 oz.	8.00--16.00
Tumbler, ftd., 10 oz.	10.00--20.00
Goblet, 9 oz.	15.00--25.00
Goblet, 10 oz.	15.00--25.00
Sherbet, tall, 7 oz.	12.00--20.00
Candy dish w/Cover 3 compartment, 7½"	35.00--55.00

MOUNT VERNON Glassware

Relish, 2 hdld., 4 compartment, 8½"	15.00--30.00
Comport, 2 hdld., 5½"	20.00--35.00

IMPERIAL HUNT

Goblet, 18 oz.	20.00--30.00
Plate, sandwich, 11½"	25.00--35.00

No. 3078 STEMWARE Line page 42

Decanter	30.00--45.00
Jug	25.00--40.00
Tumbler, 15 oz.	9.00--12.00
Tumbler, 12 oz.	8.00--10.00
Tumbler, 5 oz.	7.00-- 9.00
Tumbler, 2½ oz.	7.00-- 9.00

EVERGLADES

Creamer	12.00--30.00
Sugar	12.00--30.00
Plate, 8"	8.00--15.00
Sherbet	8.00--22.00

NARCISSUS BULB VASE

Vase, bulb	15.00--25.00

NAUTILUS WINE SET

Decanter, 28 oz.	25.00--50.00
Wine, 2 oz.	6.00-- 9.00

FLOATING ROSE BOWL

Vase	14.00--20.00

No. 3122 STEMWARE

Plain	10.00--15.00
Etched	12.00--18.00

No. 1402 TALLY HO LINE

Pitcher tankard, 74 oz.	30.00--50.00
Stein, hdld., 12 oz.	15.00--25.00

CAPRICE page 43

	Crystal	*Moonlight Blue*
Plate, dinner, 9½"	20.00--25.00	65.00--70.00
Plate, salad, 7½"	8.00--10.00	12.00--14.00
Plate, salad, 8½"	10.00--12.00	10.00--18.00
Plate, 6½"	5.00-- 6.00	10.00--12.00
Plate, 11½", 4 ftd.	15.00--17.00	20.00--22.00
Plate, torte, 14", 4 ftd.	16.00--18.00	22.00--26.00
Plate, torte, 16"	18.00--20.00	28.00--32.00
Plate, cake, ftd., 13"	40.00--45.00	
Plate, cabaret, 4 ftd., 11"	15.00--17.00	20.00--22.00
Plate, cabaret, 4 ftd., 14"	16.00--18.00	22.00--26.00
Plate, coaster, 3½"	4.00-- 5.00	12.00--14.00
Cup	10.00--12.00	30.00--35.00
Saucer	2.00-- 3.00	4.00-- 5.00
Cream, ind.	7.00-- 8.00	10.00--12.00
Cream	10.00--12.00	14.00--16.00
Sugar, ind.	7.00-- 8.00	10.00--12.00
Sugar	10.00--12.00	14.00--16.00
Tray, 6"	8.00--10.00	12.00--14.00
Tray, 9"	10.00--12.00	16.00--18.00
Bowl, belled, 4 ftd., 10½"	18.00--20.00	30.00--35.00
Bowl, belled, 4 ftd., 12½"	20.00--22.00	35.00--40.00
Bowl, crimped, 4 ftd., 10½"	18.00--20.00	30.00--35.00
Bowl, crimped, 4 ftd., 12½"	20.00--22.00	35.00--40.00
Bowl, console, oval, 11"	16.00--18.00	30.00--35.00
Bowl, shallow, 4 ftd., 11½"	16.00--18.00	35.00--40.00
Bowl, shallow, 4 ftd., 13½"	18.00--20.00	40.00--45.00

	Crystal	*Moonlight Blue*
Jug, Daulton, 9 oz.	200.00-250.00	375.00-400.00
Jug, 80 oz.	50.00--55.00	100.00-125.00
Jug, 32 oz.	45.00--50.00	125.00-135.00
Tumbler, table, 9 oz.	10.00--12.00	26.00--28.00
Tumbler, ice tea	11.00--13.00	28.00--30.00
Tumbler, 2 oz.	7.00-- 8.00	20.00--22.00
Tumbler, 5 oz.	8.00--10.00	18.00--20.00
Tumbler, 12 oz.	10.00--12.00	28.00--30.00
Tumbler, ftd., 3 oz.	12.00--15.00	16.00--18.00
Tumbler, ftd., 5 oz.	8.00--10.00	14.00--16.00
Tumbler, ftd., 10 oz.	10.00--12.00	16.00--18.00
Tumbler, ftd., 12 oz.	10.00--12.00	20.00--22.00
Goblet, 9 oz.	14.00--16.00	25.00--30.00
Goblet, cocktail, 3 oz.	14.00--16.00	22.00--25.00
Goblet, wine, 2½ oz.	16.00--18.00	30.00--35.00
Goblet, claret, 4½ oz.	18.00--20.00	35.00--40.00
Sherbet, tall, 6 oz.	14.00--16.00	28.00--30.00
Sherbet, low, 6 oz.	15.00--17.00	30.00--32.00
Fruit Cocktail or Sea Food, 4½ oz.	18.00--20.00	35.00--40.00
Salt and Pepper	10.00--12.00	20.00--22.00
Salt and Pepper, ind., (2 styles)	14:00--16.00	18.00--20.00
Salt and Pepper Set: 3 pc.	25.00--30.00	45.00--50.00
Oil and Vinegar Set: 3 pc., (tilt)	30.00--35.00	50.00--60.00
Oil, 3 oz.	20.00--25.00	35.00--40.00
Oil, 5 oz.	25.00--30.00	40.00--45.00
Celery, oblong, 12"	20.00--25.00	30.00--35.00
Pickle, 9"	10.00--12.00	16.00--18.00
Relish, 2 part, 5½"	6.00-- 9.00	12.00--14.00
Relish, 2 part, 6½"	8.00--10.00	14.00--16.00
Relish, cloverleaf, 6"	12.00--14.00	18.00--20.00
Relish, 3 compt., 8½"	12.00--14.00	18.00--20.00
Relish, 3 compt., 11½"	15.00--20.00	
Nut Dish, 2½"	10.00--12.00	15.00--17.00
Almond Dish, 4 ftd., 2"	5.00-- 7.00	15.00--17.00
Salad Dressing Set: 3 pc.	16.00--18.00	25.00--30.00
Dish, club, 6½"	18.00--20.00	25.00--30.00
Dish, heart, 6½"	18.00--20.00	25.00--30.00
Dish, diamond, 6½"	18.00--20.00	25.00--30.00
Dish, spade, 6½"	18.00--20.00	25.00--30.00
Mustard and Cover	30.00--35.00	55.00--60.00
Marmalade and Cover	32.00--37.00	60.00--65.00
Comport, low, 7"	10.00--12.00	18.00--20.00
Comport, low, 8"	10.00--12.00	16.00--18.00
Comport, tall, 7"	10.00--12.00	34.00--36.00
Bon Bon, low ftd., 6"	8.00--10.00	16.00--18.00
Bon Bon, 2 hdld., sq., 6"	8.00--10.00	16.00--18.00
Jelly, 2 hdld., 5"	6.00-- 8.00	8.00--10.00
Candy Box and Cover, 3 ftd., 6"	20.00--25.00	35.00--40.00
Candy Box and Cover, 2 pt., 6"	30.00--35.00	45.00--50.00
Candy Box and Cover, tab hdld., 6"	20.00--25.00	35.00--40.00
Ice Bucket	20.00--25.00	80.00--85.00
Decanter and Stopper	75.00--80.00	100.00-125.00
Ash Tray, 3"	6.00-- 8.00	14.00--16.00
Ash Tray, 4"	6.00-- 8.00	14.00--16.00
Ash Tray, 5"	6.00-- 8.00	16.00--18.00
Ash Tray, triangle, 3"	6.00-- 8.00	8.00--10.00
Ash Tray, triangle, 4½"	8.00--10.00	12.00--14.00
Cigarette Holder, triangle, 3" x 3"	18.00--20.00	18.00--20.00
Cigarette Holder, triangle, 2" x 2½"	12.00--14.00	16.00--18.00
Cigarette Box and Cover, 3½" x 2½"	18.00--20.00	35.00--40.00
Cigarette Box and Cover, 4½" x 3½"	20.00--22.00	30.00--35.00
Candlestick, 2½" single	8.00--10.00	16.00--18.00
Candleholder, 3 candle	14.00--16.00	20.00--22.00
Candleholder w/Prism, 7"	14.00--16.00	22.00--24.00

SEA SHELL

Highest price is for rare colors and all opaque glass.

Bowl, ftd.	85.00-150.00
Candleholders, pr.	95.00-175.00

ROSE POINT

Plate, dinner, 10½"	65.00--85.00
Plate, salad, 8"	20.00--25.00
Plate, bread and butter, 6½"	12.00--16.00
Plate, 4 ftd., 12"	30.00--40.00
Plate, torte, 4 ftd., 13"	40.00--50.00
Plate, 2 hdld., 13½"	40.00--50.00
Plate, 14"	45.00--55.00
Plate, rolled edge, 14"	45.00--55.00
Plate, 2 hdld., 6"	12.00--15.00
Plate, bon bon, ftd., 2 hdld., 8"	15.00--20.00
Cup and Saucer	35.00--40.00
Cream	18.00--22.00
Cream, ind.	20.00--22.00
Sugar	18.00--22.00
Sugar, ind.	20.00--22.00
Cream and Sugar on Tray	50.00--60.00
Cream and Sugar on Tray, ind.	50.00--60.00
Cream and Sugar Set (Gadroon Blank)	35.00--45.00
Bowl, flrd., 4 ftd., 10"	40.00--50.00
Bowl, ftd., hdld., 11½"	45.00--55.00
Bowl, flrd., 4 ftd., 12"	50.00--60.00
Bowl, 2 hdld., 11"	45.00--55.00
Bowl, oval, 4 ftd., 12"	60.00--70.00
Bowl, ftd., hdld., 7"	25.00--30.00
Bowl, fancy edge, 4 ftd., 11"	50.00--60.00
Bowl, fancy edge, flrd., ftd., 12"	65.00--75.00
Bowl, fancy edge, oblong, 4 ftd., 12"	65.00--75.00
Jug, Daulton, 80 oz.	200.00-250.00
Jug, ball, 80 oz.	150.00-180.00
Jug, 76 oz.	150.00-180.00
Jug, 32 oz.	175.00-225.00
Jug, martini, 32 oz.	1000.00-1200.00
Tumbler, 5 oz.	25.00--30.00
Tumbler, 13 oz.	35.00--40.00

3121 Blank

Tumbler, ftd., 5 oz.	28.00--32.00
Tumbler, ftd., 10 oz.	25.00--28.00
Tumbler, ice tea, ftd., 12 oz.	27.00--30.00
Goblet, 10 oz.	28.00--32.00
Goblet, cocktail, 3 oz.	35.00--40.00
Sherbet, tall, 6 oz.	20.00--25.00
Sherbet, low, 6 oz.	16.00--20.00
Goblet, cafe parfait, 5 oz.	45.00--55.00
Goblet, oyster cocktail, 4½ oz.	25.00--28.00
Goblet, claret, 4½ oz.	40.00--45.00
Goblet, wine, 3½ oz.	45.00--55.00
Goblet, cordial, 1 oz.	60.00--70.00

3500 Blank

Tumbler, ftd., 5 oz.	18.00--22.00
Tumbler, ftd., 10 oz.	18.00--20.00
Tumbler, ftd., 12 oz.	22.00--25.00
Goblet, 10 oz.	20.00--25.00
Goblet, claret, 4½ oz.	25.00--30.00
Goblet, cocktail, 3 oz.	25.00--28.00
Goblet, cocktail (plain stem) 4 oz.	20.00--24.00
Sherbet, tall, 7 oz.	18.00--20.00
Sherbet, low, 7 oz.	15.00--18.00
Goblet, oyster cocktail, 4½ oz.	20.00--24.00
Goblet, wine, 2½ oz.	30.00--35.00
Goblet, cordial, 1 oz.	40.00--45.00
Goblet, sherry, 2 oz.	35.00--40.00
Goblet, cafe parfait, 5 oz.	35.00--40.00
Goblet, 2 pc. cocktail Icer	50.00--60.00
Comport, blown, (2 styles) 5-3/8"	35.00--45.00
Comport, (2 styles) 5" x 5½"	35.00--45.00
Mayonnaise Set: 2 pc., ftd.	30.00--40.00
Mayonnaise Set: 3 pc.	55.00--60.00
Mayonnaise Set: 4 pc., 2 section bowl, 2 spoons, Plate underliner	60.00--70.00
Oil, 6 oz.	120.00-130.00
Relish or Pickle, 7"	22.00--28.00
Relish, 2 part, 7"	24.00--30.00
Relish or Celery, 5 part, 12"	70.00--75.00
Relish or Celery, 3 part, 9"	70.00--75.00
Relish or Celery, 3 part, 12"	70.00--75.00
Relish, (odd shape) 3 part, 8"	70.00--75.00
Relish, 2 part, 6"	35.00--40.00
Pickle, 9½"	35.00--40.00
Candy Box and Cover	40.00--50.00
Candy Box and Cover, blown, ftd., 5-3/8"	50.00--65.00
Candy Box and Cover, 3 part, 8"	60.00--70.00
Nite Set: 2 pc.	75.00--85.00
Cocktail Shaker, 32 oz.	300.00-400.00
Decanter, ftd., 28 oz.	200.00-300.00
Butter and Cover	145.00-160.00
Salt and Pepper	45.00--55.00
Nut Cup, 4 ftd., 3"	20.00--30.00
Candlestick, (3900) 5"	25.00--30.00
Candlestick, (646) 5"	25.00--30.00
Candlestick, (647) 2 lite, 6"	40.00--45.00
Candlestick, (3900) 2 lite, 6"	40.00--45.00
Candlestick, (1338) 3 lite, 6"	50.00--60.00
Candlestick, (3900) 3 lite, 6"	50.00--60.00
Epergne (3900/75)	80.00-100.00
Vase, cornucopia, 10"	80.00--90.00
Vase, bud, 10"	26.00--30.00
Vase, ftd., (2 styles) 11"	45.00--65.00
Vase, ftd., 13"	70.00--80.00
Vase, ftd., 12"	40.00--55.00
Vase, ftd., 9"	35.00--45.00
Vase, ftd., 8"	30.00--40.00
Vase, globe, 5"	28.00--34.00
Hurricane Lamps (3 styles)	80.00-100.00
Cigarette Box and Cover	40.00--50.00
Ash Tray, 2½"	18.00--24.00
Ash Tray Set: 5 pc. in holder	90.00-110.00

The Cambridge Glass Company

Rose Point

3400/52
5 in. Butter & Cover

3400/71
3 in. 4 Ftd. Nut Cup

3400/91
8 in. 3 part Relish

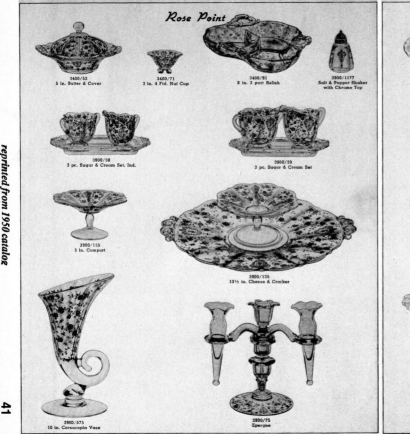

3900/1177
Salt & Pepper Shaker
with Chrome Top

3900/38
3 pc. Sugar & Cream Set, Ind.

3900/39
3 pc. Sugar & Cream Set

3900/135
5 in. Comport

3900/135
13½ in. Cheese & Cracker

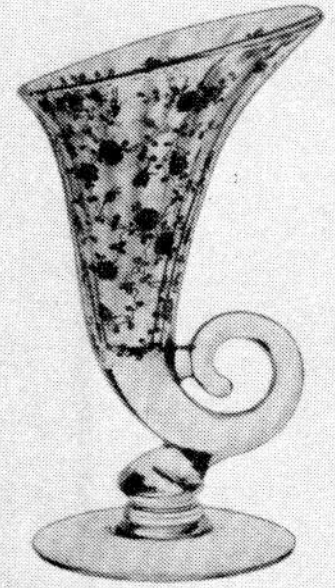

3900/575
10 in. Cornucopia Vase

3900/75
Epergne

The Cambridge Glass Company

Rose Point

3900/17
Cup & Saucer

3900/19
2 pc. Mayonnaise Set

390/20
6½ in. Bread & Butter Plate

3900/22
8 in. Salad Plate

3900/24
10½ in. Dinner Plate

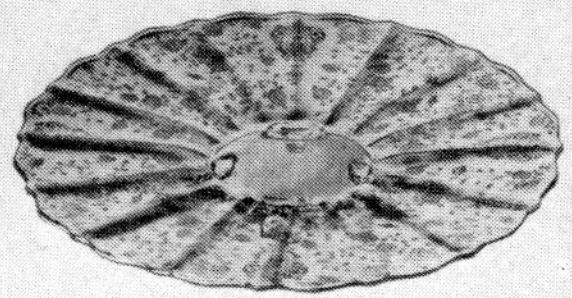

3900/26
12 in. 4 Ftd. Plate

3900/28
11½ in. Ftd. Bowl

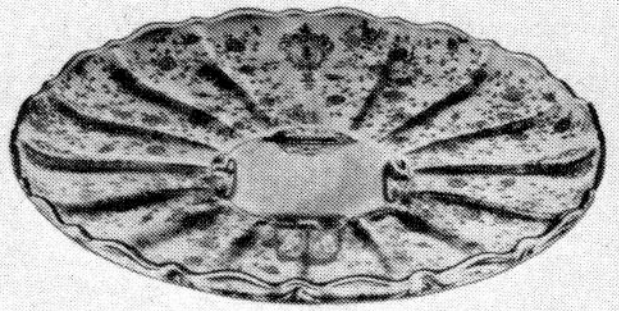

3900/33
13 in. 4 Ftd. Torte Plate, R. E.

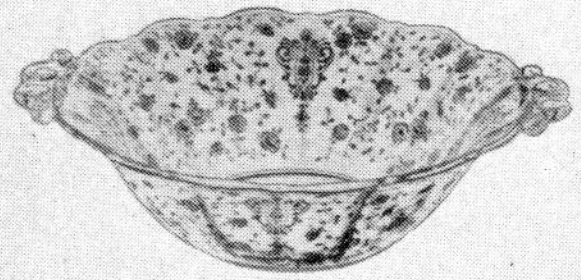

3900/34
11 in. 2 Handled Bowl

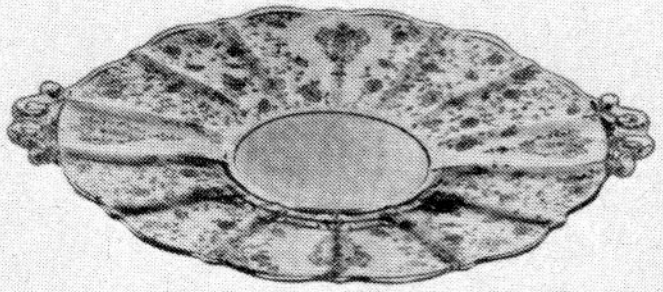

3900/35
13½ in. 2 Handled Cake Plate

3900/40
Ind. Sugar & Cream

3900/41
Sugar & Cream

The Cambridge Glass Company

Rose Point

3900/54
10 in. 4 Ftd. Bowl, flared

3900/67
5 in. Candlestick

3900/62
12 in. Ftd. Bowl, flared

3900/65
12 in. 4 Ftd. Oval Bowl

3900/72
6 in. 2 lite Candlestick

3900/111
4 pc. Mayonnaise Set.

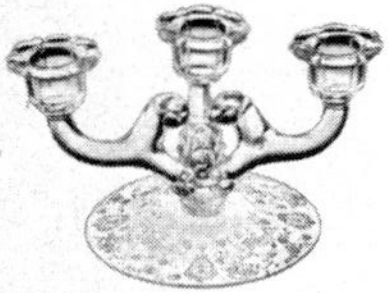

3900/74
6 in. 3 lite Candlestick

3900/100
6 oz. Oil, g. s.

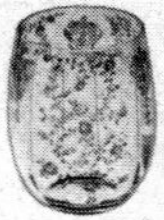

3900/115
13 oz. Tumbler

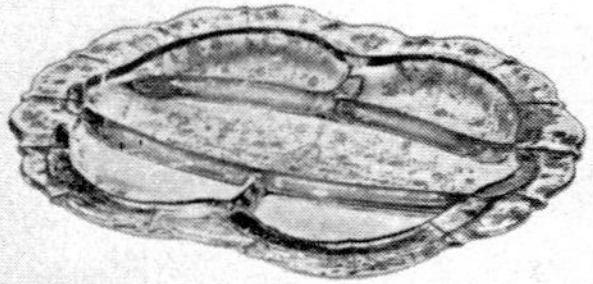

3900/120
12 in. 5 part Celery & Relish

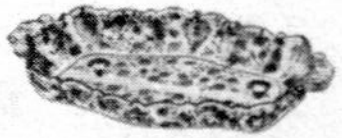

3900/123
7 in. Relish or Pickle

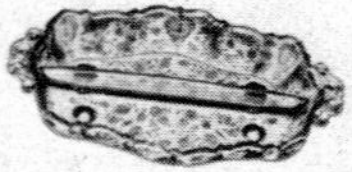

3900/124
7 in. 2 part Relish

The Cambridge Glass Company

Rose Point

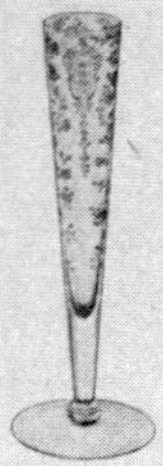

274
10 in. Bud Flower Holder

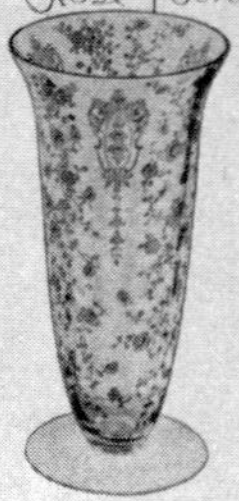

278
11 in Ftd. Flower Holder

279
13 in. Ftd. Flower Holder

1238
12 in. Ftd. Flower Holder

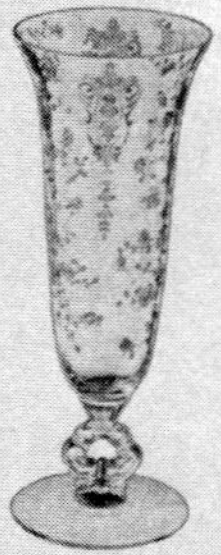

1237
9 in. Ftd. Flower Holder

1309
5 in. Globe Flower Holder

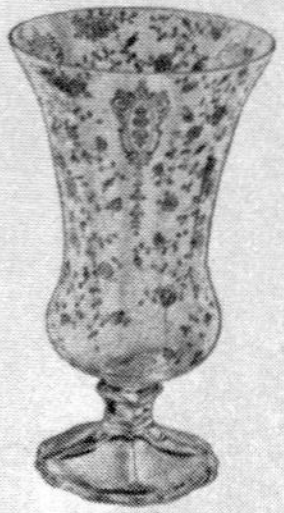

1299
11 in Ftd. Flower Holder

1603

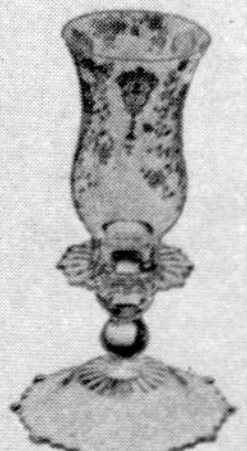

1617
Hurricane Lamp

6004
6 in. Ftd. Flower Holder

6004
8 in. Ftd. Flower Holder

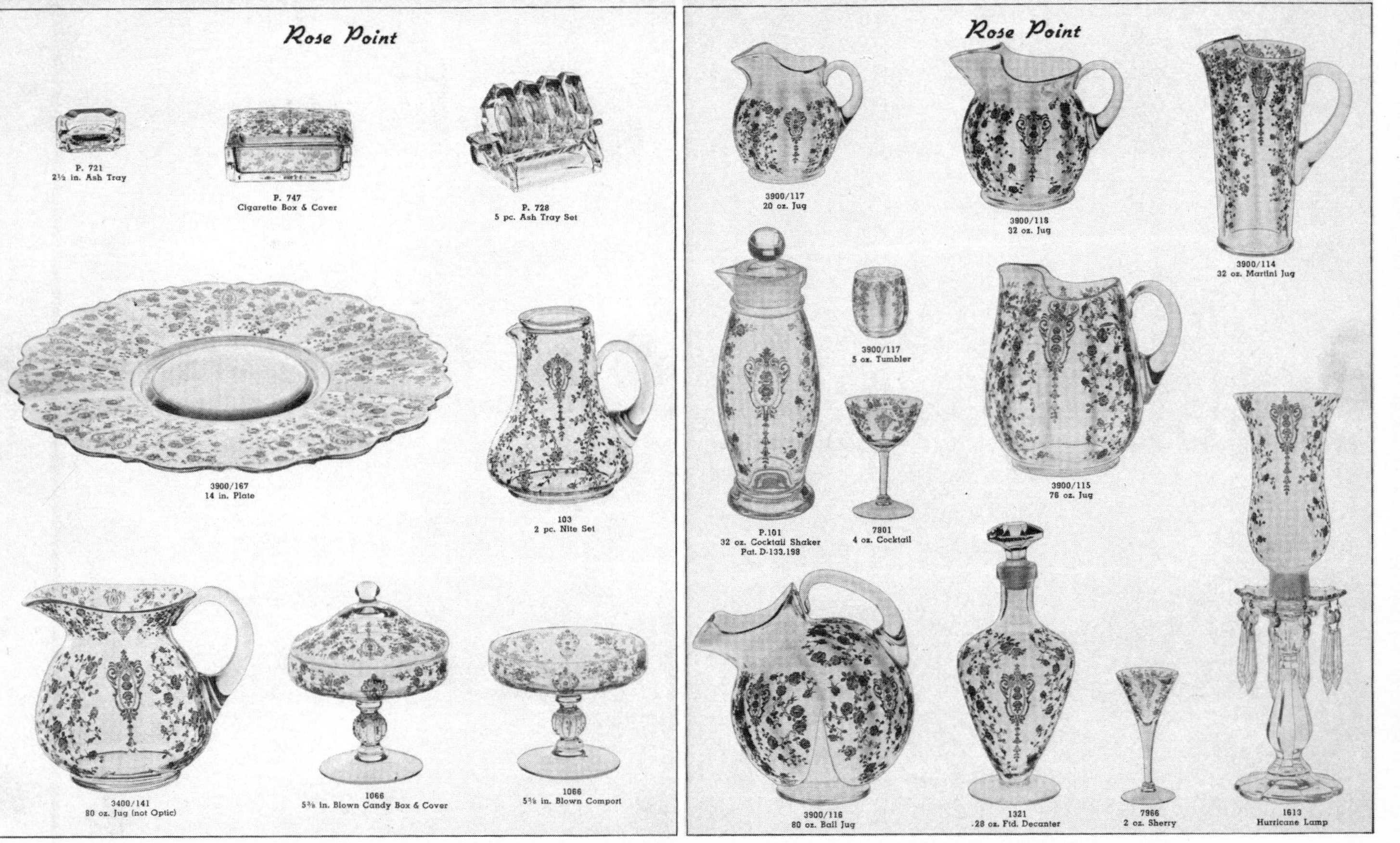
The Cambridge Glass Company
Rose Point
P. 721
2½ in. Ash Tray
P. 747
Cigarette Box & Cover
P. 728
5 pc. Ash Tray Set
3900/167
14 in. Plate
103
2 pc. Nite Set
3400/141
80 oz. Jug (not Optic)
1066
5⅜ in. Blown Candy Box & Cover
1066
5⅜ in. Blown Comport
The Cambridge Glass Company
Rose Point
3900/117
20 oz. Jug
3900/118
32 oz. Jug
3900/114
32 oz. Martini Jug
P.101
32 oz. Cocktail Shaker
Pat. D-133,198
3900/117
5 oz. Tumbler
7801
4 oz. Cocktail
3900/115
76 oz. Jug
3900/116
80 oz. Ball Jug
1321
28 oz. Ftd. Decanter
7966
2 oz. Sherry
1613
Hurricane Lamp

The Cambridge Glass Company

Rose Point

3500
10 oz. Goblet

3500
7 oz. Tall Sherbet

3500
3 oz. Cocktail

3500
12 oz. Ftd. Ice Tea

3500
10 oz. Ftd. Tumbler

3500
7 oz. Low Sherbet

3500
4½ oz. Oyster Cocktail

3500
4½ oz. Claret

3500

3500

3500

3500

3500/101

The Cambridge Glass Company

Rose Point

3900/68
5 in. Candlestick

3400/48
11 in. 4 Ftd. Bowl,
Fancy edge

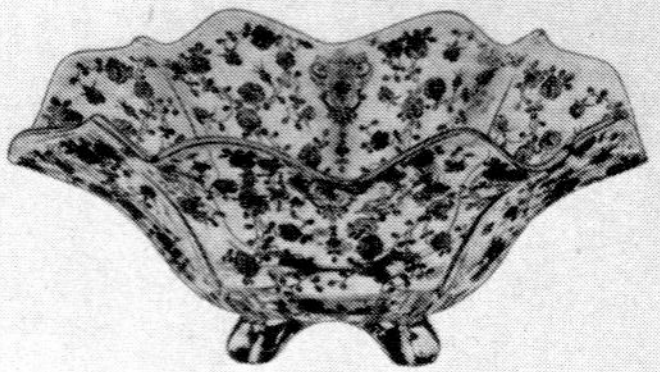

646
5 in. Candlestick

3400/160
12 in. 4 Ftd. Bowl, Oblong

647
6 in. 2 lite Candlestick

1338

3400/4
12 in. 4 Ftd. Bowl, Flared

reprinted from 1950 catalog

reprinted from 1950 catalog

Central

Alright, "FRANCES" lovers. Can you guess the news? Finally I turned up a couple of old advertisements for this elusive glass company. One was stemware and (double gasp) the other was our beloved "FRANCES" pattern, heretofore unknown. (See reprint following page). I was in a library at the time and they all thought I'd gone berserk for sure.

I'd give anything to find just ONE Central catalog now. What further treasures might it hold?

OLD CENTRAL SPIRAL	**page 44**
Candlestick, 4", 8"	15.00--25.00
"MEMPHIS"	
Console Set	40.00--60.00
"HESTER"	**page 45**
Goblet	12.00--15.00
Wine	10.00--12.00
Tumbler	12.00--14.00

"VENINGA"	
Goblet	12.00--15.00
"SHEILA"	
Goblet	12.00--15.00
"DAVID"	
Tumbler	12.00--15.00
"ZARICOR"	
Console Set	50.00--75.00

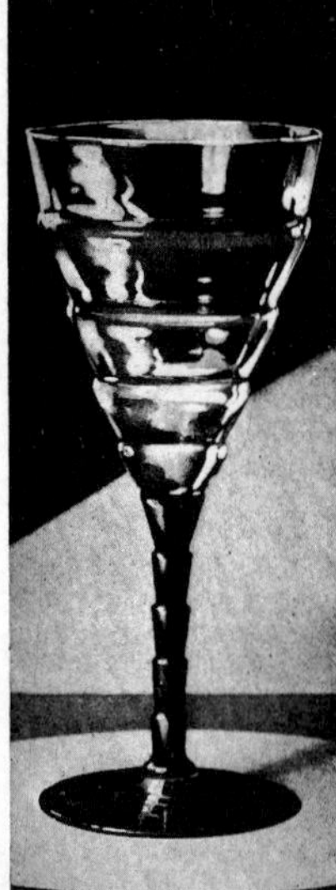

STEMWARE IN THE MODERN MANNER

Smart beyond comparison is this new optic stemware in black and crystal contrast. Crystal bowl with resonant rings leading into stem and base of ebony black—a striking play of light and shadow that adds beauty to any table setting.

What's most surprising, however, is the fact that this stemware-goblets, high and low footed sherbets, wines, cocktails, finger bowls and fruit salads, footed tumblers, may be had at attractive prices, which naturally means a real opportunity for increased sales.

CENTRAL GLASS WORKS
WHEELING, WEST VIRGINIA

REPRESENTATIVES:

New York City, A. P. Doctor, 1107 Broadway
Philadelphia, Wm. C. Byrnes, 9th and Chestnut
Chicago, Midwest, James Hutchison
New England, L. A. Bennett, 75 Hancock St., Boston
Himmelstern Bros., San Francisco, Los Angeles Seattle

SEE OUR DISPLAY at the PITTSBURGH SHOW, ROOM 872, FORT PITT HOTEL

"MODERNE" reprinted from a 1929 trade catalog

The Old Central Quality In New Modernistic Designs

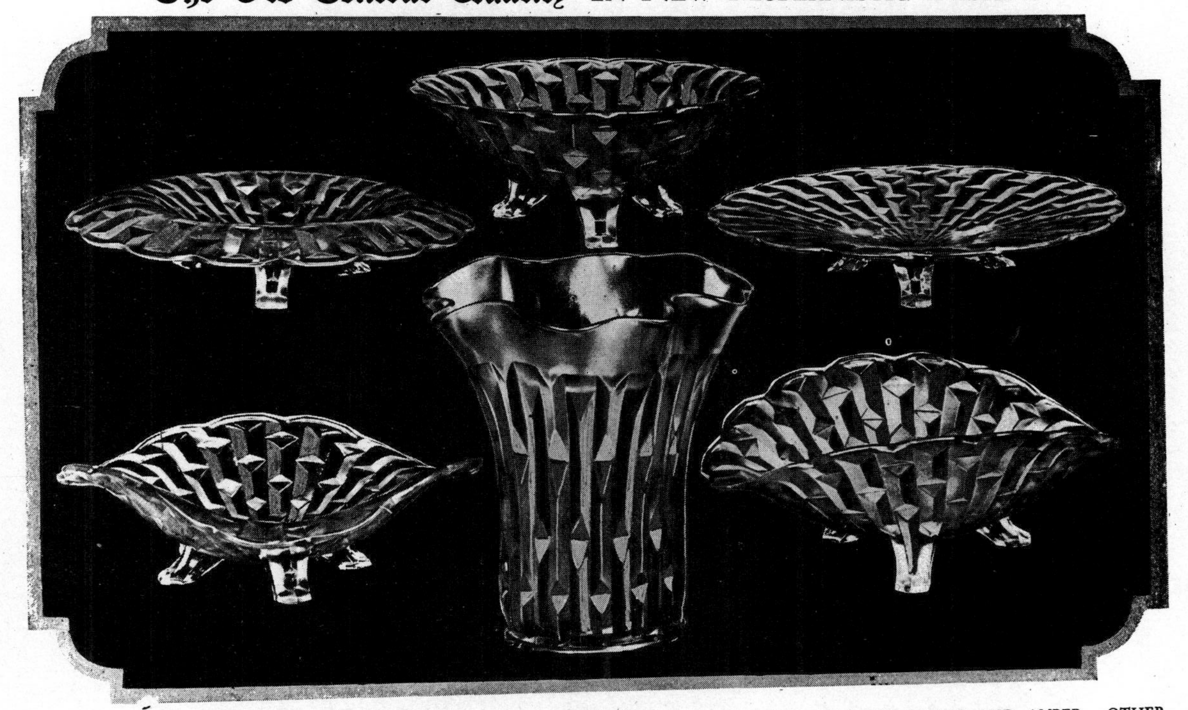

WE HAVE REPRODUCED A FEW ITEMS OF OUR 2010 LINE—MADE IN PLEASING SHADES OF ROSE, GREEN AND AMBER. OTHER ITEMS IN THIS AND OUR VARIOUS LINES OF BLOWN AND PRESSED WARE IN EXCLUSIVE SHAPES AND DESIGNS WILL BE ON DISPLAY IN PITTSBURGH, PA., AT WM. PENN HOTEL, ROOM 811, JAN. 7TH TO 19TH INCLUSIVE.

ROBERT L. HUTCHISON

WALTER F. JONES

Central Glass Works, Wheeling, W. Va.

"FRANCES" reprinted from a 1928 trade catalog

MODERNE

Goblet	12.00--15.00

"FRANCES"

Crystal, amber, green, pink, orchid, black

Vase, 7¾", 8¼", 9"	12.00--18.00
Bowl, 3 legs, 11¼"	10.00--14.00
Bowl, low, rolled, 3 legs, 11¾"	10.00--14.00
Bowl, 3 legs, elongated, 11"	10.00--14.00
Bowl, 3 legs, triangular, 10"	10.00--14.00
Bowl, berry, 9"	10.00--14.00
Bowl, berry, 4½", 5"	4.00-- 6.00
Plate, cake, 3 legs, 12"	10.00--14.00
Plate, sandwich, 12"	12.00--15.00
Cream, 5½"	15.00--20.00
Sugar, 4½"	15.00--20.00
Sandwich Server, center hdld., 10½"	15.00--20.00
Jug, ftd., 8½"	50.00--60.00
Tumbler, 4"	12.00--15.00
Goblet, 6½"	15.00--20.00
*Candy Dish	25.00--35.00
Candlesticks, pr.	25.00--30.00

**canary, satin finish (vaseline)*

Photo Courtesy Bill Newbound

"FRANCES"
cream, sugar, bowl 11¼", sandwich plate 12", bowl 11¾"

"FRANCES"

Photo by George Sionakides

Consolidated

Last year I told you about an old company catalog I found in hand painted colors that faded away upon photographing for publication.

Well, I've located another one for this year, and this you'll just have to see! Parts of it may not photo too well, but the catalog was made in 1931 and that was a long time ago.

Remember that most of those old vases thought to be Phoenix are in fact Consolidated.

MARTELE MODERNIZER page 46

Light Fixture	75.00-100.00

MARTELE page 47

Fruit and Leaf, Bird and Flower and Flower

MARTELE colors are Light Green, Russet, Pink, Orchid, Sepia, Jade Green, amethyst and blue.

The following listing was taken from a company catalog.

Plate, 6"	4.00-- 6.00
Plate, 8¼"	16.00--20.00
Plate, 12"	20.00--30.00
Plate, 13"	30.00--40.00
Bowl, fruit flrd.	30.00--40.00
Bowl, finger	6.00-- 8.00
Sandwich Tray, pear shape	15.00--18.00
Sundae	6.00-- 9.00
Cocktail, ftd., (cone shaped)	10.00--15.00
Ice Tea, ftd.	12.00--16.00
Goblet, 9 oz.	16.00--20.00
Jug, ½ gal., ftd.	75.00-100.00
Puff Box, 4", 5", 7"	30.00--50.00
Oval Box and Cover	35.00--55.00
Comport (9" ftd. bowl)	40.00--60.00
Vase, rnd.,	55.00--75.00
Vase, oblong	55.00--75.00
Vase, fan shape, 6"	25.00--35.00
Candlestick, low (pr.)	25.00--35.00
Candlestick, high (pr.)	50.00--60.00
Cigarette Box and Cover	35.00--55.00
Lamp	150.00-200.00
Ash Tray, triangle	15.00--25.00

THE MARTELE LINE (cont.)

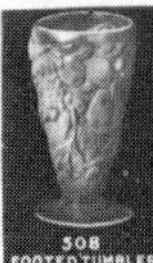

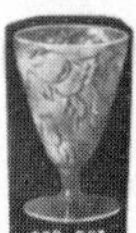

MARTELE

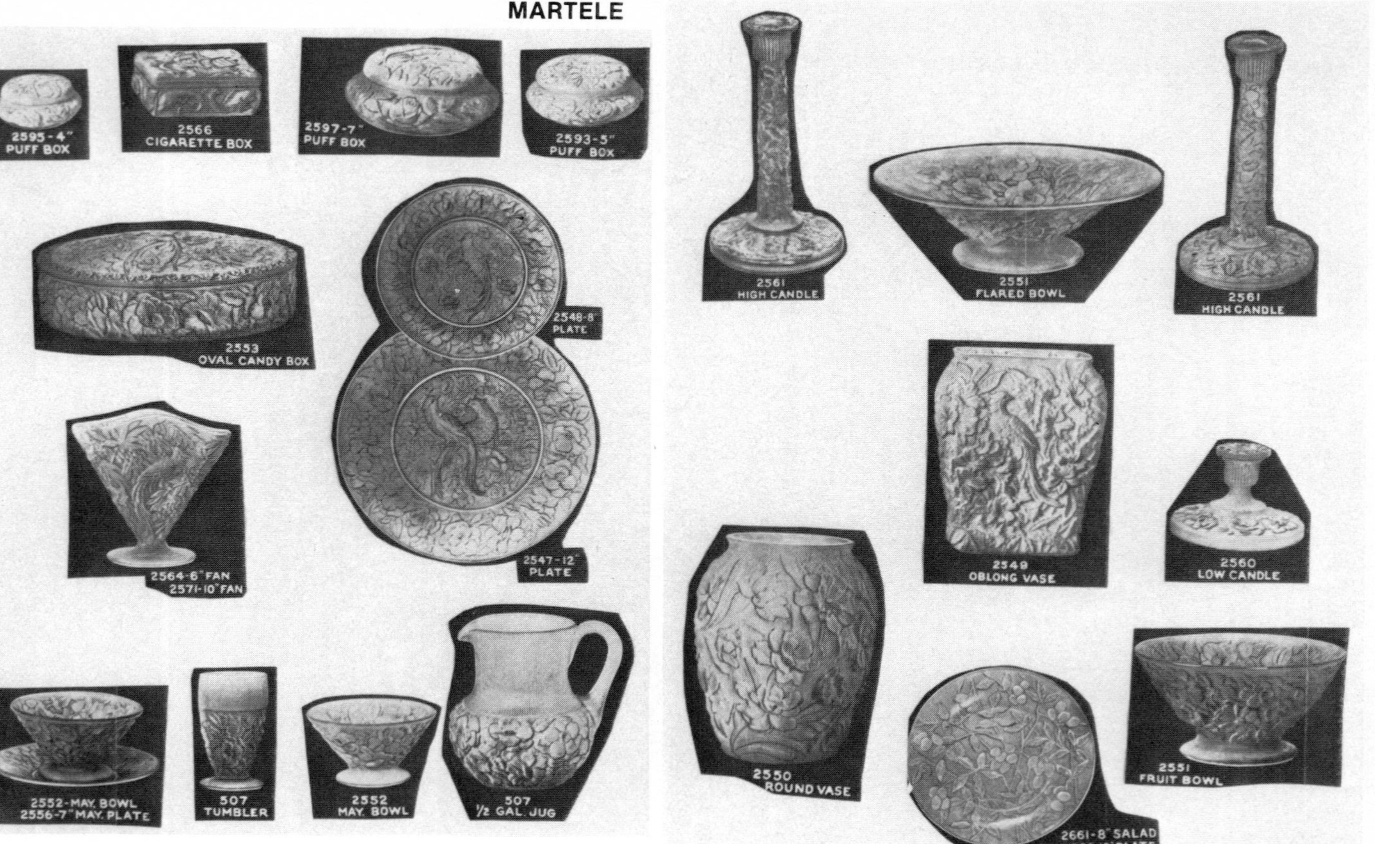

2595-4" PUFF BOX
2566 CIGARETTE BOX
2597-7" PUFF BOX
2593-5" PUFF BOX
2553 OVAL CANDY BOX
2548-8" PLATE
2547-12" PLATE
2564-6" FAN 2571-10" FAN
2552-MAY. BOWL 2556-7" MAY. PLATE
507 TUMBLER
2552 MAY. BOWL
507 1/2 GAL. JUG
2561 HIGH CANDLE
2551 FLARED BOWL
2561 HIGH CANDLE
2549 OBLONG VASE
2560 LOW CANDLE
2550 ROUND VASE
2661-8" SALAD 2669-12" PLATE
2551 FRUIT BOWL

1931 Catalog reprint

X-02753 FISH

X-2666 KATYDID

X-2550 LE FLEUR

X-2753 PINE-CONE

X-2549
BIRD OF PARADISE
X-2752
LOVE-BIRD AS LAMP
X-2787 DOG-WOOD

X-02756
SCREECH-OWL

X-2786
BITTERSWEET

X-02758
SEA-GULL

X-2587 BLACKBERRY

X-2843 DANCING GIRL

X-2754 COCKATOO

X-2785 DRAGON-FLY

X-2752 LOVE-BIRD

MARTELE (Fairy)

Bowl, flrd., 10½"	30.00--40.00
Bowl, flrd., 7"	15.00--18.00
Bowl, flrd., 5½"	8.00--10.00
Goblet, 10 oz.	12.00--15.00
Plate, 7", 8", 10"	8.00--14.00
Plate, 15"	25.00--35.00
Vase, fan shaped, 6½"	15.00--18.00
Vase, rnd., 8", 10"	30.00--45.00
Cigarette Box	20.00--25.00
Ash Tray	12.00--15.00
Finger Bowl	8.00--12.00
Sundae	10.00--14.00
Comport, 5½"	8.00--12.00
Candle	10.00--12.00
Bowl, 8", salad	15.00--18.00
Bowl, 13", 15", flrd.	35.00--50.00
Bowl, 10", fruit	25.00--30.00

MARTELE Vases *See reprint*

The old vases are certainly lovely. Be aware that replicas of them were being made as late as the 70s; the ones I've seen were translucent white glass with fired-on colors, and I don't think we will be mistaking them for the old.

DOGWOOD	125.00-175.00
LOVE BIRD	125.00-175.00
DANCING GIRL	125.00-175.00
SCREECH OWL	125.00-175.00
DOLPHIN	125.00-175.00
SEA GULL	125.00-175.00
BLACKBERRY	125.00-175.00
COCKATOO	125.00-175.00
DRAGON-FLY	125.00-175.00
BITTERSWEET	125.00-175.00
PINE-CONE	125.00-175.00
BIRD OF PARADISE	125.00-175.00
FISH	125.00-175.00
KATYDID	125.00-175.00
LE FLEUR	125.00-175.00

"DANCE of the NUDES"

Colors: Crystal, pink, med. blue green, green

Nappy, 6½"	8.00--12.00
Cup	25.00--35.00
Saucer	8.00--10.00

Saucer has a ring but is same size and shape as 6½" nappy.

Sherbet	15.00--20.00
Sherbet Plate	8.00--10.00
Tumbler, ftd., 3½", 5½"	30.00--45.00
Plate, 8¼"	18.00--26.00
Berry Dish	10.00--15.00
Plate, 10"	20.00--30.00

MARTELE (Fairy)
"Dance of the Nudes" Plate

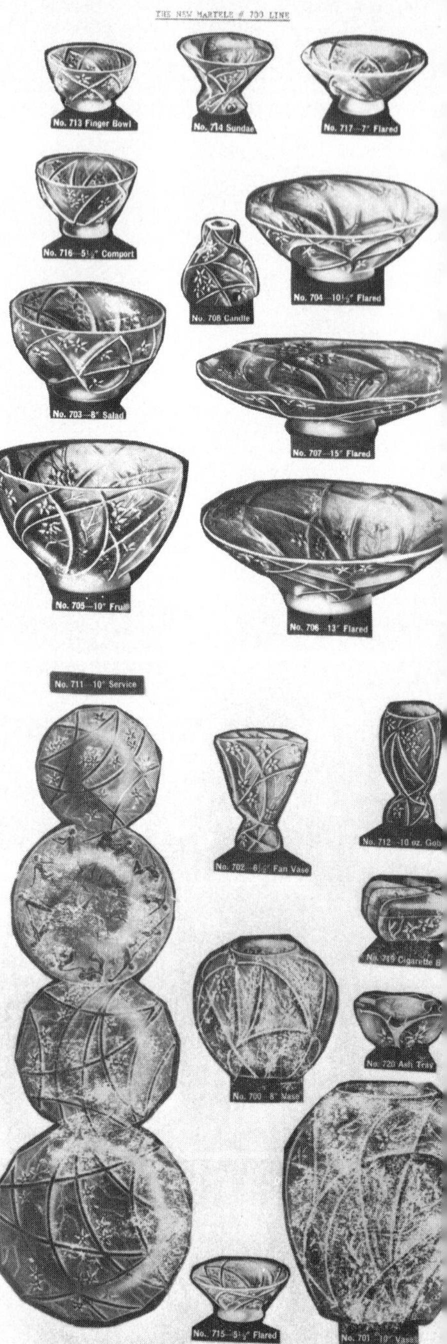

1931 Catalog Reprint

RUBA ROMBIC page 48

Colors: Dark green, emerald green, opaque, light green, topaz, dark topaz, silver, lavender.

Item	Price
Whiskey Set	150.00-200.00
Plate, 15"	15.00--25.00
Plate, salad, 8"	8.00--12.00
Plate, service, 10"	15.00--20.00
Bread & Butter, 7"	6.00--10.00
Sherbet	8.00--10.00
Bowl, finger	5.00-- 7.00
Candleholder	10.00--15.00
Bowl, flrd., 9"	20.00--25.00
Bowl, oval, 12"	24.00--30.00
Bowl, cupped, 8"	20.00--25.00
Ash Tray	10.00--15.00
Powder Box	20.00--30.00
Vase, 2 styles	30.00--45.00
Jug	60.00--85.00
Celery	10.00--15.00
Relish, divided	10.00--15.00
Bon Bon	8.00--12.00
Almond	10.00--14.00
Toilet Bottle	30.00--40.00
Bouillon, ftd.	8.00--10.00
Sundae	8.00--10.00
Compote, 7"	18.00--22.00
Sugar	12.00--16.00
Cream	12.00--16.00
Cigarette Box	20.00--30.00
Tumbler, ftd., 10 oz.	12.00--16.00
Tumbler, 12 oz., 9 oz.	10.00--14.00
Tumbler, whiskey	12.00--16.00

RUBA ROMBIC

RUBA ROMBIC LINE

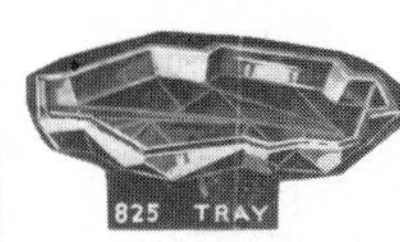

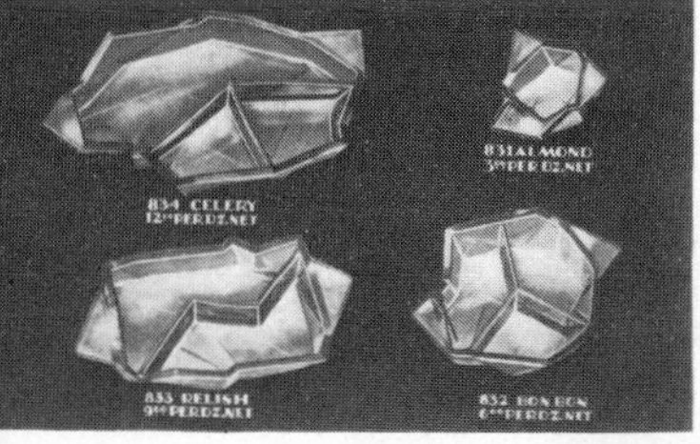

CATALONIAN

Old Spanish Glass
Remember no two pieces were made exactly the same.
This listing is taken from an old catalog, original spellings preserved.

Plate, 6"	3.00-- 5.00
Plate, bread and butter, 7"	4.00-- 6.00
Plate, salad, 8"	5.00-- 8.00
Plate, 13"	12.00--16.00
Cup	10.00--15.00
Saucer	3.00-- 5.00
Sugar, no handles	7.00--10.00
Sugar, hdld., rnd	8.00--12.00
Cream, rnd.	8.00--12.00
Cream, triangle	10.00--14.00
Sunday, low ftd., flrd., 7 oz.	5.00-- 8.00
Sundae, straight	5.00-- 8.00
Bowl, finger, flrd.	5.00-- 8.00
Bowl, finger, straight	5.00-- 8.00
Bowl, salad, flrd., 9½"	15.00--18.00
Bowl, salad, 9"	12.00--15.00
Bowl, 12¾"	18.00--22.00
Bowl, Lily, 12"	16.00--20.00
Tumbler, whiskey, 2½ oz.	7.00--10.00
Tumbler, ftd., 2½ oz.	7.00-- 9.00
Tumbler, 6 oz., 8 oz.	6.00-- 8.00
Tumbler, 9 oz., 12 oz.	7.00-- 9.00
Tumbler, tapered, 7 oz., 9½ oz.	8.00--10.00
Tumbler, ice tea, 12 oz.	9.00--11.00
Tumbler, ice tea, hdld., 12 oz.	12.00--15.00
Goblet, 10 oz.	12.00--15.00

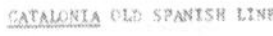
CATALONIA OLD SPANISH LINE

SWEET PEAS 1154-
1105 B-SUGAR
1103 P CREAM

1114 MAYONNAISE
1125 ASH TRAY

1176-OATMEAL DISH
CIGARETTE BOX 1107

1115 STRAIGHT SALAD

1175-TOILET BOTTLE

1105 SUGAR

2567 PUFF BOX
1124 CANDLE

1113-7" B&B PLATE
1181-6" B&B PLATE
1112-8" SALAD PLATE
1177-10" SERVICE P
1111-13" PLATE

1115 B. FLARED SALAD

1100-12 LILY BOWL

WHISKEY SET 1162

CATALONIAN

1123-7oz SUNDAE
WHISKEY 1122-2½oz
1153-FLARED VASE

VIOLET VASE 1171

1101 P-JUG

1109-JUG

1100 P-JUG

PINCH BOTTLE VASE 1166-

FOOTED FLARED VASE 1148-

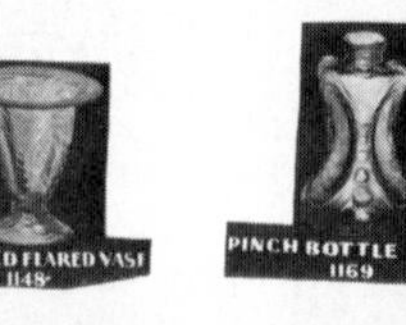
PINCH BOTTLE 1169

ICED TEA TUMBLER 1117 B-12oz

1102 P-JUG

1179-CUP
1180-SAUCER

FAN VASE
1100-B-8"
1116-B 7"

FLARED VASE
1100 C-8"
1116 C 6"

FOOTED FAN VA
1172-

1106 CREAM

1110-9oz TUMBLER

ICED TEA TUMBLER 1117-12oz

1118-7oz TUMBLER

GOBLET 1120-10oz

NASTURTIUM VASE 1170-

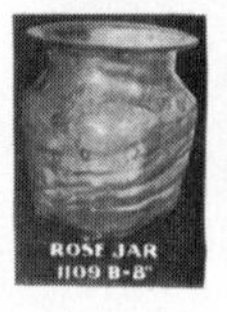
ROSE JAR 1109 B-8"

TUMBLER VASE
1100-8"
1116-7"

Dolphin Console Set

'SANTA MARIA'

1931 Catalog Reprint

THE FLORENTINE

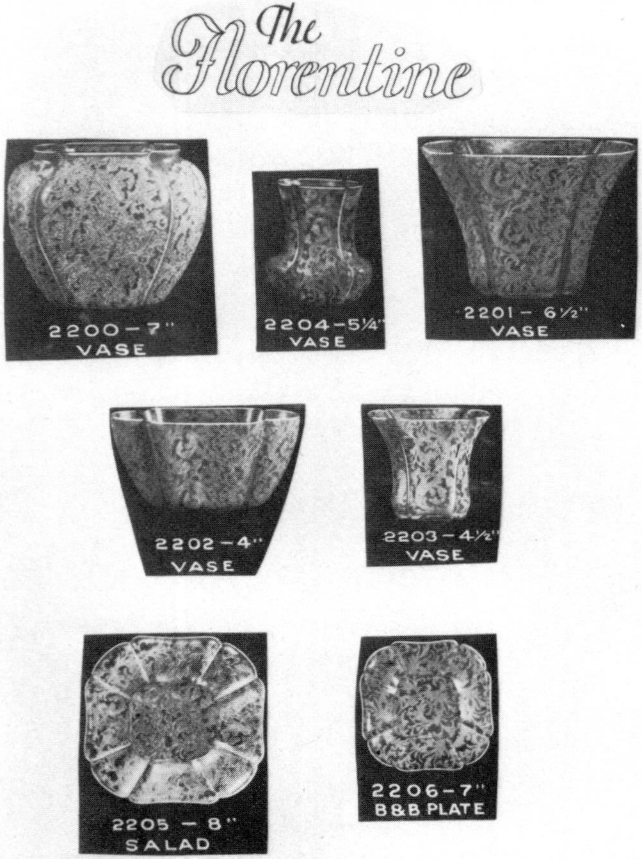
The Florentine
2200—7"
VASE
2204—5¼"
VASE
2201— 6½"
VASE
2202—4"
VASE
2203—4½"
VASE
2205 — 8"
SALAD
2206—7"
B&B PLATE

MARTELE Fishes, Birds and Flowers

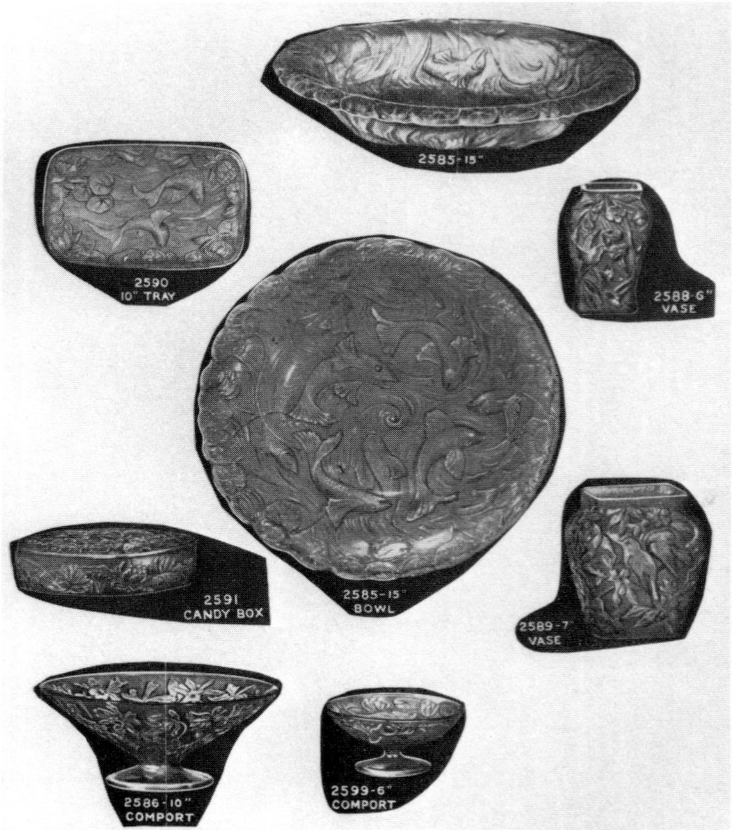
2585-15"
2590
10" TRAY
2588-6"
VASE
2591
CANDY BOX
2585-15"
BOWL
2589-7"
VASE
2586-10"
COMPORT
2599-6"
COMPORT

Goblet, low, ftd., 12 oz.	12.00--15.00
Parfait	12.00--15.00
Jug, triangle	25.00--35.00
Jug, rnd., ½ gal.	25.00--35.00
Vase, fan shaped	12.00--16.00
Vase, triangle, 4", 6"	12.00--18.00
Vase, flrd. shape, 5½", 10"	15.00--20.00
Vase, oblong	20.00--25.00
Vase, tumbler shape, small	9.00--12.00
Vase, tumbler shape, large	12.00--16.00
Vase, cupped, 6¾"	10.00--15.00
Vase, rolled	10.00--15.00
Vase, Violet	9.00--12.00
Vase, Nasturtium (4 openings)	15.00--18.00
Vase, pinch bottle	10.00--15.00
Comport, 6½"	9.00--12.00
Tray, serving, center hdld.	12.00--14.00
Guest Set	25.00--35.00
Smoker Set	20.00--30.00
Ash Tray	8.00--11.00
Whiskey Set	60.00--85.00
Candlesticks, low	8.00--12.00
Cigarette Box and Cover	15.00--20.00
Rose Jar	10.00--14.00
Ice Tub	12.00--18.00
Fish Bowl	15.00--20.00

VASES

SANTA MARIE *See reprint*

Ship Candlestick Console Set	85.00-100.00
Dolphin Console Set	100.00-125.00
Covered Cigarette Box	25.00--35.00
Footed Cigarette Holder	40.00--50.00
Tray (2572)	10.00--14.00
Covered Cigar Jar (2559)	55.00--65.00
Tray (2573)	20.00--30.00
Upright Ship Ash Tray	16.00--20.00
Covered Cigarette Jar (2558)	35.00--45.00

THE FLORENTINE *See reprint*

2200 Vase, 7"	75.00-100.00
2204 Vase, 5¼"	50.00--75.00
2201 Vase, 6½"	75.00--95.00
2202 Vase, 4"	35.00--50.00
2203 Vase, 4½"	35.00--50.00
2205 Salad, 8"	18.00--24.00
2206 B & B Plate, 7"	12.00--15.00

MARTELE (Fishes, Birds, Flowers) *See reprint*

2590 Fish Tray, 10"	25.00--30.00
2585 Fish bowl, 15"	30.00--40.00
2588 Vase, 6"	25.00--35.00
2591 Candy Box	40.00--50.00
2589 Vase, 7"	50.00--60.00
2586 Comport, 10"	20.00--30.00
2599 Comport, 6"	10.00--15.00

Co-Operative Flint

CO-OPERATIVE FLINT has always held a great deal of interest for me, and the new material I've turned up for this issue only increases the intrigue. The following pages carry much of this material, some of which I'll describe below.

#1. This is the "WIGWAM" console -- and all that time we thought it was L.E. Smith's original mold! Obviously this is not so; it must've belonged to Co-Operative first, and then when they went under during the Depression, L.E. Smith must've acquired the mold.

#3. A reader once wrote me that she had a 13" long 6" high elephant. Naturally I was flabbergated, as I'd never heard of one so large. She thought it was a fish bowl, or maybe she was just being funny. Anyway, when I located this old ad there was the size alright -- 13" x 6" -- but no mention of its ever being a fishbowl! Note all the colors it was made in, including black which I've seen and even ruby. I might mention here that elephants have been found with fired-on bright colors also.

The other reprints are probably self-explanatory, and of considerable interest too.

ITEMS IN CRYSTAL and COLORS — page 49

No. 471 Bowls	20.00--40.00
No. 449 Candlestick	20.00--30.00

FOREST TABLEWARE

Cream	9.00--12.00
Sugar	9.00--12.00
Nappy	14.00--18.00
Plate	8.00--10.00

ANIMAL FIGURES — page 50

Black and red animals will be 50% higher

Elephant and Cover	35.00--50.00
Elephant and Flower Block	35.00--50.00
Bear and Cover	35.00--55.00
Whale and Cover	35.00--55.00
Dog and Cover	35.00--55.00
Frog and Cover	35.00--55.00
Elephant container	35.00--55.00
Elephant, 13" x 6"	75.00-100.00

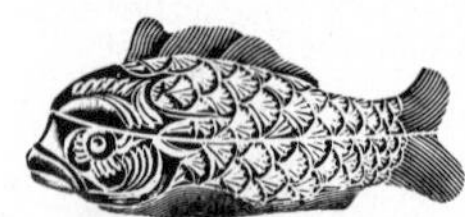

Among the many new items developed by the Co-Operative Flint Glass Co., Beaver Falls, Pa., are these pleasing novelties. The elephant in a choice of green, amber, black, blue, rose, ruby and crystal is made in two sizes, the smaller measuring about 7 x 4½ inches and the larger 13 x 6 inches. They may be put to many uses. The elephant illustrated is popular as a candy jar, for bath salts, etc. With a perforated cover for flowers, and with a cover with cigarette rests and indented for ashes, it makes a novel cigarette box. The whale is very popular as a receptacle for bath salts among other purposes. This may also be had in various colors.

NO. 587 EARLY AMERICAN PATTERN page 51

Champagne	10.00--15.00
Plate	7.00--10.00
Goblet	10.00--15.00

"POOKIE"

Decanter and 4 Tumblers	50.00--70.00

MISCELLANEOUS

No. 387 Puff Box	20.00--35.00
No. 566 Bowl, hdld., 8"	12.00--14.00
No. 574 Ivy Ball	10.00--14.00
No. 573 Flower Pot and Block	16.00--22.00

STURDY TABLE GLASS NO. 557

Goblet	12.00--18.00
Ice Tea	10.00--14.00
Tumbler, ftd.	10.00--15.00
Salt and Pepper Set	15.00--20.00

"WIG-WAM"

Console Set	30.00--45.00

"KIM"

Candy Jar	50.00--65.00

"TRAVERS"

Plate	10.00--14.00

Illustrated above is one of the most fascinating candy jars on the market, made in amber, cobalt blue, acquamarine blue, green and rose. Below is our 7" square plate, there is nothing more attractive in a square salad made. Comes in amber, cobalt blue, acquamarine blue, green, rose and black glass. An 8½" and other sizes now in preparation.

1928 journal ad
"KIM" Candy Jar
"TRAVERS" Plate

To the left: Co-Operative Flint Glass Co., Beaver Falls, Pa., offer their No. 567 modernistic design in Console bowl and candlesticks which is made in crystal, aquamarine blue, green, rose and ruby. The simplicity of its design makes it most attractive for flowers or fruit. This is only one of the many salable items shown. It is on display with the firm's New York representatives, Horace C. Gray Co., 200 Fifth Ave.

"WIG-WAM" from 1930 trade catalog

Diamond

Last time we carried news of a rib pattern "ROUND RIB" that was definitely made by this company. It was made in green, and included a center handle server.

This year some further observations about Rib patterns: Some people think "Adam's Rib" (page 393 in UNKNOWNS) belongs to Diamond. It's true it is showing up in and around Indiana PA and old worker's remember a Rib pattern. The center handle to the sandwich server matches the handle to the VICTORY sandwich server.

The only official information on a Diamond Rib pattern, however, is shown below and the handle on the sandwich server does not match the one being found with "ADAM'S RIB".

Did Diamond make two 'Ribs'? Or two different handles on sandwich servers?

EPERGNE 90.00--125.00

VICTORY page 53

Amber, pink, green, Ritz Blue, amethyst

Item	Price
Plate, 6"	4.00-- 6.00
Plate, 7", 8"	5.00-- 7.00
Plate, 9"	6.00-- 9.00
Plate, cheese and cracker, 11" Cheese Dish, 5-5/8"x2½" tall	15.00--25.00
Cup and Saucer	6.00--10.00
Cream and Sugar	12.00--18.00
Platter	14.00--18.00
Tumbler, ftd., 5"	15.00--20.00
Bowl, 6½"	6.00-- 8.00
Bowl, flat soup, 8½"	8.00--12.00
Bowl, oval veg., 9"	18.00--24.00
Bowl, console, 12"	20.00--30.00
Mayonnaise Dish, Ladle, Underplate with indent	30.00--40.00
Sandwich Server	25.00--35.00
Bon Bon, hi-footed, 5½"	18.00--24.00
Candlestick, high, 3", (pr)	15.00--25.00
Gravy Boat and Platter	70.00--75.00

VICTORY bon bon 5½"

VICTORY

NO. 99 LINE IN BLACK GLASS

Also made in amethyst

Vase	18.00--25.00
Plate	10.00--14.00
Cup and Saucer	10.00--14.00
Console Set	45.00--65.00
Bowl	30.00--40.00
Candlesticks (pr)	15.00--25.00

"ROUND RIB"

Center Handle Server	20.00--30.00
Cheese and Cracker	25.00--35.00

Glass Made In America

Diamond Glass-Ware Company

Indiana, Pa., U. S. A.

"ROUND RIB"
reprinted from a 1925 journal

Dunbar

That first reprint below -- not the most earthshaking one you've ever seen, is it? But it does provide more shapes of Dunbar liquor sets, and every little bit helps. I've seen these shapes and stoppers -- have you?

The second reprint is more like it. How many times readers have asked me who made their DOG decanter, since it was not the Cambridge or New Martinsville one. Now we know! The Dunbar DOG's ears are quite different, note. And don't miss the other surprise on that reprint, the marvelous little TOBY decanter.

REFRESHMENT SETS	**page 54**
Servette Set, 5 piece	20.00--30.00
Service Set, 12 piece	60.00--85.00
No. 4016 Iced Tea Set	35.00--45.00

GIFTS OF COLORED GLASSWARE	**page 55**
No. 6350 Water Set	25.00--35.00
No. 1223 Mayonnaise Set	18.00--24.00
No. 4089 Cheese and Cracker	16.00--20.00
Bridge Set	25.00--30.00
No. 4072 Optic Vase, 12"	15.00--18.00
No. 4077 Checo Vase	15.00--18.00
No. 4071 Cake Stand, ftd.	20.00--25.00
Trumpet Vase, 6½"	15.00--18.00
No. 1247 Servette Set	20.00--30.00
No. 4082 Nite Set	35.00--45.00
Candy Box, 7"	25.00--35.00
No. 4091, Candy Box and Cover, 3 partition	20.00--30.00
Ice Tub Set, 3 piece	18.00--24.00

RAMBLER ROSE	**page 56**
Bon-Bon Box 3 partition, covered	25.00--35.00
Sandwich Tray, hdld.	20.00--30.00
Mayonnaise Set, 3 piece	25.00--35.00
Relish Stand, ftd., 11"	30.00--40.00
Relish, flat, 10"	15.00--20.00
Relish, 6 compt., 13¼"	25.00--30.00

DECALCOMANIA	
Mayonnaise Set	18.00--24.00

"BARBRA"	
Beverage Set	50.00--65.00

VASE	
Bell Shaped	12.00--15.00

BEVERAGE SET	
Jug and Tumblers	50.00--60.00

BEVERAGE SETS LISTING	**page 57**
No. 5022 Iced Tea Set	50.00--70.00
No. 5023 Iced Tea Set	50.00--70.00
No. 5024 Iced Tea Set	50.00--70.00
No. 5025 Water Set	40.00--50.00
No. 5026 Water Set	40.00--50.00

BEVERAGES	**page 58**
"ATHOS" Beverage	20.00--25.00
"PORTHOS" Beverage	35.00--40.00
"ARAMIS" Beverage	35.00--45.00
"D'ARTAGNAN" Beverage	35.00--40.00
No. 6248 Vase, fancy shaped	15.00--20.00

MODERNIST CUTTING	
No. 6020 Beverage	35.00--40.00
No. 6114 Tumbler	5.00-- 8.00
No. 6115 Nite Set	30.00--40.00
No. 6320 Server, hdld	15.00--20.00

POINSETTIA CUTTING

No. 6010 Beverage Set	45.00--55.00
No. 6009 Beverage Set	45.00--55.00

LIQUEUR SETS

Shown below

EENEY (965 cut 2905)	30.00--35.00
MEENEY (963 D 906)	55.00--65.00
MINEY (965 D 755)	50.00--60.00
MO (3517)	30.00--35.00

DUNBAR Now Brings You—

965 cut 2095

963 D 906

965 D 755

3517

New 7 Piece Liqueur Sets . .

in a variety of colorings, cuttings and decorations

EACH AN OUTSTANDING ONE DOLLAR RETAILER!

ON DISPLAY IN ROOM 551

NEW YORK
HOUSEFURNISHING
SHOW
HOTEL PENNSYLVANIA
JULY 29 TO AUGUST 4 1934

Also Exhibiting at Chicago
1564 Merchandise Mart

Associates at Exhibit

H. F. Phillips — New York City
G. H. Krawehl — New York City
P. Messinger — New England
S. Mazabow — N. Y. & Penna.

DUNBAR GLASS CORP.

DUNBAR WEST VIRGINIA

NEW YORK OFFICE — 1107 BROADWAY
CHICAGO OFFICE — 1564 MERCHANDISE MART

CROCKERY AND GLASS JOURNAL for July, 1934

Reprinted from a 1934 trade catalog

"HI BALL" LINE	***See photo***
Ash Trays	3.00-- 5.00
Cocktail Shaker	14.00--18.00
Ice Bucket and Tongs	15.00--20.00
Tumblers	3.00-- 4.00
Jug	20.00--25.00
Plate	4.00-- 5.00
Nut Bowl	3.00-- 4.00

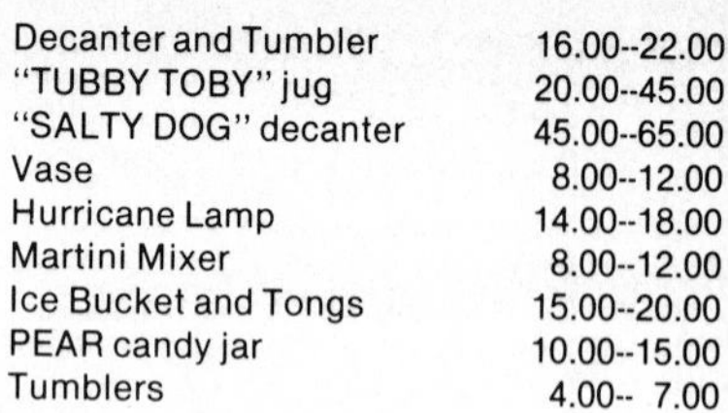

Decanter and Tumbler	16.00--22.00
"TUBBY TOBY" jug	20.00--45.00
"SALTY DOG" decanter	45.00--65.00
Vase	8.00--12.00
Hurricane Lamp	14.00--18.00
Martini Mixer	8.00--12.00
Ice Bucket and Tongs	15.00--20.00
PEAR candy jar	10.00--15.00
Tumblers	4.00-- 7.00

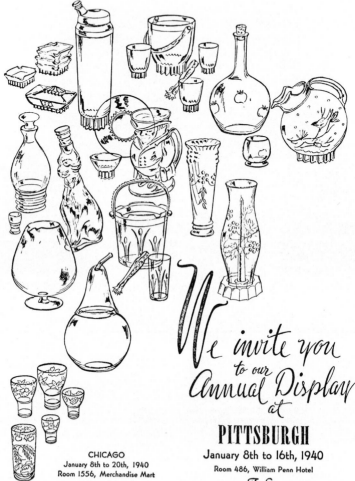

We invite you to our Annual Display at

PITTSBURGH

January 8th to 16th, 1940

Room 486, William Penn Hotel

CHICAGO
January 8th to 20th, 1940
Room 1556, Merchandise Mart

NEW YORK GIFT SHOW
Feb. 19th to 23rd, 1940
Room 916, 1107 Broadway

To See

The Most Beautiful Popular Priced Glass in America

BEVERAGE SETS • JUICE SETS • HURRICANE LAMPS
TUMBLERS • VASES • DECANTER SETS • NOVELTY ITEMS
ICE BUCKETS • COCKTAIL SETS • LIQUOR ACCESSORIES

DUNBAR GLASS CORPORATION DUNBAR **DUNBAR, WEST VIRGINIA**

Reprinted from a 1940 trade catalog

Duncan & Miller

Good news! I've acquired another old catalog. It bears no date as usual, but it is probably about 1939 or 1940 as there are no colors mentioned. We do know that some of the lines were made in color earlier, so I'm reprinting many of the lines, some of which have not been shown before.

In 1976, Gail Krause (994 Jefferson Ave., Washington PA 15301) published a book called "Encyclopedia of Duncan Glass", which includes some older pieces of George Duncan and Sons you may be interested in.

The SHIP plate shown in Book 2 isn't the real Duncan SHIP plate. The one shown here is the right one, made in 1925 and written up in several issues of the trade journals. Sorry about the error.

Lastly, I'd like to mention the National Duncan Glass Society, an organization that can be reached by writing to Box 965, Washington PA 15301.

"SPIRAL FLUTES" page 60

George Sionakides of DeWitt MI collects "SPIRAL FLUTES" and October 1977 published an article in the DAZE showing illustrations. He has loaned these pictures to me to reprint--also we have added to our listing. George points out the candleholder and 9" bowl shown in Book II aren't Duncan.

Crystal, amber, green, Rose, Canary

Plate, dinner, 10½"	10.00--12.00
Plate, luncheon, 8-3/8"	3.00-- 4.00
Plate, salad, 7½"	4.00-- 5.00
Plate, sherbet, 6"	2.00-- 3.00
Plate, sandwich, 14"	12.00--15.00
Cup	8.00--10.00
Saucer	2.00-- 4.00
Demitasse Cup and Saucer	15.00--20.00
Mug, hdld., 6½"	20.00--25.00
Mug, hdld., 7"	20.00--25.00
Bowl, nappy, 11"	20.00--25.00
Bowl, nappy, 8"	9.00--12.00
Bowl, nappy, 7"	12.00--15.00
Bowl, nappy, 5"	4.00-- 5.00
Bowl, flanged, 8½"	12.00--15.00
Bowl, flanged, 7½"	12.00--15.00
Bowl, flanged, 6¾"	3.00-- 4.00
Bowl, cream soup, 5"	12.00--15.00
Bowl, boullion, 4"	6.00-- 8.00
Bowl, finger, 4½"	5.00-- 7.00
Bowl, console, 12"	15.00--20.00
Bowl, vegetable, oval	25.00--30.00
Creamer	6.00-- 8.00
Sugar	6.00-- 8.00
Sherbet, regular, 3¾"	5.00-- 6.00
Sherbet, tall, 4¾"	6.00-- 8.00
Seafood Cocktail Cup	15.00--20.00
Grapefruit, ftd.	20.00--25.00
Tumbler, ftd., 3½"	7.00-- 9.00
Tumbler, ftd., 4½"	7.00-- 9.00
Tumbler, ftd., 5-1/8"	12.00--15.00
Tumbler, tall, ftd., 5¼"	8.00--12.00
Tumbler, flat, juice	12.00--15.00
Tumbler, flat, 4"	10.00--12.00
Tumbler, flat, ice tea, 5"	15.00--20.00

SPIRAL FLUTE
console set, jug 8½" comport 6", ladle, vase", bouillion, cream soup, finger bowl, plate 6", seafood cocktail and liner

Photo by George Sionakides

Pitcher, 8½", 60 oz.	75.00--95.00
Parfait, 5-3/8"	10.00--12.00
Goblet, 6¼"	11.00--14.00
Wine, 3¾"	11.00--14.00
Almond, ftd., 2¼"	6.00-- 8.00
Celery, 11"	12.00--15.00
Pickle, 8-5/8"	10.00--12.00
Relish, 3 pc.	30.00--40.00
Candlestick, 3½"	10.00--12.00
Candlestick, 9"	30.00--40.00
Candy Dish and Cover, ½ lb.	65.00--75.00
Comport, 4-3/8"	12.00--14.00
Vase, 6-3/8"	10.00--12.00
Vase, 8¾"	15.00--18.00
Vase, 10½"	20.00--25.00
Ice Tub	15.00--20.00
Cigarette Holder	25.00--30.00
Stand for Console Bowl	10.00--12.00

FULL SAIL page 61

Plate	16.00--20.00

See photo

"RITA"

Cheese and Cracker	25.00--35.00

"TERRI"

Center Handled Server	15.00--18.00

SANDWICH (D & M's) page 61-65

Remember Indiana Glass Company now owns the DUNCAN AND MILLER SANDWICH molds. Look on page 181 Book 2 for a resume of their activity with the Tiara Line and for Montgomery Ward.

Since then, besides making the Tiara Line in a medium dark grayed blue in 1975, Indiana made crystal SANDWICH that was marketed under the Colony label in the following pieces:

Plate, salad, 8"
Plate, torte, 16"
Plate, deviled egg, 12"
Plate, two hdld., 12"
Bowl, salad, 10"
Sugar and Creamer, ftd.
Tray, celery, 10"
Cup, 6 oz.
Goblet, stemmed, 9 oz.
Sherbet, stemmed, 5 oz.
Wine/Cocktail, 3 oz.
Old Fashion, 7 oz.
Ice Tea, ftd., 12 oz.
Relish, two/compt., 7"
Cake Stand, ftd., 13"
Candy Jar and Cover, 8½"
Epergne Set: 2-pc., 12"
Mayonnaise Set: 3-pc.
Tray, relish, 10"

Suggested prices below are for pink, green, and amber. Crystal will be 25% lower, and Chartreuse and ruby 25% to 50% higher.

Plate, salad, 8"	12.00--14.00
Plate, dinner, 9½"	25.00--30.00
Plate, dessert, 7"	10.00--12.00
Coaster, 5"	8.00--10.00
Plate, bread and butter, 6"	7.00-- 9.00
Plate, 12"	20.00--25.00
Goblet, 9 oz., 6"	15.00--18.00
Saucer Champagne, 5 oz., 5¼"	12.00--15.00
Wine, 3 oz., 4½"	15.00--18.00
Cocktail, 3 oz., 4¼"	15.00--18.00
Ice Cream, 5 oz., 3½"	10.00--12.00
Sundae, flrd., 5 oz., 3½"	10.00--12.00
Jelly, ind., 3"	7.00-- 9.00
Fruit Cup or Jello, 6 oz., 2½"	7.00-- 9.00
Oyster Cocktail, 5 oz., 3¾"	8.00--10.00
Tumbler, ice tea, 13 oz., 5¼"	12.00--14.00
Jug, ice lip, ½ gal., 8"	60.00--70.00
Ice Tea, ftd., 12 oz., 5½"	12.00--15.00
Tumbler, ftd., 9 oz., 4¾"	10.00--12.00
Orange Juice, ftd., 5 oz., 3¼"	10.00--12.00
Parfait, 4 oz., hght., 5¼"	12.00--15.00
Tea Cup and Saucer, 6 oz., 6"	16.00--20.00
Salted Almond, 2½"	7.00-- 9.00
Tray, oval, 8" x 4¾"	8.00--10.00
Salt and Pepper, 2½"	20.00--30.00
Grapefruit, fruit cup liner, 5½"	30.00--40.00
Oil and Vinegar Condiment Set: 5 pc.	60.00--90.00
Sugar and Cream Set: 3 pc., 5 oz.	30.00--35.00
Butter or Cheese and Cover, 8"	70.00--75.00
Sugar, 9 oz., 3¼"	15.00--18.00
Cream, 7 oz., 4"	15.00--18.00
Mayonnaise, ftd., 5", hgt. 2¾"	10.00--14.00
Salad Dressing Set: 3-pc., 13"	35.00--50.00
Mayonnaise Set: 3 pc.	20.00--30.00
Salad Dressing Set: 3 pc., 2 compt., 6"	25.00--35.00
Bowl, salad, shallow, 12"	15.00--20.00
Mayonnaise Set: 3 pc., 6"	18.00--22.00
Salad Set: 2 pc.	35.00--45.00
Mayonnaise Set: 2 pc., 6"	20.00--30.00

TAVERN

GEORGIAN

Salad Dressing Set:	
2 compt., 4 pc., 6"	35.00--40.00
Midnight Supper Set:	
3 pc., 12"	50.00--60.00
Bowl, fruit, crimped, ftd., 11"	25.00--30.00
Cheese and Cracker Set:	
2 pc., 13"	30.00--40.00
Cheese Stand, 5½"	8.00--10.00
Cake Salver, ftd., 13"	50.00--60.00
Cake Salver, ftd., rolled	
edge, 12"	50.00--60.00
Camelia flower pan,	
oblong, 10½"	18.00--22.00
Basket, oval, hdld., 12"	45.00--65.00
Basket, crimped, hdld., 12"	45.00--65.00
Bowl, Gardenia, 11½"	20.00--25.00
Comport, tall, 5½"	12.00--16.00
Comport, low, ftd., flrd., 6"	12.00--16.00
Grapefruit, 6"	8.00--10.00
Grapefruit w/rim liner or	
Frozen fruit server, 5½"	25.00--35.00
Fruit salad, 6"	7.00-- 9.00
Bowl, fruit, 3 compt., 10"	30.00--35.00
Bowl, fruit, flrd., 12"	25.00--30.00
Nappy, dessert, 6"	7.00-- 9.00
Nappy, fruit, 5"	6.00-- 8.00
Basket, tall, hdld., 6"	25.00--35.00
Bowl, Ivy, ftd., 5"	18.00--20.00
Vase, crimped, 4½"	12.00--16.00
Bowl, flower, crimped, 11½"	25.00--35.00
Vase, crimped, ftd., 5", 3"	15.00--20.00
Vase, ftd., 10"	25.00--40.00
Bowl, Lily, 10"	22.00--26.00
Urn and Cover, 12"	45.00--65.00
Tray, pickle, 7"	9.00--14.00
Relish, oblong, 2 compt., 7"	16.00--20.00
Celery and Relish,	
3 compt., 10"	20.00--25.00
Tray, celery, 10"	10.00--15.00
Relish, oblong, 3 compt.	20.00--25.00
Cigarette Holder, ftd., 3"	12.00--16.00
Cigarette Box and Cover,	
2¾" x 3½"	18.00--24.00
Ash Trays, ind., 2¾"	4.00-- 6.00
Tray, ice cream, 12"	22.00--28.00
Plate, deviled egg, 12"	25.00--30.00
Relish, 3 compt., 12"	25.00--30.00
Bowl, nut, cupped, 11"	22.00-28.00
Plate, flat edge, 13", also	
rolled edge	25.00--35.00
Candlestick, 2 light, 5"	18.00--24.00
Candlestick, 4" (ea.)	12.00--18.00
Bowl, oblong, 12"	25.00--40.00
Candlestick, 3 light, 5"	25.00--30.00
Candelabrum w/U Prisms	
3 light, hgt., 10"	200.00-250.00
Candelabrum w/U Prisms	
1light, hgt., 10"	50.00--60.00
Candelabrum, Hurricane Lamp	
w/Prisms, hgt., 15"	65.00--80.00
Candelabrum w/U Prisms	
3 light, hgt., 16"	250.00-350.00
Nappy, 2 compt., 5", 6"	9.00--12.00
Comport, low, crimped, 5½"	9.00--12.00
Basket, candy, hdld., 6½"	15.00--25.00
Relish, 2 compt., hdld., 5", 6"	12.00--16.00
Comport, candy,	
low, crimped, 7"	12.00--16.00
Nappy, regular, hdld., 5", 6"	12.00--16.00
Bon Bon, heart, hdld., 5", 6"	12.00--16.00
Comport, candy, low, flrd., 7"	12.00--16.00
Tray, mint, hdld., 6", 7"	11.00--14.00
Candy Box and Cover,	
rnd., 5"	25.00--35.00
Candy Jar and Cover, 8½"	35.00--45.00
Bon Bon and Cover, ftd., 5"	30.00--40.00

The following pieces were made by U.S. Glass in crystal from the Duncan and Miller molds.

See page 65 Book II

Salt and Pepper, small	14.00--18.00
Salt and Pepper, large	15.00--20.00
Salt and Pepper Set:	
3 pc., large	18.00--24.00
Oil and Vinegar Set: 3 pc.	25.00--35.00
Condiment Set: 5 pc.	45.00--55.00
Garden Epergne, 9"	30.00--35.00
Oil, 3 oz., 5¾"	12.00--15.00
Sugar or Grated Cheese	
shaker, 13 oz.	15.00--18.00
Pitcher, syrup, 13"	20.00--30.00

Additional pieces not shown in Book II

Plate, 2 hdld., 10½"	12.00--16.00
Relish 4 compt., 2 hdld., 10"	16.00--19.00
Fruit and Flower Epergne	
ftd., 14"	35.00--45.00
Candlestick, 2 light, 5"	15.00--20.00
Candelabra, w/2 Bobeches,	
2 light, hgt. 5", wdt. 9"	40.00--55.00

GEORGIAN PATTERN page 66

See reprint

Prices are for crystal, green, amber, pink. Prices for ruby and cobalt are 25% higher.

Goblet, 9 oz.	7.00--10.00
Saucer Champagne, ftd., 6 oz.	6.00-- 9.00
Ice Cream, ftd., 5 oz.	5.00-- 7.00
Jello, ftd., 5 oz.	6.00-- 9.00
Parfait	6.00-- 9.00
Wine	7.00--10.00
Ice Tea, 12 oz.	6.00-- 8.00

VICTORIAN

THE VICTORIAN PATTERN

Victorian 9 oz. Goblet

Victorian 5 oz. Saucer Champagne

Victorian 4 oz. Ice Cream

Victorian 5 oz. Parfait

Victorian 2½ oz. Cocktail or Wine

Victorian Finger Bowl and Plate

Victorian Mayonnaise

Victorian 5 in. Nappy

Victorian 8 oz. Sugar

Victorian 6 oz. Cream

Victorian 13 oz. Hi Ball

Victorian 7 oz. Old Fashioned

Victorian 12 oz. Ftd. Ice Tea

Victorian 9 oz. Ftd. Tumbler

Victorian 5 oz. Ftd. Orange Juice

Victorian 2 oz. Ftd. Tumbler

Victorian 7½ in. Plate Also made 6 in.

THE No. 102 WATERFORD PATTERN

9 oz. Goblet

5 oz. Parfait

6 oz. Saucer Champagne

6 oz. Ice Cream

3 oz. Cocktail or Wine

Finger Bowl

½ gal. Jug

14 oz. Ice Tea

12 oz. Ice Tea

9 oz. Table Tumbler

7½ oz. Hi Ball

5 oz. Orange Juice

2 oz. Tumbler

8½ in. Plate Also made 6 in.

RIPPLE

NO. 101 RIPPLE PATTERN

9 oz. Tall Goblet

9 oz. Luncheon Goblet

5 oz. Parfait

5 oz. Saucer Champagne

3 oz. Wine

3 oz. Cocktail

5 oz. Ftd. Ice Cream Also made 4 oz.

11 oz. Ftd. Ice Tea Also made 14 oz.

9 oz. Ftd. Tumbler Also made 11 oz.

5 oz. Ftd. Orange Juice

2 oz. Ftd. Tumbler

5 oz. Ftd. Jello

Finger Bowl

No. 100 12 oz. Ice Tea

No. 100 9 oz. Tumbler Also made 8 oz.

No. 100 5 oz. Orange Juice

8 oz. Hotel Sugar and Cover

6 oz. Hotel Cream

Honey Jar and Cover and 6 in. Plate

6 oz. Oil

11 in. Celery Tray Also made 8 in. Pickle Tray

Water Bottle

Ice Cocktail and Liner

8 in. Plate Also made 6 in. and 14 in.

½ gal. Pitcher

Catalog reprint c 1939-1940

Ship Plate from 1925 ad

RIPPLE PATTERN

Crystal and colors.

Goblet, tall, 9 oz.	8.00--12.00
Goblet, luncheon, 9 oz.	8.00--12.00
Parfait, 5 oz.	8.00--12.00
Saucer Champagne, 5 oz.	7.00--10.00
Wine, 3 oz.	10.00--14.00
Cocktail, 3 oz.	8.00--12.00
Ice Cream, ftd., 4 oz., 5 oz.	5.00-- 8.00
Ice Tea, ftd., 11 oz., 14 oz.	6.00-- 9.00
Tumbler, ftd., 9 oz., 11 oz.	5.00-- 8.00
Orange Juice, ftd., 5 oz.	5.00-- 8.00
Tumbler, ftd., 2 oz.	5.00-- 8.00
Jello, ftd., 5 oz.	5.00-- 8.00
Finger Bowl	5.00-- 7.00
Ice Tea, 12 oz.	5.00-- 8.00
Tumbler, 8 oz., 9 oz.	5.00-- 7.00
Orange Juice, 5 oz.	5.00-- 7.00
Hotel Sugar and Cover, 8 oz.	9.00--14.00
Hotel Cream, 6 oz.	6.00-- 9.00
Honey Jar, Cover and Plate, 6"	35.00--55.00
Oil, 6 oz.	15.00--25.00
Celery Tray, 11"	9.00--12.00
Pickle Tray, 8"	8.00--10.00
Water Bottle	18.00--24.00
Cocktail and Liner	15.00--20.00
Plate, 6", 8"	5.00-- 9.00
Plate, 14"	20.00--30.00
Pitcher, ½ gal.	25.00--35.00

VICTORIAN PATTERN

Crystal and colors.

Goblet, 9 oz.	8.00--12.00
Saucer Champagne, 5 oz.	6.00-- 8.00
Ice Cream, 4 oz.	5.00-- 7.00
Parfait, 5 oz.	8.00--10.00
Cocktail or Wine, 2½ oz.	8.00--12.00
Finger Bowl and Plate	9.00--12.00
Mayonnaise	8.00--10.00
Nappy, 5"	5.00-- 7.00
Sugar, 8 oz.	6.00-- 9.00
Cream, 6 oz.	6.00-- 9.00
Hi Ball, 13 oz.	7.00--10.00
Old Fashioned, 7 oz.	7.00--10.00
Ice Tea, ftd., 5 oz.	7.00--10.00
Orange Juice, ftd., 5 oz.	6.00-- 9.00
Tumbler, ftd., 2 oz.	7.00--10.00
Plate, 6", 7½"	5.00-- 8.00

TAVERN

Goblet, 9 oz., 5 oz., 3 oz.	6.00-- 9.00
Ice Cream, 5 oz.	5.00-- 7.00
Tumbler, 11 oz., 9 oz., 4 oz.	4.00-- 6.00
Finger Bowl, 4", 4½"	4.00-- 6.00
Custard or Punch Cups	4.00-- 5.00
Nappy, 4½"	3.00-- 4.00
Cream and Sugar	10.00--15.00
Oil and Stopper	12.00--16.00
Pitcher, ½ gal.	20.00--24.00
Water Bottle, 48 oz.	18.00--20.00
Hotel Jug, quart	20.00--24.00
Plate, 5½"	4.00-- 5.00

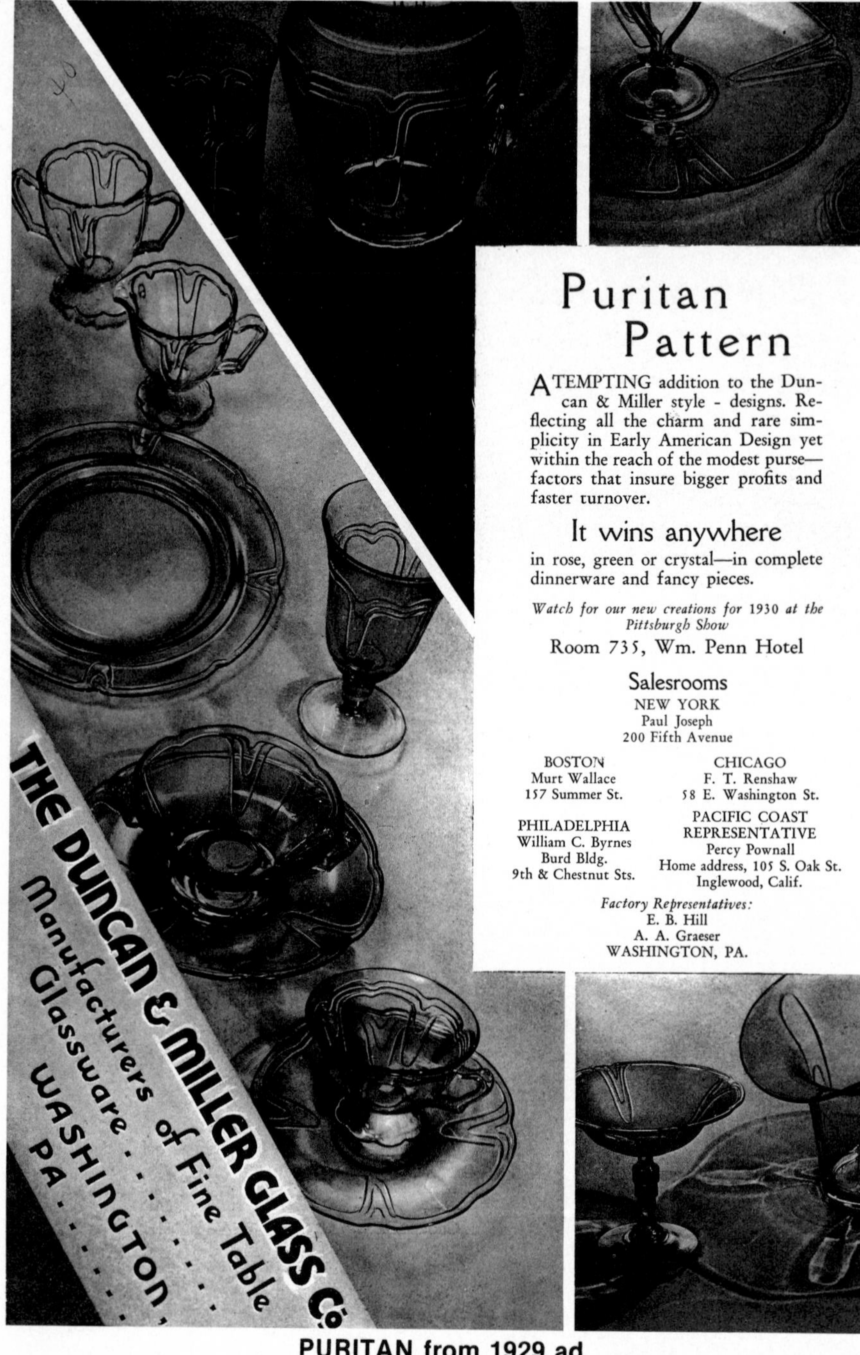

Puritan
Pattern
A TEMPTING addition to the Duncan & Miller style - designs. Reflecting all the charm and rare simplicity in Early American Design yet within the reach of the modest purse—factors that insure bigger profits and faster turnover.
It wins anywhere
in rose, green or crystal—in complete dinnerware and fancy pieces.
Watch for our new creations for 1930 at the Pittsburgh Show
Room 735, Wm. Penn Hotel
Salesrooms
NEW YORK
Paul Joseph
200 Fifth Avenue
BOSTON
Murt Wallace
157 Summer St.
CHICAGO
F. T. Renshaw
58 E. Washington St.
PHILADELPHIA
William C. Byrnes
Burd Bldg.
9th & Chestnut Sts.
PACIFIC COAST REPRESENTATIVE
Percy Pownall
Home address, 105 S. Oak St.
Inglewood, Calif.
Factory Representatives:
E. B. Hill
A. A. Graeser
WASHINGTON, PA.
THE DUNCAN & MILLER GLASS Co.
Manufacturers of Fine Table Glassware . . . . . .
WASHINGTON, PA. . . . .

PURITAN from 1929 ad

Tumbler, table, 9 oz.	5.00-- 7.00
Orange Juice, 5 oz.	5.00-- 7.00
Whiskey, 2 oz.	6.00-- 9.00
Grape Fruit	7.00-- 9.00
Nappy, 5"	4.00-- 6.00
Sugar, berry, oval	7.00-- 9.00
Cream, berry, oval	7.00-- 9.00
Ice Bucket w/ handle, 6"	18.00--24.00
Jug, ½ gal	25.00--35.00
Finger Bowl and Plate	10.00--15.00
Tea Cup and Saucer	10.00--14.00
Vase, crimped, 8"	20.00--30.00
Vase, No. 2, 8"	25.00--35.00
Plate, 14"	15.00--20.00
Plate, 9½"	12.00--15.00
Plate, 7½", 8½"	8.00--12.00
Plate, 6"	4.00-- 6.00
Console Set: 3 piece	25.00--35.00
Mug w/ colored handles	18.00--22.00
Cheese and Cracker	20.00--30.00

PURITAN

See reprint

Plate, 7½"	6.00-- 8.00
Cup	6.00-- 8.00
Saucer	3.00-- 4.00
Creamer	8.00--10.00
Sugar	8.00--10.00
Bowl, veg., oval, 9"	15.00--18.00
Comport	18.00--22.00
Cup and Saucer, demitasse	12.00--15.00
Jug	45.00--55.00
Tumbler	8.00--10.00
Center Handle Server	12.00--16.00
Cream Soup and Liner	10.00--12.00
Vase	25.00--30.00

EARLY AMERICAN HOB NAIL (old style)

Jug, ½ gal.	40.00--60.00
Tumbler	8.00--10.00
Creamer, oblong	8.00--10.00
Sugar, oblong	8.00--10.00
Plate, with sides	9.00--12.00
Vase, Ivy ball	20.00--30.00

EARLY AMERICAN HOB NAIL page 67-69

Remember, the suggested prices below are for pink, green and amber. Sapphire blue, ruby and the opalescents are from 25% to 50% higher, with opalescent being the highest.

Teacup, 6 oz.	8.00--12.00
Saucer, 5½"	4.00-- 6.00
Sugar and Cream Set: ind., 3 pc.	25.00--30.00
Sugar, 5 oz., 2¾"	8.00--10.00
Cream, 5 oz., 3"	8.00--10.00
Tray, oval, 8"	8.00--10.00
Salt and Pepper, 3"	15.00--20.00
Puff Box and Cover, 4"	20.00--30.00
Cologne and Stopper, 8 oz.	20.00--30.00
Oil and Stopper, 6 oz.	18.00--22.00
Decanter and Stopper 12 oz., 8¾"	30.00--40.00
Whiskey, 2 oz.	6.00-- 8.00
Mint Box and Cover, low, 4¾"	18.00--22.00
Flip Jug, ½ gal., 8"	65.00--75.00
Cigarette Jar and Cover, 3½"	20.00--25.00
Ash Tray, 3"	5.00-- 8.00
Relish, 2 hdld., 10"	24.00--30.00
Celery and Relish, 12"	28.00-32.00
Mayonnaise Set: 3 pc.	30.00--40.00
Bowl, salad, 12"	25.00--35.00
Bowl, salad, deep, 9"	25.00--30.00
(also 13")	35.00--55.00
Top Hat, 2½"	20.00--25.00
Top Hat, 3½"	16.00--22.00
Vase, oval, 4½"	22.00--25.00
Top Hat, 6"	20.00--30.00
Vase, crimped, 4"	18.00--24.00
Vase, Violet, ftd., 4"	20.00--25.00
Candy Jar and Cover ½ lb., 9½", also 1 lb.	25.00--35.00
Ivy Ball, ftd., 5"	25.00--30.00
Vase, Violet, ftd., 5"	25.00--30.00
Ivy Ball, ftd., 4"	20.00--30.00
Goblet, 9 oz., 6"	14.00--18.00
Saucer Champagne, 5 oz., 4¾"	12.00--16.00
Cocktail 3½ oz., 4¼"	14.00--18.00
Wine, 3 oz., 4½"	14.00--18.00
Orange Juice, 5 oz., 3¾"	8.00--12.00
Ice Tea, 13 oz., 5½"	10.00--12.00
Tumbler, table, 10 oz., 5"	10.00--12.00
Bowl, finger	8.00--12.00
Plate, for finger bowl, 6"	5.00-- 7.00
Jello, ftd., 5 oz.	8.00--10.00
Oyster Cocktail, 4 oz.	10.00--12.00
Sherbet, 5 oz.	8.00--10.00
Tumbler, ftd., 10 oz., 4¾"	10.00--14.00
Coaster, 3"	4.00-- 6.00
Sherbet, low, 6 oz.	7.00-- 9.00
Ice Tea, ftd., 13 oz., 6"	14.00-16.00
Orange Juice, ftd., 5 oz., 4½"	10.00--12.00
Nappy, reg., hdld., 5", 6"	10.00--12.00
Olive, 6"	12.00--15.00
Relish, 2 compt., 6"	12.00--15.00
Tray, mint, (also 7")	10.00--14.00
Jam Jar and Cover 6" Plate w/ring, 5½"	30.00--45.00
Bon Bon, heart shape, 6", (also 5")	12.00--15.00
Bon Bon, diamond shape, 6"	15.00--25.00
Comport, flrd., 6"	20.00--25.00
Basket, oval, 6"	20.00--25.00
Tray, 6½"	14.00--20.00
Sweetmeat, 6"	20.00--25.00
Nappy, dessert, 6" (also 5" and 7")	8.00--12.00

THE DUNCAN & MILLER GLASS COMPANY, Washington, Pennsylvania

PLAZA ("Punties")

THE DUNCAN & MILLER GLASS COMPANY, Washington, Pennsylvania

ASTAIRE (Kimberly)

Plate, salad, 8½"	25.00--35.00
Plate, bread and butter, 6"	20.00--25.00
Plate, dessert, 7½"	25.00--30.00
Plate, rolled edge, 16½" (also flat edge)	35.00--45.00
Plate, sandwich, 11"	25.00--35.00
Plate, 13" (also rolled edge)	35.00--45.00
Basket, candy, 7" (also 5")	20.00--30.00
Bowl, crimped, 9"	25.00--35.00
Vase, crimped, 6"	20.00--25.00
Basket, tall, hdld., 10"	35.00--45.00
Basket, crimped, hdld., 10"	55.00--65.00
Basket, oval, hdld., 10"	55.00--65.00
Bowl, crimped, 2 hdld., 10"	30.00--40.00
Bowl, oval, 10"	30.00--35.00
Candlestick, 4", pr.	30.00--40.00
Center Piece, flrd., 11½"	25.00--35.00
Center Piece, crimped, 12"	30.00--40.00
Candelabrum w/Prisms, 4"	25.00--30.00
Bowl, oval, crimped, 12"	30.00--40.00
Bowl, oval, 12"	30.00--40.00
Salver, ftd., 10"	40.00--60.00
Punch Set: 15 pc.	150.00-165.00
Punch Bowl, 10½"	25.00--35.00
Punch Tray, 16½"	25.00--35.00
Punch Cups	5.00-- 7.00
Punch Ladle	15.00--20.00
Cheese and Cracker Set: 2 pc.	40.00--50.00
Plate w/ring, 11"	20.00--30.00
Cheese Stand, 3¼"	15.00--20.00
Comport, low, 5½"	20.00--25.00
Comport, 5"	20.00--25.00
Comport, flrd., 4½"	20.00--25.00
Comport, 6"	20.00--25.00
Flip Vase, 8"	30.00--40.00
Flip Vase, 12"	50.00--60.00
Flip Vase, 8"	35.00--40.00

DUNCAN'S FLAIR

Bowl	20.00--25.00

PUNTIES

See PLAZA reprint

Plate, 8½"	8.00--11.00
Plate, 6½", 7½"	7.00--10.00
Plate, 10½", hdld.	15.00--25.00
Finger Bowl Plate	7.00--10.00
Cup and Saucer	8.00--12.00
Sherbet	7.00-- 9.00
Jug	40.00--50.00
Jug, flip	25.00--35.00
Tumbler, orange juice	6.00-- 8.00
Tumbler, table	6.00-- 9.00
Tumbler, ice tea	7.00--10.00
Tumbler, whiskey	7.00--10.00
Tumbler, orange juice, ftd.	7.00--10.00
Tumbler, table, ftd.	7.00--10.00
Tumbler, ice tea, ftd.	10.00--12.00
Goblet	12.00--15.00
Saucer Champagne	10.00--12.00
Parfait	10.00--12.00
Ice Cream	8.00--10.00
Wine	12.00--15.00
Cordial	15.00--18.00
Bowl, 16", flared	20.00--30.00
Bowl, 10"	18.00--22.00
Mustard and Cover	14.00--18.00
Oil	20.00--25.00
Salt and Pepper	15.00--25.00
Candlestick, twin	25.00--35.00
Vase	15.00--25.00

KIMBERLY

See ASTAIRE reprint

U.S. Glass made this pattern in crystal decorated with red, and called it KIMBERLY. Decorated in blue it was called HILTON.

Prices below are for the old pink, green and amber.

Plate, 8½"	6.00-- 9.00
Finger Bowl and Plate	10.00--15.00
Bon Bon, 6", ftd.	10.00--15.00
Tumbler, orange juice, 5 oz.	6.00-- 8.00
Tumbler, old fashioned, 7 oz.	7.00-- 9.00
Tumbler, 9 oz.	7.00-- 9.00
Tumbler, ice tea, 12 oz.	8.00--10.00
Tumbler, whiskey, 2 oz.	8.00--10.00
Goblet	12.00--14.00
Saucer Champagne, 5 oz.	9.00--11.00
Parfait, 5 oz.	9.00--11.00
Ice Cream, 5 oz., ftd.	8.00--10.00
Wine, 3 oz.	12.00--14.00
Cocktail, 3 oz.	12.00--14.00
Cordial, 1 oz.	12.00--15.00

EBONY

Some of these pieces went to Lotus for decorating, as did many other top lines of the day, and can be seen in that chapter as well.

Vase	35.00--45.00
Bon Bon, crimped	12.00--16.00
Covered Candy Box	35.00--45.00
Cigarette Box	20.00--25.00
Ash Tray (No. 18)	8.00--10.00
Ash Tray (No. 16)	7.00-- 9.00

VENETIAN page 71

Prices are for crystal. Ruby and blue 50% higher.

No. 5 Vase	20.00--25.00
No. 126 Vase	10.00--14.00
No. 28 Urn and Cover	20.00--25.00
Bowl, square, 10"	20.00--25.00

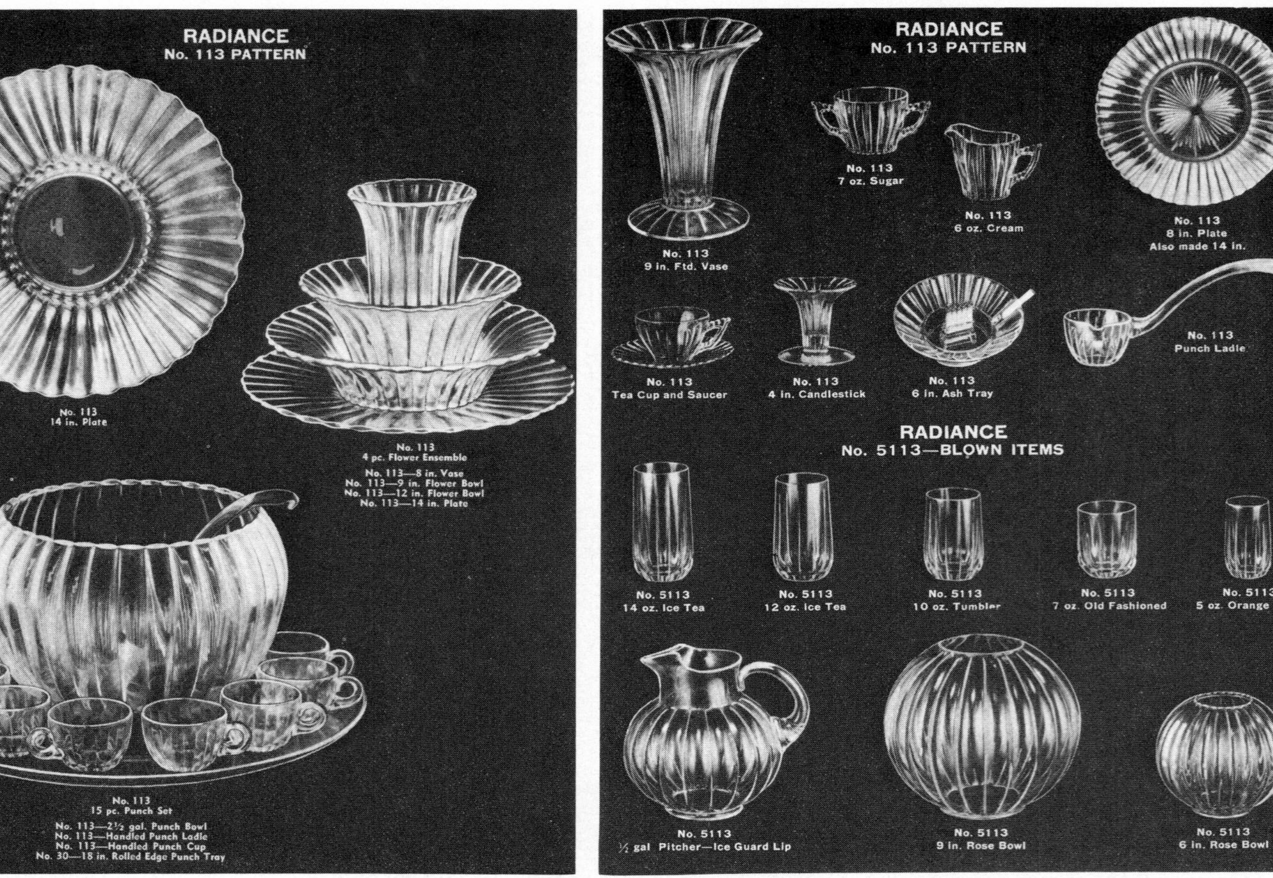
RADIANCE
No. 113 PATTERN
No. 113
14 in. Plate
No. 113
4 pc. Flower Ensemble
No. 113—8 in. Vase
No. 113—9 in. Flower Bowl
No. 113—12 in. Flower Bowl
No. 113—14 in. Plate
No. 113
15 pc. Punch Set
No. 113—2½ gal. Punch Bowl
No. 113—Handled Punch Ladle
No. 113—Handled Punch Cup
No. 30—18 in. Rolled Edge Punch Tray
RADIANCE
No. 113 PATTERN
No. 113
9 in. Ftd. Vase
No. 113
7 oz. Sugar
No. 113
6 oz. Cream
No. 113
8 in. Plate
Also made 14 in.
No. 113
Tea Cup and Saucer
No. 113
4 in. Candlestick
No. 113
6 in. Ash Tray
No. 113
Punch Ladle
RADIANCE
No. 5113—BLOWN ITEMS
No. 5113
14 oz. Ice Tea
No. 5113
12 oz. Ice Tea
No. 5113
10 oz. Tumbler
No. 5113
7 oz. Old Fashioned
No. 5113
5 oz. Orange Juic
No. 5113
½ gal Pitcher—Ice Guard Lip
No. 5113
9 in. Rose Bowl
No. 5113
6 in. Rose Bowl

Bowl, square, 8"	18.00--22.00
Bowl, round, 9"	18.00--22.00
Bcwl, round, 8"	15.00--20.00
Bowl, oval, 14"	22.00--28.00
Bowl, oval, 12"	20.00--25.00
Vase, flower holder, 6"	12.00--15.00
Vase, flower holder, 5"	12.00--15.00
Vase, crimped, 7"	12.00--15.00
Vase, regular, 7"	12.00--15.00
Vase, crimped, 8"	14.00--18.00
Vase, regular, 9"	14.00--18.00

WHITNEY

Vase	30.00--35.00
Comport	25.00--30.00

"GORDON" page 72

Decanter, 32 oz.	30.00--35.00
Whiskey, 1½ oz.	5.00-- 6.00

ASH TRAYS

No. 12 club, 5"	10.00--15.00
No. 11 Masters	10.00--14.00
No. 17 Tray, fluted	6.00--10.00
No. 16 Tray, triangular	6.00--10.00

ARLISS

Mug	20.00--25.00
Coaster/Ash Tray combination	15.00--20.00

"7-11 COCKTAIL SET" page 73

Shaker, 30 oz.	30.00--35.00
Tumbler, hdld., 4 oz.	12.00--18.00

GRANDEE

Candelabrum, pr.	70.00--75.00

EDEN (CHRYSANTHEMUM)

Bowl	80.00--90.00

FROST HIBALL LINE

Relish, 5 compt.	20.00--25.00
No. 56 Decanter, 16 oz.	30.00--35.00
No. 55 Hiball, 12 oz.	8.00--12.00
No. 55 Wine, stemmed, 3 oz.	10.00--15.00
No. 55 Decanter, 16 oz.	30.00--35.00
No. 55 Tumbler, 9 oz.	7.00-- 9.00
No. 55 Tumbler, split beer, 6 oz.	6.00-- 8.00
No. 55 Tumbler, fruit juice, 5 oz.	6.00-- 8.00
No. 55 Whiskey, 1½ oz.	7.00-- 9.00

SWAN

No. 3 Vase, 9" tall x 6½"	100.00-115.00

CHANTICLEER

Cocktail Shaker, 32 oz.	100.00-125.00
Cocktail Shaker, 16 oz.	90.00-110.00
Martini Mixer, 32 oz.	100.00-125.00
Martini Mixer, 16 oz.	90.00-110.00
Tumbler, old fashioned, 7 oz.	35.00--50.00
Tumbler, cocktail or orange, 3½ oz.	35.00--45.00

SCULPTURED GLASS page 74

Chanticleer Vase, crimped, 3½"	35.00--50.00
Chanticleer Vase, crimped, 3"	35.00--50.00
Chanticleer Vase, Tri-Cornered, 3½"	35.00--50.00
Tropical Fish Candlestick, 5"	85.00--95.00
Iris Vase, regular, 9"	75.00--85.00
Iris Vase, crimped, 9"	75.00--85.00
Dogwood Flower Bowl, 12"	75.00--85.00
Dogwood Plate, 14"	75.00--85.00
Chrysanthemum Flower Bowl, 14"	80.00--90.00
Chrysanthemum Plate, 16"	80.00--90.00

"FESTIVAL"

See RADIANCE reprint

Plate, 14"	20.00--25.00
Flower Ensemble, 4 pc.: Vase, 8", Flower Bowl, 9", Flower Bowl, 12", Plate, 14"	50.00--60.00
Punch Set, 15 pc.:	125.00-135.00
Vase, ftd., 9"	18.00--22.00
Sugar, 7 oz.	8.00--10.00
Cream, 6 oz.	8.00--10.00
Plate, 8", 14"	10.00--25.00
Tea Cup and Saucer	10.00--13.00
Candlestick, 4"	9.00--12.00
Ash Tray, 6"	8.00--10.00
Punch Ladle	12.00--15.00

RADIANCE BLOWN ITEMS

Prices are for crystal.

Ice Tea, 14 oz.	7.00-- 9.00
Ice Tea, 12 oz.	6.00-- 8.00
Tumbler, 10 oz.	6.00-- 8.00
Old Fashioned, 7 oz.	6.00-- 8.00
Orange Juice, 5 oz.	5.00-- 7.00
Pitcher, ½ gal.	20.00--25.00
Rose Bowl, 9"	15.00--20.00
Rose Bowl, 6"	10.00--15.00

MARDI GRAS

Punch bowl, w/foot	125.00-175.00

TEAR DROP pages 75-77

Couldn't resist printing all these pieces for you TEAR DROP collectors. Although the line was made primarily in crystal, a 1934 advertisement offers it "with or without colored handles". This was one of D & M's most popular patterns and was kept in production for a long time. In fact, TEAR DROP did for Duncan and Miller what AMERICAN did for Fostoria and CAPE COD for Imperial. Note that U.S. Glass made Duncan's TEAR DROP in crystal as recently as the 60s.

I will suggest prices for crystal only.

Plate, hdld., 11"	12.00--15.00
Plate, hdld., 8"	7.00-- 9.00
Plate, hdld., 6"	5.00-- 6.00
Plate, torte, rolled edge, 18"	30.00--35.00
(also 13" and 14")	18.00--22.00
Plate, 6"	3.00-- 4.00
Plate, 7½"	5.00-- 6.00
Plate, 8½"	8.00--10.00
Plate, 10½"	12.00--15.00
Plate, 14" (also 13" and 18")	22.00--35.00
Cup, demitasse, 2½ oz.	10.00--13.00
Saucer, demitasse, 4½"	4.00-- 6.00
Salt and Pepper, 3"	15.00--20.00
Cup, tea, 6 oz.	10.00--12.00
Saucer	3.00-- 4.00
Cream, 4"	8.00-- 9.00
Sugar	8.00-- 9.00
Mustard and Cover, 4¼"	12.00--14.00
Oil and Stopper, 4¾"	12.00--15.00
Oil and Vinegar Condiment Set: 5 pc.	50.00--60.00
Oil, 3 oz.	12.00--15.00
Vinegar, 3 oz.	12.00--15.00
Salt and Pepper, 3"	15.00--20.00
Tray, oval, 8"	7.00-- 9.00
Marmalade Set: 3 pc.	24.00--28.00
Marmalade and Cover, 4"	16.00--18.00
Marmalade Plate, 6"	8.00--10.00
Salt and Pepper, 5"	15.00--20.00
Pitcher, pint, 5"	12.00--15.00
Orange Juice, ftd., 4½ oz., 4"	4.00-- 6.00
Whiskey or Cocktail, ftd., 3 oz., 3"	6.00-- 8.00
Whiskey, ftd., 2 oz., 2¾"	7.00-- 9.00
Ice Tea or Hiball, ftd. 14 oz., 6" (also 12 oz., 5½")	10.00--12.00
Split or Party Glass, ftd., 8 oz., 5"	8.00--10.00
Tumbler, ftd., 9 oz., 4½"	8.00--10.00
Pitcher w/ice lip, 8½"	35.00--40.00
Whiskey, 2 oz., 2¼"	4.00-- 6.00
Orange Juice, 3½ oz., 3¼ oz.	4.00-- 6.00
Orange Juice, 5 oz., 3½"	4.00-- 6.00
Tumbler, 9 oz., 4¼"	6.00-- 8.00
Hiball, 10 oz., 4¾"	7.00-- 9.00
Hiball, 14 oz., 5¾"	9.00--11.00
Ice Tea, 12 oz., 5¼"	8.00--10.00
Split, 8 oz., 4½"	6.00-- 8.00
Old Fashioned, 7 oz., 3¼"	8.00--10.00
Goblet, 9 oz., 7"	12.00--15.00
Saucer Champagne, 5 oz., 5"	9.00--12.00
Liquor Cocktail, 3½ oz., 4½"	9.00--12.00
Claret, 4 oz., 5½"	12.00--15.00
Wine, 3 oz., 4¾"	12.00--15.00
Sherry, 1¾ oz., 4½"	12.00--15.00
Cordial, 1 oz., 4"	14.00--16.00
Bowl, finger, 4¼"	6.00-- 8.00
Goblet, luncheon, 9 oz., 5¾"	10.00--14.00
Ice Cream, 5 oz., 3½"	6.00-- 8.00
Sherbet, 5 oz.	5.00-- 7.00
Oyster Cocktail, 3½ oz., 2¾"	5.00-- 8.00
Ale Goblet, 8 oz., 6¼"	12.00--14.00
Bowl, fruit, flrd., 10"	14.00--18.00
Center Piece, 10"	15.00--18.00
Basket, 10" (also 11½", crimped)	30.00--40.00
Vase, fan shape, 9"	18.00--22.00
Bowl, low ftd., 12"	25.00--30.00
Vase, regular, 9"	15.00--20.00
Bowl, flower, flrd., 11½"	14.00--18.00
Bowl, Gardenia, 13"	15.00--20.00
Ash Tray, ind., 3"	4.00-- 6.00
Coaster or Ash Tray, 3"	4.00-- 5.00
Ash Tray, 5"	6.00-- 8.00
Bar Bottle and Stopper, 12"	30.00--40.00
Plate w/ring, canape, 6"	7.00--10.00
Cocktail, ftd., 4 oz., 3½"	6.00-- 8.00
Ice Bucket, 6½"	18.00--20.00
Comport, low ftd., 4"	9.00--12.00
Nut Dish, 6"	7.00-- 9.00
Bon Bon, 6"	7.00-- 9.00
Plate, lemon, 7"	7.00-- 9.00
Candy Dish, heart shape, 7½"	10.00--12.00
Olive, 5"	6.00-- 8.00
Relish, heart shape, 7½"	10.00--14.00
Pickle and Olive Dish, 7"	8.00--10.00
Relish, 7"	7.00-- 9.00
Relish, 9"	9.00--11.00
Olive, 6"	8.00--10.00
Pickle, 6"	7.00-- 9.00
Celery, 11"	10.00--14.00
Celery and Radish, 11"	12.00--16.00
Relish, 11"	14.00--16.00
Celery and Relish, 12"	15.00--20.00
Relish, 5 compt., 12"	18.00--22.00
(also 10")	14.00--20.00
Relish, 6 compt., 12"	22.00--25.00
(also 10")	18.00--22.00
Sweetmeat, star shape, 7"	8.00--10.00
Sweetmeat, 6½"	9.00--12.00
Basket, candy, oval, 7½"	8.00--10.00
Sweetmeat, star shape, 5½"	8.00--10.00
Basket, candy, oval, 5½"	7.00-- 9.00
Nappy, hdld., 5"	6.00-- 8.00
Candy Box and Cover, 7"	20.00--25.00

Nappy, 5"	4.00-- 5.00
Nappy, hdld., 7"	6.00-- 8.00
Nappy, 6"	5.00-- 6.00
Nappy, hdld., 9½"	12.00--16.00
Nappy, 7"	7.00-- 8.00
Cheese Stand, 3½"	12.00--15.00
Comport, ftd., 5"	12.00--14.00
Cheese and Cracker Set: 2 pc.	25.00--30.00
Plate, 11"	12.00--15.00
Cheese Stand, 3½"	12.00--15.00
Salad Set: 2 pc.	25.00--30.00
Plate w/ring, 11"	14.00--18.00
Mayonnaise, 6"	10.00--12.00
Mayonnaise Set: flrd., 3 pc.	25.00--28.00
Mayonnaise, 3"	10.00--12.00
Plate w/ring, 6"	6.00-- 8.00
Ladle	6.00-- 8.00
Bowl, salad, 12"	14.00--20.00
Mayonnaise Set: 3 pc.	25.00--30.00
Plate, 8"	7.00-- 9.00
Mayonnaise, 3"	10.00--12.00
Ladle	6.00-- 8.00
Salad Set: 2 pc.	30.00--40.00
Bowl, salad, 9"	14.00--18.00
Plate, rolled edge, 13"	18.00--22.00
(also flat edge)	15.00--20.00
Candlestick, 4", pr.	18.00--24.00
Bowl, flower, 12"	20.00--25.00
Bowl, flower, oval, 12"	20.00--30.00
Candlesticks, 2 light	20.00--25.00
Cake Salver, ftd., 13"	30.00--40.00
Mayonnaise, 4¼"	9.00--12.00
Midnight or Buffet Supper Set: 3 pc.	55.00--70.00
Plate, 18"	30.00--35.00
Relish, 6 compt., 12"	22.00--25.00
Bowl, salad dressing	9.00--12.00
Punch Set: 15 pc.	150.00-165.00
Punch Bowl, 2½ gal.	30.00--40.00
Tray, rolled edge, 18"	30.00--35.00
Punch Cups, 6 oz.	4.00-- 6.00
Ladle	10.00--15.00

TERRACE page 78

Plate, rnd., 6", 7½"	3.00-- 5.00
Plate, rnd., 8½", 10½"	8.00--14.00
Plate, square, 9"	8.00--12.00
Cup	8.00-- 9.00
Saucer, square	3.00-- 4.00
Cream	8.00-- 9.00
Sugar	8.00-- .900
Bowl, console	18.00--24.00
Bowl, salad, 12"	15.00--20.00
Goblet	12.00--14.00
Urn, covered	30.00--40.00
Sherbet	5.00-- 7.00
Comport	14.00--20.00
Relish	10.00--12.00
Plate, torte, 18"	25.00--30.00
Candlesticks, pr.	18.00--24.00

NAUTICAL

Plate, 8"	16.00--19.00
Plate, hdld., 11"	25.00--30.00

CARIBBEAN

Suggested prices are mainly for the Sapphire blue, but you may find crystal, and some pieces, such as the Tom & Jerry sets, in crystal with cobalt blue, amber, or ruby trim. You may find the smoker set in ruby, and also in dark amber.

Plate, dinner, 10½"	12.00--15.00
Plate, luncheon, 8½"	9.00--12.00
Plate, bread and butter, 6"	4.00-- 6.00
Plate, tab handles, 10¼"	15.00--20.00
Plate, 12½", 13¼" turned up edge	20.00--25.00
Cup	12.00--15.00
Saucer	6.00-- 8.00
Sugar	12.00--15.00
Cream	12.00--15.00
Bowl, 5", 1-5/8" deep	7.00-- 9.00
Bowl, salad, 9", 4½" deep	20.00--25.00
Bowl, flrd., 9", 3-5/8" deep	20.00--25.00
Bowl, console	30.00--35.00
Bowl, 5½", 3¾" deep, divided mayonnaise	30.00--35.00
Bowl, pickle, oval, 7" w/tab handles	15.00--18.00
Bowl, 5½", 3¾" deep	15.00--20.00
Relish, 4 part, 11¼"	20.00--25.00
Relish, 6 sections, 12½" turned up rim	25.00--30.00
Pitcher, 8½"	60.00--75.00
Tumbler, flat, 10 oz., 5"	12.00--16.00
Tumbler, ice tea, ftd., 6-3/8" 10 oz.	12.00--16.00
Goblet	12.00--16.00
Goblet, wine, 2½ oz., 4"	12.00--16.00
Sherbet, low, 5½ oz., 3¾"	7.00--10.00
Sherbet, high, 5½ oz., 4¾"	8.00--12.00
Vase, 6"	14.00--18.00
Vase, 10"	24.00--28.00
Vase, (mushroom shape) 2½" high	10.00--12.00
Compote	14.00--18.00
Cheese and Cracker	25.00--35.00
Salt and Pepper	25.00--35.00
Mustard	20.00--30.00
Candlesticks w/Prisms, pr.	40.00--60.00
Candy Dish and Cover 7" across, 3½" high	40.00--50.00
Smoker Set: Cigarette Holder, 2 Ash Trays stacked to look like a tumbler	15.00--25.00
Punch Bowl	50.00--60.00
Punch Cups	6.00-- 8.00
Plate, torte, 16"	25.00--35.00
Ladle	15.00--20.00

Punch Set: Bowl, 12 Cups Ladle, & Underplate	175.00-200.00
Tom and Jerry Set: Bowl, 8 Cups & Ladle	100.00-125.00
Candelabrum, 2 light	25.00--30.00
Cocktail Set: 6 Tumblers Decanter, Tray w/6 indents	100.00-125.00

MISCELLANEOUS — page 79

No. 25 Candy Jar and cover, 5"	15.00--20.00
No. 25 Nappy, 5" (also, 3½", 4", 4½" and 6")	3.00-- 7.00
No. 25 Grapefruit, ftd.	6.00-- 8.00
No. 25 Grapefruit Liner, ftd.	4.00-- 6.00
No. 26 Coaster, 3½"	3.00-- 5.00
No. 25 Cheese and Cracker Set: 2 pc.	15.00--20.00
No. 25 Cheese Plate w/ring, 11"	9.00--12.00
No. 940 Cheese Stand	6.00-- 9.00
No. 26 Nappy, 3"	2.00-- 3.00
No. 28 Candlestick, 4", pr.	12.00--15.00
No. 28 Hospital or Breakfast Tray Set:	15.00--18.00
No. 28 Sugar, 5 oz.	5.00-- 7.00
No. 28 Cream, 4 oz.	5.00-- 7.00
No. 28 Butter, 3"	3.00-- 5.00
No. 29 Nappy, 5½"	3.00-- 4.00
No. 28 Muffin Cover, 6"	10.00--14.00
No. 29 Grapefruit, 6" (also 6½")	5.00-- 6.00
No. 30 Nappy, 2 hdld., 6"	3.00-- 5.00
No. 30 Plate, 6½"	3.00-- 4.00
No. 30 Relish, 2 compt., 6"	4.00-- 6.00
No. 30 Plate, sandwich, 11"	7.00--11.00
No. 30 Ice Bucket	15.00--18.00
No. 30 Salad Dressing Set	20.00--24.00
No. 30 Flip Vase, flrd., 8"	10.00--15.00
No. 30 Celery and Relish, 12"	14.00--18.00
No. 30 Cheese and Cracker Set: 2 pc.	15.00--20.00
No. 940 Cheese Stand	7.00-- 9.00
No. 30 Plate w/ring, 2 hdld., 11"	9.00--11.00
No. 129 Perfume Set: 3 pc.	40.00--45.00
No. 129 Puff Box and Cover 5¾"	14.00--18.00
No. 129 Perfume Bottle, pr.	25.00--28.00
No. 106 Candy Box and Cover	20.00--25.00
No. 91 Nappy, 4½"	2.00-- 3.00
No. 91 Nappy, 5½"	2.00-- 4.00
No. 101 Ice Cocktail and Liner	14.00--18.00
No. 101 Ice Cocktail Goblet	7.00--10.00
No. 101 Ice Cocktail Liner	7.00-- 8.00
No. 218 Oyster Cocktail Center, 4 oz.	2.00-- 4.00
No. 219 Oyster Cocktail Center, 2½ oz.	4.00-- 5.00
No. 91 Pickle Tray, 8½"	6.00-- 9.00
No. 220 Oyster Cocktail Center, 3 oz.	4.00-- 5.00
No. 91 Celery Tray, 11"	10.00--14.00

PALL MALL — page 80

Swan prices are low prices for crystal and high for transparent colors. Pink and blue opalescent and milk glass w/green and ruby trim are much higher.

Decanter and Stopper, 32 oz., 10¾"	20.00--30.00
Plate, deviled egg, 12"	15.00--25.00
Cocktail Mixer with Spoon, 30 oz., 8¼"	20.00--25.00
Plate, torte, flat edge, 14" (also w/rolled edge)	18.00--22.00
Celery and Relish, 12"	15.00--20.00
Pimlico Celery and Relish, 12"	15.00--20.00
Vase, cornucopia, 7½"	20.00--25.00
Duck, 4", solid	20.00--40.00
Federal Mirror Bookend, 6¾", pr.	55.00--65.00
Flower Bowl or Gardenia Ring, 11½"	25.00--30.00
Sailfish, 5"	100.00-150.00
Heron, 7"	75.00--90.00
Ruffed Grouse, 6½"	375.00-400.00
Bird of Paradise, 13"	175.00-200.00
Swan, 3", solid	25.00--30.00
Swan, 5", solid	30.00--35.00
Swan, 7", solid	40.00--50.00
Swan, 7"	15.00--45.00
Swan, 6"	25.00--60.00
Swan, 3½"	25.00--60.00
Swan, 12"	55.00--75.00
Swan, 10½"	35.00--85.00

DUNCAN'S RUBY

Low price for crystal. High price for Ruby.

Duck Cigarette Box and Cover	40.00-100.00
Duck Ash Tray, 7"	45.00--80.00
Duck Ash Tray, 4"	20.00--50.00
Aladdin lamp, 7"	18.00--35.00
Plate, 8½", also made 6, 7½" and 10"	5.00--20.00
Bon Bon, hdld., 6"	10.00--30.00
Swan, 7"	20.00--45.00
Swan Candlelite Garden, 7"	25.00--50.00
Swan, 3½"	25.00--75.00
Swan Candlelite Garden, 10½"	35.00--65.00
Swan, 10½"	35.00--85.00
Swan, 6"	25.00--60.00
Cornucopia Vase, 14"	25.00--75.00
Swan, 12"	50.00--75.00

WATERFORD — page 81

Goblet, 9 oz., 6"	10.00--14.00
Saucer, champagne, 6 oz., 4½"	8.00--12.00
Wine, 3 oz., 4¼"	10.00--14.00

Cocktail, 3 oz., flrd. edge	10.00--14.00
Ice Cream, 6 oz.	6.00-- 8.00
Parfait, 5 oz., 5¼"	10.00--14.00
Ice Tea, 14 oz., 5½"	9.00--11.00
Ice Tea, 12 oz., 5¼"	8.00--10.00
Tumbler, table, 9 oz., 4¼"	7.00-- 9.00
Orange Juice, 5 oz., 4"	7.00-- 9.00
Hi Ball, 7½ oz., 5"	7.00-- 9.00
Plate, 8½"	6.00-- 9.00
Plate, 6"	3.00-- 4.00
Plate, 7½"	5.00-- 7.00
Tumbler, 2 oz., 2¾"	8.00--10.00
Bowl, finger, 4"	6.00-- 9.00
Jug, ½ gal., 8¼"	50.00--65.00

AMERICAN WAY CRYSTAL

Also flashed on red

Comport, low foot, 7½"	18.00--22.00
Comport, low foot, 7"	18.00--22.00
Relish, 3 compt., 8½"	15.00--20.00
Relish, tricorne	17.00--22.00
Plate, Hors D'oeuvre, 9½"	14.00--18.00
Candy Box and Cover, 8"	25.00--30.00
Bowl, Camelia, shallow, 8½"	14.00--18.00
Plate, star shape, 14"	30.00--35.00
Bowl, flower, 11", 3¾"	20.00--25.00
Bowl, flower, 13", 3¾"	25.00--30.00
Vase, flrd., 8"	25.00--30.00
Plate, Hors D'oeuvre, 15"	35.00--40.00
Vase, clover leaf, 6½"	28.00--32.00
Bowl, oval, 12½"	25.00--30.00
Vase, crimped, 6"	18.00--22.00
Candlestick, 2", pr.	15.00--20.00
Basket, oval, 12"	45.00--55.00
Flower Arranger, crimped, 7"	20.00--25.00
Bowl, crimped, 10½"	25.00--30.00
Vase, flrd., 6½"	25.00--30.00

DIAMOND page 82

Sweetmeat, 2 hdld., 7"	9.00--12.00
Sugar and Cream Set: ind.,	20.00--25.00
Cream, 3"	7.00-- 9.00
Sugar, 2½"	7.00-- 9.00
Tray, oval, 8"	7.00-- 9.00
Basket, oval candy, 7½"	9.00--12.00
Bon Bon, flrd., 6½"	10.00--12.00
Candy Box and Cover, 6"	20.00--25.00
Dish, mint, 2 hdld., 6½"	7.00--10.00
Bowl, salad, deep, 9½"	15.00--18.00
Bowl, salad, shallow, 12"	16.00--20.00
Salad Dressing Set: 4 pc.	35.00--45.00
Bowl, 2 compt., 6"	16.00--20.00
Plate, 2 hdld., 7½"	7.00--10.00
2 Ladles	6.00-- 9.00
Mayonnaise Set: 3 pc.	30.00--35.00
Bowl, 2 hdld.	10.00--14.00
Plate, 2 hdld., 7½"	9.00--12.00
Ladle	6.00-- 9.00
Candelabrum, 1 light w/Prisms, 8"	45.00--55.00
Candelabrum, 1 light w/Prisms, 4"	35.00--40.00
Candlestick, 1 light, 4"	10.00--15.00
Hurricane Lamp, 1 light w/Prisms, 4"	30.00--40.00
Vase or Ice Bucket, 6"	14.00--18.00
Bowl, flrd., 9½"	14.00--18.00
Flower Arranger	14.00--18.00
Bowl, flrd., 11½"	18.00--22.00
Bowl, crimped, 11½"	18.00--22.00
Bowl, 10"	18.00--22.00
Centerpiece, 2 hdld., 11"	18.00--22.00
Bowl, Sweet Pea, 8"	15.00--20.00
Goblet, 9 oz., 7¼"	11.00--14.00
Saucer, Champagne or tall Sherbet, 6 oz., 5½"	9.00--12.00
Cocktail, 3½ oz., 5"	9.00--12.00
Cordial, 1 oz., 4¼"	12.00--15.00
Wine, 3 oz., 5¾"	11.00--14.00
Claret, 5 oz., 6¾"	11.00--14.00
Goblet, low, luncheon, 9 oz., 5½"	9.00--12.00
Ice Cream, ftd., 6 oz., 3½"	7.00-- 9.00
Oyster Cocktail, 5½ oz., 3¾"	7.00-- 9.00
Orange Juice, ftd., 5 oz., 4¾"	7.00-- 9.00
Ice Tea, ftd., 12 oz., 6¼"	10.00--12.00

Pressed glass

Ice Tea, ftd., 13 oz., 6¾"	9.00--12.00
Orange Juice, ftd., 5 oz., 5"	7.00--10.00
Oyster Cocktail, 4½ oz., 4"	7.00--10.00
Bowl, finger, 4"	6.00-- 8.00
Goblet, 9 oz., 6¼"	10.00--14.00
Saucer Champagne or tall Sherbet, 6 oz., 4½"	8.00--12.00
Claret or Wine, 4 oz., 5¼"	10.00--14.00
Cocktail, 3½ oz., 4½"	9.00--12.00
Relish, 2 hdld., 6½"	9.00--12.00
Plate, rolled edge, 13"	20.00--25.00
Relish, 6½"	9.00--12.00
Celery and Relish, 11"	18.00--22.00
Hors D'oeuvre, 12"	18.00--24.00
Plate, 3 hdld., 7½"	6.00-- 9.00
Plate, torte, 13"	20.00--25.00
Plate, torte, RE, 13"	20.00--25.00
Plate, lemon, 8"	8.00--10.00
Jelly, 6"	9.00--11.00
Plate, sandwich, 12"	18.00--24.00
Olive, 6½"	9.00--12.00

CANTERBURY page 83, 84

Cup, tea, 6 oz.	9.00--12.00
Saucer, 6"	3.00-- 5.00
Sherbet, 2¾"	5.00-- 8.00
Sherbet, 4½"	6.00-- 9.00
Nappy, fruit, 5"	5.00-- 8.00
Sugar and Cream Set: ind.,	15.00--18.00
Sugar, 2½"	7.00-- 9.00
Cream, 2¾"	7.00-- 9.00
Tray, oval, 8"	7.00-- 9.00
Sugar, 7 oz., 3"	8.00--10.00
Cream, 7 oz., 3¾"	8.00--10.00

Fruit, hdld., 5½"	6.00-- 9.00
Nappy, heart shape, 5½" (also, star and square shape)	6.00-- 9.00
Fruit Set: 2 pc.	12.00--15.00
Fruit Bowl, hdld., 5½"	6.00-- 9.00
Fruit Plate, hdld., 6½"	5.00-- 7.00
Nappy, hdld., 5½"	7.00-- 9.00
Sweetmeat, star shape, 6"	8.00--10.00
Nappy, 2 hdld., 6"	8.00--10.00
Plate, 7½"	6.00-- 9.00
Plate, (finger bowl) 6"	6.00-- 8.00
Plate, 8½"	8.00--10.00
Plate, 14"	20.00--30.00
Plate, sandwich, 11"	15.00--20.00
Plate, 7½"	6.00-- 9.00
Vase, clover leaf, 3½", 4", 4½"	10.00--15.00
Vase, Violet, crimped 3", 3½", 4½"	10.00--15.00
Vase, oval, 3½", 4", 4½"	10.00--15.00
Vase, crimped, 3½", 4", 5"	11.00--15.00
Vase, clover leaf, 5", 6½"	12.00--16.00
Top Hat or Cigarette Holder	10.00--14.00
Vase, crimped, 5½", 7"	14.00--20.00
Flower Arranger, 5½", 7"	15.00--20.00
Bowl, Rose, 5"	12.00--15.00
Vase or Ice Bucket, 6", 7"	15.00--20.00
Basket, 4½" (also; 3½" size)	18.00--22.00
Basket, 3"	15.00--18.00
Basket, crimped, 3"	18.00--22.00
Basket, crimped, 4½" (also; 3½" size)	20.00--25.00
Bowl, Gardenia, 7½"	9.00--12.00
Bowl, crimped, 7½"	9.00--12.00
Bowl, flrd., 8"	14.00--18.00
Basket, 10" (also 11½")	35.00--45.00
Bowl, crimped, 8"	15.00--20.00
Bowl, Gardenia, 9"	15.00--20.00
Bowl, oval, 9"	18.00--22.00
Bowl, crimped, 9"	20.00--25.00
Bowl, oval, 10" (also; 11½")	22.00--28.00
Ash Tray, 5"	5.00-- 8.00
Cigarette Box and Cover	15.00--20.00
Club Ash Tray, 3"	6.00-- 9.00
Cigarette Jar and Cover	15.00--20.00
Club Ash Tray, 4½"	7.00--11.00
Ash Tray, 3"	5.00-- 7.00
Club Ash Tray, 5½"	8.00--12.00
Claret or Wine, 4 oz., 5"	9.00--12.00
Decanter and Stopper, 32 oz., 12"	40.00--50.00
Ice Bucket, 7" (also 6")	15.00--20.00
Goblet, 9 oz., 6"	10.00--12.00
Saucer Champagne, or tall Sherbet, 6 oz., 4½"	9.00--12.00
Claret or Wine, 4 oz., 5"	10.00--12.00
Cocktail, 3½ oz., 4¼"	10.00--12.00
Oyster Cocktail, 4½ oz., 4"	9.00--11.00
Ice Cream, 6 oz., 3¾"	7.00-- 9.00
Orange Juice, ftd., 5 oz., 4¼"	7.00-- 9.00
Goblet, luncheon, 9 oz., 5½"	8.00--10.00
Ice Tea, ftd., 13 oz., 6¼"	8.00--11.00
Ice Tea, 13 oz., 6¼"	8.00--10.00
Tumbler, table, 9 oz., 4½"	6.00-- 8.00
Orange Juice, 5 oz., 3¾"	5.00-- 7.00
Candy Box and Cover, 8"	25.00--30.00
Relish, 8"	12.00--14.00
Tray, celery, 9"	12.00--14.00
Tray, pickle and olive, 9"	12.00--14.00
Relish, 9"	12.00--14.00
Relish, rnd., 2 hdld., 6" (also; star shape)	9.00--11.00
Relish, oval, 2 hdld., 7"	9.00--12.00
Olive, oval, 6"	12.00--15.00
Celery and Relish, 2 hdld., 10½"	14.00--18.00
Goblet, 10 oz., 7¼"	11.00--14.00
Saucer Champagne, 5 oz., 5½"	10.00--12.00
Cordial, 1 oz., 4¼"	12.00--15.00
Wine, 3½ oz., 6"	11.00--14.00
Claret, 5 oz., 6¾"	11.00--14.00
Martini Mixer w/Spoon, 32 oz., 9¼"	25.00--30.00
Liquor Cocktail, 3 oz., 5¼"	12.00--15.00
Bowl, finger, 4½"	6.00-- 8.00
Martini Mixer w/Spoon, 32 oz., 9¼"	20.00--30.00
Ice Tea., ftd., 12 oz., 5¾"	7.00--10.00
Tumbler, ftd., 10 oz., 4½"	7.00-- 9.00
Orange Juice, ftd., 5 oz., 4¼"	6.00-- 8.00
Ice Cream, ftd., 5 oz., 2½"	6.00-- 8.00
Oyster Cocktail, ftd., 4 oz., 3¼"	7.00-- 9.00

THREE FEATHERS page 85

Vase, cornucopia, 8"	25.00--30. 00
Candlestick or Vase, 4", pr.	35.00--40.00
Bowl, oval, 12"	30.00--35.00
Candy Box and Cover, 7"	35.00--40.00

SWIRL

Bowl, crimped, 11"	25.00--35.00
Vase, flrd., 7½"	18.00--22.00
No. 1 Vase, cornucopia, 11"	40.00--50.00
No. 2 Vase, cornucopia, 14"	40.00--60.00
No. 3 Vase, cornucopia, 14"	40.00--60.00

MURANO

Flower Arranger, 8"	20.00--25.00
Crown Flower Holder, 5"	8.00--10.00
Flower Arranger, 5"	12.00--16.00
Plate, crimped, 8½"	8.00--10.00
Crown Candlestick, 5", pr.	20.00--24.00
Bowl, crimped, 10"	30.00--40.00
Plate, 14"	20.00--30.00
Vase, flrd., 7"	22.00--32.00
Crown Vase, 7"	22.00--32.00
Flower Arranger, 5½"	14.00--17.00
Candle Flower Arranger, 2½", pr.	25.00--30.00
Flower Arranger, 12½"	35.00--45.00

Candy Dish, 7"	12.00--15.00
Bowl, 9½"	25.00--30.00
Bon Bon, 7"	12.00--15.00

SYLVAN page 86

Prices are 50% higher for opalescent colors

Ash Tray or ind., Nut Dish, 3"	8.00--10.00
Vase or Cigarette Holder, 3½"	10.00--14.00
Ash Tray, 5½"	10.00--12.00
Swan, 12"	40.00--50.00
Swan, 7½"	30.00--40.00
Swan, 5½"	25.00--30.00
Swan, 3"	20.00--28.00
Bowl, Flower Arranger, 13"	25.00--30.00
Vase, flrd., 7"	20.00--25.00
Salad Bowl, w/mayonnaise compt., and Ladle, 11"	30.00--40.00
Bowl, fruit, 11"	25.00--30.00
Plate, salad, 7½"	10.00--15.00
Nappy, fruit, 5½"	8.00--10.00
Relish, hdld., 7½"	12.00--15.00
Plate, sandwich, 14"	30.00--40.00
Bon Bon, hdld., 5½"	8.00--10.00
Celery and Relish, 3 compt., 10"	18.00--24.00
Mayonnaise Set: 3 pc., 7½"	22.00--28.00
Candy Dish, 7½"	10.00--12.00
Oyster Cocktail, 3½ oz., 3½"	10.00--14.00
Candy Dish, 7½"	10.00-14.00
Candy Box, swan, and Cover, 7½"	45.00--55.00
Candy Box and Cover, 7½"	18.00--22.00
Candy Box, swan and cover, 7½"	35.00--45.00
Candy Box and Cover, 7½"	18.00--22.00
Tray, mint, hdld., 7½"	8.00--12.00
Candlestick, 1 light, pr. 3"	20.00--30.00
Bowl, flower, 12"	20.00--25.00
Epergne, 2 light, ftd., 5"	25.00--35.00
Bowl, fruit, deep, 12½"	20.00--25.00
Bowl, flower, flrd., 12"	22.00--26.00
Pan, flower, 14"	25.00--30.00

SANIBEL page 87

Vase, oval, ftd., 5½"	25.00--35.00
Vase, crimped, ftd., 5½"	25.00--35.00
Vase, bookend, 5¾"	25.00--35.00
Floating Garden, oblong, 13"	20.00--30.00
Floating Garden, 14"	25.00--35.00
Bowl, flower, crimped, 14"	25.00--35.00
Tray, muffin, 13"	20.00--25.00
Bowl, fruit, oval, 13"	25.00--35.00
Tray, mint, 7"	8.00--10.00
Sweetmeat, 8"	9.00--12.00
Nappy, fruit, 6"	8.00--10.00
Plate, Hors D'oeurve 14"	30.00--35.00
Bowl, salad, deep, 11"	25.00--35.00
Plate, salad, 8½"	9.00--12.00
Bowl, salad, shallow, 12½"	25.00--35.00
Candy Jar and Cover, 9"	35.00--40.00
Cigarette Jar and Cover, 5½"	25.00--30.00
Decanter, 30 oz., 9½"	35.00--45.00
Ash Tray, tropical fish, 3½"	12.00--16.00
Relish, 2 compt., 8½"	20.00--25.00
Ash Tray, life preserver, 3"	8.00--11.00
Tray, celery, 9"	14.00--18.00
Ash Tray, life preserver, 6"	14.00--16.00
Celery and Relish, oblong, 3 compt., 13"	25.00--30.00
Plate, sandwich, oblong, 13"	25.00--30.00

GRECIAN

Bowl, square hdld., 8½"	25.00--30.00
Comport, square hdld., 6"	12.00--16.00
Urn, scroll hdld., 10"	25.00--35.00
Urn, scroll hdld., 9"	25.00--35.00
Urn, swan hdld., 8"	40.00--50.00
Urn, swan hdld., 10"	50.00--60.00
Urn, square hdld., 10"	35.00--40.00
Urn, square hdld., 9½"	30.00--40.00
Urn, square hdld., 8"	25.00--35.00
Urn, square hdld., 7"	20.00--30.00

PASSION FLOWER DESIGN page 88

Candy Box and Cover, 3 compt., 8"	40.00--50.00
Candy Box and Cover, 6", 8"	35.00-45.00
Candy Box and Knob Cover, 8" (also made w/2 compt.)	35.00--45.00
Vase, cornucopia, 8"	30.00--40.00
Urn, square 2 hdld., 9½	35.00--45.00
Vase, 12", 10"	30.00--35.00
Candlestick, square 2", pr.	20.00--25.00
Floating Garden, 12"	22.00--26.00
Vase, tall, 9"	25.00--30.00
Bowl, oval, 14"	30.00--40.00
Vase, flip, flrd., 8"	20.00--30.00
Bowl, flower flrd., 12"	25.00--30.00
Bowl, oval, 10", 11½"	25.00--35.00
Bowl, crimp., 9", 10½"	22.00--28.00
Hurricane Lamp, w/Prisms, 1 light, 15"	60.00--80.00
Bowl, salad, 10½"	25.00--30.00
Plate, 14"	35.00--45.00
Plate, deviled egg, 12"	45.00--55.00

ADORATION

Goblet, 10 oz., 7½"	18.00--22.00
Saucer Champagne, or tall Sherbet, 6 oz., 6"	16.00--20.00
Cordial, 1 oz., 4½"	20.00--24.00
Cocktail, liquor, 3½ oz., 5½"	16.00--20.00
Wine, 3 oz., 6¼"	18.00--22.00
Ice Tea., ftd., 13 oz., 6¼"	14.00--18.00
Orange Juice, ftd., 5 oz., 4½"	12.00--15.00

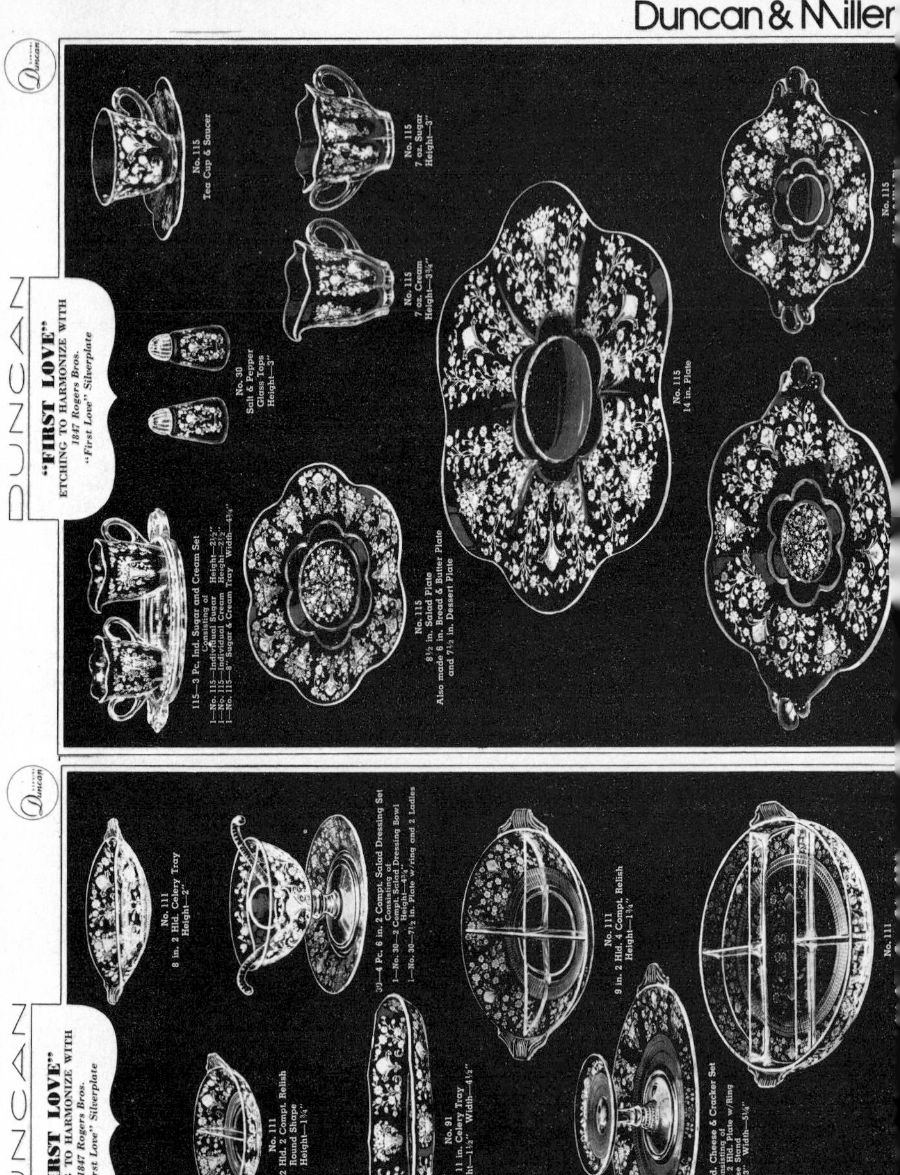
DUNCAN
"FIRST LOVE"
ETCHING TO HARMONIZE WITH
1847 Rogers Bros.
"First Love" Silverplate
No. 115
Tea Cup & Saucer
No. 30
Salt & Pepper
Glass Tops
Height—3"
No. 115
7 oz. Cream
Height—3¾"
No. 115
7 oz. Sugar
Height—3"
115—3 Pc. Ind. Sugar and Cream Set
Consisting of
1—No. 115—Individual Sugar Height—2½"
1—No. 115—Individual Cream Height—2½"
1—No. 115—8" Sugar & Cream Tray Width—4¾"
No. 115
8½ in. Salad Plate
Also made 8 in. Bread & Butter Plate
and 7½ in. Dessert Plate
No. 115
14 in. Plate
No. 115
DUNCAN
"FIRST LOVE"
ETCHING TO HARMONIZE WITH
1847 Rogers Bros.
"First Love" Silverplate
No. 111
8 in. 2 Hld. Celery Tray
Height—2"
30—4 Pc. 6 in. 2 Compt. Salad Dressing Set
Consisting of
1—No. 30—2 Compt. Salad Dressing Bowl
Height—4¾"
1—No. 30—7½ in. Plate w/ring and 2 Ladles
No. 111
9 in. 2 Hld. 4 Compt. Relish
Height—1¾"
No. 111
No. 111
6 in. 2 Hld. 2 Compt. Relish
Round Shape
Height—1¾"
No. 91
11 in. Celery Tray
Height—1½" Width—4½"
111—11 in. 2 Hld. Cheese & Cracker Set
Consisting of
111—11 in. 2 Hld. Plate w/Ring
111—Cheese Stand
Height—3" Width—5¼"
No. 111
6 in. 2 Hld. Nappy
Regular Shape
Height—1¾"
111—3 Pc. Mayonnaise Set
Consisting of
1—No. 111—5½ in. Ftd. and Hld. Mayonnaise
Height—2½"
1—No. 111—2 Hld. Plate and Ladle
No. 30
12 in. 2 Hld. Oblong Celery
and Relish Tray
Height—1½"
No. 31½

ETCHING TO HARMONIZE WITH
1847 Rogers Bros.
"First Love" Silverplate

No. 115
12 in. Flared Bowl
Height—3¼"

No. 115
13 in. Oval Bowl Flared
Height—3¼" Width—8¾"

No. 115
3 in. Low Candlestick

No. 115
10 in. Oval Hld. Basket
Height—4¼" Width—7"

No. 115
3 in. Low Candlestick

No. 30
11 in. Round Gardenia Bowl
Height—1¾"

No. 115
10½ in. Crimped Bowl
Height—5"

No. 115
11½ in. Oval Bowl
Height—5" Width—8¼"

ETCHING TO HARMONIZE WITH
1847 Rogers Bros.
"First Love" Silverplate

No. 115
6 in. 2 Hld. Oval Olive
Height—2½" Width—5¼"

No. 115
6 in. 2 Hld. Round Nappy
Height—1¾"

No. 115
6 in. 2 Hld. 2 Compt. Round Relish
Height—1¾"

115—4 Pc. 6 in. Twin Dressing Set
Consisting of
1—No. 115—6 in. 2 Compt. Salad Dressing Bowl
Height—3¼"
1—No. 115—8½ in. Plate w/ring and 2 Ladles

115—3 Pc. 5½ in. Crimped Mayonnaise Set
Consisting of
1—No. 115—5½ in. Crimped Mayonnaise
Height—3½"
1—No. 115—7½ in. 2 Hld. Plate & Ladle

No. 115
9 in. 2 Compt. Pickle & Olive
Height—1½"

No. 115
5 in. 1 Hld. Round Nappy
Height—1¾"

No. 115
5½ in. 1 Hld. Nappy, Heart Shape
Height—2"

115—11 in. Cheese & Cracker Set
Consisting of
1—No. 115—5¾" Cheese Stand Height—3½"
1—No. 115—11 in. 2 Hld. Plate w/ring

No. 115
10½ in. 2 Hld. 3 Compt. Celery & Relish
Height—1¼" Width—6"

No. 115
9 in. 3 Hld. 3 Compt. Relish
Height—1½"

Oyster Cocktail, 4½ oz., 3½" 12.00--15.00
Ice Cream, 6 oz., 3½" 10.00--12.00
Sugar, 8 oz., 2¾" 10.00--15.00
Cream, 7 oz., 3½" 10.00--15.00
Plate, sandwich, 2 hdld., 11" 15.00--20.00
Plate, salad, 8½" 10.00--14.00
Plate, dessert, 7½" 9.00--11.00
Plate, bread and butter, 6½" 6.00-- 8.00
Vase, cornucopia, 8" 30.00--40.00
Hurricane Lamp, Candelabra,
w/Prisms, 1 light, 15" 75.00--85.00
Relish, flrd., 3 hdld., 9" 18.00--22.00
Nappy, flrd., 2 hdld., 6" 7.00-- 9.00
Candlestick, 2 light, 5", pr. 35.00--50.00
Bowl, flower, 12"
(also: made crimped) 25.00--35.00
Mayonnaise Set: 3 pc. 30.00--35.00
Bowl, mayonnaise, 6" 18.00--22.00
Plate, mayonnaise 6.00-- 8.00
Ladle 6.00-- 8.00
Candy Box and Cover,
3 compt., 7" 40.00--60.00

FIRST LOVE page 89, 90

Cigarette Box and Cover, 4½" 25.00--30.00
Ash Tray, 3½" 10.00--12.00
Ash Tray, 5" 12.00--15.00
Candy Jar and Cover, ftd., 5" 50.00--60.00
Candy Box and Cover,
3 compt., 6" 50.00--60.00
Ash Tray, rect., 6½" 15.00--18.00
Candy Box and Cover,
3 hdld., 3 compt., 8" 55.00--65.00
Comport, low, 6" 20.00--25.00
Plate, deviled egg, 12" 50.00--60.00
Comport, high ftd., 5½" 25.00--30.00
Ice Bucket, hdld., and
Tongs, 6" 50.00--60.00
Cocktail Shaker, 32 oz., hgt. 9"
(also 14 oz. and 18 oz.) 75.00--95.00
Jug, ice lip, 80 oz., 9" 65.00--85.00
Urn or Vase, 7" 30.00--40.00
Vase, cornucopia, 8" 50.00--60.00
(also made in 4") 20.00--25.00
Vase or Urn, 5" 20.00--25.00
Candlestick or Vase, 4", pr. 40.00--50.00
Bowl, flower, oval, 12" 45.00--55.00
Vase, flrd., 12" 50.00--60.00
Vase, crimped, 5" 20.00--25.00
Vase, ftd., 10" 50.00--60.00
Goblet, tall, 10 oz., 6¾" 25.00--30.00
Saucer Champagne, 5 oz., 5" 22.00--26.00
Cocktail, liquor, 3½ oz., 4½" 22.00--26.00
Wine, 3 oz., 5¼" 25.00--30.00
Claret, 4½ oz., 6" 24.00--28.00
Cordial, 1 oz., 3¾" 28.00--32.00
Ice Tea, ftd., 12 oz., 6½" 18.00--22.00
Ice Tea, ftd., 14 oz., 6¾" 20.00--24.00
Goblet, luncheon, 10 oz., 5¾" 20.00--24.00
Oyster Cocktail, 4½ oz., 3¾" 16.00--20.00
Orange Juice, ftd., 5 oz., 5¼" 14.00--18.00

Ice Cream, 5 oz., 4" 11.00--14.00
Tumbler, whiskey, or cordial
1½ oz., 2" 10.00--12.00
Tumbler, cocktail, 3½ oz., 3" 8.00--10.00
Tumbler, 14 oz., 4¾" (also made
12 oz. and 10 oz.) 12.00--15.00
Bowl, finger, 4¼" 9.00--12.00
Candlestick, low, 4", pr. 26.00--30.00
Bowl, flrd., 11" 35.00--45.00
Candlestick, 2 light, 6" 35.00--40.00
Bowl, flower, flrd., 12" 40.00--50.00
Candlestick, 2 light, 5" 65.00--75.00
Candelabrum, 2 light,
w/Prisms, 6" 55.00--65.00
Bowl, oval, 14" 50.00--60.00
Breakfast Set: 3 pc., Sugar,
Cream and Butter Plate 65.00--75.00
Plate, salad, sq., 7½" 15.00--20.00
(also made 6") 12.00--15.00
Cream, 10 oz., 3" 20.00--24.00
Sugar, 10 oz., 3" 20.00--24.00
(also made w/Cover) 25.00--30.00
Plate, torte, flat edge, 13" 40.00--50.00
(also made rolled edge) 40.00--50.00
Plate, salad, round, 8½" 8.00--12.00
(also made 6" and 7") 8.00--10.00
Plate, lemon, 2 hdld., 6" 14.00--16.00
Plate, sandwich, 2 hdld., 11" 25.00--30.00
Vase, 10" 40.00--50.00
Vase, bud, ftd., 9" 20.00--25.00
Vase, ftd., 10" (also 6", 8", 12") 40.00--60.00
Vase, 9" 25.00--30.00
Vase, bud, 9" 25.00--30.00
No. 506, Vase, ftd.,
(also made 8" and 12") 40.00--50.00
Hurricane Lamp, Candelabrum
w/Prisms, 1 light, 15" 75.00--90.00
No. 505 Vase, ftd., 10" 40.00--50.00

LANGUAGE OF FLOWERS

Goblet, 10 oz., 7½" 14.00--18.00
Saucer Champagne, or tall
Sherbet, 6 oz., 4¾" 12.00--16.00
Wine, 3 oz., 5¾" 14.00--18.00
Cocktail, liquor, 3½ oz., 4½" 12.00--16.00
Cordial, 1 oz., 4¼" 16.00--20.00
Ice Tea, ftd., 13 oz., 7½" 12.00--16.00
Goblet, low, luncheon,
10 oz., 6¾" 12.00--16.00
Orange Juice, ftd., 5 oz., 5½" 10.00--14.00
Ice Cream, ftd., 5 oz., 6¾" 8.00--10.00
Oyster Cocktail, 4½ oz., 4¾" 10.00--14.00
Sugar, 7 oz., 3" 12.00--15.00
Cream, 7 oz., 3¾" 12.00--15.00
Comport, low, 6", 4¾" 15.00--18.00
Sugar, ind., 2½" 10.00--14.00
Cream, ind., 2¾" 10.00--14.00
Relish, oval, 2 hdld.,
2 compt., 7" 16.00--20.00
Marmalade Set: 3 pc., crimped 20.00--30.00
Marmalade, crimped, 4½" 11.00--14.00

Plate, 6"	5.00-- 8.00
Spoon, marmalade	5.00-- 8.00
Tray for Cream and Sugar, 8"	8.00--12.00
Relish, 3 hdld., 3 compt., 9"	20.00--25.00
Vase, crimped, 5½"	18.00--24.00
Candy Box and Cover, 3 hdld., 3 compt., 8"	35.00--45.00
Plate, 2 hdld., 7½"	10.00--13.00
Plate, 14"	30.00--35.00
Plate, 8½"	10.00--12.00
(also 7½")	8.00--10.00
Candlestick, low, 3", pr.	25.00--30.00
Bowl, oval, 10"	30.00--35.00
Candlestick, 2 light, hgt., 6"	30.00--35.00

INDIAN TREE DESIGN page 91

Goblet, 9 oz., 7¾"	15.00--20.00
Saucer Champagne or tall Sherbet, 6 oz., 6"	14.00--18.00
Liquor Cocktail, 3½ oz., 5¼"	14.00--18.00
Wine, 3 oz., 6¼"	15.00--20.00
Claret, 4½ oz., 6¾"	15.00--20.00
Cordial, 1 oz., 5"	18.00--22.00
Oyster Cocktail, 4½ oz., 4¼"	10.00--14.00
Orange Juice, ftd., 5 oz., 4¾"	10.00--14.00
Goblet, luncheon, 9 oz., 6"	12.00--15.00
Ice Tea, ftd., 13 oz., 6¾"	13.00--15.00
Sugar, 7 oz., 3"	12.00--15.00
Cream, 7 oz., 3¾"	12.00--15.00
Finger Bowl, 4¼"	8.00--10.00
Finger Bowl Plate, 6"	5.00-- 6.00
Plate, salad, 8½"	8.00--12.00
(also made 6" and 7½")	7.00-- 9.00
Sugar and Cream Set:	
3 pc., ind.	30.00--40.00
Sugar, 3 oz., 2½"	11.00--14.00
Cream, 3 oz., 2¾"	11.00--14.00
Tray, oval, 8"	9.00--12.00
Nappy, round, 2 hdld., 6"	10.00--14.00
Olive, oval, 2 hdld., 6"	10.00--14.00
Plate, sandwich, 2 hdld., 11"	15.00--20.00
Mayonnaise Set: crimped, 3 pc.	28.00--32.00
Mayonnaise Bowl, crimped	11.00--14.00
Plate, hdld., 7½"	9.00--12.00
Ladle	6.00-- 8.00
Relish, 3 hdld., 3 compt., 9"	22.00--26.00
Bowl, salad, shallow, 12"	30.00--35.00
Comport, high foot, 7"	20.00--25.00
Plate, 14"	30.00--35.00
Vase, bud, ftd., 9"	15.00--20.00
Candy Box and Cover, 3 compt., 8"	35.00--45.00
Vase, cornucopia, 8", 4¾"	30.00--40.00
Candlestick, 1 light, 3", pr.	25.00--30.00
Basket, oval hdld., 10" (also made 11½")	40.00--60.00
Candlestick, 2 light, 5", pr.	60.00--70.00
Bowl, crimped, 10½"	25.00--30.00

MALLARD DUCK DESIGN

Cigarette Box and Cover	40.00--50.00
Ash Tray, rect., 5" (also 3½" and 6½")	15.00--30.00
Ash Tray, rect., 5" (also 3½", 6½" and 8")	15.00--35.00
Cigarette Box and Cover 4½" oval (also 3½" and 7")	45.00--55.00
Ash Tray, oval, 5" (also 3½" and 7")	15.00--30.00
Ice Bucket and Tongs, 6"	55.00--65.00
Cocktail Mixer w/Spoon, hdld., 32 oz., 10¾"	55.00--65.00
Cocktail, ftd., 4 oz., 3½"	15.00--18.00
Old Fashioned Cocktail, 6½ oz., 3¼" (also 14 oz.)	15.00--20.00
Hiball, 18 oz., 7½"	24.00--28.00
Hiball, 11 oz., 5" (also 13 oz.)	22.00--26.00
Orange Juice, 5 oz., 3¼"	15.00--18.00
Old Fashioned, 7 oz., 2¾"	15.00--18.00
Decanter and Stopper, 32 oz., 9¼" (also 16 oz.)	65.00--75.00
Tumbler, 10 oz., 3¾" (also 12 oz.)	20.00--24.00
Tumbler, 14 oz., 4¼" (also 16 oz. and 18 oz.)	22.00--26.00
Martini Mixer and Spoon, 18 oz., 7¼" (also 32 oz.)	55.00--65.00
Cocktail Shaker, 14 oz., 6½" (also 28 oz., and 32 oz.)	55.00--65.00

"SWIRLED DIAMOND" Line No. 44

Console Set	65.00--85.00

Many new and striking items have been added for 1928 by the Duncan & Miller Glass Co., Washington, Pa. None are destined to attract more attention than this lovely No. 44 flower bowl with candlesticks to match in a fascinating allover diamond effect. Note the graceful scalloped, crimped bowl and well proportioned candlesticks. Made in a variety of items in green and other colors, for which this concern are noted.

"SWIRLED DIAMOND" from 1928 journal ad

Tumblers From 1939 Catalog

FOOTED TUMBLERS
Colored Foot With Novelty Cuttings
No. 500-501-502 PATTERNS

No. 500 Ftd.
14 oz Hi Ball Cut-Owl

No. 500 Ftd.
12 oz Hi Ball Cut-Fish

No. 500 Ftd.
9 oz. Tumbler Cut-Rooster

No. 500 Ftd.
8 oz. Hi Ball Cut-Walkiki

No. 500 Ftd.
7 oz. Old Fashioned
Cut-Rooster

No. 500 Ftd.
5 oz. Orange Juice

No. 8
6 in. Canape Plate—Cut-Fish
with 501 Cocktail—Cut-Fish

No. 500 Ftd.
3½ oz. Orange Juice

No. 500 Ftd.
2 oz. Whiskey

No. 500 Ftd.
Martini Mixer with
Chromium Cap and Spoon
Cut-Fish

No. 500 Ftd.
30 oz. Cocktail Shaker
Chromium Top
Cut-Sea Horse

No. 9
8 in. Coupe Plate
Cut-Sail Fish

No. 501
3 oz. Cocktail
Cut-Fish

No. 501
4 oz. Cocktail
Cut-Sea Horse

No. 502 Ftd.
14 oz. Hi Ball
Cut-Sea Horse

No. 502 Ftd.
12 oz. Hi Ball
Cut-Sail Fish

No. 502 Ftd.
10 oz. Hi Ball
Cut-Sea Horse

No. 502 Ftd.
8 oz. Hi Ball
Cut-Fish

No. 502 Ftd.
7 oz. Old Fashioned
Cut-Owl

No. 502 Ftd.
5 oz. Orange Juice

No. 502 Ftd.
2 oz. Whiskey

NOTE: Colored Foot may be Green, Amber, Royal Blue, Sapphire Blue, Ruby or all Crystal.
All items shown on this page are available with any cutting shown or plain without any cutting.

A new feature of the Duncan & Miller display is their No. 3 line of console sets, shown in four shapes. Illustrated above is their Crimp shape. The design is a lovely three leaf pattern with the stems of the leaves carried out as the feet of the bowl, shown in crystal, green and rose. It is displayed by Paul Joseph, 200 Fifth Ave.

"THREE LEAF"
Line No. 3

Console Set	45.00--65.00

"THREE LEAF" from 1929 journal

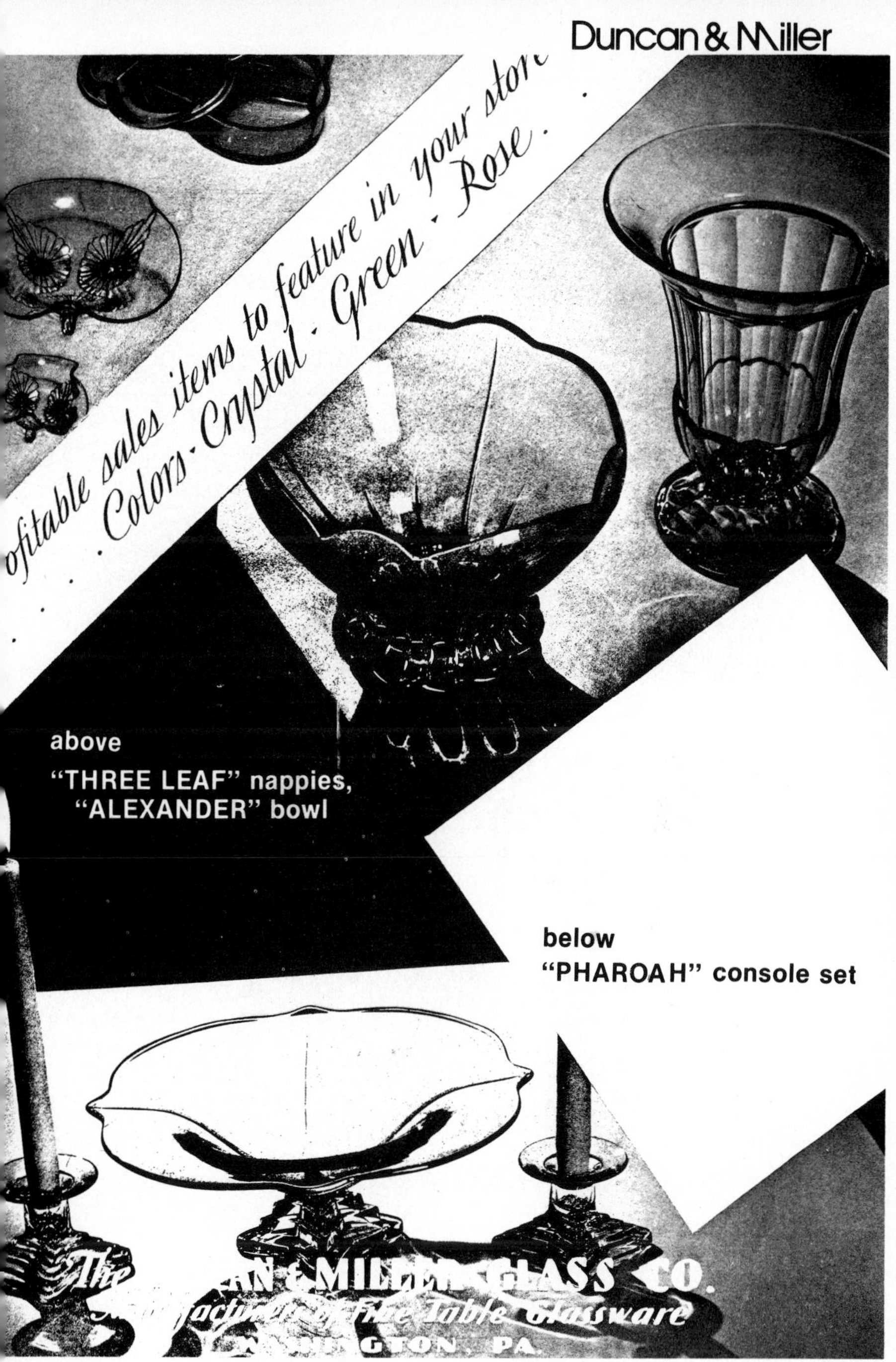

above
"THREE LEAF" nappies,
"ALEXANDER" bowl

below
"PHAROAH" console set

Miscellaneous from 1929 ad

A *Beautiful Reproduction of Venetian Glassware*

One of the newest achievements of the Duncan & Miller factory long noted for fine quality pressed ware.

In this line they have again accomplished the unusual in pressed ware in reproducing one of the loveliest and most popular Venetian glass patterns in a complete line of tableware items. The line is procurable in delectable shades of green, amber, rose, and crystal.

The Duncan & Miller Glass Co.

Manufacturers of Fine Table Glassware

Washington, Pa.

"RIBBONS AND BOWS" from 1928 journal ad

"RIBBONS AND BOWS"	
Bowl, ftd., flrd.	50.00--60.00
Finger Bowl and Plate	12.00--15.00
Vase, ftd.	40.00--50.00
Goblet	15.00--20.00
Sherbet	8.00--10.00
Sherbet Plate	4.00-- 6.00
Sugar and Cream	20.00--30.00
Tumbler, ftd.	8.00--12.00

Federal

Federal, one of the biggest Depression Era glass making machines, created many of our star Book 1 patterns. But did you know that this was once a hand house, making such items as blown jugs with stuck-on handles and needle-etched blown goblets such as those on page 95 Book 2, before turning on to automation?

Federal also pioneered the field of decorating tumblers, both hand-painted and stenciled. These can be seen in color in THE DECORATED TUMBLER book.

On January 31, 1979, Federal ceased manufacturing. We were sad to hear this news, since Federal was among our favorite companies, thanks to a most kind and helpful personnel. We will miss them.

"NEW MODE" — page 95

Goblet	8.00--12.00

No. 1 NEEDLE ETCHED

Goblet, 9 oz	8.00--12.00

THE BIG THREE

DIAMOND OPTIC, Tumbler	4.00-- 6.00
PEAR SHAPED OPTIC, Tumbler	4.00-- 6.00
POLKA DOT OPTIC, Tumbler	4.00-- 6.00

TRUMP BRIDGE LUNCHEON SET

See in color section page 16

Plate	6.00-- 8.00
Tumbler, ftd.	8.00--10.00
Sherbet, ftd.	5.00-- 7.00
Tray, sandwich, metal handle	10.00--12.00

SARACENIC

Vase, twin, (pr)	15.00--20.00

"MUTT N' JEFF" — page 96

Water Set	40.00--50.00
Jug	20.00--25.00
Tumbler, 10 oz.	4.00-- 5.00

TUDOR RING

Water Set	35.00--45.00
Jug	15.00--20.00
Tumbler	3.50-- 4.00

GRAND SLAM BRIDGE SET

Plate	5.00-- 7.00
Tumbler	8.00--10.00
Sherbet	5.00-- 7.00
Tray, sandwich,metal handle	10.00--12.00

TWISTED OPTIC

Goblet, 7½ oz.	6.00-- 8.00

CORDED OPTIC

Tumbler	4.00-- 6.00

HOSTESS LINE — page 97

No. 187 Book 1

Plate, 8"	4.00-- 6.00
Cup	4.00-- 5.00
Saucer	2.00-- 3.00

PEAR OPTIC (THUMBPRINT)

See in Book I

Plate, 8"	4.00-- 6.00
Cup	4.00-- 5.00
Saucer	2.00-- 3.00

MARY ROSE

Goblet	12.00--15.00

REAMERS

Lemon	8.00--12.00
Orange	8.00--12.00

INDIAN

Tumbler	5.00-- 8.00

CORDED OPTIC

Water Set	75.00--90.00
Jug	30.00--35.00
Tumbler, 10 oz.	8.00--10.00

TALL BOY

Ice Tea Set	55.00--65.00
Jug	20.00--25.00
Tumbler	6.00-- 7.00

DIAMOND OPTIC — page 98

Ice Tea Set	60.00--70.00
Jug and Cover	25.00--30.00
Tumbler	6.00-- 8.00

DIAMOND SQUAT

Water Set	40.00--50.00
Jug	20.00--25.00
Tumbler	4.00-- 6.00

SQUAT OPTIC

Water Set	40.00--50.00
Jug	20.00--25.00
Tumbler, 10 oz.	4.00-- 6.00

JACK FROST CRACKLED

Water Set	60.00--70.00
Jug	25.00--30.00
Tumbler	6.00-- 8.00

JACK FROST CRACKLED

Iced Tea Set	55.00--65.00
Jug and Cover	20.00--25.00
Tumbler	6.00-- 7.00

JACK FROST CRACKLED

Lemonade Set	55.00--65.00
Jug	20.00--25.00
Tumbler	6.00-- 7.00

LIDO LINE — page 99

Jug, 65 oz.	18.00--20.00
Tumbler, ftd., 15 oz.	6.00-- 8.00
Tumbler, 5, 9, 10, 12 oz.	4.00-- 6.00

TUDOR RING

Tumbler, 5, 9, 12 oz.	4.00-- 5.00
Jug, 80 oz.	18.00--22.00

PYRAMID OPTIC

Tumbler, 9 oz.	4.00-- 5.00

CROSSBAR

Tumbler, 9 oz.	3.00-- 5.00

JOHN

Jug, 80 oz.	15.00--18.00

MARY

Jug, 80 oz.	18.00--22.00

KITCHENWARE — page 100

B-10 Kitchen Bowl Set, 4 piece	
crystal	15.00--20.00
amber	35.00--40.00
pink	45.00--50.00
4 Piece Jar and Cover, square	
crystal	25.00--30.00
amber	40.00--50.00
pink	50.00--60.00
2528 Jar and Cover, round	
crystal	8.00--10.00
green	12.00--15.00

amber	12.00--15.00
pink	18.00--20.00
2524 Butter and Cover, 1/4 lb.	
crystal	8.00--10.00
green	18.00--20.00
amber	18.00--20.00
pink	30.00--35.00
2521 Orange Reamer	
crystal	3.00-- 4.00
green	10.00--12.00
amber	18.00--20.00
pink	25.00--30.00
2539 Handled Measuring Cup	
crystal	4.00-- 6.00
green	18.00--20.00
amber	30.00--35.00
pink	18.00--20.00
4 Piece Mixing Bowl set, flared	
crystal	18.00--20.00
amber	35.00--40.00
pink	45.00--50.00
2520 Lemon Reamer	
crystal	3.00-- 4.00
amber	10.00-12.00
green	8.00--10.00
pink	15.00--20.00
2523 Butter and Cover, 1 lb.	
crystal	8.00--10.00
green	22.00--25.00
amber	22.00--25.00
pink	30.00--35.00
307 Tub Butter and Cover	
crystal	4.00-- 6.00
amber	18.00--20.00
pink	25.00--30.00
Triple Lip Measuring Cup	
crystal	10.00--15.00
amber	25.00--30.00
pink	30.00--40.00

PIONEER page 101

No. 2807, Plate, 8"	5.00-- 8.00
No. 2806 Bowl, 7"	5.00-- 8.00
No. 2806½ Bowl, 7¾"	5.00-- 8.00
No. 2806½ Bowl, 11"	9.00--12.00
No. 2800 Nappy, 5-3/8"	6.00-- 8.00
No. 2800 Nappy, 5-3/8	5.00-- 7.00
No. 2806 Bowl, 10½"	9.00--12.00
No. 2806 Plate, 12"	9.00--12.00
No. 2806 Plate, 12"	8.00--10.00
No. 2806 Plate, 8"	4.00-- 6.00
No. 2806 Bowl, 10½"	8.00--10.00
No. 2806, Bowl, 11"	8.00--11.00

MISCELLANEOUS

No. 2804 Nappy, 4¼"	2.00-- 3.00
No. 2804 Nappy, 7¼"	3.00-- 4.00
No. 1914 Tumbler, etched, 9 oz.	6.00-- 8.00
No. 1914 Tumbler, etched, 9 oz.	6.00-- 8.00

**2563 – Horse Head
5½" High**

**2565 – "Mopey" Dog
3⅛" High**

1938 catalog reprint

No. 145R Tumbler, ftd., 14 oz.	5.00-- 7.00
No. 2826 Candlestick	8.00--10.00
No. 186R Tumbler, 9¼ oz	5.00-- 7.00
No. 2825 Dish, clover shaped	3.00-- 4.00

HORSE HEAD BOOKENDS

15.00--20.00

"MOPEY DOG"

6.00-- 8.00

Fenton

The Fenton Museum is located at the factory in Williamstown, W. Va. If you're vacationing that way, by all means plan to visit. It's a gorgeous display and we hope the Fentons enjoy the deluge of Depression Era glassware fans.

Then there is Mr. William Heacock's book on Fenton (O-Val Advertising Corp., P.O. Box 663, Marietta OH 45750). It includes an early history and pressed, stretched, and art glass up to 1932.

The Book 2 Fenton patterns cover the company's colored glassware from 1928 to 1940, including some later collectibles in crystal and colors.

And now there's a Fenton club for Fenton fans. It's named the Fenton Art Glass Collectors of America, Inc. and you can contact them at P.O. Box 2441, Appleton WI 54913.

The following reprints, loaned by Mr. Frank Fenton, should be of considerable interest.

MISCELLANEOUS	**page 102**
No. 232 Candlestick, 8½" (pr.)	35.00--50.00
No. 231 Cup Bowl, shallow, ftd., 10"	30.00--40.00
No. 891 Vase, 12"	75.00--95.00
No. 888 Vase, 10"	65.00--85.00
No. 887 Vase, paste mold, 8"	30.00--45.00
No. 886 Vase, paste mold, 6"	25.00--35.00
No. 885 Vase, paste mold, 5"	20.00--25.00
No. 231 Bowl, deep, cupped, ftd., 8"	30.00--40.00
No. 846 Cup Bowl and Base, flrd., 8¾"	35.00--50.00
No. 200 Guest Set, 2 pc.	45.00--55.00
No. 635 Candy Jar, ½ lb.	25.00--30.00
No. 735 Candy Jar, ½ lb.	25.00--30.00
No. 318 Butter Ball, 7"	14.00--18.00
No. 847 Vase, shell shaped, ftd., 5"	30.00--40.00
No. 2 Sugar and Cream Set	30.00--50.00
No. 847 Rose Bowl, cupped	20.00--30.00
No. 847 Bowl, nut, 6½"	20.00--25.00
No. 56 Cologne w/drip Stopper	30.00--40.00
No. 57 Powder Puff Jar	20.00--25.00
No. 401 Night Set, 2 pc.	30.00--40.00
No. 847 Bowl, shallow cup, ftd., 7"	18.00--28.00
No. 847 Bulb Bowl, ftd., 6"	18.00--28.00
No. 847 Bowl, shallow, ftd., 8"	18.00--28.00
No. 403 Ice Cream Set, 2 pc.	18.00--22.00
No. 1647 Sweetmeat Set, 2 pc.	25.00--35.00

WATER SETS	**page 103**
Water Set, 15 pc.: Jug and Cover, 76 oz. 6, hdld., Tumblers, 10 oz. 6 Tumbler Coasters 1 Jug Coaster. (Coasters & handles in Royal blue)	200.00-250.00
Lemonade Set, 14 pc: Jug, 62 oz. 6 hdld. Tumblers, 12 oz. 6 Tumbler Coasters 1 Jug Coaster. (Coasters & handles in Royal blue)	200.00-250.00

"FRANKLIN"

Highball	14.00--20.00
Table Tumbler	12.00--16.00
Juice Glass	10.00--14.00
Whiskey	14.00--20.00

GEORGIAN

These pieces are around-at least, I think that was Fenton's GEORGIAN I saw. How can we ever be certain when it's so much like Duncan and Miller's GEORGIAN? And beware of the ruby tumblers as Viking Glass at New Martinsville is making red GEORGIAN tumblers today. Red and blue are top trend.

Tumbler, 2½ oz.	10.00--14.00
Decanter	30.00--40.00
Tumbler, 5 oz.	8.00--10.00
Tumbler, 10 oz.	10.00--14.00
Jug, ½ gal.	35.00--55.00
Plate, 8"	5.00-- 8.00
Plate, 6"	4.00-- 5.00
Sherbet	4.00-- 5.00
Goblet	16.00--22.00
Ice Tea, 12 oz.	14.00--18.00

LINCOLN INN page 104, 105

	Pink, green, blue	*Ruby, Royal blue, Jade*
Plate, 8"	6.00-- 8.00	8.00--10.00
Plate, 9¼"	8.00--10.00	10.00--14.00
Plate, 12"	10.00--14.00	14.00--18.00
Cup	10.00--14.00	16.00--20.00
Saucer	3.00-- 4.00	4.00-- 5.00
Cream	9.00--12.00	12.00--16.00
Sugar	9.00--12.00	12.00--16.00
Bowl, crimped, 6"	8.00--10.00	10.00--14.00
Tumbler, 5 oz.	9.00--12.00	12.00--16.00
Tumbler, ftd., 7 oz.	9.00--12.00	12.00--16.00
Tumbler, 9 oz.	10.00--12.00	12.00--16.00
Fruit Juice, low ftd., 4 oz.	12.00--15.00	16.00--20.00
Ice Tea, ftd., 12 oz.	12.00--15.00	16.00--20.00
Highball, 12 oz.	12.00--15.00	16.00--20.00
Goblet	12.00--15.00	17.00--22.00
Sherbet	8.00--10.00	10.00--15.00
Wine or Cocktail	12.00--16.00	18.00--24.00
Comport Plate	10.00--14.00	14.00--18.00
Comport, shallow	11.00--15.00	16.00--20.00
Salt and Pepper	75.00--90.00	100.00-150.00
Dish, candy, oval, ftd.	8.00--11.00	12.00--16.00
Dish, nut ftd.	8.00--11.00	10.00--14.00
Dish, mint, ftd.	8.00--11.00	10.00--14.00
Cereal	6.00-- 8.00	8.00--12.00
Bowl, finger, and Plate	9.00--12.00	12.00--16.00
Bread and Butter, 6"	3.00-- 4.00	4.00-- 6.00
Dish, olive, hdld.	8.00--10.00	10.00--14.00
Dish, Bon Bon, square, hdld.	8.00--10.00	10.00--14.00
Dish, Bon Bon, oval, hdld.	8.00--10.00	10.00--14.00
Saucer, fruit, 5"	4.00-- 6.00	6.00-- 9.00
Bowl, ftd., 9¼"	15.00--20.00	25.00--30.00
Bowl, ftd., 10½"	20. 00--25.00	30.00--35.00
Snack Set, 2 pc.	15.00--18.00	20.00--25.00
Relish	8.00--10.00	12.00--16.00
Ashtray, 5 pc. set	12.00--16.00	18.00--24.00

PLYMOUTH page 105

Amber, Steigel green, Royal blue, Ruby

Plate, salad, 8"	8.00--12.00
Plate, bread and butter	4.00-- 6.00
Sherbet	8.00--12.00
Tumbler, liquor, 2½ oz.	10.00--15.00
Tumbler, orange juice, 5 oz.	8.00--12.00
Tumbler, table, 5 oz.	8.00--12.00
Tumbler, hiball, 9 oz.	8.00--12.00
Tumbler, ice tea, 12 oz.	10.00--15.00
Tumbler, old fashioned	10.00--15.00
Tumbler, pilsner, ftd.	15.00--20.00
Goblet, wine	16.00--20.00
Goblet	15.00--20.00
Decanter	50.00--60.00
Cocktail Shaker	40.00--50.00
Ice Bucket	35.00--50.00
Jigger	20.00--25.00

SHEFFIELD LINE page 106

Mermaid blue, gold and ruby

Vase, cupped, 8"	18.00--24.00
Vase, flrd., 8"	18.00--24.00
Vase, straight, 8"	18.00--24.00
Bowl, crimped, 11"	20.00--25.00
Bowl, flrd., 11"	20.00--25.00
Candleholders	20.00--25.00
Bowl, flrd., 13"	24.00--28.00
Bon Bon, shallow, 3 ftd., 7½"	8.00--12.00
Vase, regular, 6½"	14.00--18.00
Bowl, flrd., 3 ftd., 7"	12.00-15.00
Vase, flrd., 6¼"	14.00--18.00
Vase, Tulip, 6¼"	14.00--18.00
Bon Bon, covered, 3 ftd.	22.00--28.00
Vase, cupped, 6¼"	14.00--18.00
Bon Bon, triangular, 3 ftd.	8.00--12.00
Bon Bon, cupped, 3 ftd	9.00--14.00
Bon Bon, club, 6½"	9.00--14.00
Plate, 3 ftd., 8¼"	8.00--12.00
Vase, Crimped, 6¼"	14.00--18.00

MISCELLANEOUS page 107

Crystal, pink, green, ruby, Royal blue

Dish, Bon Bon	12.00--24.00
Candleholders (pr.)	15.00--25.00
FRANKLIN Decanter	30.00--50.00
Whiskey, small	14.00--20.00
Relish, 3 compt., hdld.	14.00--22.00
Dish, leaf shaped	8.00--14.00
Plate, fruit design	5.00-- 8.00
Cigarette Box	12.00--18.00
Ashtray	4.00-- 8.00
Dish, leaf shaped	8.00--14.00

MING

Crystal, pink, green

Bowl, cupped, and Base	20.00--25.00
Jar, ginger, and Base	30.00--40.00
Liquor Set	60.00--90.00
Bowl, console, 12" with candleholders	30.00--40.00
Bowl, salad, and Plate	20.00--25.00
Pitcher and Tumbler	35.00--55.00

PEACOCK BOOKENDS

Book-ends	75.00-100.00

MISCELLANEOUS *See Photos*

1502A Bowl, flrd., cup, 8"	15.00--20.00
1502A Bowl, cupped, 7"	25.00--30.00
1502A Bowl, crimp., 9"	30.00--35.00
1503A Bowl, roll edge, 8½"	30.00--35.00
1503A Bowl, cupped, 7"	25.00--30.00
1502A Bowl, roll edge, 8½"	30.00--35.00
1502 Bowl, flrd., cup, 8½"	25.00--35.00
1502 Bowl, roll edge, 14"	16.00--24.00
1503 Candlestick, pr.	20.00--25.00
1503 Bowl, flrd., 10"	25.00--35.00
1502 Bowl, roll edge, 10"	14.00--18.00
1502A Bowl, flrd., 10"	25.00--35.00
1502 Bowl, deep cup, 8"	15.00--20.00
1623 Candlestick, pr.	20.00--25.00
1503A Bowl, flrd., 10"	15.00--20.00
1503A Bowl, shallow cup, 9"	25.00--30.00
1502 Guest Set, 2 pc.	20.00--25.00
1502 Goblet, bridge, 11 oz.	9.00--12.00
1502 Goblet, bridge, 9 oz.	8.00--11.00
1502 Finger Bowl and Plate	8.00--10.00
1502 Cup and Saucer	12.00--14.00
1502 Plate., oct., 6"	3.00-- 4.00
1503 Plate, spiral optic, 8"	4.00-- 6.00
1503 Sherbet, spiral optic	6.00-- 9.00
1503 Goblet, 9 oz.	10.00--14.00
1502 Vase, roll edge, 7"	12.00--15.00
1502 Vase, crimp top, 8"	12.00--18.00
1502 Vase, fan, 8½"	12.00--18.00
1502 Vase, dolphin fan. hdld., 6"	22.00--26.00
1502 Vase, dolphin fan, hdld., 5¼"	20.00--24.00
1502 Vase, flrd., 6"	8.00--11.00
1502 Vase, flrd., 8¼"	12.00--16.00
1502 Bon Bon, comport, 7½"	20.00--24.00
1502 Bon Bon, oval, 7½"	20.00--24.00
1502 Bon Bon, flrd., 6"	20.00--24.00
1502 Bon Bon, crimp top, 7½"	20.00--24.00
1502 Dresser Set: 3 pc.	70.00--80.00
53 Dresser Set: 4 pc.	80.00--90.00
1502 Console Set: 3 pc. roll edge bowl, 12"	25.00--35.00

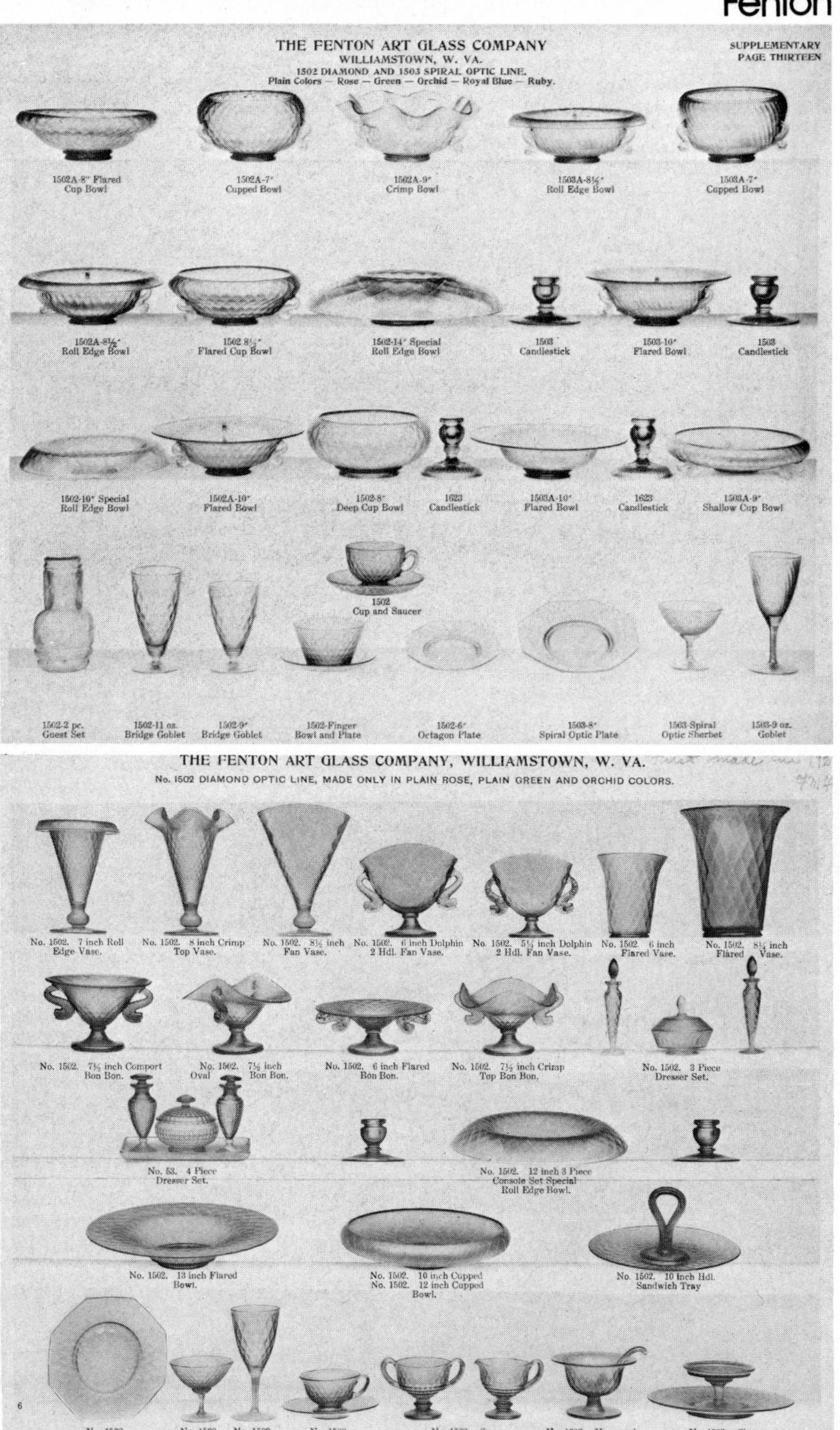

THE FENTON ART GLASS COMPANY
WILLIAMSTOWN, W. VA.
1502 DIAMOND AND 1503 SPIRAL OPTIC LINE.
Plain Colors — Rose — Green — Orchid — Royal Blue — Ruby.

SUPPLEMENTARY
PAGE THIRTEEN

1502A-8" Flared Cup Bowl
1502A-7" Cupped Bowl
1502A-9" Crimp Bowl
1503A-8½" Roll Edge Bowl
1503A-7" Cupped Bowl

1502A-8½" Roll Edge Bowl
1502 8½" Flared Cup Bowl
1502-14" Special Roll Edge Bowl
1503 Candlestick
1503-10" Flared Bowl
1503 Candlestick

1502-10" Special Roll Edge Bowl
1502A-10" Flared Bowl
1502-8" Deep Cup Bowl
1623 Candlestick
1503A-10" Flared Bowl
1623 Candlestick
1503A-9" Shallow Cup Bowl

1502 Cup and Saucer

1502-2 pc. Guest Set
1502-11 oz. Bridge Goblet
1502-9" Bridge Goblet
1502-Finger Bowl and Plate
1502-6" Octagon Plate
1503-8" Spiral Optic Plate
1503-Spiral Optic Sherbet
1503-9 oz. Goblet

THE FENTON ART GLASS COMPANY, WILLIAMSTOWN, W. VA.
No. 1502 DIAMOND OPTIC LINE, MADE ONLY IN PLAIN ROSE, PLAIN GREEN AND ORCHID COLORS.

No. 1502. 7 inch Roll Edge Vase.
No. 1502. 8 inch Crimp Top Vase.
No. 1502. 8½ inch Fan Vase.
No. 1502. 6 inch Dolphin 2 Hdl. Fan Vase.
No. 1502. 5½ inch Dolphin 2 Hdl. Fan Vase.
No. 1502. 6 inch Flared Vase.
No. 1502. 8½ inch Flared Vase.

No. 1502. 7½ inch Comport Bon Bon.
No. 1502. 7½ inch Oval Bon Bon.
No. 1502. 6 inch Flared Bon Bon.
No. 1502. 7½ inch Crimp Top Bon Bon.
No. 1502. 3 Piece Dresser Set.

No. 53. 4 Piece Dresser Set.
No. 1502. 12 inch 3 Piece Console Set Special Roll Edge Bowl.

No. 1502. 13 inch Flared Bowl.
No. 1502. 10 inch Cupped
No. 1502. 12 inch Cupped Bowl.
No. 1502. 10 inch Hdl. Sandwich Tray

6

No. 1502 8 inch Octagon Salad Plate.
No. 1502 Footed Sherbet.
No. 1502 Goblet
No. 1502 Cup and Saucer
No. 1502. Sugar and Cream Set.
No. 1502. Mayonnaise and Ladle.
No. 1502. Cheese and Cracker.

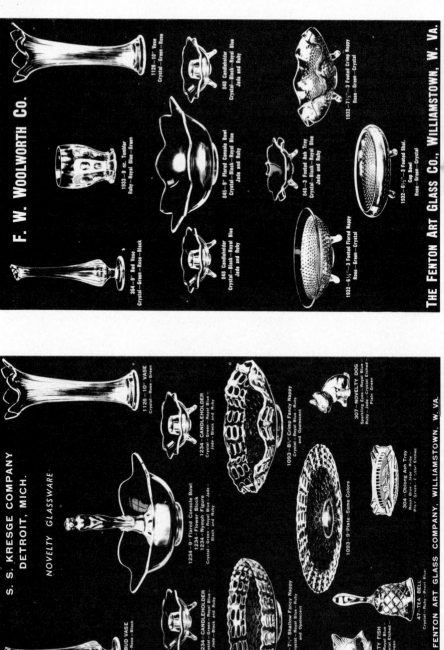

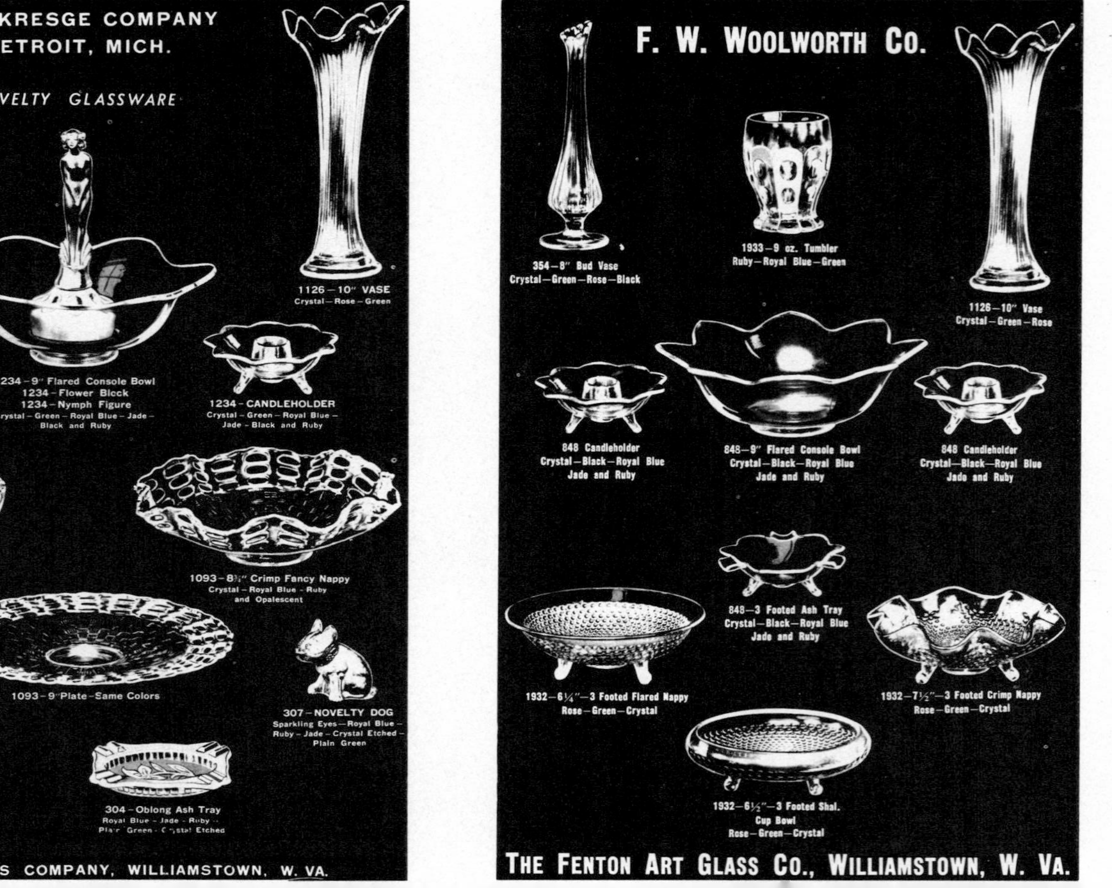
S. S. KRESGE COMPANY
DETROIT, MICH.
NOVELTY GLASSWARE
354-8"-9" BUD VASE
Crystal-Green-Rose-Black
1234-9" Flared Console Bowl
1234-Flower Block
1234-Nymph Figure
Crystal-Green-Royal Blue-Jade-Black and Ruby
1126-10" VASE
Crystal-Rose-Green
1234-CANDLEHOLDER
Crystal-Green-Royal Blue-Jade-Black and Ruby
1234-CANDLEHOLDER
Crystal-Green-Royal Blue-Jade-Black and Ruby
1093-7½" Shallow Fancy Nappy
Crystal-Royal Blue-Ruby and Opalescent
1093-8½" Crimp Fancy Nappy
Crystal-Royal Blue-Ruby and Opalescent
1093-9" Plate-Same Colors
307-NOVELTY DOG
Sparkling Eyes-Royal Blue-Ruby-Jade-Crystal Etched-Plain Green
306-NOVELTY FISH
Sparkling Eyes-Royal Blue-Ruby Jade-Crystal Etched-Plain Green
47-TEA BELL
Crystal-Ruby-Royal Blue
304-Oblong Ash Tray
Royal Blue-Jade-Ruby-Plain Green-Crystal Etched
FENTON ART GLASS COMPANY, WILLIAMSTOWN, W. VA.
F. W. WOOLWORTH CO.
354-8" Bud Vase
Crystal-Green-Rose-Black
1933-9 oz. Tumbler
Ruby-Royal Blue-Green
1126-10" Vase
Crystal-Green-Rose
848 Candleholder
Crystal-Black-Royal Blue
Jade and Ruby
848-9" Flared Console Bowl
Crystal-Black-Royal Blue
Jade and Ruby
848 Candleholder
Crystal-Black-Royal Blue
Jade and Ruby
848-3 Footed Ash Tray
Crystal-Black-Royal Blue
Jade and Ruby
1932-6¼"-3 Footed Flared Nappy
Rose-Green-Crystal
1932-7½"-3 Footed Crimp Nappy
Rose-Green-Crystal
1932-6½"-3 Footed Shal. Cup Bowl
Rose-Green-Crystal
THE FENTON ART GLASS CO., WILLIAMSTOWN, W. VA.

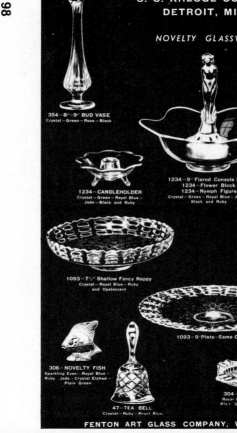

ADDITIONAL NEW PIECES NOT ILLUSTRATED IN CATALOG.
1602-10¼" Crimp Footed
1531-16" Vase
1530-12" Vase
1535-10" Crimp Top Vase
354-8" Bud Vase
847-6" Fan Vase
1615 Ice Jar
835-½ lb. Candy Jar
1608-10½" Oval Footed Bowl
1604-11" Oval Footed Bowl
1601-10¾" Flared Footed Bowl
1600-10¼" Roll Edge Footed Bowl
844-1 lb Candy Jar Flower Top
1618-Elephant Flower Bowl
1634-7 piece Water Set
1635-7 piece Water Set
1636-7 piece Ice Tea Set
1569-Cigarette Box and Ash Tray
847-7" Shallow Bowl
574-Crimp Flared Bon Bon
16-17-54-4 piece Bath Room Set
1554-Flower Pot and Saucer
1555-Flower Pot and Saucer
The Fenton Art Glass Co., Williamstown, W. Va.
Swan Console Set and Novelties Crystal Satin Finish.
Sp. 487.4
No. 6. Candlestick.
No. 6. 11" Square Swan Bowl.
No. 6. Candlestick.
No. 4 Swan.
No. 4 Swan.
No. 4 Swan.
No. 6. 12" Tulip Swan Bowl.
No. 4 Swan
No. 5 - 6" Satin Finish Flared Swan Handled Bon Bon.
No. 5. 5½" Crimped Swan Handled Bon Bon.
No. 5 - 5" Square Swan Handled Bon Bon.
No. 5 - 5" Oval Swan Handled Bon Bon

1502 Bowl, flrd., 13"	15.00--20.00
1502 Bowl, cupped, 10", 12"	15.00--20.00
1502 Sandwich tray, hdld., 10"	10.00--14.00
1502 Plate, salad, oct., 8"	4.00-- 6.00
1502 Sherbet, ftd.	6.00-- 9.00
1502 Goblet	10.00--14.00
1502 Cup and Saucer	12.00--15.00
1502 Sugar and Cream	25.00--30.00
1502 Mayonnaise and Ladle	16.00--18.00
1502 Cheese and Cracker	12.00--16.00

MISCELLANEOUS

354 Bud Vase, 8", 9"	9.00--12.00
1933 Tumbler, 9 oz.	8.00--12.00
1126 Vase, 10"	12.00--15.00
848 Candleholder, pr.	9.00--12.00
848 Bowl, console, flrd., 9"	15.00--20.00
1932 Nappy, ftd., flrd., 6¼"	6.00-- 8.00
848 Ash Tray, ftd.	5.00-- 7.00
1932 Nappy, ftd., crimped, 7½"	7.00-- 9.00
1932 Bowl, ftd., cupped, 6½"	6.00-- 8.00
1234 Bowl, console, flrd., 9"	15.00--20.00
1234 Flower Block and Nymph Figure	100.00-150.00
1093 Nappy, shallow, 7¾"	17.00--22.00
1093 Candleholder, pr.	12.00--15.00
1093 Nappy, crimped, 8¾"	18.00--26.00
1093 Plate, 9"	15.00--20.00
306 Novelty Fish	15.00--30.00
307 Novelty Dog	15.00--30.00
47 Tea Bell	20.00--30.00
304 Ash Tray, oblong	6.00-- 9.00

MISCELLANEOUS

1602 Compote, ftd., crimped 10¼"	35.00--45.00
1531 Vase, 16"	35.00--45.00
1530 Vase, 12"	25.00--30.00
1535 Vase, crimp, 10"	20.00--25.00
354 Vase, bud, 8"	10.00--12.00
847 Vase, fan, 6"	10.00--14.00
1615 Ice Jar	18.00--26.00
835 Candy Jar, ½ lb.	20.00--25.00
1608 Bowl, ftd., oval, 11"	55.00--65.00
1601 Bowl, ftd., flrd., 10¾"	40.00--50.00
1600 Bowl, ftd., roll edge, 10¼"	40.00--50.00
844 Candy Jar, flower top, 1 lb.	25.00--30.00
1618 Elephant Flower Bowl	150.00-200.00
1634 Water Set: 7 pc.	70.00--85.00
1635 Water Set: 7 pc.	70.00--85.00
1636 Water Set: 7 pc.	70.00--85.00
1569 Cigarette Box and Ashtray	10.00--14.00
847 Bowl, shallow, 7"	8.00--10.00
574 Bon Bon, flrd., crimped	10.00--15.00
16-17-54 Bath Room Set: 4 pc.	25.00--35.00
1554 Flower Pot and Saucer	12.00--16.00
1555 Flower Pot and Saucer	12.00--16.00

SWAN LAKE

No. 6 Candlestick, pr.	30.00--40.00
No. 6 Bowl, sq., 11"	50.00--60.00
No. 4 Swan	30.00--40.00
No. 6 Bowl, Tulip, 12"	50.00--60.00
No. 5 Bon Bon, flrd., hdld., satin finish, 6"	20.00--30.00
No. 5 Bon Bon, hdld., crimped, 5½"	20.00--30.00
No. 5 Bon Bon, hdld., sq., 5"	20.00--30.00
No. 5 Bon Bon, hdld., oval, 5"	20.00--30.00

TURTLE AQUARIUM

See in Color Section

Aquarium	15.00--20.00
Turtle	70.00--80.00
Turtle Aquarium	85.00-100.00

Fostoria

Book 2 is very minimal in the area of Fostoria because the big book, FOSTORIA: ITS FIRST FIFTY YEARS (Glassbooks) covers the subject so thoroughly. At least 50 patterns were made in color by this great company and I can't imagine anyone missing seeing them. Fostoria is a glass go-ers paradise!

Supplementing the big book is the price guide, FOSTORIA PRICE WATCH, which lists each piece to each pattern, and includes a special section on identifying, at a glance, the many, many Fostoria stems made from 1900 to 1978.

The area continues to incline steadily upwards, with many dealers now specializing in Fostoria and the glass always eliciting much excitement at shows.

Following are the current suggested prices for the four (quite highly representative) patterns shown in Book 2.

JUNE	page 110
Plate, cake, hdld., 10"	20.00--30.00
Comport, 6"	25.00--30.00
Shaker, ftd., pr.	70.00--90.00
Ice Dish and T.J. Liner	25.00--30.00

TROJAN	
Plate, dinner, 9"	12.00--15.00
Sherbet, high, 6 oz.	15.00--18.00
Goblet, 9 oz.	20.00--25.00
Cup and Saucer	15.00--20.00
Tumbler, ftd., 9 oz.	12.00--15.00

VERSAILLES	
Plate, cake, hdld., 10"	20.00--25.00
Ice Bucket	60.00--80.00
Cream	15.00--20.00
Sugar	15.00--20.00
Sweetmeat	15.00--20.00

MANOR	
Plate, dinner, 9"	12.00--18.00
No. 6007 Goblet, 10 oz.	16.00--18.00
Cup and Saucer	14.00--18.00
No. 6003 Goblet, 10 oz.	18.00--22.00

Fry

In the 20s Fry advertised "A Dish for Every Oven Use" and featured a line made in their PEARL ware tint. Shown below are a few examples of them and their suggested prices.

James Lafferty (P.O. Box 1025, Barstow CA 92311) published a book in 1967 called FRY'S PEARLWARE or PEARL ART GLASS FOVAL that shows the Fry Foval Pearl glass with blue, green, jade and amethyst trim.

MISCELLANEOUS	page 111
No. 40007 Sugar	12.00--15.00
No. 40007 Cream	12.00--15.00
Tray, spice, hdld.	18.00--22.00
Reamer, fruit	35.00--45.00
Cigarette Holder and Ash Tray	50.00--65.00
No. 7542 Goblet	20.00--24.00
No. 7542 Pitcher	85.00-100.00

REED	
Pitcher	100.00-150.00
Tumbler, ftd.	20.00--26.00

BRIDGE SET	
Plate, large	20.00--25.00
Plate, small	12.00--16.00
Sherbet, low ftd.	7.00-- 9.00
Tumbler, low ftd.	9.00--12.00

PEARL BAKEWARE	
Oval Casserole	20.00--30.00
Measuring Cup	20.00--25.00
Pie Plate	10.00--15.00
Oblong Baker	15.00--20.00
Custard Cups	4.00-- 6.00

Hazel-Atlas

Hazel Atlas' major patterns such as ROYAL LACE, the FLORENTINES, MODERNTONE, CLOVERLEAF and others are in Book 1. This didn't leave us much for Book 2, did it? As you know, HA was a machine house and most of their major lines were made in quantities.

I'm printing a few more pieces at the end of the chapter.

We know that HA did enamel decorations on colored glass as well as on crystal in the early 30s. These you can see in THE DECORATED TUMBLER book in color.

PLATONITE KITCHENWARE page 115

No. 02015-2015½ Refrigerator Bowl, square	8.00--10.00
No. 03060-1742 Dripping Bowl, round	10.00--12.00
No. 03153-3160 Refrigerator Bowl, round	7.00-- 9.00
No. 0759-759½ Refrigerator Bowl, round	8.00--10.00
No. 03127 Kitchen Set (shakers)	18.00--22.00
No. 03027 Milk Pitcher	6.00-- 8.00

KITCHENWARE page 116

Green glass

No.G773-4-5-6-7, Mixing Bowl Set, 5 pc.	50.00--60.00
No. G2015-2015½ Refrigerator Sets	15.00--20.00
No. G2528 Percolator Top	2.50-- 3.50
No. G3040 Measuring Cup	15.00--18.00
No. G13000 Cream	8.00--10.00
No. G13001-13001½ Sugar and Lid	10.00--14.00
No. G1738-1738½ Butter Dish	28.00--32.00
No. G13063 Sherbet	3.00-- 4.00
No. G763 Nappy, 4"	4.00-- 5.00
No. G766 Nappy, 7"	10.00--12.00
No. G732 Nappy, fancy, 8"	8.00--10.00
No. G730 Nappy, fancy, 4"	3.00-- 4.00
No. G386 Beverage Shaker	10.00--12.00
No. G758 Ash Tray	6.00-- 9.00
No. G751 Beater Bowl	10.00--12.00
No. G908-909 Combination Cigarette Jar and Ash Tray	15.00--18.00

PLATONITE KITCHENWARE

No. 02013-13½ Butter Dish oblong	18.00--22.00
No. 0155½ Kitchen Set (shakers), square	20.00--24.00
No. 072 Fruit Reamer	12.00--16.00
No. 0358 Tumbler, 8 oz.	8.00--10.00
No. 0773-4-5-6-7, Mixing Bowls, 5 pc. set	14.00--20.00
No. 03038 Measuring Pitcher pint, three lipped	40.00--50.00
No. 03042-2954 Measuring Pitcher, w/perforated Reamer	24.00--26.00
No. 0364 Tumbler, 12 oz.	8.00--10.00

KITCHENWARE page 117

All green

No. 1818 Pitcher, blown, 80 oz. (FLORENTINE)	65.00--75.00
No. G1488 Pitcher, pressed ice-lip, 54 oz.	15.00--18.00
No. G1819 Pitcher, blown, 80 oz.	18.00--20.00
No. G1489 Pitcher, pressed ice-lip, 54 oz., (FLORENTINE)	40.00--45.00

No. G3025 Pitcher, pressed, 44 oz.	15.00--18.00
No. G3026 Pitcher, pressed, 41 oz.	15.00--18.00
No. G13025 Pitcher, pressed, 44 oz.	15.00--18.00
No. G1933 Pitcher, pressed, ice-lip, 44 oz.	15.00--18.00

KITCHENWARE page 118

All green

No. G1816 Pitcher, blown, 80 oz.	15.00--20.00
No. 1821 Wine Decanter and Stopper, 32 oz.	15.00--20.00
No. 1820 Wine Decanter and Stopper, 16 oz.	14.00--18.00
No. G1049 Coaster, scalloped edge, 3-7/8"	4.00-- 5.00
No. G115 Candy Tray, 3 compt. 5"	6.00-- 8.00
No. G703 Coaster, 3-3/8"	4.00-- 5.00
No. GK865 Wine Decanter and Stopper, 32 oz.	15.00--20.00

KITCHENWARE page 119

All green

No. G3036 Sherbet, 4 oz.	2.00-- 4.00
No. G1883 Sherbet, 3¾ oz.	3.00-- 4.00
No. G3051 Sherbet, 5½ oz.	2.00-- 3.00
No. G766 Nappy, 7"	10.00--12.00
No. G767 Nappy, 8"	12.00--14.00
No. G765 Nappy, 6"	5.00-- 6.00
No. G764 Nappy, 5"	4.00-- 5.00
No. G763 Nappy, 4"	3.00-- 4.00
Mixing Bowl Set, 5 pc. rolled edge	50.00--60.00
No. G1573, dia. 5½"	6.00-- 8.00
No. G1574, dia. 6½"	7.00-- 9.00
No. G1575, dia. 7½"	8.00--10.00
No. G1576, dia. 8½"	10.00--12.00
No. G1577, dia. 9½"	12.00--16.00
also a 10½"	18.00--20.00
No. G751 Beater Bowl	10.00--12.00
No. G2013-G2013½ Butter covered w/two handy grips	24.00--28.00

KITCHENWARE page 120

Green or crystal

No. G759, G759½ round Refrigerator Bowl w/knob Cover, 5¾"	15.00--18.00
No. G780, G752½ high Refrigerator Bowl w/flat Cover, 5¾"	15.00--20.00
No. G759, 752½ Refrigerator Bowl, rnd., w/flat Cover, 5¾"	12.00--15.00
No. G2015, G2015½ Refrigerator Bowl, oblong, 4½" wide by 5" long	12.00--15.00

UTILITY JAR
Cobalt, with "COFFEE" insignia

No. GK345-G796½ Utility Jar, w/glass Cover. 32 oz.	18.00--22.00
No. GK802 Oil Bottle or Vinegar Cruet, 8 oz.	15.00--20.00
No. G1095 Mixing Bowl w/lip, 7"	12.00--15.00
No. GK866 Syrup Pitcher w/top, 11 oz.	18.00--22.00

KITCHENWARE page 121

Green

No. G3042 Measuring Pitcher, 32 oz.	22.00--26.00
No. G3043, G2954 Reamer Set (measuring pitcher & reamer)	28.00--32.00
No. G175 Reamer, lemon	8.00--10.00
No. G2954 Reamer, perforated	8.00--10.00
No. G72 Reamer, orange	10.00--12.00
No. G1102 Vase, crimped top, 6¾" *(also made in white)*	8.00--10.00
No. G1950 Egg Cup, 5½ oz.	3.00-- 4.00
No. G3027 Pitcher, 19½ oz. *(also made in white)*	10.00--14.00
No. G1491 Salt Shaker, 4½"	15.00--20.00
No. G1491 Pepper Shaker, 4½"	15.00--20.00
No. G1491 Sugar Shaker, 4½"	15.00--20.00
No. G1491 Flour Shaker, 4½"	15.00--20.00

CRISSCROSS page 122

Crystal, pink, green
(Ritz blue prices are below)

Mixing Bowl, 6½, 7½, 8½, 9½, 10½ ea.	6.00--15.00
Reamer, orange	15.00--20.00
Reamer, lemon	9.00--12.00
Sugar and Cover	10.00--15.00
Creamer	7.00-- 9.00

Jug, 54 oz., ice lip	50.00--75.00
Tumbler, 9 oz.	10.00--15.00
Butter, ¼ lb.	15.00--30.00
Butter, 1 lb.	15.00--30.00
Water Bottle, 32 oz., 1 qt.	15.00--25.00
Water Bottle, 64 oz., 2 qt. (w/black screw top)	15.00--30.00
Refrigerator Dish, rnd., 6"	10.00--15.00
Refrigerator Dish, sq., (8" X 8")	15.00--35.00
Refrigerator Dish, sq., (4" X 4")	10.00--15.00
Refrigerator Dish, oblong (4" X 8")	15.00--25.00

Ritz blue

Mixing Bowl, 6½, 7½, 8½, 9½, 10½, ea.	10.00--25.00
Reamer, orange	120.00-130.00
Reamer, lemon	60.00--70.00
Sugar and Cover	40.00--50.00
Creamer	30.00--35.00
Jug, 54 oz., ice lip	125.00-150.00
Tumbler, 9 oz.	20.00--25.00
Butter, ¼ lb.	30.00--35.00
Butter, 1 lb.	50.00--55.00
Water Bottle, 32 oz., 1 qt.	40.00--50.00
Water Bottle, 64 oz., 2 qt. (w/black screw top)	40.00--50.00
Refrigerator Dish, rnd., 6"	20.00--25.00
Refrigerator Dish, sq., (8" X 8")	45.00--55.00
Refrigerator Dish, sq., (4" X 4")	15.00--20.00
Refrigerator Dish, oblong, (4" X 8")	35.00--40.00

MISCELLANEOUS page 123

Crystal, pink, green, Ritz blue

No. 1709 Tumbler, table, 9 oz.	4.00-- 6.00
No. 1876 Pitcher, water, pressed, ice lip, 54 oz.	18.00--22.00
No. 372 Tumbler, table, 9 oz.	4.00-- 6.00
No. 9526 Tumbler, table, 9 oz.	4.00-- 6.00
No. 9937 Pitcher, water, blown, tilt style, 42 oz., 80 oz. ***(FINE RIBBED 217 Book 1)*** ***Also made in fired on colors***	30.00--35.00
No. 485 Pitcher, water, blown, tilt style, 40 oz.	12.00--16.00
No. 486 Pitcher, water, blown, tilt style, 80 oz.	15.00--20.00
No. 367 Pitcher, water, blown, 70 oz.	15.00--18.00
No. 9939 Tumbler, table, 5 oz., 9 oz., 13 oz. ***(FINE RIBBED 217 Book 1)*** ***Also made in fired on colors***	4.00-- 6.00
No. 9870 Pitcher, water, blown, ice lip, 80 oz.	18.00--24.00
No. 9908 Pitcher, water, blown, ice lip, 80 oz.	16.00--20.00
No. 9878 Salt and Pepper ¾ oz., (w/molded ruby tops)	8.00--12.00
No. 311 Ice Tea, 12 oz.	6.00-- 8.00
No. 9891 Milk Pitcher 20 oz., 5"***(FINE RIBBED 217 Book 1)***	15.00--20.00

MISCELLANEOUS page 124

Crystal, pink, green

No. 9776 Tumbler, bulged, 12 oz.	2.50--3.00
No. 9585 Tumbler, GEORGIAN 5 oz.	3.00-- 4.00
No. 1877 Tumbler, GEORGIAN 9 oz.	3.00-- 4.00
No. 9820 Tumbler, GEORGIAN 9 oz.	3.00-- 4.00
No. 1564 Tumbler, table, 9 oz.	4.00-- 5.00
No. 1552 Tumbler, table, 9 oz.	4.00-- 5.00
No. 232 Dish, rnd., divided, 6½"	4.00-- 6.00
No. 248 Dish, candy, sq., 6¼"	4.00-- 6.00
No. 254 Dish, olive, hdld., 8"	4.00-- 6.00
No. 259 Dish, Bon Bon, 3 sided, 7"	4.00-- 6.00
No. 263 Tray, mint, 7"	4.00-- 6.00
No. 264 Dish, nut, fan-shaped	4.00-- 6.00
No. 572 Dish, three partition, 7"	4.00-- 6.00
No. 573 Dish, rnd., divided, 6¾"	4.00-- 6.00
No. 574 Dish, candy, sq., 6"	4.00-- 6.00
No. 575 Tray, rnd., 7"	4.00-- 6.00
No. 576 Dish, olive, hdld., 8½"	4.00-- 6.00
No. 577 Tray, preserve, hdld., 6"	4.00-- 6.00
No. 1533 Shaker, ¾ oz., pr.	6.00-- 9.00
No. K966/5 Shaker, ¾ oz., pr.	4.00-- 6.00
No. K477/8 Shaker, 7/8 oz., pr.	6.00-- 8.00
No. 3530 Shaker, 1 oz., pr.	6.00-- 9.00
No. 1875 Shaker, 1¼ oz., pr.	4.00-- 6.00
No. K491/2 Shaker, 1-5/8 oz., pr.	7.00-- 9.00
No. K-468/2 Shaker, 2 oz., pr.	7.00-- 9.00
No. K474/2 Shaker, 2 oz., pr.	8.00--12.00
No. K488/2 Shaker, 2-1/8 oz., pr.	4.00-- 6.00
No. 9629 Shaker, 2¼ oz., pr.	6.00-- 9.00
No. K-472/5 Shaker, 2½ oz., pr.	4.00-- 6.00
No. 9833 Shaker, 1 oz., pr.	3.00-- 5.00
No. 757½ Ash Tray, 4"	8.00--10.00
No. 9785 Ash Tray, 4¼"	8.00--12.00
No. 9786 Ash Tray, 4¼"	2.00-- 4.00
No. 788 Ash Tray, 5"	3.00-- 5.00
No. K422 Nurser, oval, 4 oz.	3.00-- 4.00
No. K410 Nurser, oval, 8 oz.	11.00--14.00
No. K413 Nurser, rnd., 8 oz.	5.00-- 7.00
No. K970 Nurser, rnd., 8 oz.	14.00--16.00

NEWPORT page 125

Plain and fired on, pink, Platonite
(Ritz blue and Burgandy prices are below)

Plate, luncheon, 8½"	3.00-- 4.00
Plate, sherbet, 6"	2.00-- 2.50
Plate, sandwich, 11½"	4.00-- 6.00
Cup	2.50-- 4.00
Saucer	1.50-- 2.50

Bowl, nappy, 4¼"	1.50-- 2.50
Bowl, nappy, 5½"	2.00-- 4.00
Bowl, nappy, 8¼"	8.00--12.00
Bowl, cream soup, 4¾"	4.00-- 5.00
Platter, 11¾"	8.00--10.00
Sugar	3.50-- 4.50
Creamer	3.50-- 4.50
Sherbet	2.00-- 3.50
Tumbler, 4½"	4.00-- 6.00
Salt and Pepper	12.00--15.00

Ritz blue, Burgandy

Plate, luncheon, 8½"	4.00-- 6.00
Plate, sherbet, 6"	2.50-- 3.50
Plate, w/rays in center, 10¼"	12.00--15.00
Plate, sandwich, 11½"	14.00--16.00
Cup	4.00-- 6.00
Saucer	2.00-- 2.50
Bowl, nappy, 4¼"	6.00-- 8.00
Bowl, nappy, 5½"	10.00--12.00
Bowl, nappy, 8¼"	18.00--24.00
Bowl, cream soup, 4¾"	8.00--10.00
Platter, 11¾"	18.00--22.00
Sugar	8.00--10.00
Sugar, w/metal Cover	14.00--18.00
Creamer	8.00--10.00
Sherbet	6.00-- 8.00
Tumbler, 4½"	15.00--18.00
Salt and Pepper	30.00--35.00
Plate, cake, 11" turned up edge	18.00--22.00

WHITE SHIP

Tumbler, 5, 9 oz.	7.00-- 9.00
Tumbler, 10, 12 oz.	7.00-- 9.00
Whiskey, 2½ oz.	25.00--35.00
Jug, 80 oz.	30.00--35.00

"X DESIGN"

(No. 165 Book 1)

Butterdish and Cover	25.00--30.00
Candy Dish and Cover	15.00--20.00

COLONY

Tumbler, 4½"	4.00-- 6.00
Jug, 6½"	15.00--18.00

SHAKERS

Salt and Pepper	8.00--10.00

MISCELLANEOUS

WHITE SHIP Cocktail Mixer and Stirrer	15.00--18.00
ROLY POLY Tumbler	6.00-- 7.00
WHITE SHIP Whiskey Tumbler	25.00--35.00
Ash Tray w/metal sail	15.00--20.00
WHITE SHIP Ice Tub	12.00--15.00
AFGHAN and SCOTTIE DOG Tumbler	5.00-- 8.00
POLO Tumbler	4.00-- 6.00
WHITE SHIP Cocktail Shaker	20.00--22.00
WHITE SHIP Plate	10.00--12.00
ANGEL FISH Cocktail Shaker	12.00--15.00
WINDMILL Cocktail Shaker	12.00--15.00
WINDMILL Tumbler	4.00-- 5.00
Ice Bowl in metal holder w/Tongs (No. 196 Book 1)	15.00--20.00

FLORAL STERLING page 126

Plate, 8"	4.00-- 6.00
Cup	3.50-- 4.50
Saucer	2.00-- 2.50
Cream	6.00-- 8.00
Sugar	6.00-- 8.00
Salt and Pepper	25.00--28.00
Candlesticks	12.00--14.00
Sherbet	5.00-- 6.00
Sherbet Plate	2.50-- 3.50

MISCELLANEOUS

JINGLE BELLS Punch Sets: 9" Bowl and 6 Punch Cups, red and green trim	15.00--18.00
"WINTER SCENE" Mug	3.00-- 4.00
"INDIAN" Mug, fired on mulberry color	4.00-- 6.00
"HOPALONG CASSIDY" Mugs, green, red and black trim	10.00--12.00
TOM and JERRY Set: 9" Bowl and 6 Punch Cups, red and green trim	15.00--18.00
"DUTCH" Cookie Jar, 7½" high, fired-on white and blue	10.00--15.00
"DUTCH" Kitchen Shakers	4.00-- 5.00
EGG NOG Set: 9¾" bowl and 6 Punch Cups, red and green trim	17.00--20.00

(NOTE: Some of these have been found marked HA. The DUTCH cookie jar was made by Bartlett-Collins. See in THE DECORATED TUMBLER BOOK page 41.)

FORGET-ME-NOT page 127

You may find these blanks decorated with other stripes, geometrical designs, flowers and fruit, or fired-on solid colors.

Ovide Cup and Saucer	3.00-- 4.00
Bowl, vegetable	6.00-- 8.00
St. Denis Cup and Saucer	3.00-- 4.00
Platter	6.00-- 8.00
Plate, dinner, 9"	3.50-- 4.50
Cream and Sugar	5.00-- 7.00

Nappy	2.00-- 2.50
Plate, salad, 7"	3.00-- 4.00

DUTCH DESIGN

Mixing Bowl Set: 5 pc. 5", 6", 7", 8" and 9" bowls	20.00--25.00
Jars, refrigerator, covered, 6"	8.00--10.00
Bowls, utility, covered, 5"	8.00--10.00
Shakers	4.00-- 6.00

"LOONEY TUNES"

Infant's Ware

No. 03211 Deep Plate	10.00--15.00
No. 03421 Divided Plate	10.00--15.00
No. 03404 Milk Mug	8.00--10.00
No. 03422 Cereal Bowl	6.00-- 8.00

SHIRLEY TEMPLE Creamer (G1300), cobalt, only a few of this second style	150.00-200.00
Cocktail Set, Moroccan amethyst, Cocktail 6¼", Tumbler 2½"	8.00--10.00
Batter Bowl, green, 7"	30.00--35.00
Canister Set, fired on green with black lettering	35.00--40.00

SHIRLEY TEMPLE Creamer

COCKTAIL SET

BATTER BOWL

CANISTER SET

Heisey

"Heisey News" is the official publication of Heisey Collectors of America, who also offer for sale about a dozen books on Heisey Glass. Write them at P.O. Box 27, Newark OH 43055 for a list.

This past summer I acquired four Heisey catalogs dated 1947, 1948, 1949 and 1950 which show the patterns of those years. I'm reprinting only the Heisey ROSE and the figurines as my space is limited. These are the items showing up most often at our glass shows.

One final reminder: do not pass Ohio without going directly to the absolutely marvy Heisey Museum in Newark. A monopoly of beauties!

ASH TRAY page 130

Cigarette Holder and Ash Tray	25.00--50.00

TWIST STEMWARE

Goblet	25.00--35.00
Saucer Champagne	20.00--30.00
Wine	25.00--35.00
Sherbet, tall	15.00--25.00
Sherbet, reg.	15.00--20.00

DIAMOND OPTIC Tableware

Plate, 6"	4.00-- 5.00
Goblet (both styles)	15.00--20.00
Saucer Champagne (both styles)	12.00--16.00
Sherbet	8.00--12.00
Parfait	15.00--18.00
Cream Soup and Plate	15.00--20.00
Cup and Saucer	12.00--15.00
Jug	65.00--75.00
Comport	20.00--25.00
No. 4204 Vase	30.00--40.00
No. 3359 Vase	25.00--30.00

THUMB PRINT page 13

Design No. 1404

Plate, 8"	15.00--25.0
Plate, 6"	8.00--12.0
Tumbler, ftd., 10 oz.	15.00--25.0
Goblet, 10 oz.	20.00--35.0
Soda, 8 oz.	16.00--24.0
Ice Tea, ftd., 12 oz.	18.00--28.0
Sherbet	10.00--15.0
Pitcher, ½ gal. jug	65.00--85.0
Sundae	10.00--15.0

EARLY AMERICAN SCROLL

Design No. 1405

Sherbet, 4 oz.	12.00--18.0
Saucer Champagne, 4 oz.	15.00--25.0
Goblet, 10 oz.	20.00--30.0
Plate, 7", 8"	15.00--25.0
Soda, 10 oz.	15.00--25.0
Soda, 8 oz.	12.00--20.0
Soda, 5 oz.	12.00--20.0

NO. 1252 TWIST page 13

Cream	20.00--30.0
Sugar	20.00--30.0

French Dressing Bottle	40.00--50.00
Tumbler, 8 oz.	12.00--18.00
Nasturtium Bowl, 8"	25.00--40.00
Ice Tub	30.00--50.00

NO. 1401 EMPRESS

Plate, 7"	10.00--15.00
Plate, 8"	15.00--20.00
Plate, square	15.00--20.00
Celery, 13"	20.00--30.00
Flower Bowl, 11"	35.00--45.00
Salt Shaker	15.00--25.00
Mint Dish, 6"	12.00--18.00
Mayonnaise, 5½"	25.00--35.00
Nut Dish, ind.	12.00--15.00
No. 4164 Jug	50.00--75.00
No. 3381 Sodas, ftd.	20.00--30.00

SATURN

Salad Bowl and Platter	45.00--65.00

1949 Catalog Reprint

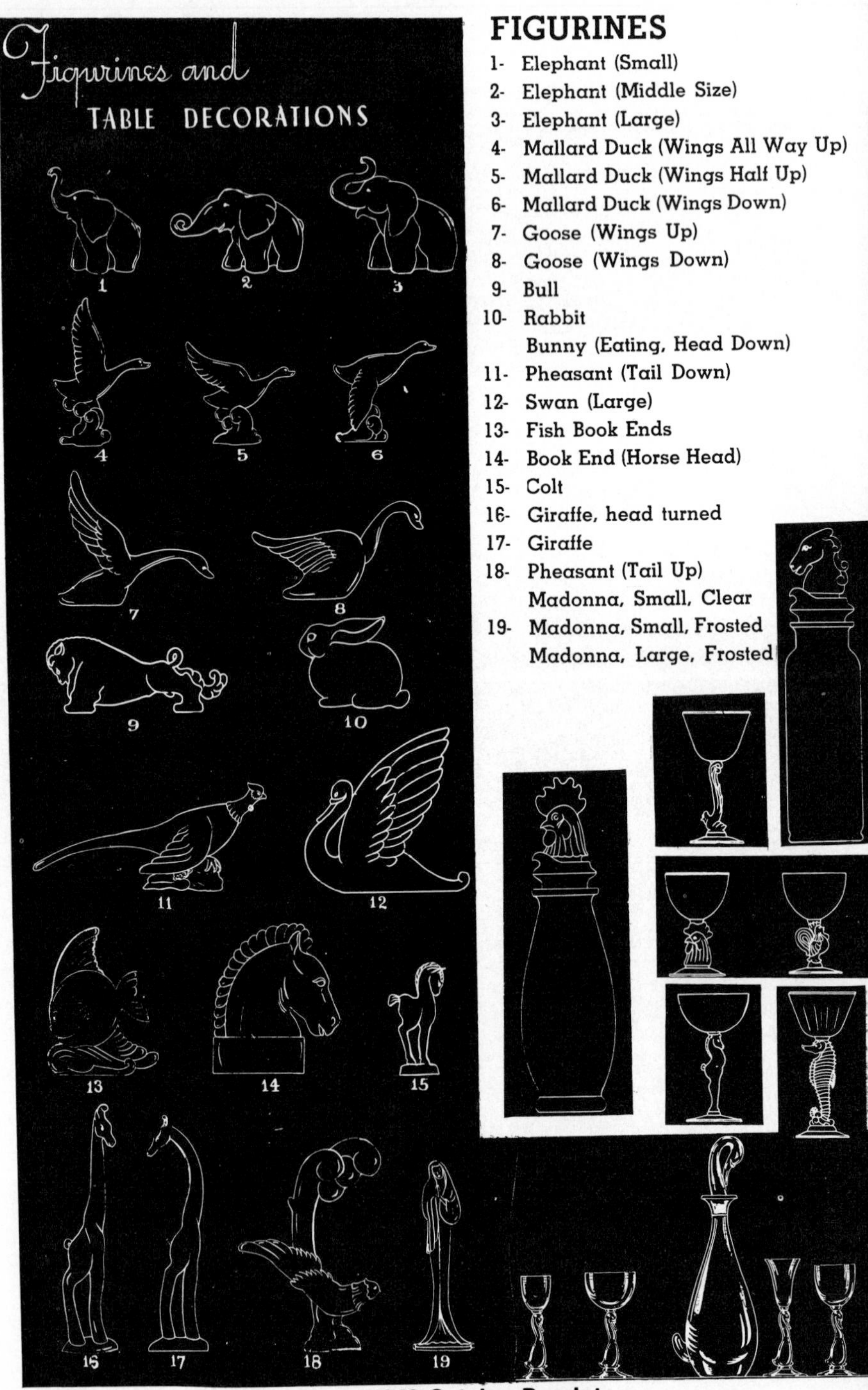

FIGURINES

1- Elephant (Small)
2- Elephant (Middle Size)
3- Elephant (Large)
4- Mallard Duck (Wings All Way Up)
5- Mallard Duck (Wings Half Up)
6- Mallard Duck (Wings Down)
7- Goose (Wings Up)
8- Goose (Wings Down)
9- Bull
10- Rabbit
Bunny (Eating, Head Down)
11- Pheasant (Tail Down)
12- Swan (Large)
13- Fish Book Ends
14- Book End (Horse Head)
15- Colt
16- Giraffe, head turned
17- Giraffe
18- Pheasant (Tail Up)
Madonna, Small, Clear
19- Madonna, Small, Frosted
Madonna, Large, Frosted

Hocking/ Anchor Hocking

Don't forget that Book I, COLORED GLASSWARE OF THE DEPRESSION ERA, presents over a dozen major patterns made by Hocking and Anchor Hocking glass companies. Such lines as CAMEO, PRINCESS, MAYFAIR, MISS AMERICA, BLOCK, LACE EDGE, COLONIAL, QUEEN MARY, and MANHATTAN are fully illustrated, listings the pieces and giving the history of each.

What Book 2 features is the remainder of this factory's activities, and together the picture is really quite complete. Reprinted here are just a couple of reprints that didn't fit in Book 2.

NOW -- if you want to see the panorama of tumblers decorated by Hocking, starting in 1933 and continuing to 1960, find THE DECORATED TUMBLER book! They're all there, and many were designed to complement the Hocking dishware patterns.

CIRCLE page 140

(No. 218 Book I)
Crystal and green

Jug w/reamer	25.00--35.00
Tumbler	6.00-- 8.00
Decanter and Tumblers	50.00--60.00

HOCKING's GEORGIAN

(No. 215 Book I)

Tumbler (also Royal Ruby)	8.00--12.00
Decanter	20.00--35.00
Sherbet	4.00-- 6.00
Sherbet Plate	3.00-- 4.00
Pitcher (also Royal Ruby)	30.00--40.00

MISCELLANEOUS

Optic Tumblers, wide, straight Nos. 60, 64, 65, 66, 63, 61, 67, 69	3.00-- 6.00
Spiral Optic Tumblers Nos. 409, 406, 414, 401, 403, 405, 404, 400	4.00-- 8.00
Wide Optic Tumblers, hand blown, Nos. 900, 904, 905, 903, 901, 906, 909	8.00--14.00
No. 940 Plate, salad, 8"	4.00-- 6.00
No. 944 Plate, sandwich, 10"	10.00--14.00
No. 980 Wine, ftd.	10.00--16.00
No. 981 Tumbler, ftd.	9.00--12.00
No. 988 Ice Tea, ftd.	10.00--14.00
No. 934 Sundae	9.00--12.00
No. 930 Wine	12.00--16.00
No. 933/929 Sherbet and 6" plate	6.00-- 8.00
No. 942 Goblet	10.00--14.00
No. 138 Goblet, 20 oz.	8.00--10.00
No. 654 Jug	20.00--24.00
No. 401 Tumbler	4.00-- 6.00
No. 53 Crackled Tumbler	4.00-- 6.00
No. 065 Hog Tumbler	6.00-- 8.00
No. 2 Decanter and Stopper	16.00--20.00
No. 0203 Tumbler, beverage 5 oz.	6.00-- 8.00

KITCHENWARE page 141

Green and pink

Utility Set:	
Coffee, sugar, cereal, flour, ea	25.00--30.00
Shaker Set:	
Spice, salt, pepper, sugar, ea.	10.00--12.00
Refrigerator Jar and Cover	
Small	12.00--15.00
Medium	20.00--25.00
Large	30.00--35.00
Mixing Bowl, (No. 278 Book I) ea.	6.00--15.00
Measuring Cup	18.00--20.00
Caster	2.50-- 3.00
Ashtray	8.00--10.00
Syrup	22.00--25.00
Salt and Pepper	5.00-- 7.00
Percolater Top	2.00-- 3.00
Reamer Set	25.00--30.00
Cookie Jar w/metal lid	25.00--30.00
Refrigerator Jar and Cover, sq.	10.00--12.00
Butter and Cover, 1 lb. oblong	28.00--32.00
Water Bottle	12.00--15.00
Reamer	10.00--14.00

BEER AND PRETZEL SET

Green and pink

Pretzel Jar and Cover	35.00--45.00
Jug, 80 oz.	18.00--22.00
Beer Mug, 12 oz.	10.00--20.00

NEW PINCH LINE

Green and pink

No. G124 Beverage, 1½ oz.	4.00-- 6.00
No. G125 Wine, 2½ oz.	4.00-- 6.00
No. G123 Fruit Juice, 5 oz.	4.00-- 6.00
No. 126 Tumbler, tall, 10 oz.	4.00-- 6.00
No. 128 Ice Tea, 13 oz.	6.00-- 8.00
No. 180 Jug, 75 oz.	15.00--18.00
No. 151 Shaker, cocktail w/alum. top	18.00--24.00
No. 102 Decanter w/drop stopper	20.00--26.00

STRIPE page 142

Applied bands of red and white

A Tumbler, 3 sizes, ftd.	4.00-- 6.00
B Tumbler, 6 sizes	4.50-- 5.50
C Cup and Saucer	4.00-- 6.00
D Mixer	10.00--12.00
E Stemware, 4 sizes	4.00-- 8.00
F Sherbet and plate	3.00-- 4.00
G Ice tub	6.00-- 9.00
H Decanter and stopper	9.00--12.00
J Shaker, cocktail w/metal lid	8.00--10.00
K Plate	2.50-- 3.00
L Pitcher	12.00--16.00

BEVERAGE SETS

ARCTIC	25.00--30.00
POLAR BEAR	30.00--35.00
CHARIOT	30.00--35.00

"RING DING"

Decoration 88

Yellow, orange, green, red painted -bands

Tumblers: 6 oz., 7 oz., 8 oz., 10 oz., 12 oz., 14 oz., 16 oz., 18½ oz.	4.00-- 6.00
Tumblers: 7½ oz., 1½ oz., 9 oz., 1½ oz., 2½ oz., 4½ oz., 9 oz., 10 oz., 12 oz.	4.00-- 6.00
No. 33 Sherbet	2.00-- 3.00
No. 729 Plate, 6"	1.50-- 2.00
No. 32 Cocktail	6.00-- 8.00
No. 30 Wine	6.00-- 8.00
No. 34 Saucer Champagne	5.00-- 7.00
No. 142 Goblet	6.00-- 8.00
No. 182 Cocktail, 3 oz.	5.00-- 7.00
No. 181 Tumbler, 10 oz.	5.00-- 7.00
No. 188 Ice Tea, 15 oz.	5.00-- 7.00
No. 40 Plate, 8"	2.50-- 3.00
No. 170 Cocktail Mixer	7.00-- 9.00
No. 702 Decanter w/ground stopper, 32 oz.	9.00--12.00
No. 752 Shaker, 32 oz.	8.00--10.00
No. 780 Jug, 80 oz.	12.00--16.00
No. 754 Jug, 60 oz.	10.00--14.00

"PANELLED RING-DING"

No. 63 Juice, fruit, 5 oz.	4.00-- 6.00
No. 61 Tumbler, 9 oz.	4.00-- 6.00
No. 68 Ice Tea, 12 oz.	4.00-- 6.00
No. 181 Tumbler, ftd.	5.00-- 7.00
No. 729 Plate, 6"	1.50-- 2.00
No. 134 Sherbet, high	5.00-- 7.00
No. 188 Ice Tea, ftd.	5.00-- 7.00
No. 740 Plate, 8"	2.50-- 3.50
No. 142 Goblet	8.00--10.00

SHAKERS page 143

Shakers in Crystal and green

"WREN" shaker	6.00--10.00
DOVE shaker (*same as shown in Book 1 with PRINCESS*)	12.00--15.00
"QUAIL" shaker	6.00--10.00
"CROW" Vinegar w/cork stopper (*I've only seen this in crystal*)	16.00--18.00

LAKE COMO

Cup, two styles	4.00-- 5.00
Saucer	1.50-- 2.00

Plate, dinner, 9¼"	4.00-- 5.00
Plate, bread and butter or salad, 7¼"	2.50-- 3.50
Creamer	5.00-- 6.00
Sugar	5.00-- 6.00
Vegetable, 9½"	9.00--11.00
Platter, 11"	8.00--10.00
Salt and Pepper	20.00--25.00
Bowl, rnd.	9.00--11.00

"FLOWER RIM" VITROCK TABLEWARE page 144

(No. 237 Book I)

Plate, dinner, 10"	4.00-- 6.00
Plate, luncheon, 8¾"	3.00-- 5.00
Soup, cream	5.00-- 7.00
Dessert, 4"	3.00-- 4.00
Sugar	5.00-- 7.00
Cream	5.00-- 7.00
Cup	5.00-- 6.00
Saucer	1.50-- 2.50
Fruit, 6"	4.00-- 6.00
Cereal, 7½"	5.00-- 7.00
Bowl, vegetable, 9½"	8.00--10.00
Platter, meat, 11½"	8.00--10.00
Plate, bread or cream soup 7¼"	3.00-- 4.00
Plate, soup, 9"	6.00-- 8.00

VITROCK KITCHENWARE

Reamer, orange	8.00--10.00
Jar and Cover, left-over, rnd.	10.00--12.00
Salt and Pepper, pr.	8.00--10.00
Ashtray	2.00-- 4.00
Mixing Bowl Set, 6 pc.:	35.00--45.00
6½", 7½", ea.	3.00-- 6.00
8½", 9½", 10½", 11½", ea	8.00--12.00
Sugar, Flour and Spice, ea. *(not pictured)*	4.00-- 5.00
Egg Cup *(not pictured)*	6.00-- 8.00

"FISHCALE" page 145

Cup and Saucer	6.00-- 8.00
Plate, dinner, 9¼"	4.00-- 6.00
Cereal, 5½"	4.00-- 6.00
Dessert, 5½"	4.00-- 6.00
Plate, soup, 7½"	4.00-- 6.00
Platter, 11¾"	7.00-- 9.00
Bowl, vegetable, 8¾"	8.00--10.00

ST. DENIS Line

Ivory, undecorated or with red and - black lines

Cup and Saucer (2 styles)	3.00-- 4.00
Plate	3.00-- 4.00
Bowl	5.00-- 7.00
Salt, Pepper and Range Jar decorated with black and red green or blue	15.00--20.00

LEAF AND BLOSSOM DESSERT SET

Dessert Set	6.00-- 8.00

LITTLE BO-PEEP INFANTS WARE

Orange and green decorations

Plate, divided, 7¾"	9.00--12.00
Cereal, 5½"	6.00-- 8.00
Mug	8.00--10.00

FIRE KING page 146

Blue, Jad-ite, and Ivory

Roaster, 10¾" x 5½"	40.00--50.00
Casseroles, Knob Covers, 1 pt., 1 qt., 2 qt.	8.00--18.00
Open Bakers, 1 pt. 1 qt., 1½ qt., 2 qt.	6.00--10.00
Casseroles, Pie Plate Covers, 1 qt., 2 qt.	10.00--16.00
Pie Plates, 8-3/8", 9", 9-5/8"	5.00-- 8.00
Cake Pan, 8¾"	8.00--10.00
Deep Loaf Pan, 9-1/8"	10.00--12.00
Utility Pan, 10½"	10.00--12.00
Refrigerator Jar, sq., 1 pt.	5.00-- 7.00
Refrigerator Jar and Cover, 4½" x 5"	8.00--10.00
Refrigerator Jar, oblong, 5-1/8" x 9-1/8"	10.00--12.00
Individual Casserole and Cover, 10 oz.	6.00-- 8.00
Deep Pie Dish, 5-3/8"	5.00-- 7.00
Nursing Bottles, 4 oz., 8 oz.	15.00--25.00
Percolator Top, 2-1/8"	3.00-- 4.00
Custard Cups, Ind. Bakers, 5 oz. shallow, 6 oz. deep, 6 oz. regular	3.00-- 4.00
Measuring Cup	15.00--18.00
Hot Plate w/handles	10.00--12.00
Coffee Mug, 7 oz.,(2 styles)	16.00--19.00
Mixing Bowls, 6-7/8" 8-3/8", 10-1/8"	8.00--18.00
Measuring, Mixing Bowl w/tab handles	25.00--35.00

"PHILBE"

Crystal, pink, green, blue

Plate, 8"	15.00--25.00
Plate, 10½"	20.00--30.00
Plate, grill, 10½"	15.00--25.00

Service Plate, 11-5/8"	20.00--30.00
Bowl, oval, 9"	30.00--40.00
Soup, 7¼"	35.00--45.00
Cereal, 5½"	15.00--25.00
Creamer	35.00--50.00
Sugar	35.00--50.00
Platter	45.00--55.00
Tumbler, ftd., 6½"	45.00--55.00
Tumbler, ftd., 5½"	35.00--45.00
Juice, ftd., 3½"	75.00--90.00
Tumbler, 4"	60.00--70.00
Tumbler, 5"	65.00--75.00
Cookie Jar	150.00-250.00
Candy Dish, low	100.00-150.00
Cup	50.00--75.00
Saucer	15.00--20.00
Pitcher, juice, 6"	200.00-300.00
Pitcher, 8½"	300.00-400.00

ROYAL RUBY OR FOREST GREEN page 147

With crystal

Serva-Snack Set, oblong	5.00-- 8.00
"DEMON" Cigarette Set	20.00--25.00
Serva-Snack Set, fan shaped	5.00-- 8.00
Serva-Snack Set, square	5.00-- 8.00

LUNCHEON SET

Square shape
Forest Green, Royal Ruby

Cup	2.50-- 3.50
Saucer	1.00-- 1.50
Dessert or Cereal, 4¾"	2.00-- 3.00
Soup, 6"	4.00-- 6.00
Plate, salad, 6-5/8"	2.50-- 3.50
Plate, luncheon, 8-3/8"	3.50-- 4.00
Bowl, 7-3/8"	6.00-- 9.00
Platter, 11"	5.00-- 7.00
Sugar (no red)	3.00-- 4.00
Cream (no red)	3.00-- 4.00

"BOOPIE"

Tumbler, 9 oz., 4 oz. 3½ oz., 6 oz.	6.00-- 9.00

"WHIRLY-TWIRLY" SETS

Forest Green

Tumbler, 5 oz., 9 oz., 12 oz.	3.00-- 4.00
Pitcher, 3 qt.	12.00--18.00

"BURPLE" DESSERT SETS

Crystal, Forest Green, Royal Ruby

Bowl, 4-5/8"	3.00-- 4.00
Bowl, 8½"	6.00-- 9.00

"BIBI"

Bon Bon, 6½"	2.50-- 3.00

SERVA-SNACK SETS

Crystal, Forest Green or Royal Ruby Cups

Fan Shape	5.00-- 8.00
Square Shape	5.00-- 8.00

VASES

"WILSON" Ivy ball, 4", 4¾"	4.00-- 5.00
"HARDING" Vase, 6-3/8"	4.50-- 6.00
"COOLIDGE" Vase, 6-3/8"	4.50-- 6.00
"HOOVER" Vase, 9"	8.00--10.00
"ROOSEVELT" Vase, 3¾"	3.00-- 4.00
15 HOUR CANDLE Tumbler	2.50-- 3.50

ROYAL RUBY page 148

"RACHAEL" Bowl, 11"	15.00--18.00
Nappy, 5¼"	4.00-- 6.00
Plate, serving, 14½"	11.00--14.00
Vase, 9"	14.00--16.00
"MONARCH" Tumbler, 5-3/8"	7.00--10.00
ROYAL RUBY Sugar and Cover w/hole	10.00--12.00
ROYAL RUBY Creamer	5.00-- 7.00
Bottle, 7 oz. (3 sizes)	8.00--12.00
HOCKING HOBNAIL Water Set:	
Jug, 8"	15.00--20.00
Tumbler, 4¼"	4.00-- 6.00
HIGH POINT Water Set:	
Jug, 80 oz.	20.00--25.00
Tumbler, 5, 9 and 12 oz.	4.00-- 6.00

"ALICE"

Plate, 8½"	4.00-- 4.50
Cup	2.50-- 3.00
Saucer	1.50-- 2.00

"JANE RAY"

Cup	1.50-- 2.00
Saucer	.75-- 1.00
Dessert, 4-7/8"	2.00-- 3.00
Cereal or Oatmeal, 5-7/8"	3.00-- 4.00
Plate, 6¼"	1.50-- 2.00
Plate, salad, 7¾"	2.00-- 2.50
Plate, dinner, 9-1/8"	3.00-- 4.00
Soup, 7-5/8"	4.00-- 6.00
Bowl, vegetable, 8¼"	5.00-- 7.00
Platter, 12"x 9"	5.00-- 7.00
Sugar and Cover	3.00-- 4.00
Cream	2.00-- 3.00
Demitasse Cup and Saucer	6.00-- 8.00

'RACHAEL" vase 9"

INFANTS DECORATED TABLEWARE

Furnished in either blue or pink colors. Attractively decorated in black with figures to appeal to children. Items which now, for the first time, can be retailed at low prices. Fast-moving—sell all the year round.

DEC. 177—BLUE
DEC. 178—PINK

350—MUG, DEC. 177-178
Packed 4 doz. ctn.—wt. 25 lbs.

329—6¾" PLATE DEC. 177-178
Packed 4 doz. ctn.—wt. 31 lbs.

391—5¼" CEREAL DEC. 177-178
Packed 4 doz. ctn.—wt. 21 lbs.

343—7¾" DIVIDED PLATE DEC. 177-178
Packed 4 doz. ctn.—wt. 47 lbs.

SPECIFY COLOR DESIRED

(One color only packed to a carton)

1934 catalog reprint

INFANTS DECORATED TABLEWARE

No. 350 Mug	6.00-- 8.00
No. 329 Plate, 6¾"	8.00--10.00
No. 391 Cereal, 5¼"	4.00-- 6.00
No. 343 Plate, divided, 7¾"	9.00--12.00

VEGETABLE FRESHENER

Tray and Cover	50.00--65.00

THE HOCKING GLASS CO., LANCASTER, OHIO
VEGETABLE FRESHENER
VEGETABLE
FRESHENER

VEGETABLE FRESHNER from 1933 catalog

Huntington

We've been hunting hard for these lil' rascals and I'm happy to say our search has turned up quite a few. The few Huntington stems and shapes shown in Book 2 have been a lifesaver. And the "Lil' Rascals" themselves -- would you believe they turned out to be enamel silkscreen decorated tumblers?

STEMWARE	page 149
"NOVA"	10.00--12.00
"AVON"	10.00--12.00
"DING"	12.00--15.00
"DONG"	12.00--15.00
"GRACIOUS"	11.00--14.00
No. 2701 Goblet, low square ftd., 12 oz.	8.00--14.00

"LIL' RASCALS"	
"SPANKY"	3.00-- 5.00
"FARINA"	3.00-- 5.00
"ALFALFA"	3.00-- 5.00
"BULLSEYE"	3.00-- 5.00
"BUCKWHEAT"	3.00-- 5.00

"TIP TOE" GOBLET	
Goblet	11.00--14.00

ILLUSTRATING a new creation for 1930—our 4416 goblet in 303 all polished cutting. This and other striking designs and shapes will be introduced at the Pittsburgh Show in

Room 736
Wm. Penn Hotel

Huntington Tumbler Company
Huntington, W. Va.

"TIP TOE" goblet from 1930 ad

Imperial

Many pieces come in colors not noted on the original catalog reprints, especially Golden Green in the earlier pieces. You may also find dark blue, light blue, blue-green and topaz, and some black glass as well. Know, too, that most old Imperial pieces have ground bottoms.

A book on Imperial Glass from 1904 to 1938 is available at the factory or can be ordered from the authors, Margaret and Douglas Archer (P. O. Box 423, Ballwin MO 63011).

And the fans have formed a club. For information write the Imperial Glass Collectors' Society, P. O. Box 4012, Silver Springs, Maryland 20904.

VIKING — page 151

Rose and green

Plate	5.00-- 7.00
Mayonnaise and Ladle	18.00--20.00
Sugar	8.00--10.00
Cream	8.00--10.00
Bowl	10.00--12.00
Service Plate	8.00--10.00

EARLY AMERICAN HOBNAIL — pages 151, 152

Crystal, amber, blue, Golden Ophir, green, rose, ruby and black.
Sea Foam in Harding blue, Moss green, and Burnt Almond tints.

Flip Vase	20.00--25.00
Table Tumbler	9.00--11.00
Pitcher	35.00--50.00
Salver, 10"	20.00--25.00
Toilet Water Bottle	15.00--25.00
Puff or Vanity Box and Cover	20.00--25.00
Tumbler	9.00--12.00
Sherbet	6.00-- 8.00
Goblet	15.00--20.00
Ivy Ball	15.00--20.00
Jardiniere	9.00--12.00

MISCELLANEOUS — page 152

Intaglio white etched Fruit Plates	8.00--10.00
Console Set: large Saucer Candlesticks	30.00--35.00
Sandwich Tray, black handle and crystal Platter	20.00--25.00

CAPE COD

See listing page 111

"SPUN" (officially Imperial's REEDED pattern)

Crystal, amber, red, blue-green, cobalt, fired on pastels

Plate, salad, 8"	6.00-- 8.00
Plate, cupped edge, 13½"	18.00--20.00
Plate, 14"	14.00--16.00
Cup	5.00-- 8.00
Saucer	3.00-- 3.50
Bowl, fruit, 4½"	4.00-- 5.00
Bowl, nappy, 7"	8.00--10.00
Bowl, salad, deep 8"	14.00--16.00
Bowl, ball, deep, 2½", 4", 6"	4.00-- 7.00
Cream	8.00--10.00

Sugar	6.00--10.00
Tumbler, cocktail, 3½ oz.	5.00-- 7.00
Tumbler, juice, 5 oz.	5.00-- 7.00
Tumbler, old fashioned, 7 oz.	7.00-- 9.00
Tumbler, highball, 12 oz.	8.00--10.00
Tumbler, ice tea, 12 oz.	8.00--12.00
Jug, ice lip, 80 oz.	20.00--30.00
Cocktail Shaker, 36 oz.	18.00--24.00
Ice Tub	10.00--15.00
Cigarette Holder, 2½" ball	6.00-- 8.00
Ball 2 pc. Smoker	8.00--10.00
Ash Tray, 2½"	2.00-- 3.50
Candle Holder, 2½" ball	4.00-- 6.00
Muddler, 4½"	5.00-- 7.00
Vase, bud, 5"	5.00-- 7.00
Vase, Rose bowl, 5"	6.00-- 8.00
Vase, Rose bowl (ball), 6"	6.00-- 9.00
Bitters w/metal tube	7.00--10.00
Vanity Set: 2 Colognes and Powder Box	25.00--35.00

(see "SPINNERS" page 396 Book II)

"SPUN" bowl, 8"

NO. 678 PART-CUT "D'ANGELO" page 153

Rose Marie, Imperial Green

Water Set: 7 pc., Pitcher and 6 Tumblers	100.00-125.00
Sugar, oval	9.00--12.00
Cream, oval	9.00--12.00
Berry Set: 7 pc., 1 Bowl, 8¾" and 6 Berry, 4¼"	50.00--60.00
Bowl, orange, oval, 11"	40.00--50.00
Candy Jar and Cover	30.00--40.00
Nappy, 2 hdld., 6"	12.00--15.00
Tray, celery, 10"	15.00--20.00
Vase, oval, 10"	30.00--40.00
Bowl, tall, ftd., 6"	20.00--25.00
Bon Bon, 1 hdld., 5¼"	10.00--15.00
Pickle Boat, 6"	10.00--12.00

ROSE MARIE GLASS, NUCUT DESIGN page 154

No. 91/506 Tray sandwich, 12"	18.00--24.00
No. 91/750 Bowl, fruit, 12"	30.00--40.00
No. 91/2929C Bowl, orange, 12"	35.00--45.00
No. 91/587 Fern Dish, 7½"	20.00--30.00
No. 91/534/9A Bowl, salad, rnd., 9¼"	20.00--25.00
No. 91/4828 Bowl, salad, deep, 8½"	20.00--25.00
No. 91/502 Bowl, salad, 9"	20.00--25.00
No. 91/571 Nappy, shallow, 10¼"	18.00--24.00
No. 91/460 Bowl, berry, 8"	15.00--20.00
No. 91/5338S Bowl, berry, square, 7½"	16.00--22.00
No. 91/466 Tray, celery, 11"	12.00--16.00
No. 91/485/2 Comport, partitioned, rnd., 2 hdld., 7¼"	20.00--25.00
No. 91/737A Bowl, salad, ftd., 8½"	25.00--30.00
No. 91/607 Bowl, oval, ftd., 2 hdld., 9½" long	25.00--30.00
No. 0464, Punch Set: 8 pc. Bowl, dia. 15", 15" tall on foot, Cups, reg. size, ground bottoms	150.00-200.00
No. 0500, Punch Set: 8 pc., Bowl, dia. 13", 13½" tall on foot, Cups, reg. size ground bottoms	135.00-175.00
No. 4040B Bowl, orange, 11"	30.00--40.00
No. 4822 Bowl, tall ftd., 8½"	30.00--35.00
No. 750 Bowl, fruit, ftd., 12"	35.00--45.00

ROSE MARIE GLASS, NUCUT DESIGN page 155

No. 91/564 Pickle Boat, 8"	12.00--16.00
No. 91/452B Bowl, ftd., 7"	20.00--30.00
No. 91/538 Dish, oval, 7½"	15.00--20.00
No. 91/555 Sugar, berry	11.00--15.00
No. 91/555 Cream, berry	11.00--15.00
No. 91/555 Mayonnaise and Plate Set, oval	25.00--30.00
No. 91/555 Vase, 6¼"	16.00--19.00
No. 91/555 Bon Bon Dish hdld., rnd., 5½"	12.00--15.00
No. 91/555A Nappy, rnd, 6½"	10.00--14.00
No. 91/511 Jelly, ftd., 4½"	15.00--20.00
No. 91/5316A Nappy, rnd., 6½"	10.00--14.00
No. 91/460D Plate, 10½"	16.00--22.00
No. 91/555 Pickle Dish, 7¾"	12.00--15.00
No. 91/360C Bowl, fruit, oval, 13"	40.00--50.00
No. 91/537 Jelly, ftd., 4½"	10.00--14.00
No. 91/485/1 Nappy, 2 hdld., 7¼"	12.00--15.00
No. 91/498 Dish, berry, hdld., 5½"	10.00--14.00
No. 91/4742 Salad, square, 9"	20.00--25.00
No. 91/4826 Bowl, berry, deep, 6½"	10.00--15.00
No. 91/466 Bowl, berry, 9"	20.00--30.00
No. 91/4048 Bowl, berry, deep, grnd. bottom, 8½"	20.00--25.00
No. 91/484 Bowl, berry, 5"	6.00-- 8.00

No. 91/466 Bowl, berry, 5"	6.00-- 8.00
No. 91/475 Bowl, berry, melon shaped, 5"	6.00-- 8.00
No. 91/4044 Bowl, berry, grnd. bottom, 4"	6.00-- 8.00
No. 91/484 Bowl, berry, 8"	20.00--25.00
No. 91/475 Bowl, berry, melon shaped, 8"	20.00--25.00
No. 91/497 Plate, ice cream, 6"	9.00--12.00
No. 91/497 Tray, ice cream, 10½"	14.00--20.00
No. 91/4821 Bowl, ftd., 6½"	20.00--25.00
No. 91/4047 Bouquet, 13"	30.00--40.00
No. 91/4743 Vase, 12"	30.00--40.00
No. 91/482 Bowl, heavy, ftd., 8½"	35.00--45.00
No. 91/404 Bouquet, 9"	20.00--25.00
No. 91/387 Bouquet, 7"	15.00--20.00

FANCY COLONIAL — page 156, 157

Crystal, Rose Marie

You will find some pieces in blue-green.

Bon Bon, hdld., 5½"	10.00--12.00
Olive, hdld., 5"	10.00--12.00
Table Butter and Cover, 4¼"	40.00--50.00
Plate, 5¾"	3.00-- 5.00
Salt and Pepper Shaker	25.00--35.00
Bowl, ftd., 2 hdld., 5"	11.00--14.00
Custard	5.00-- 8.00
Punch Cup	5.00-- 8.00
Table Salt, hdld.	10.00--15.00
Tray, celery, 12"	15.00--18.00
Nappy, 3½", 4½", 5", 6"	6.00--10.00
Nappy, 7",8"	12.00--18.00
Mayonnaise and Plate, 5"	12.00--16.00
Salad and Plate, 8"	18.00--22.00
Tray, pickle, oval, 8",	12.00--15.00
Tray, spoon, oval, 8"	14.00--20.00
Berry, 4¼", 5", 7", 8", 9"	6.00--20.00
Bowls, nut, 5", 6", 7", 8"	7.00--18.00
Berry, 2 hdld., 7½"	14.00--16.00
Cocktail, 3 oz., 4½ oz.	14.00--18.00
Saucer Champagne, 6 oz.	14.00--18.00
Cafe Parfait	14.00--18.00
Tumbler, 10, 8, 6, 5, 4½ oz.	7.00--14.00
Whiskey, 2 oz.	12.00--14.00
Ice Tea, 12 oz., 14 oz.	10.00--14.00
Bell Tumbler, 8 oz.	10.00--12.00
Bowl, ftd., 4", 5¼", 6¼"	10.00--16.00
Plate, salad, 7½"	5.00-- 8.00
Plate, cake, 10½"	10.00--15.00
Oil Bottles, 6¼, 5½ oz.	30.00--40.00
Vase, 8"	12.00--15.00
Vase, Rose, 10"	15.00--18.00
Water Bottle, pressed	15.00--20.00
Tumbler, table	7.00-- 9.00
Jug, 3 pint	50.00--60.00
Cordial, 1 oz.	18.00--24.00
Wine, 2 oz.	18.00--24.00
Port, 3 oz.	18.00--24.00
Burgandy, 4 oz.	18.00--24.00
Claret, 5 oz.	18.00--24.00
Champagne, 6 oz.	18.00--24.00
Goblet, 8 oz., 10 oz.	18.00--24.00
Egg Cup	16.00--20.00
Sherbets	6.00-- 9.00
Jelly, ftd., 4¼"	8.00--12.00
Spoon holder	14.00--16.00
Cream	14.00--16.00
Butter and Cover	60.00--70.00
Sugar and Cover	30.00--40.00
Sugar, ftd.	12.00--15.00
Cream, ftd.	12.00--15.00
Bowl, fruit, 10"	20.00--25.00

"TWISTED OPTIC" — page 158

No. 313 Tray, sandwich, hdld., 10"	12.00--15.00
No. 3134D Plate, 6"	3.00-- 4.00
No. 803/3 Tumbler, ice tea, blown, 14 oz.	4.00-- 6.00
No. 313 Cup and Plate	8.00--10.00
No. 313D Plate, salad, 8"	3.00-- 5.00
No. 3132 Comport, covered	20.00--25.00
No. 313 Powder Box, covered	15.00--20.00
No. 313 Candy Jar, covered	20.00--25.00
No. 645/3 Candy Box, covered	20.00--25.00
No. 148/1 Candy Box, covered	20.00--25.00
No. 615/3 Sugar	5.00-- 7.00
No. 615/3 Cream	5.00-- 7.00
No. 685/1 Candy Jar, covered	20.00--25.00

"PACKARD"

No. 320 Console Set: 3 pc., oval, Candlestick, 8¼", oval Base, oval Bowl, 10½"	30.00--45.00
No. 3130/715/3 Console Set: 3 pc., Candlesticks, 3½", Bowl, oval, 10½"	30.00--35.00

VASES

No. 313R rolled top, 7¼"	12.00--14.00
No. 313B flrd. top, 8"	12.00--15.00
No. 313P fan shaped, 8"	12.00--15.00
No. 6001 rnd., 10"	14.00--18.00
No. 5982 square, 10½" *(inside Optic Flute)*	14.00--18.00
No. 6002 rnd., 9"	14.00--18.00

ICE TEA SETS — page 159

No. 83/3 Set: 7 pc., "TWISTED OPTIC"	40.00--50.00
83/3 Jug, blown, ½ gal.	16.00--20.00
803/3 Tumblers, ice tea, blown, 14 oz.	4.00-- 5.00

No. 6003 Ice Tea Set: 8 pc.	
"CHESTERFIELD",	85.00--95.00
06003 Jug, tankard,	
covered, ½ gal.	30.00--40.00
600 Tumbler, hdld.,	
pressed, 10 oz.	7.00-- 9.00

CONSOLE SETS

Amber, green, Rose Marie

No. 808/30/637/3 Console Set:	
5 pc.	30.00--40.00
637/3 Candlestick, pr.	12.00--15.00
808/3Q Bowl, console, 10¼"	12.00--15.00
No. 3139B/635/3 Console Set:	
4 pc.	35.00--45.00
635/3 Candlestick, 8¼", pr.	20.00--25.00
3139B Bowl, console	
on back Base, 11½"	15.00--20.00
No. 675R Console Set: 5 pc.	40.00--45.00
675 Candlestick, pr.	10.00--12.00
675R Bowl, console, 9½"	15.00--20.00
No. 6567/2B/635 Console Set:	
4 pc.	35.00--45.00
635 Candlestick, 8¼", pr.	20.00--25.00
6567/2B Bowl, console,	
on back Base, 9½"	15.00--20.00

BASKETS

Measurements include handle

No. 300 10½"	20.00--25.00
No. 714 10"	25.00--30.00
No. 252 13"	30.00--40.00
No. 698 10"	20.00--25.00
No. 313 10"	20.00--25.00

MISCELLANEOUS page 160

Amber, green, Rose Marie

No. 629D "STRAWFLOWER"	
Plate, salad, ftd. bottom, 7½"	6.00-- 8.00
No. 682D Plate, square, ftd.	
bottom, 7¾"	5.00-- 6.00
No. 704 "WOODBURY"	
Plate, salad, 8"	6.00-- 8.00
No. 706 "BLAISE"	
Plate, salad, 8"	6.00-- 8.00
No. 200 Tall Caster Set: 3 pc.	20.00--25.00
No. 428 Basket Caster Set:	
3 pc.	18.00--22.00
No. 313 "TWISTED OPTIC"	
Mayonnaise Set: 3 pc.	18.00--22.00
No. 629B "STRAWFLOWER"	
Mayonnaise Set: 3 pc.	16.00--20.00
No. 682 Mayonnaise Set:	
square, 3 pc.	16.00--20.00
No. 602 Mayonnaise Set: 3 pc.	12.00--16.00
No. 602/5 "DIAMOND QUILTED"	
Mayonnaise Set: 3 pc.	16.00--20.00

No. 12 GUEST ROOM SET:	
3 pc.	20.00--26.00
Pitcher, pt.	10.00--14.00
Tumbler, 6 oz.	3.00-- 4.00
Plate, oval	6.00-- 8.00
No. 600 "ZAK", Wine Set:	
9 pc. Tray; Decanter, blown;	
Tumblers, pressed	45.00--55.00
No. 505 "ROXY", Wine Set:	
9 pc; Tray; Decanter, blown;	
Tumbler, pressed	55.00--65.00
No. 650 Guest Room Set: 2 pc.	
Pitcher, blown	
with pressed tumbler	20.00--30.00

VASES

No. 294 Vase, bud, 5" to 8"	6.00-- 8.00
No. 6924 Vase, bud, 11"	7.00-- 9.00
No. 304 Vase, bud, 10" to 12"	9.00--12.00
No. 6922 Vase wide, 7" to 9"	6.00-- 8.00
No. 6923 Vase, tall, 9" to 10"	8.00--12.00
No. 6932C Vase, crimped,	
5" high	6.00-- 8.00
No. 6931 Vase, Sweet Pea, 4"	6.00-- 8.00
No. 6935 Vase, wide, 8" to 9"	10.00--15.00

MISCELLANEOUS page 161

Amber, green, Rose Marie

No. 313 "TWISTED OPTIC"	
Cup and Plate (saucer) set	8.00--10.00
No. 313 "TWISTED OPTIC"	
Sherbet and Plate Set	5.00-- 8.00
No. 91/625/5 "DIAMOND QUILTED",	
Punch Set: 8 pc.	150.00-200.00
Bowl and Foot	100.00-150.00
Punch Cups	5.00-- 6.00
No. 4142R Bowl, ftd., 7¼"	15.00--20.00
No. 4146D Salver, 8¼"	18.00--24.00
No 4146F Bowl, ftd., 7½"	15.00--20.00
No. 4146A Bowl,	
ftd., covered, 6¼"	35.00--40.00
No. 6067/5X Bowl, ftd., 9"	20.00--25.00
No. 6067/5W Bowl, 9"	20.00--25.00
No. 6067/5R Bowl, ftd., 8¾"	20.00--25.00
No. 6067/5D Salver, 10"	25.00--30.00

(See more "DIAMOND QUILTED" on page 124)

WATER SETS

No. 414 Set: 7 pc.	50.00--60.00
Jug, ½ gal., hand made	
handle, 79 oz.	25.00--30.00
Tumblers, blown table	4.00-- 6.00
No. 6983 Set: 7 pc.	45.00--55.00
Pitcher, ½ gal.	20.00--25.00
Tumbler, table, 9½ oz.	4.00-- 6.00

'OMERO" page 162

4mber, Rose Marie, green

No. 6155NC/25 Lily Bowl	6.00-- 8.00
No. 609/25 Sugar, 2 hdld.	5.00-- 8.00
No. 609/25 Cream	5.00-- 8.00
No. 6152/25 Berry, 2 hdld.	5.00-- 8.00
No. 6674/25 Berry, 1 hdld.	5.00-- 7.00
No. 6165A/25 Berry, 5¾"	4.00-- 6.00
No. 615/25 Pickle, 2 hdld.	7.00-- 9.00
No. 599/25 Jelly, ftd.	7.00-- 9.00
No. 692/25 Vase, 7½"	10.00--12.00
No. 692/25 Vase, 5"	10.00--12.00
No. 499B/25 Sherbet	4.00-- 5.00
No. 499/25 Plate, sherbet	2.00-- 3.00
No. 6250/25 Tray, celery, 2 hdld.	8.00--10.00
No. 6156A/25 Berry, 7"	8.00--10.00
No. 646B/25 Nappy, 8"	10.00--14.00
No. 6253/25 Bon Bon, ftd., 2 hdld.	11.00--14.00
No. 6158/25 Berry, 2 hdld.	7.00-- 9.00
No. 6934/25 Vase, tall, 12"	14.00--17.00
No. 6935/25 Sweet Pea Vase, 7½"	12.00--15.00
No. 456/25 Celery, tall	14.00--18.00

'FLORA"

4mber, Rose Marie, green

No. 6253/205 Bowl, ftd., 5¼"	11.00--14.00
No. 606/205 Sugar, open	5.00-- 7.00
No. 606/205 Cream	5.00-- 7.00
No. 771/205 Bowl, Rose, blown, 6"	9.00--11.00
No. 6935/205 Vase, wide, 8" to 10" high	12.00--15.00
No. 648B/205 Bowl, salad, 10"	12.00--15.00

'ELIZABETH"

4mber, Rose Marie, green

No. 169R/206 Mayonnaise Set: 3 pc.	16.00--20.00
No. 664/206 Tray, sandwich, center hdld., 10"	12.00--15.00
No. 6567R/206 Bowl, salad, 8½"	12.00--15.00
No. 645/206 Candy Box and Cover	20.00--25.00
No. 300/206 Basket, 10" including handle	25.00--35.00
No. 223/206 Vase, blown, 9½"	12.00--15.00

MISCELLANEOUS page 163

Crystal, Rose Marie, green

No. 300/cut 2 Basket	25.00--35.00
No. 805/cut 217 2 pc. Night Set	20.00--25.00
No. 650/cut 2 2 pc. Guest Room Set	25.00--35.00
No. 6247/cut 63, Candlestick, square base, 7"	12.00--15.00
No. 6249/cut 63 Candlestick, square base, 9"	15.00--18.00
No. 62412/cut 66 Candlestick, square base, 12"	18.00--24.00

CONSOLE SETS

Amber, Rose Marie, green

No. 715/cut 200 "ROMA", 3 pc.	25.00--30.00
No. 715 Candlestick, oval	5.00-- 6.00
No. 320 Bowl, oval, 10½"	15.00--20.00
No. 6569Q/718R/cut 201 "ITALIA" 5 pc.	30.00--40.00
No. 718R Candlestick, pr.	10.00--12.00
No. 6569Q Bowl, 13½"	12.00--15.00
No. 320/cut 15 "SUSIE", 3 pc.	35.00--40.00
Candlestick, oval, 8¼"	10.00--12.00
Bowl, oval, 10½"	15.00--18.00
No. 718R/cut 19 "APPIANO" 5 pc.	30.00--40.00
Candlesticks, low, pr.	10.00--12.00
Bowl, rnd., 11"	12.00--15.00
No. 6569R/637/cut 16 "MONACO" 5 pc.	35.00--45.00
No. 637 Candlestick, low, pr.	10.00--12.00
No. 6569R Bowl, rnd., 11½"	16.00--20.00
No. 75Q/718R/cut 202 "MT. MARIA" 5 pc.	30.00--40.00
No. 718R Candlestick, low, pr.	10.00--12.00
No. 75Q Bowl, rnd., 12¼"	14.00--18.00

"MONACO" Cut 16 page 164

Amber, Rose Marie, green

No. 118 Bowl, blown, 8"	10.00--14.00
No. 641 Cheese and Cracker: Set, 2 pc., 10"	14.00--16.00
No. 664 Tray, sandwich, center hdld., 10"	12.00--14.00
No. 169R Mayonnaise Set: 3 pc.	16.00--20.00
No. 717 Candy Box and Cover	20.00--25.00
No. 770 Bowl, Rose, blown, 8"	12.00--15.00
No. 79F Bowl, ftd., 7½"	14.00--17.00
No. 170 Comport, ftd., and Cover	20.00--25.00
No. 790 Oval Cake and Sherbet Set: 2 pc.	9.00--11.00
No. 615 Cup and Plate (saucer)	5.00-- 7.00
No. 645 Candy Box and Cover	15.00--20.00
No. 79 Sherbet and Plate	5.00-- 7.00
No. 2428 Plate, salad, 8"	3.50-- 4.50
No. 169 My Lady Set: 5 pc.	30.00--35.00
Tray, rnd.	5.00-- 6.00
Bottle, cologne and stopper	15.00--18.00
Powder Box and Cover	10.00--12.00

"NAVONA"

Rose Marie only—Cut 207

No. 6569R Bowl, 11½"	14.00--18.00
No. 637 Candlestick	6.00-- 8.00
No. 664 Tray, sandwich, center hdld., 10"	10.00--14.00
No. 803 Saucer, berry, 4¾"	4.00-- 5.00
No. 615 Cup and Plate (saucer)	5.00-- 7.00
No. 802 Tumbler, table, blown	4.00-- 6.00
No. 84 Pitcher, blown, ½ gal.	18.00--22.00
No. 6567R Bowl, rol'd edge, 9"	12.00--14.00
No. 169R Mayonnaise Set: 3 pc.	16.00--20.00
No. 79 Sherbet and Plate	5.00-- 7.00
No. 609 Sugar, open	5.00-- 8.00
No. 609 Cream	5.00-- 8.00
No. 641 Cheese and Cracker Set: 2 pc.	12.00--16.00
No. 77 Plate, salad, 8¼"	3.50-- 4.50

"FRANCESCO" page 165

Rose Marie only—Cut 204

No. 718R Candlestick, pr.	12.00--16.00
No. 75X Center Bowl, 12½"	15.00--20.00
No. 602 Mayonnaise Set: 3 pc.	12.00--16.00
No. 6567B Bowl, salad, 9½"	11.00--14.00
No. 45B Fruit Salad and Plate	9.00--11.00
No. 6567Q Bowl, rolled edge, 10"	10.00--12.00
No. 664 Tray, sandwich, center hdld, 10"	12.00--15.00
No. 841B Dish, preserve, 3 ftd., 7½"	8.00--10.00
No. 6150 Tray, celery, 10" long including 2 handles	8.00--10.00
No. 6253 Bon Bon, ftd., 2 hdld., 5½"	10.00--12.00
No. 169 Candy Jar and Cover, 9" high including cover	20.00--25.00
No. 641 Cheese and Cracker Set: 2 piece, 10"	12.00--16.00
No. 242 Plate, 12"	10.00--12.00
No. 6067R Bowl, high ftd., hgt. 8", dia. 9"	14.00--18.00
No. 77 Plate, salad, 8¼"	3.50-- 4.50

"ANDREA"

Rose Marie, amber, green—Cut 9

No. 5737B Bowl, salad, 9½"	11.00--14.00
No. 169 Candy Jar and Cover, ftd.	20.00--25.00
No. 169R Mayonnaise Set: 3 pc.	16.00--20.00
No. 300 Basket	25.00--30.00
No. 664 Tray, sandwich, center hdld., 10"	11.00--14.00

"NANCY" page 16

Crystal, green, Rose Marie

No. 664 Tray, sandwich, center hdld., 10"	11.00--14.0
No. 641 Cheese and Cracker Set: 2 pc., 10"	12.00--16.0

"KAROLA"

Crystal, green, Rose Marie—Cut 10

No. 664 Tray, sandwich, center hdld., 10"	11.00--14.
No. 641 Cheese and Cracker Set: 2 pc., 10"	12.00--16.

SATIN IRIDESCENT GLASS

Hand cut rose ice and blue iridescent colors

No. 169R/cut 105 Comport and Plate	25.00--35.0
No. 664/cut 12 Tray, sandwich, hdld., 10"	20.00--25.0
No. 641/cut 103 Cracker and Cheese Set: 2 pc., 10"	20.00--25.0
No. 6641 cut 30 Bowl fruit, hdld., 9"	22.00--28.

VASES

Green, Rose Marie, crystal

No. 6944/cut 90 Vase, wide, 8" to 11"	12.00--16.0
No. 6945/cut 20 Vase, tall, 11" to 14"	18.00--24.0
No. 6944/cut 88 Vase, wide, 8" to 11"	12.00--18.0

"ROSETTA"

Green, Rose Marie, crystal—Cut 20

No. 664 Tray, sandwich center hdld., 10"	15.00--20.0
No. 641 Cheese and Cracker Set: 2 pc., 10"	15.00--20.0

"JULIANA"

Cut 13

No. 664 Tray, sandwich center hdld., 10"	15.00--20.0
No. 641 Cheese and Cracker Set: 2 pc., 10"	15.00--20.0

MISCELLANEOUS page 167

(First 4 items in amber, green, Rose Marie)

No. 169/cut 216 My Lady Set:	
5 pc.	30.00--40.00
Tray, rnd.	5.00-- 7.00
Cologne Bottle and Stopper	15.00--20.00
Powder Box and Cover	12.00--14.00
No. 771/cut 212 Rose Bowl blown, 6"	11.00--14.00
No. 78/cut 51 Relish Dish 4 pc., (rnd. dish with 3 movable compartments)	18.00--24.00
No. 766/cut 208 Vase, 12"	16.00--20.00

(Next 5 items in crystal, amber, green, Rose Marie)

No. 2428/cut 2 Plate, 8"	4.00-- 6.00
No. 2428/cut 18 Plate, 8"	4.00-- 6.00
No. 77/cut 9 Plate, 8¼"	4.00-- 6.00
No. 2428/cut 30 Plate, 8"	4.00-- 6.00
No. 2428/cut 20 Plate, 8"	4.00-- 6.00

VASES

No. 729/cut 214, 7½"	40.00--50.00
No. 731/cut 213, 7½"	40.00--50.00
No. 119/cut 215, 7½"	40.00--50.00
No. 768/cut 12, 9"	75.00--85.00
No. 771/cut 12, 6"	70.00--80.00
No. 223/cut 12, 9½"	75.00--85.00
Class C, 8¼"	40.00--50.00
Class C, 8½"	75.00--85.00
Class A, 11"	100.00-125.00
Class B, 10"	100.00-125.00
Class B, 10"	85.00--95.00

MONTICELLO page 168

No. 6988N Lily Bowl, 8"	10.00--12.00
No. 6987N Lily Bowl, 7"	9.00--11.00
No. 6986N Lily Bowl, 6"	6.00-- 8.00
No. 6985N Lily Bowl, 5"	5.00-- 7.00
No. 6988 Pitcher, ice lip, 52 oz.	20.00--25.00
No. 6988D Plate, rnd., 12"	8.00--10.00
No. 6987D Plate, rnd., 10½"	6.00-- 8.00
No. 698 Plate, square, 10½"	6.00-- 8.00
No. 698 Bowl, square, 7½"	5.00-- 6.00
No. 6981 Vase, 10½"	12.00--15.00
No. 6982 Vase, 6"	6.00-- 8.00
No. 6987N Flower Bowl, 7"	12.00--15.00
No 698 Basket, 10"	20.00--25.00
No. 698 Relish, divided, square, 8¼"	11.00--13.00
No. 698 Goblet	8.00--10.00
No. 698 Cocktail or Wine	8.00--10.00
No. 698 Sherbet	4.00-- 6.00
No. 6983D Plate, bread and butter, 6"	1.50-- 2.50
No. 6980D Plate, salad, 8"	3.50-- 4.50
No. 6981D Plate, dinner, 9"	6.00-- 8.00
No. 699 Coaster, 3¼"	3.00-- 4.00
No. 698 Tumbler, water, 9 oz.	4.00-- 6.00
No. 698 Ice Tea or Hi Ball, 12 oz.	5.00-- 7.00
No. 6982 Cup and Saucer	5.00-- 7.00
No. 6980 Sugar, open	5.00-- 7.00
No. 6980 Cream	5.00-- 7.00
No. 698 Soup, cream, 5½"	4.00-- 6.00
No. 698 Mayonnaise Set: 3 pc.	12.00--16.00
No. 6981W Butter Tub, 5½"	10.00--12.00
No. 698 Dish, pickle, oval, 6"	5.00-- 7.00
No. 698 Tray, celery, oval, 9"	6.00-- 8.00
No. 6981W Vegetable, rnd., 8"	7.00-- 9.00
No. 698 Bon Bon, 1 hdld., 5½"	4.00-- 6.00
No. 698 Bowl, finger, 4½"	3.00-- 5.00
No. 698 Cheese Dish, covered	25.00--35.00
No. 698 Salt and Pepper w/glass tops	12.00--16.00
No. 698X Compote, 5¾"	6.00-- 8.00
No. 698 F Compote, 5¼"	6.00-- 8.00

"HUCKABEE"

Salt or Pepper, aluminum tops	20.00--25.00
Sherbet, 3½"	4.00-- 6.00
Plate, sherbet, 6"	2.50-- 3.00
Oil Bottle and Stopper, 6 oz.	25.00--30.00
Salver, 7¾"	9.00--11.00
Bowl, ftd., 7¼"	9.00--11.00
Saucer, fruit, 4¾"	3.00-- 4.00
Bowl, fruit, 8½"	11.00--14.00
Celery, tall	18.00--22.00
Cream	7.00-- 9.00
Butter and Cover	35.00--45.00
Tumbler, table	4.00-- 6.00
Pitcher, 51 oz.	25.00--35.00
Pitcher, 22 oz.	15.00--25.00
Sugar and Cover	12.00--16.00
Spoon Holder	12.00--15.00

"BEADED BLOCK"

No. 710 Sugar, open	12.00--15.00
No. 710 Cream	12.00--15.00
No. 710 Jelly, 2 hdld., 4¾"	10.00--12.00
No. 710 Pickle, 2 hdld., 6½"	10.00--12.00
No. 710 Olive, 1 hdld., 5½"	9.00--12.00
No. 710 Tray, celery, 8½"	12.00--15.00
No. 710 Bouquet, 6", Vase	14.00--18.00
No. 7105B Nappy, 6½"	9.00--12.00
No. 710 Dish, square, 5½"	8.00--10.00
No. 710 Plate, square, 7¾"	8.00--10.00
No. 710 Plate, round, 8¾"	10.00--12.00
No. 710 Comport, deep, 5¼"	10.00--15.00
No. 710 Berry, 7"	12.00--15.00
No. 710 Jelly, ftd., 4"	12.00--15.00
No. 7101 Jug, large pint	100.00-125.00
No. 7106N Lily Bowl, 6"	10.00--15.00
No. 7106B Bowl, salad, 7½"	12.00--15.00

"AMELIA" page 169

No. 6715N Lily Bowl, 5"	5.00-- 8.00
No. 671 Pickle, oval, 6¼"	6.00-- 8.00
No. 671 Cup, custard	4.00-- 6.00
No. 6715B Nappy, 6½"	4.00-- 6.00
No. 671 Nappy, 2 hdld., 5"	6.00-- 8.00
No. 671 Tumbler, table, 9 oz.	5.00-- 7.00
No. 671 Ice Cream, tall, 6 oz.	4.00-- 6.00
No. 671 Candlestick, 7"	10.00--12.00
No. 671 Tumbler, ice tea, 12 oz.	7.00-- 9.00
No. 671 Plate, 6"	3.00-- 4.00
No. 671C Jelly, crimped, 5½"	9.00--12.00
No. 671 Goblet, 8 oz.	9.00--11.00
No. 671 Dish, square, 5½"	6.00-- 8.00
No. 671 Comport, deep, 5½"	7.00-- 9.00
No. 6716F Nappy, shallow, 8½"	8.00--11.00
No. 671 Dish, oval, 7"	8.00--10.00
No. 6816B Bowl, salad, 7½"	9.00--12.00
No. 671B Preserve, 5"	5.00-- 7.00
No. 671 Bouquet, 6"	7.00-- 9.00
No. 671 Tray, celery, 8"	9.00--12.00
No. 671 Sugar and Cover	15.00--18.00
No. 671 Cream	6.00-- 8.00
No. 671 Butter and Cover	30.00--35.00
No. 671 Spoon Holder	10.00--12.00
No. 671 Jug, milk, large pint	20.00--30.00
No. 671 Celery Holder, tall	15.00--20.00

"DIAMOND BLOCK"

(No. 34 Book I) Pink, green, blue, black, ruby, milk and iridescent.

No. 3306B Berry, 7½"	10.00--14.00
No. 330 Dish, honey, sq., 5½"	6.00-- 9.00
No. 3305B Nappy, 6½"	6.00-- 8.00
No. 330 Bouquet, 6"	9.00--11.00
No. 3301 Jug, tall, tankard	50.00--75.00
No. 330B Jelly, ftd., 5"	10.00--12.00
No. 330 Tray, celery, 8½"	9.00--11.00
No. 330 Sugar, open	10.00--14.00
No. 330 Cream	10.00--14.00
No. 330 Dish, jelly, 1 hdld., 4¾"	9.00--11.00
No. 3306N Lily Bowl, 6"	6.00-- 9.00
No. 330 Dish, pickle, 2 hdld., 6½"	7.00-- 9.00

"DIAMOND QUILTED"

DIAMOND QUILTED in Book I

Rose pink, green, light blue, also pieces in black and ruby.

No. 625/5 Goblet, 9 oz.	8.00--10.00
No. 414 Goblet, 8 oz.	7.00-- 9.00
No. 625/5 Sherbet, 6 oz.	6.00-- 8.00
No. 414B Jelly or Fruit Salad, ftd., 4¾"	7.00-- 9.00
No. 625/5 Ice Tea, 12 oz.	7.00-- 9.00
No. 625/5 Tumbler, 8 oz.	6.00-- 8.00
No. 625/5 Parfait, 6 oz.	6.00-- 8.00
No. 6675/5 Jelly, 1 hdld., 5½"	6.00-- 8.00
No. 6152/5 Olive, or Bon Bon, 2 hdld., 4¾"	6.00-- 9.00
No. 4141 Dish, covered, 3-toed, 6¼"	18.00--24.00
No. 414 Tumbler, blown, 9 oz.	4.00-- 6.00
No. 414 Ice Tea, blown, 12 oz.	6.00-- 8.00
No. 414 Jug, blown, ½ gal.	25.00--30.00
No. 6253/5 Bon Bon, 5½"	10.00--14.00
No. 414N Bowl, flower, 3-toed, 5½"	10.00--14.00
No. 414B Dish, preserve, 3-toed, 7½"	12.00--15.00
No. 499/5 Sherbet and Plate	6.00-- 8.00
No. 414R Candle Holder	8.00--10.00
No. 4149Q/75 Bowl, flower	16.00--20.00
No. 4149Q/75 Flower Block	6.00-- 7.00
No. 414/1 Candle Holder	7.00-- 9.00
No. 4145W Nappy, 7"	7.00--10.00
Plate, 7", 8"	4.00-- 6.00
Plate, 14"	9.00--12.00
Cup and Saucer	7.00-- 9.00
Sugar and Creamer	14.00--18.00

"LINDBURGH"

Saucer, berry, 5"	2.50-- 3.50
Bowl, berry, 9"	9.00--12.00
Plate, cake, 10½"	9.00--12.00
Bowl, Lily, 7"	9.00--12.00
Saucer, berry, 4¾"	2.50-- 3.50
Bowl, berry, 8½"	9.00--12.00
Comport, 7"	10.00--14.00
Salver, cake, ftd., 10"	12.00--15.00
Saucer, berry, 4½"	2.50-- 3.50
Bowl, berry, 8"	9.00--12.00
Comport, 8¾"	12.00--15.00
Sugar and Cover	10.00--14.00
Sugar, open	5.00-- 7.00
Cream	5.00-- 7.00
Pitcher, 1 qt.	15.00--20.00
Pitcher, 1 pt.	15.00--20.00

SCROLL FLUTED page 170

Saucer, berry, 4¾"	3.00-- 4.00
Saucer, berry, 4½"	3.00-- 4.00
Saucer, berry, 5"	4.00-- 5.00
Bowl, berry, 8½"	10.00--12.00
Bowl, berry, 8" (7217A)	10.00--12.00
Bowl, 9"	11.00--13.00
Plate, cake, 10½" (7217D)	11.00--14.00
Bowl, square, 7"	11.00--13.00
Bowl, flower, 7"	10.00--12.00
Sugar and Cream Set	10.00--12.00
Pitcher, 1 pt.	20.00--30.00
Pickle, 7"	10.00--14.00

NO. 7387

Bowl, square, 7"	8.00--12.00
Bowl, Lily, 7"	7.00--10.00

Bowl, berry, 8"	7.00--10.00
Nappy, shallow, 9"	7.00-- 9.00
Bowl, fruit, 9"	8.00--11.00
Plate, cake, 10½"	7.00--10.00

MISCELLANEOUS

Rose pink and crystal

No. 460 Bowl, berry, 9"	20.00--30.00
No. 485/2 Relish, partitioned 7½"	20.00--25.00
No. 737A Comport, 8½"	20.00--25.00
No. 607 Bowl, oval, ftd., 2 hdld., 9½"	20.00--30.00
No. 5338S Bowl, square, 7½"	18.00--24.00
No. 466 Bowl, celery, oval, 11"	15.00--18.00
No. 4828 Bowl, salad, deep, 8½"	20.00--25.00
No. 572 Nappy, shallow, rnd., 10¾"	18.00--24.00
No. 587 Dish, fern, 3 ftd., 8"	20.00--25.00
No. 502 Bowl, salad, 9"	20.00--25.00
No. 4821 Bowl, tall ftd., 6½"	25.00--30.00
No. 5349A Bowl, fruit, 9¼"	20.00--25.00

MISCELLANEOUS

Rose pink only

No. 64/6751G Bowl, flower deep, dia. 8"	8.00--12.00
No. 64/6751D Plate, ftd., 12"	8.00--10.00
No. 64/360C/Bowl, fruit, oval crimped, 13"	30.00--35.00
No. 64/252 Basket, large, 13" tall, including handle	30.00--40.00
No. 64/4892C Bowl, fruit, 3 ftd., crimped, 11"	35.00--40.00
No. 64/4892B Bowl, fruit, 3 ftd., rnd., 11"	30.00--40.00
No. 64/4822 Bowl, tall ftd., 8½"	25.00--35.00
No. 64/2929C Bowl, orange, 12"	35.00--40.00
No. 64/750A Bowl, fruit, 12"	30.00--35.00
No. 564 Pickle Boat, 8"	10.00--12.00
No. 555 Bon Bon, 1 hdld., 5½"	10.00--12.00
No. 5316A Nappy, 6½"	10.00--14.00
No. 555 Mayonnaise, oval with Plate, 2 pc., 7"	18.00--25.00
No. 555A Nappy, 6½"	10.00--14.00
No. 452B Bowl, ftd., 7"	12.00--16.00
No. 538 Dish, oval, 7½"	12.00--14.00
No. 511 Jelly, ftd., 4½"	12.00--16.00
No. 555 Sugar	8.00--12.00
No. 555 Cream	8.00--12.00
No. 555 Bouquet, 6¼"	16.00--18.00
No. 4742 Salad, square, 9"	20.00--25.00
No. 485/1 Nappy, 7½", 2 hdld.	12.00--15.00
No. 466 Bowl, fruit, 9"	20.00--25.00
No. 466 Saucer, fruit, 5"	7.00-- 9.00
No. 404 Bouquet, 9"	18.00--22.00
No. 4743 Vase, 12"	30.00--35.00
No. 4047 Bouquet, 13"	30.00--35.00

"MOLLY" page 171

Crystal, rose pink, green, blue, opalescent, ruby.

Cup w/ground bottom saucer	6.00-- 9.00
Boullion w/ground bottom saucer	7.00-- 9.00
A.D. Cup w/ground bottom saucer	8.00--10.00
Sugar, Cream and Tray Set: Style "B"	15.00--20.00
Sugar and Cream Set: Style "A"	10.00--14.00
Plate, 8"	4.00-- 6.00
Plate, oval, 9½"	7.00-- 9.00
Plate, oval, 11"	9.00--11.00
Salt or Pepper, cast silver top	12.00--18.00
Goblet, 9 oz.,	7.00-- 9.00
Pitcher, ½ gal.	18.00--24.00
Bowl, oval, 10"	10.00--12.00
Bowl, oval, 8"	9.00--11.00
Soup, covered cream and Plate	12.00--16.00
Soup, coup, 7"	6.00-- 8.00
Tray, sandwich or lunch, center hdld., 12"	10.00--14.00
Tray, fruit, center hdld., 11"	11.00--14.00
Tray, Bon Bon, center hdld., 7½"	5.00-- 7.00
Tray, mint, center hdld., 8½"	6.00-- 9.00
Mayonnaise Set (727R)	12.00--16.00
Mayonnaise Set (7255W)	12.00--16.00
Mayonnaise Set (38)	14.00--16.00
Sandwich Set (40)	15.00--18.00
Sandwich Set (20)	12.00--16.00
Ladle, glass	6.00-- 8.00
Mayonnaise Set, oval (7270)	14.00--18.00
Mayonnaise Set, rnd. (727/9)	11.00--14.00
Roquefort Cheese and Cracker Set w/covered Bowl	16.00--20.00
Cheese and Cracker Set (727)	11.00--14.00
Cheese and Cracker Set (72581)	11.00--14.00
Marmalade Set: 3 pc.	14.00--17.00
Ice Tub, nickle plated hdld., and tongs, 5½"	14.00--18.00
Bowl, Rose, 7"	8.00--11.00
Bowl, nut, 8½"	8.00--11.00
Bowl, fruit, 8½"	11.00--14.00
Comport, 10½"	12.00--16.00
Plate, salad, 8"	3.00-- 5.00
Tray, octagon, 2 hdld., 10½"	7.00-- 9.00
Bowl, flower, 11"	12.00--16.00
Dish, muffin, 12"	12.00--16.00
Plate, cake, ftd., 12"	11.00--14.00
Comport, covered, 6¼"	14.00--18.00
Nut Box, covered, 3-partitions, 6¼"	16.00--20.00
Nut Box, covered, no partitions, 6¼"	12.00--16.00

Candy Box and Cover, 5¼"	16.00--20.00
Dish, covered, 3 legs, 6¼"	16.00--20.00
Casserole, covered, 8"	18.00--24.00
Candy Box, covered, 5¼"	12.00--15.00
Glass Bell, metal clapper	15.00--25.00
Dish, olive, 4¾"	6.00-- 8.00
Bowl, rnd., bulb, 8"	10.00--14.00
Dish, 3 legs, 8"	12.00--15.00
Dish, preserve, 3 legs, 7½"	10.00--12.00

Console Sets:

No. 727R Candleholder	6.00-- 8.00
No. 72710Q Bowl, center, 13"	14.00--18.00
No. 727L Candleholder	6.00-- 8.00
No. 39L Bowl, center, 11"	12.00--15.00
No. 39 Candleholder	5.00-- 7.00
No. 39X Bowl, flower	12.00--16.00
No. 727R Candleholder	6.00-- 8.00
No. 7277B Bowl and glass Base	11.00--14.00
No. 727R Candleholder	6.00-- 8.00
No. 7277R Bowl and glass Base	11.00--14.00
No. 727L Candleholder	6.00-- 8.00
No. 72710S Bowl, center, 13"	12.00--16.00

EARLY AMERICAN HOBNAIL PATTERN — page 172

Ruby and Cobalt will be somewhat higher

Tumbler, table	9.00--11.00
Pitcher, pressed, 55 oz.	30.00--50.00
Plate, salad, 8"	4.00-- 6.00
Ice Tea, pressed, 12 oz.	7.00--10.00
Tumbler, pressed, 9 oz.	6.00-- 9.00
Sherbet, 9 oz.	6.00-- 8.00
Plate, salad, square, 8"	4.00-- 7.00
Flip Vase, 8"	20.00--25.00
Ivy Ball, ftd.	14.00--18.00
Ivy Ball, blown and Chain	11.00--14.00
Nappy, square, 7"	9.00--12.00
Toilet, Dresser or Bath Set: 6 pc.	60.00--70.00
Cologne and Stopper	15.00--25.00
Puff Box and Cover	20.00--25.00
Plate, cake, 4 toed, 10" (Salver)	20.00--25.00
Ice Tea, blown, 12 oz.	7.00-- 9.00
Pitcher, blown, ½ gal.	35.00--55.00
Tumbler, table, 10 oz.	8.00--10.00
Ice Tea, 13 oz.	10.00--12.00
Compote, 7"	12.00--15.00

EMPIRE

No. 779 Cologne, 5 oz.	15.00--20.00
No. 7796N Bowl, flower w/double deck wire holder	8.00--10.00
No. 779S Vase, square, 10"	12.00--15.00
No. 779 Candy Box, w/Cover	14.00--18.00
No. 699 Cologne, square, 6 oz.	14.00--18.00
No. 779SC Bowl, square, fancy shape, 12"	12.00--16.00
No. 799 Relish, oval, divided, 9"	8.00--10.00
No. 779S Salad Set: square 2 pc., Bowl and Plate	14.00--17.00
No. 779S Bowl, square, 8"	7.00-- 9.00
No. 779S Bowl, square, 5"	3.00-- 4.00
No. 7792 Ash Tray, 5½"	4.00-- 5.00
No. 779 Ash Receiver, 3 ftd., 4"	5.00-- 7.00
No. 779S Mayonnaise Set: 3 pc.	12.00--16.00
No. 779 Candlestick, square, 5", (pr.)	20.00--25.00
No. 799S Plate, square, 7"	3.50-- 4.00
No. 799 Canape Set: 2 pc. Glass and Plate	6.00-- 9.00
No. 779S Console Set: 3 pc.	30.00--35.00
No. 779S Bowl, square, 8"	8.00--10.00
No. 779S Candlestick, square, 5", (pr.)	20.00--25.00

CAPE COD — page 173

Prices below are for crystal. Some pieces were made in ruby, cobalt and amber and these prices will be somewhat higher.

No. 1604½X Bowl, fruit 6"	3.50-- 5.00
No. 1604½A Bowl, finger, 4½"	4.00-- 5.00
No. 160 Cup, custard, hdld.	3.00-- 4.00
No. 1601 Coaster, ground bottom, 4¼"	4.00-- 5.00
No. 1604W Nappy, fruit, 4½"	3.00-- 4.00
No. 1605W Bowl, fruit, 6¾"	4.00-- 5.00
No. 160 Cup and Saucer	5.00-- 7.00
No. 1605P Nappy, shallow, 7"	6.00-- 8.00
No. 160 Goblet	7.00-- 9.00
No. 160 Sherbet	3.50-- 5.00
No. 160B Cocktail	6.00-- 8.00
No. 160 Ice Tea or Hiball, 12 oz.	6.00-- 8.00
No. 160 Ginger Ale, 6 oz.	5.00-- 7.00
No. 160 Old Fashion, 7 oz.	5.00-- 7.00
No. 160 Wine	6.00-- 9.00
No. 160 Whiskey	6.00-- 8.00
No. 1604½ Plate, 7"	3.00-- 4.00
No. 1605D Plate, salad, 8"	3.50-- 4.50
No. 160 Cup and Saucer	5.00-- 7.00
No. 1601W Jelly, ind. 3¾"	4.00-- 5.00
No. 1604W Bowl, fruit, 4½"	3.00-- 4.00
No. 1604½X Nappy, 6"	4.00-- 5.00
No. 160 Decanter and Stopper	15.00--18.00
No. 160 Mayonnaise Set, 3 pc.	12.00--16.00
No. 1605W Nappy, flrd., 6¾"	4.00-- 5.00
No. 1605F Nappy, shallow, 7"	6.00-- 8.00
No. 1604½A Bowl, finger, 4½"	3.50-- 5.00
No. 1601R Coaster, 4½"	4.00-- 5.00
No. 160 Sugar, ftd.	6.00-- 8.00
No. 160 Cream, ftd.	6.00-- 8.00
No. 160F Compote, 5¼"	7.00-- 9.00
No. 160X Compote, 5¾"	7.00-- 9.00
No. 160U Relish, divided, 9½"	12.00--14.00

No. 16010V Plate, cupped edge, 16"	12.00--15.00
No. 16010B Bowl, fruit, bell shaped, 12"	14.00--18.00
No. 1608V Plate, cupped edge, 13½"	10.00--12.00
No. 16010V Buffet Set: 3 pc.	20.00--25.00
No. 16010A Bowl, round, 11"	12.00--14.00
No. 1608X Bowl, flanged edge, 11"	12.00--14.00
No. 16010D Plate, flat edge, 17"	16.00--20.00
No. 16010 Punch Set: 15 pc.	75.00--85.00
No. 1608A Bowl, round, 10"	10.00--12.00
No. 1608X Bowl, fruit, 11½"	11.00--14.00
No. 1608A Bowl, salad, 11"	11.00--14.00
No. 1608F Plate, torte, 13½"	10.00--13.00
No. 160 Whiskey Set: 8 pc.	60.00--65.00
No. 160 Wine Set: 8 pc.	65.00--75.00
No. 165 Ice Pitcher	24.00--28.00
No. 160 Refrigerator Jug	24.00--28.00

TRADITION page 174

No. 1655D Plate, salad, 8"	3.50-- 4.50
No. 165 Goblet, 10 oz.	6.00-- 8.00
No. 165 Sherbet, 6 oz.	3.50-- 4.50
No. 165 Ice Tea, 12 oz.	6.00-- 7.00
No. 165 Pitcher, ice lipped	24.00--28.00
No. 1655W Nappy, flrd., 6¾"	3.50-- 4.50
No. 1654½A Bowl, finger, 4½"	3.00-- 4.00
No. 1654½X Bowl, baked apple, 6"	4.00-- 5.00
No. 1655F Nappy, shallow, 7"	5.00-- 7.00

OLD ENGLISH

No. 1664½D Plate, 7"	3.00-- 4.00
No. 1664½X Bowl, baked apple, 6"	3.50-- 4.50
No. 1664½W Nappy, 6"	4.00-- 5.00
No. 166 Compote, 4¼"	4.00-- 5.00
No. 1346N Bowl, flower, 7"	8.00-- 9.00
No. 1664½A Bowl, finger, 4¼"	3.00-- 4.00
No. 166 Sherbet and Plate Set	6.00-- 7.00
No. 166 Cocktail, 5 oz.	3.00-- 4.00
No. 166 Tumbler, water, 9 oz.	3.00-- 4.00
No. 166 Ice Tea, 12 oz.	4.00-- 5.00
No. 134 Mug, 10 oz.	6.00-- 8.00
No. 1346A Comport or Bowl, 9"	8.00--10.00

MOUNT VERNON

No. 699 Bottle, Oil and Stopper, 6 oz.	15.00--20.00
No. 699 Jar, Pickle and Cover, tall	15.00--20.00
No. 699 Syrup with Lock Cover, 8½ oz.	20.00--25.00
No. 699 Sugar and Cover	10.00--12.00
No. 699 Cream	4.00-- 6.00
No. 6991 Sugar and Cream Set: covered	12.00--16.00
No. 699 Celery Holder, tall	12.00--15.00
No. 699 Butter and Cover	20.00--30.00
No. 699 Spoon Holder	12.00--14.00
No. 69910X Console Set:	20.00--25.00
Candlestick, 9", pr.	12.00--15.00
Bowl, console, 12"	8.00--10.00
No. 699 Wine Set: 8 pc.	40.00--50.00
Decanter, w/pressed stopper, 36 oz.	20.00--25.00
Wines, pressed, 2 oz.	4.00-- 5.00
No. 6995 Nappy and Cover, 2 hdld., 5¾"	8.00--10.00
No. 6991 Dish, butter, covered, 5"	15.00--20.00

"IDA"

Stiegel green, Ritz blue, ruby

No. 85 Plate, 6", 6½", 8½", 10½", 14"	3.00--12.00
No. 242/2 Cup and Saucer ground bottom	4.00-- 7.00
No. 78 Tray, relish, ground bottom, 10"	8.00--12.00
No. 757/1 Box, covered, no partition, 7"	10.00--15.00
No. 757/2 Box, covered, with partitions, 7"	10.00--15.00
No. 7723 Sugar, Cream and Tray Set, (crystal)	8.00--12.00
No. 46 Cocktail Set: 2 pc.	6.00--10.00
No. 231/5 Soup, cream, 5"	4.00-- 6.00
No. 85X Soup, ground bottom, 7½"	6.00-- 9.00
No. 86X Baked Apple, ground, 6½"	5.00-- 8.00

"MUNSEL"

Rose pink, green, Ritz blue, Stiegel green, Ruby

No. 728 Candleholder, (pr.)	14.00--20.00
No. 7287A/728 Bowl, console, 10½"	15.00--20.00
No. 727 Vase, 8"	12.00--18.00
No. 727/2 Tray, relish, partitioned, ground bottom, 11"	10.00--15.00
No. 727/1 Tray, celery, ground bottom, 11"	10.00--14.00
No. 725/8 Cream	6.00-- 9.00
No. 725/8 Sugar, open, no hdls.	6.00-- 9.00
No. 728 Bouquet, 6"	10.00--12.00

"GENIE" page 175

Crystal, Stiegel green, Ritz blue, amber, Rose pink, Imperial green

Vases, 5", 5½", 4½", 5¼"	12.00--16.00

CHICKEN-ON-NEST

Crystal glass w/painted red comb

No. 145	12.00--15.00

"SUGAR CANE" LINE

Crystal, Stiegel green, Ritz blue, amber, Rose pink, Imperial green

Plate, 7½"	5.00-- 8.00
Bowl, basket, 5"	7.00--10.00
Nappy, belled, 6½"	7.00--10.00
Nappy, shallow, 6¾"	8.00--12.00

"KATY"

See "KATY BLUE" at end of chapter.

No. 7499D Plate, 14"	10.00--15.00
No. 7499B Bowl, orange, 12"	20.00--25.00
No. 7499F Bowl, fruit, 13"	23.00--27.00
No. 7499N Bowl, flower, 8½"	12.00--16.00
No. 7498R Bowl, flower and Holder, 7½"	12.00--16.00
No. 7498K Rose Bowl and Holder, 7½"	12.00--16.00
No. 7498N Bowl, flower, 7½"	12.00--14.00
No. 7497D Plate, 11"	12.00--14.00
No. 7497E Bowl, basket, 9½"	15.00--25.00
No. 7498B Bowl, 10"	15.00--25.00
No. 7497F Bowl, 9½"	15.00--20.00
No. 7497K Rose Bowl and Holder, 6½"	10.00--13.00
No. 7497 Bowl, flower and Holder, 6½"	10.00--13.00
No. 7498D Plate, 12"	12.00--15.00
No. 7497B Bowl, 9"	12.00--15.00
No. 7497N Bowl, flower, 6½"	9.00--12.00
No. 1346N Rose Bowl and Holder, 7"	9.00--12.00
(OLD ENGLISH pattern)	
No. 770/2 Rose Bowl, blown, 8"	8.00--10.00
No. 7498F Bowl, 11"	11.00--15.00

CONSOLE SETS

Twin Candlestick (pr.) (same shaped candlesticks used with various "KATY" Bowls)	15.00--18.00
No. 7499B Bowl, 12"	15.00--20.00
No. 7499F Bowl, 13"	20.00--25.00
No. 7498B Bowl, 10"	15.00--20.00
No. 7498F Bowl, 11"	18.00--22.00
No. 7497B Bowl, 9"	14.00--18.00
No. 7497F Bowl, 9½"	14.00--18.00
No. 1537 Bowl, console, oval "NEWBOUND"	15.00--20.00
No. 153 Candlestick, twin (pr.)	12.00--15.00
No. 648B Bowl, console, rnd., 11"	12.00--15.00
No. 169 Candlestick, twin, (pr.)	12.00--15.00
No. 153B Bowl, console, rnd., "NEWBOUND"	15.00--20.00
No. 153 Candlestick, twin, (pr.)	12.00--15.00
No. 6567 Bowl, console, 9½"	12.00--15.00
No. 169 Candlestick, twin, (pr.)	12.00--15.00
(Crystal Stiegel green, Ritz blue, amber and Imperial green.)	
No. 147 Swan *(all six colors)*	30.00--40.00
No. 60 Honey Pot or Preserve Jar and Cover	30.00--35.00
No. 739 Holder, cigarette or playing cards *(all six colors)*	14.00--20.00
No. 7112 Tumbler, CALIENTE, 9 oz., *(all six colors)*	6.00-- 7.00
No. 741 Tumbler, HOBNAIL, 9 oz. *(all six colors)*	6.00-- 9.00

"NEWBOUND"

Crystal, Stiegel green, Ritz blue, amber, Rose pink, Imperial green.

No. 153B Bowl, belled console or fruit, 10"	15.00--20.00
No. 153 Candlestick, twin, (pr.)	12.00--15.00

PILLAR FLUTE page 176

Sugar and Cream Set	10.00--14.00
Vase, bouquet, 6"	8.00--10.00
Tray, celery, oval, 8½"	9.00--11.00
Mayonnaise Set	10.00--14.00
Bowl, flared, 7"	6.00-- 8.00
Plate, square, 8"	4.00-- 5.00
Dish, square, 5½"	4.00-- 5.00
Nappy, belled, 6½"	5.00-- 6.00
Pickle, 2 hdld., 6¼"	5.00-- 7.00
Jelly, 2 hdld., 4¾"	5.00-- 7.00
Nappy, 1 hdld., 4½"	5.00-- 7.00
Bon Bon, crimped, 7"	6.00-- 8.00
Relish, partitioned, 2 hdld., 6½"	6.00-- 8.00
Compote, 4½"	8.00--10.00
Bowl, flower, 5"	6.00-- 8.00
Cup and Saucer	6.00-- 8.00
Plate, salad, 8"	3.50-- 4.50
Plate, cake, 12"	8.00--10.00
Bowl, salad, 10"	12.00--14.00
No. 682F Compote	6.00-- 8.00

MISCELLANEOUS

No. 323 Bitter and Tube Bottle	6.00-- 8.00
No. 142 Cocktail, 3⅓ oz.	3.00-- 4.00
No. 142 Cocktail Shaker	12.00--15.00
No. 625 Decanter and Stopper	15.00--20.00
No. 84 Ice Tub, blown	8.00--10.00
No. 158 Canape Set: 2 pc.	5.00-- 7.00
No. 142 Canape Set: 2 pc. *(Fish Shaped Plate)*	9.00--12.00
No. 100 Whiskey, boot shaped, 1¼ oz.	10.00--12.00

No. 451 Ash Tray, 3½"	3.00-- 4.00
No. 658 Old Fashioned and Muddler	7.00-- 9.00
No. 160 Old Fashioned and Muddler	8.00--10.00
No. 756 Old Fashioned and Muddler	7.00-- 9.00
No. 699 Old Fashioned and Muddler	8.00--10.00
Vase, 7½"	7.00-- 9.00
Bowl, Rose, blown, 6"	7.00-- 9.00
Vase, 9½"	7.00-- 9.00
No. 355 Liquor, 1¼ oz.	4.00-- 6.00
No. 3551 Decanter and Stopper, 18 oz.	12.00--16.00
No. 355 Tumbler, 12 oz.	4.00-- 5.00
No. 355 Jug, 100 oz.	18.00--24.00
Decanter and Stopper	15.00--20.00
Cocktail Shaker	12.00--16.00
Pitcher, ice lip, 80 oz.	18.00--24.00
Tumbler, 12½ oz.	5.00-- 6.00
Tumbler, 9¾ oz.	4.00-- 5.00
Tumbler, 5½ oz.	3.00-- 4.00
Liquor, 2½ oz.	4.00-- 6.00
No. 144 Fruit, ftd.	2.50-- 4.00
Tumbler, ftd., 5 oz.	3.00-- 4.00
Tumbler, ftd., 9 oz.	4.00-- 5.00
Tumbler, ftd., 12 oz.	5.00-- 6.00
Cordial	6.00-- 8.00
Wine	6.00-- 8.00
Oyster	5.00-- 7.00
Cocktail	6.00-- 8.00
Sherbet, low	3.00-- 4.00
Sherbet, tall	4.00-- 5.00
Goblet	6.00-- 8.00

"SHAEFFER"

Crystal, Stiegel green, Ritz blue, amber, ruby

Decanter Set: blown w/1½ oz. Jigger Stopper, pressed, 34 oz. and 6 Tumblers	40.00--60.00
Rose Bowl, blown	10.00--12.00
Tumbler, 5½, 9½, and 12½ oz.	4.00-- 9.00
Pitcher, blown, 80 oz.	15.00--25.00

CANDLEWICK page 177

Although Imperial is still making CANDLEWICK in crystal, many of the earlier pieces have long since been discontinued, making them collectible. Mary Wetzel (Box 594, Notre Dame, IN 46556-0594) has thoroughly researched this pattern, compiling a listing of over 700 pieces made since 1936, the year it was introduced. Her publication tells when each piece was made and discontinued, and gives a history of the line. Virginia Scott (275 Milledge Terrace, Athens GA 30606) also has a book on CANDLEWICK and publishes a newsletter, both very informative. Write to either or both for more info!

66B Comport, 5½"	12.00--15.00
63B Comport, 4½"	20.00--22.00
88 Cheese and Cracker Set: 2 pc., 10"	35.00--40.00
36 Canape Set: 2 pc.	15.00--20.00
87F Vase, fan shape, 8"	18.00--22.00
87R Vase, 7"	18.00--22.00
40 Mayonnaise Set: 3 pc.	25.00--30.00
74B Nappy, 4 ftd., 8½"	12.00--15.00
86 Candleholder, pr.	16.00--20.00
81 Candleholder, 1 hdld., 3½", pr.	18.00--22.00
34 Ash Tray, 4½"	6.00-- 8.00
74SC Dish, 4 ftd., fancy square shape, 9"	15.00--18.00
74J Bowl, Lily, 4 ftd., 7"	16.00--18.00
80 Candleholder, 3½", pr.	16.00--20.00
67D Cake Stand, 10"	25.00--35.00
13B Centerbowl, 11"	13.00--16.00
67B Bowl, ftd., 9"	17.00--19.00
8013B Console Set: 3 pc.	30.00--35.00
8613B Console Set: 3 pc.	30.00--35.00
72E Tray, 2 hdld., 10"	25.00--28.00
62E Tray, 2 hdld., 8½"	20.00--25.00
52E Tray, 2 hdld., 7"	18.00--22.00
42E Tray, 2 hdld., 5½"	15.00--18.00
72B Bowl, 2 hdld., 8½"	13.00--15.00
*62B Bowl, 2 hdld., 7"	15.00
52B Nappy, 2 hdld., 5½"	9.00--11.00
42B Bowl, fruit, 2 hdld., 4½"	7.00-- 9.00
42D Plate, 2 hdld., 5½"	9.00--11.00
52D Plate, 2 hdld., 7"	11.00--13.00
62D Plate, 2 hdld., 8½"	12.00--14.00
72D Plate, 2 hdld., 10"	15.00--17.00
34 Coaster, 4½"	6.00-- 8.00
1D Plate, 6"	6.00-- 8.00
*3D Plate, 7"	14.00
*5D Plate, 8"	17.00
7D Plate, 9"	15.00--18.00
33 Jelly, individual, 4"	4.50-- 5.50
3F Nappy, 6"	6.00-- 7.00
*1F Nappy, 5"	8.50
5F Nappy, 7"	7.00-- 9.00
51 Nappy, hdld., 5"	11.00--13.00
7F Nappy, 8"	8.00--10.00
17D Plate, 14"	20.00--24.00
13D Plate, 12"	16.00--19.00
13F Nappy, 10"	10.00--12.00
17F Nappy, 12"	13.00--15.00
31 Sugar and Cream Set	18.00--22.00
35 Cup and Saucer	16.00--18.00
Goblet	6.00-- 8.00

****Still in production, prices set by Imperial***

CANDLEWICK (crystal)

The following are pieces and their retail prices being made January 1, 1982.

7" Plate (400/3D)	14.00
8½" Plate (400/5D)	17.00
10½" Plate (400/10D)	21.00
12½" Torte Plate (400/75V)	25.00
12" 2-Handled Plate (400/145D)	29.00
Saucer (400/35)	10.00
Cup & Saucer (400/37)	19.00
Cup (400/37)	9.00
Salt & Pepper Set (400/96)	9.00
Salt & Pepper Set (400/247)	9.00
Sugar & Cream Set (400/30)	18.00
Sugar & Cream & Tray (400/29/30)	26.00
7" Oblong Tray (400/29)	8.00
5" Nappy (400/1F)	8.50
6" Bowl (400/85)	12.00
5" Handled Bon Bon (400/40H)	15.00
3 pc. Mar. Set (400/289)	11.00
6½" Relish (400/54)	14.00
8½" 4-Part Relish (400/55)	20.00
8" 2-Part Relish (400/268)	12.00
11" 2-Part oval Relish (400/256)	18.00
7" Butter and Cover (400/161)	15.00
6½" Handled Basket (400/40/0)	22.00
7" 2-Handled Bowl (400/62B)	15.00
8½" Bowl (400/69B)	19.00
10" 2-Handled Bowl (400/145B)	23.00
2 Pc. Hurricane Lamp (10/22)	20.00
2 Pc. Hurricane Lamp	21.00
3½" Candleholder (400/170)	10.00
Punch Ladle (400/91)	12.00

CANDLEWICK STEMWARE

3400 9 oz. Goblet	16.00
3400 6 oz. Dessert	16.00
3400 4 oz. Wine	16.00
3400 12 oz. Iced Beverage	16.00

MISCELLANEOUS

No. 550/12 Console Set: 5 pc. *blown and hand cast feet*	25.00--30.00
701/10 Ball, ftd., 4"	8.00--10.00
7850/3 Cigarette Set: 6 pc. pressed *(4 ash trays and box w/cover)*	18.00--22.00
550/3 Ball, ftd., 3¼"	5.00-- 7.00
7012 Cocktail, 3½ oz.	5.00-- 7.00
701/8 Candleholder	8.00--10.00
550/1 Candleholder	7.00-- 9.00
7012 Cocktail Shaker Set: 36 oz. w/chrome top	35.00--50.00
550/2 Ball, ftd., 7"	10.00--12.00
701/7 Ball, ftd., 6"	10.00--12.00
701/9 Ball, ftd., 3"	4.00-- 6.00
701/78 Console Set: 5 pc. *Blown and Cast Feet*	25.00--35.00
No. 136 Tumbler, 5 oz.	3.00-- 4.00
No. 136 Tumbler, 10 oz.	4.00-- 5.00
No. 136 Tumbler, 13 oz.	5.00-- 6.00
No. 136 Tumbler, 16 oz.	6.00-- 7.00
No. 136 Jug, 8 oz.	20.00--25.00

TUMBLERS page 178

No. 1748

Tumbler, old fashioned cocktail, 7 oz. Decorations of: Lamb, Elephant, Mouse, Parrot, Duck, Rabbit, Cat, Turtle, Ape, Crow, Lady Bug, Rooster	5.00-- 7.00
No. 103/86 Full Sham Tomato, 5 oz.	4.00-- 6.00
No. 103/85 Full Sham Rooster, 5 oz.	4.00-- 6.00
No. 103/87 Full Sham orange, 5 oz.	4.00-- 6.00
No. 8701 Happy Hour Mixer, blown, 12 oz.	9.00--12.00

MISCELLANEOUS

No. 775 Vase, plain, blown, 10" and 12"	14.00--18.00
No. 7751 OPTIC Vase, blown, 10"	14.00--18.00
No. 488 Vase, blown, 12"	30.00--35.00
No. 1 Flower Pot and Saucer, 2 pc., pressed	10.00--14.00

MISCELLANEOUS

(Crystal, Stiegel green, Ritz blue, amber, ruby)

No. 11/7455G Bowl, basket, 5"	9.00--11.00
No. 11/7455B Nappy, belled, 6½"	10.00--12.00
No. 11 Nappy, shallow, 6½"	8.00--11.00
No. 11 Plate, 7½"	5.00-- 7.00
No. 11/4732L Vase, 7½"	12.00--15.00
No. 11/4732N Vase, 6"	11.00--14.00
No. 11 Vase	11.00--14.00
No. 169 Compote, high stem 6¾"	12.00--15.00
No. 2428 Plate, ground bottom, 8"	4.00-- 5.00
No. 46 Saucer Foot Syrup Jug	15.00--20.00
No. 637D Candleholder, low rnd., pr.	10.00--14.00
No. 75X Bowl, console, 4 ftd., rnd., flanged, 12½"	14.00--20.00

CUT 600 page 179

Hand cut pattern on genuine Ruby glass.

No. 10/7257W Bowl, 2 hdld., 9"	15.00--18.00
No. 10/717 Candy Box and Cover	25.00--30.00

No. 10/760/2 Tray, square, lunch, 10½"	15.00--20.00
No. 10/760 Sugar and Cream Set	16.00--22.00
No. 10/7255W Mayonnaise Set: 3 pc.	18.00--24.00
No. 10/7287Y Bowl, Rose, 7"	16.00--20.00
No. 10/7257D Plate, cake, 10½"	15.00--18.00
No. 10/7287X/728 Console Set: 3 pc.	35.00--40.00
728 Candleholder	15.00--20.00
7287X Bowl, console, 11"	15.00--20.00

CUT 256 LAUREL

Crystal, Rose pink, green, topaz

No. 728 Tray, sandwich, center hdld., 10"	11.00--14.00
No. 7286A Comport, 9"	12.00-15.00
No. 7257W Bowl, two hdld., 9"	10.00--12.00
No. 7286D Plate, ftd., 10"	11.00--14.00
No. 7286Y Bowl, Rose, 6"	10.00--12.00
Bowl w/Ladle, ftd.	12.00--15.00
Candy Box and Cover	15.00--20.00
Plate, two hdld.	10.00--12.00

CHARDON PATTERN

Crystal, Rose pink, green, Topaz

No. 7251/1 Bon Bon Tray, center hdld., 7½"	10.00--12.00
No. 7605W Nappy, square, 6½"	7.00-- 9.00
No. 5991 Comport, 5¼"	7.00-- 9.00
No. 615 Tray, pickle or relish, 2 hdld., 8½"	7.00-- 9.00
No. 7275W Nappy, octagon, 7"	6.00-- 8.00
Plate, 2 hdld.	6.00-- 8.00
Bowl, 2 hdld., (fits plate)	7.00-- 9.00
Vase	10.00--14.00

"MOLLY"

OCTAGON and Square Luncheon Sets, hand made.
See page 110.

"HAZEN"

Luncheon Set: 15 pc. square	50.00--60.00
No. 7885D Plate, salad, 8"	3.00-- 4.00
No. 760 Cup and Saucer	5.00-- 6.00
No. 760 Sugar and Cream	10.00--12.00
No. 7608D Tray, square, 13"	10.00--12.00

"KATY BLUE"

Opalescent blue, Opalescent green

Plate, luncheon, 12"	12.00--15.00
Plate, dinner, 10"	12.00--14.00
Plate, salad, 8"	6.00-- 8.00
Plate, bread and butter, 6½"	4.00-- 6.00
Sugar	12.50--15.00
Cream	12.50--15.00
Cup	8.00--10.00
Saucer	4.00-- 6.00
Tumbler, 9 oz.	14.00--16.00
Bowl, soup, 7"	12.00--15.00
Bowl, fruit, 4½"	6.00-- 8.00
Mayonnaise Set: 3 pc.	25.00--30.00
Bowl, oval veg., 11"	15.00--20.00
Bowl, oval, divided veg., 11"	15.00--20.00
Platter, 13"	15.00--20.00
Bowl, round, 9"	15.00--20.00
Tid Bit Set	25.00--35.00
Ash Receiver, 3 toed	8.00--10.00
Mayonnaise Set: 3 pc.	18.00--24.00
Decanter, 11"	25.00--30.00

Blue-green decanter 11"

Blue-green Decanter, 11" **25.00--30.00**

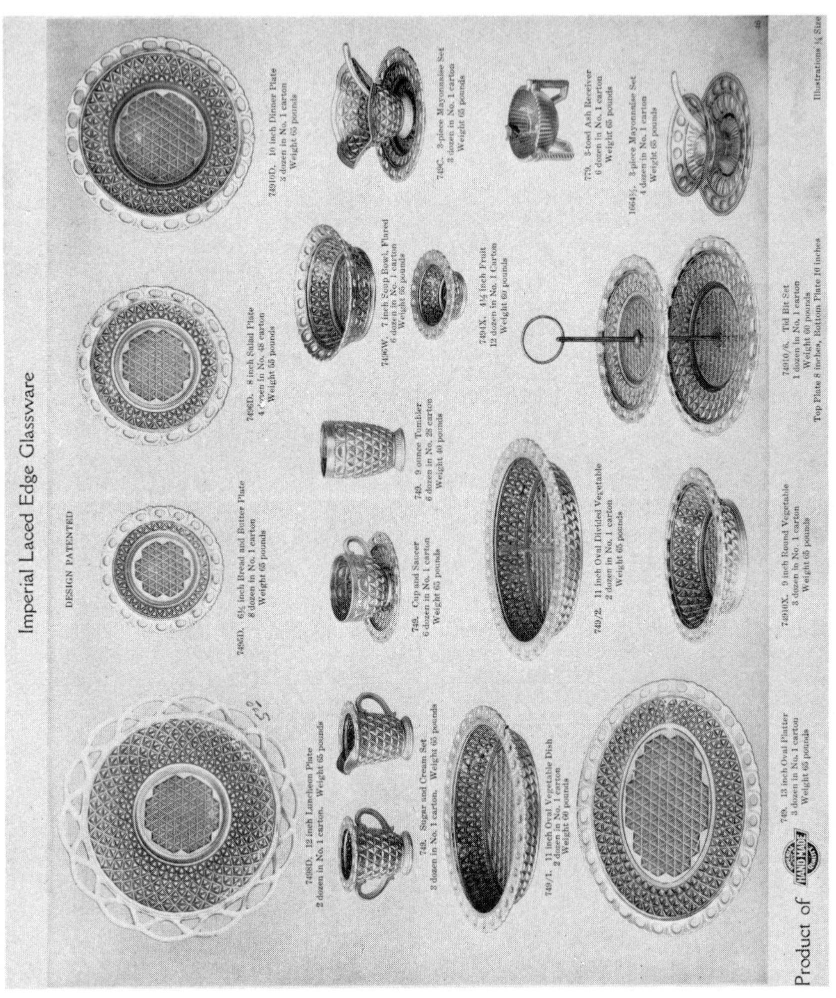

Imperial Laced Edge Glassware

DESIGN PATENTED

7498D. 12 inch Luncheon Plate
2 dozen in No. 1 carton. Weight 65 pounds

7495D. 6½ inch Bread and Butter Plate
8 dozen in No. 1 carton
Weight 65 pounds

7496D. 8 inch Salad Plate
4 dozen in No. 48 carton
Weight 55 pounds

74910D. 10 inch Dinner Plate
3 dozen in No. 1 carton
Weight 65 pounds

749. Sugar and Cream Set
3 dozen in No. 1 carton. Weight 65 pounds

749. Cup and Saucer
6 dozen in No. 1 carton
Weight 65 pounds

749. 9 ounce Tumbler
6 dozen in No. 28 carton
Weight 40 pounds

7496W. 7 inch Soup Bowl, Flared
6 dozen in No. 1 carton
Weight 65 pounds

749C. 3-piece Mayonnaise Set
3 dozen in No. 1 carton
Weight 65 pounds

7494X. 4½ inch Fruit
12 dozen in No. 1 Carton
Weight 60 pounds

749/1. 11 inch Oval Vegetable Dish
2 dozen in No. 1 carton
Weight 60 pounds

749/2. 11 inch Oval Divided Vegetable
2 dozen in No. 1 carton
Weight 65 pounds

779. 3-toed Ash Receiver
6 dozen in No. 1 carton
Weight 65 pounds

1664½. 3-piece Mayonnaise Set
4 dozen in No. 1 carton
Weight 65 pounds

Product of HAND MADE

749. 13 inch Oval Platter
3 dozen in No. 1 carton
Weight 65 pounds

74910X. 9 inch Round Vegetable
3 dozen in No. 1 carton
Weight 65 pounds

74910/6. Tid Bit Set
1 dozen in No. 1 carton
Weight 60 pounds
Top Plate 8 inches, Bottom Plate 10 inches

Illustrations ½ Size

"KATY BLUE" reprinted from an Imperial catalog

Indiana GLASS

Indiana

The big news this year is another "Rib" identified. This one is "Zipper Rib", formerly of the Unknowns, and now sure of its Indiana origins. Being printed below is an old company sheet, dated late 20s, that is green in color and therefore not easy to reproduce. You will also find pieces with fired on orange, yellow, blue, etc. as the mold was made and used before pink and green became popular.

When Federal Glass Co. closed in 1979 many of their molds were purchased by Indiana glass. Indiana is producing glass from some of them, including the Recollection series, which as you know was a copy of Federal's old 1936 MADRID. To date the acquired molds have only been issued in crystal, and it is not dated as the late Federal issue in amber was.

Indiana also makes glass for "Tiara Exclusives". Again this year they are marketing AVOCADO and SANDWICH in Burnt Honey. Last year they sold the Humpty Dumpty Child's Mug and the "See Saw" child's plate and a set of four NURSERY RHYME plates and tumblers, all in Burnt Amber.

Then, I've acquirea another old Indiana catalog circa 1940, and am printing a few lines even though they are crystal because some pieces have been made in colors, most notably pastel topaz and blue. Each line was made in many pieces but for lack of space I'm printing only a few pieces of each.

Last but not least, many pieces of old Indiana glass can be viewed at the new museum in Dunkirk, Indiana!

OLD ENGLISH **page 183**

Green, pink, amber

Item	Price
Candy Jar and Cover, ½ lb.	35.00--40.00
Comport, ruffled	14.00--17.00
Candlestick, 4", pr.	22.00--28.00
Sugar and Cover	25.00--30.00
Creamer	10.00--14.00
Tumbler, 4½"	10.00--14.00
Tumbler, 5½"	12.00--16.00
Jug, 9"	35.00--45.00
Jug and Cover	85.00-100.00
Bowl, fruit, ftd., 11"	20.00--25.00
Bowl, berry	12.00--14.00
Bowl, Master berry	22.00--28.00
Cheese and Cracker	25.00--35.00
Server, sandwich center handle	20.00--25.00
Sherbet	10.00--12.00
Vase	25.00--35.00
Candy Jar in metal holder	30.00--35.00

"SODA FOUNTAIN" page 184

Tumbler, 6", 8½ oz.	6.00-- 9.00
Sundae, low ftd.	4.00-- 6.00
Sundae, tall ftd.	5.00-- 7.00
Goblet	9.00--11.00
Coca Cola, ftd., 6 oz.	8.00--10.00
Tumbler, service, ftd. 8 oz.	8.00--10.00
Ice Tea, ftd., 10 oz.	8.00--10.00
Malted Milk, ftd., 12 oz.	9.00--12.00
Cream, berry	8.00--10.00
Sugar, berry	8.00--10.00
Oil, 4 oz.	20.00--25.00
Relish, dish, 4-7/8"	6.00-- 8.00
Bowl, finger	6.00-- 8.00
Banana Split, ftd.	14.00--18.00
Plate, 6"	4.00-- 6.00
Shaker, Salt and Pepper	25.00--30.00
Plate, 8½"	6.00-- 8.00

"TEA ROOM" page 185,186,187

Crystal, pink, green, amber

Plate, hdld., 10½"	25.00--35.00
Plate, 8¼"	25.00--40.00
Plate, 6½"	10.00--15.00
Cup	20.00--25.00
Saucer	10.00--12.00
Sherbet, ice cream, ftd.	15.00--25.00
Sherbet, sundae, low ftd.	14.00--20.00
Sherbet, sundae, tall ftd.	30.00--45.00
Parfait	25.00--35.00
Glace, 7 oz., 6½ oz.	25.00--35.00
Bowl, finger	12.00--15.00
Bowl, deep berry, 8½"	35.00--55.00
Bowl, deep oval, 9½"	35.00--50.00
Banana Split, ftd.	40.00--45.00
Bowl, banana split, 7½"	25.00--35.00
Pickle, 8½"	8.00--10.00
Relish, 2-part, 8½"	14.00-18.00
Sugar and Cream	24.00--30.00
Cream and Sugar, oval w/hdld. tray	50.00--65.00
Sugar and Cream, berry, center hdld., tray	30.00--35.00
Sugar, plain or slotted cover	50.00--75.00
Tumbler, table, 8½ oz.	30.00--45.00
Tumbler, Coca Cola, ftd., 6 oz.	16.00--24.00
Tumbler, service, ftd., 8 oz.	20.00--30.00
Tumbler, ice tea, ftd., 11 oz.	20.00--35.00
Tumbler, malted milk, 12 oz.	28.00--40.00
Goblet, 9 oz.	30.00--45.00
Pitcher, ½ gal. jug	100.00-125.00
Ice Bucket	50.00--60.00
Candlestick, low, pr.	25.00--45.00
Salt and Pepper, pr.	35.00-50.00
Sandwich Server, center hdld.	35.00--55.00
Mustard, plain or slotted cover	50.00--75.00
Vase, plain 11"	50.00--65.00
Vase, plain or ruffled 9"	28.00--36.00
Lamp, 9", pr.	65.00--75.00

(page 16 Book II)

AVOCADO page 188

Indiana has made the ½ gallon jug and footed tumbler in a new pink, a topaz, an amethyst and a green. This year they are making a dark amber called Burnt Honey.

Cream, berry, hdld.	25.00--30.00
Jelly, hdld., 7"	16.00--20.00
Sugar, berry, hdld.	25.00--30.00
Bowl, salad, 9"	80.00--90.00
Plate, 5½"	8.00--10.00
Cup and Saucer	45.00--55.00
Jug, ½ gal.	600.00-900.00
Pickle, 2 hdld., 8"	18.00--22.00
Plate, salad, 8¼"	15.00--20.00
Relish, ftd., 6"	18.00--24.00
Plate, 2 hdld., 10"	30.00--35.00
Olive, 2 hdld., 5¼"	16.00--20.00
Plate, cheese, 6½"	14.00--18.00
Preserve, shallow, 7¼"	18.00--22.00
Sundae, ftd. (pink highest)	50.00--80.00
Tumbler	90.00-110.00

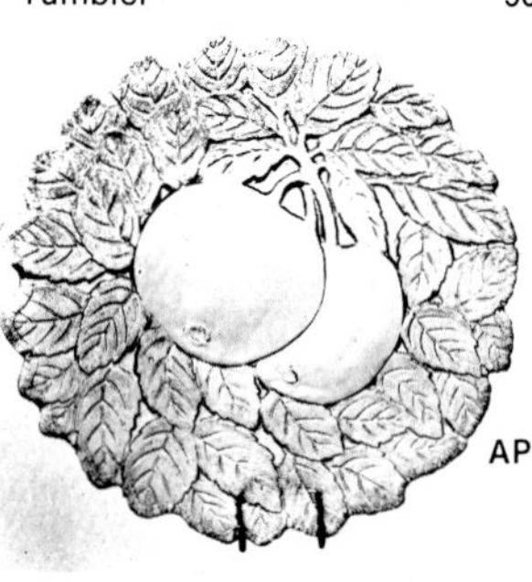

APPLE plate 8" 9.00--12.00

605 "LILY PONS" page 189

Prices not for recent crystal

Cream, hdld.	6.00-- 8.00
Sugar, hdld.	6.00-- 8.00
Pickle, 2 hdld., 8½"	8.00--10.00
Fruit Cocktail and Plate Set	9.00--12.00
Plate, 6"	6.00-- 8.00
Nappy, 7"	8.00--10.00
Bon Bon, ftd., 6½"	8.00--10.00
Plate, salad, 8½"	6.00-- 8.00
Preserve, 7"	8.00--10.00

606 "LOGANBERRY"

Bon Bon, ftd. 7"	10.00--14.00
Plate, service, 9"	12.00--15.00

607 "DUNKIRK"

Plate, salad, 8¼"	12.00--16.00

608 "ARTURA" page 190

Cream, hdld.	5.00-- 6.00
Cup and Saucer	6.00-- 8.00

Sugar, hdld.	5.00-- 6.00
Tumbler, ftd.	6.00-- 8.00
Sandwich, hdld.	12.00--16.00
Plate, salad, 7½"	4.00-- 6.00

"TWIGGY"

Jelly, 8"	7.00-- 9.00
Relish, 2-part, 8", 10"	8.00--10.00
Plate, 5½", 8"	4.00-- 8.00
Nappy, 4½", 8"	5.00-- 9.00
Plate, snack, 10"	6.00-- 8.00

"JOYCE"

Dish, nut, 6"	8.00--10.00
Individual Nuts, 3"	3.00-- 4.00

"CHARLIE"

Dish, candy, 7"	8.00--10.00

"PYRAMID" page 191

(No. 43 Book 1)

Prices below are for crystal, pink and green. Topaz prices are 25% higher

Tumbler, tea serv., ftd., 11 oz.	35.00--45.00
Cream, berry, hdld.	15.00--20.00
Sugar, berry, hdld.	15.00--20.00
Ice Tub with handle	70.00-100.00
Ice Tub with Cover	175.00-200.00
Tumbler, service, ftd., 8 oz.	30.00--35.00
Jug, ½ gal.	150.00-300.00
Bowl, oval, 9½"	35.00--45.00
Pickle, 9½"	25.00--35.00
Berry, 4¾"	15.00--20.00
Sugar and Cream Set, 3 piece	40.00--60.00
Berry, 8½"	30.00--45.00
Relish, 4 part, 8½"	30.00--45.00

"BANANAS" page 192

Cream, berry, hdld.	6.00-- 8.00
Sugar, berry, hdld.	6.00-- 8.00
Tray, oblong, 8"	10.00--12.00
Coca Cola, ftd., 6 oz.	8.00--10.00
Tumbler, service, ftd., 8 oz.	10.00--12.00
Tea, service, ftd., 12 oz.	10.00--12.00
Malted Milk, ftd., 12 oz.	12.00--14.00

"KING ARTHUR"

Plate, 6-5/8"	3.00-- 5.00
Plate, 7"	4.00-- 6.00
Platter, meat, 11"	9.00--12.00
Dish, oblong or veg., 9"	12.00--14.00
Platter, meat, 9"	8.00--12.00

"INDIANA CUSTARD" page 193

(No. 239 Book 1)

Plate, 9", 9¾"	10.00--14.00
Plate, salad, 7½"	6.00-- 8.00
Plate, sherbet, 6"	3.00-- 4.00
Cup and Saucer	20.00--25.00
Platter, 12"	18.00--22.00
Cream	10.00--12.00
Sugar and Cover	18.00--24.00
Sherbet	50.00--60.00
Bowl, nappy, 5½"	5.00-- 6.00
Bowl, nappy, 6"	10.00--12.00
Bowl, 9"	24.00--28.00
Bowl, vegetable, oval, 9½"	24.00--28.00
Bowl, soup, 7½"	14.00--17.00
Butterdish and Cover	40.00--50.00

ORANGE BLOSSOM

Plate	4.00-- 6.00
Cup	4.00-- 5.00
Saucer	2.00-- 3.00
Dessert	3.00-- 5.00
Sugar	4.00-- 6.00
Cream	4.00-- 6.00

"PRETZEL" page 194

(No. 153 Book 1) (also with fruit)

Cream, hdld.	5.00-- 7.00
Cup and Saucer	5.00-- 7.00
Sugar, hdld.	5.00-- 7.00
Soup, coupe, 7½"	4.00-- 6.00
Berry, 9-3/8"	6.00-- 8.00
Plate, sandwich or cake, 11½"	8.00--10.00
Plate, dinner, 9-3/8"	5.00-- 7.00
Plate, salad, 8-3/8"	4.00-- 6.00
Plate, 6"	2.00-- 3.00
Olive, hdld., 7"	4.00-- 6.00
Cup, fruit,	3.00-- 4.00
Plate, fruit cup or cheese	3.00-- 4.00
Pickle, 2-hdld., 8½"	4.00-- 5.00
Tray, celery, 10¼"	5.00-- 7.00
Tumbler, 5 oz.	6.00-- 8.00
Tumbler, 9 oz.	6.00-- 8.00
Tumbler, 12 oz.	8.00--10.00
Jug, 39 oz.	24.00--30.00

GARLAND page 195

Console Set, 3 piece	35.00--45.00

INTAGLIO

(No. 68 Book 1 Section)

Dish, relish, 3 part., etched, 7¼"	14.00--18.00
Dish, relish, 5 part., etched, 10"	18.00--22.00

"CRACKED ICE"

Tumbler, ftd., 5"	6.00-- 8.00
Sugar and Cover	8.00--12.00
Sherbet	4.00-- 6.00
Cream	6.00-- 8.00
Plate, 6½"	3.00-- 4.00

MISCELLANEOUS

17½—Bon Bon, covered.

Hen-on-Nest.

Crystaleaf Punch Set

No. 6 — Crystaleaf Punch Set

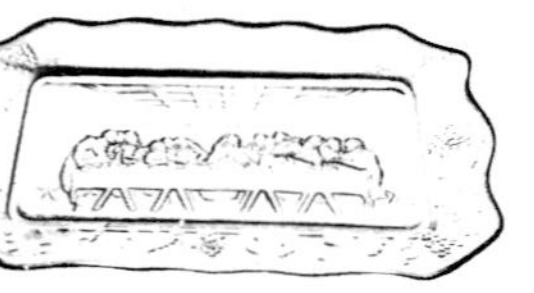

100—Cake Plate—11½-inch.

Lord's Supper Plate.

"GLORIA ANNE"

7—Plate—10-inch.

Horse Head Book Ends

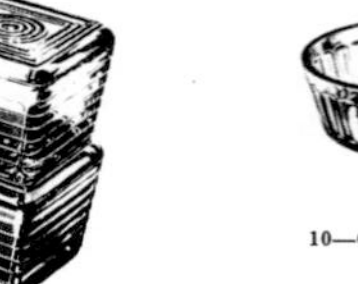

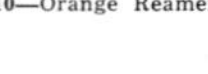

10—Orange Reamer.

4—Lemon Reamer.

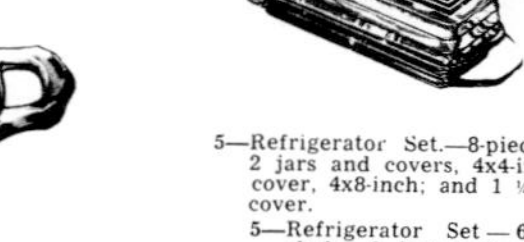

No. 8 — 5½" 2-Handled Olive

"KILLARNEY"

Duck and Cover

5—Refrigerator Set.—8-piece set includes 2 jars and covers, 4x4-inch; 1 jar and cover, 4x8-inch; and 1 ¼-lb. butter and cover.

5—Refrigerator Set — 6-piece set includes 2 jars and covers, 4x4-inch, and 1 jar and cover, 4x8-inch.

5—Refrigerator Jar and Cover — 4x4-inch.

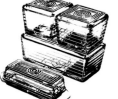

5—Refrigerator Jar and Cover — 4x8-inch.

5—Butter Dish and Cover—¼-lb.

12—Candy Tray, oblong, 8-inch.

Indiana Glass

reprinted from 1950 catalog

Indiana Glass Co.

Dunkirk, Indiana

Manufacturers of

Pressed and Blown Glassware

:-: Colored :-:

"DOILY" plate

Made in Crystal, Amber or Green

Reprinted from 1926 trade journal

Pigeon Book Ends

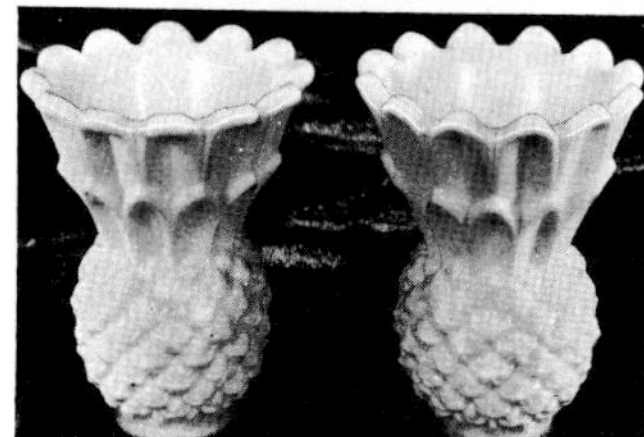

Pineapple Vase, Candlesticks

MISCELLANEOUS *See reprints*

Crystal

CRYSTALEAF punch set	20.00--30.00
"GLORIA ANNE" 10" plate	7.00--10.00
HORSE HEAD bookend	8.00--10.00
DUCK and Cover	10.00--14.00
"KILLARNEY" 5½" olive	5.00-- 8.00
Bon Bon, covered	5.00-- 8.00
Hen-On-Nest	10.00--12.00
Cake Plate (100) 11½"	10.00--12.00
Lord's Supper Plate	8.00--10.00
Refrigerator Set:	
Jar and Cover, 4" x 8"	6.00-- 9.00
Jar and Cover, 4" x 4"	5.00-- 8.00
Butter Dish and Cover, ¼ lb.	6.00-- 8.00
Orange Reamer	8.00--12.00
Lemon Reamer	7.00-- 10.00
Candy Tray, oblong, 8"	6.00-- 8.00
"DOILY" plate	6.00-- 8.00
PIGEON bookends	15.00--25.00
PINEAPPLE vase candlesticks	12.00--15.00
LAMPS (1, 2, 3)	20.00--30.00

See reprint next page

Sanitary refrigerator jar	15.00--25.00
Ash Tray w/metal top	9.00--12.00
Relish, 4 part, 7"	5.00-- 7.00
Butter, 1 lb. oblong	20.00--30.00
Rolling Pin	20.00--30.00
Refrigerator Set w/ball bearing tray	25.00--35.00
Condiment Set	30.00--40.00
Measuring Cup (15, 16, 17)	25.00--35.00
Measuring Glass	6.00-- 9.00
Measuring Pitcher	20.00--25.00
Reamers, ea.	7.00--15.00

"ZIPPER RIB" (No. 4 Pattern)

Amber, green, pink

Comport, 9"	11.00--14.00
Sandwich Plate, 11½"	12.00--15.00
Plate and Sherbet, 8"	8.00--10.00
Covered Candy Box, 1 lb.	18.00--24.00
Vase, blown, 5½"	7.00-- 9.00
Vase, pressed 8¼"	12.00--16.00
Vase, fan	10.00--14.00
Covered Candy Box, ½ lb.	16.00--20.00
Comport, tall, 6½"	9.00--12.00
Cabarette, low foot, 11"	10.00--14.00
Footed Salad, 8¼"	10.00--14.00
Mayonnaise and Spoon	12.00--15.00
Vase, blown, 7½"	8.00--10.00
Bon Bon, ftd., covered, 6¼"	18.00--22.00
Candy Jar and Cover, ½ lb.	18.00--22.00

See reprint next page

"ZIPPER RIB"

No. 4 PATTERN
Amber, Green or Pink
9"—Comport
11½"—Sandwich Plate
8"—Plate and Sherbet
1 lb.—Covered Candy Box Oval
5½"—Blown Vase
8¼"—Pressed Vase
Fan Vase
11"—Low Foot Cabarette
6½"—Tall Comport
½ lb.—Covered Candy Box Oval
7½"—Blown Vase
6¼"—Footed Covered Bon Bon
½ lb.—Candy Jar

REFRIGERATOR JAR AND COVER

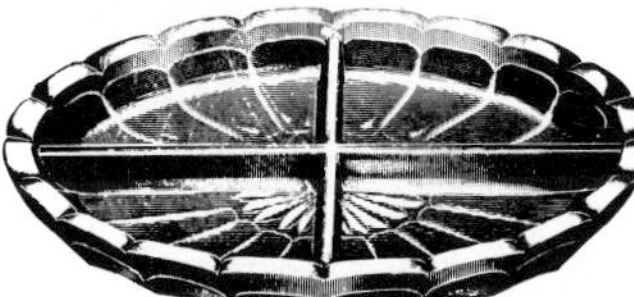

NO. 232—7-IN. 4 PART RELISH

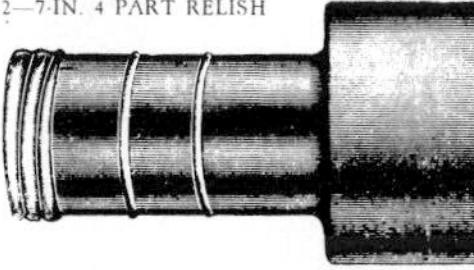

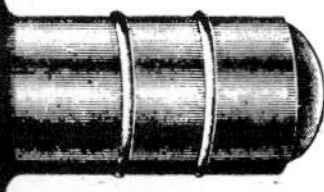

INDIANA GLASS CO.

REFRIGERATOR SET
NO 500

STRAIGHT "EASY CLEAN" JAR
WIDE MOUTH
FLAT COVER
HANDLED JAR
EASY TURNING TRAY

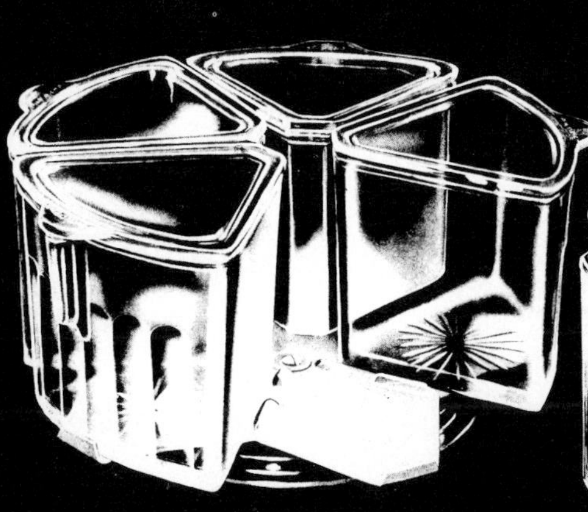

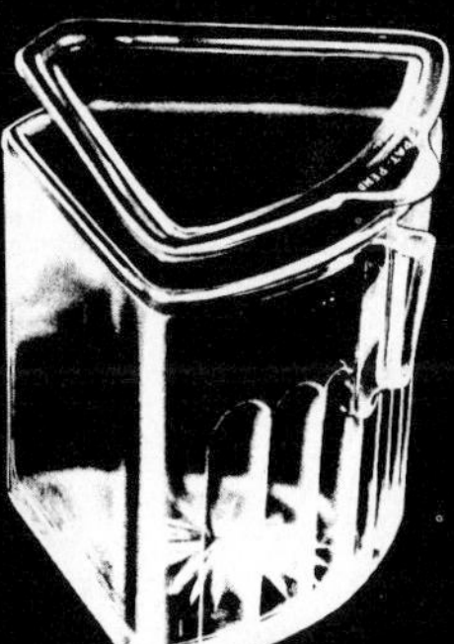

1 - BALL BEARING TRAY
5 - GLASS JARS OVER 32 OZ. CAPACITY EACH
5 - GLASS COVERS
ONE SET TO SHIPPING CARTON WEIGHT 14 LBS.

PATENTS PENDING

No. 15—Measuring Cream

Medicine or Extract Measuring Glass

No. 16—Measuring Cup

Quart Measuring Pitcher with well assorted measuring tables and other information that is helpful. Illustration shows only half the story told by this useful article.

No. 17—Measuring Cream

NO. 9—ORANGE REAMER

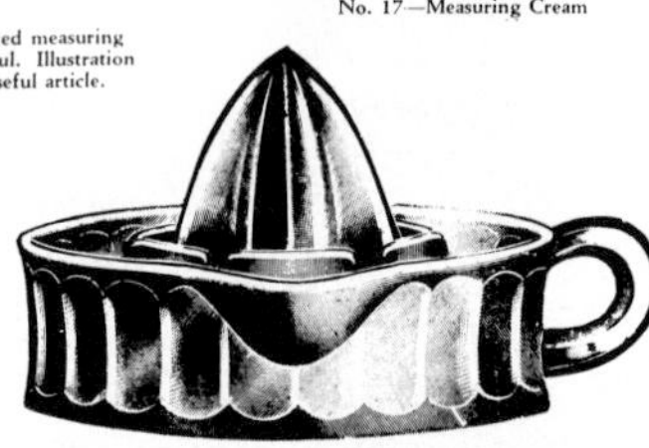

No. 8 Orange Reamer

Reamers

No. 7 Orange Reamer

No. 17

NO. 4—LEMON REAMER

No. 1 A or No. 6

NO. 10—6½" ORANGE REAMER

1940 Catalog Reprint

Catalog reprint c. 1939-1940

Pattern No. 1005

NO. 1006

Pattern No. 1007

Pattern No. 1008

Pattern No. 1009

Laurel

PATTERN NO. 1010

Teardrop

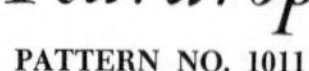

PATTERN NO. 1011

Coronation

PATTERN NO. 1016

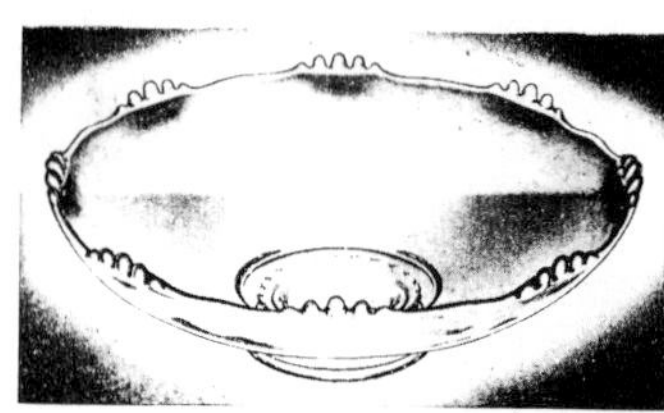

Catalog reprint c.1939-1940

Jeannette

You will find most of Jeannette's major patterns, such as ADAM, CHERRY BLOSSOM, DORIC AND PANSY, WINDSOR, etc. in Book 1.

Notice the new listing of the PETALWARE wall vase in the Shell Pink Milk Glass. Other pieces such as the NATIONAL candy bottom, and vases made for Napco Ceramics of Cleveland, Ohio, may be found.

MISCELLANEOUS page 200

Console Sets:	
No. 26/49 3 piece	40.00--50.00
No. X-31 Console Set, amber, 3 piece	35.00--45.00
Automobile Vases:	
No. 5155 cut crystal w/nickel plated holder	14.00--16.00
No. 5265 Amber iridescent w/nickel plated holder	15.00--20.00
Sugar and Cream Sets:	
No. X-35	10.00--15.00
No. X-50	8.00--12.00

"BRIDGET"

Green and topaz

Plate	2.00-- 3.00
Cup	2.00-- 3.00
Saucer	1.00-- 1.25
Cream	3.00-- 4.00
Sugar	3.00-- 4.00
Server, sandwich	7.00-- 9.00

MISCELLANEOUS page 201

Crystal and green

No. X-33 Wine Set, Ringed design	40.00--55.00
No. X-32 Water Set, crystal, fluted design	30.00--35.00

CONSOLE SETS

No. 127-99:	
Bowl, square, ftd.	10.00--14.00
Candleholder, square base, tall, pr.	16.00--20.00
No. X-69:	
Bowl, rnd., flrd.	8.00--12.00
Candleholder, low, pr.	9.00--11.00
No. 127-37:	
Bowl, square, ftd.	10.00--14.00
Candleholder, sq. base, low, pr	9.00--11.00
No. X-67:	
Bowl, rnd., flrd., 4 toed	10.00--14.00
Candleholder, low, pr.	9.00--11.00
No. 26-97:	
Bowl, ftd.	10.00--12.00
Candleholder, tall, pr.	16.00--22.00
No. X-68:	
Bowl, rnd., flrd., toed.	10.00--14.00
Candleholder, low, pr.	9.00--11.00

"DAISY J"

Green, amber and pink
The #95 Candy Jar to this pattern is shown in color section page 16.

Cheese and Cracker	10.00--14.00
Cream and Sugar	9.00--12.00
Plate	3.00-- 4.00
Server, sandwich	9.00--12.00
Candy Jar and Cover	15.00--20.00
Bowl, console	10.00--14.00
Bowl and Plate Set	15.00--20.00
Candlestick, pr.	16.00--20.00

KITCHENWARE page 202

Green and pink (pink is highest)

Kitchen Salt or Sugar Shaker *(J-in-triangle in bottom)*	35.00--45.00
Reamer, lemon	15.00--35.00
Berry Set *(#142 Book l; I have creamer in this pattern but find none listed)*	18.00--22.00
Jug*(note sunflower motif in bottom)*	15.00--25.00
Mixing Bowl Set:	35.00--50.00
Bowl, ea.	6.00--18.00
Butter Box, 2 lb.	18.00--22.00
Utility Crock w/Cover	20.00--25.00
Salt Box	55.00--75.00
Reamer, orange	20.00--35.00

JADITE

Listed in KITCHENWARE - page 204 Book 2

KITCHENWARE AND MISCELLANEOUS GLASSWARE page 203

No. 253 Ash Tray	6.00--10.00
*No. 254 Ash Tray	6.00--10.00
No. 1102 Ash Tray	5.00-- 9.00
No. 287 Jug, 33 oz.	20.00--25.00
No. 289 Tumbler, 9 oz.	6.00-- 8.00
No. 68 Tumbler, 8½ oz.	3.00-- 5.00
No. 352 Refrigerator Tray and Cover, square	45.00--50.00
No. 393/4 Dish, relish, w/nickel plated band	10.00--12.00
No. 5175 Butter and Cover	30.00--35.00
No. 379 Reamer, orange	15.00--20.00
No. 37 Cigarette Jar	4.00-- 6.00
No. 207 Cigarette Jar	5.00-- 8.00
No. 2051 Salt or Sugar Shaker w/aluminum top	35.00--45.00
No. 516 Mug, 16 oz.	18.00--20.00
No. 300 Sugar Dispenser w/aluminum top	50.00--55.00
No. 780/735 Cocktail Set Tray w/4 Tumblers	60.00--65.00
No. 517 Cup, measuring, 16 oz.	18.00--22.00
No. 69 Puff Box	6.00-- 8.00
No. 353 Large Refrigerator Tray and Cover, oblong	60.00--65.00

**Ultra-Marine*

"JENNY WARE"

(No. 195 Book l) Crystal, pink and Ultra-Marine

Refrigerator Set: rnd.	
Jar and Cover, 16 oz.	8.00--12.00
Jar and Cover, 32 oz.	12.00--15.0
Jar and Cover, 70 oz.	20.00--25.0
Refrigerator Set: square	
Jar and Cover, 4½" x 9"	15.00--20.0
Jar and Cover, 4½" x 4 ½"	10.00--15.0
Jug, 37 oz.	25.00--30.0
Tumbler, 8 oz.	6.00--10.0
Butter Box and Cover	15.00--25.0
Reamer, lemon	50.00--65.0
Mixing Bowl Set:	
Bowl, 26 oz.	10.00--15.0
Bowl, 64 oz.	15.00--20.0
Bowl, 120 oz.	20.00--25.0
Measuring Cup Set: ¼ cup, 1/3 cup, ½ cup, full cup	40.00--50.0
No. 490 Range Set: (salt and pepper)	20.00--25.0

KITCHENWARE page 20

Made in both Jadite and Delfite Some of these were in the numbered sec-tion of Book l; they are repeated here.

Bath Room Set, 5 pc.	40.00--45.0
Beater Bowl	6.00-- 8.0
Bud Vase	5.00-- 6.0
Tumbler, 8 oz.	5.00-- 8.0
Jar and Cover, rnd., 32 oz.	12.00--14.0
Ash Tray	8.00--10.0
Jar and Cover, square, 29 oz.	14.00--16.0
No. X6 Refrigerator Set	25.00--30.0
No. X7 Refrigerator Set	20.00--25.0
Crock and Cover, rnd.	15.00--18.0
Butter Box and Cover	30.00--35.0
Ice Box Jug and Cover	60.00--65.0
Reamer, orange	15.00--25.0
Jug, 33 oz.	18.00--20.0
Egg Cup	5.00-- 7.0
"Matches" *(See in color section)*	15.00--20.0
Salt Box and Cover	65.00--70.0
Measuring Cup Set	30.00--35.0
(in original box)	35.00--40.0
Measuring Cup with spout, lg.	8.00--12.0
Mixing Bowl Set, 6", 7", 8", 9"	????
Reamer	7.00-- 9.0
No. X45 Refrigerator Set	25.00--30.0
No. X20 Cereal Set	75.00--80.0
Range Set, rnd., 5 pc.	35.00--40.0
Range Set, square, 4 pc.	28.00--32.0
Spice Set, 4 pc. *(Also found in child's set with Cocoa, sugar, flour, cereal)*	50.00--60.0
No. X10 Cereal Set	50.00--60.0
(FLORAL design on cover)	90.00-100.0

500 PATTERN page 205

Tumbler, ftd., 9 oz.	4.00-- 6.0
Tumbler, ftd., 14 oz.	6.00-- 8.0
Jug, tilt, ice lip, 80 oz.	15.00--20.0

WAFFLE PATTERN

Nappy, crimped, 5"	1.50-- 2.00
Tumbler, 9 oz.	2.00-- 3.00
Nappy, crimped, 9"	6.00-- 8.00
Creamer	3.00-- 4.00
Sugar	3.00-- 4.00
Tumbler, 12½ oz.	2.50-- 3.50
Butter, covered	15.00--20.00
Toast and Jam Set, 4 piece	25.00--30.00
Berry Set, 7 piece	12.00--18.00

"HARP"

Plate, 7"	3.00-- 4.00
Cup and Saucer	4.00-- 5.00
Coaster Ash Tray, 4", 3¼"	3.00-- 4.00
Plate, cake, ftd., 9"	10.00--12.00
Coaster	2.00-- 3.00
Vase, 7½"	7.00-- 9.00
Tray, hdld., 12½" x 9¾"	10.00--12.00

DEWDROP

Cup	1.50-- 2.50
Sugar and Cover	6.00-- 8.00
Creamer	3.00-- 4.00
Butter and Cover	10.00--15.00
Dish, Maple Leaf, 8"	4.00-- 6.00
Candy Jar and Cover, 7"	8.00--10.00
Tumbler, 9 oz.	3.00-- 4.00
Ice Tea, 15 oz.	4.00-- 5.00
Nappy, 4¾"	2.00-- 3.00
Nappy, 8½"	6.00-- 9.00
Jug, 60 oz., 64 oz.	12.00--16.00
Bowl, 10-3/8"	8.00--11.00
Tray, Lazy Susan, 13½"	9.00--12.00
Plate, 11½"	6.00-- 9.00
Bowl, punch, w/Base, 6 qt.	10.00--15.00
Plate, snack, and Cup	4.00-- 6.00

CHANTILLY page 206

Jug, 9"	15.00--20.00
Tumbler, 2½", 3½", 5", 5¼"	4.00-- 6.00

CAMELLIA

Plate, dinner	3.00-- 5.00
Plate, salad	2.00-- 4.00
Cup and Saucer	3.50-- 4.50
Sugar and Cream	8.00--10.00
Bowl, 8-7/8"	7.00-- 9.00
Bowl, 11½"	9.00--11.00
Sandwich Tray, 12"	7.00-- 9.00
Candle holder, 2¾"	2.00-- 4.00
Relish, 6¾" x 11¾"	7.00-- 9.00

COSMOS

Jug, water, ice lipped, 60 oz.	10.00--14.00
Tumbler, 11½" oz.	2.50-- 3.00

NATIONAL

Berry Set	8.00--10.00
Tray	3.00-- 5.00
Candy Jar	5.00-- 8.00
Vase	2.00-- 4.00
Relish Set	6.00-- 9.00
Cup	1.00-- 1.50
Saucer	.50-- 1.00
Cigarette Set	7.00-- 9.00
Milk Pitcher	6.00-- 8.00
Jug, ice lip	7.00-- 9.00
Table Set	10.00--14.00

SHELL PINK MILK GLASS page 207

Cookie Jar and Cover	40.00--50.00
Dish, candy, nut, ftd.	6.00-- 8.00
Candy Jar and Cover, square	12.00--15.00
Florentine Dish, ftd.	16.00--20.00
Gondola fruit Bowl/Planter	12.00--15.00
Vineyard Dish, w/partitions, octagonal	12.00--16.00
Lazy Susan	18.00--22.00
Juice Set, 5-pc.	40.00--50.00
Sherbet, 5 oz.	5.00-- 8.00
Thumb Print, 8 oz. Goblet	6.00-- 9.00
Tray, oval, w/partitions, 15¾" long	12.00--16.00
Sugar and Cover, 10 oz.	12.00--15.00
Creamer, 6½ oz.	5.00-- 8.00
Eagle Candle Holder	18.00--20.00
Lombardi Bowl, 4-toe	12.00--15.00
Candlestick 2-light, pr.	15.00--20.00
Punch Set, Feather design	55.00--75.00
Snack Set, 8-pc.	20.00--24.00
Bowl, ftd., 10½" ***(HOLIDAY pattern)***	15.00--20.00
Bowl, fruit, ftd., 9"	7.00-- 9.00
Beverage Tray, 12½ X 9¾"	10.00--15.00
Venetian Tray, 16½"	12.00--15.00
Celery and Relish Dish	10.00--14.00
Wedding Bowl and Cover, 8"	12.00--15.00
Wedding Bowl and Cover, 6½"	11.00--14.00
Candy Jar and Cover, ½ lb.	9.00--12.00
Salver, cake, ftd., 10"	12.00--15.00
Pheasant Bowl, 8"	12.00--15.00
Pheasant Candleholders	20.00--25.00
Powder Jar and Cover	12.00--15.00
Butterfly Cigarette Set	25.00--30.00
Bee Hive Jar and Cover	12.00--15.00
Compote, 6"	6.00-- 8.00
Vase, heavy bottom, 9"	7.00--10.00
Vase, 7"	6.00-- 9.00
Vase, cornucopia, 5"	7.00--10.00
Ash Tray	5.00-- 8.00
PETALWARE wall vase, 7"	20.00--25.00
NATIONAL candy bottom	5.00-- 7.00

See in Color Section

Jenkins

My favorite Jenkins' pieces have always been the plates,-"SEASIDE", "TWIN DOLPHIN", "FIELDCREST", and "JENKINS' BASKET". Maybe because I own all of them?

Now Demetra Ferguson of Sonora, Kentucky, tells me she has a Jenkins' BASKET plate in topaz with a label saying "Hand Made by John E. Kemple, Kenova, W. Va.". It has the slightest variation in the rows of dots.

Maybe Kemple Glass Company acquired the old mold after Jenkins folded.

JENKINS' SANDWICH PLATES page 208

Crystal, green, iridescent amber

"SEASIDE"	15.00--20.00
"TWIN DOLPHIN"	15.00--20.00
"JENKINS BASKET"	12.00--15.00
"FIELDCREST"	10.00--12.00

JENKINS' "HOB" page 209

Green

Butter and Cover	28.00--34.00
Bon Bon and Cover, 4½"	15.00--18.00
Sundae	4.00-- 6.00
Spoon	12.00--16.00
Cream	8.00--10.00
Sugar and Cover	10.00--14.00
Custard, hdld.	3.50-- 4.00
Nappy, hdld.	8.00--10.00
Pickle	8.00--10.00
Celery	9.00--11.00
Nappy, 4½"	4.00-- 5.00
Nappy, 6"	4.00-- 6.00
Nappy, 7"	8.00--10.00
Nappy, 8"	12.00--16.00
Plate, salad	4.00-- 6.00
Wine	9.00--12.00
Cup and Saucer	10.00--12.00
Sugar, berry	8.00--10.00
Cream, berry	8.00--10.00
Goblet	9.00--12.00
Tumbler	8.00--10.00
Jug	30.00--40.00
Vase	10.00--14.00
Jelly and Cover, ftd.	18.00--24.00

VASES

No. 980 Vase, 80 oz.	12.00--16.00
No. 981 Vase, 80 oz.	12.00--16.00
No. 982 Vase, 80 oz.	12.00--16.00
No. 983 Vase, 80 oz.	12.00--16.00
No. 984 Vase, 80 oz.	12.00--16.00
No. 985 Vase, 80 oz.	12.00--16.00

MISCELLANEOUS

No. 121 Ash Tray, 4½"	8.00--10.00
No. 477 Tray, relish, 6½"	7.00-- 9.00
No. 470 Tray, sandwich, plain	12.00--15.00
No. 471 Tray, sandwich, optic	12.00--15.00
No. 181 Reamer Set, 4 oz.	20.00--25.00

WATER AND BEVERAGE SETS

Crystal and green

No. 980 Jug w/Cover 80 oz.	20.00--25.00
No. 980 Tumbler, 9 oz.	4.00-- 6.00
No. 980 Ice Tea, 12 oz.	5.00-- 7.00
No. 981 Jug w/Cover, 80 oz.	20.00--25.00
No. 981 Tumbler, 9 oz.	4.00-- 6.00

No. 981 Ice Tea, 12 oz. 5.00-- 7.00
No. 982 Jug w/Cover, 80 oz. 20.00--25.00
No. 982 Tumbler, 9 oz. 4.00-- 6.00
No. 982 Ice Tea, 12 oz. 5.00-- 7.00
No. 983 Jug w/ Cover, 80 oz. 20.00--25.00
No. 983 Tumbler, 9 oz. 4.00-- 6.00
No. 983 Ice Tea, 23 oz. 5.00-- 7.00
No. 984 Jug w/Cover, 80 oz. 20.00--25.00
No. 984 Tumbler, 9 oz. 4.00-- 6.00
No. 984 Ice Tea, 12 oz. 5.00-- 7.00
No. 985 Jug w/Cover, 80 oz. 20.00--25.00
No. 985 Tumbler, 9 oz. 4.00-- 6.00
No. 985 Ice Tea, 12 oz. 5.00-- 7.00

FISH GLOBES

No. 1 5 qt., ½ gal., 1 gal., 2 gal. 9.00--18.00
No. 2 pt., 7 pt., 6 qt., ½ gal., 1 gal., 2 gal., 3 gal., 6 gal. 9.00--25.00
No. 3 2 gal., plain, 2 gal., optic, 1 gal., plain, 1 gal., optic, 1 gal., plain 9.00--18.00
No. 4 1 qt., 3 pt., ½ gal., 1 gal., 2 gal., 3 gal., 9.00--20.00
No. 5 2 gal. 15.00--18.00
No. 6 2 gal. base 5.00-- 7.00
No. 7 3 gal. 15.00--20.00
No. 8 2 gal. 12.00--16.00
No. 9 1 qt., ½ gal., 1 gal., 2 gal. 12.00--16.00
No. 10 1 qt., ½ gal., 1 gal., 2 gal. 15.00--20.00
No. 11 2 gal. 15.00--20.00

JUGS OR PITCHERS

No. 10 1 quart 8.00--10.00
No. 66 w/Cover, ½ gal. 12.00--15.00
No. 8½ 3 pt. 12.00--15.00
No. 70 w/ice lip, ½ gal. 16.00--18.00
No. 70 regular, ½ gal. 14.00--16.00
No. 72 w/Cover, ½ gal. 20.00--25.00
No. 90 w/Cover, 3 pints and ½ gal. 20.00--25.00
No. 80 w/Cover, ½ gal. 18.00--22.00
No. 77 w/Cover, ½ gal. 18.00--22.00
No. 85 w/Cover, 10 oz. 1 pt., 3 pt., ½ gal. 15.00--25.00
No. 96 3 pt. 12.00--15.00
No. 111 ½ gallon 12.00--16.00
No. 800 w/Cover, 10 oz., 1 pt., 1 qt., 3 pt., ½ gal., 3 qts. 15.00--20.00
No. 950 w/Cover, 1 pt., ½ gal. 20.00--25.00
No. 975 3 pt. 8.00--10.00

OCEAN WAVE page 210

Tumbler, water, 9 oz. 6.00-- 8.00
Jug, 3 pint 24.00--28.00
Plate, tall, ftd., 5" 7.00-- 9.00
Plate, low, ftd., 5" 7.00-- 9.00
Cup 5.00-- 7.00
Saucer 2.00-- 3.00
Plate, service, 11" 8.00--10.00
Plate, salad, 8" 4.00-- 6.00
Sugar 8.00--10.00
Cream 8.00--10.00
Nappy, berry, 4" 3.00-- 4.00
Dish, berry, 8" 10.00--14.00
Dish, berry, 8" 10.00--14.00
Sundae, tall 5.00-- 7.00
Sundae, tall 5.00-- 7.00
Sundae, low 4.00-- 6.00
Sundae, low 4.00-- 6.00
Soda, ftd., or Malted Milk, 12 oz. 12.00--14.00
Soda, ftd., or Lemonade, 10 oz. 10.00--12.00
Soda, ftd., or Beverage Tumbler, 6 oz. 8.00--10.00
Soda, ftd., or Beverage Tumbler, 8 oz. 8.00--10.00
Parfait, 5 oz. 10.00--12.00
Tumbler, 6 oz. Beverage or Water 6.00-- 8.00

"ARCADIA LACE" page 211

Crystal (No. 202)

Spoon 10.00--14.00
Sugar and Cover 8.00--12.00
Cream 6.00-- 8.00
Butter and Cover 20.00--25.00
Nappy, straight, 8" 7.00-- 9.00
Nappy, flared, 8" 7.00-- 9.00
Nappy, flared, 4" 3.00-- 4.00
Nappy, cupped, 8" 7.00--10.00
Plate, 6" 3.00-- 4.00
Nappy, striaght, 4" 3.00-- 4.00
Plate, 11" 7.00-- 9.00
Nappy, cupped 4" 3.00-- 4.00
Jelly and Cover, ftd. 12.00--16.00
Jelly, open, ftd. 8.00--10.00
Wine 7.00-- 9.00
Celery, tall 10.00--15.00
Ice Tea, 12 oz. 6.00-- 8.00
Tumbler, table 4.00-- 6.00
Jug, 3 pint 14.00--20.00
Vase, flared, 10" 12.00--16.00
Vase, flared, 6" 7.00-- 9.00
Vase, cupped, 6" 7.00-- 9.00
Nappy, hdld., 5" 5.00-- 8.00
Pickle, 8" 5.00-- 8.00
Bon Bon and Cover 10.00--14.00
Vase, cupped, 10" 12.00--16.00

"DAHLIA" page 212

Crystal, green (No. 286)

Butter and Cover 35.00--45.00
Sugar 8.00--10.00

Cream	8.00--10.00
Spoon	14.00--18.00
Jelly, "A", ftd.	12.00--16.00
Tumbler	10.00--12.00
Jug	35.00--50.00
Vase, 6", 10"	15.00--25.00
Jelly, "B", ftd.	12.00--16.00
Jelly, "C", ftd.	12.00--16.00
Nappy, straight, 8"	16.00--20.00
Nappy, flrd., 8"	16.00--20.00
Nappy, cupped, 8"	16.00--20.00
Nappy, straight, 4"	5.00-- 8.00
Nappy, cupped, 4"	5.00-- 8.00
Nappy, flrd., 4"	5.00-- 8.00
Sundae, ftd., or Mayonnaise straight	9.00--12.00
Sundae, ftd., or Mayonnaise, flrd.	9.00--12.00
Bowl, mayonnaise	8.00--10.00
Plate, mayonnaise	6.00-- 8.00

"KOKOMO" page 213

This is a crystal pattern except for pieces in 'doped ware' which I've seen. (No. 400)

Cream	4.00-- 7.00
Sugar, covered	8.00--11.00
Tray, pickle, 8"	4.00-- 6.00
Nappy, hdld., 5"	3.00-- 5.00
Tumbler, table	4.00-- 5.00
Spoon Holder	8.00--10.00
Butter, covered	15.00--18.00
Bowl, jelly, ftd., 5"	5.00-- 7.00
Jug, 3 pt.	12.00--18.00
Bowl, jelly, and Cover, ftd., 5"	10.00--14.00
Nappy, deep, 4½"	3.00-- 4.00
Casserole and Cover, 4½"	10.00--14.00
Nappy, 5"	3.00-- 4.00
Nappy, 8"	7.00-- 9.00
Nappy, covered, deep, 4½"	6.00-- 9.00

"LATTICE"

In crystal and 'doped ware'

Jug and Cover, ½ gal.	12.00--15.00
Tumbler, blown	3.00-- 4.00
Jelly, ftd.	3.00-- 4.00
Jelly and Cover, ftd.	6.00-- 9.00
Casserole and Cover	7.00--10.00
Jug, ½ gal.	10.00--12.00
Spoon Holder	6.00-- 8.00
Sugar and Cover	6.00-- 9.00
Butter and Cover	15.00--18.00
Cream	4.00-- 6.00
Nappy, 8"	7.00-- 9.00
Nappy, 4"	2.00-- 3.00
Nappy, 5"	3.00-- 4.00
Nappy, hdld.	4.00-- 6.00
Pickle	4.00-- 6.00

MISCELLANEOUS page 214

No. 10 Mug, childs	20.00--25.00
No. 42 Cup, sherbet	1.50-- 2.00
No. 96 Cup, sherbet	20.00--25.00
No. 807 Mug, childs	20.00--25.00
No. 40 Cup	12.00--15.00
No. 925 STRAWBERRY Design, Can	45.00--60.00
No. 910 Cup	3.00-- 4.00
No. 150 Mug, 4 oz.	6.00-- 9.00
No. 209 Mug	6.00-- 9.00
No. 475 Mug, childs	20.00--25.00
No. 360 Nappy and Cover, 4½"	8.00--12.00
No. 199 Cover, cake, 9"	18.00--22.00
No. 460 Dish, swan, 12 oz.	18.00--24.00
No. 180 Marmalade Jar w/Cover, 9 oz..	4.00-- 6.00
No. 215 Tray, candy, 7¼" X 5½" X 7/8"	8.00--12.00
No. 209 Tray, candy, oblong, 8" X 5" X 2"	10.00--15.00
No. 211 Tray, candy, 7¼" X 5½" X 7/8"	8.00--12.00
No. 175 Sundae, crimped, 6½"	6.00-- 9.00
No. 320 Comport, straight, 11 oz.	6.00-- 9.00
No. 320 Comport, flrd., 11 oz.	6.00-- 9.00
No. 320 Tray, candy, ftd., 7½"	7.00--10.00
No. 66 Jar, 14 oz.	15.00--20.00
No. 77 Jar, 18 oz.	18.00--24.00
No. 290 Jar, 1 qt.	12.00--16.00
No. 355 Jar, 1 qt.	14.00--20.00
No. 356 Jar, 2 qt.	18.00--24.00
Percolator Top, large	2.50-- 3.50
Percolator Top, small	2.00-- 3.00
No. 44 Jars, 2 gal. w/hinged aluminum Cover	15.00--30.00
No. 39 Bowl, mixing, 9"	9.00--11.00
No. 38 Bowl, mixing, 8"	8.00--10.00
No. 1 Dipper, pickle, 9½" long	12.00--16.00
No. 88 Jar, tilted drum, 2 gal. w/hinged aluminum Cover	8.00--12.00
No. 210 Jar,vertical drum, 2 gal. w/hinged aluminum Cover	7.00--10.00
No. 211 Jar, 1 gal. w/hinged aluminum Cover	6.00-- 9.00
No. 85 Jar, 2 gal. w/hinged aluminum Cover	10.00--14.00
No. 86 Jar, 1½ gal. w/hinged aluminum Cover	12.00--16.00

ANTENNAE INSULATORS

No. 1, 3½" X 1-1/8"	4.00-- 6.00
No. 3, 4¼" X 1½"	4.00-- 6.00
No. 9, 3-1/8" X 1-3/8"	4.00-- 6.00
No. 4, 3-1/8" X 1-1/8"	4.00-- 6.00

FUNNELS

No. 6 Plain, qt. size	10.00--14.00
No. 12 Plain, pt. size	10.00--14.00
No. 13 Optic, qt. size	10.00--15.00
No. 14 Optic, pt. size	10.00--15.00
No. 116 Chick Fountain & Base	20.00--25.00

LEMON AND ORANGE REAMERS

No. 160 Lemon	8.00--10.00
No. 170 Lemon w/seed catcher	10.00--14.00
No. 180 Orange	12.00--16.00

"YO-YO" page 215

(No. 560)

Sugar, covered	8.00--12.00
Butter, covered	15.00--25.00
Cream	6.00-- 9.00
Spoon Holder	9.00--12.00
Jelly, ftd., 4½"	10.00--14.00
Nappy, 7½"	6.00--10.00
Nappy, 4½"	2.00-- 5.00
Jug, covered, 1 pt.	15.00--25.00
Jug, covered, qt.	15.00--25.00
Jug, covered, ½ gal.	20.00--30.00

WATER JUGS

No. 55 Ice, ½ gal.	20.00--25.00
No. 55 Regular, ½ gal.	20.00--25.00
No. 55 w/reamer Cover, ½ gal.	25.00--30.00
No. 220 Jug, ½ gal.	16.00--22.00
No. 560 1 pt., 1 qt., ½ gal.	15.00--25.00
No. 570 1 pt., 1 qt., ½ gal.	15.00--30.00

"HUCK FINN"

(No. 921)

Sugar and Cover	9.00--12.00
Butter and Cover	15.00--18.00
Nappy, 8", 4"	3.00-- 7.00
Cream	5.00-- 7.00
Spoon Holder	8.00--12.00
Jug, 1 qt., 1 pt.	10.00--14.00

"YOO-HOO"

(No. 570)

Sugar, covered	8.00--12.00
Butter, covered	15.00--25.00
Cream	6.00-- 9.00
Spoon Holder	9.00--12.00
Jelly and Cover ftd., 4"	15.00--25.00
Nappy, 7½"	6.00--10.00
Nappy, 4½"	2.00-- 5.00
Jug and Cover, 1 pt.	15.00--25.00
Jug and Cover, 1 qt.	15.00--25.00
Jug and Cover, ½ gal.	25.00--30.00

FLOWER VASES

You may find these vases in 'doped - ware'

No. 330 Plain Vase w/bird design, 10½"	12.00--16.00
No. 331 Stippled Vase w/bird design, 10½"	12.00--16.00
No. 310 Vase, 7-1/8"	5.00-- 8.00
No. 311 Vase, 7-3/8"	5.00-- 8.00
No. 312 Vase, 7-1/8"	8.00--11.00
No. 313 Vase, 7½"	7.00--10.00

LAMPS

No. 330 Lamp w/bird design	30.00--40.00
No. 370 Lamp	25.00--30.00
No. 312 Lamp	30.00--40.00

Kopp

Do you have time for a little side-trip?

As you know from Book 2, Kopp Glass makes most of our traffic lights in this country, as well as for the rest of the world. While Annette and I were visiting the company, we were each given an ashtray. Mine was red, made of the exact glass used in all the red-lights you stop for. Hers was blue. the glass used for green lights.

"Green lights!" we cried in disbelief. "This blue is blue." Our hosts played the trick they loved best. Lighting a match, they held it behind the blue ashtray. Lo and behold. our familiar go-green!

They explained the phenomenon. "Tax-payers' dollars can only afford so much light. It takes a lot of light to illuminate green glass. We had to come up with a quality of glass that would respond to low-intensity illumination with a brilliant green. We did it. But the particular glass material looks as blue as blue, in everyday light."

So, the next time you breeze through one—remember the blue in it.

LAMP page 216

No. 1210 Ruby, emerald or topaz	200.00--300.00

LIGHT FIXTURE

No. 920-N	20.00--30.00
No. 909 10"X 4"	12.00--18.00
No. 910 16"X 6"	15.00--20.00

GOBLET

No. 1929 patent	9.00--12.00

"MODERNISTIC" GLASS VASES

The dainty pink #401 vase, marked -KG- in the bottom was given to me by George and Janet Gerloch, Warren MI.

No. 400, 8½"	12.00--16.00
No. 401, 6½"	10.00--14.00

MODERNISTIC PORTABLE LAMP

No. 1225, 18" high	75.00-100.00

Lancaster

One of the easiest things collectors can do is get Hocking's "LACE EDGE" confused with the Lace Edged pattern by Lancaster we call "OPEN WORKS". It helps to remember that most Lancaster pieces have a ground or polished off bottom rim and are hand-pressed, whereas Hocking's pieces are machine-made.

Most all Lancaster pieces were made at one time in colors other than the ones listed on the catalog reprints. These I have noted, in italics, where possible in the listings that follow. But not every case is reported. That will take time.

Notice that on page 218 is Monongah glassware. These pages were originally printed with LANCASTER GLASS COMPANY across the top; our printer had to cut this off to make it fit in the layout. As explained in the Book 2 Monongah history, Lancaster handled the sales and distribution of Monongah glassware at about this time, 1929-1930.

The Lancaster reprints are being shown again this year at the end of this chapter.

CANDY JAR AND COVER page 217

No. 83	15.00--20.00

"JANE" page 218

Pink, green, topaz

No. 1500/2 Bowl, 8"	9.00--11.00
No. 71 D/272 Mayonnaise Set: 3 pc.	12.00--16.00
No. 82 B Bowl, 12"	11.00--14.00
No. 351 Comport, high ftd.	10.00--13.00
No. 88 Sandwich Tray, center hdld., 10½"	11.00--14.00
No. 85 Salver, 10"	11.00--14.00
No. 88 Cheese and Cracker, 2 pc.	10.00--13.00
No. 85D Bowl, salver, ftd., 10"	12.00--16.00
No. 652 Sugar and Cream	10.00--15.00
No. 854 Candlestick, low	12.00--14.00
No. 945 Relish and Cover	12.00--16.00
No. 83 Candy Jar and Cover	14.00--18.00

"YUCCA"

In Ivory, green amber, and Orchid.

No. 1 Dresser Set: 4 pc.	45.00--55.00
Powder Box w/Cover	12.00--15.00
Cologne Bottles, and Stopper, ea	12.00--16.00
Tray, rnd.	7.00-- 9.00
No. 788 Candy w/Cover, ½ lb.	15.00--20.00
No. 941 Candy Box and Cover	15.00--20.00

MONONGAH STEMWARE

Optic, green or amber trimmed

Goblet	11.00--14.00
Saucer or High Sherbet	10.00--12.00
Sherbet, low	9.00--11.00

Cocktail	10.00--12.00
Wine	11.00--14.00
No. 6107	
Goblet	11.00--14.00
Saucer or High Sherbet	10.00--12.00
Sherbet, low	8.00--10.00
Cocktail	10.00--12.00
Wine	11.00--14.00
Parfait	10.00--12.00
No. 6108	
Goblet	11.00--14.00
Saucer or High Sherbet	10.00--12.00
Sherbet, low	8.00--10.00
Cocktail	10.00--12.00
Wine	11.00--14.00
No. 6120	
Spiral Optic, green trimmed	
Goblet	11.00--14.00
Saucer or High Sherbet	10.00--12.00
Sherbet, low	8.00--10.00
Cocktail	10.00--12.00
Wine	11.00--14.00
Parfait	10.00--12.00

SPIRAL OPTIC

Rose or green trimmed

Goblet	11.00--14.00
Saucer or High Sherbet	10.00--12.00
Sherbet, low	8.00--10.00
Cocktail	10.00--12.00
Wine	11.00--14.00
Parfait	11.00--14.00
Whiskey	7.00-- 9.00
Seltzer	4.00-- 5.00
Table	5.00-- 6.00
Ice Tea	7.00-- 9.00
Bowl, finger, ftd.	3.00-- 4.00
No. 20 Jug, ftd.	25.00--35.00
No. 10304 Plate, (Diamond Optic) 7½"	4.00-- 5.00

OPENWORK page 219

Pink and green

Cheese Comport	5.00-- 8.00
Comport, rnd, 6½"	6.00-- 9.00
Comport, "D", 7½"	6.00-- 9.00
Salver w/handle, 8"	7.00--10.00
Plate w/handle, 9"	7.00--10.00
Nappy, "B", 8"	6.00-- 8.00
Nappy, rnd., 7½"	6.00-- 9.00
Nappy w/handle, "D", 8"	8.00--11.00
Nappy w/handle, "B", 9½"	8.00--12.00
Nappy w/handle, "D", 10"	10.00--13.00
Plate w/handle, 10½"	10.00--13.00
Nappy, rnd., 8½"	8.00--11.00
Comport, "D", 11"	10.00--14.00
Salver, "A", 10"	10.00--14.00
Candy Jar	12.00--16.00
Bowl w/handle, "B", 12"	10.00--15.00
Plate w/handle, 14"	12.00--16.00
Mayonnaise Set: 3 pc.	12.00--16.00
Bowl w/handle, rnd., 11"	11.00--14.00
Salver, 12"	12.00--15.00
Sandwich Tray, center handle, 12"	10.00--14.00
Cheese and Cracker	9.00--11.00
Fruit, center handle, 11"	10.00--14.00
Candleholder, pr.	40.00--50.00

MISCELLANEOUS

Decoration 55 pink only

1907-B Nappy, 9"	9.00--13.00
1907 Nappy, rnd., 8"	9.00--13.00
1907 Plate, 10½"	10.00--12.00
1907-D Nappy, 10"	10.00--14.00

"WIG-WAG"

1716/1 Nappy, 9"	8.00--11.00
1716/3 Tray, hdld, 10½"	8.00--11.00
1716/6 Bowl, oval, 10"	9.00--12.00
1716/4 Plate, 10½"	8.00--11.00

"DARLENE"

Decoration 55 pink only

1675/1 Bowl, ftd., 9"	6.00-- 9.00
1675/3 Bowl, 9¾"	6.00-- 9.00
615 Candleholder	6.00-- 8.00
607 Powder Box or Candy Box	10.00--16.00
1923/1 Nappy, hdld, 9"	6.00-- 9.00
612 "D" Bowl, 11"	10.00--15.00
923 Mayonnaise Set: 3 pc.	12.00--16.00
612 Plate, 12"	8.00--11.00
605 Comport, 10"	10.00--13.00
602 Plate, sandwich, center hld., 11"	8.00--12.00
620 Salver, ftd., 11"	10.00--14.00
1923/4 Plate, hdld, 10½"	7.00--10.00

"CAROL" page 220

869/1 Bowl, Rose, 9"	8.00--11.00
869/8 Bowl, Rose, 10¼"	8.00--11.00
868/1 Bowl, 8¼"	8.00--11.00
868/8 Bowl, 10½"	8.00--11.00

"DART"

867/1 Bowl, salad, 9"	8.00--11.00
867/4 Plate, sandwich, 11"	8.00--11.00
378/9 Bowl, 12"	12.00--16.00

"MILLY"

886-141 Console Set: 3 pc.	15.00--20.00

"AMY"

378/1 Bowl, 13½"	12.00--16.00
382/1 Bowl, Rose, 11"	10.00--12.00
382/7 Plate, cupped, 11½"	10.00--12.00

"BETH"

R1830/1 Bowl, legs, 6"	5.00-- 8.00
R1830/7 Plate, cupped, toed, 8"	5.00-- 8.00
R1660/B Plate, toed, 8½"	5.00-- 8.00
1660/D Bowl, 7"	5.00-- 8.00
T898/4 Tray, hdld., 10"	8.00--10.00
R1786/4 Plate, hdld., 11"	8.00--11.00
T1894/7 Plate, cupped, 7"	6.00-- 8.00

"JO"

T1894/1 Bowl, 6"	3.50-- 5.00
T898/1 Bowl, 8"	6.00-- 8.00
T1894/4 Plate,7½"	4.00-- 6.00
R1786/1 Bowl, 9"	9.00--12.00

"AMY"

T382/4 Plate, 11½"	6.00-- 9.00
T3821/1 Bowl, 11"	8.00--11.00
T382/7 Plate. cupped, 11"	8.00--11.00

MISCELLANEOUS

R381/1 Bowl, salad, 11"	8.00--12.00
T381/4 Plate, sandwich, 11¼"	8.00--12.00
T899/4 Tray, hdld., 10"	6.00-- 9.00
R1660/D Nappy, ftd.	5.00-- 7.00
T1831/6 Bowl, Rose, ftd., 6"	8.00--10.00
T1831/7 Tray, 10"	5.00-- 7.00
R1830/1 Bowl, 6"	4.00-- 6.00
R1831/3 Bowl, crimped, 9"	7.00--10.00
T378/1 Bowl, 13½"	8.00--12.00
T378/3 Bowl, crimped, 13"	8.00--12.00
T1377/9 Bowl, 6¼"	3.50-- 5.00
T378/12 Vase, 9" X 6¼"	7.00--10.00

"BANGLE"

3-ftd., rose color

R/1 Bowl, cupped, 9½"	14.00--18.00
R/1 Bowl, flrd., 10½"	14.00--18.00
R/7 Bowl, shallow, 10½	14.00--18.00

"CAROLYN" page 221

Topaz or rose

381/1 Bowl, salad	6.00-- 9.00
381/7 Tray, 11½"	5.00-- 8.00
381/4 Plate, sandwich, 11½"	6.00-- 9.00

"LANDRUM"

767/6 Bowl, Rose, 6"	8.00--10.00
767/1 Bowl, ftd., 8¼"	10.00--14.00
767/3 Bowl, crimped, ftd., 9"	10.00--13.00
767/7 Tray, ftd., 10"	8.00--12.00
765/1 Bowl, salad, 9"	8.00--11.00
765/4 Tray, sandwich, hdld., 11"	8.00--11.00

MISCELLANEOUS

901/8 Bowl, hdld, 9¼" (black decoration 78)	7.00--10.00
901/4 Tray, hdld., 9½" (black decoration 78)	7.00--10.00

"LANDRUM"

T767/1 Bowl, ftd., 8¼"	10.00--15.00
R765/1 Bowl, salad, hdld., 9"	8.00--11.00
T767/3 Bowl, crimped, ftd., 9"	10.00--15.00
R767/4 Tray, ftd., 10"	8.00--12.00
R767/6 Bowl, Rose, ftd,, 6"	8.00--10.00
T765/4 Tray, sandwich, 11"	8.00--12.00

"JODY"

353/1 Nappy, 7"	5.00-- 7.00
353/3 Nappy, 7"	5.00-- 7.00
353/4 Nappy, 7"	5.00-- 7.00
353/5 Nappy, 6"	4.00-- 6.00
355/3 Candleholder, Dec. 27	6.00-- 9.00
354/3 Bowl, 12", Dec. 27	10.00--14.00
354/1 Bowl, 12", Dec. 25	10.00--14.00
354/4 Bowl, 11½", Dec. 26	10.00--14.00
354/5 Bowl, 10", Dec. 25	9.00--12.00

"LANA"

Pink satin finish

731/1 Bowl, hdld., 9"	7.00--10.00
731/3 Tray, hdld., 10"	7.00--10.00
731/6 Bowl, oval, hdld, 10"	7.00--10.00
731/4 Plate, hdld., 10½"	6.00-- 9.00
735 Candlestick, low, pr.	10.00--14.00
737 Sugar and Cream Set	10.00--14.00
734 B Bowl, 12"	9.00--12.00
733 Tray, sandwich, center handled 11"	9.00--12.00
734 Plate, 14"	9.00--12.00

"FRANJAY" page 222

All black

901/8 Bowl, 9¼", Dec. 104D	8.00--10.00
901/4 Tray, 9½", Dec. 104D	8.00--10.00
901/8 Bowl, 9¼", Dec. 78	8.00--10.00
901/4 Tray, 9½", Dec. 78	8.00--10.00

BLACK VASES

53 Vase, 9", Dec. 104D	12.00--15.00
H21 Vase, 10", Dec. 80A	10.00--13.00
437 Vase, 10", Dec. 104D	12.00--15.00
213 Vase, 12", Dec. 80B	14.00--18.00
117 Vase, 12", Dec. 78	16.00--20.00
117 Vase, 12", Dec. 100A	16.00--20.00

"CIRCUS"

All black

901/8 Bowl, 9¼", Dec. 80A	7.00-- 9.00
901/4 Tray, 9½", Dec. 80A	7.00-- 9.00
901/8 Bowl, 9¼", Dec. 80B	7.00-- 9.00
901/4 Tray, 9½", Dec. 80B	7.00-- 9.00

MISCELLANEOUS

No. 533 Black Shaker Set: 4 pc. silver decoration salt, pepper, flour, sugar	16.00--20.00
No. 174 Cookie Jar Set: decoration 125-A, B, C	30.00--36.00

JUBILEE page 223

Plate, 8¾"	12.00--15.00
Plate, salad, 7"	8.00--12.00
Cup	8.00--10.00
Saucer	3.00-- 4.00
Goblet	16.00--20.00
Sugar	8.00--10.00
Creamer	8.00--10.00
Tray, sandwich, cake, 11"	14.00--20.00
Tray, sandwich or salad 13½"	20.00--25.00
Bowl, hdld., fruit, 9"	12.00--15.00
Mayonnaise Set: 3 pc.	30.00--35.00
Tray, sandwich, center hdld.	20.00--25.00
Cheese and Cracker	35.00--45.00

"PATRICK" page 224

Topaz or rose

Kathe Karstens, Portland OR, writes she found a 19-pc. luncheon set in pink in the original packing box. It was shipped via Railway Express dated 9-19-31. Now we know the likely date that this pattern was made.

1955 Goblet, luncheon	10.00--14.00
1952 Sherbet	6.00-- 8.00
896 Plate, sherbet, 7"	3.00-- 5.00
1956 Juice, fruit	9.00--12.00
1953 Cocktail	10.00--14.00
795/96 Cup and Saucer	6.00-- 9.00
8967 Plate, salad, 7½"	3.00-- 5.00
898 Plate, luncheon, 8¼"	6.00-- 8.00
895/1 Bowl, fruit, hdld., 9"	12.00--15.00
889/890/131 Mayonnaise Set: 3 pc.	16.00--20.0
895/4 Plate, sandwich, hdld., 11"	10.00--12.0
879 Sugar	7.00-- 9.0
879 Cream	7.00-- 9.0
5205 Candy Bowl and Cover	20.00--25.0
885 Tray, sandwich, center hdld., 11"	11.00--15.0
833 Candlestick, pr.	12.00--14.0
886/11 Bowl, 11½"	11.00--14.0
882/888 Cheese and Cracker Set: 2 pc.	15.00--25.0

DISPLAY STAND

No. 450/11 2 pc. Crystal Bowl, 19" w/black Base	25.00--35.0

OIL LAMP

Rose glass base, green and rose shades. The oil lamp bottom right page 224, Boo II is the pink one in the color section o Book II.

No. 686-F	45.00--60.0

1933'S LAMP page 22

No. 287 Lamp	25.00--35.0

TUBULAR PEDESTAL AQUARIUM

Crystal

Ht., 30", Bowl, dia., 9½" Base, dia., 7" Aquarium	35.00--45.0

"SPHINX"

Design found on green and yellow Lan caster blanks

Bowl, ruffled, 9"	14.00--18.0
Bowl, flrd., 12"	14.00--18.0
Vase, 12"	14.00--18.0

"LOOKING GLASS LINE"

Tumbler, ftd., 12 oz.	6.00-- 8.0
Tumbler, ftd., 10 oz.	5.00-- 7.0
Tumbler, ftd., 6 oz.	5.00-- 7.0
Tumbler, ice tea, 12 oz.	5.00-- 8.0
Tumbler, 9 oz.	4.00-- 6.0
Tumbler, 6 oz.	3.00-- 4.0
Goblet	7.00-- 9.0
Parfait	7.00-- 9.0
Oil	16.00--20.0
Sherbet	3.00-- 4.0

"LOOKING GLASS LINE" from 1933 catalog

Banana Split	4.00-- 6.00
Salt	5.00-- 7.00
Pepper	5.00-- 7.00
Sugar	6.00-- 8.00
Cream	6.00-- 8.00

CONSOLE BOWLS

86/952 Console Set, Dec. 03	35.00--50.00
86/952 Console Set, Dec. 01	35.00--50.00
86/952 Console Set, Dec. 54	35.00--50.00
86/950 Console Set, Dec. 52	35.00--50.00

LAMPS

291 Lamp, Dec. 17-C	20.00--30.00
291 Lamp, Dec. 18-R	20.00--30.00
291 Lamp, Dec. 20-A	20.00--30.00
291 Lamp, Dec. 19-G	20.00--30.00

"IVY"

891/1 Bowl, legged, 6"	5.00-- 8.00
891/3 Bowl, crimped, 6"	6.00-- 8.00
891/4 Tray, legged, 8"	7.00-- 9.00
891/7 Plate, cupped, 8"	7.00-- 9.00
892/4 Tray, 14", Dec. 26	10.00--12.00
892/7 Tray, legged, 13", Dec. 25	8.00--10.00
892/1 Bowl, leg'd, 12", Dec. 25	10.00--14.00
892/3 Bowl, crmp'd, 12", Dec 26	11.00--15.00
892/5 Bowl, Rose, 9½"	12.00--16.00

"PANSY"

1831/1 Bowl, legged, 8¼", Dec. 31-A	9.00--11.00
1675/7 Tray, ftd., 9½" Dec. 31-A	8.00--10.00
1832/1 Bowl, legged, 8¼", Dec. 25-A	9.00--11.00
1676/7 Tray, ftd., 9½", Dec. 25-A	8.00--10.00
1831/3 Bowl, legged, 9", Dec. 31-A	9.00--11.00
1675/5 Bowl, ftd., Dec. 31-A	8.00--10.00
1832/3 Bowl, legged, 9", Dec. 25-A	10.00--13.00
1676/5 Bowl, ftd., 6½", Dec. 25-A	6.00-- 8.00
1831/7 Tray, legged, 10", Dec. 31-A	10.00--13.00
1675/1 Bowl, ftd., 9", Dec. 25-A	10.00--13.00
1832/7 Tray, legged, 10", Dec. 25-A	9.00--11.00
1676/1 Bowl, ftd., 9", Dec. 25-A	10.00--14.00

No. 86/952. Console Set.
Dec. 03

No. 86/952. Console Set.
Dec. 01

No. 86/952. Console Set.
Dec. 54

No. 86/950. Console Set.
Dec. [illegible]

CONSOLE SETS from 1933 catalog

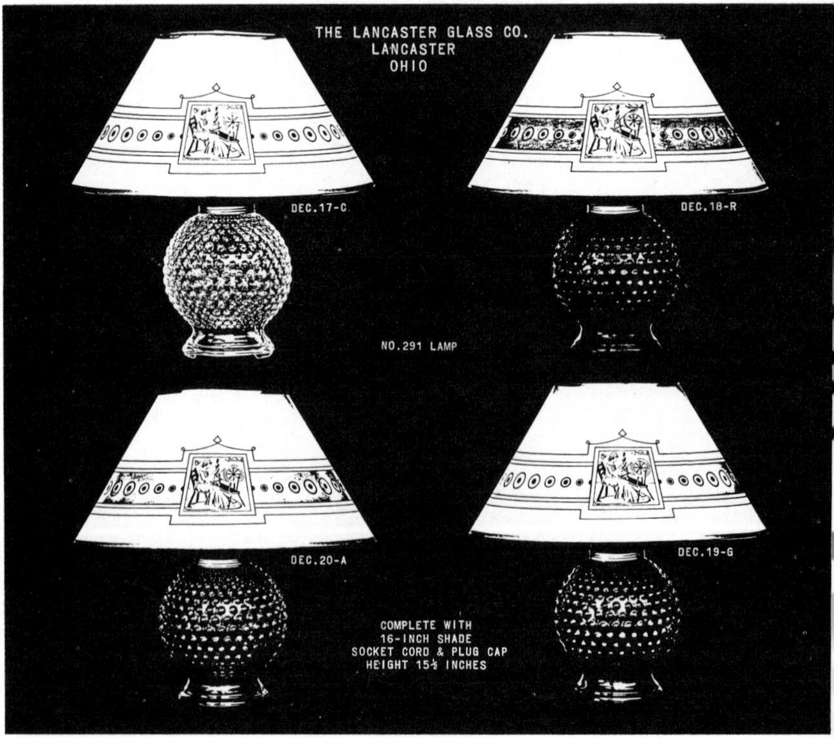

THE LANCASTER GLASS CO.
LANCASTER
OHIO

DEC.17-C

DEC.18-R

NO.291 LAMP

DEC.20-A

DEC.19-G

COMPLETE WITH
16-INCH SHADE
SOCKET CORD & PLUG CAP
HEIGHT 15½ INCHES

"LAMPS" from 1933 catalog

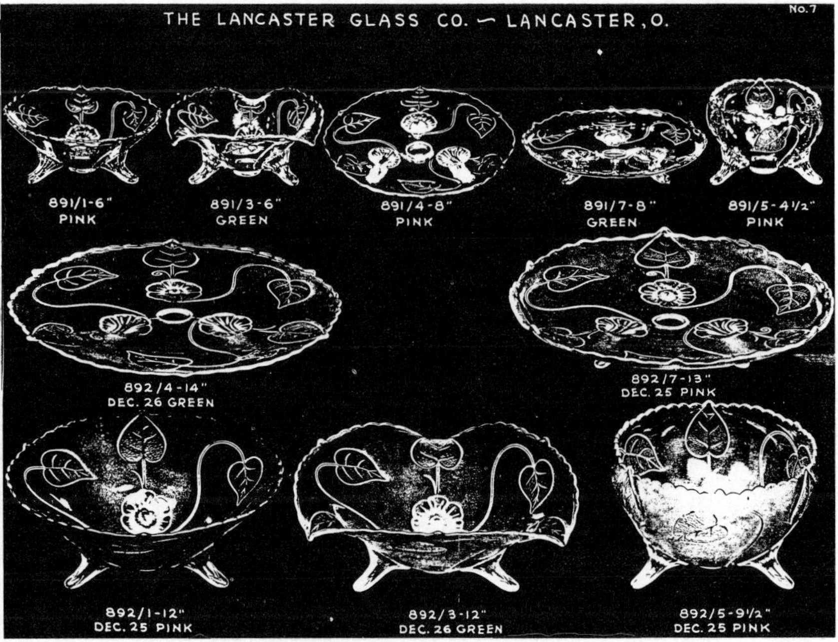

THE LANCASTER GLASS CO. — LANCASTER, O.

No. 7

891/1-6" PINK	891/3-6" GREEN	891/4-8" PINK	891/7-8" GREEN	891/5-4½" PINK

892/4-14" DEC. 26 GREEN	892/7-13" DEC. 25 PINK

892/1-12" DEC. 25 PINK	892/3-12" DEC. 26 GREEN	892/5-9½" DEC. 25 PINK

"IVY" from 1933 catalog

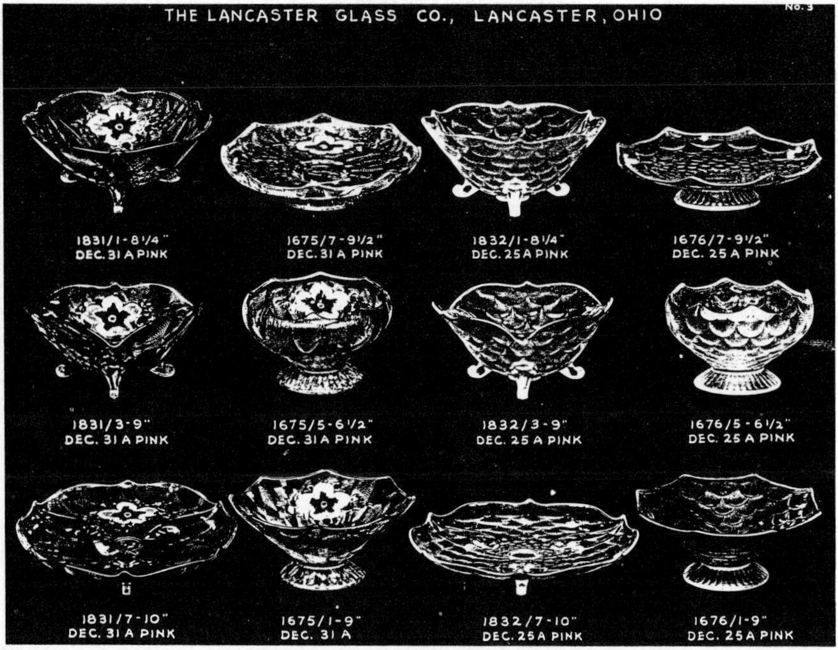

THE LANCASTER GLASS CO., LANCASTER, OHIO

No. 3

1831/1-8¼" DEC. 31 A PINK	1675/7-9½" DEC. 31 A PINK	1832/1-8¼" DEC. 25 A PINK	1676/7-9½" DEC. 25 A PINK
1831/3-9" DEC. 31 A PINK	1675/5-6½" DEC. 31 A PINK	1832/3-9" DEC. 25 A PINK	1676/5-6½" DEC. 25 A PINK
1831/7-10" DEC. 31 A PINK	1675/1-9" DEC. 31 A	1832/7-10" DEC. 25 A PINK	1676/1-9" DEC. 25 A PINK

"PANSY' from 1933 catalog

Libbey

While researching for THE DECORATED TUMBLER book I had the chance to look into the Libbey archives, which of course I did, at long last. And I found nothing but crystal and a few plain colored tumblers. If anything else turns up in color you'll be the first to know!

The old Libbey tumblers are usually offered for sale for $4 to $6.

Most Libbey tumblers have the L on the bottom, as does the Ship tumbler in pink (page 121 THE DECORATED TUMBLER).

MOIRE, MORNING, FILIGREE	page 227
Jug	75.00-100.00
Tumbler	14.00--18.00
Bowl	40.00--50.00
Candy Jar	35.00--50.00
Decanter, small	25.00--35.00
Decanter, large	40.00--60.00
Candy Dish, ftd.	40.00--50.00
Cocktail Set	100.00-150.00

Liberty Works

If you remember, last time I wrote in these pages that surely some Egg Harborite would be writing in to enlighten us as to other pieces of this company's ware. So far, no new lines have been reported but several people have reported new color news.

EGG HARBOR has been found, for example, in black glass, including the center handle server; and AMERICAN PIONEER is being found in amber. AMERICAN PIONEER continues to be our big Liberty pattern; additional pieces illustrated last year are being repeated plus another reprint showing the shape of the 1 lb candy jar and cover and the 8 oz. goblet.

I also saw the drip plate this past year. They are 6¼" x 8" plates, round, with indentions that fit the bottom of the covered urns.

"DANNY" JUG — page 228

Tankard and Cover	20.00--30.00

"SUE" CHEESE DISH

Covered Cheese and Cracker Dish	20.00--30.00

"EGG HARBOR" LINE — page 229

Also made in black

Plate, 8"	5.00-- 8.00
Cup	4.00-- 6.00
Saucer	3.00-- 4.00
Nappy, fruit	4.00-- 6.00
Double Egg Cup	15.00--20.00
Sugar	7.00--10.00
Cream	7.00--10.00
Salt and Pepper	20.00--25.00
Server, center handle	18.00--22.00

"CRACKERJACK"

Ice Pail	18.00--24.00
Ice Tub	16.00--22.00
Cookie Jar and Cover	25.00--30.00

BAMBOO OPTIC AND WHIST SET — page 230

Plate	5.00-- 8.00
Cup	4.00-- 6.00
Saucer	2.00-- 3.00
Cream	7.00--10.00
Sugar	7.00--10.00
Sandwich Server	10.00--14.00
Sherbet	4.00-- 6.00
Goblet	8.00--12.00
Cheese and Cracker, covered	20.00--30.00

"JEAN"

Flower Pot	15.00--20.00

"TRUMAN"

Plate, square	6.00-- 9.00
Plate, round	6.00-- 9.00
Platter, hdld., 12"	9.00--12.00

"PAULA" — page 231

Console Set	25.00--45.00

"ROBIN"

Salad Set	25.00--50.00

"LAWRENCE"

Tumbler	9.00--12.00
Sherbet	6.00-- 8.00

"COLLINS"

Console Set	25.00--35.00

AMERICAN PIONEER

Be sure to view the additional pieces of American Pioneer in the Color Section of Book 2. A few pieces have been found in amber.

Printed here is a photo of extra pieces that didn't make it into Book 2.

See in Color Section

Plate, 8"	6.00-- 9.00
Plate 6"	4.00-- 6.00
Plate, sandwich, hdld., 11"	10.00--15.00
Cup	8.00--11.00
Saucer	3.00-- 5.00
Cream, 2¾", 3½"	10.00--14.00
Sugar, 2¾", 3½"	10.00--14.00
Sherbet, tall	12.00--18.00
Bowl, hdld., 5"	8.00--10.00
Bowl, hdld., 9"	12.00--16.00
Bowl w/Cover, hdld., 9"	60.00--90.00
Bowl w/Cover, 8¾"	60.00--90.00
Bowl, console, 10-3/8"	30.00--45.00
Tumbler, 4", 5"	22.00--28.00
Goblet, 8 oz., 6"	25.00--35.00
Goblet, wine, 3 oz., 4"	25.00--35.00
Urn, covered, 5"	100.00-140.00
Urn, covered, 7"	125.00-175.00
Drip Plate	35.00--45.00
Ice Pail, 6"	30.00--45.00
Candy Jar and Cover, 9-5/8", 1½ lb.	50.00--80.00
Candy Jar and Cover, 11", 1 lb.	50.00--80.00
Comport, Mayonnaise, 4½" tall, 6½" wide w/Ladle and Underplate	20.00--40.00
Comport, 3½" tall, 4" wide	10.00--20.00
Cheese and Cracker Set: 11"hdld., plate w/indention and shallow comport, 3½"	20.00--35.00
Vase, 7"	35.00--65.00
Ivy Ball Vase (pattern only on top half)	50.00--70.00
Lamp, 8½"	50.00--70.00
Lamp, ball, 5¼" high, 3 legged	60.00--80.00
Coaster, 3½"	10.00--15.00
Candlestick, 6-3/8" high, pr.	40.00--60.00
Dresser Set: 2 bottles, 4½", low jar and cover, 3½" on rnd. tray w/indentions, 7½"	65.00--80.00

AMERICAN PIONEER coaster, candy jar 11", tumbler, tall sherbet, mayonnaise or comport, bowl 9" and candlestick

Lotus

As we know, Lotus is a decorating company only, adding their own patterns to the fine glass blanks made by such other companies as Cambridge, Duncan, Fostoria, Heisey, Paden City, and other hand houses. The Lotus catalogs as reprinted in Book 2 have been a big help to the glass world, assigning to Lotus many familiar-looking lines we could not pin down elsewhere.

Remember that we can be sure only that the colored lines are old; decorations such as Grecian Gold and others have continued to be in the Lotus production up to the present time.

"MAE WEST"	page 233
Cheese and Cracker, 10"	20.00--25.00
Comport, 10"	25.00--30.00
Plate, cake, hdld., 10"	16.00--20.00
Comport, low, 5"	14.00--18.00
Candlestick, 9", pr.	25.00--35.00
Bowl and Base, 10"	20.00--30.00
Comport, tall, 7"	18.00--22.00

MARIE	
Goblet, 9 oz.	8.00--10.00
Sherbet, low, 5½ oz.	5.00-- 7.00
Sherbet, high, 5½ oz.	6.00-- 8.00
Parfait, 5 oz.	8.00--10.00
Cocktail, 3½ oz.	8.00--10.00
Wine, 3 oz.	8.00--10.00
Plate, 7½"	3.00-- 4.00
Jug, 4 pt.	18.00--24.00
Jug, 3 pt.	15.00--20.00
Decanter, 1 qt.	22.00--26.00
Ice Tea, ftd., 12 oz.	7.00-- 9.00
Tumbler, ftd., 9 oz.	6.00-- 8.00
Whiskey, ftd., 2½ oz.	7.00-- 9.00
Tumbler, 5 oz.	4.00-- 5.00
Tumbler, 9 oz.	4.00-- 6.00
Ice Tea, 11 oz.	5.00-- 8.00

"XENIA"	page 234
Salver, 10"	20.00--25.00
Tray, cake, hdld., 10"	20.00--25.00
Whip Cream Set: 3 pc.	25.00--30.00
Cheese and Cracker, 10"	25.00--30.00
Candy Box, w/Cover, 6"	25.00--30.00
Candlestick, 9¼", pr.	25.00--35.00
Bowl and Base, 10"	20.00--30.00
Bowl, ftd., 10"	15.00--20.00

BUTTERFLY	
71797 Comport	16.00--20.00
75797 Vase	35.00--45.00
80797 Candlestick, pr.	28.00--34.00
81797 Bowl, crimped	25.00--30.00
62797 Bowl, Rose	20.00--25.00
91797 Relish, covered	30.00--35.00
95797 Candlestick, pr.	15.00--20.00
74797 Bowl, console	25.00--30.00
98797 Cake, hdld.	15.00--20.00
73797 Bowl, console	25.00--35.00
98797 Plate, hdld.	16.00--20.00
97797 Cheese and Cracker	20.00--25.00
60797 Bowl, rolled edge	20.00--25.00
99797 Whipped Cream Set	25.00--30.00
88797 Bowl, hdld.	15.00--20.00

GENE CUTTING NO. 10

Tub w/Cover, lemon, 4½"	15.00--20.00
Bon Bon, hdld., 5¾"	4.00-- 6.00
Sugar, ftd.	5.00-- 8.00
Cream, ftd.	5.00-- 8.00
Cheese, hdld., 6½"	4.50-- 6.00
Mint, hdld., 6½"	4.00-- 6.00
Ice Tub, hdld., 4"	12.00--16.00
Mayonnaise, hdld., 5½"	8.00--10.00
Tray, cake, hdld., 10"	10.00--14.00
Cheese and Cracker, 10"	10.00--14.00
Basket, 4"	12.50--15.00
Basket, 5"	15.00--20.00
Comport, LF, 6½"	6.00-- 8.00
Candlestick, low, 3½", pr.	10.00--12.00
Bowl, RE, 10"	8.00--12.00
Canoe, 8½"	6.00-- 8.00
Basket, 6"	16.00--20.00

"PEARL"

Relish and Cover, 6½"	15.00--20.00
Sugar	5.00-- 8.00
Cream	5.00-- 8.00
Comport, low	8.00--12.00
Candy Jar w/Cover, 1 lb.	15.00--20.00
Cheese and Cracker, 10"	10.00--13.00
Candle, 3½", pr.	8.00-- 9.00
Bowl, RE, 9"	8.00--10.00
Salver, 10"	10.00--14.00
Tray, cake, hdld., 10½"	9.00--12.00
Candlestick, 5"	10.00-12.00
Bowl, RE, 12"	11.00--14.00
Comport, 7½"	6.00-- 8.00

SPECIAL SALE ITEMS page 235

Candlestick, low, 3½"	10.00--12.00
Bowl, RE, 12"	10.00--14.00
Cake Plate, hdld., 10"	9.00--12.00
Mayonnaise Set: 3 pc.	11.00--13.00
Cheese and Cracker, 10"	10.00--12.00

SPECIAL SALE ITEMS NEW OCTAGONAL ASST.

Candlesticks, low, 4¾" pr.	10.00--12.00
Bowl, RE, 12"	9.00--11.00
Relish, covered, 3 section	16.00--22.00
Cheese and Cracker, 10"	11.00--14.00
Whipped Cream Set: 3 pc.	14.00--18.00
Plate, sandwich, hdld., 10"	9.00--12.00

CUTTING NO. 15

Rose and green

Goblet, 9 oz.	10.00--12.00
Sherbet, high, 5½ oz.	5.00-- 8.00
Sherbet, low, 5½ oz,	4.00-- 6.00
Parfait, cafe, 5 oz.	10.00--12.00
Cocktail, 3½ oz.	10.00--12.00
Wine, 2½ oz.	10.00--12.00
Cordial, ¾ oz.	12.00--14.00
Tumbler, ftd., 2½ oz.	4.00-- 6.00
Tumbler, ftd., 5 oz.	4.00-- 6.00
Tumbler, ftd., 9 oz.	5.00-- 7.00
Ice Tea, ftd., 12 oz.	6.00-- 8.00
Ice Tea, 12 oz.	5.00-- 8.00
Tumbler, table, 9 oz.	4.00-- 5.00
Tumbler, tall, 8 oz.	4.00-- 5.00
Tumbler, 5 oz.	3.00-- 4.00
Whiskey, 2½ oz.	4.00-- 6.00
Jug, tankard, 3 pt.	18.00--22.00
Jug, ice tea, covered, 4 pt	22.00--28.00
Cup and Saucer	5.00-- 7.00
Plate, 6"	2.00-- 3.00
Plate, 7½"	3.00-- 4.00
Plate, 8"	4.00-- 5.00
Plate, 9"	6.00-- 8.00

GENE CUTTING NO. 10

Rose and green Stem and Foot

Goblet, 9 oz.	10.00--12.00
Sherbet, high, 5½ oz.	5.00-- 8.00
Sherbet, low, 5½ oz.	4.00-- 6.00
Oyster Cocktail, 3½ oz.	8.00--10.00
Wine, 2 oz.	10.00--12.00
Cocktail, 3½ oz.	10.00--12.00
Ice Tea, ftd., 12 oz.	6.00-- 8.00
Tumbler, table, ftd., 10 oz.	5.00-- 7.00
Tumbler, ftd., 7 oz.	4.00-- 6.00
Tumbler, ftd., 2½ oz.	4.00-- 6.00
Jug, 3 pt.	18.00--24.00
Decanter, 1 qt.	20.00--25.00
Cup and Saucer	5.00-- 7.00
Plate, 6"	2.00-- 3.00
Plate, 7½"	3.00-- 4.00
Plate, 8"	3.50-- 5.00

"SOPHIA" page 236

Vase, tall, ftd., 9"	35.00--45.00
Pastry, hdld., 12"	15.00--20.00
Comport, tall, 7"	14.00--18.00
Candle, low, 3½", pr.	12.00--15.00
Bowl, flrd., 13"	18.00--24.00
Relish, covered, 3 sect., 6"	20.00--25.00
Tray, celery, 2 hdld., 11"	11.00--14.00
Whipped Cream Set: 3 pc.	18.00--22.00
Bowl, flrd., 6 toed, 12½"	20.00--25.00
Ice Tub, oblong, 2 hdld., 4"	20.00--25.00
Bowl, flrd., 12½"	24.00--28.00
Candle, tall, 5½"	18.00--24.00
Bowl, fruit, ftd., 12½"	25.00--30.00
Cheese and Cracker, 10"	16.00--20.00
Sandwich, 2 hdld., 11"	14.00--17.00
Cake, hdld., 10"	12.00--16.00
Bowl, Rose, 8¾"	18.00--22.00
Vase, flat rim, 3 ftd., 12"	35.00--40.00
Vase, large, flrd., ftd.	35.00--45.00

Candlestick, tall, 5¼", pr.	18.00--24.00
Bowl, crimped, ftd., 12"	20.00--25.00
Platter, oblong, 12½"	15.00--20.00
Sugar	8.00--10.00
Cream	8.00--10.00
Bowl, oblong, 11"	15.00--20.00
Ice tea, ftd., 12 oz.	10.00--12.00
Tumbler, ftd., 9 oz.	9.00--11.00
Tumbler, ftd., 6 oz.	8.00--10.00
Tumbler, ftd., 2½ oz.	9.00--12.00
Cocktail, 3½ oz.	15.00--18.00
Wine, 2½ oz.	15.00--18.00
Cordial, ¾ oz.	15.00--18.00
Fruit Salad, ftd.	5.00-- 7.00
Plate, salad, 7½"	4.00-- 6.00
Sherbet, high, 5½ oz.	12.00--15.00
Sherbet, low, 5½ oz.	6.00-- 8.00
Cup and Saucer	7.00--10.00
Decanter, 1 qt.	25.00--35.00
Plate, dinner, 9"	7.00--10.00
Goblet, 9 oz.	15.00--18.00
Jug, 48 oz.	50.00--60.00

GRECIAN GOLD page 237

Whipped Cream Set	18.00--22.00
Comport, tall, 7"	14.00--18.00
Bowl, nut, hdld., 10"	14.00--18.00
Candle, low, 3½", pr.	12.00--15.00
Bowl, flrd., 13"	18.00--22.00
Relish, covered	20.00--25.00
Ice Tub, hdld., 4"	15.00--18.00
Cheese and Cracker, 10"	12.00--15.00

FLATWARE DEC. 0889G13

Relish, covered, 3 sect., 6"	15.00--20.00
Plate, sandwich, 2 hdld., 11"	10.00--14.00
Candy Jar, 1 lb.,	16.00--20.00
Cheese and Cracker, 10"	12.00--15.00
Candlestick, low, 3½" pr.	12.00--15.00
Bowl, flrd., 13"	18.00--22.00
Candlestick, low, 4" pr.	18.00--22.00
Bowl, oval boat, 11"	20.00--25.00
Ice Tea Tub, 4"	15.00--18.00
Bowl, RE, 10"	9.00--12.00
Bowl, nut, hdld., 10"	10.00--14.00
Bowl, Lily, 10"	12.00--14.00
Comport, tall, 7"	14.00--18.00

DECORATION NO. 889

Bowl, flrd.	22.00--26.00
Bowl, Rose	18.00--24.00
Bowl, RE	18.00--22.00
Candlestick, tall, pr.	20.00--25.00
Bowl, crimped	18.00--22.00
Bowl, RE	10.00--14.00
Muffin, hdld., 10½"	10.00--12.00
Bowl, flrd.	18.00--22.00

DECORATION NO. 0889G13

Bowl, ftd., 10"	14.00--18.00
Salver, 10"	12.00--16.00
Tray, muffin, 2 hdld., 10½"	10.00--12.00
Bell Bowl, 2 hdld., 9"	12.00--14.00
Salad Set, 14"	20.00--25.00
Cake, hdld., 10"	10.00--12.00
Whipped Cream Set: 3 pc.	18.00--22.00
Candlestick, tall, 5¾" pr.	20.00--25.00
Bowl, oval, 10½"	20.00--25.00
Candy Box, LF, 6"	20.00--25.00

FUCHSIA page 238

Bowl, nut, hdld., 10"	10.00--14.00
Whipped Cream Set	18.00--22.00
Cake, hdld., 10"	10.00--14.00
Comport, tall, 7"	14.00--18.00
Relish, covered, 6 sect.	20.00--25.00
Candle, low, 3½", pr.	12.00--15.00
Bowl, 6 ftd., 12½"	18.00--24.00
Ice Tub, oblong, 2 hdld.	20.00--25.00
Cheese and Cracker, 10"	12.00--15.00
Muffin, 2 hdld., 10"	10.00--12.00
Sandwich, 2 hdld., 11"	10.00--14.00
Bell Bowl, 2 hdld., 9"	12.00--15.00

FUCHSIA ETCHING

Plate, salad, 7½"	4.00-- 6.00
Plate, salad, 8"	6.00-- 8.00
Whipped Cream Set: 3 pc.	18.00--22.00
Sugar	6.00-- 9.00
Cream	6.00-- 9.00
Goblet, 9 oz.	16.00--18.00
Sherbet, high, 5 oz.	12.00--14.00
Sherbet, low, 5 oz.	8.00--10.00
Cocktail, 3 oz.	16.00--18.00
Ice Tea, ftd., 12 oz.	11.00--14.00
Tumbler, ftd., 10 oz.	10.00--12.00
Cup and Saucer	8.00--10.00
Candy Box, covered, 6"	20.00--25.00
Cake, hdld., 10"	10.00--14.00
Candle, low, 3½" pr.	12.00--15.00
Bowl, 6 ftd., 12"	22.00--26.00
Jug, 4 pt.	40.00--50.00

"PARSON"

Bowl, RE, 10"	11.00--14.00
Tray, muffin, 2 hdld., 10½"	10.00--12.00
Bowl, Lily, 10"	11.00--14.00
Flower Block, Crystal, 4"	4.00-- 6.00
Candlestick, low, 3½" pr.	12.00--14.00
Bowl, flrd., 13"	18.00--22.00
Bell Bowl, 2 hdld., 9"	10.00--14.00
Cheese and Cracker, 10"	12.00--16.00
Plate, sandwich, 2 hdld., 11"	10.00--14.00

DECORATION NO. 902

Bowl, RE,	15.00--20.00
Bowl, Rose	20.00--25.00
Bowl, flrd.	20.00--25.00
Tray, celery, 2 hdld.	10.00--14.00
Pastry, hdld., 12"	12.00--15.00
Celery Boat	10.00--14.00
Bowl, oblong	12.00--15.00
Sugar	7.00-- 9.00
Cream	7.00-- 9.00
Platter, oblong	15.00--20.00

REVERE page 239

No. 24

Goblet	14.00--17.00
Sherbet, high	12.00--15.00
Sherbet, low	10.00--12.00
Cocktail	12.00--15.00
Wine	14.00--17.00
Ice Tea, ftd., 12 oz.	10.00--12.00
Tumbler, ftd., 10 oz.	8.00--10.00
Tumbler, ftd., 7 oz.	7.00-- 9.00
Whiskey, 2¾ oz.	10.00--12.00
Sugar and Cream	15.00--18.00
Cup and Saucer	8.00--10.00
Fruit Salad	5.00-- 7.00

No. 22

Goblet	15.00--18.00
Sherbet, high	14.00--16.00
Wine	14.00--18.00
Cocktail	14.00--18.00
Oyster Cocktail	10.00--14.00
Plate, 7½"	6.00-- 8.00
Decanter, 1 qt.	35.00--45.00
Jug	50.00--60.00

LA FURISTE page 240, 241

Bowl, flrd., 12½ X 3½"	22.00--26.00
Bowl, Rose, 8¾ X 5½"	24.00--30.00
Bowl, rolled edge, 12 X 3½"	22.00--26.00
Relish, covered, 3 sect., 6"	20.00--25.00
Pastry, hdld., 12"	14.00--20.00
Comport, tall, 7"	14.00--18.00
Ice Tub, 2 hdld., 4"	15.00--20.00
Whipped Cream Set: 3 pc.	18.00--22.00
Cake, hdld., 10"	10.00--14.00
Goblet, 9 oz.	14.00--18.00
Sherbet, high, 6½ oz.	12.00--16.00
Sherbet, low, 6½ oz.	8.00--10.00
Cocktail, 3½ oz.	14.00--18.00
Wine, 2¾ oz.	14.00--18.00
Cordial, 1½ oz.	18.00--20.00
Fruit Salad	6.00-- 8.00
Cup and Saucer	9.00--12.00
Ice Tea, ftd., 12 oz.	10.00--14.00
Tumbler, ftd., 10 oz.	9.00--11.00
Tumbler, ftd., 6 oz.	6.00-- 9.00
Tumbler, ftd., 2½ oz.	9.00--12.00
Jug, 4 pt.	45.00--60.00
Decanter, 1 qt.	32.00--42.00
Plate, bread and butter, 6"	3.00-- 4.00
Plate, salad, 7½"	4.00-- 6.00
Plate, salad, 8"	5.00-- 7.00
Plate, dinner, 9"	7.00--11.00
Plate, service, 12"	12.00--14.00
Bowl, rolled edge, 10"	10.00--14.00
Muffin, 2 hdld., 10½"	8.00--12.00
Bowl, nut, hdld., 10"	10.00--14.00
Celery, 2 hdld., 4½", 12¼"	9.00--12.00
Bowl, flrd., 13"	22.00--26.00
Celery Boat, 4½", 10½"	9.00--12.00
Candlestick, low, 3½", pr.	12.00--15.00
Bell Bowl, hdld., 9"	10.00--14.00
Cheese and Cracker, 10"	15.00--20.00
Sandwich, 2 hdld., 11"	12.00--14.00
Bowl, 3 ftd., flrd., 12"	20.00--25.00
Bowl, Rose, 3 ftd., 7¾ X 5½"	18.00--22.00
Bowl, rolled edge, 3 ftd., 11¼"	14.00--18.00
Bowl, crimped, 3 ftd., 12"	18.00--24.00
Candle, semi tall, 5½", pr.	20.00--25.00
Platter, oblong, 12½ X 10"	15.00--20.00
Bowl, oblong, 11 X 8½"	18.00--22.00
Sugar and Cream	16.00--20.00

"CALL OF THE WILD" page 242

No. 1850 1750 Dish, small	8.00--10.00
No. 2650 Cigarette holder	25.00--35.00
No. 2050, 2150, 2250 Ashtray	8.00--10.00
No. 1950 Tray	14.00--18.00
No. 1650 Ashtray	10.00--12.00
No. 2450 Cigarette Box	25.00--30.00
No. 2850 Comport	14.00--18.00
Brandy and Soda, 12 oz.	15.00--20.00
Hiball, 8 oz.	14.00--18.00
Tumbler, ftd., 9 oz.	14.00--18.00
Cocktail, 4 oz.	14.00--18.00
No. 2350 Jar and Cover	25.00--35.00
No. 2550 Box and Cover	20.00--25.00
No. 0650 Cocktail Shaker	35.00--45.00
No. 1150 Bottle	45.00--60.00
No. 0750 Bitters Bottle	40.00--50.00
No. 0850 Ice Tub	25.00--30.00
No. 0950 Decanter	40.00--50.00
No. 7350 Bowl, 12"	35.00--40.00
No. 7250 Bowl, cupped, 8¾"	35.00--45.00
No. 7450 Bowl, 12½"	35.00--45.00
No. 3050 Vase, 8"	30.00--40.00
No. 6850 Candlestick, 5½", pr.	35.00--45.00
No. 6950 Console	40.00--50.00
No. 2950 Vase, 6"	25.00--30.00
No. 9150 Dish, candy, 6"	50.00--60.00
No. 9850 Server, hdld., 10"	25.00--35.00
No. 9750 Cheese and Cracker	25.00--35.00
No. 6450 Mayonnaise and Plate	30.00--35.00
No. 8050, 9550, 6650 Candlestick, pr.	20.00--40.00
No. 5050 Candy Dish and Cover	40.00--50.00

No. 6550 Candleholder, 2 branch, pr.	35.00--40.00
No. 6750 Bowl, legged	60.00--70.00
No. 7550 Vase	50.00--60.00
No. 7650 Vase, hat shaped	50.00--60.00
No. 7150 Comport	24.00--30.00
Jug, 8"	100.00-150.00

POPPY

Chocolate Box, 6"	35.00--40.00
Flower Block, 3½", 4", 5"	5.00-- 8.00
Tray, card, 7"	10.00--14.00
Ash Tray and Cigarette Box, 5¾"	20.00--25.00
Bowl, bulb, 6"	10.00--14.00
Comport, LF, 8½"	18.00--22.00
Cheese and Cracker, 10"	22.00--26.00
Comport, HF, 7½"	16.00--20.00

STERLING SILVER DEPOSIT Page 243

Bowl, Rose	25.00--30.00
Flower, flat rim	35.00--40.00
Vase, lg., flrd.	25.00--35.00
Whipped Cream Set: 3 pc.	22.00--26.00
Candle, 5½", pr.	20.00--25.00
Bowl, fruit, ftd.,	30.00--35.00
Relish, covered, 3 sect.	30.00--35.00
Cake, hdld., 10"	20.00--25.00
Cheese and Cracker, 10"	25.00--30.00
Lily Pan	25.00--30.00

STERLING SILVER DEPOSIT

Bowl, 6 ftd., 12½"	25.00--35.00
Candle, 5½", pr.	22.00--28.00
Bowl, crimped	25.00--35.00
Vase, ftd., 9"	30.00--35.00
Candle, 2 light	20.00--25.00
Candle, low, 3½", pr.	18.00--22.00
Bowl, flrd., 13"	20.00--25.00
Candle, (12)	20.00--25.00
Bowl, oblong	15.00--25.00
Platter, oblong	15.00--20.00
Bowl, flrd.	25.00--30.00

EBONY SILVER LOLA

1800 Cheese and Cracker	25.00--35.00
1900 Chocolate Box	28.00--34.00
2324/4 Candlestick, pr.	20.00--25.00
12 Vase	35.00--40.00
1900 Bowl, flrd.	25.00--35.00

EBONY SILVER LOLA

1450 Cream and Sugar	22.00--28.00
2427 Cigarette Box	25.00--35.00
1849 Server, hdld.	20.00--25.00
1211 Ice Bucket	30.00--40.00
4105 Vase	30.00--40.00
2297/12 Bowl, flrd.	30.00--40.00

STERLING SILVER DEPOSIT

Vase, FR, 11½"	30.00--40.00
Candle, 2 light, 4¾, pr.	25.00--30.00
Comport, tall, 7"	20.00--25.00
Bowl, Rose, 8¾"	35.00--45.00
Cheese and Cracker, 10"	25.00--30.00
Candle, low, 3½", pr.	18.00--24.00
Bowl, flrd., 6 ftd., 12"	25.00--35.00
Bell Bowl, 2 hdld., 9"	18.00--24.00
Sandwich, 2 hdld., 11"	18.00--24.00
Tray, cake, hdld., 10"	20.00--25.00

SYLVANIA page 244

Candy, 3 section, 6"	25.00--30.00
Candle, tall, 5", pr.	25.00--35.00
Bowl, cupped, 3 ftd., 9"	28.00--32.00
Sugar and Cream	22.00--25.00
Candle, tall, 5", pr.	25.00--30.00
Bowl, flrd., 12"	30.00--35.00
Mayonnaise Set: 3 pc.	20.00--25.00
Platter, oblong, 12½"	20.00--25.00
Bowl, oblong, 11"	20.00--25.00
Vase, tall ftd., 9"	30.00--35.00

AVALON

Tray, cake, hdld., 10"	20.00--25.00
Cheese and Cracker, 0"	25.00--35.00
Candle, low, 3½", pr.	18.00--24.00
Candy, 3 section, 6"	25.00--35.00
Sandwich, 2 hdld., 11"	20.00--25.00
Bell Bowl, 2 hdld., 9"	20.00--25.00
Bowl, oblong, 11"	20.00--25.00
Platter, oblong, 12½"	20.00--25.00
Candle, tall, 5", pr.	25.00--30.00
Vase, FR, 11½"	30.00--35.00
Vase, tall ftd., 9"	28.00--38.00
Bowl, 6 ftd., flrd., 12"	30.00--35.00
Bowl, flrd., 12"	25.00--30.00
Bowl, Rose, 8¾"	25.00--30.00
Comport, tall, 7"	18.00--24.00
Bowl, cupped, 3 ftd., 9"	28.00--34.00
Candle, tall, 5", pr.	25.00--30.00
Candle, 2 light, 4¾", pr.	25.00--30.00
Vase, ftd., 10"	30.00--40.00
Sugar and Cream	22.00--26.00

"McGUIRE"

Plate, dinner, 9"	12.00--15.00
Plate, salad, 7", 8"	8.00--12.00
Sugar and Cream	22.00--26.00
Goblet, ftd., 9 oz.	14.00--16.00

Tumbler, ftd., 8 oz.	10.00--12.00
Sherbet, ftd., 5½ oz.	8.00--10.00
Cocktail, 3 oz.	10.00--12.00
Wine, ftd., 2 oz.	10.00--12.00
Cup and Saucer	9.00--12.00
Candy Box, covered, 3 section, 6"	25.00--35.00
Cake, hdld., 10"	20.00--25.00
Candle, low, 3½", pr.	20.00--24.00
Bowl, console, 6 ftd., 12"	25.00--30.00

FLANDERS page 245

Ice Tea, ftd., 12 oz.	10.00--14.00
Tumbler, ftd., 10 oz.	9.00--12.00
Tumbler, ftd., 5 oz.	9.00--12.00
Tumbler, ftd., 3 oz.	9.00--12.00
Claret, 5 oz.	14.00--18.00
Wine, 2½ oz.	14.00--18.00
Cocktail, 3½ oz.	14.00--18.00
Saucer Champagne, 5½ oz.	12.00--16.00
Sherbet, low, 5½ oz.	8.00--12.00
Plate, oct., 6"	3.00-- 4.00
Cocktail, ¾ oz.	16.00--20.00
Parfait, 5 oz.	12.00--16.00
Fruit Salad	8.00--12.00
Plate, oct., 8"	7.00-- 9.00
Plate, oct., 7½"	4.00-- 6.00
Goblet, 9 oz.	14.00--18.00
Jug, 4 pt.	35.00--50.00

"YODEL"

Cheese, 2 hdld., 6½"	6.00-- 8.00
Mint, 2 hdld., 6"	6.00-- 8.00
Mayonnaise	10.00--14.00
Bon Bon, flrd., 6½"	6.00-- 8.00
Bon Bon, 2 hdld., 6½"	6.00-- 8.00
Cheese and Cracker, 10"	12.00--15.00
Bon Bon, crimped, 6½"	7.00-- 9.00
Bell Bowl, hdld., 9"	10.00--14.00
Cake, hdld., 10"	10.00--14.00
Sandwich, 2 hdld., 11"	10.00--14.00
Goblet, 9 oz.	14.00--18.00
Sherbet, low, 5 oz.	8.00--12.00
Sherbet, high, 5 oz.	12.00--16.00
Cocktail, 3½ oz.	14.00--18.00
Wine, 2½ oz.	14.00--18.00
Cup and Saucer	9.00--12.00
Plate, salad, 8"	6.00-- 8.00
Decanter, 1 qt.	30.00--40.00
Jug, 4 pt.	35.00--50.00
Sugar and Cream	15.00--20.00
Ice Tea, ftd., 12 oz.	10.00--14.00
Tumbler, ftd., 10 oz.	9.00--12.00
Tumbler, ftd., 7 oz.	8.00--11.00
Tumbler, ftd., 2¾ oz.	9.00--12.00
Celery, 2 hdld., 7", 11"	9.00--12.00

BUTTERFLY page 246

Goblet, 9 oz.	15.00--20.00
Sherbet, high, 5½ oz.	12.00--16.00
Sherbet, low, 5½ oz.	10.00--14.00
Cocktail, 3½ oz.	15.00--20.00
Wine, 2½ oz.	15.00--20.00
Cordial, ¾ oz.	18.00--24.00
Fruit Salad	8.00--10.00
Ice Tea, ftd., 12 oz.	14.00--18.00
Tumbler, ftd., 10 oz.	12.00--16.00
Tumbler, ftd., 7 oz.	10.00--14.00
Tumbler, ftd., 2¾ oz.	10.00--14.00
Cup and Saucer	10.00--15.00
Plate, dinner, 9"	9.00--12.00
Plate, salad, 8", 7"	6.00-- 9.00
Plate, bread and butter, 6"	4.00-- 5.00
Sugar and Cream	18.00--24.00
Salt and Pepper	25.00--35.00
Bowl, 6 ftd., 12"	25.00--30.00
Candle, low, 3½", pr.	20.00--25.00
Tray, cake, hdld., 10"	14.00--18.00
Candy, covered, 3 sect.	25.00--30.00
Whipped Cream Set: 3 pc.	20.00--25.00

LOUISE

Plate, dinner, 9"	8.00--10.00
Plate, salad, 7½", 8"	6.00-- 8.00
Sugar and Cream	18.00--22.00
Bread and Butter, 6"	3.00-- 5.00
Cup and Saucer	9.00--12.00
Salt and Pepper	20.00--25.00
Tumbler, ftd., 2¾ oz.	8.00--12.00
Tumbler, ftd., 7 oz.	7.00--11.00
Tumbler, ftd., 10 oz.	8.00--12.00
Ice Tea, ftd., 12 oz.	10.00--14.00
Goblet, 9 oz.	14.00--18.00
Saucer Champagne, 5½ oz.	12.00--14.00
Sherbet, low, 5½ oz	8.00--10.00
Wine	14.00--18.00
Cocktail	14.00--18.00
Cordial	18.00--20.00
Fruit Salad	5.00-- 8.00

DRESDEN

Ice Tea, ftd., 12 oz.	9.00--12.00
Tumbler, ftd., 10 oz.	8.00--10.00
Tumbler, ftd., 5 oz., 3 oz.	7.00-- 9.00
Claret, 5 oz.	14.00--17.00
Wine, 2½ oz.	14.00--17.00
Cocktail, 3½ oz.	14.00--17.00
Saucer Champagne, 5½ oz.	12.00--15.00
Sherbet, low	8.00--10.00
Plate, oct., 6"	3.00-- 4.00
Cordial, ¾ oz.	16.00--18.00
Parfait, 5 oz.	9.00--12.00
Fruit Salad	5.00-- 7.00
Plate, oct., 8", 7½"	5.00-- 7.00
Goblet, 9 oz.	14.00--17.00
Jug, 4 pt.	35.00--45.00

"WANDA" page 247

Bowl, salad, 2 hdld.	12.00--15.00
Mayonnaise Set: 3 pc.	20.00--25.00
Comport, tall	12.00--16.00
Bowl, crimped, 2 hdld.	12.00--16.00
Sugar and Cream	14.00--20.00
Candle, tall, 5", pr.	20.00--30.00
Bowl, console	15.00--25.00
Comport, low	10.00--12.00
Cheese and Cracker	18.00--22.00
Candy Box and Cover	20.00--30.00
Cake Tray, hdld.	12.00--16.00
Sandwich, 2 hdld.	10.00--15.00

"NELL"

Bowl, salad, 2 hdld.	16.00--20.00
Mayonnaise Set: 3 pc.	20.00--30.00
Comport, tall	16.00--20.00
Bowl, crimped	16.00--20.00
Sugar and Cream	20.00--24.00
Candle, tall, 5", pr.	20.00--30.00
Bowl, console	18.00--26.00
Comport, low	10.00--14.00
Cheese and Cracker	20.00--25.00
Candy Box and Cover	20.00--30.00
Tray, cake, hdld.	14.00--18.00
Sandwich, 2 hdld.	12.00--16.00

LOWELL

Bell Bowl, 2 hdld., 11"	14.00--18.00
Candy and Cover, 3 ftd., 7"	25.00--35.00
Plate, fruit, 2 hdld., 10"	10.00--15.00
Sugar and Cream	18.00--22.00
Mayonnaise Set: 3 pc.	18.00--24.00
Sandwich, 2 hdld., 11"	10.00--14.00
Plate, cake, hdld., 11½"	12.00--16.00
Cheese and Cracker, 11"	18.00--22.00

NON-TARNISH SILVER DEPOSIT

Springtime Decoration 65

Vase	25.00--30.00
Tray, cake, hdld.	15.00--20.00
Sandwich, 2 hdld.	12.00--16.00
Comport, tall, 7"	14.00--18.00
Sugar and Cream	18.00--22.00
Candle, tall, 6", pr.	20.00--30.00
Bowl, console, 12"	20.00--28.00
Candy Box, 3 part	25.00--35.00
Candy Box, 2 part	25.00--35.00
Mayonnaise Set: 3 pc.	20.00--25.00
Comport, low, 7"	10.00--14.00
Cheese and Cracker, 10"	20.00--25.00

CLASSIC page 248

Mary Thompson of East Meadows NY has enlightened us as to this pattern. She says the stemware is Heisey's CARCASSONNE and the tableware is Heisey's EMPRESS.

Goblet, TF, 9 oz.	25.00--30.00
Sherbet, 5½ oz.	15.00--20.00
Ice Tea, ftd., 12 oz.	20.00--25.00
Tumbler, ftd., 8 oz.	15.00--20.00
Soda, ftd., 5 oz.	15.00--20.00
Cocktail	20.00--25.00
Wine	20.00--25.00
Cordial	25.00--35.00
Plate, square, 6"	8.00--10.00
Preserve, ftd., 2 dld., 5"	15.00--20.00
Jelly, ftd., 2 hdld., 6"	15.00--20.00
Cream Soup and sq. Plate, 5"	15.00--20.00
Salt and Pepper	25.00--35.00
Plate, salad, square, 8"	10.00--15.00
Sugar and Cream, ftd.,	35.00--45.00
Tray, oblong, 6" X 11"	10.00--15.00
Cup and Saucer	20.00--25.00
Decanter, tall	75.00-100.00
Relish, 3 comp., 10"	25.00--35.00
Relish, 3 comp., 7"	20.00--25.00
Candy and Cover, ftd., 6"	45.00--65.00
Comport, oval, 6"	25.00--30.00
Mayonnaise and Ladle, ftd., 5"	20.00--30.00
Candlestick, 6", pr.	35.00--50.00
Bowl, ftd., flrd., 11"	35.00--50.00
Lemon and Cover, oval 6 X 4¾"	35.00--40.00
Sandwich, hdld., sq., 11"	20.00--30.00
Candle, twin light	40.00--50.00
Plate, dinner, square, 10½"	20.00--25.00

Louie

Lots of beautiful 'Louie Blue' jugs have been reported this past year. At least, we presume they are Louie jugs. The reports indicate many variations from the four "Marxes" in Book 2. Makes life interesting.

"BRENNER"	page 249
Stemware	8.00--12.00

"SEMPER"	
Refreshment Set	60.00--65.00

"GROUCHO" REFRESHMENT SET	
Jug	20.00--25.00
Tumbler	6.00-- 8.00

"HARPO" REFRESHMENT SET	
Jug	20.00--25.00
Tumbler	6.00-- 8.00

"CHICO" REFRESHMENT SET	
Jug	20.00--25.00
Tumbler	6.00-- 8.00

"ZEPPO" REFRESHMENT SET	
Jug	20.00--25.00
Tumbler	6.00-- 8.00
Bowl, flared	14.00--18.00

Macbeth-Evans

Looking at Book 2's Macbeth-Evans chapter, one might think this company made very little colored glass, but that's certainly not the case. Macbeth was one of the most important contributors of Depression Glass and most of its main paths were followed in Book 1.

Major Book 2 coverage centers on the CHINEX and CREAMAX patterns of the early 40s, and area of quickening interest. The lines are beautiful, and very fun to collect right now as the prices are still reasonable.

At the end of this chapter is one little goodie I found to show you.

DIAMOND DART — page 254

Jug, 54 oz.	16.00--20.00
Tumbler, 5 oz., 9 oz., 12 oz.	5.00-- 7.00

"DIXIE"

Jug (Topaz, pink, green)	18.00--22.00
Jug (Ruby)	30.00--35.00
Tumbler, 10 oz., 12 oz.	5.00-- 7.00
Vase	12.00--15.00

SPINDLE

Jug	15.00--18.00

"MacHOB"

Crystal, pink, monax

Jug	20.00--30.00
Tumbler, 5, 9, 12 oz.	5.00-- 7.00

CRYSTAL LEAF

Jug, 8½"	18.00--22.00
Tankard, 8"	15.00--20.00
Tumbler, 5, 8, 12 oz.	6.00-- 8.00
Nite Set	25.00--30.00

page 255

Moire Rose, Moire Gold, and Moire Green

No. 8156 Lamp Base	20.00--25.00
No. 8154 Lamp Base	20.00--25.00
No. 8199 Vase	14.00--18.00
No. 8157 Vase	14.00--18.00
No. 8150 Vase	14.00--18.00

"DIAMOND LATTICE"

(No. 51 in Book l)

Cake Plate	15.00--18.00

"RINGED TARGET" Ice Tea Set

(No. 205 in Book l)

Jug	20.00--24.00
Tumbler, 10 oz.	5.00-- 8.00

SILVERED GAZING BALL

Ball	14.00--18.00

UTILITY SET, 3 piece

Jars	10.00--12.00

TUMBLERS

Crystal, pink, green and ruby.

These tumblers and jug are the blanks used for DOGWOOD and S-PATTERN

Tumbler, 5, 9, 12 oz. *(ruby is highest)*	5.00-- 8.00
Jug	20.00--25.00

"YANKEE" WATER SET

Jug	12.00--15.00
Tumbler, 9 oz.	3.00-- 4.00

"DIXIE" WATER SET

Jug	18.00--22.00
Tumbler, 10 oz.	5.00-- 7.00

"SCRABBLE" ICE TEA SETS AND TUMBLERS

Jug	12.00--16.00
Tumbler, 8 oz.	3.00-- 5.00
No. 7059 Tumbler, 12 oz.	5.00-- 7.00
Tumbler, 5 oz.	3.00-- 4.00
Tumbler, 9 oz.	4.00-- 6.00
No. 7507 Tumbler, 12 oz.	6.00-- 8.00

"SQUIRT" WATER SETS

Jug	12.00--16.00
No. 7553-8254 Tumbler	4.00-- 6.00
No. 7553-8249 Tumbler	3.00-- 5.00

ROLY POLY TUMBLERS page 256

2½ oz.	4.00-- 6.00
5 oz.	5.00-- 8.00
12 oz.	6.00-- 9.00

HOSTESS

Pitcher	50.00--75.00
Cocktail Shaker	30.00--35.00

"FANFARE"

Plate, 6"	3.00-- 4.00

"APRIL"

Sherbet	2.50-- 3.5

MISCELLANEOUS

Pink, green, topaz

The little No. 7541-A ashtray has bee named "MAC-B". It's the one originall promoted with DOGWOOD an S-PATTERN as shown in compan catalogs. Fern's Antiques, Mansfiel MO, has one in topaz. The usual color are pink and green.

Ash Tray (7541-A)	3.00-- 5.0
Ash Tray Set	12.00--18.0
Coaster	2.00-- 4.0
Ash Tray, Shur-Out	4.00-- 7.0
Electric Shade, 2¼" fitter	11.00--14.0

CLASSIC pages 257, 25

Chinex—Plain, Princess, Bouquet, Windsor Decoration (brown, blue)

Plate, 6¼"	2.00-- 3.0
Dish, utility, covered (Butter Dish)	45.00--55.0
Bowl, 7"	7.00-- 9.0
Soup, coupe, 7½"	10.00--12.0
Sherbet	6.00-- 8.0
Bowl, 9", 12"	9.00--14.0
Plate, dinner, 9¾"	4.00-- 6.0
Dish, dessert, 6"	3.00-- 5.0
Cream and Sugar	9.00--12.0
Cup and Saucer	5.00-- 8.0
Salver, 12"	7.00-- 9.0

"PIE CRUST" pages 259, 26

Cremax—Plain, Bordette, Rainbow, Windsor, Princess and Flora Decoration

Sandra Handler of Ontario, Canad writes to tell us that Corning Glass work of Canada, Ltd., made the light blu opaque "PIECRUST" in 1949 and continued for two or three years. The piece all appear to carry the trademark "Pyre in Canada" on their undersides.

Salver, 12"	4.00-- 8.0
Plate, dinner, 9¼"	3.00-- 5.0
Cup and Saucer	4.00-- 7.0
Dish, cereal or dessert, 5-7/8"	2.00-- 4.0
Plate, bread and butter, 6¼"	1.00-- 2.0
Bowl, 5"	2.00-- 4.0
Soup, coupe	8.00--10.0
Sugar and Cream	8.00--10.0
Sherbet	3.00-- 4.0
Bowl, 7", 9"	6.00-- 9.0
Cup and Saucer, demi-tasse	5.00-- 7.0
Dessert, 6"	3.00-- 4.0
Tumbler, 9 oz.	4.00-- 6.0

OXFORD page 261

Plain, Bordette, Rose and Red Band Decoration

Mary Frances Jenkins of Mobile AL has sent me the OXFORD sugar in Ritz Blue. It's the 'real' blue, not painted-on blue.

Salver, 12"	4.00-- 7.00
Plate, dinner, 9¼"	3.00-- 5.00
Dish, dessert, 6"	2.00-- 4.00
Plate, bread and butter, 6"	1.00-- 2.00
Cup and Saucer	4.00-- 7.00
Soup, coupe, 7½"	8.00--10.00
Bowl, 9"	6.00-- 9.00
Tumbler, crystal, decorated, 9 oz.	3.00-- 5.00

SHEFFIELD page 262

Plate, dinner, 9¼"	3.00-- 4.00
Dish, dessert, 6"	2.00-- 3.00
Bowl, 7"	5.00-- 7.00
Cup and Saucer	3.50-- 5.00
Plate, 6¼"	2.00-- 3.00

UTILITY CUPS

All Colors	3.00-- 5.00

"SWAN-SONG"

Bowl, flower	10.00--12.00

"BIANCA"

White, Ivory, fired on pastels

Vase, flower, 3-1/8"	5.00-- 7.00
Vase, flower, 7"	12.00--14.00

UTILITY TRAYS

All Colors	4.00-- 6.00

"GLASS DRIP"

Coffee Pot	15.00--20.00

Courtesy Macbeth-Evans

New shapes for glass drip coffee pots

"GLASS DRIP" 1934 ad

McKee

On the following pages are reprints of more ROCK CRYSTAL Design from the c. 1924 company catalog we printed last year. Then, later in the chapter, we have repeated a selection of miscellaneous pieces, and lastly are some McKee lamps which were made in the mid-20s and are being found in color.

Once again we want to remember the late E.L. Healy, who originally contributed the extensive ROCK CRYSTAL FLOWER listing below.

ROCK CRYSTAL FLOWER	page 264
Console Set: 4 pc.	75.00-100.00

CAKE PAN	
Optic Tube	22.00--26.00

VIRGINIA	
Lunch Plate	16.00--20.00

ROCK CRYSTAL FLOWER — **page 264, 265**

	Crystal	*Pink, Green, Amber*	*Ruby, Cobalt*
Plate, custard, 5½", SE	4.00-- 6.00	5.00-- 8.00	10.00--12.00
Saucer, cup, 5½", SE	4.00-- 6.00	5.00-- 8.00	10.00--12.00
Plate, sundae/B&B, 6". SE	4.00-- 6.00	5.00-- 8.00	10.00--12.00
Plate, oval, 7"	7.00-- 9.00	8.00--12.00	15.00--20.00
Plate, salad, 7½", SE, PE	6.00-- 8.00	8.00--10.00	14.00--18.00
Plate, luncheon, 8", SE	6.00-- 8.00	8.00--12.00	15.00--20.00
Plate, salad, 8½", SE, PE	8.00--10.00	8.00--10.00	18.00--22.00
Plate, cake, 9", SE	10.00--12.00	10.00--12.00	22.00--25.00
Plate, cake, 10½", SE	12.00--15.00	22.00--25.00	28.00--34.00
Plate, dinner, 10½", SE	20.00--25.00	30.00--35.00	50.00--60.00
Plate, dinner, 11", PE	20.00--25.00	30.00--35.00	50.00--60.00
Plate, cake, 11½", SE	15.00--20.00	24.00--28.00	30.00--35.00
Plate, finger bowl, 7", SE	8.00--10.00	11.00--14.00	12.00--15.00
Stand, cake, 11"	20.00--25.00	30.00--40.00	55.00--65.00
Plate, server, 10½", Metal hdld.	18.00--24.00	25.00--35.00	35.00--45.00

FINE AMERICAN "PRESCUT" GLASS
ROCK CRYSTAL DESIGN
SCALE, HALF SIZE.

Sugar and Cover
Packs 5 doz. to bbl.

Spoon
Packs 9 doz. to bbl.

4 Piece Set Packs 1½ doz. to bbl.

Butter and Cover
Packs 4½ doz. to bbl.

Nappy
4 in. Packs 24 doz. to bbl.
4½ in. Packs 18 doz. to bbl.
7-Piece Berry Set Packs 1½ doz. to bbl.

Cream
Packs 8 doz. to bbl.

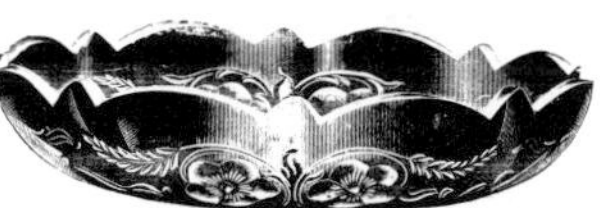
Round Saucer
5 in. Packs 18 doz. to bbl.
8 in. Packs 5 doz. to bbl.

7, 8, and 9 Inch Nappy, Round
Also make Belled, Crimped and Square
Packs 5 doz. 7 in.; 4 doz. 8 in.; and 3 doz. 9 in. to bbl.
5, 6, 8, 9, and 10½ in. Shallow Nappy
Shallow Nappies Pack 25 doz. 5 in.; 20 doz. 6 in.;
5 doz. 8 in.; 3½ doz. 9 in., 3 doz. 10½ in. to bbl

Whiskey Tumbler
Bell or Crimp
Packs 50 doz. to bbl.

12 in. Oblong Ice Cream Tray
Packs 2½ doz. to bbl.

Large Goblet
Packs 8 doz. to bbl.
Small Goblet
Packs 10 doz. to bbl
Claret
Packs 18 doz. to bbl

Large Wine
Packs 28 doz. to bbl.
Small Wine
Packs 34 doz. to bbl.

Cordial
Packs 60 doz. to bbl.

Cocktail
Packs 17 doz. to bbl.

Saucer Champagne
Packs 11 doz. to bbl.

c. 1924 catalog reprint

FINE AMERICAN "PRESCUT" GLASS
ROCK CRYSTAL DESIGN
SCALE, HALF SIZE.

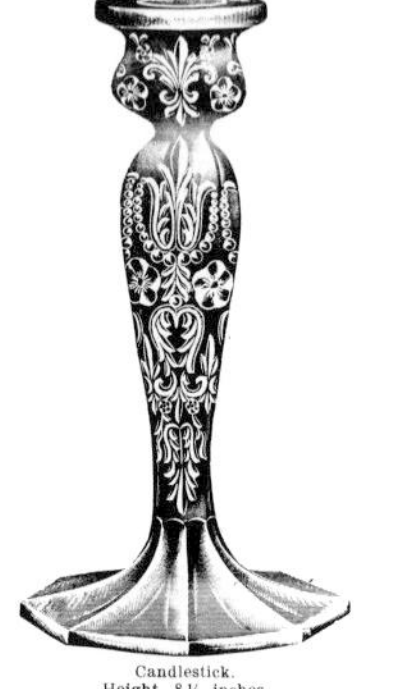

Candlestick.
Height, 8¼ inches.
Packs 3 doz. to bbl.

Banana Split.
Length 7 inches; Width 4½ inches.
Packs 12 doz. to bbl.

Ice Tea Tumbler.
Packs 12 doz. to bbl.

Footed Jelly Bowl.
Packs 6 doz. to bbl.

12 in. Footed Punch Bowl.
Capacity, 6 Quarts.
Packs ½ doz. to bbl.
13-Piece Punch Set Packs ½ doz. to bbl.

Footed Sherbet
or Egg.
Packs 22 doz. to bbl.

Custard.
Packs 24 doz. to bbl.

Finger Bowl.
Also make Finger Bowl Plate.
Finger Bowls Pack 16 doz. to bbl.
Finger Bowl Plates Pack 20 doz. to bbl.

5 inch Handled Nappy.
Packs 12 doz. to bbl.
Also Make no Handl.
Packs 20 doz. to bbl.

7 in. Footed Comport.
Packs 3½ doz. to bbl.

Champagne or Grape
Juice Tumbler.
Packs 27 doz. to bbl.

Footed Sundae.
Packs 14 doz. to bbl.

12 inch Vase.
Packs 1⅔ doz. to bbl.
Also make Crimped, Square and Belled.

c. 1924 catalog reprint

FINE AMERICAN "PRESCUT" GLASS
ROCK CRYSTAL DESIGN
SCALE, HALF SIZE.

Berry Sugar and Cover, Footed.
Packs 7 doz. to bbl.

Berry Cream, Footed.
Packs 10 doz. to bbl.

Quart Jug.
Packs 4½ doz. to bbl.

High Foot Bon Bon.
Packs 3½ doz. to bbl.

Pickle Tray.
Packs 12 doz. to bbl.

Whiskey Tumbler, Crimped
or Toothpick.
Packs 46 doz. to bbl.

Celery Tray or Comb and Brush Tray.
Packs 5 doz. to bbl.

Oil.
Packs 10 doz. to bbl.

Mayonnaise Bowl and Plate.
Packs 6 doz. to bbl.

Plate.
5½ in. Packs 30 doz. to bbl.
6 in. Packs 25 doz. to bbl.
7 in. Packs 15 doz. to bbl.
9 in. Packs 7 doz. to bbl.
10½ in. Packs 5 doz. to bbl.
11½ in. Packs 4 doz. to bbl.

No. 2 Cut Shut
Salt or Pepper.
Packs 36 doz. to bbl.

No. 1 Salt
or Pepper.
Packs 36 doz. to bbl.

Molasses Can.
Packs 9 doz. to bbl.

c. 1924 catalog reprint

FINE AMERICAN "PRESCUT" GLASS
ROCK CRYSTAL DESIGN

SCALE, HALF SIZE.

All Glass Center Piece consisting of 1 Large Vase and 4 Small Vases and 4 Glass Chains.
Packs 1 doz. Sets in bbl.

No. 2 Concave
Cupped Tumbler.
Packs 18 doz. to bbl.

No. 1 Taper Tumbler.
Packs 16 doz. to bbl.

No. 2 Concave
Bell Tumbler.
Packs 18 doz. to bbl

Fancy Jug Tankard.
Packs 1½ doz. to bbl.

Low Foot Goblet.
Packs 9 doz. to bbl.

½ Gallon Jug.
Packs 2 doz. to bbl.
7-Piece Lemonade or Water Set Packs 1 doz. to bbl.

c. 1924 catalog reprint

	Crystal	Pink, Green, Amber	Ruby, Cobalt
Plate, server, 10½", center hdld.	22.00--25.00	25.00--30.00	35.00--50.00
Plate, server, 12¾", w/base, SE	20.00--24.00	24.00--30.00	30.00--40.00
Tray, pickle/spoon, 7", SE	8.00--12.00	14.00--18.00	20.00--25.00
Tray, celery/comb., 10", SE	10.00--14.00	15.00--20.00	25.00--30.00
Tray, ice cream, 12", SE	12.00--14.00	20.00--24.00	26.00--30.00
Tray, relish, 11½", PE	14.00--18.00	20.00--24.00	35.00--45.00
Tray, relish, 11", PE	14.00--18.00	20.00--24.00	25.00--35.00
Tray, relish, 14", SE, PE	20.00--25.00	25.00--35.00	50.00--60.00
Insert, cup relish	6.00-- 9.00	10.00--12.00	12.00--15.00
Tray, roll, 13", PE	15.00--20.00	20.00--30.00	40.00--50.00
Nappy, w/Base, 4", SE	10.00--12.00	15.00--18.00	18.00--22.00
Nappy, 4½"	8.00--10.00	9.00--12.00	12.00--15.00
Nappy, 7", crimp, sq., rnd., bell	12.00--15.00	15.00--20.00	20.00--30.00
Nappy, 8", crimp, sq., rnd., bell	12.00--15.00	15.00--20.00	30.00--35.00
Nappy, 9", crimp, sq., rnd., bell	14.00--18.00	20.00--25.00	40.00--45.00
Nappy, shallow, 5", 6"	9.00--12.00	15.00--20.00	15.00--20.00
Nappy, shallow, 8", 9", 10½", w/base	12.00--18.00	18.00--34.00	30.00--50.00
Nappy, hdld., 5"	9.00--11.00	12.00--15.00	20.00--25.00
Bowl, finger, 4¾", PE	8.00--10.00	10.00--14.00	15.00--18.00
Bowl, icer, 4¾", PE and Cup insert, 3½", PE	15.00--20.00	20.00--30.00	40.00--45.00
Bowl, console, 12¼", SEB	25.00--30.00	50.00--60.00	90.00-100.00
Saucer, ice cream, 5", 8", SE	6.00-- 8.00		
Bowl, punch, 14", SE, w/base	200.00-225.00		
Bowl, punch/fruit, 12", SEF	60.00--70.00	70.00--85.00	85.00-100.00
Bowl, comport, 6½", REF	10.00--15.00		
Bowl, comport, high, 8½", REF	12.00--18.00	25.00--35.00	45.00--50.00
Bowl, salad, low, 10½", 12", REF	12.00--16.00	25.00--30.00	40.00--50.00
Bon Bon, high, 7½", SEF	15.00--20.00	20.00--25.00	30.00--40.00
Vase, 12", SEF, PEF, SQF	25.00--35.00	60.00--80.00	85.00-100.00
All Glass Center Piece	150.00-200.00		
1 large vase, 4 small vases and 4 glass chains			
Jar, candy, w/foot, tall, 1 lb., 10¼"	30.00--40.00	60.00--90.00	150.00-200.00
Candy Box w/Lid, 7"	25.00--30.00	40.00--60.00	90.00-110.00
Lamp, base elect., F 10"	60.00--80.00	200.00-225.00	350.00-400.00
Bowl, comport, 7", SEF	15.00--18.00	25.00--30.00	35.00--40.00
Mayonnaise and liner	20.00--25.00	25.00--35.00	35.00--45.00
Bon Bon, high, SEF	12.00--15.00	15.00--25.00	25.00--35.00
Vase, Cornucopia	25.00--35.00		
Candle, 3 lite, oval base, 5¼"	40.00--45.00	55.00--85.00	150.00-165.00
Candle, 2 lite, rnd. base, 5¼"	35.00--40.00	50.00--65.00	90.00-100.00
Candle, 1 lite, tall, 8¼"	40.00--45.00	55.00--65.00	90.00-100.00
Candle, 1 lite, 5½", SEF	20.00--25.00	25.00--40.00	60.00--70.00
Bon Bon, low, 2 hdld.	10.00--15.00		
Nut Bowl, low, 2 hdld.	10.00--15.00		
Bon Bon, low	10.00--15.00		
Nut Bowl, low	10.00--15.00		
Nut Bowl, glass hdld., 10", CTR	30.00--35.00	50.00--60.00	90.00-100.00
Banana Split	25.00--35.00		
Dish, butter, w/Cover, SE	150.00-200.00		
Spooner, 2 hdld.	25.00--35.00		
Cream, 10 oz., SE	12.00--15.00	15.00--20.00	25.00--35.00
Sugar, w/Lid, 10 oz., SE	30.00--40.00	60.00--80.00	100.00-125.00
Sugar, 9 oz., SEF	15.00--20.00		
Cream, 9 oz., SEF	15.00--20.00		
Salt and Pepper, straight	60.00--75.00		
Salt and Pepper, concave	60.00--75.00	75.00-100.00	
Tops, cast nickle, embossed, silver plated, glass			
Salt Dip	15.00--20.00		
Cruet, oil w/Stopper, 6 oz., DS, GS, CS	60.00--70.00	75.00-100.00	

	Crystal	Pink, Green, Amber	Ruby, Cobalt
Jug, syrup, plated or cast top	60.00--75.00		
Jug, tankard, applied hdld., 10"	80.00--90.00		
Jug, tankard, pressed. hdld.,8¼"	70.00--80.00		
Jug, w/lid, 9"	100.00-150.00	200.00-300.00	900.00-1000.00
Jug, qt., SE	60.00--80.00		
Jug, ½ gal., SE	70.00--90.00		
Plate, deviled egg, 11"	20.00--25.00		
Cordial, 1 oz., PEF	20.00--25.00	25.00--30.00	55.00--60.00
Wine, small, 2 oz., PEF	20.00--25.00	25.00--30.00	35.00--40.00
Wine, large, 3 oz., PEF	20.00--25.00	25.00--30.00	35.00--40.00
Claret, PEF	20.00--25.00	25.00--30.00	35.00--40.00
Goblet, low, 7½ oz., PEF	10.00--15.00	15.00--20.00	30.00--35.00
Goblet, tall, 9 oz., PEF	15.00--20.00	20.00--25.00	40.00--45.00
Champagne, saucer, 6 oz., PEF	12.00--15.00	15.00--20.00	25.00--30.00
Cocktail, 4¼", 3½ oz., PEF	12.00--15.00	15.00--20.00	20.00--25.00
Egg Cup/Sherbet, 3½ oz., PEF	12.00--15.00	15.00--20.00	18.00--22.00
Sherbet, 3½", PEF	12.00--15.00	15.00--18.00	25.00--30.00
Sundae, 3½ ", 6 oz., PEF	12.00--15.00	15.00--18.00	25.00--30.00
Jelly w/foot, 6 oz.	15.00--18.00	18.00--24.00	25.00--30.00
Ice Tea, low, 11 oz., PEF	12.00--15.00	15.00--20.00	40.00--45.00
Champagne, 3½"	10.00--14.00	15.00--20.00	30.00--35.00
Parfait, 5¼", 3½ oz.	12.00--15.00	15.00--20.00	30.00--35.00
Tumbler, 4", 9 oz.	12.00--15.00	15.00--20.00	35.00--45.00
Tumbler, ice tea, 5", 12 oz.	16.00--20.00	20.00--25.00	35.00--45.00
Tumbler, cup in, 4", 8 oz.	12.00--15.00	15.00--20.00	35.00--40.00
Tumbler, bell out, 4", 9 oz.	12.00--15.00	15.00--20.00	35.00--40.00
Tumbler, whiskey, bell or crimp 2½ oz.	15.00--20.00	25.00--30.00	35.00--40.00
Tumbler, tooth pick	15.00--20.00	25.00--30.00	35.00--40.00
Tumbler, ice tea, 10 oz.	12.00--15.00	15.00--20.00	35.00--40.00
Tumbler, champagne/juice, 5 oz.	12.00--15.00	15.00--20.00	35.00--40.00
Tumbler, old fashioned, 5 oz.	12.00--15.00	15.00--20.00	35.00--40.00
Cup, custard/punch, 7 oz.	9.00--12.00	10.00--14.00	18.00--22.00
Cup, coffee	10.00--14.00	15.00--20.00	25.00--30.00

MISCELLANEOUS page 266, 267

"GLENDALE" COMPORT	35.00--45.00
CRACKLED ICE TEA SET	80.00-110.00
"WIGGLE" WATER SET	50.00--80.00
"HANSEN" SANITARY DISPENSER	40.00--60.00
"THOMAS" KEG SET	60.00--80.00
GLASBAKE BAKE DISH	20.00--28.00
GLASBAKE SERVER	15.00--20.00
APOLLO ROSE VASE	15.00--20.00
MAYFLOWER LAMP	40.00--60.00
TAMBOUR ART GLASS MANTLE CLOCK	350.00-450.00
BETTY JANE SET	25.00--30.00
GLASBAKE TOY PUDDING SET	18.00--22.00
BAKING DISH AND COVER	12.00--16.00
TWO PIECE BRIDGE SET	20.00--25.00
CRACKLED SATIN FINISH WARE BOWL AND BASE	30.00--40.00
BOWL, FOOTED	20.00--30.00
"CUNNINGHAM" SERVER	15.00--20.00
REBECCA TWO HANDLED VASE	25.00--35.00
THE LIFE SAVER 8 PIECE DECANTER SET	65.00--95.00
DANSE DE LUMIERE LAMPS	100.00-150.00

SCALLOP EDGE page 268

Plate, lunch, hdld., 11"	11.00--14.00
Bowl, nut, hdld., 10"	12.00--15.00
Candy Jar and Cover	20.00--30.00
Sugar	5.00-- 8.00
Cream	5.00-- 8.00
Candlestick, RE, pr.	10.00--15.00
Bowl, console, RE	10.00--12.00
Cheese and Cracker, 11"	18.00--20.00
May. Comport and Plate	16.00--20.00
Bowl, salad, 2 hdld., 9"	15.00--20.00
May. Bowl and Plate	12.00--15.00
Comport, cone shape, 10"	18.00--20.00
Candlestick, flat	12.00--15.00
Plate, salad, 2 hdld., 11"	10.00--14.00
Sherbet Plate, 5½"	3.00-- 4.00
Plate, salad, 6½"	3.00-- 4.00
Plate, salad, 7½"	4.00-- 5.00
Plate, salad, 8½"	4.00-- 6.00
Bowl, 9"	12.00-16.00
Candy Box and Cover	20.00--30.00

OCTAGON EDGE

Plate, lunch, hdld., 11"	11.00--14.00
Cream Soup and Plate, 2 hdld.	8.00--12.00
Sugar and Cream and Tray	12.00--15.00
Ice Cream, ftd.	3.00-- 4.00
Bowl, nut, hdld., 10"	12.00--15.00
Plate, sherbet, 5½"	3.00-- 4.00
Plate, salad, 6½"	3.00-- 4.00
Plate, salad, 7½"	4.00-- 5.00
Plate, salad, 8½"	4.00-- 6.00
Cheese and Cracker, 11"	15.00--20.00
May. Bowl and Plate, 2 hdld.	12.00--15.00
Bowl, 2 hdld.	14.00--18.00
Cup and Saucer	7.00-- 9.00
Comport, cone shape, 10"	18.00--20.00
Swung Vases, 10", 12", 14"	10.00--18.00
Center Bowl, flrd. edge, 12"	11.00--14.00
Center Bowl, flrd. edge, 14"	12.00--15.00
Candy Jar and Cover	20.00--30.00
Plate, salad, 2 hdld., 11"	10.00--14.00
Demitasse Cup and Saucer	8.00--10.00
Candlestick, 3 ftd., pr.	12.00--15.00
Candy Box and Cover, 7"	20.00--30.00
Dish, nut, 3 ftd.	5.00-- 7.00
Candlestick, pr. RE	12.00--15.00
Bowl, console, 12", 13", RE	10.00--12.00
Salver, ftd., 11"	12.00--14.00
Tumbler, ftd., 9 oz.	7.00-- 9.00
Platter, meat, 12"	10.00--14.00
Platter, meat, 14"	12.00--15.00
Salt and Pepper	10.00--12.00

BROCADE page 269

Comport, flrd. edge, 10"	20.00--25.00
Candlestick, pr.	14.00--18.00
Candy Jar and Cover	25.00--35.00
Cheese and Cracker	18.00--24.00
Candy Box and Cover	25.00--35.00
Center Bowl, roll edge, 12"	15.00--20.00
Mayonnaise Comport, Plate and Ladle	20.00--25.00
Bowl, nut, hdld.	14.00--18.00
Salver, ftd.	14.00--18.00
Center Bowl, flrd. edge, 12"	15.00--20.00
Comport, cone shaped	12.00--16.00
Plate, lunch, hdld.	15.00--20.00
Cream and Sugar	15.00--20.00

CLICO

Plate	6.00-- 8.00
Tumbler, ftd.	7.00--10.00
Cream	8.00--10.00
Sugar	8.00--10.00
Sherbet	5.00-- 7.00

JADE GREEN page 270

Bowl and Plate	9.00--12.00
Vase	12.00--15.00
Bowl, ftd.	14.00--18.00

REFRIGERATOR AND KITCHEN PIECES

Stokie green, Chalaine blue, Seville yellow

Kitchen Shaker Set: 4 pc.	25.00--35.00
*Sunkist Orange Reamer	25.00--35.00
Mixing Bowl Set: 3 pc.	20.00--25.00
Food Preserver Set	20.00--25.00
Salt Box	25.00--30.00
Jug, batter, graduated qt.	20.00--25.00
Butter Box, covered	20.00--25.00
Utility Jar Set: 4 pc.	100.00-120.00

****Blue $125.00***

VASES

Jardinere, 3 ftd., 5½" high	12.00--15.00
Bulb Bowl, 5½"	9.00--12.00
Bulb Bowl, 7"	11.00--14.00
Cookie Jar and Cover, 3 ftd., 5½" high	20.00--30.00
Vase, ftd., 8½" high	16.00--20.00
Vase, triangle, 8½" high	65.00--75.00

LENOX page 271

My pieces have "McK" on the bottom.

Sherbet	3.50-- 5.00
Wine or Cocktail	6.00-- 8.00
Goblet	7.00--10.00
Tumbler	5.00-- 7.00
Jug	20.00--30.00
Plate, 6¾"	2.00-- 3.00
Nappy, 4½"	3.00-- 4.00

SARAH

Vase	15.00--25.00

GEORGE WASHINGTON CHERRY LINE

Goblet	14.00--18.00
Sherbet, tall	9.00--12.00
Bowl and Plate	10.00--12.00

BOTTOMS UP

Tumbler	20.00--30.00
Coaster	12.00--20.00
Tumbler and Coaster	40.00--60.00

"AUTUMN" page 272

Bowl, console, 8½", 10"	14.00--20.00
Candlesticks, pr.	18.00--22.00

"FLOWER BAND"

Bowl, 9½"	10.00--14.00
Tumbler, ftd., 3½"	6.00-- 9.00

LAUREL

No. 238 in Book 1

Plate, dinner	9.00--12.00
Plate, salad	7.00-- 9.00
Plate, grill	6.00-- 8.00
Plate, 6"	3.00-- 5.00
Platter, oval	10.00--14.00
Candlestick, pr.	20.00--25.00
Dish, fruit, 5"	4.00-- 6.00
Sherbet, ftd.	6.00-- 8.00
Sugar and Cream, (2 styles)	15.00--18.00
Cup and Saucer	12.00--14.00
Bowl, 9"	12.00--16.00
Bowl, oval, 9¾"	15.00--18.00
Tumbler, 5"	18.00--24.00
Goblet, cocktail, 4"	25.00--30.00
Goblet, wine, 4½"	25.00--30.00
Jelly, 3 toe.	6.00-- 8.00
Cheese Plate and Cover	40.00--50.00
Salt and Pepper	30.00--40.00
Bowl, utility, legged, 11"	18.00--22.00
Cereal, 6"	8.00--11.00
Plate, soup, 9"	10.00--12.00

CHILD's LAUREL TEA SET

(Prices higher on the Scotty Dog decoration and the red, green or orange band decoration)

Plate	7.00-- 9.00
Cup	12.00--15.00
Saucer	4.00-- 6.00
Cream	18.00--22.00
Sugar	18.00--22.00
14 Piece Set	125.00-135.00

TOM AND JERRY SETS page 273

Bowl and 8 cups.

Sled Scene	35.00--45.00
Tom and Jerry w/scroll	30.00--40.00
Tom and Jerry w/o scroll	30.00--40.00

"KIDDIE CARNIVAL"

Dish and Cup, child's, 7"	20.00--25.00

MISCELLANEOUS

UTILITY SET: 48 oz., Cereal, Tea, Coffee, Flour, Sugar	100.00-120.00
CADDY SET: 28 oz., Coffee, Tea, Sugar, Cereal	90.00-100.00
SHAKER SET: Salt, Pepper, Sugar, Flour	30.00--35.00
ART NUDE VASE, 8½"	65.00--75.00
LAMP, 8½"	65.00--75.00
SOUVENIR SHAKER, 4¾"	15.00--20.00
TUMBLER, 3¾"	6.00-- 8.00
BOWL, 4¼"	4.00-- 6.00
SHALLOW BAKER, 7" x 4¾"	5.00-- 8.00
BOTTOMS UP TUMBLER AND COASTER	40.00--60.00
BOWL, 8½"	8.00--10.00
BUTTERDISH, 1 lb	30.00--35.00
SNACK TRAY	6.00-- 9.00
CASSEROLE AND COVER AND NO. 12 CHROME TRAY	15.00--20.00

LOUVRE page 274

Vase	12.00--15.00
Bowls	12.00--18.00

"BIG JUG"

WATER JAR AND COVER, 1 gal., (jade)	75.00-100.00

BEACON INNOVATION

This is only one of the many McKee's INNOVATION patterns of the 20s that was made in pink, green, blue and amber pieces.

Sugar	6.00-- 9.00
Cream	6.00-- 9.00
Nappy, 3 ftd., 8"	30.00--40.00
Basket, 10"	30.00--40.00
Apple Bowl	40.00--60.00
Rose Bowl, 3 ftd., 8"	30.00--40.00
Fern and Liner	30.00--40.00
Orange Bowl, oval, 4 ftd.	30.00--40.00
Orange Bowl, ftd., 14½"	50.00--60.00
Nut Bowl	20.00--30.00
Bowl, 8"	20.00--30.00
Vase, cylinder, 12"	25.00--35.00
Vase, square, 12"	25.00--35.00
Vase, square, 10"	20.00--30.00
Orange Bowl, 14½"	35.00--45.00
Tray, 3 ftd., 12"	25.00--35.00

LAMPS

Electroliers	200.00--400.00

MISCELLANEOUS (in photos)

Item	Price
*LION Window Box	20.00--25.00
CAKE ICING TRAY	12.00--15.00
BOTTOMS DOWN Beer Mug	90.00-100.00
*NUDE VASE	65.00--75.00
NUDE CANDY JAR and Cover	70.00--80.00
JOLLY GOLFER Set	85.00-100.00

**Also in Black*

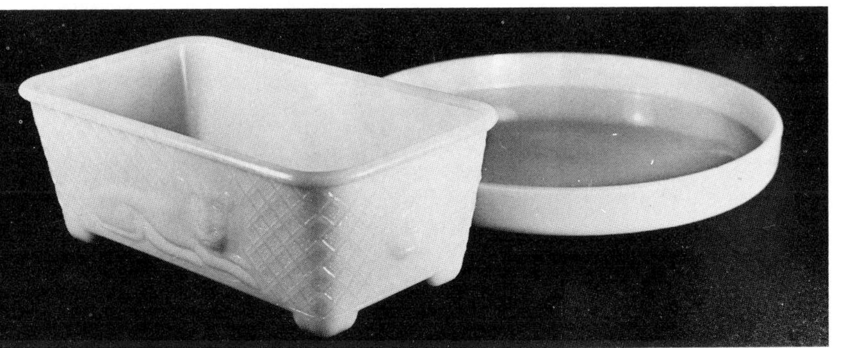

LION window box 9" x 5", Cake ICING TRAY 10½"

14 piece "Jolly Golfer" set designed by Tony Sarg, made of velvety satin-finish opaque glass in rose pink, blue, white, green and combinations.

JOLLY GOLFER

Reprinted from 1929 trade catalog

BOTTOMS DOWN beer mug, NUDE vase or lamp 8½" NUDE candy jar and cover 7½"

ELECTROLIERS COMPLETELY EQUIPPED WITH SOCKET, CORD AND ATTACHMENT PLUG.
NO BULBS FURNISHED EXCEPT ON SMALL ELECTROLIERS.

Dimac. 10 in. Height, 20 inches
Dimac. 8 in. Height, 17 inches
Dimac. 6 in. Height, 12¾ inches
(Full Cut Potash Lead Blank)

Aztec. 18¾ inches High

18 inches High
Rotec "A" Fitting 1 Light
(Sold either cut or uncut)

Rotec "B" Fitting 2 lights
16 inches High (Sold either cut or uncut)

No. 414, 6 inch
Height 12¾ inches
(Innovation Cutting)

No. 412, 6 inch
Height 12¾ inches (Innovation Cutting)

No. 407, 6 inch
Height 12¾ inches (Innovation Cutting)

McKee, 6 inch
Height 12½ inches
(Sold either cut or uncut)

1924 catalog reprint

Monongah

We don't see very much Monongah, but what we do see is beautiful -- especially in the SPRINGTIME pattern, the one our CAMEO was copied from. I doubt we will find any more examples of this company's wares, other than the one old catalog I reprinted in Book 2.

SPRINGTIME pages 275 & 276

Item	Price
Sugar	8.00--12.00
Cream	8.00--12.00
Decanter, Cut Stopper, 26 oz.	35.00--50.00
Almond, Ind., 1½ oz.	6.00-- 9.00
Almond, ftd., 9 oz.	6.00-- 9.00
Confection Stand, 6"	12.00--16.00
Bowl, finger	6.00-- 9.00
Plate, 6½"	3.00-- 5.00
Plate, 8½"	5.00-- 8.00
Parfait, 5½ oz.	12.00--15.00
Goblet, 9 oz.	14.00--18.00
Sherbet, HF, 5½ oz.	8.00--12.00
Sherbet, LF, 5½ oz.	5.00-- 8.00
Claret, 4 oz.	14.00--18.00
Wine, 2½ oz.	14.00--18.00
Cocktail, 2¾ oz.	14.00--18.00
Brandy, ¾ oz.	16.00--20.00
Ice Tea, hdld., 13 oz.	14.00--18.00
Ice Tea, 13 oz.	10.00--14.00
Ice Tea, 10 oz.	8.00--10.00
Water, 9 oz.	7.00-- 9.00
Water, 8 oz.	7.00-- 9.00
Ginger Ale, 7 oz.	7.00-- 9.00
Grape Juice, 5 oz.	7.00-- 9.00
Whiskey, 2½ oz.	10.00--14.00
Jug, water, 60 oz.	40.00--60.00
Ice Tea, 60 oz.	45.00--65.00
Grape Juice, 30 oz.	40.00--60.00
Jug, water, 50 oz.	40.00--60.00
Plate, 5½"	2.00-- 3.00
Plate, 7"	3.00-- 5.00
Bowl, finger	4.00-- 6.00
Grape Fruit, 30 oz.	7.00--10.00
Comport, ftd., 5", 7"	7.00--10.00
Confection Stand, 6"	7.00--10.00
Jug, 67 oz.	20.00--25.00

"ROSELAND" page 277

Item	Price
Goblet, 10 oz.	7.00--10.00
Sherbet, Saucer, or Hi., 5½ oz.	6.00-- 8.00
Sherbet, 5 oz.	4.00-- 6.00
Cocktail, 3½ oz.	7.00--10.00
Parfait, 6 oz.	7.00--10.00
Sherbet, 6½ oz.	4.00-- 6.00
Sherbet, Saucer or Hi., 6 oz.	6.00-- 8.00
Tumbler, 5 oz.	5.00-- 7.00
Tumbler, 9 oz.	5.00-- 7.00

GOLD BAND DECORATION NO. 200

Item	Price
Ice Tea, hdld., 13 oz.	5.00-- 8.00
Ice Tea, 13 oz.	4.00-- 6.00
Tumbler, 9 oz.	2.00-- 4.00
Tumbler, 10 oz.	2.00-- 4.00
Tumbler, 8 oz.	2.00-- 4.00
Tumbler, 7 oz.	2.00-- 4.00
Grape Juice, 5 oz.	2.00-- 4.00
Sugar	5.00-- 7.00
Cream	5.00-- 7.00
Grape Juice, 30 oz.	12.00--15.00
Ice Tea, 60 oz.	14.00--18.00
Water Jug, 50 oz.	9.00--12.00

GOLD ENCRUSTED DECORATION NO. 251

Item	Price
Bowl, finger	2.50-- 3.50
Parfait, 4½ oz.	5.00-- 8.00
Goblet, 8 oz.	5.00-- 8.00
Sherbet, HF, 5 oz.	4.00-- 6.00
Sherbet, LF, 5 oz.	3.00-- 4.00
Claret, 4 oz.	5.00-- 8.00
Wine, 2½ oz.	5.00-- 8.00
Cocktail, 2¾ oz.	5.00-- 8.00

"KEY BLOCK"

Item	Price
Goblet, 10 oz.	8.00--12.00
Saucer, or Hi Sherbet, 6 oz.	5.00-- 8.00
Sherbet, low, 5½ oz.	4.00-- 6.00
Cocktail, 3 oz.	8.00--12.00

Wine, 2½ oz.	8.00--12.00
Parfait	8.00--12.00
Whiskey, 1¾ oz.	7.00-- 9.00
Seltzer, 4½ oz.	6.00-- 8.00
Table, 9 oz.	6.00-- 8.00
Ice Tea, 12 oz.	7.00-- 9.00

SALAD PLATES, FTD. FINGER BOWLS AND FTD. JUGS page 278

Plate, salad, 7½"	2.00-- 4.00
Bowl, finger, ftd.	3.00-- 5.00
Jug	18.00--22.00
Jug, w/top	20.00--30.00

"DIAMOND CLASSIC"

Goblet, 9 oz.	8.00--12.00
Sherbet, high, 5½ oz.	6.00-- 9.00
Sherbet, low, 5½ oz.	4.00-- 6.00
Wine, 2½ oz.	8.00--12.00
Cocktail, 2¾ oz.	8.00--12.00
Parfait, 5½ oz.	8.00--12.00
Ice Tea, 13 oz.	6.00-- 9.00
Water, 9 oz.	5.00-- 8.00
Grape Juice, 5 oz.	5.00-- 8.00
Whiskey, 2½ oz.	6.00-- 9.00
Bowl, finger	2.00-- 4.00

DIAMOND OPTIC, OPTIC, AND HERRINGBONE OPTIC

Goblet, 9 oz.	10.00--14.00
Saucer or high Sherbet, 5½ oz.	8.00--10.00
Sherbet, low, 5 oz.	6.00-- 8.00
Cocktail, 2½ oz.	10.00--14.00
Wine, 2 oz.	10.00--14.00
Parfait, 4½ oz.	10.00--14.00
Goblet, 9 oz.	10.00--14.00
Saucer or high Sherbet, 5½ oz.	8.00--10.00
Sherbet, low, 5 oz.	6.00-- 8.00
Wine, 2 oz.	10.00--14.00

ROSEPINK 13 OPTIC CUT

Goblet	8.00--12.00
Sherbet, high	6.00-- 9.00
Sherbet, low	4.00-- 6.00
Cocktail	8.00--12.00
Wine	8.00--12.00
Parfait	8.00--12.00
Plate, 7½"	3.00-- 5.00
Bowl, finger, ftd.	3.00-- 5.00
Seltzer, ftd., 4 oz.	4.00-- 6.00
Table, ftd., 9 oz.	4.00-- 6.00
Ice Tea, ftd., 12 oz.	6.00-- 9.00
Jug and Cover, ftd., 58 oz.	22.00--28.00

BO-PEEP page 279

Goblet	12.00--15.00
Sherbet, high	8.00--12.00
Sherbet, low	6.00-- 8.00
Cocktail	12.00--15.00
Wine	12.00--15.00
Bowl, finger, ftd.	6.00-- 8.00
Plate, 7½"	5.00-- 7.00
Vase, 9"	20.00--26.00
Parfait	12.00--15.00
Seltzer, ftd.	7.00--10.00
Table, ftd.,	7.00--10.00
Ice Tea, ftd.,	9.00--12.00
Jug and Cover, ftd.	35.00--45.00

"ARLENE"

Goblet	10.00--14.00
Saucer Champagne	8.00--10.00
Sherbet	5.00-- 7.00
Cocktail	10.00--14.00
Wine	10.00--14.00
Parfait	10.00--14.00
Seltzer, ftd., 4 oz.	6.00-- 9.00
Table, ftd., 9 oz.	6.00-- 9.00
Ice Tea, ftd., 12 oz.	7.00--10.00
Bowl, finger, ftd.	5.00-- 7.00
Plate, salad, 7½"	4.00-- 6.00
Jug and Cover, ftd., 58 oz.	30.00--40.00

"MAXWELL"

Goblet	10.00--14.00
Saucer Champagne	8.00--10.00
Sherbet	5.00-- 7.00
Cocktail	10.00--14.00
Wine	10.00--14.00
Plate, salad, 7½"	4.00-- 6.00
Bowl, finger, ftd.	5.00-- 7.00
Seltzer, ftd., 4 oz.	6.00-- 8.00
Table, ftd., 9 oz.	6.00-- 8.00
Ice Tea, ftd., 12 oz.	7.00-- 9.00
Jug and Cover, ftd., 58 oz.	30.00--40.00

"VIDA"

Goblet	10.00--14.00
Saucer or high Sherbet	8.00--10.00
Sherbet, low	5.00-- 7.00
Cocktail	10.00--14.00
Wine	10.00--14.00
Parfait	10.00--14.00
Seltzer, ftd., 4 oz.	6.00-- 8.00
Table, ftd., 9 oz.	6.00-- 8.00
Ice Tea, ftd., 12 oz.	7.00-- 9.00
Jug, ftd.	25.00--30.00
Jug and Cover, ftd.	30.00--40.00
Bowl, finger, ftd.	5.00-- 7.00
Plate, salad, 7½"	4.00-- 6.00

Morgantown

As we mentioned in the historical introduction to this company in Book 2, Old Morgantown Glassworks was once the Economy Glass Company.

Printed at the end of chapter are two early ads, showing etching #751 MEDALLION and a small group of miscellaneous items made in 1927 and 1928 by Economy before the name was changed to Old Morgantown. The other reprints will be familiar to you from Book II; they are the "OLD ENGLISH" line of candy jars and the 1932 liquor sets.

"KRINKLE"	page 281
Sherbet, tall	6.00-- 9.00
Tumbler, juice	5.00-- 7.00
Tumbler, hdld.	6.00-- 9.00
Tumbler, regular	5.00-- 7.00
Candy Jar and Cover	15.00--20.00

PALM OPTIC	
Plate	4.00-- 6.00
Goblet	10.00--14.00
Sherbet, tall	8.00--10.00

"PRIMROSE LANE"	
Plate	3.00-- 5.00
Goblet	10.00--12.00
Sherbet, tall	8.00--10.00

"SQUARE"	
Goblet	10.00--15.00

MARILYN	
Plate	4.00-- 6.00
Goblet	10.00--14.00
Sherbet, tall	8.00--10.00

PINEAPPLE OPTIC	
Plate	3.50-- 5.00
Goblet	10.00--12.00
Sherbet, tall	6.00-- 9.00
Tumbler, ftd.	6.00-- 8.00

ART MODERNE	
Goblet	10.00--14.00
Wine	10.00--14.00
Sherbet, tall	8.00--12.00

"BUTTON"	page 282
Goblet	12.00--15.00
Sherbet, tall	9.00--12.00
Goblet, claret	12.00--15.00

"MORGANA"	
Goblet	10.00--14.00
Sherbet, tall	8.00--12.00
Tumbler, ftd.	8.00--10.00

SIMPLICITY	
Goblet	10.00--14.00
Sherbet, tall	8.00--12.00
Tumbler, ftd.	8.00--10.00

OLD ENGLISH

Goblet, luncheon	12.00--15.00
Parfait, tall	12.00--15.00
Wine, 10 oz.	12.00--15.00
Sherbet	10.00--12.00
Goblet	12.00--15.00
Candy Jar	20.00--30.00

"WILLOW"

Goblet	10.00--12.00
Sherbet, tall	8.00--10.00
Tumbler, ftd.	7.00-- 9.00

PEACOCK OPTIC

Plate	4.00-- 6.00
Goblet	10.00--14.00
Sherbet, tall	8.00--10.00
Jug	20.00--30.00
Tumbler	8.00--10.00

TUMBLERS page 283

Water, 9 oz.	6.00-- 8.00
Iced Tea, 12 oz.	7.00-- 9.00
Juice, orange, 5 oz.	6.00-- 8.00
Sundae or Sherbet, 5½ oz.	6.00-- 8.00
Cocktail, 2½ oz.	4.00-- 6.00

VASES

Witch Ball	15.00--25.00
Ivy Ball	12.00--18.00

MISCELLANEOUS

No. 59 Vase	10.00--14.00
No. 18 Bowl, 9"	12.00--16.00
No. 14½ Vase, 10"	12.00--16.00
Goblet, 9 oz.	10.00--12.00
Saucer Champagne, 6 oz.	8.00--10.00
Jug, square	15.00--25.00
Tumbler, 12 oz.	4.00-- 8.00
Goblet, 9 oz.	12.00--15.00

DUCAL

Goblet	14.00--18.00

SUPERBA

Goblet	15.00--20.00

SAN TOY

Goblet	12.00--16.00

FAIRWIN

Goblet	14.00--18.00

OLD BRISTOL page 284

Jug	25.00--35.00
Tumbler, ftd.	9.00--12.00

"CONNOISSEUR"

No. 7662 Goblet	8.00--12.00
No. 606 Tumbler	6.00-- 8.00
No. 7954 Compote	9.00--12.00
No. 7675 Goblet	10.00--14.00
No. 544 Jug	18.00--24.00
No. 7955 Bowl, 10½"	12.00--15.00
No. 7955 Bowl, 12" with bubble stem	16.00--24.00
No. 7667 Goblet	10.00--14.00

FERNLEE

Goblet	14.00--18.00

ROSALIE

Goblet	10.00--14.00

CARLTON

Goblet	12.00--15.00

PRICILLA

Goblet	11.00--14.00

FONTINELLE

Goblet	15.00--20.00

LIQUOR SETS page 285

"LITTLE KING"	50.00--70.00
SPARTA	50.00--70.00
"TINKLE"	40.00--60.00

VASES

No. 76	15.00--20.00
No. 75	15.00--20.00
No. 73	15.00--20.00
No. 77	12.00--16.00

GOBLETS

No. 7690 "Carlos" cut	12.00--15.00
No. 7660 "American Beauty" etched	12.00--15.00

No. 7684 Yale Shape	12.00--15.00
No. 7604½ "Dawn" cut	12.00--15.00
No. 7688 No. 795 etching	12.00--15.00
No. 7682 "Mt. Vernon" cut	12.00--15.00

MISCELLANEOUS page 286

Hand blown Stems	8.00--14.00

SPARTA

Goblet	15.00--20.00

DANCING GIRL (Sunrise)

Goblet	12.00--15.00

"MEDALLION"

Goblet	15.00--20.00

FAUN

Goblet	15.00--20.00

"RADIANT RUBY"

Goblet	12.00--15.00

VASES

A, 10½"	20.00--25.00
B, 11"	20.00--25.00
C, 6"	10.00--12.00
D, 8"	14.00--16.00
E, 4"	10.00--12.00
F, 4"	10.00--12.00

"SOMMERSET" BEVERAGE SET page 287

Pitcher	20.00--30.00
Tumbler, ftd.	4.00-- 7.00

"LANGSTON" BEVERAGE SET

Jug, ftd.	25.00--35.00
Ice Tea, ftd.	8.00--10.00

"HUGHES" BEVERAGE SET

Jug, square, dished sides	25.00--35.00
Tumbler, dished sides	6.00--10.00

"MILLAY" BEVERAGE SET

Jug, ftd.	25.00--35.00
Tumbler, 12 oz., ftd.	8.00--10.00

"MELON" BEVERAGE SET

Jug	35.00--45.00
Tumbler, ftd.	10.00--12.00

BRIDGE SET

Comes in two shapes--octagonal or the embellished square

Ice Tea	8.00--10.00
Cup and Saucer	6.00-- 9.00
Plate, salad	5.00-- 8.00

"MR. NATURAL" REFRESHMENT SET

Pitcher	20.00--30.00
Tumbler, 12 oz.	5.00-- 7.00

1928 ad

SPARKLING GIFTS FOR SPRIGHTLY SALES!

THESE glass jars with their quaint knobbed covers will intrigue many feminine shoppers by their rich tones of ruby, Ritz Blue or Black, enhanced by dancing lights from the cut crystal knobs. Though they are particularly attractive as candy jars, they may be used also to hold powder and a puff, or what you will.

MORGANTOWN GLASS WORKS
MORGANTOWN, W. VA.

—SALES OFFICES—

80 SUMMER ST., BOSTON
1007 FILBERT ST., PHILA.
308 W. RANDOLPH ST., CHICAGO
1604 ARAPAHOE ST., DENVER
731 FOLSOM ST., SAN FRANCISCO
200 FIFTH AVENUE, NEW YORK
110 HOPKINS PLACE, BALTIMORE
838 RAYMOND AVE., ST. PAUL
410 HOLLAND BLDG., SEATTLE
TRANSPORTATION BLDG., LOS ANGELES

"TURNOVER TOPICS" tells how to sell glass Mailed monthly to dealers who request it.

Tell our advertisers you saw it in THE CROCKERY AND GLASS JOURNAL

Old English 1931 ad

ANOTHER
ETCHING
BY
ECONOMY

7604 LINE
WITH ETCHING NO. 751

PLEASING design in contrasting treatments applied to rich lead blanks in wide optic effect. Is furnished in all-crystal blanks as illustrated and with Fancy Stems in Golden Amber or Apple Green colors with crystal bowls.

The service is complete with Salad Plates, Handled Lunch Tray, Cheese and Cracker Set and other items of Stemware, of course.

ECONOMY
REPRESENTATIVES

Chicago—Earl W. Newton
Baltimore—John A. Dobson & Co.
Columbus—A. L. Reber
St. Louis—W. L. Meakin
Los Angeles—The Myers Co.
New York—D. King Irwin
Philadelphia—Fred Stott
Kansas City—Walter C. Reel
St. Paul—Richard A. Walker
San Francisco—F. M. Smith

BOSTON—THOMAS F. O'HARA

New Sample Room Just Opened
At 111 SUMMER ST.

ECONOMY GLASS CO.
MORGANTOWN, W. VA.

"Egyptian Girl" 1927 ad

Ultra-Modern LIQUOR SETS . . .

featuring Platinum Decoration at its best

Here are six brilliant conceptions from the hands of expert designers—flawlessly blown in the famous Old Morgantown manner—decorated with bands of gleaming platinum that never lose their lustre (an exclusive Old Morgantown quality that will please your patrons).

Each "set" you sell will consist of a Bottle and Stopper, six Hi Ball Glasses and six Liquor Glasses (or a bottle with six glasses). Your choice of Black, Ritz Blue, Stiegel Green, Ruby or Crystal—with Crystal Stoppers. Attractive prices. Write us!

No. 24-24 Decanter; No. 9719-3 Tumbler; platinum decorated rings.

Old Made in U.S.A. Morgantown

No. 9719-12 Hi Ball; platinum decorated rings.

MORGANTOWN GLASS WORKS
Morgantown, W. Va.

No. 2 Decanter, P/D791
9051-1½ Tumbler, P/D791
8701-14 Hi Ball, P/D791

No. 10½ Bar Bottle, P/D Sparta
9051-1½ Tumbler, P/D Sparta
8071-14 Hi Ball, P/D Sparta

No. 10½ Bar Bottle, P/D Flora
9051-1½ Tumbler, P/D Flora
8071-14 Hi Ball, P/D Flora

No. 21-24 Decanter, P/D Roses
9051-1½ Tumbler, P/D Roses
8701-14 Hi Ball, P/D Roses

No. 10½ Bar Bottle, P/D Roses
9051-1½ Tumbler, P/D Roses
8701-14 Hi Ball, P/D Roses

1932 ad

New Martinsville

The gorgeous rubies, amethysts, and Ritz blues of New Martinsville practically electrify collectors. MOONDROPS and RADIANCE have such a fascination that they continue to draw a train of followers despite their ultra-scarce availability.

How much longer can the MOONDROPS list get? That's anybody's guess, but for sure we want to thank Kevin Kiley of West Orange, NJ, for this year's update on pieces and prices. He's an expert!

Finally, we have the four company catalog pages, circa 1938, to reprint again at the end of the section. Many of these items have shown up in colors.

POWDER PUFF BOX	page 289
Box and Cover	25.00--30.00

BRIDGE SET	
Sugar and Cream	20.00--25.00

"GENE"	
Liquor Set	75.00--85.00

"DAVIDA"	
No. 149-3 Candy Jar	18.00--20.00

"PATTI"	
Console Set	50.00--65.00

"WISE OWL"	page 290
In color section; has inverted tumbler for a cover	
Jug and Tumbler	60.00--80.00

"SILLY TOBY"	
Decanter	60.00--80.00

"ALLAH"	
Cigarette Set	30.00--45.00

"VOLSTEAD PUP"	
Decanter, dog	65.00--75.00
Decanter, cat	65.00--75.00

"MARTY"	
Liquor Set	75.00--85.00

"VAN'S OWN"	page 291
Cigarette Holder	30.00--35.00

CONSOLE SETS	
No. 10-10 Console Set: 3 pc.	75.00--85.00
No. 10-21 Console Set: 3 pc.	75.00--85.00

SALAD SETS

No. 160-12 Bowl and Plate	20.00--35.00
No. 160-8 Plate	10.00--12.00
No. 728-12 Bowl and Plate	20.00--35.00
No. 728-7½ Plate	10.00--12.00

RELISH DISHES

No. 10 Relish Dish and Liner: 5 pc.	20.00--30.00

CANDY JARS

No. 149-2 Candy Jar and Cover	35.00--45.00
No. 10 Candy Box and Cover	30.00--40.00
No. 149-3 Candy Jar and Cover	30.00--35.00

QUEEN ANNE

No. 10-2 Dresser Sets	70.00--85.00

MISCELLANEOUS page 292

No. 10-1-282 Wine Set	80.00--95.00
No. 140-1 Guest Jug and Tumbler	40.00--45.00
No. 723-8 Bud Vases	14.00--16.00
No. 190-4 Ice Tea Jug	30.00--45.00
No. 113 Tumbler, 12 oz.	6.00-- 8.00
No. 198-7 Water Jug	30.00--40.00
No. 82 Tumbler	6.00-- 8.00
No. 725 Vase, fan, 11"	40.00--50.00
No. 725 Vase, fan, 8"	30.00--40.00
No. 725 Vase, fan, 6"	25.00--35.00
Console Set	75.00--85.00
No. 10-2 Candlestick	20.00--25.00
No. 10-12 Princess Bowl and Foot	35.00--40.00
No. 2001 Vanity Set	40.00--50.00
No. 1926 Vanity Set and Tray	60.00--75.00
No. 2003 Smoker Set	35.00--45.00
No. 20 Ash Tray	25.00--30.00
No. 149-2 Cigarette Holder	20.00--30.00
No. 10-2 Cigarette Set	30.00--40.00

MISCELLANEOUS page 293

No. 728 Ash Tray	6.00-- 8.00
No. 10-3 Candlestick, 3"	12.00--15.00
No. 728 Match Stand	10.00--14.00
No. 10 Candlestick, 4"	15.00--20.00
No. 725 Tobacco Jar with Ash Tray Cover	35.00--45.00
No. 725 Cigarette Jar with Ash Tray Cover	20.00--30.00
No. 2001 Vanity Set: 3 pc	40.00--50.00
No. 1926/3001 Vanity Set: 3 pc	50.00--60.00
No. 728/3006 Guest Set	45.00--55.00
No. 511/3055 Bud Vase, 10"	13.00--15.00
No. 149/4/3020 Cigarette Holder	30.00--40.00
No. 149/2/3019 Cigarette Holder	30.00--40.00
No. 10/3016 Ash Tray Set	18.00--24.00
No. 160/3019 Lemon Plate and Fork	8.00--10.00
No. 10/2/3000 Smoker Set	35.00--45.00
No. 150/3010 Sweet Pea Vase	15.00--20.00
No. 10 Plate 6"	3.00-- 4.00
No. 10 Plate, 8½"	5.00-- 6.00
No. 10 Plate, 7½"	4.00-- 5.00
No. 10 Plate, 10"	8.00--12.00
No. 1926 Candy Box	18.00--22.00
No. 728 Guest Set	45.00--55.00

"GENEVA" page 294

Vanity Set	50.00--60.00

"OSCAR"

Refreshment Set	45.00--55.00

"MICHAEL"

Liquor Service	65.00--85.00

"JUDY"

Vanity Set	60.00--70.00

"SWEETHEART"

Lamp	25.00--35.00

"MOONDROPS" page 295

	Amber, Pink Green, Evergreen	*Ritz Blue Ruby, Amethyst*
Plate, dinner, 9½"	8.00--12.00	12.00--15.00
Plate, luncheon, 8½"	6.00-- 8.00	10.00--12.00
Plate, 6", off center indent	8.00--10.00	12.00--14.00
Plate, 7-1/8", salad	8.00--10.00	12.00--14.00

This pressed decanter looks like a large goblet when it first comes from the mold. It is then cupped and finished by a patented tool that gives it a bottle neck

1933 journal ad

MOONDROPS

tumbler w/tripod base, candlestick w/metal base, goblet w/metal base, sherbet, mayonnaise and low comport

Photo Courtesy Bill Newbound

"MOONDROPS"
comport 11½", crimped vase, winged bowl, cocktail shaker, handled tumbler and candlestick

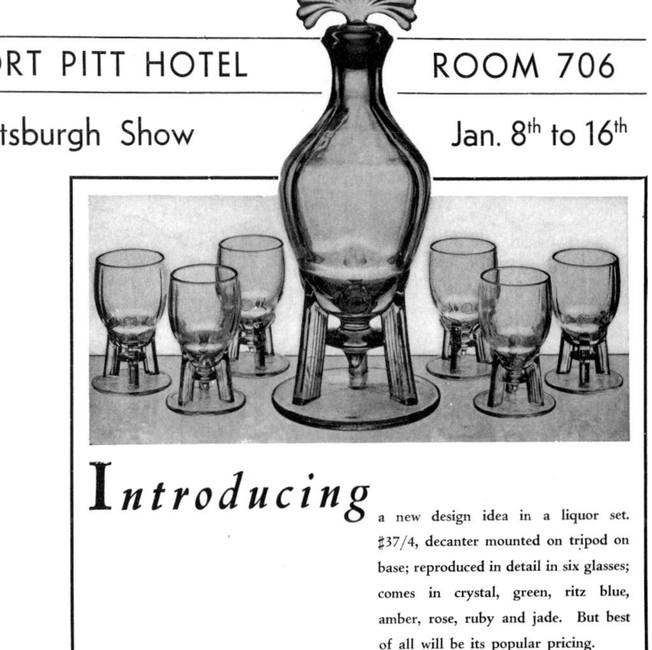

FORT PITT HOTEL
ROOM 706
Pittsburgh Show
Jan. 8th to 16th
Introducing
a new design idea in a liquor set. #37/4, decanter mounted on tripod on base; reproduced in detail in six glasses; comes in crystal, green, ritz blue, amber, rose, ruby and jade. But best of all will be its popular pricing.

MOONDROPS
TUMBLER w/tripod base, decanter w/tripod base

	Amber, Pink Green, Evergreen	*Ritz Blue Ruby, Amethyst*
Plate, 7-1/8", underplate	8.00--10.00	12.00--14.00
Plate, 13½" sandwich	16.00--20.00	25.00--28.00
Plate, 11¼", 3 ftd. cake	18.00--22.00	28.00--30.00
Plate, sherbet or bread and butter, 6¼"	3.00-- 4.00	6.00-- 8.00
Plate, 15"	20.00--25.00	30.00--40.00
Cup and Saucer, 5¾ oz.	8.00--12.00	12.00--16.00
Sugar, 3¼"	7.00-- 9.00	10.00--14.00
Creamer, 3½"	7.00-- 9.00	10.00--14.00
Sugar and Cream, individual, 2-5/8"	15.00--20.00	20.00--25.00
Sherbet, low ftd., 6 oz., 2-5/8"	5.00-- 8.00	10.00--12.00
Sherbet, tall, 4-3/8"	9.00--12.00	14.00--16.00
Sherbet Set: edge plate and sherbet, 5 oz.	10.00--15.00	15.00--20.00
Bowl, nappy, 5¼"	8.00--10.00	16.00--18.00
Bowl, oval vegetable, 9¾"	12.00--16.00	22.00--28.00
Bowl, oval 9¾" on base with cover	80.00-100.00	120.00-150.00
Bowl, cream soup, 4-3/16"	20.00--25.00	30.00--35.00
Bowl, soup 6-5/8"	7.00--10.00	14.00--16.00
Bowl, centerpiece or salad, 12"	15.00--20.00	30.00--35.00
Bowl, rd., 3 legged, curved in top, 8½"	15.00--20.00	30.00--35.00
Bowl, 8¼", 2 handle w/without divide	20.00--25.00	35.00--40.00
Bowl, 3 ftd., concave, 7"	20.00--30.00	35.00--40.00
Bowl, 10", 3 ftd., console	15.00--20.00	25.00--30.00
Bowl, 10", 3 ftd., ruffled	20.00--25.00	35.00--40.00
Bowl, console w/wings, 13"	25.00--30.00	60.00--70.00
Platter, oval, 12"	15.00--20.00	20.00--25.00
Tumbler, 1 oz., 1¾"	10.00--15.00	15.00--20.00
Tumbler, 2 oz., 2¾"	8.00--10.00	10.00--12.00
Tumbler, w/handle, 2 oz., 2¾"	8.00--10.00	10.00--12.00
Tumbler, 5 oz., 3-5/8"	6.00-- 8.00	8.00--10.00
Tumbler, 5 oz., 3-5/8", w/handle	15.00--20.00	25.00--30.00
Tumbler, 7 oz., 4-3/8"	8.00--10.00	10.00--12.00
Tumbler, 9 oz., 4¾"	8.00--10.00	9.00--12.00
Tumbler, w/handle, 9 oz., 4¾"	15.00--20.00	25.00--30.00
Tumbler, 10 oz., 4-7/8"	8.00--10.00	9.00--12.00
Tumbler, 12 oz., 5-1/8"	8.00--10.00	12.00--15.00
Tumbler, w/handle, 12 oz., 5-1/8"	15.00--20.00	25.00--30.00
Tumbler, ftd., 3 oz., 3-3/8"	10.00--12.00	15.00--18.00
Tumbler, tripod base, 4½"	20.00--30.00	40.00--50.00
Goblet, ¾ oz., 3" liqueur	12.00--15.00	18.00--22.00
Goblet, 4 oz., 4" cocktail; 4¾" wine	10.00--12.00	14.00--18.00
Goblet, 9 oz., 6¼"	15.00--20.00	25.00--30.00
Goblets w/ metal base		
3 oz., 5¼"	7.00--10.00	10.00--12.00
4 oz., 5½" wine	7.00--10.00	10.00--12.00
9 oz., 5-7/8" water	10.00--14.00	15.00--18.00
Pitcher, jug, 24 oz., 7"	65.00--75.00	145.00-160.00
Pitcher, jug, 32 oz., 8"	60.00--80.00	150.00-170.00
Pitcher, jug, bulbous, 56 oz., 8¼"	60.00--80.00	150.00-175.00
Butter Dish and Cover	150.00-200.00	350.00-400.00
Decanter w/Stopper, 7¾" or 9"	30.00--35.00	40.00--45.00
Decanter, 8¾"	30.00--35.00	45.00--50.00
Decanter on tripod base, 9¼"	100.00-150.00	200.00-225.00
Decanter, 11"	35.00--40.00	55.00--60.00
Cocktail Shaker, w/without handle	25.00--35.00	35.00--50.00
Candlestick, metal stem, 8", pr.	15.00--25.00	30.00--40.00
Candlestick, 5", pr.	20.00--30.00	45.00--55.00
Candlestick, low ruffled, 2", pr.	12.00--16.00	24.00--28.00
Candlestick, triple, 5¼"	40.00--60.00	75.00--90.00
Candlestick, 2" comport style, pr.	12.00--16.00	24.00--28.00
Candlestick, 2", curved up edge, pr.	15.00--18.00	25.00--30.00
Candlestick, 2-5/8", sherbet style, pr.	12.00--16.00	24.00--28.00

	Amber, Pink Green, Evergreen	Ritz Blue Ruby, Amethyst
Relish or Candy Dish, 3 legged, 8½" rd. divided, w/metal handle	20.00--30.00	30.00--40.00
Relish, oval, divided, w/handle	20.00--25.00	35.00--40.00
Pickle Dish, 7½"	15.00--20.00	25.00--30.00
Celery Dish, 11½"	20.00--25.00	30.00--40.00
Dish, round, 3 ftd., shallow, 5¼"	10.00--15.00	18.00--22.00
Dish, round, flat top, 3 ftd., 5½"	10.00-15.00	18.00--22.00
Candy Dish, 8¼", 3 ftd., open	20.00--25.00	30.00--40.00
Candy Dish, 8", triangular, 3 ftd., open	25.00--30.00	35.00--45.00
Mayonnaise, 3", 3 ftd.	25.00--35.00	40.00--50.00
Vase, flared, tripod base, 8"	65.00--85.00	100.00-125.00
Vase, 8", ruffled	35.00--50.00	75.00--85.00
Vase, 7", curved in top	25.00--30.00	45.00--50.00
Vase, bud w/tripod base	50.00--60.00	90.00-100.00
Tray, 7½"	20.00--25.00	35.00--45.00
Tray, sandwich, 2 hdld., oblong, 15"	25.00--35.00	50.00--60.00
Comport, 11½"	30.00--35.00	50.00--60.00
Comport, 2", low	8.00--12.00	14.00--16.00
Comport, 4", stemmed	10.00--12.00	16.00--20.00
Jelly, ftd., 5"	10.00--14.00	15.00--20.00
Perfume Bottle with fan Stopper	40.00--60.00	80.00--90.00
Ash Tray, 6"	10.00--15.00	20.00--35.00
Ash Tray, 4"	10.00--15.00	15.00--20.00
Fingerbowl, 4", 1½" deep	10.00--14.00	18.00--20.00
Grapefruit, stemmed, 4¾"	12.00--16.00	22.00--25.00
Gravy, 3", 12 oz., 3 ftd.	75.00-100.00	125.00-150.00

"MOONDROPS" page 296

Wine Set	125.00-150.00

"LEOTA"

Vanity Set	40.00--50.00

"MORNING DOVE"

Vase, 9"	45.00--60.00

"ROBERTO"

Liquor Service	55.00--70.00

THE HOSTMASTER page 297

Stems	8.00--15.00
Tumblers	6.00--10.00
Bar Bottle	20.00--30.00
Bitters Bottle	20.00--30.00
Jigger	15.00--20.00

WAFFLE SET

Jugs and Tray	35.00--45.00

"SIR COCKTAIL"

Shaker Set	35.00--50.00

"COZY CORDIAL"

Decanter Set	65.00--75.00

FIGURINES page 298

No. 761 Pelican	40.00--55.00
No. 435 Baby Seal	35.00--45.00
No. 452 Seal	30.00--40.00
No. 670 Squirrel w/base	35.00--45.00
No. 668 Rooster	45.00--60.00
No. 674 Squirrel, no base	40.00--50.00
No. 508 Cigarette Cart	15.00--18.00
No. 737 Wheelbarrow	15.00--18.00
No. 733 Police Dog	35.00--40.00
No. 716 Wolfhound	55.00--60.00
No. 488 Mama Bear	35.00--45.00
No. 487 Baby Bear	30.00--40.00
No. 489 Papa Bear	40.00--45.00
No. 76 Porpoise	55.00--65.00
No. 764 Large Rabbit	45.00--55.00
No. 765 Small Rabbit (3 shapes)	20.00--30.00
No. 669 Hen	30.00--40.00
No. 667 Chicks	20.00--30.00
No. 762 Large Pig	45.00--55.00
No. 763 Small Pig	20.00--30.00

Vases

No. 135 Jug w/handle, 20 oz.	12.00--15.00
No. 650 Vase, cornucopia, 6"	15.00--20.00
No. 651 Vase Bookend, cornucopia, 5"	18.00--24.00

No. 134 Vase, square, 6"	10.00--12.00
No. 772 Flower Cart, 7"	15.00--25.00
No. 770 Ivy Vase w/peg, 4"	7.00-- 9.00
No. 131 Vase, square, 8"	12.00--16.00
No. 132 Basket, square, 14"	20.00--35.00
No. 4221 Ball Vase, 9"	15.00--25.00
No. 136 Basket, square, 11"	18.00--26.00

MISCELLANEOUS page 299

We've found an official name to one of the popular miscellaneous lines, No. 18. A glass journal describes the pattern this way in February 1936:

Crystal Eagle is the particularly descriptive name which the New Martinsville Glass Mfg. Co. has given to its new pressed design, with its flaring ridges curving in wing-like effect. Among the numerous items made in this interesting design are an oval bowl and oval platter, two-light candlesticks, a service set with a tray, cream and sugar, salt and pepper; and many other articles.

Note too that I've given 'popular' names to other New Martinsville lines and sets. We are finding so many that we need names.

No. 36 Relish, 3 compt., 8"	12.00--16.00
No. 38 Relish, 3 compt. 9"	14.00--18.00
No. 2019 Jelly, 2 hdld., 6"	8.00--12.00
No. 105 Cigarette Set: 7 pc.	20.00--25.00
No. 125 "JASPER" Cocktail Shaker	30.00--40.00
No. 125 "JASPER" cocktail	6.00-- 8.00
No. 15 "PAPPY" Wine Set: 8 pc.	75.00--85.00
No. 112 "CAESAR" Cordial Set: 7 pc.	45.00--50.00
No. 606 "GIRAFFE" Cordial Set: 7 pc.	65.00--75.00
No. 111 "PET" Cordial Set: 7 pc.	55.00--65.00
No. 28 "SHINING STAR" Vanity Set: 4 pc.	60.00--70.00
No. 18/2 CRYSTAL EAGLE Vanity Set: 4 pc.	60.00--70.00
No. 25 "JERRY" Vanity Set: 4 pc.	60.00--70.00
No. 15 "GENEVA" Vanity Set: 4 pc.	50.00--60.00
No. 2019 Bon Bon, 2 hdld., 6"	8.00--10.00
No. 2019 Plate, 2 hdld., 6"	8.00--10.00
No. 140/1 Guest Set	40.00--45.00
No. 103 Candy Box and Cover, 3 compt.	35.00--40.00
No. 190/0 Syrup and Plate	35.00--45.00
No. 18/728 CRYSTAL EAGLE Service Set: 5 pc.	35.00--45.00

No. 34 KAY	
Plate, 14"	10.00--14.00
Sugar and Cream	15.00--18.00
Cup and Saucer	6.00-- 8.00
Plate, salad, 8"	6.00-- 8.00
No. 18 CRYSTAL EAGLE Candelabra w/u Prisms	25.00--40.00
No. 18 CRYSTAL EAGLE Bowl, oval, 15"	25.00--35.00
No. 18 CRYSTAL EAGLE Plate, 17"	25.00--35.00

JANICE PATTERN

No. 4532 Sugar and Cream	20.00--25.00
No. 4520 Plate, 2 hdld., 7"	8.00--12.00
No. 4529 Plate, 2 hdld., 12"	10.00--14.00
No. 4521 Celery, 11"	14.00--16.00
No. 4517 Nappy, 2 hdld., 6"	8.00--12.00
No. 4524 Bon Bon, 2 hdld.	10.00--14.00
No. 4534 Relish, 2 compt., 6"	8.00--12.00
No. 4527 Vase, flrd., 8"	25.00--35.00
No. 4513 Bowl, flrd., 12"	20.00--30.00
No. 4522 Mayonnaise Set: 3 pc.	25.00--35.00
No. 4515 Bowl, crimped, 12"	20.00--30.00
No. 4533 Bowl, fruit, 12"	20.00--30.00
No. 4518 Bon Bon, 6"	8.00--12.00
No. 4514 Bowl, salad, 12"	20.00--30.00
No. 4512 Bowl, fruit, 11"	25.00--35.00
No. 4526 Vase, 8"	25.00--35.00
No. 4511 Bowl, flrd., 11"	25.00--35.00
No. 4510 Bowl, flrd., 11"	25.00--35.00
No. 4525 Bon Bon, 2 hdld.	10.00--14.00
No. 4516 Plate, 13"	20.00--30.00
No. 4530 Plate, 11"	18.00--24.00

ETCHED NO. 30 WILD ROSE PATTERN

No. 4536 Candlestick, 2 light	16.00--18.00
No. 4554 Candlestick, 5"	14.00--16.00
No. 42 Celery, 10"	14.00--16.00
No. 4460 Bowl, fruit, 12"	25.00--30.00
No. 18 Hurricane Candlestick, single	40.00--50.00
No. 4462 Plate, 2 hdld., 12"	18.00--20.00
No. 4459 Bowl, flrd., 12"	20.00--25.00
No. 4463 Bowl, salad, 11"	16.00--19.00
No. 4461 Plate, 14"	20.00--25.00
No. 4464 Plate, 13"	18.00--24.00

SHELL candlestick

25.00--35.00

RADIANCE LINE NO. 42

page 300

A glass journal reviews the new line in February of 1937:

RADIANCE, a new pressed design in swirl effect created with graduated series of jewel-like studdings--done in sky tint, amber, ruby, and crystal, the latter plain or etched in the MEADOW WREATH pattern is a line wide and varied in scope...

	**Amber, Sky Blue*	*Ruby*
No. 42 Mayonnaise Set: 3 pc.	25.00--35.00	60.00--70.00
No. 4252 Compote, crimped, 6"	8.00--12.00	10.00--14.00
No. 4251 Compote, 6"	8.00--10.00	10.00--12.00
No. 4248 Bon Bon, ftd., 6"	8.00--10.00	10.00--12.00
No. 4236 Mint or Compote, ftd., 5"	10.00--12.00	12.00--14.00
No. 4246 Bon Bon, flared, 6"	8.00--10.00	10.00--12.00
No. 4247 Bon Bon, crimped, 6"	8.00--10.00	10.00--12.00
No. 42 Service Set: 5 pc.	85.00--95.00	100.00-135.00
No. 4233 Bon Bon, covered, 6"	65.00--75.00	125.00-135.00
No. 42 Condiment Set: 5 pc.	160.00-170.00	200.00-225.00
No. 4253 Salver, ftd., 8"	15.00--20.00	35.00--40.00
No. 42 Bowl, flared, 10"	14.00--18.00	15.00--18.00
No. 4220 Bowl, crimped, 10"	14.00--18.00	15.00--18.00
No. 4214 Candlestick w/u Prisms, 8"	14.00--18.00	25.00--30.00
No. 18 Candelabra w/u Prisms, 2 light	14.00--18.00	25.00--30.00
No. 42 Candlestick, 2 light, pr.	40.00--50.00	95.00-100.00
No. 4212 Bowl, crimped, 12"	10.00--20.00	25.00--30.00
No. 4211 Bowl, crimped, 12"	10.00--20.00	25.00--30.00
No. 4219 Bowl, crimped, ftd., 10"	10.00--15.00	25.00--30.00
No. 4221 Ball Vase or Punch Bowl, 9"	40.00--50.00	65.00--75.00
No. 4218 bowl, flared, ftd., 10"	10.00--15.00	25.00--30.00
No. 4250 Pickle, 7"	12.00--15.00	15.00--18.00
No. 42, Candy box and cover, 3 compt.	30.00--40.00	70.00--80.00
No. 42 Celery, 10"	15.00--20.00	18.00--22.00
No. 42 Plate, 17"	30.00--40.00	50.00--60.00
No. 42 Sugar and Cream	25.00--30.00	25.00--30.00
No. 42 Cup and Saucer	8.00--10.00	10.00--12.00
No. 42 Plate, salad, 8"	6.00-- 8.00	8.00--10.00
No. 42 Jug, 4pint	100.00-150.00	150.00-200.00
No. 42 Tumbler, 9 oz.	12.00--15.00	12.00--15.00
No. 4232 Vase, crimped, 10" (also 12", 8")	18.00--24.00	35.00--45.00
No. 42 Vase, flared, 10", (also 12")	18.00--22.00	30.00--40.00
No. 4224 Relish, 2 compt., 7"	10.00--12.00	12.00--15.00
No. 4223 Relish, 2 compt., 7"	10.00--12.00	12.00--15.00
No. 4222 Relish, 2 compt., 7"	10.00--12.00	12.00--15.00
No. 4238 Mint, 2 hdld., 5"	8.00--10.00	10.00--14.00
No. 42 Sugar, Cream and Tray	45.00--50.00	55.00--60.00
No. 4237 Mint, 2 hdld., 5"	8.00--10.00	10.00--12.00
No. 4228 Relish, 3 compt., 8"	8.00--10.00	10.00--12.00
No. 4227 Relish, 3 compt., 8"	8.00--10.00	10.00--12.00
No. 4226 Relish, 3 compt., 8"	8.00--10.00	10.00--12.00
No. 42 Honey Jar and cover	50.00--60.00	75.00--85.00
No. 42 Covered Butter or Cheese	350.00-375.00	600.00-700.00
No. 42 Cheese and Cracker Set: 2 pc. 11"	25.00--30.00	35.00--45.00
No. 42 Plate, 11"	15.00--20.00	20.00--25.00
No. 4213 Bowl, flared, 12"	9.00--12.00	15.00--20.00
No. 42 Bowl, fruit, flared, 12"	9.00--12.00	15.00--20.00
No. 42 Plate, 14"	25.00--30.00	45.00--55.00
No. 42 Salt and Pepper	30.00--45.00	90.00-100.00

**Amber prices will be much lower than the Sky Blue.*

ETCHED No. 29 FLORENTINE PATTERN

37/29 12" 3 Compt. Relish

44/29 14" Plate
44/29 11" Plate

44/29 Cheese & Cracker

44/29 11" Hdl. Sandwich

44/29 3 Pc. Mayonnaise Set

44/29 11" Hdl. Nut Bowl

44/29
Sugar, Cream & Tray

44/29
3 Compt. Candy Box & Cover

44/29
11" Cake Salver

4457/29 2 light Candlestick

4456/29 13" Flared Bowl

4457/29 2 light Candlestick

4453/29 6" Candlestick

4454/29 13" Flared Bowl

4453/29
6" Candlestick

44/29
10" Flared Bowl
44/29
11" Plate

NEW MARTINSVILLE GLASS COMPANY

New Martinsville, W. Va.

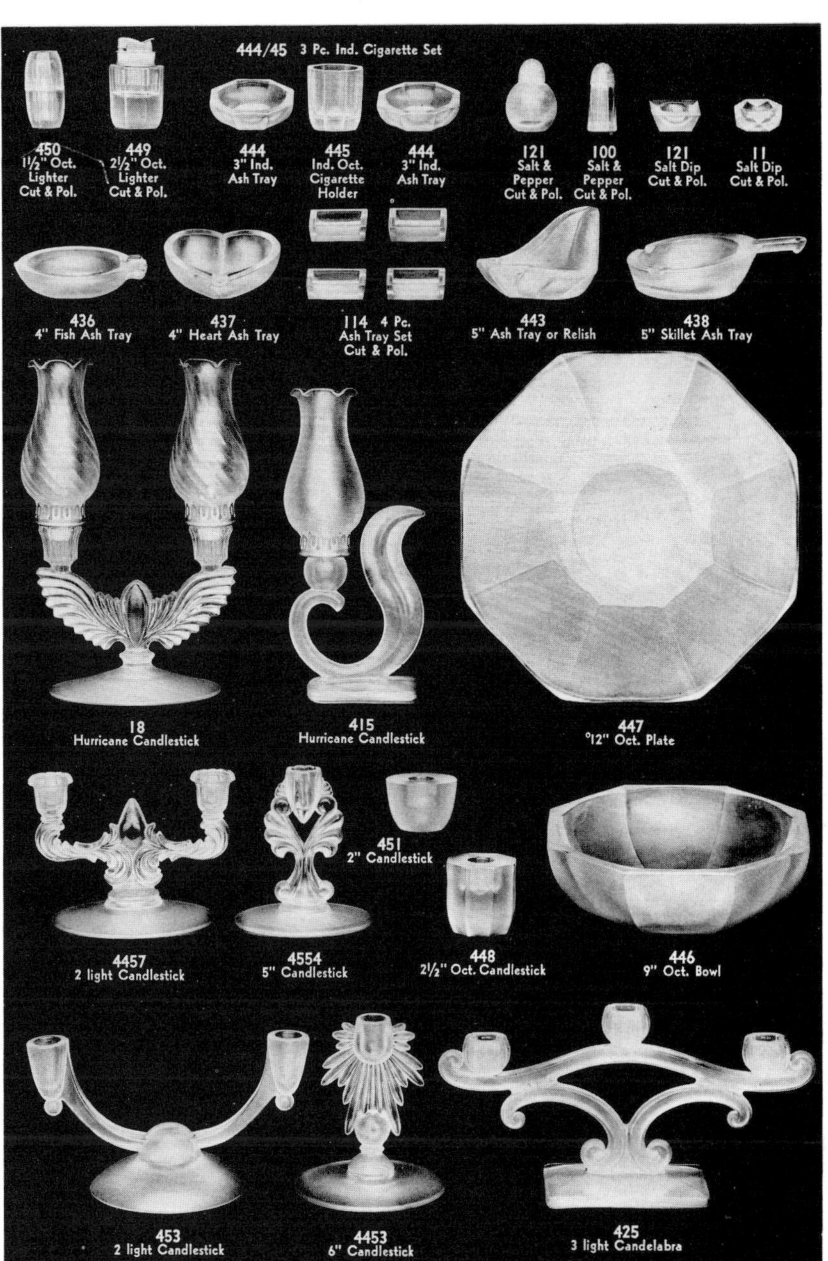
444/45 3 Pc. Ind. Cigarette Set
450
1½" Oct.
Lighter
Cut & Pol.
449
2½" Oct.
Lighter
Cut & Pol.
444
3" Ind.
Ash Tray
445
Ind. Oct.
Cigarette
Holder
444
3" Ind.
Ash Tray
121
Salt &
Pepper
Cut & Pol.
100
Salt &
Pepper
Cut & Pol.
121
Salt Dip
Cut & Pol.
11
Salt Dip
Cut & Pol.
436
4" Fish Ash Tray
437
4" Heart Ash Tray
114 4 Pc.
Ash Tray Set
Cut & Pol.
443
5" Ash Tray or Relish
438
5" Skillet Ash Tray
18
Hurricane Candlestick
415
Hurricane Candlestick
447
°12" Oct. Plate
4457
2 light Candlestick
4554
5" Candlestick
451
2" Candlestick
448
2½" Oct. Candlestick
446
9" Oct. Bowl
453
2 light Candlestick
4453
6" Candlestick
425
3 light Candelabra

NEW MARTINSVILLE GLASS COMPANY New Martinsville, W. Va.

BOOK ENDS

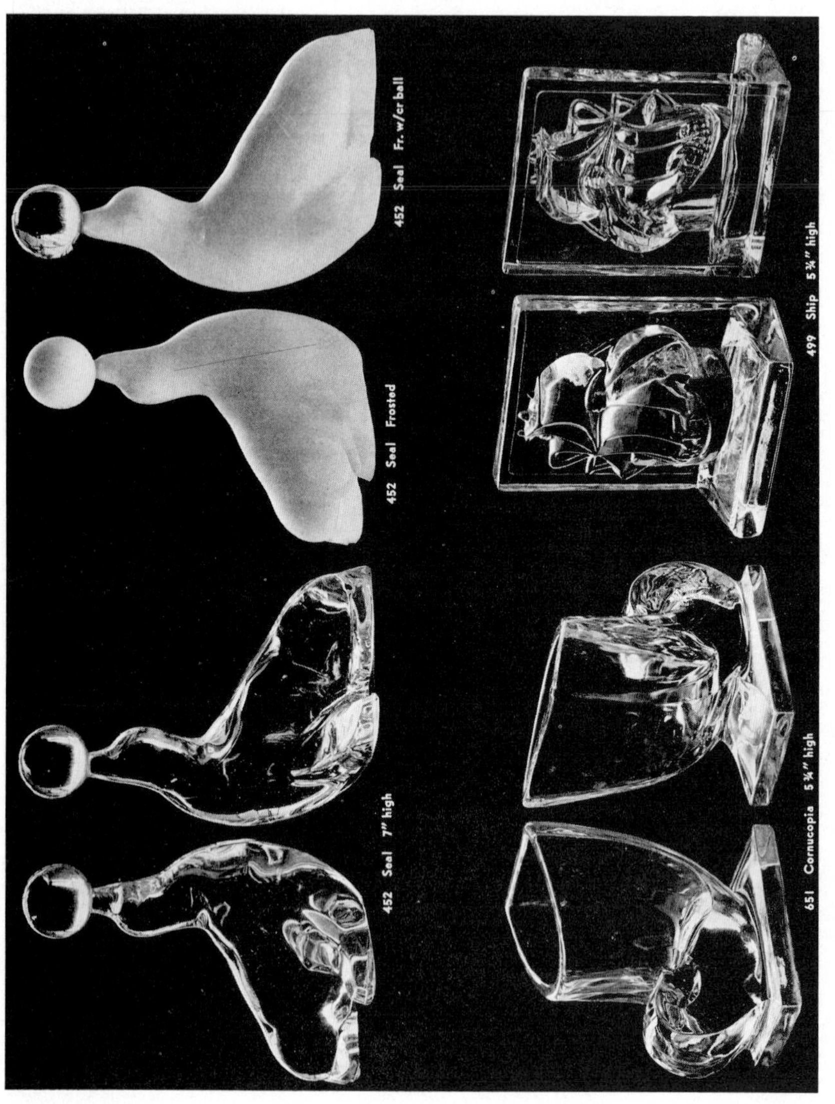

452 Seal Fr. w/cr ball

452 Seal Frosted

452 Seal 7" high

499 Ship 5¾" high

651 Cornucopia 5¾" high

BOOK ENDS (Continued)

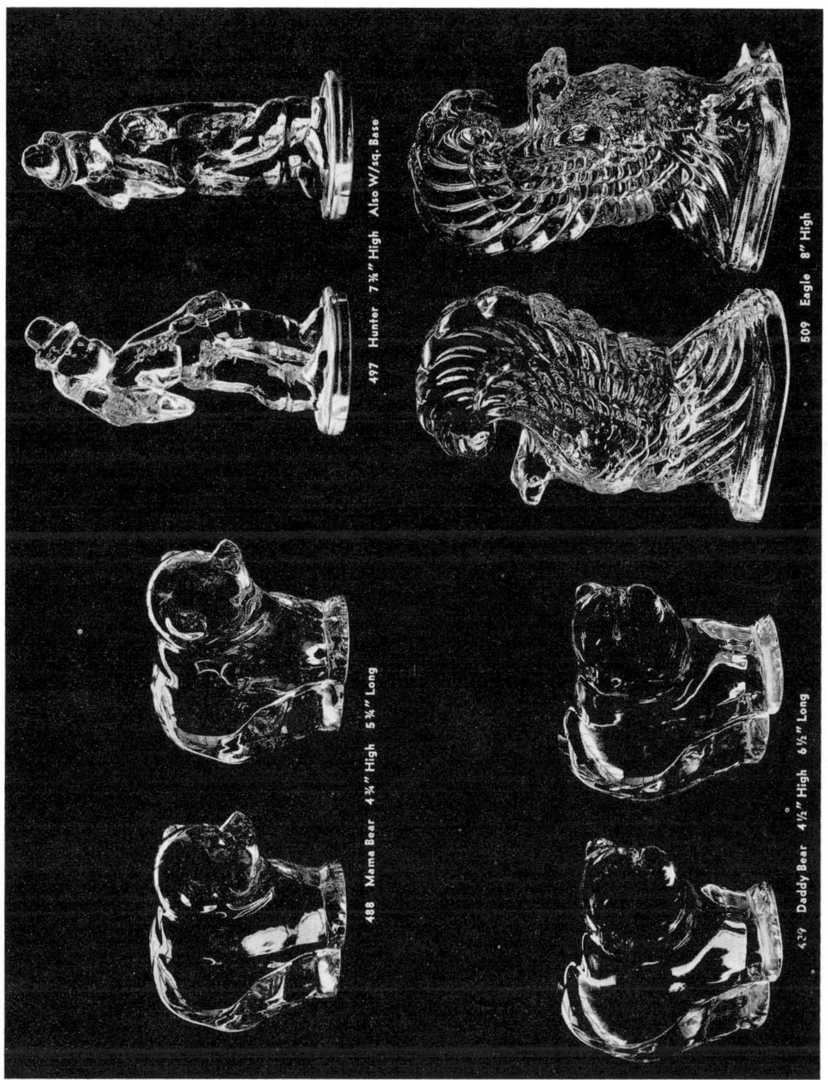

MADE BY THE
NEW MARTINSVILLE GLASS CO.

VIKING

NEW MARTINSVILLE
WEST VIRGINIA

MEADOW WREATH *Etched No. 26*

Vase, 10", ftd.	22.00--26.00
Punch Bowl, 5 qt.	40.00--50.00
No. 42/26 Punch Cup, 4 oz.	3.00-- 5.00
No. 42/26 Punch Ladle	35.00--50.00
No. 42/26 Plate, 11"	10.00--14.00
No. 4223/26 Relish, 2 compt., 7"	7.00--10.00
No. 4220/26 Bowl, crimped, 10"	12.00--15.00
No. 4266/26 Bowl, crimped, 11"	18.00--20.00
No. 4222/26 Relish, 2 compt., 7"	7.00--10.00
No. 42/26 Celery, 10"	8.00--11.00
No. 4212 Bowl, crimped, 12"	15.00--18.00
No. 4265/26 Bowl, flrd., 11"	17.00--20.00
No. 42/26 Bowl, flrd., 12"	15.00--18.00
No. 4213/26 Bowl, flrd., 12"	15.00--18.00

ETCHED NO. 29 FLORENTINE PATTERN

37/29 Relish, 3 compt., 12"	16.00--20.00
44/29 Cheese and Cracker	20.00--25.00
44/29 Plate, 14"	20.00--25.00
44/29 Plate, 11"	16.00--19.00
44/29 Sandwich, hdld., 11"	20.00--24.00
44/29 Mayonnaise Set: 3 pc.	20.00--25.00
44/29 Nut Bowl, hdld., 11"	22.00--26.00
44/29 Sugar, Cream and Tray	18.00--22.00
44/29 Candy Box and Cover, 3 compt.	25.00--30.00
24/29 Cake Salver, 11"	25.00--30.00
4457/29 Candlestick, 2 light	18.00--20.00
4456/29 Bowl, flrd., 13"	15.00--18.00
4453/29 Candlestick, 6"	16.00--19.00
4454/29 Bowl, flrd., 13"	14.00--17.00
44/29 Bowl, flrd., 10"	12.00--15.00
44/29 Plate, 11"	10.00--12.00

MISCELLANEOUS

450 Lighter, oct., 1½"	15.00--18.00
449 Lighter, oct., 2½"	15.00--18.00
444 Ash Tray, 3"	4.00-- 6.00
445 Cigarette Holder, oct.	6.00-- 8.00
121 Salt and Pepper	5.00-- 8.00
100 Salt and Pepper	5.00-- 7.00
121 Salt Dip	4.00-- 6.00
11 Salt Dip	6.00-- 8.00
436 Fish Ash Tray, 4"	6.00-- 9.00
437 Heart Ash Tray, 4"	7.00--10.00
114 Ash Tray Set: 4 pc.	8.00--10.00
443 Ash Tray or Relish, 5"	10.00--12.00
438 Skillet Ash Tray, 5"	12.00--14.00
18 Hurricane Candlestick	40.00--50.00
415 Hurricane Candlestick	35.00--40.00
447 Plate, oct., 12"	10.00--12.00
4457 Candlestick, 2 light	16.00--18.00
4554 Candlestick, 5"	12.00--15.00
451 Candlestick, 2"	6.00-- 8.00
448 Candlestick, oct., 2½"	6.00-- 9.00
446 Bowl, oct.,9"	12.00--15.00
453 Candlestick, 2 light	16.00--18.00
4453 Candlestick, 6"	12.00--16.00
425 Candlestick, 3 light	18.00--22.00

BOOK ENDS

Prices are for pairs.

452 Seal, 7" high	75.00--85.00
452 Seal, frosted, 7" high	75.00--90.00
651 Cornucopia, 5¾" high	35.00--45.00
499 Ship, 5¾" high	50.00--60.00
488 Mama Bear, 4¾" high, 5¾" long	100.00-125.00
497 Hunter, 7¾" high (also with square base)	100.00-125.00
429 Daddy Bear, 4½" high, 6½" long	100.00-125.00
509 Eagle, 8" high	100.00-150.00

PIECES SELECTED FROM TWO NEW LINES *just brought out by the New Martinsville Glass Mfg. Co., shown below, now on view at the salesroom of Frederick Skelton, 200 Fifth Ave., New York. Both have immediate sales appeal and offer outstanding values that alone should place them on retail tables throughout the country. At the left is a deep plate etched lace-like design at once attractive. It features a 14 point edge and shallow flute and is full fire polished. It comes in pink, green, black and amber in bridge sets, also 11, 9, 7, and 6 inch plates, vases and various other pieces. At the right is a wonderful dollar assortment on a new shape in a well executed and very pleasing light cut design. The items are mostly larger pieces such as console set, sandwich tray, salver, handled nut bowl, etc. It is made in pink and green.*

"LORELIE LACE" and "JOLENE" from 1930 trade catalog

Paden City

Following are reprints from a Paden City catalog circa 1933, as published here previously. Following that, other new lines which are of interest are shown.

Paden City closed in 1951, and most of their old molds were sold to the Canton Glass Company of Marion, Indiana. The following lines were shown in a 1954 catalog and I'm reprinting them here, since the line numbers match those of Paden City ware. Of these, "CROW'S FOOT" is the most often found today, but the others are also turning up and should be properly identified as belonging to this company.

Further information on Paden City wares may be found in the new newsletter being published by Michael Krumme of 1611 Brockton Ave. #6, West Los Angeles CA 90025. It's called "Paden City Party Line."

FLAPPER"	page 302
uest Set	40.00--50.00

PARTY LINE"	
:e Tea Set	50.00--60.00

SPEAKEASY"	
ocktail Shaker	20.00--30.00

SHEBA"	
onsole Set	25.00--30.00

SHEIK"	
efreshment Set	15.00--20.00

VAMP"	
resser Set	40.00--60.00

PARTY LINE"	page 303
oblet, 9 oz.	8.00--12.00
Coca Cola, 5, 6, 7, 8, 10, 12 oz.	6.00-- 9.00
Ice Tea, 12, 14 oz.	8.00--10.00
Tumbler, blown, 8, 10, 12 oz.	6.00-- 8.00
Tumbler, 7, 9 oz.	6.00-- 8.00
Plate, 6", 8"	4.00-- 7.00
Sherbet, LF, 4½, 3½ oz.	5.00-- 7.00
Sherbet, HF, 6 oz.	6.00-- 8.00
Sugar	6.00-- 8.00
Cream	6.00-- 8.00
Banana Split, 8¼"	10.00--14.00
Crushed Fruit and Cover, high	25.00--30.00
Tulip Sundae	8.00--10.00
Tumbler, 1½ oz.	4.00-- 6.00
Parfait, 5 oz.	7.00-- 9.00
Water Bottle	18.00--22.00
Candy Jar and Cover, ½ lb.	18.00--24.00
Cup, hdld., 6 oz.	4.00-- 7.00
Saucer, 5¾"	2.00-- 3.00
Cigarette Holder and Cover	20.00--30.00
Soda, ftd., 10, 12 oz.	6.00-- 9.00
Grape Juice, ftd., 6 oz.	4.00-- 6.00
Cocktail, ftd., 3½ oz.	5.00-- 7.00
Berry, 4½"	3.00-- 5.00
Berry, 8", 9"	10.00--15.00
Champagne, HF, 6 oz.	8.00--10.00
Tumbler, pressed, 7, 9 oz.	7.00-- 8.00
Comport, LF, flrd., or RE, 11", 14"	20.00--24.00
Jug and Cover, 70 oz.	45.00--55.00

Tumbler, blown, 10, 12 oz.	6.00-- 8.00
Cocktail, ftd., 18 oz.	35.00--40.00
(Shaker, Aluminum top)	
Cheese and Cracker, 10½", 12"	25.00--35.00
Tray, sandwich, 10", 12"	14.00--18.00
Comport, LF, flrd., RE, 9"	15.00--20.00
Wine Bottle, 22 oz.	25.00--35.00
Tumbler, wine, 3 oz.	3.00-- 4.00
Mayonnaise, ftd., flrd., RE, 6"	8.00--11.00
Bowl, flrd., 9", 11"	20.00--25.00
Bowl, HF, flrd., or reg., 10½"	20.00--30.00
Fan Vase, 6", 7"	12.00--16.00
Wine, ftd., 1½, 2½ oz.	4.00-- 5.00
Ice Tub, deep, 6½"	10.00--14.00
Sundae, crimped, 9 oz.	8.00--12.00
No. 5 Cologne, 1½ oz.	15.00--20.00
Salt Shaker	8.00--12.00
Sugar Shaker	18.00--26.00
Marmalade and Cover, 12 oz.	25.00--30.00
Syrup and Cover, 12 oz.	30.00--40.00
Molasses Can, nickel top, 8 oz.	25.00--35.00
Custard, 6 oz.	4.00-- 6.00
Orange Juice, 4½ oz.	4.00-- 5.00
Mixing Bowl, 7", 8", 9", each	8.00--12.00
Butter Box and Cover	20.00--30.00
Measuring Cup and No. 10 Reamer	35.00--40.00
Measuring Jug, 36 oz. and Juice Extractor, 5½"	55.00--65.00
Ice Tub and Pail, No. 2	20.00--25.00
Flower Holder, 4"	10.00--12.00
Sweet Pea Vase	10.00--15.00
Globe Vase	20.00--25.00
Console Bowl, 11"	20.00--25.00
Ice Tub, 7¾" dia.	12.00--16.00
Nappy and Cover, 4½"	8.00--12.00
Box and Cover, round	15.00--20.00
Sugar Server, 4½", 12 oz.	20.00--25.00
Beer Mug, 10 oz., 12 oz.	15.00--20.00
Plate, serving, 10"	10.00--13.00
Candlestick, 3½"	6.00-- 9.00
Cocktail Liner, 3½ oz.	4.00-- 5.00
Cocktail, 2½ oz.	6.00-- 8.00

NO. 300 LINE page 304

Candy Box and Cover, 6", 7"	25.00--35.00
Mayonnaise Set: 3 pc.	20.00--25.00
Comport, LF, 8", 10"	15.00--25.00
Comport, HF, 8"	20.00--25.00
Tray, sandwich, center hdld., 11"	12.00--16.00
Plate, cake, LF, 10"	14.00--18.00
Plate, cake, ftd., 9"	16.00--20.00
Cream, 5, 7 oz.	7.00-- 9.00
Sugar, 5, 7 oz.	7.00-- 9.00
Candlesticks, pr.	15.00--20.00
Bowl, console, No. 5, 11", 14" (Also No. 3 flrd. shape)	20.00--30.00
Ice Tub, 6"	15.00--20.00
Nappy and Cover, 3 part, 6½" (Also 2 part, & w/o partition)	20.00--30.00
Cheese and Cracker, 10½"	20.00--25.00
Bowl, HF, 8"	14.00--18.00
Candy Tray, center hdld., 11"	12.00--15.00
Goblet, 8 oz.	6.00-- 9.00
Cup	4.00-- 6.00
Saucer	2.00-- 3.00
Sherbet, LF, 5 oz.	4.00-- 5.00
Vase, 8"	10.00--15.00
Vase, bud, 9"	8.00--10.00
Vase, fan, 8½"	15.00--20.00
Oyster Plate, 10½"	9.00--12.00
Butter Tub and Cover, 5"	18.00--22.00
Plate, 11"	10.00--15.00
Bowl, salad, flrd., 9" (Also made RE)	16.00--22.00

"PEACOCK AND ROSE"

Comport, ftd., 6½"	25.00--35.00
Tray, sandwich, hdld., 11"	20.00--25.00
Sugar and Cream Set, 4"	25.00--30.00
Bowl, ftd., 8½"	25.00--30.00
Plate, cake, ftd., 10"	25.00--35.00
Mayonnaise Set: 3 pc.	25.00--35.00
Relish and Cover, 3 part, 6½"	30.00--40.00
Candy Box and Cover, ftd., 7"	35.00--45.00
Bowl, fruit, hdld., 8½"	25.00--30.00
Bowl, fruit, oval	25.00--30.00
Bowl, fruit, 10½"	25.00--30.00
Ice Bucket, 5¾"	25.00--30.00
Bowl, console, RE, 11"	20.00--25.00
Candlesticks, rolled top, 5" across, pr.	20.00--25.00
Vase, 10", 12"	35.00--45.00
Vase, 8¼" (same style as ORCHID Vase)	40.00--45.00

"ORCHID" page 305

Vase, 8¼"	40.00--45.00

"DELILAH BIRD"

Vase, 6½"	30.00--35.00
Candleholder, pr.	25.00--30.00
Bowl, console, w/handles, 13¾"	30.00--35.00

"LELA BIRD"

You may find other pieces not listed.

Vase, 10"	40.00--45.00
Jug, 7"	50.00--60.00
Vase, 5"	35.00--40.00
Comport, 6½"	30.00--35.00
Cream and Sugar	22.00--28.00
Fruit Bowl, oval shaped	30.00--40.00
Mayonnaise Set	30.00--40.00

Sandwich Tray, 10"	16.00--22.00
Candlestick pr.	20.00--25.00
Cake Plate, ftd.	20.00--30.00

"NORA BIRD" page 306

You may find more pieces in this pattern

Plate, 8"	6.00-- 9.00
Tumbler, 3", 4"	10.00--12.00
Tumbler, ftd., 4¾"	10.00--13.00
Cup and Saucer	12.00--16.00
Cream and Sugar	16.00--22.00
Cream and Sugar, (2nd. style)	16.00--22.00

"CUPID"

You will find other pieces in this pattern.

Plate, 10"	16.00--24.00
Cream and Sugar	22.00--28.00

"CALIFORNIA POPPY"

Vase, 12"	35.00--45.00

"LAZY DAISY" page 307

Pink, green.

Plate	3.00-- 5.00
Cup	3.00-- 5.00
Saucer	2.00-- 3.00
Sugar	5.00-- 8.00
Cream	5.00-- 8.00
Candy Box and Cover, ftd., 6½", 7"	18.00--22.00
Candlestick, RE, 3", pr.	15.00--20.00
Candlestick, cupped, 3½"	18.00--22.00
Cake Plate, low ftd., 10"	15.00--20.00
Nappy and Cover, 3 compt., 6½", 7"	16.00--22.00
Candy Tray, hdld., 10"	14.00--18.00
Comport, flrd., low ftd., 10"	15.00--20.00
Cheese and Cracker, 11"	15.00--20.00
Mayonnaise Set: 3 pc.	20.00--24.00
No. 5 Bowl, console, 12"	20.00--25.00
No. 2 Bowl, console, 12"	20.00--25.00
Tray, sandwich, hdld., 11"	12.00--16.00
Candy Jar and Cover, ½ lb.	18.00--24.00

"POPEYE AND OLIVE" page 307

	Colors	Ruby, Royal Blue
Tulip Sundae, 7 oz.	8.00--10.00	11.00--14.00
Claret, 3½ oz.	6.00-- 8.00	9.00--11.00
Sherbet, LF	3.00-- 5.00	6.00-- 8.00
Sherbet, HF	4.00-- 6.00	8.00--10.00
Goblet, 10 oz.	7.00-- 9.00	9.00--12.00
Wine, 2½ oz.	6.00-- 8.00	8.00--10.00
Orange, 5 oz.	4.00-- 6.00	6.00-- 8.00
Tumbler, 9 oz.	4.00-- 6.00	8.00--10.00
Ice Tea, 12 oz., 17 oz.	7.00--10.00	10.00--14.00
Cup and Saucer	5.00-- 8.00	10.00--12.00
Sugar	7.00-- 9.00	9.00--12.00
Cream	7.00-- 9.00	9.00--12.00
Finger Bowl and Plate	7.00-- 9.00	9.00--12.00
Plate, salad, 8", 6"	3.50-- 5.00	4.00-- 6.00
Tray, sandwich, hdld., 10½"	11.00--14.00	15.00--20.00
Bowl, 8"	10.00--13.00	14.00--18.00
Vase, regular, 7"	8.00--10.00	11.00--15.00
Vase, crimped top, 7"	8.00--10.00	11.00--15.00
Bowl, salad, 2 hdld., 8" and 10" plate	15.00--20.00	20.00--28.00
Decanter, with jigger Stopper, 36 oz.	30.00--35.00	35.00--45.00
Jug, stuck handle, 48 oz.	20.00--25.00	35.00--40.00

"PENNY" LINE page 308

	Colors	Ruby, Royal Blue
Tumblers (3 sizes)	5.00-- 7.00	7.00--10.00
Nappy	4.00-- 5.00	4.00-- 6.00
Cup and Saucer	10.00--12.00	12.00--15.00
Sherbet (2 sizes)	6.00-- 8.00	8.00--10.00
Goblet, wine	6.00-- 8.00	8.00--10.00
Goblet, low stem	6.00-- 8.00	8.00--10.00
Goblet, tall	7.00-- 9.00	9.00--11.00

"WOTTA" LINE

(Also with IRWIN etching)

	Colors	Ruby, Amethyst Royal Blue
Plate, luncheon, 2 hdld., 13"	12.00--15.00	15.00--20.00
Cup	4.00-- 6.00	8.00--10.00
Saucer	2.00-- 3.00	3.00-- 4.00
Cream	6.00-- 8.00	8.00--10.00
Sugar	6.00-- 8.00	8.00--10.00
Bowl, cream soup and Plate	8.00--10.00	15.00--18.00
Bowl, salad, 2 hdld., 11"	10.00--14.00	15.00--20.00
Candy Box and Cover, 3 part, 6", 7"	15.00--20.00	25.00--35.00
Nut Tray, hdld., 10"	10.00--15.00	20.00--25.00
Comport, HF and LF, 7"	12.00--15.00	16.00--22.00
Mayonnaise Set: 3 pc.	16.00--22.00	22.00--28.00
Comport, LF, 10"	18.00--22.00	20.00--26.00
Candlestick, 6", pr.	22.00--25.00	40.00--50.00
No. 2 Bowl, console, 12" (Also RE and flrd.)	14.00--20.00	25.00--30.00
Salver, LF, 10½"	12.00--16.00	15.00--25.00
Tray, sandwich, hdld., 10½"	10.00--14.00	15.00--20.00

BATTER SETS page 309

Batter Jug, Syrup Jug, and Tray	40.00--60.00

ROUND RELISH

3 Part	14.00--20.00

WINGED RELISH

3 Part, hdld.	15.00--25.00

"ARISTOCRAT"

Old Fashioned, 6 oz.	6.00-- 9.00
Bar Bottle w/Stopper, 23 oz.	25.00--35.00
Whiskey and Soda, 12 oz.	10.00--12.00
Cocktail Shaker, chromium topped	30.00--40.00
Tumbler, "Georgian", 9 oz.	6.00-- 8.00
Tumbler, 5 oz., 7 oz., 9 oz.	6.00-- 8.00
Tumbler, Hi Ball, 8 oz.	6.00-- 8.00
Tumbler, Ice Tea, 11 oz.	8.00--10.00
Whiskey, 3 oz.	7.00-- 9.00
Goblet, 5 oz.	8.00--10.00
Goblet, 8 oz.	8.00--10.00
Goblet, high foot, 9 oz.	8.00--10.00
Goblet, low foot, 10 oz.	9.00--11.00
Shaker	10.00--12.00
Plate, oval, 8½" X 12"	15.00--20.00
Bowl, oval, 7½" X 10½"	15.00--20.00
Oil, 6 oz.	25.00--35.00
Nappy, 6", 7"	6.00--10.00
Plates, 6", 6½", 8½"	4.00-- 8.00
Oil, 3 oz.	25.00--30.00
Tulip Sundae, 5½ oz.	8.00--10.00
Peach Melba, 10 oz.	9.00--11.00
Soda, 14 oz.	8.00--10.00
Soda, ftd., 8 oz.	8.00--10.00
Parfait, 5 oz.	8.00--10.00
Sherbet, 5 oz.	4.00-- 6.00
Sherbet, or Cocktail, 3½ oz.	6.00-- 8.00
Sherbet, reg., 4 oz.	4.00-- 6.00
Banana Split	8.00--10.00
Finger Bowl, 4"	6.00-- 8.00
Finger Bowl Plate, 6"	3.00-- 4.00
Jug, 60 oz.	40.00--45.00
Vase, 5"	8.00--10.00
Ash Tray, 4½"	5.00-- 6.00
Wine, 2½ oz.	8.00--10.00
Marmalade and Cover, 12 oz.	28.00--32.00
Syrup and Cover, 12 oz.	30.00--35.00
Ice Tea, 12 oz.	8.00--10.00

"SUNSET"

Vanity Set	35.00--55.00

"MOON SET"

Vanity Set	35.00--55.00

MISCELLANEOUS

500 Cologne, 1 oz.	15.00--20.00
502 Cologne, 1 oz.	15.00--20.00
501 Cologne, I oz.	15.00--20.00
503 Puff Box and Cover	12.00--16.00
198 Puff Box and Cover	12.00--16.00
209 Puff Box and Cover	12.00--16.00
201 Puff Box and Cover	12.00--16.00
207 Sugar and Cover, ftd.	12.00--16.00
207 Jam Dish and Cover, ftd.	14.00--18.00

207 Cream, ftd.	8.00--10.00
191 Candlestick, 4½"	15.00--20.00
700 Sandwich Tray, oval, hdld., 12½"	10.00--14.00
700 Puff Box and Cover	10.00--14.00
700 Cheese and Cracker, oval, 13"	12.00--16.00
700 Candy Jar & Cover, ½ lb.	12.00--16.00
503 Candy Box and Cover, low foot, 6"	20.00--25.00
198 Nappy and Cover, 3 part, 6½"	15.00--20.00
198 Candy Box & Cover, 6½"	15.00--20.00
189 Jug and Cover	35.00--45.00
116 Candlestick, 7"	15.00--18.00
706 Goblet, 9½ oz.	8.00--12.00
207 Sherbet, ftd., 5 oz.	5.00-- 8.00
102 Cocktail, 3 oz.	5.00-- 8.00
326 Oyster Plate, 8¼"	6.00-- 8.00
400 Relish Tray, 4 compt., 10"	10.00--15.00
499 Vanity Tray, 10"	12.00--15.00
2 Flower Block, 3"	3.00-- 5.00
5 Ash Tray	10.00--15.00
405 Oil, square, 5 oz.	15.00--25.00
192 Candlestick, 3½"	6.00-- 8.00
7 Cigarette Jar	20.00--25.00
8 Childs Mug, 5 oz.	15.00--20.00
6 Toy Mug, 1 oz.	4.00-- 6.00
7 Toy Mug, 1 oz.	6.00-- 8.00
136 Shaker	8.00--10.00
300 Water Bottle	10.00--14.00
401 Jug, 3 qt.	20.00--25.00
902 Tray, round, 9½"	8.00--10.00
207 Nappy, 4½"	3.00-- 4.00
404 Sugar and Cover	12.00--15.00
207 Nappy, 9"	8.00--12.00
701 Candy Jar and Cover, ½ lb.	15.00--25.00
6 Percolator, 56 oz.	75.00-100.00

MISCELLANEOUS VASES

300 Fan Vase, 8½"	15.00--20.00
191 Flower Holder, 4"	10.00--12.00
191½ Vase, Sweet Pea	10.00--15.00
191 Globe Vase	20.00--25.00
503 Fan Vase, 8½"	20.00--25.00
180 Vase, 12"	25.00--30.00
192 Vase, 8"	12.00--15.00
182 Vase, oval, 8"	20.00--25.00
Water Bottle	15.00--20.00
195 Vase, 12"	20.00--25.00

Following are reprints of company catalog

PADEN CITY GLASS MFG. CO., Paden City, W. Va., U. S. A.

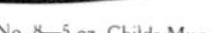

No. 8—5 oz. Childs Mug

No. 6—1 oz. Toy Mug

No. 7—1 oz. Toy Mug

No. 136—Shaker

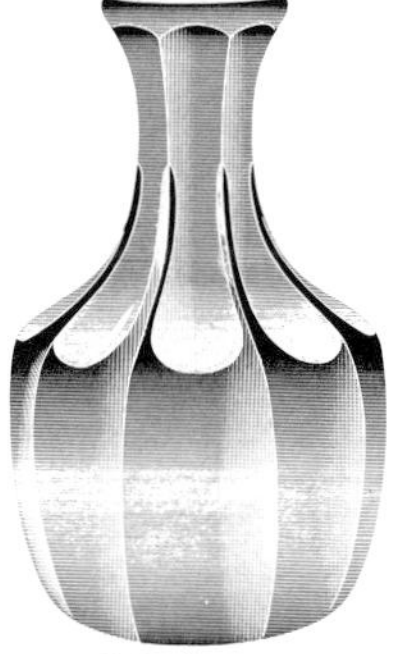

No. 300—Water Bottle

No. 401—3 Qt. Jug

PADEN CITY GLASS MFG. CO., Paden City, W. Va., U. S. A.

No. 902—9½ in. Round Tray
Also made in 8½ inch

No. 404 Sugar & Cover

No. 207—4½ in. Nappy

No. 6—56 oz. Percolator
Complete

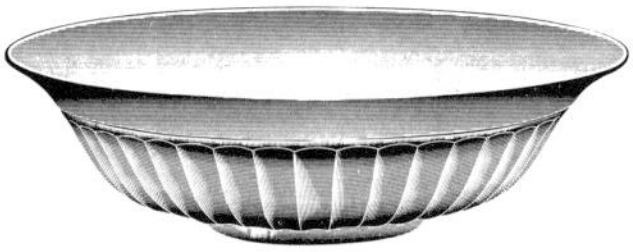

No. 207—9 in. Nappy
Also made in 8 inch

No. 701—½ lb. Candy Jar & Cover

PADEN CITY GLASS MFG. CO., Paden City, W. Va., U. S. A.

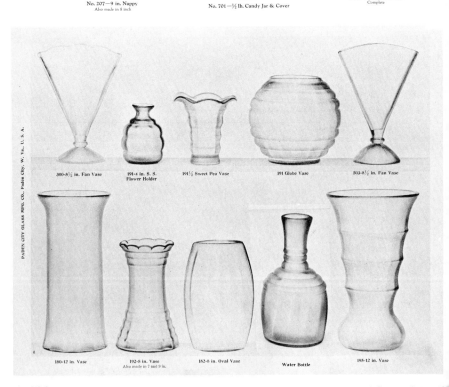

300-8½ in. Fan Vase

191-4 in. S. S. Flower Holder

191½ Sweet Pea Vase

191 Globe Vase

503-8½ in. Fan Vase

6

180-12 in. Vase

192-8 in. Vase
Also made in 7 and 9 in.

182-8 in. Oval Vase

Water Bottle

195-12 in. Vase

69-9 oz. Peach Melba

69-9 oz.-Goblet

69½ Sherbet

69-12 oz. Tumbler

69-9 oz. Tumbler

69-2½ oz. Wine

"ARISTOCRAT"

69-12 oz. Marmalade and Cover

69-12 oz. Syrup and Cover

69 Finger Bowl and 6 in. Plate

"LAZY DAISY"

701-½ lb. Candy Jar and Cover

701 Cup and Saucer

701 Sugar
also made optic

701 Cream
also made optic

69½-12 oz. Ice Tea

69-60 oz. Jug and Cover

701 LINE

3½ in. Cupped Candlestick

10 in. L. F. Cake Plate

3 in. R. E. Candlestick

"LAZY DAISY"

7 in. 3 Comp. Nappy and Cover
Also made 6½ in. Size

7 in. Ftd. Candy Box and Cover
Also made 6 in. Size.

12 in. No. 5 Console Bowl
Also made Flared and Reg.

10 in. Hld. Candy Tray

10 in. L. F. Comport Flared
Also made R. E. and No. 2 Shape

12 in. No. 2 Shape Console Bowl

11 in. Cheese and Cracker

3 piece Mayonnaise Set

11 in. Hld. Sandwich Tray

No. 300 LINE

PADEN CITY GLASS MFG. CO., Paden City, W. Va., U. S. A.

8 in. High Foot Comport Flared
Also made R. E.

11 in. Sandwich Tray

3 in. Candlestick

6 in. Ice Tub

6 in. L. F. Candy Box

3 Piece Mayonnaise Set

5 oz. Sugar
Also made 7 oz.

5 oz. Cream
Also made 7 oz.

6½ in. 3 Part. Nappy and Cover
Also made 2 part. and without partition

10 in. L. F. Comport R. E.
Also made Flared and Regular

1

10½ in. Cheese and Cracker

14 in. Console Bowl No. 5 Shape
Also made No. 3 and Flared Shape

10 in. L. F. Cake Plate

No. 300 LINE

PADEN CITY GLASS MFG. CO., Paden City, W. Va., U. S. A.

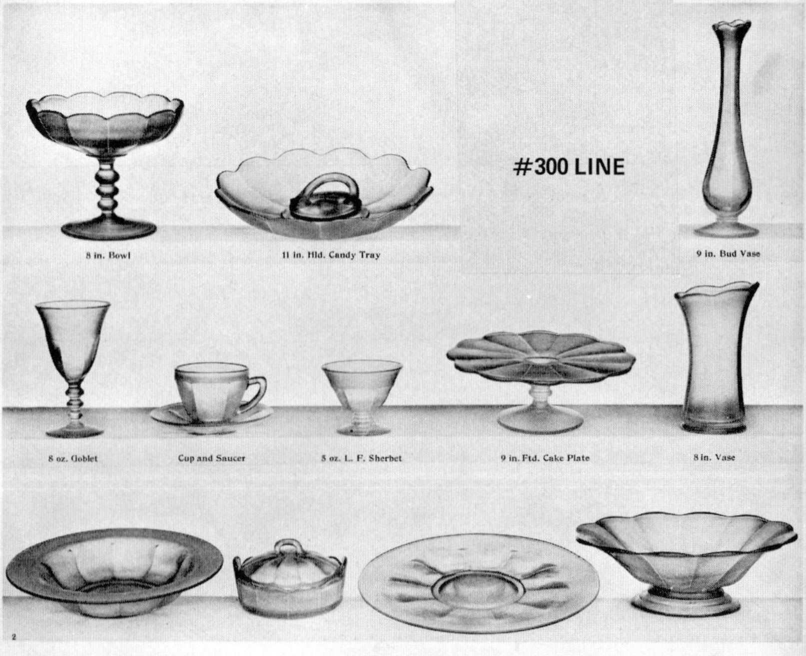

#300 LINE

8 in. Bowl

11 in. Hld. Candy Tray

9 in. Bud Vase

8 oz. Goblet

Cup and Saucer

5 oz. L. F. Sherbet

9 in. Ftd. Cake Plate

8 in. Vase

2

10½ in. Oyster Plate

5 in. Butter Tub and Cover

11 in. Plate

9 in. Oval Salad Bowl, Flared
Also made R. E.

No. 994 LINE (Green) "POPEYE & OLIVE"

7 oz. Tulip Sundae | 3½ oz. Claret | L. F. Sherbet | H. F. Sherbet | 10 oz. Goblet | 2½ oz. Wine | 5 oz. Orange | 9 oz. Tumbler | 12 oz. Ice Tea Also Made 17 oz.

Cup and Saucer | Sugar | Cream | Finger Bowl and Plate

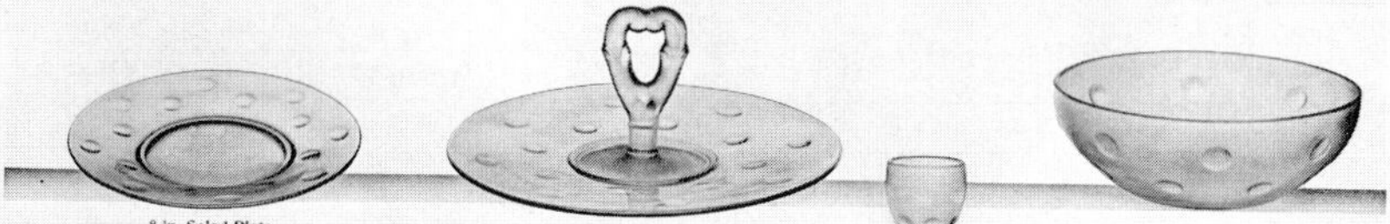

8 in. Salad Plate Also Made 6 in. Plate | 10½ in. Hld. Sandwich Tray | 8 in. Bowl

7 in. Vase, regular Also Made Crimped Top | 8 in. 2 Hld. Salad Bowl 10 in. 2 Hld. Plate | 36 oz. Decanter With Jigger Stopper | 48 oz. Stuck Handle Jug

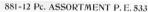

PADEN CITY GLASS MFG. CO., Paden City, W. Va., U. S. A.

11

881-12 Pc. ASSORTMENT P. E. 533

7 in. 3 Part Candy Box and Cover Also Made 6 in. | 10 in. Hld. Nut Tray | 7 in. H. F. Compote Also Made Low Foot | 3 pc. Mayonnaise Set | Sugar | Cream

"WOTTA" LINE *with IRWIN etching*

10 in. L. F. Comport | 6 in. Candlestick | 12 in. 2 Console Bowl Also Made R. E. and Flared | 6 in. Candlestick | 11 in. 2 Hld. Salad Bowl

10½ in. L. F. Cake Salver | 10½ in. Hld. Sandwich Tray | 13 in. 2 Hld. Plate

PADEN CITY GLASS MFG. CO., Paden City, W. Va., U. S. A.

12

catalog reprint c. 1933

As explained in the chapter heading, these are lines and pieces that once belonged to Paden City. They are reprinted from a 1954 Canton company catalog. Some of them you'll find in the Book 2 patterns and some are shown for the first time here.

"BRETON"
Line 90 CHAVALIER

Tumbler, 5 oz.	6.00-- 8.00
Tumbler, 9 oz., 12 oz.	7.00-- 9.00
Tumbler, Ice Tea, 12 oz.	7.00-- 9.00
Whiskey, 2 oz.	6.00-- 8.00
Jug, ice lip, 44 oz.	30.00--40.00
Goblet, 10 oz.	9.00--11.00
Nappy, 4½", 8" flrd., or cup't.	4.00--10.00
Sugar, 6 oz.	6.00-- 8.00
Cream, 6 oz.	6.00-- 8.00
Plate, 6", 8", 11"	3.00--12.00
Sherbet, low foot, 4 oz., 4½ oz.	4.00-- 5.00
Decanter, square, 24 oz.	25.00--30.00
Decanter, round, 24 oz.	25.00--30.00
Cordial, 1¼ oz.	9.00--10.00
Wine, 2½ oz.	9.00--10.00
Claret, 3½ oz.	9.00--10.00
Cocktail, ftd., 3 oz.	6.00-- 9.00
Champagne, 3½ oz.	6.00-- 9.00

"LULI"
Line 330

Low prices are for crystal. High prices are for Ruby.

Nappy, 6"	4.00-- 6.00
Nappy, hdld., 6", 9"	7.00--12.00
Nappy, hdld., 2 part, 6"	7.00-- 9.00
Mayonnaise, 4"	7.00-- 9.00
Bowl, reg. and flrd.	10.00--12.00
Plate, 6", 8", 12"	3.00--12.00
Plate, crimped	6.00-- 9.00
Cup & Saucer	9.00--15.00
Plate, hdld., 13"	15.00--25.00
Cheese and Cracker, covered, 12½"	25.00--40.00
Cheese Sherbet, 5½"	10.00--12.00
Candlestick, 6½"	12.00--18.00
Bowl, shallow, 10"	15.00--25.00
Console, 12½"	15.00--30.00
Console Bowl, 3 toed, 11"	15.00--25.00
Bowl, salad, 8½"	12.00--20.00
Relish, 3 part, 7"	10.00--20.00
Bowl, hdld., 11"	15.00--30.00
Plate, 3 toed, 13½"	15.00--25.00
Plate, pan, 3 toed, 12"	15.00--25.00

"VALE"
Line 444

Plate, hdld., 10½"	9.00--11.00
Cheese and Cracker, covered, 12"	15.00--20.00
Cracker Plate, 10½"	9.00--11.00
Plate, 10½"	9.00--11.00
Plate, 15"	10.00--14.00
Bowl, shallow, 9"	9.00--11.00
Bowl, deep, 8½"	11.00--13.00
Bowl, shallow, 12"	12.00--14.00
Console Bowl, 12½"	12.00--15.00
Cheese Sherbet, 5"	6.00-- 8.00
Comport, high foot, 7"	20.00--25.00
Candy Box and Cover, 3 part, 6"	15.00--20.00
Candy Bowl and Cover, 6"	20.00--25.00
Candlestick, 6"	10.00--12.00
Candlestick, 2 way, 5"	12.00--14.00
Ice Tub	8.00--11.00
Ash Tray, round, 3¾"	4.00-- 6.00
Bowl, hdld., 8½"	9.00--11.00

FUTURA
Line 836

Goblet, 10 oz.	7.00-- 9.00
Beverage, 6 oz.	5.00-- 7.00
Tumbler, 9 oz.	5.00-- 7.00
Tumbler, Ice Tea, 12 oz.	6.00-- 8.00
Sherbet, low foot, 5 oz.	4.00-- 6.00
Sherbet, high foot, 6 oz.	5.00-- 7.00
Soda, ftd., 10 oz., 12 oz.	6.00-- 8.00
Parfait	6.00-- 8.00
Cup, 7 oz.	4.00-- 6.00
Saucer	1.00-- 2.00
Wine, 3 oz.	7.00-- 9.00
Sugar	5.00-- 7.00
Cream	5.00-- 7.00
Plate, 8"	3.00-- 4.00
Wine Cordial, 3 oz.	7.00-- 9.00

"PLUME"
Line 888

Sugar	7.00-- 8.00
Cream	7.00-- 8.00
Relish, 3 part, reg., or crimped, 7"	8.00--12.00
Marmalade and Cover, 7 oz.	12.00--16.00
Sandwich Tray, hdld., 11"	10.00--14.00
Relish, 4 part, 10"	12.00--15.00
Cheese and Cracker, covered, 12"	18.00--24.00
Candy Box and Cover, 3 part, 7"	15.00--20.00
Cake Salver, 11"	12.00--18.00
Comport, 10"	12.00--16.00

"NADJA" Line 900

Prices are for crystal.

Bowl, shallow, crimped, bell	4.00-- 5.00
Nappy, 5"	4.00-- 5.00
Nappy, stuck hdld., flat rim, 5"	5.00-- 8.00
Nappy, stuck hdld., crimped rim, 5"	5.00-- 8.00
Sugar	5.00-- 7.00
Cream	5.00-- 7.00
Candy Box and Cover, 3 part, 7"	12.00--15.00
Relish, crimped, 3 part, 7"	7.00-- 9.00
Relish, 4 part, 10"	8.00--12.00
Dressing Bowl Plate	3.00-- 4.00
Dressing Bowl, 2 part, 5"	6.00-- 9.00
Plate, 7"	3.00-- 4.00
Plate, 15"	10.00--14.00
Plate, pan, 14"	9.00--12.00
Candlestick, 4½"	7.00--10.00
Comport, high foot, 8"	12.00--16.00
Marmalade and Cover, 7½ oz.	10.00--14.00
Candlestick, 2 way, 6"	10.00--12.00
Cake Salver, low foot, 11"	12.00--15.00
Bowl, hdld., 11"	8.00--10.00
Plate, hdld., 12"	7.00-- 9.00
Comport, low foot, 10"	10.00--14.00
Nappy, 3 toed, flrd., or crimped	6.00-- 9.00

"TRANCE" Line 1503

Prices are for crystal.

Cream Soup, hdld., 4½"	4.00-- 5.00
Nappy, hdld., 4½", 6", 7"	3.00-- 8.00
Nappy, hdld., 2 part, 4½", 6"	3.00-- 7.00
Nappy, hdld., 2 part, 6"	4.00-- 5.00
Nappy, hdld., 5½", 7-3/8"	4.00-- 7.00
Cream	3.00-- 5.00
Sugar	3.00-- 5.00
Nappy, 3 part, hdld., 7"	7.00-- 9.00
Nappy, oval, 9"	7.00-- 9.00
Relish, oval, 2 part, 7"	6.00-- 8.00
Candlestick, 2¾"	5.00-- 7.00

"CHAUCER" Line 1504

Prices are for crystal.

Nappy, 5"	3.00-- 4.00
Nappy, hdld., 8"	7.00--10.00
Mayonnaise Bowl	5.00-- 7.00
Mayonnaise Plate	2.00-- 3.00
Cream	3.00-- 5.00
Sugar	3.00-- 5.00
Cheese Sherbet, 5½"	4.00-- 6.00
Relish, 3 part, 11½"	7.00--10.00
Soda, 8 oz.	2.00-- 4.00
Soda, 16 oz.	3.00-- 5.00
Relish, 3 part, crimped, 6¾"	5.00-- 7.00
Salver, 8", 10"	9.00--12.00
Comport, low foot, 6", 7"	5.00-- 7.00
Sandwich Tray, hdld., 11"	6.00-- 9.00
Nut Tray, hdld., 10"	6.00-- 9.00
Cheese Plate, 10½"	8.00--10.00
Cheese and Cracker, covered, 12"	14.00--20.00

CANDY BOXES AND COVERS

Low prices are for colors. High prices are for Ruby and Cobalt and etched.

"VAARA"	
411 Candy Box and Cover, sq., 2 part, 7"	25.00--40.00
411 Candy Box and Cover, sq., 3 part, 7"	25.00--40.00
"CROW'S FOOT"	
412½ Candy Box and Cover, 3 part	25.00--40.00
"VALE"	
444 Candy Bowl and Cover, 6"	15.00--30.00
444 Candy Box and Cover, 3 part, 6"	15.00--25.00
466 Candy Box and Cover, 3 part, 7"	15.00--25.00
"PLUME"	
888 Candy Box and Cover, 3 part, 7"	20.00--30.00
"NADJA"	
900 Candy Box and Cover, 3 part, 7"	20.00--30.00
"TRANCE"	
1503 Candy Box and Cover, 3 part, 6½"	20.00--30.00
"CHAUCER"	
1504 Candy Box and Cover, 3 part, 7"	15.00--25.00

BOWLS

"CROW'S FOOT"	
412 Bowl, low foot, 6"	9.00--12.00
"VALE"	
444 Bowl, flrd., 5½"	6.00-- 9.00
444 Bowl, shallow, 9", 12"	12.00--15.00
444 Bowl, hdld., 8½"	10.00--15.00
444 Console Bowl, 12½"	10.00--15.00
"PLUME"	
888 Console, 12"	12.00--16.00
888 Lily Bowl, 13"	14.00--18.00
888 Bowl, hdld., 11"	10.00--15.00
888 Console, 3 toed, 11"	12.00--18.00
"CROW'S FOOT"	
890 Bowl, hdld., 10"	15.00--18.00
"NADJA"	
900 Lily Bowl, 13"	10.00--14.00
900 Console, flrd., or shallow, 12"	10.00--15.00

"ARISTOCRAT"

69 LINE

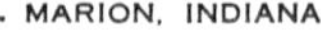
MARION, INDIANA

69 - 9 oz "Georgian" Tumbler
Ht. 4 1/16" Diam. 2 15/16"

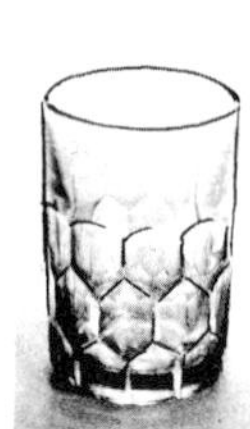
69½ - Tumbler
5 oz Juice Ht. 3 5/16"
7 oz Tumbler Ht. 4"
9 oz Tumbler Ht. 4"

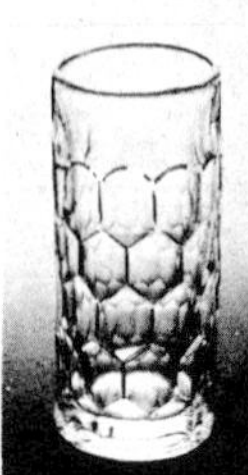
69 - Hi Ball
8 oz - Ht. 5"

69 - Ice Tea
11 oz - Ht. 5⅝"

69 - Whiske
3 oz

69 - 5 oz Goblet
Ht. 4¼"

69 - 8 oz Goblet
Ht. 6"

69 - 9 oz HF Goblet
Ht. 5 13/16"

69½ - 10 oz Low Ft. Goblet - Ht. 5 3/16"

69 - S & P Shaker
No Top - Ht. 3

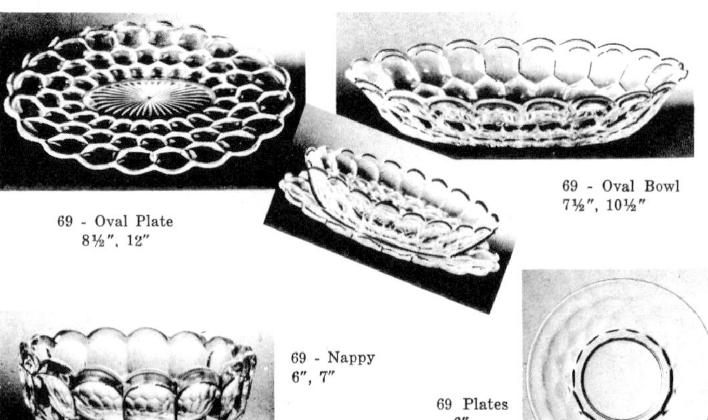
69 - Oval Plate
8½", 12"

69 - Oval Bowl
7½", 10½"

69 - Nappy
6", 7"

69 Plates
6"
6½"
8½"

69 - 6 oz Oil
Ht. 4⅝"

69 - 3 oz Oil
Ht. 3½"

Reprinted from 1954 Canton Catal

ARISTOCRAT"

69 LINE
Con't.

MARION · INDIANA

69 - 5½ oz Tulip Sundae
Ht. 5¼" Diam. 4⅜"

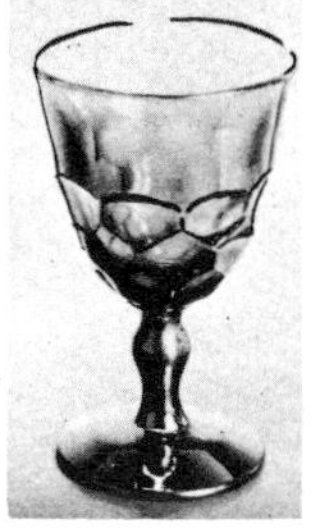

69 - 10 oz Peach Melba
Ht. 5 13/16" Diam. 3 7/16"

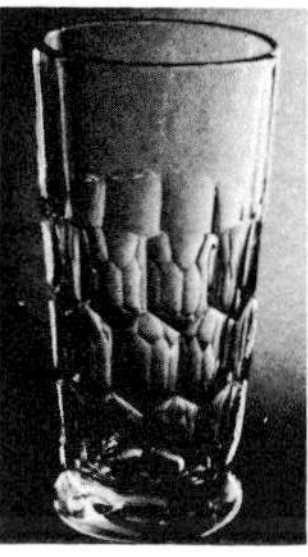

69 - 14 oz Soda
Ht. 6" Diam. 3⅛"

69 - Low Ftd.
Ftd. Soda 8 oz
Ht. 5¼" Diam. 3¾"

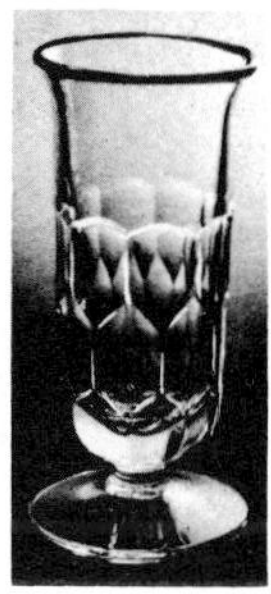

69 - 5 oz Parfait
Ht. 5½"

69 - 5 oz HF Sherbet
Ht. 3⅞" Diam. 3¾"
69 - 3½ oz LF Sherbet or Cocktail
Ht. 3¼" Diam. 3⅜"

69 - 4 oz Reg. Sherbet
Ht. 3" Diam. 3 3/16"

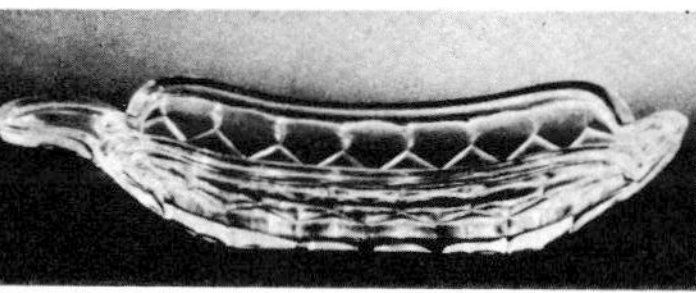

69 - Banana Split

69 - Finger Bowl - 4"
69 - Finger Bowl Plate - 6"

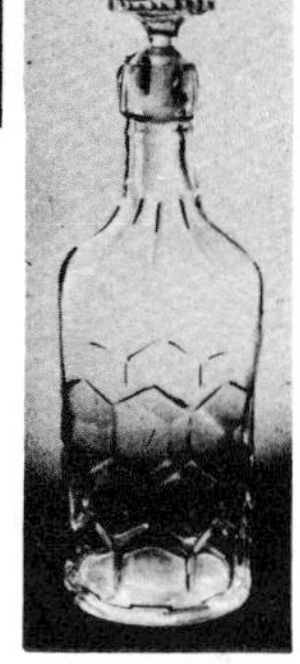

69 - 23 oz Bar Bottle
Ht. 10¼"

69 - 60 oz Jug

69 - Vase - Ht. 5"

69 - 4½" Ash Tray

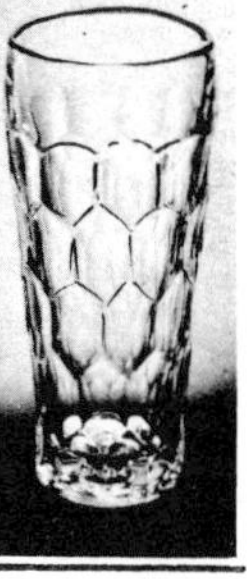

Ht. 8¼"
Diam. 3⅝"
69 - 30 oz Cocktail Shaker

"BRETON"

90 LINE

MARION, INDIANA

90 - 5 oz Tumbler
Ht. 3⅜"

90 - Tumbler
9 oz - Ht. 3⅞"
12 oz - Ht. 4 13/16"

90 - Ice Tea
12 oz - Ht. 5⅝"

90 Whiskey
2 oz

90 - 44 oz Ice Lip Jug

90 - 10 oz Goblet
Ht. 6¼"

90 - Nappy
4½" - 8" Fld. or Cup't

90 - 6 oz Sugar
90 - 6 oz Cream

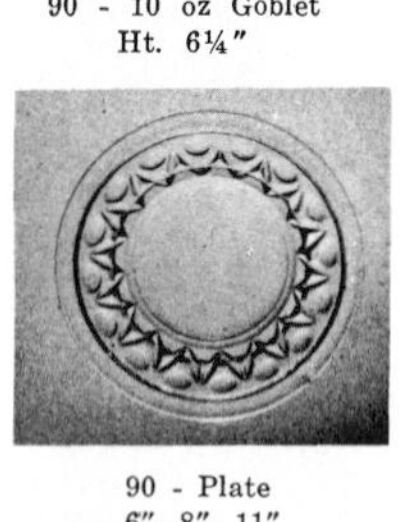

90 - Plate
6", 8", 11"

90 - Low Ftd. Sherbet
4 oz - 4½ oz
Ht. 3" Diam. 3⅜"

90 - 24 oz
Square
Decanter

90 - 24 oz
Round
Decanter

90 - Cordial
1¼ oz

90 - Wine
2½ oz

90 - Claret
3½ oz

90 - Ftd. Cocktail
3 oz

90 - Champagne
3½ oz

191 LINE

PARTY" LINE

MARION · INDIANA

)1 - 11" Console Bowl
)1 - Ice Tub, Ht. 4¾" Diam. 7¾"

191 - Mixing Bowls, 7", 8", 9"

191 - 80 oz Hi Crushed Fruit Bowl & Cover
Ht. 9 5/16" - Diam. 6½"

191 - 4" Round Box and Cover

191 - 4½" Nappy and Cover

191 - 5½" Round Box and Cover

191 - 6 oz Hld. Cup
191 - 5½" Saucer

. - S & P Shaker
Top - Ht. 3¼"

191 - Sugar Server
12 oz No Top - Ht. 4½"

191 - Molasses Can
No Top - Ht. 4⅛"
8 oz

191 - Sugar Shaker
No Top - Ht. 4⅜"

191½ - Beer Mug
10 oz, 12 oz - Ht. 5½"

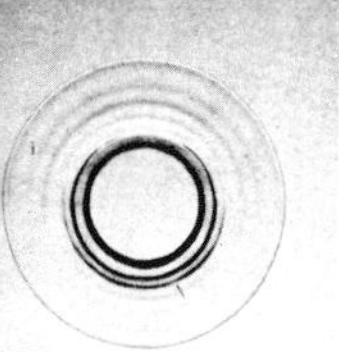

191 - Plate - 6" Reg.
10" Serving

192 - 3½" Candlestick

191½ - 3½ oz Cocktail Liner

192 - 2½ oz Cocktail

·printed from 1954 Canton Catalog

"LULI"

330 LINE

MARION, INDIANA

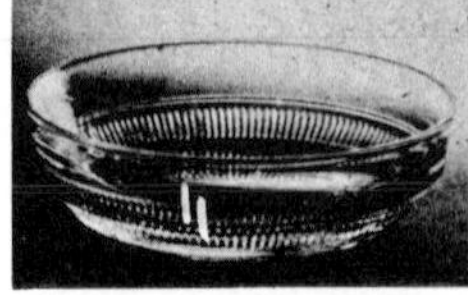

330 - 6" Nappy

330 - Handled Nappy
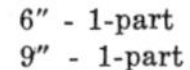
6" - 1-part
9" - 1-part
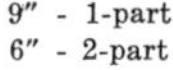
6" - 2-part

330 - Tid Bit Tray
(Reg. or with center hole)
6", 8¼", 9"

330 - 11" 2-Hld. Tray

330
4" Mayonnaise
Bowl - Regular & Flared

330 Plate
6", 8", 12"

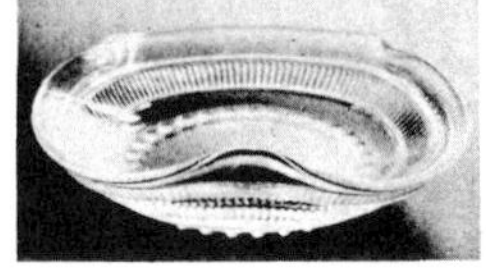

(330 Plates
Crimp't)

330 - 5½ oz Cup
330 - Saucer

Items not illustrate
in relative proporti

Highest Quality
Pot Glass

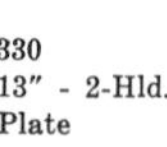

330
13" - 2-Hld.
Plate

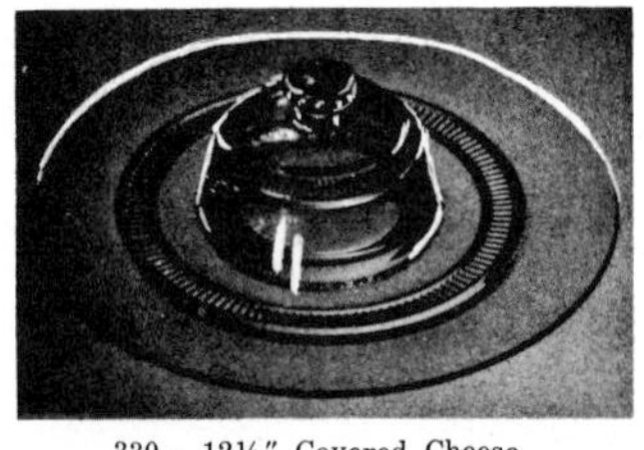

330 - 12½" Covered Cheese
and Cracker Plate

330 - 5½" Cheese Sherbet

330 - 6½" Sing
Candlestick

Reprinted from 1954 Canton Cat

LULI"

330 LINE

Con't.

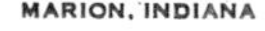

MARION, INDIANA

QUALITY ALWAYS FIRST

330 - 10" Shallow Bowl

330 - 12½" Console Ass't Shapes

330 - 11" 3-toed Console Bowl

330 - 8½" Salad Bowl

330 - 7" 3-part Relish

330 - 11" 2-Hld. Bowl - Ass't Shapes

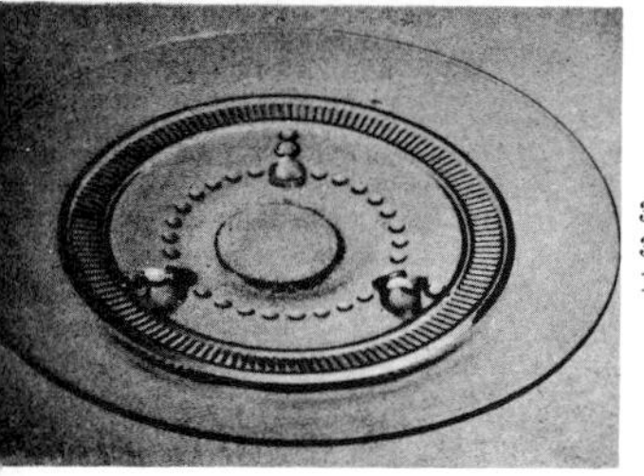

330 3-toed 13½" Plate

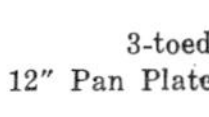

3-toed 12" Pan Plate

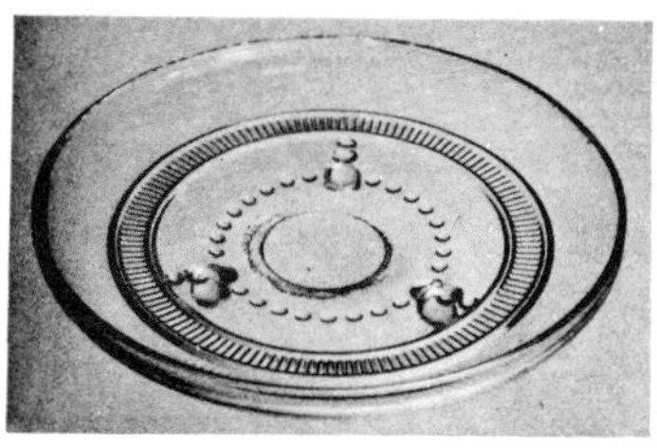

"VALE"

444 LINE

Con't.

MARION, INDIANA

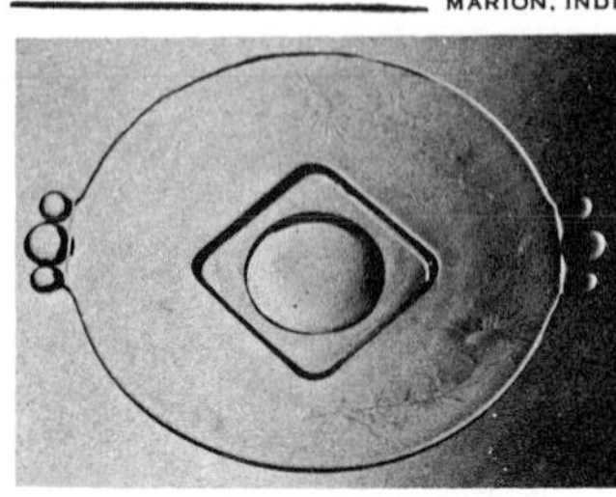

444 - 10½"
2-Hld.
Plate

444
12" Covered
Cheese &
Cracker
10½" Cracker
Plate

Decoration not standard

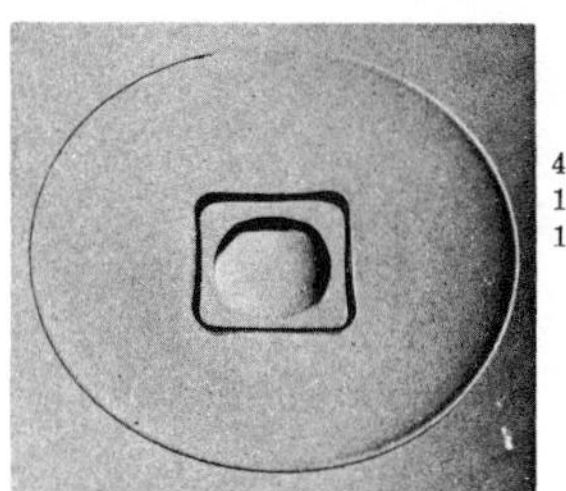

444
10½" Plate
15" Plate

444 - 9"
Shallow
Bowl

444 - 8½"
Deep Bowl

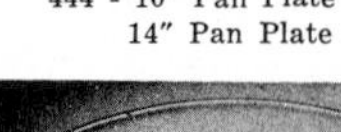

444 - 10" Pan Plate
14" Pan Plate

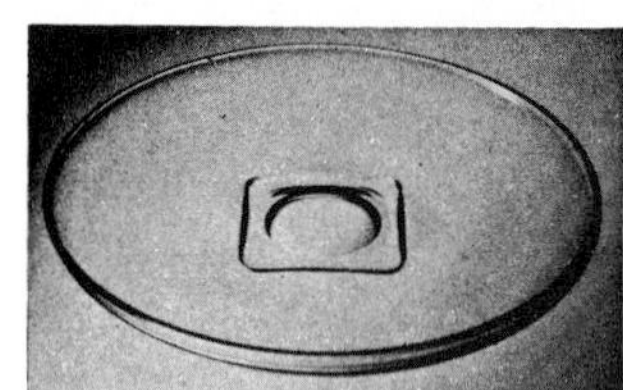

Highest Quality Pot Glass

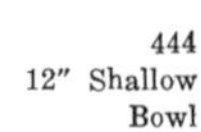

444
12" Shallow
Bowl

444 - 12½"
Console Bowl
Ass't Shapes

CON'T NEXT PAGE

VALE"

444 LINE

Con't.

MARION, INDIANA

444 - 5" Cheese Sherbet

444 - 7" HF Comport
(with or without cover)

444 - 6" 3-part Candy
Box and Cover

444 - 6" Candy Bowl
and Cover

444 - 6" Candlestick
Single

444 - 5" 2-way
Candlestick

444 - Ice Tub
Ht. 5½" Diam. 8½"

444 - 3¾" Round
Ash Tray

444 - 8½" 2-handled
Bowl

Items not illustrated
n relative proportions

Decoration
not standard

Highest Quality
Pot Glass

"FUTURA"

836 LINE

MARION, INDIANA

836¾ - Goblet
10 oz - Ht. 5⅜"

836 - Beverage
6 oz - Ht. 4 $\frac{9}{16}$"

836 - Tumbler
9 oz - Ht. 4⅛"

836 - Ice Tea
12 oz - Ht. 5 $\frac{11}{16}$"

836 - Low Foot
Sherbet - 5 oz
Ht. 2⅝" Diam. 3¼

836 - High Foot
Sherbet - 6 oz
Ht. 3¾" Diam. 3½"

836 - Ftd. Soda
10 oz - Ht. 5½"
12 oz - Ht. 5⅞"

836 - Parfait
Ht. 5 $\frac{3}{16}$"

836 - 7 oz Cup
836 - Saucer

836 - 3 oz W
5 oz Champag

Items not illustrated in relative proportions

836 - 5 oz Sugar

836 - 5 oz Cream

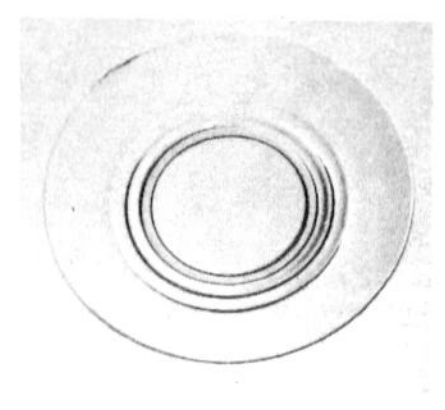
836 - 8" Plate

991
3 oz HF Wi
Cordial

PLUME"

888 LINE

MARION, INDIANA

888 - 5½ oz Sugar

888 - 5 oz Cream

888 - 7" 3-part Relish
Regular or Crimpt

888 - 7 oz Marmelade
and Cover

888 - 11" Hld. Sandwich Tray

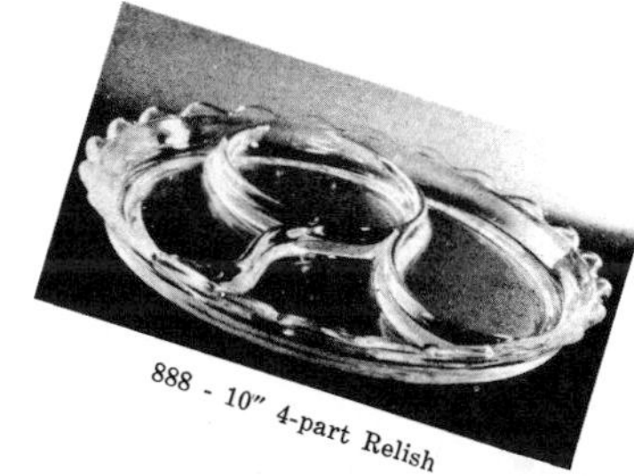

888 - 10" 4-part Relish

888 - 12" Cov'd Cheese & Cracker

888 - 7" 3-part Candy Box
and Cover

**Highest Quality
Pot Glass**

888
11" LF
Cake
Salver

888 - 10" LF Comport

"NADJA"

900 LINE

MARION, INDIANA

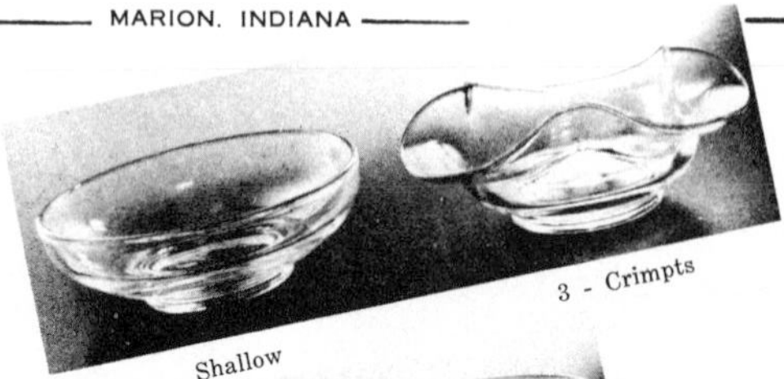

Shallow

3 - Crimpts

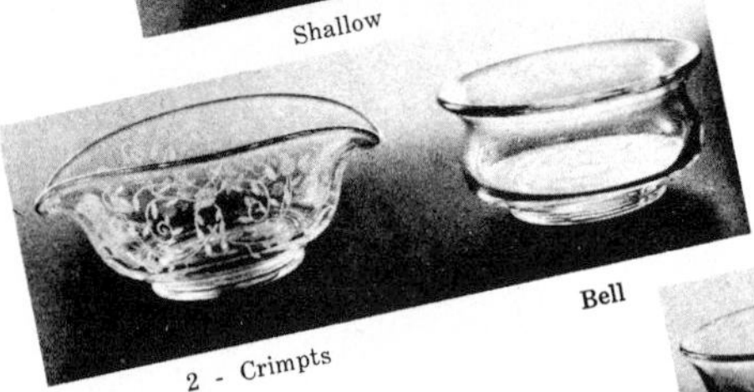

2 - Crimpts

Bell

900 - 5″ NAPPY

Regular
or
Mayonnaise Bowl

900 - 5″ Nappy
1. Flat rim, stuck handle
2. 1-Crimpt, stuck handle

Decoration not standard

900 - 5½ oz Sugar

900 - 5 oz Cream

Items not illustrated in relative proportions

900 - 7″
3-part Cand
Box & Cove

900 - 7″ 3-part Relish, Crimpt

900 - 10″ 4-part Relish

Dressing
Bowl
Plate

900 - 5″ 2-part Dressing Bowl

Reprinted from 1954 Canton Catal

"NADJA"

900 LINE

Con't.

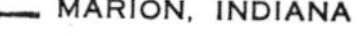
MARION, INDIANA

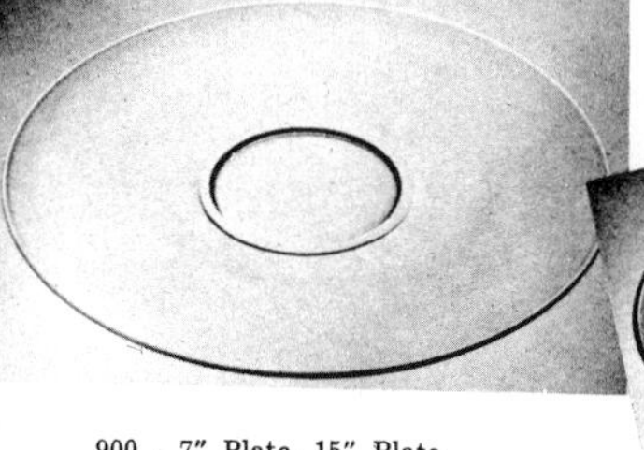

900 - 7" Plate, 15" Plate

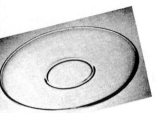

900 - 14" Pan Plate

900 - 4½"
Candlestick - Single

900 - 8" HF Comport

900 - 7½ oz
Marmelade & Cover

900 - 2-way Candlestick
6"

900 - 11" LF Cake Salver

900 - 11" 2-Hld. Bowl

900 - 12" 2-Hld. Plate (not illustrated)

900 - 10" LF Comport

900 - 3-toed Nappy, Flared or Crimpt

"TRANCE"

1503 LINE

MARION, INDIANA

1503 - 4½" 2-Hld.
Cream Soup

1503 - 2-Hld. Nappy
4½", 6", 7"

1503 - 2-part, 2-Hld. Nappy
4½", 6"
1503½ - 6" 2-part
2-Hld. Nappy
(not shown)

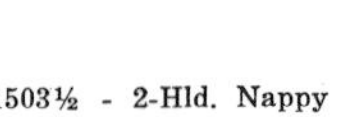

1503½ - 2-Hld. Nappy
5½", 7⅜"
(Both sizes in assorted shapes)

Highest Quality Pot Glass

1503 - Cream

Items not illustrated in relative proportions

1503 - Sugar

1503 - 7" 3-part 2-Hld. Nappy

1503 - 2¾" Single
Candlestick

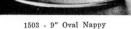

1503 - 9" Oval Nappy

1503 - 7" 2-part Oval Relish

Reprinted from 1954 Canton Catalog

"CHAUCER" 1504 LINE

MARION, INDIANA

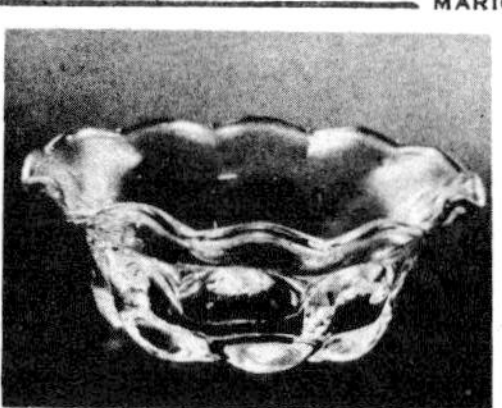

1504 - 5" Nappy

1504 - 8" 2-Hld. Nappy

1504 - Mayonnaise Bowl
1504 - Mayonnaise Plate

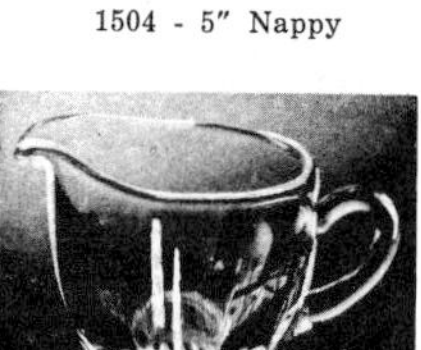

1504 - 5½" Cheese Sherbet

1504 - 11½" 3-pt. Relish

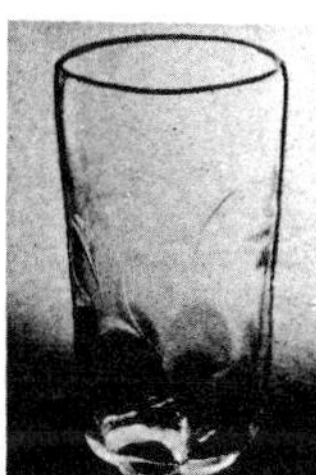

1504
8 oz Soda
16 oz Soda

1504 - 7 oz Cream and Sugar

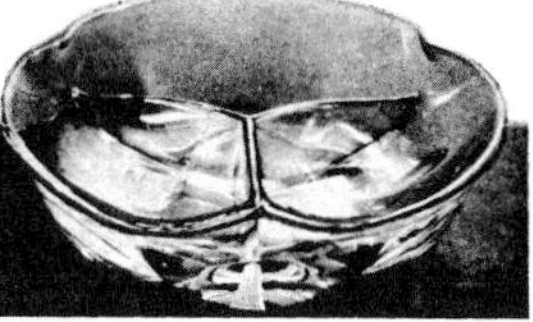

1504 - 6¾" 3-part Relish, Crimpt

1504 - 8" Salver
10" Salver

Decoration not standard

1504 - 6" LF Comport
7" LF Comport
Assorted Shapes

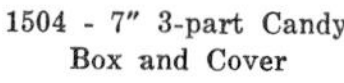

1504 - 7" 3-part Candy Box and Cover

1504 - 11" Hld. Sandwich Tray
10" Hld. Nut Tray

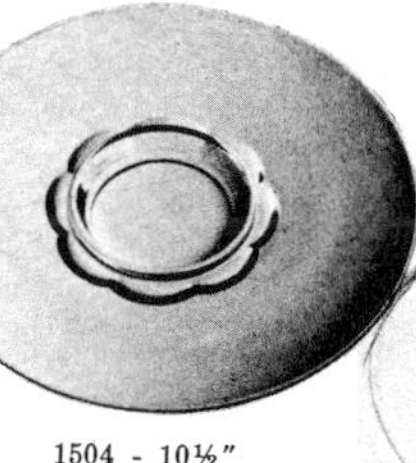

1504 - 10½" Cheese Plate

1504 - 12" Cov'd. Cheese & Cracker

"VAARA" (411)
"CROW'S FOOT" (412)

CANDY BOXES
and COVERS

MARION · INDIANA

411 - 7" Sq. 2-part Candy Box and Cover
411 - 7" Sq. 3-part Candy Box and Cover

412½ - 3-part Candy Box and Cover

444 - 6" Candy Bowl and Cover

444 - 6" 3-part Candy Box and Cover
(Cutting shown - not standard)

466 - 7" 3-part Candy Box and Cover

888 - 7" 3-part Candy Box and Cover

900 - 7" 3-part Candy Box and Cover

1503 - 6½" 3-part Candy Box and Cover

1504 - 7" 3-part Candy Box and Cover

CON'T NEXT PAGE

HANDMADE

"CROW'S FOOT" (412)
"VALE" (444)
"PLUME" (888)

BOWLS

MARION · INDIANA

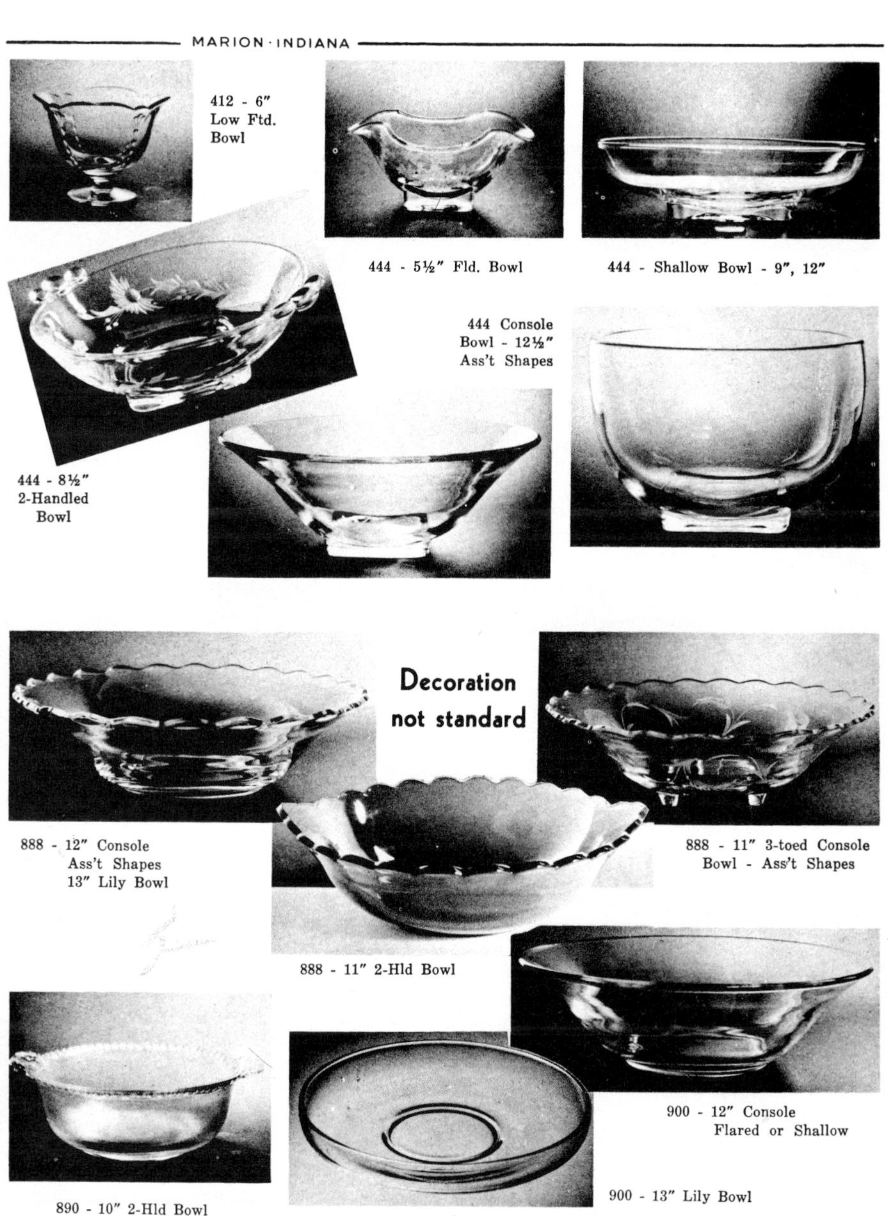

412 - 6" Low Ftd. Bowl

444 - 5½" Fld. Bowl

444 - Shallow Bowl - 9", 12"

444 Console Bowl - 12½" Ass't Shapes

444 - 8½" 2-Handled Bowl

Decoration not standard

888 - 12" Console Ass't Shapes 13" Lily Bowl

888 - 11" 3-toed Console Bowl - Ass't Shapes

888 - 11" 2-Hld Bowl

900 - 12" Console Flared or Shallow

900 - 13" Lily Bowl

890 - 10" 2-Hld Bowl

"SECRETS" (777)
"CROW'S FOOT" (890)
"NADJA" (900)

RELISH-SERVING and MISC. TRAYS

MARION · INDIANA

777 - 8″ 3-part Relish-crimpt

777 - 10″ 4-part Relish

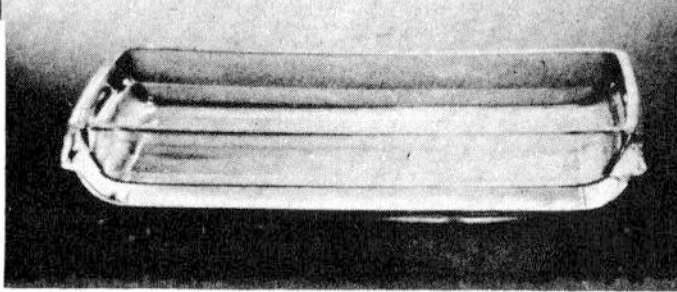

799 - 9″ Oblong Tray

862 - 5½″ 2-part 3-toed round Relish

888 - 7″ 3-part Relish Reg. or Crimpt

888 - 10″ 4-part Relish

890 - 11″ 3-part oblong Relish

890 - 11½″ 2-part Celery Dish Tray

900 - 7″ 3-part Relish Reg. or Crimpt

900 - 10″ 4-part Relish

1175 - 7½″ 4-part & center Relish

Reprinted from 1954 Canton Catalog

"SKIDOO" (211)
"CITY LIGHTS" (100)
"CANTINA" (220)
"HOTCHA" (215)
"S.S. DREAMSHIP" (221)

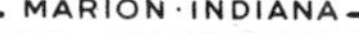

211 - 7 oz Sugar

211 - 7 oz Cream

211 - 7½ oz Large Cream

211 - 8 oz Large Sugar

100 - 5 qt, 13" Bowl
100 - 18" Plate

215

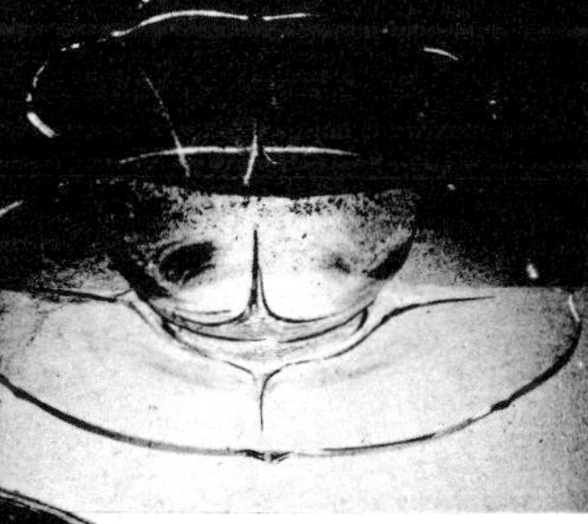
211 - 7 qt, 14" Punch Bowl
211 - 19" Punch Bowl Plate

211 ½ - 7 qt, 14" Punch Bowl
211 ½ - 19" Punch Bowl Plate

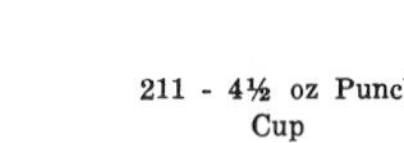
211 - 4½ oz Punch Cup

215 - 5" Candlestick

215 Nappy - 5½" Available in special shapes

220 - 6" Deep - 7½" Regular Nappy

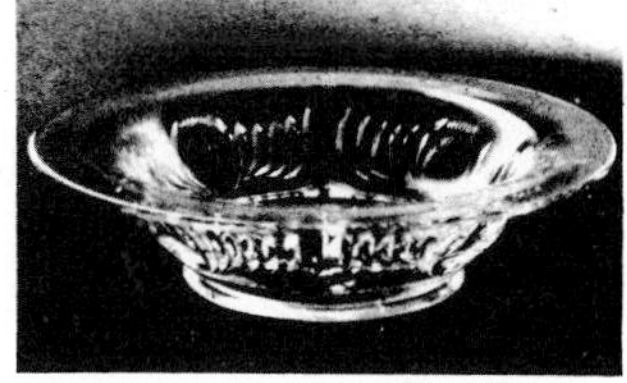
221 - 7" Nappy (shown flared)

"SECRETS" (777)
"WOTTA" LINE (881)
"CROW'S FOOT" (890)
"VERMILION" (555)
"POPEYE & OLIVE" (994)

MARION · INDIANA

702 - 3" Flat Cheese Nappy

702 - 3½" Flat Cheese Nappy

777 - Nappy - 4¾" Reg., 5" Ass't Shapes 5½" Flared, 6" Shallow

881 - 9 oz Tumbler

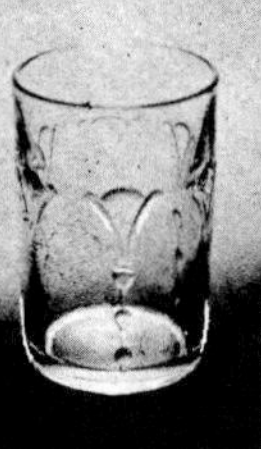

890 - Tumbler 9 oz - Height 4¼"

555 - 7½" Square 2-part Relish

555 - 9" Tray

555 - 10½" 5-part round Relish

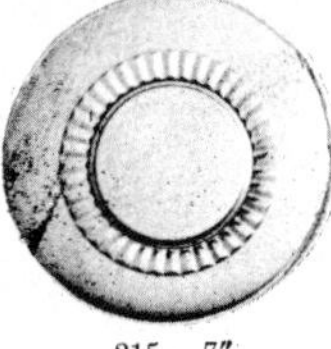

215 - 7"

555 - 11" 3-part round Relish

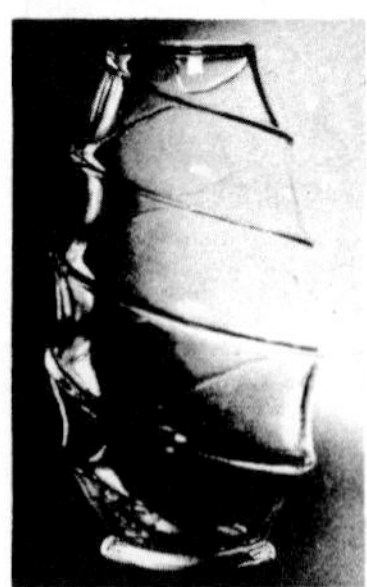

2001 - Swirl Vase Height 10"

994 - Lg. Vase - Ht. 7"

502 - Fan Vase - Ht. 8"

991 - 22 oz Wine Ht. 10¼" Diam. 4⅞"

Reprinted from 1954 Canton Catalog

'PENNY" LINE (991)
'SKIDOO" (211)
'HOTCHA" (215)
'NADJA" (900)
'WOTTA" LINE (881)

MARION · INDIANA

991 - 7 oz Cream

991 - 7 oz Sugar

211 - 27 oz
Cordial

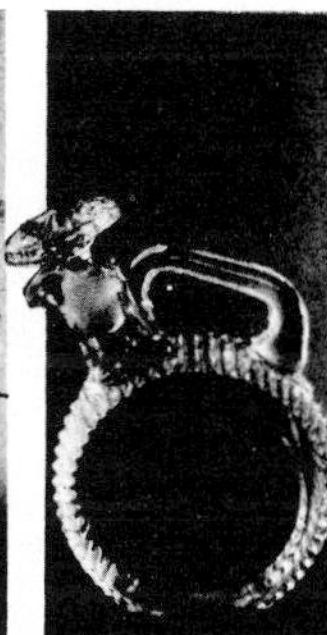

215½ - 12 oz
Cordial

215 - 7 oz Cream

215 - 7 oz Sugar

900
11"

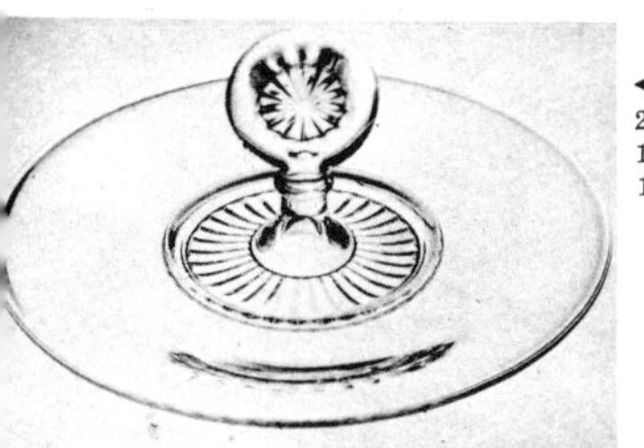

215
11" Sandwich
10" Nut Tray

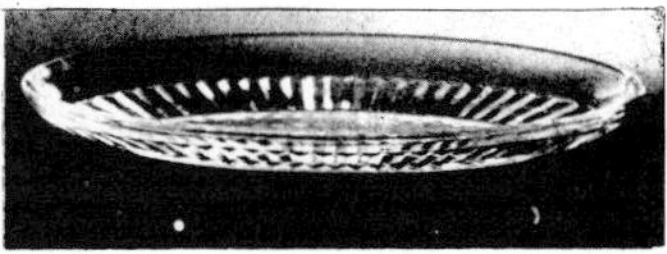

881 - 2-Hld. Cream Soup

FC-1 - "Chil-Cup" Cry. or Black
Diam. 6¼" Height 1¾"

CB-1 "Chil-Bowl"
Outside Diam. 6¼" Height 2⅜"
Glass Insert Diam. 2⅜"

215 - 11" Celery Tray

eprinted from 1954 Canton Catalog

RELISH-SERVING AND MISC. TRAYS

"SECRETS"	
777 Relish, 3 part, crimped, 8"	15.00--20.00
777 Relish, 4 part, 10"	15.00--20.00
799 Tray, oblong, 9"	10.00--14.00
862 Relish, rnd., 2 part, 3 toed, 5½"	8.00--10.00
"PLUME"	
888 Relish, reg. or crimped, 3 part, 7"	9.00--12.00
888 Relish, 4 part, 10"	10.00--15.00
"CROW'S FOOT"	
890 Relish, oblong, 3 part, 11"	10.00--14.00
890 Celery Dish Tray, 2 part, 11½"	15.00--20.00
"NADJA"	
900 Relish, reg. or crimped, 3 part, 7"	9.00--12.00
Relish, 4 part, 10"	10.00--14.00
1175 Relish, 4 part and center, 7½"	10.00--14.00

MISCELLANEOUS

"SKIDOO"	
211 Sugar	7.00-- 9.00
211 Cream	7.00-- 9.00
211 Cream, large	7.00--10.00
211 Sugar, large	7.00--10.00
"CITY LIGHTS"	
100 Bowl, 5 qt., 13"	15.00--20.00
100 Plate, 18"	15.00--20.00
"HOTCHA"	
215 Shaker	9.00--12.00
215 Nappy, 5½"	6.00--10.00
215 Candlestick, 5"	12.00--18.00
"SKIDOO"	
211 Punch Bowl, 7 qt., 14"	15.00--30.00
211 Punch Bowl Plate, 19"	18.00--28.00
211½ Punch Bowl, 7 qt., 14"	15.00--30.00
211½ Punch Bowl Plate, 19"	18.00--28.00
211 Punch Cup, 4½ oz.	3.00-- 5.00
"CANTINA"	
220 Nappy, deep, 6"	15.00--25.00
220 Nappy, reg., 7½"	15.00--25.00
"S.S. DREAM SHIP"	
221 Nappy, 7"	15.00--25.00
702 Nappy, flat cheese, 3"	3.00-- 5.00
702 Nappy, flat cheese, 3½"	3.00-- 5.00
"SECRETS"	
777 Nappy, reg, 4¾", 5"	10.00--20.00
777 Nappy, flrd., 5½"	10.00--20.00
777 Nappy, shallow, 6"	10.00--20.00
"WOTTA LINE"	
881 Tumbler, 9 oz.	8.00--12.00
"CROW'S FOOT"	
890 Tumbler, 9 oz.	15.00--25.00
"VERMILION"	
555 Relish, sq., 2 part, 7½"	10.00--20.00
555 Tray, 9"	10.00--20.00
555 Relish, rnd., 5 part, 10½"	12.00--22.00
555 Relish, rnd., 3 part, 11"	12.00--24.00
"HOTCHA"	
215 Plate, 7"	6.00-- 8.00
2001 Vase, swirl, 10"	15.00--25.00
"POPEYE AND OLIVE"	
994 Vase, 7"	10.00--15.00
502 Fan Vase, 8"	12.00--16.00
"PENNY LINE"	
991 Wine Decanter, 22 oz.	25.00--40.00
991 Cream	8.00--12.00
991 Sugar	8.00--12.00
"HOTCHA"	
215 Cream	8.00--12.00
215 Sugar	8.00--12.00
215 Sandwich Tray, 11"	11.00--16.00
215 Nut Tray, 10"	11.00--16.00
215 Celery Tray, 11"	9.00--12.00
"SKIDOO"	
211 Cordial, 21 oz.	20.00--30.00
215½ Cordial, 12 oz.	20.00--30.00
"NADJA"	
900 Sandwich Tray, 11"	11.00--16.00
FC-1 Chil-Cup, cry., or black, 6¼"	8.00--12.00

PADEN CITY GLASS MFG. CO.

See This Showing

Room 707—Fort Pitt at Pittsburgh

Paden City W. Va.

"BONNIE" decanter, 3 styles wines

CB-1 Chil-Bowl, outside 6¼", insert 2-3/8"	8.00--12.00
"WOTTA LINE"	
881 Cream Soup, hdld.	8.00--12.00
"BONNIE"	
Decanter	25.00--30.00
Wines	6.00-- 8.00

"CROW'S FOOT"

Amber, pink, Steigel green, topaz, Ritz blue, amethyst and ruby.

After six years of research I have decided to attribute this pattern to Paden City. For some time I had been ruling out companies, with my attention coming to rest on Paden City. Then knowledgeable Mr. Hanse of Lotus Glassware told me he, too, would attribute it to Paden City.

When it didn't show up in the Paden City company catalogs, I was dis-illusioned. But then the Canton catalogs came to light with the explanation that Canton had bought and used Paden City molds (see chapter heading). No. 412 and 890 both look like they could be "CROW'S FOOT". So it looks like the evidence comes round in the end!

The pattern has been found mostly in ruby, but we are finding amethyst, Ritz blue, amber, pink, topaz and Steigel green.

Some pieces have ground bottoms and some do not.

It was made in two shapes, round and square. Some pieces apparently fit both variations. When I find pieces in the mysterious square shape, I'm calling it "BEE'S KNEES". I hope soon to distinguish between the two modes of this pattern.

Plate, 6"	3.00-- 5.00
Plate, round, 8"	6.00-- 9.00
Plate, square, 8½"	5.00-- 9.00
Plate, hdld., 10½"	10.00--15.00
Cup	6.00-- 9.00
Saucer, round, square.	3.00-- 5.00
Cream (2 styles)	8.00--12.00
Sugar (2 styles)	8.00--12.00
Bowl, oblong	16.00--22.00
Bowl, cream soup	10.00--13.00
Bowl, square, hdld., 10"	15.00--25.00
Bowl, comport,round, ftd., 10"	25.00--35.00
Bowl, console, square, 11½"	25.00--35.00
Platter	15.00--25.00
Comport, 7"	17.00--24.00
Candy Box and Cover	20.00--40.00
Whipped Cream w/Liner	25.00--35.00
Candlestick, pr.	35.00--45.00
Vase, 10"	25.00--35.00
Cheese and Cracker	20.00--30.00
Sandwich Server, center hdld.	15.00--25.00
Tumbler, 4¼"	15.00--25.00

"CROW'S FOOT" 10" comport, 4¼" tumbler, 5" cheese stand, 10" handled bowl and 11½" console bowl.

Photo 1, 2 & 3 "CROW'S FOOT" vase, plate, sugar (style 1 w/ground bottom), cup, saucer, plate, cream,

Photo courtesy J. C. Cox

"CROW'S FOOT" and "BEE'S KNEES" handled plate, cream soup, candlesticks, comport, whipped cream w/liner, plate and cup and saucer.

Seneca

This past summer I revisited the interesting Seneca factory and again went through all the old catalogs they had. As you know, Seneca is known for its beautiful cuttings and etchings on crystal, and that is mostly what I found. They don't, at the factory, have a catalog of the color period, if ever they made one. This doesn't mean to say I've stopped looking!

"GERMANA" page 310

Goblet	10.00--15.00
Goblet, champagne	9.00--12.00
Goblet, wine	10.00--15.00

STREAMLINE TUMBLER

101 R	6.00-- 8.00

"BAUBLES" page 311

Goblet, brandy	10.00--14.00
Goblet, cordial	10.00--14.00
Goblet, cocktail	10.00--14.00

"SLIM"

Tumbler, 5, 10, 16 oz., ea.	10.00--16.00

"ALLEGHENY" Beverage Set

Jug and Cover	20.00--30.00
Tumblers, ftd.	6.00-- 9.00
Sherbet	5.00-- 7.00
Decanter	25.00--35.00

"CANDLEWICK"

Goblet	8.00--14.00
Sherbet	6.00--10.00

NAOMI Line page 312

Goblet	12.00--15.00
Saucer Champagne	10.00--12.00
Sherbet	6.00-- 8.00
Cocktail	10.00--12.00
Cordial	12.00--15.00
Wine	11.00--14.00
Parfait	11.00--14.00
Tumbler, ftd., 9 oz.	8.00--12.00
High Ball, 9 oz.	12.00--14.00
High Ball, 12 oz.	11.00--15.00
Bud Vase	10.00--14.00
Sugar	9.00--11.00
Cream	9.00--11.00
Finger Bowl	6.00-- 8.00
Jug, covered	35.00--45.00
Wine Set	85.00-100.00
Plate, 8"	6.00-- 9.00
920 Vase, 10"	22.00--28.00
Candlestick, pr.	20.00--25.00
Console Bowl	18.00--26.00
925 Vase, 10"	22.00--28.00

MISCELLANEOUS

492 Goblet, Cut 286	12.00--18.00
482 Goblet, Cut 259	12.00--18.00
492 Goblet, Cut 261	12.00--18.00
482 Goblet, Cut 218	12.00--18.00
515 Goblet, Cut 374	12.00--18.00
475 Goblet, Cut 258	12.00--18.00
499 Goblet, Cut 371	12.00--18.00
492 Goblet, Cut 300	12.00--18.00
903 Goblet, Cut 338	12.00--18.00
492 Goblet, Cut 308	12.00--18.00
482 Goblet, Cut 64	12.00--18.00

"ANAIS" *see next page*

Tumblers and stems	6.00--10.00

1925 ad

"ANAIS" LINE

"FESTUS" No. 484 Line	Etch 631
Goblet	12.00--15.00
Saucer Champagne	10.00--12.00
Sherbet	8.00--10.00
Cordial	12.00--15.00
Finger Bowl	6.00-- 8.00
Cocktail	10.00--12.00
Parfait	12.00--15.00
Wine	12.00--15.00
Tumbler, ftd., 12 oz.	11.00--14.00
Plate, 6"	3.00-- 4.00
Plate, 7", 8"	5.00-- 8.00
Candlestick, pr.	16.00--22.00
Bowl, console, 12"	20.00--30.00

ESTES No. 499 Line	*See next page*
Goblet	12.00--15.00
Saucer Champagne	10.00--12.00
Finger Bowl	6.00-- 8.00
Cocktail	10.00--12.00
Cordial	12.00--15.00
Tumbler, ftd., 12 oz.	11.00--14.00
Sherbet	8.00--10.00
Wine	11.00--14.00
Jug	30.00--40.00
Parfait	12.00--15.00
Plate, 8"	6.00-- 8.00
Candlestick, pr.	16.00--22.00
Bowl, console, 12"	20.00--30.00

No. 484 LINE OPTIC DEEP ECTH 631

Page 33

No. 484. FINGER BOWL

No. 484. SHERBET

No. 484. COCKTAIL

No. 484. WINE

No. 484. PARFAIT

No. 484. 12 oz. Ftd. TUMBLER

No. 484. SAU. CHAMP.

No. 484 GOBLET

No. 484. CORDIAL

No. 30. 8 in. PLATE

No. 30. 6 in. PLATE

No. 30. 7 in. PLATE

No. 3. CANDLESTICK

No. 3. 12 in. CONSOLE BOWL

No. 3. CANDLESTICK

"FESTUS"

SENECA GLASS COMPANY, MORGANTOWN, W. VA.

1935 Catalog reprint

No. 499 LINE OPTIC P/D ESTES

Page 28

No. 499. FINGER BOWL
Optic, P/D Estes

No. 499. COCKTAIL
Optic, P/D Estes

No. 499. CORDIAL
Optic, P/D Estes

No. 499. 12 oz. Ftd. TUMBLER
Optic, P/D Estes

No. 499. GOBLET
Optic, P/D Estes

No. 499. SAU. CHAMP.
Optic, P/D Estes

No. 900. JUG
Optic, P/D Estes

No. 499. PARFAIT
Optic, P/D Estes

No. 499. SHERBET
Optic, P/D Estes

No. 499. WINE
Optic, P/D Estes

No. 30. 8" PLATE
P/D Estes

No. 30. CANDLESTICK
P/D Estes

No. 1. 12" CONSOLE BOWL
P/D Estes

No. 30. CANDLESTICK
P/D Estes

"ESTES"

SENECA GLASS COMPANY, MORGANTOWN, W. VA.

L.E. Smith

The name 'L.E. Smith' bounces around a lot; one reason is that L.E. Smith is a name practically synonymous with black glass, and black glass is always bouncing around everywhere. Now that the Art Deco black-and-white or black-and-silver schemes are stylish with moderns again, our Depression black is more popular than ever.

People often ask me, "What's black amethyst?" meaning that kind of black that shows through amethyst when held up to a bright light. Or "What is it when we see red showing through? or green?" And some black, of course, is dead black through any light.

The glass companies tell me they never paid any attention to what the final show-through color turned out to be. They aimed for black glass, and got it by various ways and recipes. The translucency of the end black, including whatever color tints were inherent in it, was entirely incidental.

I feel the same way on this question. Black glass by any other glow is still black glass to me, and I value it equally. You may think differently, and that's okay too!

MISCELLANEOUS	page 313
Lemon Juicer and Cup	20.00--30.00
Universal Percolator Top	2.00-- 3.00
Wall Safety Match	15.00--20.00
Sanitary Sugar Bowl	40.00--60.00

GLASS SANITARY DRINKING FOUNTAIN	page 314
Chick Waterer	15.00--25.00

CRUCIFIX	
Candlestick, 9"	20.00--30.00
Candlestick, 5"	15.00--20.00

SANITARY BUTTER	
Dish and cover	15.00--25.00

KING FISH AQUARIUM	
Bowl, high base, 15" x 10"	200.00-250.00
Bowl, ftd., 15" x 7¼"	200.00-250.00
Bowl, 15" x 7¼" (shown)	100.00-125.00

"QUEEN FISH" aquarium

"SODA SHOP" page 315

Jumbo Soda	9.00--12.00
Parfait	4.00-- 6.00
Tulip Sundae, 5-5/8" high	6.00-- 9.00
Tulip Sundae, 6" high	6.00-- 9.00
Smith's Sanitary Sugar Pour	75.00--85.00
Low Sundae	3.00-- 4.00
Banana Split	4.00-- 6.00
Napkin Holder	35.00--40.00
No. 509 Ash Tray	4.00-- 6.00
No. 1000 Ash Tray	4.00-- 6.00
No. 503 Ash Tray	6.00-- 9.00

"BY CRACKY"

Candle Holder, pr.	8.00--10.00
Flower Block, 3"	3.00-- 4.00
Plate, octagonal, 8" (Also rnd.)	4.00-- 6.00
Luncheon Set w/Sherbet	9.00--12.00
Cup	4.00-- 5.00
Plate, cake, 3 legged	10.00--12.00

"HOMESTEAD"

You may find other pieces not listed.

Plate, octagon, rnd., 8"	3.00-- 6.00
Plate, 11½"	8.00--10.00
Plate, grill, 9"	4.00-- 6.00
Cream and Sugar	12.00--16.00
Tumbler, ftd., 4½"	5.00-- 8.00
Sherbet on Tray	9.00--12.00
Cup and Saucer	5.00-- 7.00

"MELBA" page 316

Plate, 9"	4.00-- 6.00
Plate, 7"	3.00-- 4.00
Plate, 6"	2.00-- 2.50
Dessert	3.00-- 4.00
Cup and Saucer	5.00-- 7.00
Cream and Sugar	9.00--12.00
Platter, oval, 11½"	9.00--12.00
Baker, oval vegetable, 9½"	9.00--12.00
Plate, serving, hdld.	8.00--10.00
Bowl, ruffled, 10½"	9.00--12.00
Candle Holder, pr.	8.00--12.00
Candy Dish and Cover (2 sizes) No. 78 in Book I	10.00--14.00
Flower Block	5.00-- 7.00

"BY CRACKY" "ROMANESQUE" AND MISCELLANEOUS page 317

No. 100 Bowl and Base, octagonal, 12"	12.00--16.00
No. 105 Candy Jar	12.00--16.00
Luncheon Set: 2 pc.	9.00--12.00
No. 100 Plate, octagonal	4.00-- 5.00
Plate, cake ftd.	6.00-- 9.00
Plate, crackled, octagonal	4.00-- 6.00
No. 100 Plate, round	4.00-- 6.00
Plate, crackled, round	4.00-- 5.00
No. 88 Sherbet, octagonal or round	3.00-- 5.00
Tea Cup	3.00-- 4.00
No. 91 Cake Plate	10.00--13.00
No. 30 Candy Box	10.00--14.00
No. 110 Candle Holder	4.00-- 5.00
No. 77 Violet Bowl	6.00-- 8.00
No. 133 Candle Holder	7.00-- 9.00
No. 100 Fan Vase	8.00--10.00

"ROMANESQUE"

Plate, octagonal and round	4.00-- 5.00
Plate, cake, hdld., w/ship	12.00--15.00
Console Bowl on Base, 10½"	10.00--14.00
Console Bowl, (base like No 81 in Book I)	10.00--14.00
Candle Holder, pr.	9.00--11.00
Sherbet, (fits on snack tray same as No. 154 in Book I)	3.00-- 5.00
Fan Vase, 7½"	8.00--10.00

"DO-SI-DO" page 318

Plates are "MOUNT PLEASANT" style. You may find pieces with gold trim; maybe that's what the ad means by 'illuminated'.

Plate, 8"	5.00-- 7.00
Cup	3.00-- 4.00
Saucer	2.00-- 3.00
Cream and Sugar	8.00--10.00
Cake Plate, hdld.	12.00--14.00

"MOUNT PLEASANT"

The MT. PLEASANT pattern has certainly caused a stir--and a rumble. What is, and what isn't, MT. PLEASANT? Clearly the pattern is not well defined. As you can see, its shapes and similar shapes, with the shield emblem and without, are scattered throughout the L.E. Smith Book 2 Chapter, appearing, re-appearing, and in the case of the elusive shield, even disappearing randomly on the various catalog page reprints and ads.

In other words, don't look at me, folks! the company had a will and an inimitable way with this pattern making it all the merrier for us.

My solution is fantastic. I say, collect MT. PLEASANT in any way, shape or form you want to, so long as it's black, L.E. Smith, and has at least one of the following: shields, scallops, or matching curvatures of the spine. You can't go wrong because it all looks great together.

Cobalt prices may be a little higher in your area.

Plate, 8"	7.00-- 9.00
Plate, 2 hdld.,	12.00--15.00
Cup	8.00--10.00
Saucer	2.50-- 4.00
Cream	9.00--12.00
Sugar	9.00--12.00
Cream and Sugar; Salt and Pepper on Tray	60.00--70.00
*Bowl, hdld., 8"	10.00--15.00
Bowl, 3 ftd.	9.00--12.00
Bowl, cupped, 6¼", 8¼"	9.00--12.00
Sherbet (No. 200 in Book I)	8.00--10.00
Candlestick, 2 candle, pr.	25.00--30.00
Candlestick, pr.	14.00--18.00
Salt and Pepper	35.00--45.00

**This bowl and other pieces have been found with a DOGWOOD motif in black.*

COOKIE JARS AND COVER

No. 1 Cookie Jar	30.00--50.00
No. 3 Cookie Jar	30.00--50.00
No. 4 Cookie Jar	30.00--50.00

Wonder what No. 2 looks like!

NO. 55 DECORATION page 319

No. 200 Plate, hdld.	6.00-- 9.00
No. 200 Mayonnaise Bowl	5.00-- 8.00
No. 575 Bowl, cupped	8.00--10.00
No. 200 Plate, salad,2 hdld.	10.00--14.00
No. 521 Bowl, flrd.	12.00--16.00
No. 525 Bowl, flrd.	10.00--12.00
No. 527 Bowl, cupped	12.00--16.00
No. 1 Fern Bowl	8.00--12.00
No. 515 Bowl, flrd.	12.00--16.00
No. 200 Nut Dish, center hdld.	8.00--11.00
No. 525 Bowl, round	8.00--10.00
No. 516 Nut Bowl, ftd.	10.00--14.00

SILVER-ON-BLACK ASS'T

No. 102 Vase	9.00--12.00
No 2000 Plate, salad, 2 hdld.	12.00--15.00
No. 410 Bowl, salad, 2 hdld.	12.00--15.00
No. 433 Vase, 2 hdld.	15.00--20.00
No. 327 Bowl, cupped, 3 ftd.	12.00--16.00
No. 505 Bowl, salad, 2 hdld.	14.00--20.00

KENT ASS'T

Bowl, round, 3 ftd.	10.00--14.00
Candlestick, pr.	10.00--14.00
Bowl, flrd., 3 ftd.	10.00--14.00
No. 102 Vase, 2 hdld.	9.00--11.00
Tray, center hdld.	8.00--10.00
Cream	6.00-- 8.00
Sugar	6.00-- 8.00
No. 711 Vase,	6.00-- 9.00
Fern Bowl	10.00--12.00
Bulb Bowl	9.00--11.00
Mayonnaise, ftd.	9.00--12.00

FLORAL ASS'T

Plate, salad, 2 hdld.	9.00--12.00
Pilsner Glass	6.00-- 8.00
Vase, 2 hdld.	12.00--18.00
Tea Room Glass, 7 oz.	6.00-- 8.00
No. 410 Bowl, salad,	10.00--14.00
No. 505 Bowl, salad	10.00--14.00

MISCELLANEOUS page 320

Fern Bowl, 3 ftd.	10.00--12.00
Bon Bon Dish, flrd., 3 ftd.	10.00--12.00
Bowl, triangle, 3 ftd.	10.00--12.00
Bowl, mayonnaise, ftd., square	10.00--12.00
Salt and Pepper	15.00--20.00
Relish Dish, fancy crystal, 11½"	12.00--15.00
Candlestick Holder, double	12.00--14.00
Bowl, fruit, 2 hdld.	25.00--35.00
Bowl, console, 3 ftd.	10.00--15.00
Vase, crimped top, 2 hdld., ftd.	10.00--14.00
Vase, fancy, 2 hdld.	9.00--12.00
Vase, flrd., top, 2 hdld., ftd.	12.00--15.00
No. 432/5 Vase, fancy crimped top, 2 hdld., ftd.	20.00--25.00
No. 433 Vase, fancy crimped top, 2 hdld., ftd.	18.00--24.00
Ivy Ball, Hobnail, ftd.	8.00--10.00
Fern Bowl, 3 ftd.	12.00--16.00
Bon Bon Dish, 2 hdld., ftd.	7.00-- 9.00
Cockeral Ash Tray	7.00--10.00
Scotty Dog Ash Tray	7.00--10.00
Flower Pot and Saucer	6.00-- 9.00

MISCELLANEOUS page 321

Also made in black.

Swan dish, large	25.00--40.00
Swan Dish, small	20.00--30.00
Bulb Bowl	8.00--10.00
Candlestick, pr.	9.00--12.00
Hobnail Vase	9.00--12.00
Urn Vase, ftd.	10.00--14.00
No. 2-H/10 Fern Bowl, 3 ftd.	6.00-- 9.00
No. 2/10 Fern Bowl, 3 ftd.	6.00-- 9.00
No 1/10 Fern Bowl, 3 ftd.	8.00--12.00
No. 405/10 Window Box, large	14.00--18.00

Levay Glass Co., Edwardsville IL., has made this piece in Honey Persimmon Carnival. They call it "Dancing Ladies".

No. 9/10 Window Box, small	9.00--12.00
Bowl, triangle, 3 ftd.	7.00--10.00

Violet Bowl and Block	8.00--12.00
Vase, 6"	8.00--10.00
No. 300/4 Flower Pot	7.00--11.00
No. 67/4 Flower Pot	7.00--11.00
No. 66/4 Flower Pot	6.00--10.00
No. 201/4 Flower Pot	6.00--10.00
No. 3/4 Swan Dish	40.00--50.00
No. 90/4 Ash Tray	9.00--12.00
Cocktail Tray, 15" x 6"	8.00--10.00
Cocktail Tray, crystal, 15" x 6"	5.00-- 8.00

SPECIAL LISTING WITH F.W. WOOLWORTH CO. page 322, 323

No. 1/4 Fern Bowl	12.00--16.00
No. 2/4 Fern Bowl	9.00--12.00
No. 2-H/4 Fern Bowl	8.00--11.00
No. 77-H/4 Violet Bowl and Block	10.00--14.00
No. 4/4 Flower Block	3.00-- 4.00
No. 600/4 Twin Candle Holder	9.00--12.00
No. 1022/4 Console Bowl	12.00--15.00
No. 805/4 Candle Holder, pr.	10.00--12.00
No. 27/4 Candlestick, pr.	8.00--11.00
No. 99-H/4 Vase	12.00--15.00
No. 800/4 Urn Vase, ftd.	14.00--18.00
No. 433/4-F Vase, 2 hdld.	20.00--25.00
No. 433/4-C Vase, 2 hdld.	20.00--25.00
No. 102/4 Vase, 6¼"	9.00--12.00
No. 1020/4 Ash Tray	9.00--12.00
No. 1000/4 Ash Tray	7.00--10.00
No. 1000-P Ash Tray	7.00--10.00
No. 365/4 Ash Tray, (rooster or dog)	6.00-- 8.00
No. 405/4 Window Box, large	16.00--22.00
No. 9/4 Window Box, small	10.00--14.00
No. 50/4 Bulb Bowl, 5¾"	8.00--10.00
No. 525-H/4 Bowl, triangle	7.00-- 9.00
No. 505 Sandwich Tray, 1 hdld.	18.00--22.00
No. 505 Salad Bowl, 2 hdld.	12.00--15.00
No. 505 Nut Dish, 1 hdld., 8¼"	12.00--15.00
No. 505 Salad Tray, 2 hdld.,	12.00--15.00
No. 309 Console bowl, flrd.,	15.00--20.00
No. 309 Cupped Bowl, large	15.00--20.00
No. 327 Cupped Bowl, small	10.00--14.00
No. 404 Window Box and Block	20.00--25.00
No. 515 Nut Bowl, ftd., 9" dia.	15.00--20.00
No. 1 Fern Bowl, 5½" high	9.00--12.00
No. 515 Cake, ftd., 10½" dia.	20.00--25.00
No. 515 Cupped Bowl, ftd.	11.00--14.00
No. 1000 Vase, flrd.	15.00--18.00
No. 1000 Cupped Vase	12.00--15.00
No. 1000 Fan Vase	15.00--18.00
No. 1931 Vase, 7¾ high	15.00--18.00

CONSOLE SETS page 324

No. 309/38 Console Set: 3 pc. crimped	15.00--25.00
No. 982 Console Set: 3 pc.	15.00--25.00
No. 982 Console Set: 7 pc.	30.00--40.00
No. 1/18 Console Set: 3 pc.	22.00--25.00
No. 1/308 Console Set: 3 pc.	22.00--25.00

"WIG-WAM" page 325

See in Co-Operative chapter.

Bowl	20.00--25.00

ROOSTER

No. 208 Rooster, 9"	25.00--35.00

"PUNCH"

Dresser Set	35.00--40.00

VASE

No. 905 Vase, 10"	18.00--24.00

BLACK SILVER DECORATED ITEMS

No. 49 Vase	12.00--16.00
No 432 Vase	18.00--22.00
"Scotty" Ash Tray	7.00--10.00
"Cockeral" Ash Tray	7.00--10.00
Jardiniere, 3 ftd., small	10.00--13.00
Jardiniere, 3 ftd., large	14.00--18.00
Flower Block	3.00-- 4.00
Beer Mug, crystal, polished bottom, 12 oz.	7.00-- 9.00

GREENSBURG GLASS WORKS page 326

Vase, 7", 9", 11"	9.00--14.00
Candlestick, pr.	10.00--15.00
Flower Bowl	12.00--16.00
Flower Block, 16 holes	7.00-- 9.00
Decorated Vase	7.00--12.00
Dog Cigarette Box	15.00--20.00
Elephant Cigarette Box	15.00--20.00
Elephant Ash Tray	12.00--15.00
Dog Ash Tray	12.00--15.00
Cordial Tray	10.00--12.00
Bon Bon	8.00--10.00
Bottle Caster Set w/Tray	11.00--14.00
Celery Dish, 9½"	9.00--12.00
Candlestick, pr.	8.00--12.00
Mayonnaise Set: 3 pc. Bowl, Plate, Ladle	18.00--22.00
Sugar Bowl and Cover, 2 hdld.	8.00--10.00
Cream, hdld.	4.00-- 6.00
No. 3 Flower Block	2.00-- 3.00
No. 1019 Vase	9.00--12.00
Cookie Jar	40.00--50.00
Beverage Tray, center hdld.	12.00--16.00
Tumbler Tray, center hdld.	18.00--24.00
Butter Tub and Cover	10.00--14.00

Standard

If you think your pattern ought to be here, and it isn't, turn to the Lancaster chapter. The two companies, both subsidiaries of Hocking after 1924, often shared molds.

We're taking this opportunity to reprint a Standard pattern that wouldn't edge sideways into Book 2. It concludes the section.

MARTHA WASHINGTON	page 327
Plate, salad	4.00-- 6.00
Cup	3.00-- 4.00
Saucer	1.50-- 2.00
Tumbler, ftd.	7.00-- 9.00
Sugar	6.00-- 8.00
Creamer	6.00-- 8.00
Plate, sandwich	7.00--10.00

"GRAPE"	page 328, 329
Water Sets	50.00--60.00
Plate, 6"	1.50-- 2.00
Plate, 8"	4.00-- 5.00
Plate, sherbet, 6"	1.50-- 2.00
Cup and Saucer	5.00-- 7.00
Cream	5.00-- 8.00
Cream, cone shaped	7.00-- 9.00
Sugar	5.00-- 8.00
Sugar, cone shaped	7.00-- 9.00
Sherbet, regular	3.50-- 4.00
Sherbet, low	3.50-- 4.00
Sherbet, tall	5.00-- 7.00
Tumbler, 2½, 5, 9, 10, 12 13, 15 oz.	4.00-- 8.00
Tumbler, ftd., 10 oz.	7.00-- 9.00
Ice Tea, ftd.	6.00-- 8.00
Juice, fruit, ftd.	5.00-- 7.00
Tumbler, barrel, 9 oz.	6.00-- 9.00
Salt and Pepper, pr.	14.00--18.00
Salt and Pepper, fat, pr.	14.00--18.00
R-23 Salt and Pepper, ftd., pr.	14.00--18.00
Goblet	10.00--12.00
Cocktail	10.00--12.00
Sundae	8.00--10.00
Vase	8.00--12.00
Nite Set	25.00--35.00
Jug, 56 oz.	18.00--22.00
Jug, 80 oz.	20.00--25.00
Jug, 57 oz.	18.00--22.00

"ROSE"	page 329
Plate, 8"	3.00-- 5.00
Tumbler, 10 oz.	4.00-- 6.00
Tumbler, ftd., 10 oz.	5.00-- 7.00
Ice Tea, 12 oz.	5.00-- 7.00
Ice Tea, ftd., 15 oz.	6.00-- 8.00
Juice, fruit, 5 oz.	4.00-- 5.00
Sherbet, high	5.00-- 7.00
Goblet	9.00--11.00
Cup and Saucer	5.00-- 7.00
Cream and Sugar	8.00--12.00
Jug, 54 oz.	16.00--20.00

MISCELLANEOUS	
Tumbler, Cut 3001, 6, 7, 8, 10, 12 oz.	3.00-- 6.00
Tumbler, Cut 2, 5, 9, 13, 15 oz.	3.00-- 6.00
Bowl, Cut 400	3.00-- 5.00

REFRESHMENT SET	page 330
Jug, 80 oz.	20.00--25.00
Ice Tea, 12 oz.	5.00-- 7.00
Juice, fruit, 5 oz.	4.00-- 5.00

ICE TEA SET	
Jug, 80 oz.	20.00--25.00
Ice Tea, 15 oz.	6.00-- 8.00

GENUINE ROCK CRYSTAL Cut 7

Goblet, 9 oz.	9.00--12.00
Saucer Champagne	7.00--10.00
Plate, 6"	2.00-- 3.00
Plate, 8"	4.00-- 6.00
Sherbet, 6 oz.	5.00-- 7.00
Wine, 2½ oz.	8.00--10.00
Cocktail, 3 oz.	8.00--10.00
Wine, ftd.	5.00-- 7.00
Tumbler, ftd.	7.00-- 9.00
Ice Tea, ftd.	8.00--10.00

NO. 380 CRYSTAL ASSORTMENT

Orange Bowl, 12"	14.00--18.00
Sandwich Tray, 11"	10.00--12.00
Fruit Bowl, 14½"	15.00--20.00
Console Bowl, 11"	10.00--14.00
Candlestick, pr.	10.00--14.00

"TRUDY" page 331

604-D Comport	6.00-- 8.00
648 Sugar	5.00-- 8.00
648 Cream	5.00-- 8.00
Vase	7.00-- 9.00
852 Candle, pr.	8.00-- 9.00
86-B Bowl	8.00--10.00
Plate, ftd.	8.00--10.00
Comport, ftd.	6.00-- 9.00
Plate, salad	4.00-- 6.00
619-D Comport	7.00-- 9.00
Bowl, 9"	10.00--12.00
Cheese and Cracker	10.00--13.00
Tray Sugar and Cream	12.00--16.00
Mayonnaise Set	12.00--15.00
Candy and Cover	15.00--18.00
611 Candle	6.00-- 8.00
Bowl, 12"	9.00--12.00
Bon Bon and Cover	15.00--20.00
Plate, cake	7.00-- 9.00
Bowl, ftd.	10.00--12.00
Sandwich Tray	10.00--13.00
Salver, ftd.	10.00--14.00

"BLANCHE"

Goblet	10.00--12.00
Saucer Champagne	8.00--10.00
Sherbet	6.00-- 8.00
Wine	10.00--12.00
Sugar	5.00-- 8.00
Cream	5.00-- 8.00
Candy and Cover	15.00--20.00
Candlestick	5.00-- 7.00
Nappy, flrd., 7"	6.00-- 9.00
Plate, 8"	4.00-- 6.00
Shaker, pr.	15.00--20.00
Syrup and Plate	15.00--20.00

"FAITH" page 332

Plate, sandwich, 13"	14.00--18.00
Tray, sandwich, 13"	14.00--18.00
Stand, cake, 13½"	12.00--15.00
Bowl, orange, 11"	10.00--14.00
Tray: 3 pc.	
Sugar and Cream Set	15.00--20.00
Candlestick, pr.	10.00--14.00
Bowl, console, 12"	10.00--14.00

"TYRUS"

Salver, 14"	12.00--15.00
Bowl, console	10.00--14.00
Candlestick	10.00--12.00
Center Piece	10.00--14.00
Bowl, crimp	10.00--14.00
Bowl, orange	10.00--14.00
Bowl, flower	10.00--14.00

"HOFFMAN"

Sugar	5.00-- 8.00
Cream	5.00-- 8.00
Syrup	10.00--15.00
Bon Bon, 7"	6.00-- 8.00
Fruit, 8½"	8.00--11.00
Relish, deep, 7½"	8.00--10.00
Jelly, 8"	7.00-- 9.00
Comport, 9"	8.00--12.00
Plate, fudge, 8"	6.00-- 8.00

BUD VASES CUT 9

150, 250, 151, 252, 152, 252	10.00--14.00

"CORONA" page 333

Bowl, ftd., 11"	11.00--15.00
Mayonnaise Set: 3 pc., 10½"	12.00--15.00
Nappy	6.00-- 8.00
Candy Box and Cover	16.00--22.00
Candlestick, pr.	15.00--20.00
Bowl, fruit, 12"	11.00--14.00
Sandwich, 12"	10.00--14.00
Plate, salad, 9"	4.00-- 6.00
Tray, nut, hdld., 11"	10.00--14.00

"HARLOW"

Goblet	10.00--12.0[illegible]
Saucer Champagne	8.00--10.0[illegible]
Sherbet	6.00-- 8.0[illegible]
Wine	10.00--12.0[illegible]

"BRINK"

Goblet	9.00--11.0[illegible]
Saucer Champagne	7.00-- 9.0[illegible]
Sherbet	5.00-- 7.0[illegible]

Wine	9.00--11.00
Cocktail	8.00--10.00
207 Wine	4.00-- 6.00
Tumbler, ftd.	5.00-- 7.00
Ice Tea	7.00-- 9.00

"XAVIER"

Bowl, ftd., 11"	10.00--12.00
Bowl, 9¾"	8.00--10.00
Oval 11"	10.00--12.00
Bon Bon, covered, 6"	15.00--20.00
Candlestick, pr.	10.00--14.00
Bowl, 12"	10.00--14.00
Bowl, 13½"	11.00--14.00
Plate, 10½"	7.00-- 9.00
Tray, sandwich, 11"	10.00--14.00

ROSE CUT 106 — page 334

Wine, 2½ oz.	3.00-- 5.00
Juice, fruit, 5 oz.	3.00-- 5.00
Tumbler, 9 oz.	4.00-- 6.00
Tumbler, 10 oz.	5.00-- 7.00
Jug	20.00--25.00

CRYSTAL CUT 113

Wine, 2½ oz.	3.00-- 4.00
Tumbler 9 oz.	3.00-- 4.00
Ice Tea, 12 oz.	4.00-- 6.00

"CHARLES"

Bowl, orange, 10"	12.00--15.00
Bowl, fruit, 9"	10.00--14.00

"YUMMY"

Vase, 6½"	6.00-- 9.00
Tray, 13½"	10.00--14.00
Candlestick, 2½", pr.	10.00--14.00
Bowl, 13½"	12.00--14.00
Bowl, 13½"	14.00--16.00
Bowl, 13"	14.00--16.00

"BARNES"

Mayonnaise Set: 2 pc.	8.00--10.00
Salad Set: 2 pc.	15.00--18.00
Candy Jar and Cover	15.00--20.00
Candlestick, 2½", pr.	10.00--14.00
Bowl, console, 11"	9.00--12.00
Sugar and Cream	10.00--15.00
Tray, sandwich, 11"	10.00--14.00
Tray, roll, 10½"	8.00--12.00

"BEADLES" — page 335

Bowl, 3 toed, 9"	8.00--10.00
Fruit, 3 toed, 9½"	8.00--10.00
Crimp, 3 toed, 8½"	9.00--11.00
Fruit, ftd., 9"	9.00--11.00
Comport, ftd., 9"	9.00--11.00
Rose Bowl, ftd., 7"	8.00--10.00

"TWINKLE"

Bowl, orange, ftd., 12"	10.00--14.00
Bowl, flower, ftd., 9"	9.00--12.00
Bowl, crimp, ftd., 12"	10.00--14.00
Salver, ftd., 14"	12.00--15.00
Center Piece, ftd., 13"	11.00--14.00
Bowl, console, 13"	12.00--15.00

"PAULINE"

Plate, fudge, 8¼"	7.00-- 9.00
Bowl, candy, 7"	7.00-- 9.00
Relish, deep, 6¼"	6.00-- 8.00
Bowl, Violet, 6¼"	6.00-- 8.00
Plate, 8¼"	5.00-- 7.00
Bowl, fruit, ftd., 6½"	5.00-- 7.00
Sweetmeat, ftd., 8"	5.00-- 8.00
Dish, crimped almond, ftd., 6¾"	6.00-- 8.00

"TAT"

Goblet	9.00--11.00
Saucer Champagne	6.00-- 9.00
Wine	9.00--11.00
Sherbet	4.00-- 6.00
Plate, sherbet, 6"	2.00-- 3.00
Juice, fruit	4.00-- 6.00
Tumbler, ftd.	5.00-- 7.00
Ice Tea, ftd.	7.00-- 9.00
Plate, 8"	4.00-- 6.00
Vases, bud, R-250, R-252, R-251, 59	10.00--14.00

"MARY ELIZABETH"

See following reprints

Tumbler, 9 oz.	4.00-- 6.00
Tumbler, ice tea, 14 oz.	6.00-- 8.00
Tumbler, bell, 8 oz.	4.00-- 6.00
Sherbet, 5 oz.	4.00-- 6.00
Goblet, saucer champagne, 5 oz.	7.00-- 9.00
Goblet, wine, 3 oz.	9.00--11.00
Tumbler, beverage, 1½ oz.	5.00-- 7.00
Goblet, 9 oz.	9.00--11.00
Tumbler, fruit juice, 5 oz.	3.00-- 4.00
Sugar	6.00-- 9.00
Cream	6.00-- 9.00
Pitcher, syrup and plate	15.00--18.00
Nappy, ftd., 6"	6.00-- 8.00
Vase, 6"	6.00-- 9.00
Nappy, hdld, heart, 6"	6.00-- 9.00
Vase, 9½"	8.00--11.00
Plate, deep, 10"	10.00--13.00
Salt and Pepper, pr.	15.00--20.00
Nappy, hdld., 6"	6.00-- 9.00
Comport, 6"	5.00-- 8.00
Salt and Pepper, pr.	15.00--20.00
Oil	14.00--18.00
Tumbler, 9 oz.	4.00-- 6.00
Vase, ftd., 6"	8.00--10.00
Bowl, RE, 7"	7.00-- 9.00

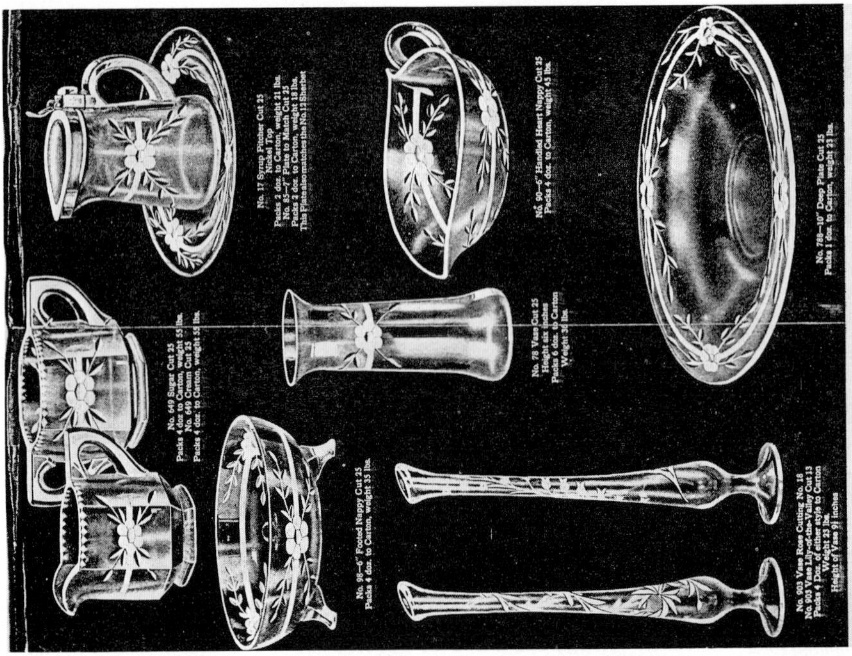

No. 20 Salt and Pepper Shaker C N T
Cut 25
Packs 12 doz. to Carton(½ Salt-½ Pepper)
Weight 40 lbs.

No. 702—6" Handled Nappy Cut 25
Packs 4 doz. to Carton, weight 50 lbs.

No. 20 Salt and Pepper Shaker A. T.
Cut 95
Packs 12 doz to Carton, weight 38 lbs

No. 788-6" Comport Cut 25
Packs 4 doz. to Carton, weight 55 lbs.

No. 9 Oil and Stopper Cut 25
Packs 4 doz. to Carton, weight 40 lbs.

No. 1-9 oz. Optic Table Tumbler
Cut 95
Straight Shape—Thin Blown
Packs 12 doz. to Carton
Weight 48 lbs.

No. 83—6" Footed Bowl or Vase
Cut 25
Packs 3 doz. to Carton, weight 35 lbs.

No. 788—7" Rolled Edge Bowl Cut 25
Packs 4 doz. to Carton, weight 60 lbs.

No. 649 Sugar Cut 25
Packs 4 doz to Carton, weight 55 lbs.
No. 649 Cream Cut 25
Packs 4 doz. to Carton, weight 55 lbs.

No. 17 Syrup Pitcher Cut 25
Nickel Top
Packs 2 doz. to Carton, weight 21 lbs.
No. 85—7" Plate to Match Cut 25
Packs 2 doz. to Carton, weight 18 lbs.
This Plate also matches the No. 12 Sherbet

No. 98—6" Footed Nappy Cut 25
Packs 4 doz. to Carton, weight 35 lbs.

No. 78 Vase Cut 25
Height six inches
Packs 6 doz. to Carton
Weight 36 lbs.

No. 90—6" Handled Heart Nappy Cut 25
Packs 4 doz. to Carton, weight 45 lbs.

No. 903 Vase Rose Cutting No. 18
No. 903 Vase Lily-of-the-Valley Cut 13
Packs 4 Doz. of either style to Carton
Weight 23 lbs.
Height of Vase 9½ inches

No. 788—10" Deep Plate Cut 25
Packs 1 doz. to Carton, weight 23 lbs.

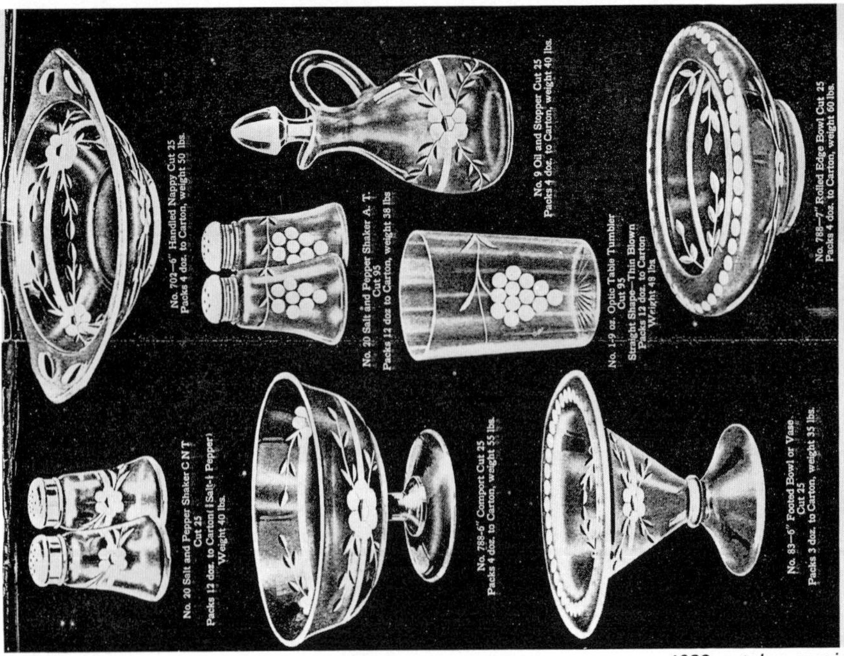

"MARY ELIZABETH"

1933 catalog reprin

U.S. Glass

My Find of the Year in U.S. Glass: The Black Satin frog candleholders which are viewable in this edition's color section.

Several reprints follow the end of this chapter. The first is of a kitchen line, in U.S.'s light green, that I found this past year. Of the pieces shown, to date I've only seen the jug and tumblers and the cream and sugar (also shown in the color section).

Following that is a reprint showing the various U.S. Lamps. Note the two sizes of PARROT lamps. The large one is shown, too, in this year's color section.

Next is a page from an old 1920 crystal catalog showing some reamers and a salt box that were later made in milk white and green. The green one's in the color section.

Finally, there's a reprint of some of the later stems of U.S. Glass.

1924 U.S. ITEMS **page 337**

MILADY'S

Ring Holder	12.00--16.00

COLOGNES

Each	30.00--40.00

CENTER SERVER

Server	18.00--26.00

STIPPLE OR CRACQUELLED

Jug Set	40.00--60.00

CHEESE AND CRACKER

Stand	25.00--35.00

CRAQUEL

Water Set	40.00--60.00

KITCHEN ITEMS

Reamers	12.00--18.00
Measurers	18.00--24.00
Mixing Bowls	6.00--12.00
Jug	9.00--12.00

CONSOLE SET

No. 15319	25.00--35.00

SLICK **page 338**

Shakers, ea.	4.00-- 6.00

ECHEL

Comport	20.00--30.00
Vase	20.00--30.00

TAPESTRY

Jug and Tumbler	40.00--50.00

BOUDOIR LAMP

Lamp	40.00--60.00

Photo Courtesy L.C. Cox

"FLOWER GARDEN AND BUTTERFLIES"

candy jar and cover, plate, candlestick with glass candle, console bowl on stand, console bowl with pattern on inside, center handled server, cream, sugar, and ash tray

VANITY SET

Set	40.00--50.00

STIPPLED

Candy Jar and Cover	25.00--40.00
Cheese and Cracker	18.00--28.00
Cake Plate, hdld.	15.00--25.00

SMOKER'S page 339

Tray	15.00--25.00

LEEDS

Bowl	15.00--25.00

FISH BOWL

Bowl	10.00--20.00

GLASS SALAD SET

Set	15.00--20.00

"FLOWER GARDEN AND BUTTERFLIES"

Most pieces were made in black. They will be 50% to 75% higher.

Plate, 7¼"	15.00--20.00
Plate, 8"	15.00--20.00
Plate, 9"	25.00--30.00
Plate, 10"	30.00--40.00
Cup	90.00-110.00
Saucer	25.00--30.00
Cream	100.00-125.00
Sugar	100.00-125.00
Bowl, console, ftd., 10"	75.00--95.00
Tray, 5½ x 10"	20.00--25.00
Tray, 7½ x 11¾"	25.00--35.00
Dresser Set	200.00-300.00
Candy Dish and Cover, 8" high	85.00--95.00
Candy Dish and Cover, 6" high	45.00--55.00
Powder Jar and Cover, flat	25.00--35.00
Cheese and Cracker	40.00--50.00
Server, center hdld., 10½"	40.00--50.00
Candy Dish and Cover, flat, 6-3/8"	150.00-200.00
Bon Bon, stemmed, 6"	20.00--30.00
Candlestick, 8", pr.	75.00--85.00
Candlestick, 3¼", pr.	50.00--60.00
Candlesticks, 6", pr.	65.00--75.00
Mayonnaise Set, 3 pc.	80.00-100.00
Vase, 6"	30.00--35.00
Vase, 10"	65.00--75.00
Wall Vase	50.00--60.00
Ash Tray w/match holder	100.00-150.00
Bowl, console, 10½", 4½" high (Black w/pattern on the inside)	80.00-100.00
Candy Dish, heart shape	200.00-300.00
Cigarette Box and Cover	45.00--65.00

PARAKEET LINE page 340

Salty and Peppy, pr.	20.00--30.00
Vase, wall	10.00--15.00
Candy Jar	15.00--20.00
Candleholder	8.00--10.00

VASES

9723	7.00-- 9.00
16212	9.00--12.00
310	12.00--15.00
6149	12.00--16.00
185	7.00-- 9.00
15021	10.00--20.00
152	12.00--15.00
328	25.00--35.00
320	10.00--13.00
165	20.00--30.00
16261	14.00--18.00
15162	20.00--30.00

ENGLISH LAMP

Lamp	25.00--35.00

GALLEON

Ash Tray, 3" (9389)	8.00--12.00
Ash Tray, 3", 6"	12.00--16.00

BEE HIVE LINE page 341

Goblet, Sherbets, Tumblers, etc.	8.00--12.00

KIMBERLY

Console Set	50.00--70.00

"ELYSIUM"

Bulb Box	20.00--25.00
Candleholders, pr.	8.00--12.00

CLASSIC SIMPLICITY

Set	35.00--50.00

ETCHED "PSYCHE"

Plate, 6", 8", 10"	4.00--12.00
Cream and Sugar	20.00--25.00
Bon Bon	8.00--12.00
Bud Vase	10.00--13.00
Jug with Cover	35.00--50.00
Jug without Cover	30.00--40.00
Tumbler	8.00--10.00
Oyster Cocktail	9.00--12.00
Finger Bowl	6.00-- 8.00

Goblet	16.00--20.00
Cafe Parfait	16.00--20.00
Saucer Champagne	14.00--18.00
Wine	18.00--22.00
Cocktail	16.00--20.00

GOBLETS page 342

002, 014, 199, 015	9.00--12.00

MILADY DRESSER SET

Dresser Set	35.00--50.00

"TWIRL"

Jug	35.00--45.00
Tumbler	6.00-- 9.00
Goblet	9.00--12.00

LADY NICOTINE

Set	20.00--25.00

SANTA CLAUS

Lamp	150.00-175.00

TORCHIERE

Lamp	75.00-100.00
Vase	50.00--75.00

FLANDERS page 343

Plate	8.00--10.00
Goblet	20.00--25.00

HELIO

Console Set	24.00--28.00

WALL VASE

Vase	15.00--25.00

"TOP O' THE MORNING"

Sets	35.00--50.00

SANDWICH OR CAKE

Plate	9.00--11.00

"DINER"

Plate	4.00-- 6.00
Goblet	10.00--12.00

FRUIT JUICE EXTRACTORS

Extractors	15.00--25.00

OCTAGON BRIDGE SET page 344

Tumbler, ftd.,	6.00-- 8.00
Server, sandwich, center hdld.,	9.00--12.00
Plate	3.50-- 4.50
Cup and Saucer	5.00-- 8.00
Cream and Sugar	15.00--18.00

MISCELLANEOUS

Smokers Set	20.00--30.00
Juicer Set	25.00--35.00
Breakfast Set	25.00--35.00
Cocktail Set	25.00--35.00
Nite Set	25.00--35.00
Vinegar and Oil Set	30.00--40.00

"UPSY DAISY" page 345

Console Set	20.00--35.00

"POPPY"

Vase	25.00--35.00

"UNCLE SAM"

Cocktail Set	65.00--75.00

BATH SALT

Jar with Cover	25.00--35.00

CANDY JAR

Jar with Cover	30.00--40.00

"ROSEMARY" ETCHING

Mint Wafer, ftd.	8.00--12.00
Marmalade, ftd.	10.00--14.00

SYLVAN

Goblet	10.00--15.00
Tumbler	8.00--12.00

U.S. KITCHENWARE page 346

Refrigerator Set: 6 pc.	70.00--75.00
Reamer Sets	40.00--45.00
Refrigerator Jars and Covers, ea.	10.00--15.00

Mixing Bowl, slick hdld., ea.	10.00--25.00
"TICK-TAC-TOE" Ice Bucket	15.00--25.00
"ACORN" Salver	10.00--14.00
"STAG" Ashtray	20.00--25.00
"KING TUT" Bowl, 3 ftd.	12.00--16.00
"SHAGGY DAISY" Cake Plate	15.00--20.00

U.S. ITEMS page 347

Slick Cup	3.00-- 5.00
SNOWFLAKE Measuring Jug	25.00--30.00
SLICK Measuring Cup	25.00--35.00
U.S. Mixing Bowl	8.00--12.00
SLICK Batter	18.00--22.00
"JUMBO" Mixing Bowl	30.00--35.00
"BIMBO" Mixing Bowl	35.00--40.00
SLICK Plate	3.00-- 5.00
"SCROLL" Plate	3.00-- 5.00

"ROSE BURR"

Utility or Cake Plate	15.00--20.00

"WALLFLOWER"

Utility Plate	12.00--16.00
Bowl and Cover, ea.	20.00--35.00

"SHAGGY ROSE"

Cake Plate, 10"	15.00--20.00

"POPPY-COCKLEBURR"

Refrigerator Dish and Cover	12.00--16.00

SLICK page 348

Reamer, orange, large	15.00--25.00

"BRILLE"

Tumbler	7.00-- 9.00
Sugar	8.00--10.00
Cream	8.00--10.00

"BURNISH"

Bowl	20.00--25.00

"HOT CAKES"

Plate and Cover	20.00--30.00

SLICK

Condiment Holder	15.00--20.00

"EVE"

Cosmetic Set	30.00--40.00

"ROSE AND THORN"

Marsha Newhart, DeWitt MI reminds us that the "Rose and Thorn" bowl also was made with a "Donna" rim

Bowl, 11"	10.00--16.00
Nappy	5.00-- 7.00

"TENDRIL"

Plate	6.00-- 9.00

"TITA"

Water Set	20.00--25.00

"DONNA"

Bowl	10.00--16.00

"BOWMAN"

Console Set	14.00--18.00

"PEEP-HOLE"

Bowl	9.00--12.00

PARAMOUNT SERVICE

Napkin Holder	35.00--50.00

U.S. CAT page 349

Cat, 11", (also in white)	85.00-100.00
Cat, 6"	85.00-100.00

U.S. MOOSE

Ash Tray	20.00--25.00

U.S. BRIDGE SET

Ash Tray Coaster w/Tumbler	16.00--22.00

"U.S. BIG CHIEF"

Goblet	12.00--15.00
Sherbet, tall	10.00--12.00
Tumbler, ftd.	8.00--10.00
Plate	4.00-- 6.00

U.S. LOVEBIRD

Lamp	100.00-150.00

U.S. PARROT *See in Color Section*

Lamp, 13"	150.00-175.00
Lamp, 14", large base	200.00-250.00

"LARIETTE"

Server, sandwich, center hdld.	15.00--20.00
Sugar	8.00--10.00
Cream	8.00--10.00
Nappy	6.00-- 8.00
Plate	5.00-- 7.00

PRIMO page 350

Plate, dinner, 10"	8.00--10.00
Plate, grill, 10"	6.00-- 8.00
Plate, tea, partitioned w/cup ring, 10"	8.00--10.00
Plate, salad, 7½"	4.00-- 6.00
Plate, sherbet, 5½"	2.00-- 3.00
Plate, cake, 2 hdld., 10½"	9.00--12.00
Cup	4.00-- 6.00
Saucer	2.00-- 3.00
Sherbet, 5½ oz.	6.00-- 8.00
Bowl, berry, 4½"	4.00-- 6.00
Bowl, berry, 3 toed, 11", flng.	12.00--15.00
Bowl, nappy, 6", baked apple	6.00-- 8.00
Bowl, nappy, 8"	12.00--16.00
Cream	7.00-- 9.00
Sugar	7.00-- 9.00
Tumbler, ftd., 9½ oz., 5¾"	9.00--11.00
Coaster/Ashtray	12.00--15.00
Cake plate, 3 toed, salver, 10"	10.00--14.00

PARADE

Liqueur Set	55.00--65.00

SPIRIT OF ST. LOUIS

Pink, green, blue, canary
Inscribed "Patented in 1927"

Decanter, 8" high, 14" long	300.00-400.00

ARTICLES FOR KITCHEN USE

Lemon Reamer	12.00--20.00
Measuring Cups	15.00--20.00
Lemon Juice Set	20.00--25.00
Funnels	10.00--18.00
Fruit Jar Filler and Strainer	12.00--15.00
Rolling Pin	15.00--25.00
Salt Box, wooden cover	40.00--65.00
Kitchen Measuring Pitcher	20.00--35.00

See reprint next page

ALL GLASS BOUDOIR AND NOVELTY LAMPS

Fruit or Flower Console Lamp	45.00--65.00
Boudoir Lamps	35.00--55.00
Torchiere Lamp	25.00--40.00

The Shield of a Great Name Protects the Buyer

Three Graces

ETCHED "JULIA" Crystal Optic Bowl Amber Stem and Foot

CUT NO. 405 Crystal Optic Bowl Amber Stem and Foot

CUT NO. 406 Crystal Optic Bowl Light Green Stem and Foot

These decorations show only three of the many available in our fine lines of lead blown tableware—HAND CUT; NEEDLE or PLATE ETCHED; GOLD ENCRUSTED AND DECORATED; SAND BLASTED. *The range of shapes and patterns is wide—plain and all optics; crystal and solid colors; combinations of crystal bowls and colored stems and feet, and colored bowls with contrasting colors in the trim.*

United States Glass Company

PITTSBURGH, PA.

Our Salesmen can give any required information about these lines, and a full exhibit of samples can be seen at our sales and Display Rooms — conveniently located in all principal cities

1926 ad

Fruit or Flower Basket Lamp	45.00--65.00
Perfume Lamp	35.00--45.00
Parrot Lamp (E6)	150.00-175.00
Owl Lamp	110.00-135.00
Lovebird Lamp	100.00-150.00
Elk Lamp	50.00--60.00
Rabbit Lamp	100.00-125.00
Girl Lamp	50.00--75.00
Parrot Lamp (E13)	200.00-250.00

See in Color Section

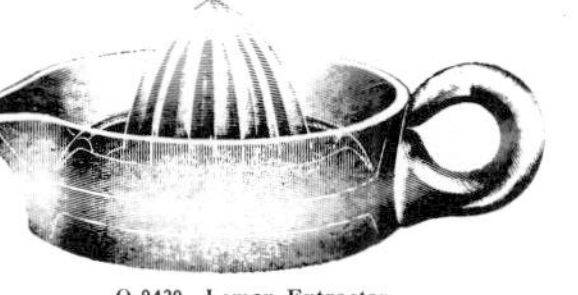

O 9429—Lemon Extractor

No. 9431—Lemon Juicer
Also made for Orange and Grape Fruit

No. 9436—Lemon Juicer

No. 9437—Orange Reamer
6½ doz. to bbl. Wt. 115 lbs.

F 3879—Measuring Cup

O 3870—Lipped Measuring Cup

9416—Lemon Juicer Set
1 Juicer, 1 measuring Cup
12 doz. to bbl. Wt. 165 lbs.

O 9416—Lemon Juicer

No. 14400—Funnel

Glass Funnel

Fruit Jar Filler and Strainer
10 doz. to bbl. Wt. 120 lbs.

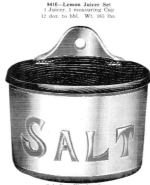

Salt Box, Wooden Cover
Made in Crystal and Opal Glass

Kitchen Measuring Pitcher
A most useful article adapted to practical use in the kitchen of private house and public institutions.
It measures—
From 2 ounces to 48 ounces
From ¼ cup to 6 cups
From 1 pint to 3 pints
From ¼ lb. sugar to 2 lbs. sugar
From ¼ lb. Flour to 1 lb. Flour
2 doz. to bbl.—Wt. 110 lbs.

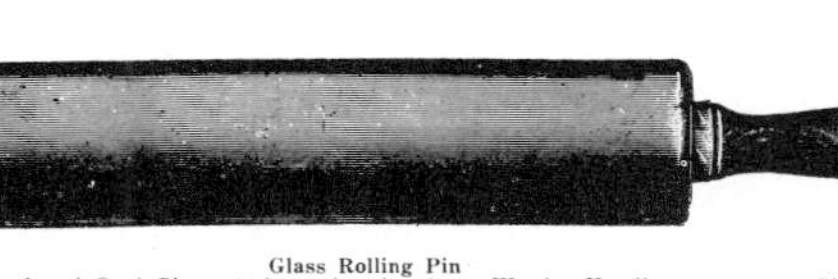

Glass Rolling Pin
Made in Crystal and Opal Glass—10-in. and 12-in sizes—Wooden Handles screw on to Glass

KITCHEN ITEMS From 1922 U.S. Glass Items

Decorated All-Glass Boudoir and Novelty Electric Lamps
Lamparas Electricas

LAMPS From 1926 U.S. Glass Catalog

JUST a few of the many new United States Glass items that will bring bigger business and bigger profits to many wide awake dealers during the coming Spring and Summer months.
Let us send you, gratis, the Glass Outlook, published monthly
United States Glass Company, Pittsburgh, Pa.
SALES OFFICES IN ALL LARGE CITIES

1925 ad

The Colonial Dame

Portable Lamp

A memory of Colonial days that blends harmoniously with the old four poster and the rag rugs of the boudoir of 1800. Gives a soft diffused light and serves admirably on dresser or bedside table. Hand decorated in soft tints—pink, green, and yellow. Base is lustrous black glass.

Lamp is complete with cord and plug in individual carton. No orders accepted for less than six.

UNITED STATES GLASS COMPANY

General Offices and Salesrooms

South Ninth and Bingham Sts., Pittsburgh, Pa.

New York: 1107 Broadway. E. T. W. Craig, Representative
Philadelphia: 10th and Market Sts. J. A. Hemple, Representative
San Francisco: 682 Mission Street, F. M. Dunn, Representative
Boston: 99 Bedford Street, M. A. Lovell, Representative
Los Angeles: 643 South Olive Street, J. F. Stirk, Representative
Dallas: Southland Hotel Building. D. D. Otstott, Inc., Representative
Baltimore: 110 Hopkins Place, John A. Dobson Co., Representative
Chicago: 30 East Randolph Street, F. T. Renshaw, Representative
Denver: 404 Jacobson Building, Norton C. Boyer, Representative
St. Louis: 1017 Olive Street. J. Donald Fisher, Representative

1923 ad

NEW SHIP DESIGN BOOK ENDS—NO. 9352

All-glass book ends combining beauty and utility are now available in an artistic ship design that is enhanced by the lustrous satin finish, black or amber.

Made to retail for $2.00 to $2.50 a pair, east of the Mississippi.

UNITED STATES GLASS COMPANY

PITTSBURGH, PENNSYLVANIA

OFFICES IN ALL PRINCIPAL CITIES

Visit Our New Display and Sales Rooms—Pottery & Glass Bldg., 954 Liberty Ave., Pittsburgh, Pa.

1925 ad

SPIRIT OF ST. LOUIS

Four stunning 1928 *stemware creations by the United States Glass Co., Pittsburgh. From left to right: No.* 032*—a fetching, festoon optic glass with shirred and button stem, rose bowl, with green stem and foot. Arcadian—twisted green stem, green foot, wide optic crystal bowl, deep plate etched basket design, set in satin finished medallion. Empire—rose colored goblet with deep plate etched bird medallions in satin finish, shirred stem, medium optic. Fallaje—tall optic crystal bowl, cut leaf and floral spray, satin leaves, polished flowers, cut stem, with fluted button, green foot.*

1928 ad

An Invitation

When visiting the New York China and Glass Show at the New Yorker Hotel, July 29th to August 4th or the Housefurnishing Show at the Pennsylvania Hotel same date, it will be to your advantage to call at our New York Sales Room, 1107 Broadway, where is displayed a complete line of bar, hotel, restaurant and soda fountain glassware; also the famous Tiffin line of Department Store items, attractive wine and liquor sets and occasional and decorative pieces.

1934 journal ad

NO. 330—7 IN. VASE

"POPPY" DECORATION

ON LIGHT GREEN SATINED GLASS

A fascinating novelty, developed especially for fine retail and gift shop trade.

The decoration, in vivid coloring, applied by hand to this lustrous ware, has a compelling appeal.

Covered Candy Boxes and Bon Bon Dishes; Dresser, Smoking and Night Cap Sets; Vases, Baskets and Candleholders; are among the articles available, either singly or as an assortment (No. 22074-1) which gives variety.

PITTSBURGH, PA.

1926 ad

"Cricket" Water Set From 1933 Company Brochure

NO.352-19 PIECE-BEVERAGE SET

"CRICKET" Water Set

Jug	15.00--20.00
Tumbler	4.00-- 6.00
Sugar and Cream Set	10.00--14.00

See in Color Section

REAMER SETS

Reamer Sets	40.00--45.00

6456-2 Piece Comb. Reamer Set

6460-2 Piece Comb. Reamer Set

6489-2 Piece Comb. Reamer Set

6478-2 Piece Comb. Reamer Set

6492-2 Piece Comb. Reamer Set

Tiffin's Stemware Blanks From 1940-1960

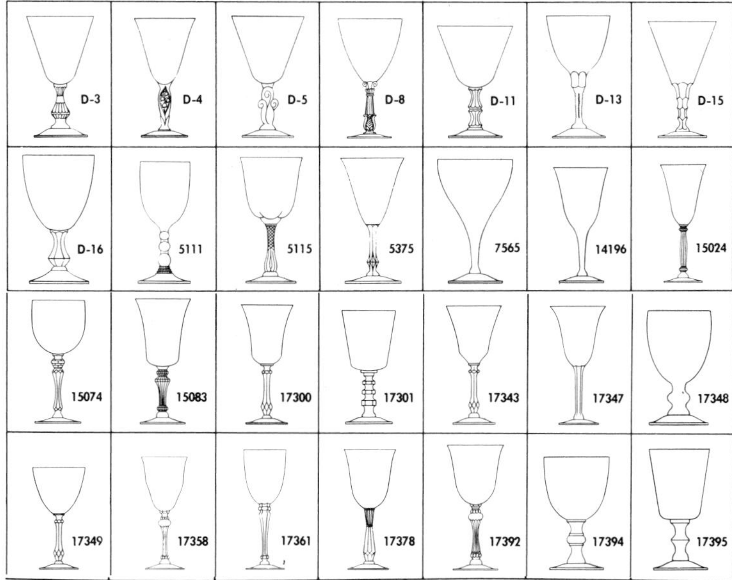

Tiffin's Stemware Blanks From 1940-1960

17397	17399	17403	17406	17418	17431	17434
17439	17440	17441	17442	17453	17454	17457
17458	17467	17474	17476	17477	17480	17489
17490	17491	17492	17500	17501	17502	17503
17505	17507	17524	17525	17528	17536	17540
17542	17544	17546	17547	17548	17549	17551
17552	17553	17566	17568	17574	17576	17578
17581 *	17586	17588	17589	17591	17593 *	17594 *
17595 *	17596 *	17597	17598	17601	17602	17603 *

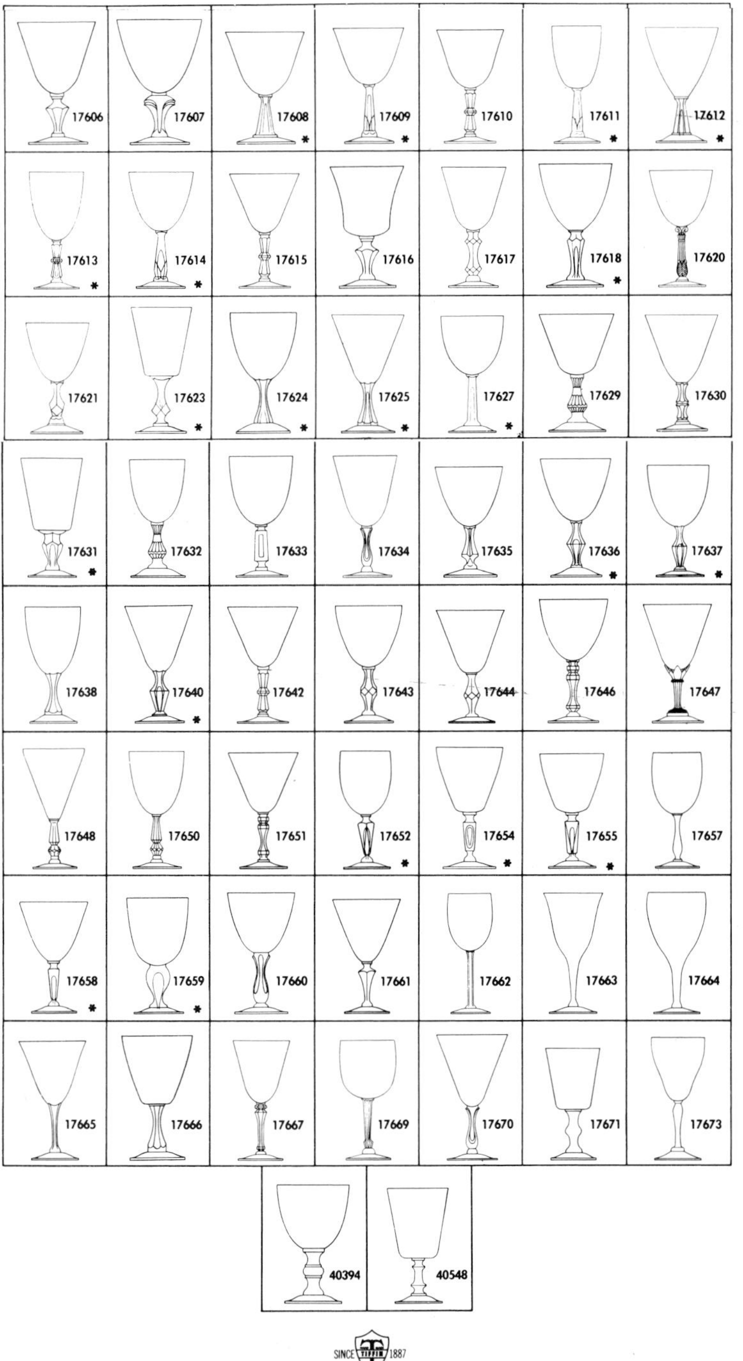

TIFFIN IS FOREVER—*Patterns Produced Since 1887 Available Today*

Van Deman

We now know that BLACK FOREST comes in crystal, amber, pink, green and cobalt as well as black. We also know some BLACK FOREST was re-issued in 1976. Two pieces, a goblet and a comport, were made in amber, a pale blue and a ruby red. As Nora Koch wrote in a February 1976 DAZE article, "The squarish knob in the stem has a pressed starred effect. This motif is repeated around the base of the tumbler below the etching, and of course appears on the bottom of the comport."

Nothing to worry about, really; the crystal, pink, green, cobalt and black are definitely of the original issue. But be alert for the new.

"BAGHEERA"	**page 351**
Bowl	15.00--20.00

BLACK FOREST	
Plate, 10-1/8"	12.00--16.00
Plate, 8-3/8"	8.00--12.00
Plate, 7-3/8"	7.00--10.00
Plate, 6 ¾"	5.00-- 7.00
Cup	12.00--15.00
Saucer	5.00-- 6.00
Tumbler, ftd., 5¾"	12.00--15.00
Tumbler, flat, 9 oz., 3¾"	14.00--16.00
Candlestick, pr.	20.00--30.00
Sugar and Cream Set, (two styles)	18.00--26.00
Plate, cake, ftd., hdld., 11"	18.00--26.00
Bowl, console, 14"	20.00--30.00
Bowl, console, rolled ege, 12½"	20.00--30.00
Bowl, ftd., rolled edge, 9"	18.00--24.00
Bowl, flrd., 11¼"	18.00--26.00
Bowl, hdld., 9"	18.00--24.00
Bowl, hdld., 8¼"	18.00--24.00
Candy Box, covered	25.00--35.00
Candy Box, covered, ftd. "PARTY" line blank	45.00--65.00
Sandwich Server, center hdld.	14.00--20.00
Cheese and Cracker	20.00--28.00
Comport, ftd. rolled edge, 3¼"	14.00--20.00
Comport, ftd., flrd., 4½"	16.00--20.00
Comport, tall, 5½"	16.00--20.00
Jug, 56 oz. 8"	65.00--75.00
Jug, 8", 40 oz. *(you will find other styles/sizes)*	60.00--85.00
Ice Tub, tab hdld., 4"	18.00--24.00
Salt and Pepper Shakers	25.00--30.00
Vase, 10"	25.00--30.00
Vase, 6"	14.00--18.00
Decanter and Stopper, 10¾"	30.00--40.00

Vineland

I've done no further study of Durand Art Glass, so I'm not prepared to suggest prices. It is not, of course, considered Depression Glass as such, but it's of the era and most interesting to see in comparison.

"POLA"	page 352
Lamp	16.00--20.00

"PICKFORD"	
Lamp	16.00--20.00

"KEATON"	
Lamp	16.00--20.00

"CHAPLIN"	
Lamp	18.00--22.00

Westmoreland

ENGLISH HOBNAIL, the well-known Book 1 pattern, is still out front for Westmoreland, and you"ll find a complete listing with suggested prices in the Book 1 PRICE TRENDS.

This past year, Westmoreland Glass Co. was sold to Grossman Designs of St. Louis. We will miss our good friends Mr. and Mrs. Brainard, now retired, who were always there these past years to welcome us.

Although it was thought the Westmoreland factory would be doing business as usual, the glassmaking part of the plant is closed this summer, and we hope it will re-open soon. The gift shop is open now but best you call or check before making plans for a visit in the near future.

NOVELTIES page 359

U.S. Hat	12.00--15.00
Soldier Hat	15.00--18.00
Straw Hat	12.00--15.00

"ORPHAN ANNIE"

Goblet	5.00-- 7.00
Plate, sherbet	1.50-- 2.00
Plate, luncheon	3.00-- 4.00
Plate, dinner	4.00-- 5.00
Nappy	3.00-- 4.00
Cream	5.00-- 6.00
Sugar	5.00-- 6.00
Cup and Saucer	5.00-- 6.00

PICKLE JARS

1926 Jar, 9"	20.00--30.00
12"	25.00--35.00
15"	35.00--45.00
1929 Jar	30.00--35.00
1927 Jar, 13"	30.00--35.00
15"	40.00--50.00

"LAZY SUSAN" page 360

18" or 20", ftd.	25.00--30.00

DELLA ROBBIA

See page 269, 270

DOLPHIN CONSOLE

3 piece set	100.00-150.00

"WOOLWORTH"

Plate, round or ruffled	6.00-- 9.00
Cream and Sugar	15.00--18.00
Nappy, 1 hdld., 5½"	8.00--10.00
Nappy, square, 6"	6.00-- 9.00
Nappy, rnd., 8" x 1¾"	10.00--12.00
Basket, low hdld., 5½"	12.00--16.00

LAMPS page 361, 362

No. 1904 Dice Lamp	20.00--30.00
No. 1905 Water Lamp	15.00--25.00
No. 1049/2 Dolphin Lamp	45.00--55.00
No. 1049/1 Dolphin Lamp	75.00--90.00
No. 1900 Water Lamp	20.00--25.00
No. 1901 Water Lamp	15.00--20.00
No. 1902 Water Lamp	20.00--25.00
No. 1903 Water Lamp	20.00--25.00
No. 1505 Lamp	20.00--25.00
No. 1017 Lamp	20.00--25.00

No. 555 Lamp, 9¼"	75.00-100.00
No. 185 Lamp	25.00--30.00
No. 1917 Lamp w/Fixtures, 9"	15.00--20.00
No. 1707 Spiral Lamp w/Fixtures, 8", 12"	15.00--20.00
No. 1911 Lamp w/Fixtures	25.00--35.00
No. 1918 Lamp w/Fixtures, 9"	25.00--30.00
No. 1921 LOTUS Lamp w/Fixtures	30.00--40.00

LAMPS page 363

Prices suggested for pink, green, and blue. Crystal and milk glass are late issue and much lower priced. Lamp No. 1955 has been found in black glass and No. 555, 9¼", has been found in amethyst.

Fairy Lamp	30.00--35.00
No. 185 Whale Lamp	25.00--35.00
No. 1955 Lamp w/Fixtures	40.00--50.00
No. 555 Candlestick Lamp, 9"	25.00--30.00
No. 55 Vanity Lamp, 8"	25.00--30.00
No. 300 Lamp, 8"	100.00-150.00
No. 1920 Lamp	30.00--35.00
No. 555/1 Lamp, 6½"	50.00--65.00
No. 555 Lamp, 9¼"	75.00-100.00

"OCTAVIA ROSE" page 364

Console Set	30.00--35.00

NOVELTY ITEMS

Hen on a Nest	20.00--25.00
Swan Server	15.00--18.00
Camel Container	40.00--60.00
Tea Tray, center hdld.	6.00-- 9.00
Bridge Service Tray, hdld.	12.00--14.00
Service Tray, center hdld.	12.00--14.00
Salt and Pepper Set: 3 pc.	12.00--16.00
Cheese Tray and Cover	25.00--35.00

"CAMEO DIAMOND"

See more "CAMEO DIAMOND" page 270

Jelly, 6½"	4.00-- 6.00
Bon Bon, 7"	5.00-- 7.00
Plate, 8½"	4.00-- 5.00
Cheese, 8"	5.00-- 7.00

WATERFORD

Pink, green, amber, and crystal w/black feet.

Westmoreland has re-issued this No. 300 line off and on since 1931, and even today is making a few pieces with fired-on red trim.

From a very interesting 1930 trade journal write-up:

Westmoreland Glass Co. is now showing a most attractive assortment of Old Waterford glass reproductions. Naturally, the name "Waterford" when applied to glass immediately brings to mind the beauty and charm found in ware of this kind, and the Westmoreland creations live up to this reputation in every sense of the word.

The line is offered in combinations of crystal and amber and crystal and black, and may also be had in rose, green or plain crystal. This glass is carried out in a general line of stemware, plates, and decorative pieces.

For instance, illustrated is their 15" covered urn which is an excellent example of the line. The shape of this, as may be seen, is perfect in its grace of line, while a pleasing touch of contrast is added by the square amber foot.

Line No. 300

Plate	5.00-- 8.00
Cream	9.00--11.00
Sugar	9.00--11.00
Goblet	10.00--12.00
Wine	10.00--14.00
Cordial	10.00--14.00
Tumbler, ftd.	9.00--11.00
Urn, covered, tall, 11¾", 15"	75.00-100.00
Candy Jar, covered	35.00--50.00
Candlestick, pr.	35.00--50.00
No. 300 Lamp	100.00-150.00

WAKEFIELD page 365

Crystal

Urn, 12½"	25.00--30.00
Nappy, heart shaped, 5"	4.00-- 5.00
Mint	6.00-- 8.00
Nappy, cupped, 6"	5.00-- 6.00
Candy, crimped	6.00-- 8.00
Candy, covered	15.00--20.00
Sugar	6.00-- 8.00
Cream	6.00-- 8.00
Compote, crimped	8.00--10.00
Salver, cake, 12"	15.00--20.00
Celery, 12"	10.00--12.00
Nappy, heart shaped, 8"	9.00--11.00
Bowl, lipped, 12"	12.00--15.00
Bowl, turned edge, 13"	14.00--18.00
Bowl, cupped, 10"	12.00--15.00
Plate, 14"	10.00--12.00
Candlestick, 6"	18.00--24.00
Bowl, bell, ftd., 12"	15.00--20.00
Goblet, 10 oz.	7.00--10.00
Sherbet	5.00-- 6.00
Wine, 2 oz.	10.00--12.00
Ice Tea, ftd., 12 oz.	7.00-- 9.00
Plate, 8½"	3.50-- 5.00

PRINCESS FEATHER page 366

Remember amber was made in the 60s

Nappy, rnd., 5", 6"	5.00-- 7.00
Finger Bowl Plate, 6½"	3.00-- 4.00
Finger Bowl, 4½"	4.00-- 5.00
Puff Box, flat	10.00--12.00
Ginger Ale, 5 oz.	6.00-- 8.00
Nappy, rnd. 12"	16.00--19.00
Ice Tea, 10 oz.	8.00--10.00
Tumbler, ftd., 8 oz., 9 oz., 12 oz.	8.00--12.00
Champagne HF	7.00-- 9.00
Cocktail, 3 oz.	8.00--10.00
Sherbet HF	7.00-- 9.00
Wine	10.00--12.00
Service Plate, 10½"	8.00--10.00
Sherbet	4.00-- 6.00
Goblet, 8 oz.	10.00--12.00
Plate, 8", 7"	6.00-- 8.00
Grapefruit, 6½"	7.00-- 9.00
Plate, 13"	12.00--15.00
Salt and Pepper	20.00--25.00
Server, 3 tier	20.00--25.00
Cup and Saucer	8.00--10.00
Cream and Sugar	15.00--18.00
Jug, 54 oz.,	35.00--45.00
Jelly and Cover, ftd. 5"	20.00--25.00
Basket, 6½", 7", 8"	15.00--30.00
Bon Bon, 1 handle	12.00--15.00
Banana Dish, ftd.	25.00--30.00
Bowl, ftd., 9", 9½", cupped	20.00--25.00
Bowl, 2 hdld. oval, 7¼", 10½" 11"	15.00--25.00
Plate, 18"	18.00--24.00
Candelabra, 2 lite	15.00--20.00
Candlestick, pr.	15.00--18.00
Light Fixture, 17½"	35.00--45.00

MISCELLANEOUS page 367

No. 1900 Sugar and Cream	6.00-- 8.00
No. 100 Wing Sugar and Cream	10.00--15.00
No. 1820 Sugar and Cream	10.00--12.00
No. 1825 Domino Sugar and Cream	8.00--10.00
No. 1800 Sugar and Cream	8.00--10.00
No. 1715 Mayonnaise Set: 3 pc.	15.00--18.00
No. 1701 Dresser Set	30.00--35.00
No. 73 Orange Juicer	14.00--18.00
No. 1855/1 Chocolate Box and Cover	12.00--16.00
No. 908 Honey Dish and Cover	15.00--18.00
No. 1854-1 Chocolate Box	15.00--20.00
No. 1854-2 Chocolate Box	18.00--24.00
No. 101 Semi Cut Bowl, 8"	10.00--14.00
No. 102 Semi Cut Bowl, 8"	10.00--14.00
No. 100 Semi Cut Vase, 10"	25.00--35.00
No. 103 Vase, 12½"	20.00--30.00
No. 102 Vase, 9½"	20 00--30.00
No. 104 Vase, 15"	35.00--50.00
No. 349 Cigarette Holder and Ash Tray	15.00--20.00
No. 352 Cigarette Holder	20.00--25.00
No. 205 Butter or Ash Tray, ind.	4.00-- 6.00
No. 1603 coaster	2.00-- 3.00
No. 350 Ash Tray	4.00-- 5.00
No. 1850/344 Snuffer and Tray	15.00--20.00
No. 343 Ash Tray, 3 cigar rests	8.00--10.00
No. 353 Ash Tray	4.00-- 6.00
No. 1800 Tray, 3 cornered	4.00-- 6.00
No. 454 Pin or Ash Tray, 4"	3.00-- 5.00
No. 346 Safety Ash Tray	6.00-- 8.00
No. 1835 Ash Tray Nest, 4 pc.	9.00--11.00
No. 337 Safety Ash Tray	4.00-- 6.00
No. 454 Ash or Pin Tray, 3"	3.00-- 5.00
No. 351 Ash Tray	6.00-- 8.00
No. 1834 Ash Tray Nest, 4 pc.	9.00--11.00
No 347 Cigarette Ash Tray, 4" x 3"	6.00-- 8.00
No. 334 Coaster	3.00-- 4.00
No. 345 Coaster	3.00-- 4.00
No. 348 Candle Ash Tray, 6" x 4"	8.00--12.00

MISCELLANEOUS page 368

No. 1 Sanitary Spoon Holder	12.00--15.00
No. 515 Goblet	6.00-- 8.00
No. 3 Toy Chick	14.00--18.00
No. 334 Domino Sugar Holder	12.00--15.00
No. 61 Tooth Pick Holder	11.00--14.00
No. 1302 Eye Cup	6.00-- 8.00
No. 1 Butter Drainer	8.00--10.00
ABC Plate, 7"	9.00--12.00
No. 2 Medium Hen	15.00--20.00
No. 2 Butter Drainer	10.00--12.00
No. 1026 Card Holder	6.00-- 8.00
No. 1028 Card Holder	6.00-- 7.00
No. 30 Heel Rest	7.00-- 9.00
No. 1027 Card Holder, 1¾"	6.00-- 8.00
Ice Cubes; No. 103, 104, 105 ea.	3.00-- 5.00
No. 1048 Shelf Support, 7", 12"	10.00--15.00
No. 1049 Shelf Support, 9", 12", 15"	15.00--18.00
No. 555 Nut and Card Holder	12.00--15.00
No. 1 Knife Rest	9.00--12.00
No. 1801 Fruit Knife	10.00--15.00
No. 1800 Sanitary Fruit Knife	12.00--16.00
No. 1801 Salad Fork	5.00-- 8.00
No. 2 Knife Rest	5.00-- 8.00
No. 3 Knife Rest	6.00-- 8.00
No. 1801 Salad Spoon	5.00-- 8.00
No. 1709 Mustard Spoon	6.00-- 8.00
No. 1 Mustard Spoon	6.00-- 8.00
No. 1801 Mustard Spoon	6.00-- 8.00
No. 1800 Whip'd Cream Ladle	7.00--10.00
No. 1800 Mayonnaise Ladle	7.00--10.00
No. 1837 Mayonnaise Ladle	7.00--10.00
No. 1838 Mayonnaise Ladle	7.00--10.00
No. 1839 Mayonnaise Ladle	7.00--10.00
No. 750 Basket	20.00--30.00
No. 752 Basket	25.00--35.00
No. 755 Basket	25.00--35.00

MISCELLANEOUS page 369

Owl Book End, pr.	25.00--30.00
Ash Tray	4.00-- 6.00
Hi-Hat	6.00-- 9.00
Owl	12.00--16.00
Flask	4.00-- 5.00
Dog Door Stop	30.00--35.00
Small Dog	12.00--18.00
Large Key	20.00--25.00
Duck Salt, ind.	9.00--12.00
Salt, large, ind.	4.00-- 6.00
Salt, small, ind.	4.00-- 5.00
Camel	40.00--60.00
Tumbler, 6 oz.	2.00-- 3.00
Ice Tub, 40 oz.	7.00-- 9.00
Bowl, ftd., 10"	20.00--25.00
Sherbet	3.00-- 4.00

"ROCKER"

Ice Tub, low, pressed	10.00--14.00
Jug, covered	25.00--30.00
Tumbler, 9 oz., 12 oz.	5.00-- 7.00
Ice Tub, high blown, 6"	10.00--15.00

MISCELLANEOUS

Canoe Dish	15.00--20.00
Celery Pan	15.00--20.00
Shell Nappy	7.00--10.00
Tray, round	6.00-- 8.00
Bell Bowl	25.00--30.00
Shell Comport	25.00--35.00
Breakfast Set	25.00--35.00
Condiment Set	20.00--25.00
Mustard	10.00--15.00
Sugar and Cream Set	15.00--20.00

MISCELLANEOUS page 370

Puff Box, flat	6.00-- 8.00
No. 1801 Puff Box and Cover	8.00--12.00
No. 1105 Puff Box and Cover	8.00--12.00
No. 1828 Cigarette Box	12.00--16.00
No. 800 Cigarette Set	8.00--12.00
No. 1913 Puff Box, 3 ftd.	10.00--15.00
No. 1804 Puff Box	8.00--12.00
No. 752 Cigarette Box and Cover	12.00--16.00
No. 1857 Heart Candy Box	16.00--22.00
No. 1860 Chocolate Box	10.00--15.00
No. 1856 Triangle Candy Box	9.00--12.00
No. 1062 Candlestick, pr.	10.00--15.00
No. 1067 Candlestick, pr.	10.00--15.00
No. 1066 Candlestick, pr.	10.00--12.00
No. 1061 Candlestick, pr.	8.00--10.00
No. 1053 Candlestick, pr.	10.00--12.00
No. 1063 Candlestick, pr.	15.00--18.00
No. 1060 Candlestick, pr.	15.00--18.00
No. 1059 Candle Ash Tray	6.00-- 8.00
No. 1049 Dolphin, 4" Candlestick, pr.	20.00--25.00
No. 1058 Candlestick, pr.	10.00--15.00
No. 1057 Candlestick, low, pr.	7.00-- 9.00
No. 1064 Candlestick, pr.	10.00--14.00

"MARGUERITE"

Candlestick, 4¼", pr.	10.00--14.00
Bowl, round and Bell, 9"	12.00--15.00
Plates, 11", 14", (also made w/Cntr. Ring for Mayo. Bowl)	10.00--14.00
Bell Bowl, 12"	12.00--15.00
Tray, sandwich, hdld., 11"	12.00--14.00
Cheese and Cracker, 11"	14.00--16.00
Goblet, 8 oz.	8.00--10.00
Champagne, HF	6.00-- 8.00
Tumbler, ftd.	5.00-- 8.00
Cocktail, 4 oz.	6.00-- 8.00
Wine, 2 oz.	8.00--10.00
Ice Tea, 12 oz.	6.00-- 8.00
Sherbet and Plate	5.00-- 8.00
Mayonnaise Bowl and Plate	10.00--14.00
Finger Bowl and Plate	6.00-- 8.00
Cup and Saucer	5.00-- 8.00
Nappy, rnd., 4½", 5¾", 6¾"	3.00-- 5.00
Plate, 8½"	4.00-- 5.00
Plate, bread & butter, 6¼"	2.00-- 3.00
Sugar and Cream Set	12.00--16.00

"ROSELIN" page 371

Cream	7.00-- 9.00
Sugar	7.00-- 9.00
Comport, rnd., 5½"	8.00--11.00
Bell Comport, 6"	8.00--11.00
Bon Bon, hdld.	8.00--11.00
Plate, 10½", 8", 6½"	6.00--12.00
Bell Bowl	10.00--15.00
Bowl, flange, 12"	10.00--15.00
Mayonnaise, 5½"	6.00-- 9.00
Bowl,RE, 7"	6.00-- 8.00
Candlestick, low, pr.	12.00--16.00
Nappy, ftd., 10"	10.00--15.00
Nappy, bell, 9"	10.00--15.00
Nappy, rnd., 5", 4½", 6"	4.00-- 8.00
Nappy, rnd., 8"	10.00--12.00
Nappy, square, 5", 6"	6.00-- 9.00
Bowl, ftd., 7"	8.00--10.00
Nappy, Bell, 6", 5", 7"	4.00-- 9.00
Nappy, rnd., 6"	6.00-- 8.00
Nappy, square, 6"	7.00-- 9.00
Plate, 8"	4.00-- 6.00
Nappy, Bell, 7"	7.00-- 9.00
Pickle, 8"	10.00--12.00

DELLA ROBBIA page 372

Plate, service, dinner, 10½"	18.00--22.00
Plate, luncheon, 9"	12.00--14.00
Plate, salad, 7½"	10.00--12.00
Plate, bread and butter, 6"	5.00-- 7.00
Plate, torte, rnd., 14"	15.00--20.00

Plate, rnd., turned edge, 14"	18.00--22.00
Plate, rnd., 18"	30.00--35.00
Plate, rnd., turned edge, 18"	30.00--35.00
Platter, oval, 14"	35.00--40.00
Salver, cake, ftd., 14"	30.00--35.00
Plate, rnd., revolving hndl., 9"	35.00--40.00
Plate, rnd., hndl., turned up on sides, 9"	22.00--26.00
Cup	8.00--10.00
Saucer	3.00-- 5.00
Salt and Pepper, chrome tops	20.00--25.00
Sugar	10.00--12.00
Cream	10.00--12.00
Tray, sugar and cream	25.00--30.00
Finger Bowl and Liner, 5"	10.00--12.00
Nappy, cupped, 4½"	5.00-- 7.00
Nappy, 4½"	5.00-- 7.00
Nappy, cupped, 6"	9.00--11.00
Nappy, bell, 6"	9.00--11.00
Nappy, cupped, loop hndl., 6½"	18.00--22.00
Nappy, bell, 6½"	18.00--22.00
Nappy, 7½"	18.00--22.00
Nappy, bell, loop hndl., 8"	25.00--28.00
Nappy, heart, loop hndl., 8"	25.00--28.00
Nappy, 9"	25.00--28.00
Bowl, bell, 12"	16.00--20.00
Bowl, bell, ftd., 12"	26.00--30.00
Bowl, comport, rolled edge, 13"	16.00--20.00
Bowl, comport, rolled edge, ftd., 13"	25.00--30.00
Bowl, bell, 15"	60.00--70.00
Bowl, punch, 15"	60.00--70.00
Nappy, turned edge, 8"	14.00--18.00
Bowl, oval, turned up w/scalloped edge, 12"	35.00--40.00
Bowl, oval w/scalloped edge, 14"	30.00--35.00
Jug, 32 oz.	55.00--65.00
Goblet, tall, 8 oz.	12.00--15.00
Goblet, short, 8 oz.	10.00--12.00
Sherbet, tall, 5 oz.	8.00--10.00
Sherbet, short, 5 oz.	6.00-- 8.00
Champagne, tall, 5 oz.	12.00--15.00
Cocktail, claret, tall, 3¼ oz.	12.00--15.00
Wine, tall, 3 oz.	12.00--15.00
Goblet, ice tea, short, 11 oz.	10.00--12.00
Tumbler, juice, 5 oz.	8.00--10.00
Tumbler, ice tea, bell or straight, 12 oz.	8.00--10.00
Tumbler, ice tea, ftd., 12 oz.	10.00--12.00
Mayonnaise Set: Bowl, Plate Ladle	15.00--20.00
Chocolate Box, rnd., covered	30.00--35.00
Candy Jar, scalloped edge, dome cover, low, ftd.	20.00--25.00
Sweetmeat, bell or straight, tall, 8"	35.00--40.00
Comport, crimped, ftd., 6½"	25.00--30.00
Comport, mint, ftd., 6½"	10.00--15.00
Candlestick, pr., 4"	15.00--20.00
Candlestick, double, pr., 4"	40.00--45.00
Basket, rnd., 8½"	40.00--45.00
Basket, rnd., 9"	50.00--60.00
Basket, rnd., 12"	60.00--70.00
Basket, rnd., 12½"	70.00--75.00
Punch Set: 15 pc., pedestal, ladle	100.00-125.00

CAMEO DIAMOND

Bon Bon, 2 hdld., 7"	5.00-- 7.00
Mint, 2 hdld., 7"	4.00-- 6.00
Cheese, 2 hdld., 8"	5.00-- 7.00
Plate, 8½"	5.00-- 7.00
Nappy, rnd., 7"	4.00-- 6.00
Jelly, 2 hdld.	4.00-- 6.00
Bell Bowl, 2 hdld., 9" (also made in 8" rnd. bowl)	6.00-- 9.00
Plate, 2 hdld., 10½"	6.00-- 9.00

SHELL DOLPHIN

Dolphin Shell, 12"	50.00--75.00
Dolphin Lamp, No. 1	75.00--90.00
Dolphin Shell, 8"	25.00--35.00
Dolphin Lamp, No. 2	45.00--55.00
Dolphin Candlestick, 9"	30.00--35.00
Dolphin Comport, 7", 11"	40.00--60.00
Dolphin Oval, 16"	35.00--45.00
Dolphin Sandwich	30.00--40.00

"DOREEN" page 373

Mint, 2 hdld.	3.00-- 4.00
Custard Cup	2.50-- 3.50
Cup and Saucer	4.50-- 6.00
Bon Bon, 2 hdld., 7"	4.00-- 5.00
Jelly, 2 hdld., 6½"	4.00-- 5.00
Ice Tub w/Metal hndl., 5 x 6"	10.00--14.00
Sweetmeat, ftd., 7½"	7.00-- 9.00
Cheese, 2 hdld., 8"	4.00-- 6.00
Sugar	5.00-- 7.00
Cream	5.00-- 7.00
Tumbler, blown, 8 oz.	3.00-- 4.00
Tray, 10 x 6¼"	5.00-- 8.00
Mayonnaise, ftd.	5.00-- 7.00
Puff and Cover, 4½"	10.00--12.00
Cigar Tray, 5½"	7.00--10.00
Cologne, ½ oz.	12.00--16.00
Puff and Cover, 5"	10.00--14.00
Toothbrush Holder	12.00--15.00
Open Soap	8.00--12.00
Bell Bowl, 2 hdld., 11"	10.00--12.00
Candlestick, 2 hdld., 4", pr.	10.00--14.00
Comport, 2 hdld., 13", LF	12.00--16.00
Candlestick, 3", pr.	9.00--12.00
Plate, sandwich, 2 hdld., 13"	7.00-- 9.00
Mayonnaise Bowl and Plate, 6"	8.00--11.00
8 Part Relish and Cocktail Center, 13"	18.00--24.00
Plate, 3 ftd., 8"	7.00-- 9.00
Grapefruit, low, 7"	4.00-- 5.00
Butter Ball, 6"	7.00-- 9.00

Bread and Butter Plate	1.50-- 2.50
Candy Jar, ½ lb.	12.00--16.00
Candy Box	10.00--14.00
Candy Jar, 1 lb.	14.00--20.00

"HUXFORD" page 374, 375

Claret, 3½ oz.	6.00-- 8.00
Sherbet, LF	2.50-- 3.50
Goblet, 8 oz.	6.00-- 8.00
Salt and Pepper, ftd., silver plated Top, sm., med., and large	15.00--20.00
Sherbet, HF	4.00-- 6.00
Cream	5.00-- 7.00
Sugar	5.00-- 7.00
Chocolate Box, oval, (also made w/part. in ct.)	15.00--18.00
Mayonnaise Set: 3 pc.	12.00--16.00
Cocktail, ftd.	4.00-- 6.00
Plate, optic, 5½"	1.50-- 2.50
Candy Jar, ¼ lb.	10.00--14.00
Candy Jar and Cover, plain and optic, ½ lb., 1 lb.	14.00--20.00
Wall Vase, 9"	10.00--14.00
Comport, ftd., 13"	15.00--18.00
Jug, 5 pt. (also made w/Cover)	15.00--20.00
Bedroom Set	20.00--25.00
Flower Pot and Saucer, 5"	5.00-- 8.00
Asparagus Dish, 8 x 12"	7.00--10.00
Vase, Violet, 3"	4.00-- 6.00
Cocktail Shaker w/metal Top	12.00--16.00
Waffle Jug and Cover, 3 pt.	15.00--20.00
Vase, optic, blown, 11", 8", 9"	8.00--16.00
Bowl, cupped, 3 ftd., 11½"	12.00--15.00
Bowl, 3 ftd., RE, 13"	12.00--15.00
Oval, SE, 10½ x 13½"	14.00--18.00
Ice Tub, high, w/metal Handle 5 x 6", (also other sizes)	10.00--14.00
Ice Tub, high, w/metal Handle, 6 x 4½"	10.00--14.00
Ice Tub, low, w/metal Handle, 6 x 7"	16.00--22.00

MISCELLANEOUS page 375

1803 Coaster, 3½"	2.00-- 4.00
1803 Cocktail, 2½ oz., MC	3.00-- 4.00
1800 Nappy, 5", 5½" and 6"	3.00-- 4.00
1856 Cologne, 1 oz.	15.00--20.00
3000 Flower Pot	6.00-- 8.00
1800 Grapefruit and Liner	6.00-- 9.00
200 Icicle Sugar and Cream Set	6.00-- 9.00
1708 Vase, ftd., 7"	9.00--11.00
1709 Vase, 8" (Also made "Umbrella" style w/hdl.)	12.00--20.00
200 Icicle Ice Tub, 6"	12.00--16.00
1900/1 Puff Box, 3½"	8.00--10.00
1900/2 Puff Box, 4¼"	10.00--12.00
1900 Puff and Powder Box	12.00--16.00
1900 Coaster, 3¼"	2.00-- 4.00
1900 Comport, LF, 8"	8.00--10.00
1900 Bowl and Stand, RE, 7"	9.00--12.00
1900/2 Cream Soup Set: 2 hdld.	6.00-- 8.00
1900 Comport, HF, 7½"	9.00--12.00
1900 Sweetmeat, HF, RE, 8½"	10.00--14.00
1900 Sweetmeat, HF, SE, 8½"	10.00--14.00
74 Orange Juicer, 2 pc.	20.00--25.00
15 Cocktail Shaker	14.00--20.00
300 Jar, covered	50.00--75.00
176 Tumbler	4.00-- 6.00
1930 Candlestick, 3", pr.	12.00--15.00
1930 Bowl, 9"	12.00--16.00
1931 Shaker, 2/B top	7.00--10.00
1930 Shaker, SPT	9.00--12.00

WAGNER page 376

Sugar	5.00-- 7.00
Cup and Saucer	6.00-- 8.00
Mug, hdld., 6½ oz.	6.00-- 9.00
Cream	5.00-- 7.00
Plate, bread and butter, 6"	2.00-- 2.50
Nappy, 4½"	2.00-- 4.00
Tumbler, 8 oz.	3.00-- 5.00
Ice Tea, hdld.	6.00-- 9.00
Jug, ½ gal.	18.00--22.00
Jug, pint	16.00--18.00
Cologne, ½ oz.	15.00--20.00
Fan Vase, 6"	6.00-- 9.00
Finger Bowl and Plate	5.00-- 8.00
Candy Jar, ½ lb.	12.00--16.00
Tray, sandwich, 11½"	10.00--14.00
Candlestick, 3", pr.	10.00--14.00
Cheese and Cracker	8.00--10.00
Vase, 6½"	5.00-- 8.00
Candlestick, 9", pr.	18.00--24.00
Bowl, RE, 11"	9.00--12.00
Bowl, cupped, 10"	9.00--12.00
Bowl, bell, 11", 13"	10.00--15.00
Comport and Cover, 6½"	14.00--20.00
Grapefruit, 6½"	4.00-- 6.00
Plate, 9"	3.50-- 5.00
Sherbet	3.00-- 4.00
Plate, 14"	9.00--12.00
Plate, 7"	2.50-- 3.50
Goblet, 8 oz.	5.00-- 7.00
Ice Tea, 10½ oz.	4.00-- 6.00

"SCRAMBLE" page 377

Cream	5.00-- 8.00
Sugar	5.00-- 8.00
Sherbet	2.00-- 4.00
Jug and Cover, ½ gal.	20.00--25.00
Ice Tea, 12 oz. (1800)	4.00-- 6.00
Jug, 60 oz. (1801)	15.00--20.00
Ice Tea, 12 oz., (1821)	4.00-- 6.00
Bowl, 10½"	10.00--14.00
Cologne, 1 oz.	15.00--20.00
Mayonnaise Bowl	6.00-- 9.00
Finger Bowl, 5½"	3.00-- 4.00
Bowl, RE, 13"	10.00--15.00

Bowl, bell, 13"	10.00--15.00
Ice Tea Set, covered, ½ gal.	45.00--60.00
Plate, 14"	10.00--14.00
Plate, 9"	4.00-- 6.00
Plate, 6"	2.00-- 3.00
Plate, octagon, 9"	4.00-- 6.00
Plate, 8½"	3.00-- 5.00
Candlestick, 9", pr.	20.00--30.00
Bowl, low ftd., 10"	16.00--20.00

LOTUS page 378

Remember price suggestion only for color.

Candy Jar, ½ lb.,	18.00--24.00
Sugar	8.00--10.00
Cream	8.00--10.00
Mayonnaise, bell, ftd.	10.00--14.00
Lily Bowl, 6"	8.00--10.00
Sherbet, tulip bell	6.00-- 8.00
Plate, salad, 8½"	4.00-- 6.00
Comport, 12"	20.00--30.00
Comport, 8"	16.00--20.00
Candlestick, pr.	15.00--20.00
Mayonnaise, flrd., ftd.	10.00--14.00
Bowl, cupped, 9"	20.00--30.00
Candlestick, tall, 9", pr.	25.00--30.00
Lotus Flower and Plate, cupped, 4"	9.00--11.00
Plate, flrd., 13"	15.00--20.00
Individual Salt	8.00--10.00
Mayonnaise and Plate, 8¾"	10.00--12.00
Cologne, ½ oz.	15.00--20.00
Tray, lemon, hdld., 6"	6.00-- 8.00
Puff Box and Cover, 5"	12.00--15.00
Honey, 6½"	6.00-- 8.00
Salt and Pepper, silver plated top, pr.	22.00--28.00
Coaster or Ash Tray, 5½"	3.00-- 5.00

MISCELLANEOUS

1923 Leaf Salad, 9"	6.00-- 9.00
Cologne, 1 oz., (1901)	15.00--20.00
Tie Back, 2¼"	3.00-- 5.00
Tie Back, 3"	4.00-- 6.00
Tie Back, 4½"	6.00-- 8.00
Flower Block, 5¾"	8.00--10.00
Flower Block, 4½", Turtle	14.00--18.00
Tree Holder, 2½", 3½", 5¾"	7.00--12.00
Flower Block, 4½", 5½"	6.00--10.00
Tray, 3¼" x 5½"	3.00-- 4.00
Bowl, 3 ftd., 5½"	3.00-- 5.00
Stand, 5"	4.00-- 6.00
Tray, 6½" x 10½"	5.00-- 8.00

"BRAMBLE" page 379

Flange Bowl, 11½"	12.00--15.00
Bowl, RE, 11½"	15.00--18.00
Bell Bowl, 11"	15.00--18.00
Plate, 13½"	11.00--14.00
Mayonnaise, RE, ftd.	8.00--10.00
Sugar	6.00-- 9.00
Cream	6.00-- 9.00
Nappy, round	4.00-- 6.00
Plate, 8½"	4.00-- 6.00
Comport, HF	10.00--15.00
Chocolate Box	15.00--20.00
Vase, 9"	15.00--20.00

"ZEBRA"

Bell Bowl, ftd., 9½"	10.00--12.00
Candlestick, 4", pr.	9.00--14.00
Cheese and Cracker, 11"	9.00--12.00
Tray, sandwich, 11"	9.00--12.00
Sugar	5.00-- 7.00
Cream	5.00-- 7.00
Jug, ftd., ½ gal.	16.00--20.00
Ice Tea, ftd., 13 oz.	4.00-- 6.00
Bowl, ftd., RE, 10½"	10.00--14.00

PLATES

No. 1901 6", 8½", 14"	3.00--10.00
No. 1901 Mayonnaise Plate, 8½"	4.00-- 6.00
No. 1902 7½" Star Bottom	3.00-- 4.00
No. 1903 6", 8", 13"	3.00-- 9.00
No. 1929 Plate, square, 9"	4.00-- 6.00
No. 1904 6", 9", 14"	3.00--11.00

"THUMBELINA" page 380

Crystal, pink, milk white

Sugar	8.00--12.00
Cream	8.00--12.00
Spoon	8.00--12.00
Butter	14.00--18.00
Toy Punch Set	25.00--40.00

Note: Westmoreland made this Toy Punch Set and Toy Water Set in 1976-1982 in iridescent, pink, cobalt and other colors.

"LITTLE JO"

Toy Water Set	20.00--25.00
Jug	8.00--10.00
Tumbler	2.00-- 3.00

MISCELLANEOUS TOYS

Revolver	15.00--20.00
Card Set	8.00--10.00
Berry Set, 7 pc.	12.00--18.00
Condiment Set	15.00--25.00

CLASSICS IN GLASS

Item	Price
Top Hat	6.00-- 8.00
Piano	8.00--10.00
Mail Box	8.00--10.00
Boy on Drum	10.00--12.00
Mug	2.00-- 3.00
Small Container	6.00-- 8.00
Thimble	4.00-- 5.00
Clock	8.00--10.00
Wash Boiler	10.00--12.00
Dog in House	8.00--10.00
Creamer	4.00-- 5.00
Toy Gun	15.00--20.00
Bank	8.00--10.00
Egg	8.00--10.00

Presenting

"Classics in Glass"

by

WESTMORELAND

This grouping—typical of wares produced by Colonial Craftsmen—is offered in Commemoration of America's First Industry—200 years of Classics in Handmade Glass:

1973 ITEMS, PRICES & MINIMUMS

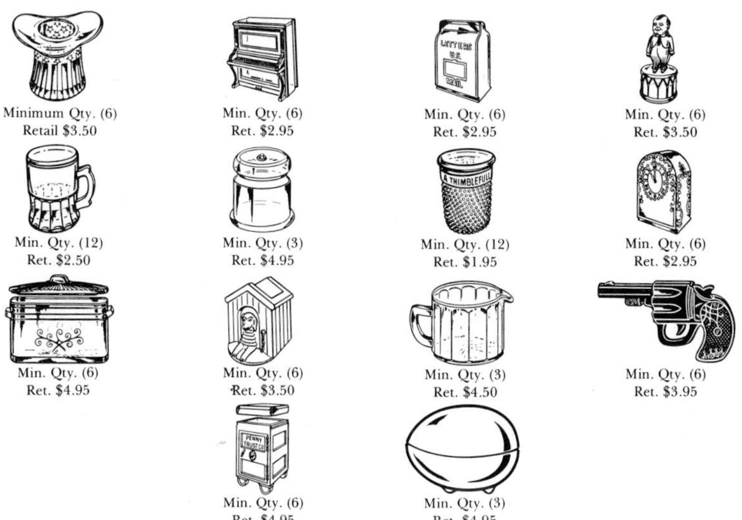

WESTMORELAND GLASS COMPANY

GRAPEVILLE, PA. 15634

Reprint of Westmoreland brochure

LACE EDGE Compote	8.00--10.00
"LUNAR" Lamp	25.00--35.00
FIFTH AVENUE LINE	
Candlestick, pr.	10.00--14.00
Comport	8.00--10.00
Mayonnaise w/ladle	10.00--14.00
Console Bowl	15.00--20.00
Celery Dish	9.00--12.00
Sandwich Server, center hdld.	11.00--16.00
"JOKER" Console Set w/glass leaves	30.00--35.00
SHELL Dish	6.00-- 8.00
WATERFORD Cream and Sugar	20.00--25.00
"ZEBRA" Lamp	20.00--28.00

No. 1916 Lamp with fixture

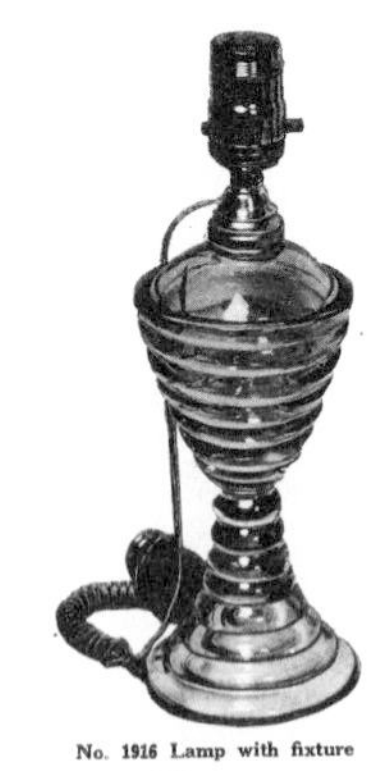

"ZEBRA" lamp from 1929 ad

WESTMORELAND GLASS CO.
GRAPEVILLE, PA.
Manufacturers of Plain-Cut and Decorated Glassware for Table Service, Gift Shops, Florist

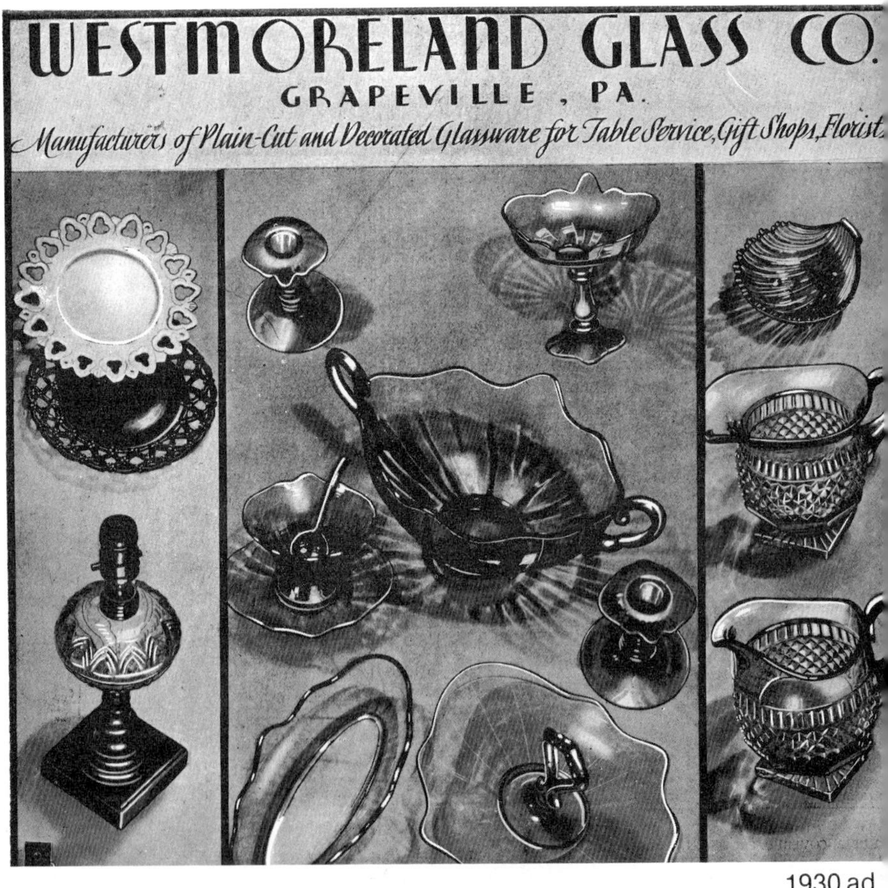

1930 ad

"FIFTH AVENUE" LINE

1000 EYE LINE

Item	Price
Ice Tea, ftd., 12 oz.	6.00-- 8.00
Tumbler, ftd. 5, 7, 9 oz.	4.00-- 7.00
Parfait	6.00-- 8.00
Ice Tea, 12 oz.	5.00-- 7.00
Tumbler, 8 oz.	4.00-- 6.00
Ginger Ale, 5 oz.	4.00-- 5.00
Cocktail, 6 oz.	5.00-- 8.00
Whiskey, 1½ oz.	5.00-- 8.00
Cordial, 1 oz.	8.00--10.00
Wine, 2 oz.	8.00--10.00
Cocktail, 3½ oz.	6.00-- 8.00
Sherry, 3 oz.	6.00-- 8.00
Sherbet, high ftd.	6.00-- 8.00
Sherbet, low ftd.	4.00-- 6.00
Claret, 5 oz.	6.00-- 8.00
Goblet, 8 oz.	7.00--10.00
Basket, oval, hdld, 8"	9.00--12.00
Relish, rnd., 10"	10.00--14.00
Ash Tray	4.00-- 6.00
Cup and Saucer	7.00-- 9.00
Cigarette Box and Cover	9.00--12.00
Nappy, 4½", 5½"	3.00-- 4.00
Sugar and Cream Set	10.00--14.00
Nappy, bell, hdld., 7½"	6.00-- 9.00
Comport, high ftd., 5"	7.00-- 9.00
Salt and Pepper	12.00--16.00
Mayonnaise and Ladle, ftd.	10.00--14.00
Bowl, hdld., 10"	14.00--18.00
Bowl, flrd., 12"	15.00--18.00
Candelabra, pr.	18.00--22.00
Jug, ½ gal.	22.00--28.00
Candlestick, 5", pr	12.00--16.00
Bowl, bell, 11"	12.00--16.00
Bowl, rnd., 11"	12.00--16.00
Bowl, triangular, 11"	14.00--18.00
Bowl, crimped, oblong, 11"	14.00--18.00
Plate, 6", 7"	2.00-- 4.00
Plate, 8½", 10"	4.00-- 9.00
Plate, 14", 18"	12.00--18.00

Have You Seen Our Glass Leaves?

Westmoreland's latest novelty. Made in refreshing green (satin finish) to match flower block. See how artistic they are—they hold flowers up that are inclined to droop. Harmonize with natural or artificial flowers. Shown in connection with our lovely new 1211 /13" bowl with candlesticks to match. In roselin green or amber.

Westmoreland Glass Co.

GRAPEVILLE, PA.

"JOKER" console set w/glass leaves **from 1929 journal**

WESTMORELAND GLASS CO., GRAPEVILLE, PA.

1000 EYE LINE

1000/12 oz. Ftd. Ice Tea

1000/9 oz. Ftd. Tumbler also 7 oz. & 5 oz.

1000/Parfait

1000/12 oz. Ice Tea

1000/8 oz. Tumbler

1000/5 oz. Ginger Ale

1000/6 oz. O. F. Cocktail

1000/1½ oz. Whiskey

1000/1 oz. Cordial

1000/2 oz. Wine

1000/3½ oz. Cocktail

1000/3 oz. Sherry

1000/H. F. Sherbet also Low Foot

1000/5 oz. Claret

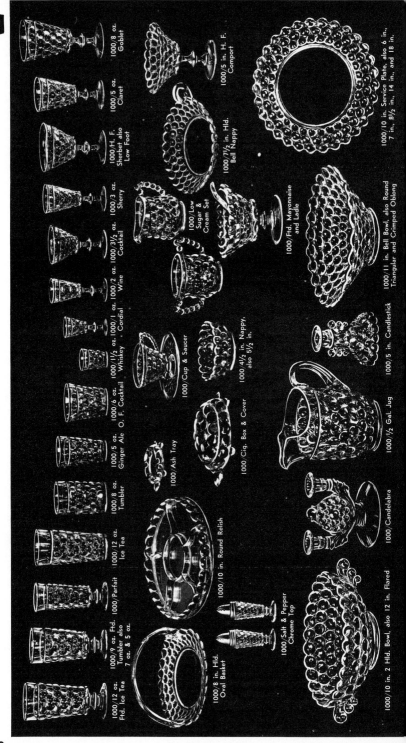

1000/8 oz. Goblet

1000/8 in. Hld. Oval Basket

1000/10 in. Round Relish

1000/Ash Tray

1000/Cup & Saucer

1000/Low Sugar & Cream Set

1000/7½ in. Hld. Bell Nappy

1000/5 in. H. F. Comport

1000/Salt & Pepper Chrome Top

1000/Cig. Box & Cover

1000/4½ in. Nappy, also 5½ in.

1000/Ftd. Mayonnaise and Ladle

1000/10 in. 2 Hld. Bowl, also 12 in. Flared

1000/Candelabra

1000/½ Gal. Jug

1000/5 in. Candlestick

1000/11 in. Bell Bowl, also Round Triangular and Crimped Oblong

1000/10 in. Service Plate, also 6 in., 7 in., 8½ in., 14 in., and 18 in.

"XYZ"

The entries in this chapter consolidate the remainder of those companies making glass for the Depression Era. Many of these were but small contributors; about others, we have but small knowledge. This chapter, then, as you might well could guess, is far from 'complete'.

TULIP BY DELL page 381

Cup	3.50-- 5.00
Saucer	1.50-- 2.00
Plate, 6"	2.00-- 3.00
Plate, 7¼"	3.00-- 5.00
Plate, 9"	6.00-- 9.00
Cream	5.00-- 7.00
Sugar	5.00-- 7.00
Wine Decanter	20.00--25.00
Tumbler, whiskey	8.00--10.00
Nappy, 6"	4.00-- 6.00
Console, oblong, 13¼" x 2½" deep, 6" wide	12.00--16.00
Vase or Bowl, 4¾" wide 2½" deep	6.00-- 8.00
Fruit Cup, 3¾" x 1¾"	3.00-- 4.00
Candleholders, pr. (same as fruit cup)	8.00--12.00
Candleholders, pr. (reg.)	10.00--14.00

See in Color Section

OWENS-ILLINOIS GLASS CO.

Hope the trademark in the book has helped you identify all these dark green shakers and other kitchen items that this company made.

OWENS Shakers, pr.	10.00--12.00
Water Bottle, 2 qt.	15.00--18.00
7-UP Bottle (old style green bottle with OWENS ILLINOIS on bottom.)	10.00--15.00

"RUFF N' READY" RANGE SET

Coffee, Sugar, Flour or Cereal, ea.	14.00--18.00
Tea or Rice, ea.	15.00--20.00
Salt, Pepper, or Flour Shaker, ea.	6.00-- 8.00

STEUBEN GLASS WORKS page 382

Vases	35.00-150.00

HOUZE GLASS COMPANY

Lamp	25.00--35.00

MISSISSIPPI GLASS COMPANY "STRIPPLE"

Tray, sq.	8.00--12.00
Bowl, console	10.00--14.00
Nappy	5.00-- 8.00

NORTHWOOD COMPANY

Candlestick, pr.	30.00--50.00
Bowl, console	25.00--40.00

TULIP BY DELL *fruit cup, whiskey, oblong console and vase or bowl*

BISON DECORATING page 384

Candlestick, pr.	10.00--12.00
Bowl, console, rolled edge	8.00--12.00
Sandwich Tray, center handle	9.00--12.00
Candy Jar, low ftd.	12.00--16.00
Candy Jar, high ftd.	15.00--18.00
Cheese and Cracker	10.00--14.00
Candy Jar	12.00--15.00
Salver, cake	9.00--12.00
Mayonnaise Set w/ Ladle	12.00--16.00
Comport, low ftd.	9.00--12.00
Sugar and Cream	10.00--14.00
Bowl	9.00--12.00

IDEAL DOLPHIN LAMP

Lamp	30.00--40.00

NATIONAL SILVER DEPOSIT WARE CO., INC.

Plate, luncheon	7.00-- 9.00
Sandwich Tray	14.00--18.00
Cream and Sugar	15.00--20.00
Cup	5.00-- 7.00
Saucer	3.00-- 4.00

"ESSEN" Liquor Set page 385

Decanter and Tumblers	40.00--60.00

PREMIER WATER SET

Jug and Tumblers	50.00--60.00

MARY RYAN ORGANIZATION

Pebbled Elephants	
small	30.00--40.00
medium	30.00--40.00
large	30.00--40.00
Myran Turtle	25.00--35.00

FLORADORA

Tumbler	5.00-- 7.00
Sherbet	3.50-- 4.50
Tumbler, ftd., 3¾", 2½ oz.	5.00-- 7.00
Tumbler, ftd., 5½"	6.00-- 8.00
Finger Bowl and Plate	5.00-- 8.00

"SWEDA" Water Set

Jug and Tumblers	45.00--55.00

CANTON GLASS CO. page 386

Goblets	4.00-- 6.00
Beer Mugs, hdld.	4.00-- 6.00
Whiskey	3.00-- 4.00
Tumbler	3.00-- 4.00

UTILITY GLASS WORKS, INC. "CAMBODIA"

Goblet	8.00--10.00
Wine	8.00--10.00
Sherbet, low ftd.	4.00-- 5.00
Nappy	3.00-- 4.00
Saucer	1.00-- 2.00
Tumbler	4.00-- 5.00

ZITRONENPRESSER

Reamers	10.00--20.00

SPICER STUDIOS page 387

Honey Jar	14.00--20.00
Sugar and Cream	10.00--15.00
Vase (2 styles)	12.00--16.00
Cigarette Holder (2 styles)	25.00--30.00
Tray	6.00-- 8.00

POTOMAC GLASS CO.

Candlestick, pr.	9.00--12.00

McDONALD GLASS WORKS, Inc.

Goblets (3 styles)	8.00--12.00

MEASURING CUP *see photo*

Plain or lipped	20.00--25.00

FUTURA

See next page

MANNY REAMERS

No. 1, No. 2	10.00--15.00

SAF-KLIP BATHROOM FIXTURES

Toothpaste and Tooth Brush Holder	20.00--30.00
Soap Dish	15.00--20.00
Tumbler Holder	15.00--20.00
Tumbler	3.00-- 4.00

BIRD BATH AND SEED CUPS

Matthews Patent Perch Bird Bath	5.00-- 7.00
No. 2307 Bird Bath	2.00-- 4.00
Perfection Bird Seed Cup	2.00-- 4.00
No. 2307 Bird Bath	4.00-- 6.00
No. 2310 Bird Seed Cup	2.00-- 4.00

FISH GLOBES

No. 20154, 20128, 20148, 20127	10.00--20.00

THE SANITARY WAY

TWO STYLES OF **Kanton Kitchen Kups**

No. 1150—Graduated Cooking Cup, Plain.
Made with finished or unfinished edge.
Packed 18 dozen in barrel.

No. 1150—Graduated Cooking Cup, Lipped.
Made with finished edge only.
Packed 18 dozen in barrel.

c. 1930 brochure

FUTURA

Trade Mark Registered

Article	Size	Dozen Per Bbl.	Approx. Wt. Per Bbl.
Plate	8 in.	12	140
Saucer	6 in.	40	170
Sugar	—	25	150
Cream	—	25	150
Cup	6 oz.	30	150
No. 2 Tumbler	9 oz.	18	155
No. 1 Sherbet 5 oz. (Short)	5 oz.	30	150
No. 2 Sherbet 6 oz. (Tall)	6 oz.	18	140
Ice Tea	12 oz.	12	140
Footed Soda	10 oz.	12	110
Footed Soda	12 oz.	10	120
836¾ Goblet	10 oz.	6 doz. per cart.	50
Footed Parfait	4½ oz.	25	140
Coca Cola	6 oz.	30	160
No. 1 Wine	3 oz.	25	140
No. 2 Cocktail	3 oz.	25	140

CANTON GLASS CO. - Marion, Indiana

c. 1954 Canton Cata

CANTON GLASS CO.
MARION, INDIANA

No. 1 Manny

Here are the two best Lemon Juice Extractors on the market.

No. 2 Manny

Speedy Simple Sanitary

CANTON GLASS CO.
MARION, INDIANA

No. 1—PATENT MANNY Lemon Juice Extractor

Packed in ⅛ doz. pasteboard boxes, 2 gross to the barrel.

This is a light, handy article ingeniously constructed so as to let the juice pass readily through apertures at the base of the cone, while the extractor rests on the top of the tumbler. No pulp or seeds can drop through. The base is flanged so as to rest firmly on any ordinary drinking glass.

We will be pleased to quote you our best prices on application.

CANTON GLASS CO.

No. 2—PATENT MANNY Lemon Juice Extractor

Packed in ½ doz. pasteboard boxes 1 gross to the crate.

This extractor represents the highes type of lemon juice reamers yet devised The corrugated glass cone squeezes ou every drop of the juice in the fruit an the close set teeth surrounding the bas of the cone collect all the pulp and seeds The pure juice flows into the saucer o the extractor and can then be poure into any kind of receptacle. The Mann No. 2 is the most substantial glass ex tractor made.

Kindly state the quantity desired.

CANTON GLASS CO

c. 1930 brochure

MADE of the finest opaque glass in modern designs, SAF-KLIP Bathroom Fixtures lead the field. Supplied in an assortment of colors to harmonize with bathroom color scheme - Alice Blue, Nile Green, Black, Opal. SAFE-KLIP sets are sturdy and sanitary and excel because the patented attachment holds them firmly to the wall.

● Priced to retail for 15c each, including metal attachment. ●

Combination Tooth Paste and Tooth Brush Holder.

This Name

SAF-KLIP

on your bathroom fixtures means

SATISFACTION

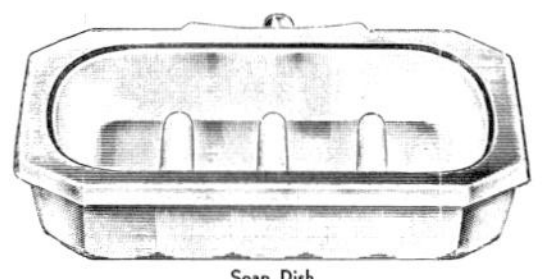

Soap Dish

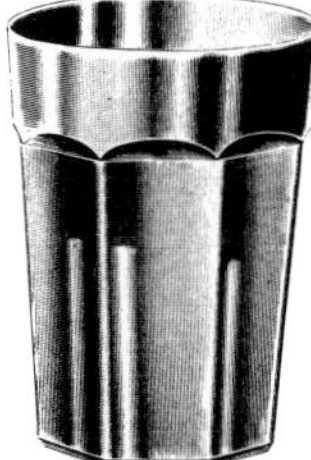

Bath Room Tumbler.

Tumbler Holder

The Patented Attachment

This ingenious device consists of a rust-proof KLIP which is screwed to the wall. The Bathroom Fixtures have a moulded slot at the back which slips over the flange of the KLIP and a spring at the top presses against the fixture keeping it firmly in place. Accidental blows will not dislodge the fixture, yet by pressing back the spring the fixture can be removed easily for cleansing.

The Saf-Klip Attachment

Patents protect SAF-KLIP. This valuable feature cannot be obtained on any other type of fixture.

● ● ● ●

Manufactured by

CANTON GLASS CO.

MARION, INDIANA

MATTHEWS PATENT PERCH BIRD BATH

Size of same is 5¼" long, 3 13/16", 1¾" high.

Made in Following Colors, Glass—Opal, Jade Green, "Baby" Blue.

Always packed 3 dozen in cell corrugated cartons. Average gross weight is 25 lbs. per carton

No. 2308 BIRD BATH

Size is 5¼" long, 3 13/16" wide, 1⅝" high

Made in Following Colors, Glass—Opal, Crystal, Black, Jade Green and "Baby" Blue.

Always packed 3 dozen in cell corrugated carton. Average gross weight per carton is 22 lbs.

PERFECTION BIRD SEED CUP

Size is 3" long, 2½" wide, 1½" high

Made in Following Colors, Glass—Crystal, Opal, Black, Jade Green and "Baby" Blue.

Packed 6 dozen bulk in cell corrugated carton. Average gross weight above is 19½ lbs. Also may be packed in 1 dozen pasteboard carton and 6 dozen to master corrugated carton. Average gross weight of same, 21 lbs.

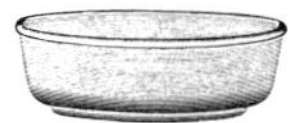

No. 2307 BIRD BATH

Size is 4¾" long, 3½" wide, 1 7/16" high

Made in Following Colors, Glass—Opal, Crystal, Black, Jade Green, "Baby" Blue.

Always packed 3 dozen in cell corrugated carton. Average gross weight, per carton is 17½ lbs.

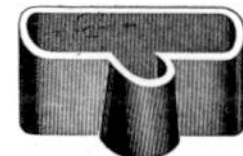

No. 2310 BIRD SEED CUP

Size 3 1/16" long, 1 3/16" wide, 1 5/16" high.

Always made in Opal or Crystal Glass.

Packed 6 dozen in cell corrugated carton. Average gross weight is 17 lbs.

No. 20154

No. 20128

No. 20148

No. 20127

c. 1934 company brochure

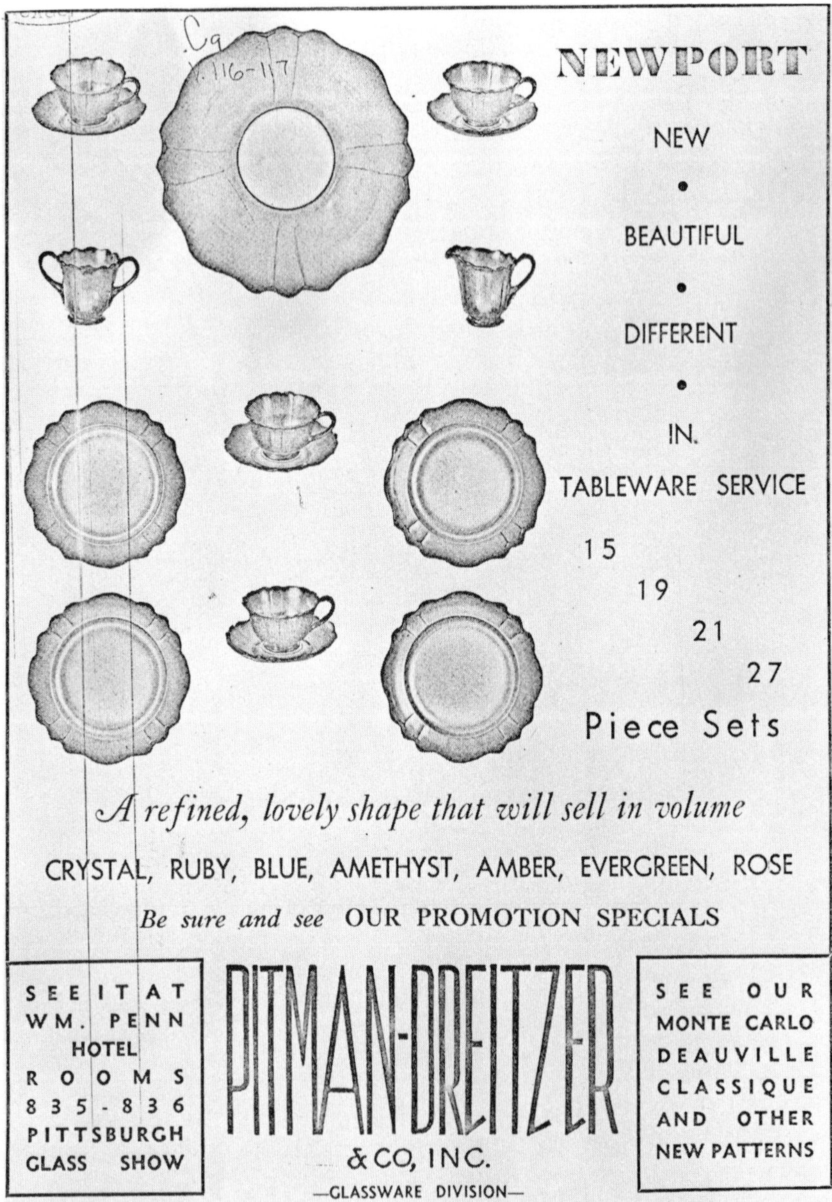

1935 ad

NEWPORT

Cup	4.00-- 6.00
Saucer	2.00-- 3.00
Sandwich Plate	10.00--14.00
Cream	7.00-- 9.00
Sugar	7.00-- 9.00
Plate, luncheon	6.00-- 8.00

The UFO's

This chapter, formerly known as "The Unknowns" in Book 2, contains lines and pieces found in Depression colors but which had not, at the time of Book 2, been identified as to manufacturer.

By this time, however, we've traced or by chance discovered many of the missing makers. One heretofore Unknown, the well-known "FRANCES" pattern, has after years of hovering finally landed on home base: Central Glass Company. You'll find it in that chapter.

"ZIPPER RIB" has moved in with Indiana, and the "PEANUT" vase has been restored to Hocking and its set-mate, the "RACHAEL" bowl.

We now know that U.S. Glass made our STRAWBERRY, CHERRY-BERRY, our UNKNOWN SWIRL, and our "AUNT POLLY."

Fenton made "SWAN LAKE", the "MAISY DAISY" mug, and the "ABBY" nappy. Hocking made the "LEXINGTON" console set and the SWIRL jug. Jeannette made the "COCKLESHELL" berry set. Hazel Atlas made "DRIP DROP" and called it CAPRI.

I found the "DOILY" plate advertisement by Indiana and Mr. Harshman said Indiana made the STRAWHOLDER, the "ROSANNA" and "STARWHIRL" plate, the "ALTON" set, the "ANITA" chicken waterer and the HUMPTY DUMPTY mug.

Macbeth made the "SHIRLEY" water set. Imperial made the "SPINNER" powder jar. "LAKE SPRINGFIELD" is on a U.S. Glass blank. Canton made the toothbrush holder and the "JOHANNA" bird feeder.

"S & R" stands for Sears and Roebuck on the ovenware pieces; don't miss the reprints of these plus the Flamex Top-of-Stove cookware at the end of this chapter.

ASHTRAYS	page 388
"Caravan", 4½"	6.00-- 9.00
"Moondance", 4½"	6.00-- 9.00
"Into The Mistic", 4½"	6.00-- 9.00

"DOMINO"	
Smoker Set	20.00--25.00

"ST. DOMINICS"

Candle Tumbler	6.00-- 9.00

CYPRUS OWL

Pitcher and Tumbler	35.00--45.00

ASTRAL OWL

Bookend	20.00--25.00

"BELFAST TURTLE"

Turtle	35.00--40.00

UNKNOWN SWIRL page 389

Made by U.S. Glass

Butter Dish and Cover	30.00--35.00
Sugar and Cover	12.00--15.00
Cream	8.00--10.00
Tumbler, 4½"	4.00-- 6.00
Dish and Cover, 5¾" x 2"	12.00--16.00

(It's not SWIRL but note the same style handles.)

Plate, 8"	3.00-- 4.00

"FLORAL AND DIAMOND BAND"

No. 155 Book 1. Made by U.S. Glass.

Butter Dish and Cover	75.00-100.00
Sugar and Cover, large	25.00--35.00
Cream, large	9.00--12.00
Sugar, small	8.00--10.00
Cream, small	8.00--10.00
Tumbler, 4", 5"	10.00--14.00
Jug, 8"	60.00--80.00
Plate, 8¼"	4.00-- 6.00
Bowl, nappy, 8"	8.00--12.00
Comport, 4"	12.00--14.00
Bowl, 4½"	5.00-- 8.00
Bowl, nappy, hdld., 5-5/8"	8.00--10.00
Sherbet	6.00-- 8.00

"AUNT POLLY"

Made by U.S. Glass

Blue is most prevalent and highest-priced.

We have something further on "AUNT POLLY", a most popular pattern in blue. It dates back to 1927, when it was advertised in green tableware pieces only in a Sears catalog. This makes it a very early D.G. pattern. The spoon holder shown is a flat boat shaped bowl (looks like a long relish) with ends turned up and in, like a canoe.

Shown here are the real "AUNT POLLY" shakers. Smaller, thinner shakers are being found in blue and thought to belong to this pattern, they may be Cambridge or Fostoria.

"AUNT POLLY" shakers

20-Piece Green Colored Glassware Set

Clear transparent green colored fire polished press glass in colonial and diamond design. The set consists of pieces that are useful every day in the year.

1 Seven-Piece Water Set.
1 Covered Butter Dish, (2 pieces)
1 Cream Pitcher
1 Seven-Pc. Berry Set
1 Covered Sugar Bowl (2 pieces)
1 Spoon Holder

Weight, packed, 25 pounds.
35K6817—Per set.................... $2.50

1927 Sears catalog reprint

"AUNT POLLY"

Also shown is a reprint from a 1927 Sears, Roebuck catalog. It shows the "AUNT POLLY" spoon holder, which no one to my knowledge, has found. Who will be the lucky one?

"AUNT POLLY"

Made by U.S. Glass

Butter Dish and Cover	125.00-150.00
Sherbet Plate	4.00-- 6.00
Sherbet	8.00--10.00
Comport, hdld., (ftd. Jelly), 5¼"	15.00--20.00
Tumbler, 8 oz., 3¾"	12.00--15.00
Tumbler, ftd., 6½"	20.00--25.00
Pickle Dish, 7¼"	14.00--18.00
Sugar	12.00--15.00
Sugar and Cover	50.00--60.00
Cream	20.00--25.00
Nappy, 4-3/8"	7.00--10.00
Nappy, 7-7/8"	15.00--25.00
Jug, 8"	130.00-140.00
Plate, 8"	10.00--12.00
Salt and Pepper, pr.	150.00-175.00
Bowl, oval veg., 8-3/8"	30.00--40.00
Spoon Holder	30.00--40.00

"STRAWBERRY" and "CHERRYBERRY" page 390

Made by U.S. Glass

Plate, salad, 7½"	12.00--15.00
Plate, sherbet, 6"	6.00-- 8.00
*Bowl, berry, 4"	11.00--14.00
Bowl, salad, deep, 6½"	10.00--14.00
*Bowl, berry, deep, 7½"	12.00--16.00
Sugar	14.00--17.00
Cream	14.00--17.00
Sugar and Cover, large, 5½"	25.00--30.00
Cream, large, 4-5/8"	14.00--18.00
Sherbet	8.00--10.00
*Pitcher, jug, 7¾"	125.00-150.00
Tumbler, 9 oz., 3½"	15.00--20.00
Olive Dish, 1 hdld., 5"	9.00--12.00
Pickle Dish, oval, 8¼"	9.00--12.00
Butter Dish and Cover	100.00-125.00
Comport, 5¾"	12.00--15.00

**Iridescent*

"FRUITS"

FRUITS is also in Book 1, remember. As for who made it, evidence (and strong intuition!) still leads to Hazel Atlas, but we have no proof.

Plate	6.00-- 8.00
Cup & Saucer	6.00-- 8.00
Bowl, nappy, 8"	35.00--40.00
Bowl, nappy, 4"	10.00--12.00
Tumbler, cherries only, 4¼"	18.00--20.00
Pitcher, jug, cherries only, 7"	85.00--95.00
Tumbler, grapes and leaves, 4¼"	7.00-- 9.00
Tumbler, grapes and leaves, 4"	7.00-- 9.00

"ROXANNA"

Plate, sherbet, 6"	2.00-- 2.50
Bowl, nappy, 5"	3.00-- 4.00
Bowl, opaque white, 4¼" x 2½"	3.00-- 4.00
Bowl, nappy, 6"	5.00-- 7.00
Saucer, 5½"	1.50-- 2.50
Sherbet	3.00-- 4.00
Tumbler, 4", 9 oz.	5.00-- 7.00

S AND R OVENWARE page 391

See reprint. Made for Sears as early as 1943.

A. Covered Roaster	25.00--35.00
B. Covered Loaf Pan	15.00--20.00
C. Oblong Utility Roaster	12.00--15.00
D. Covered Casseroles, 1 qt., 1½ qt., 2 qt., 3 qt. ea.	12.00--20.00
E. Round Baking Dishes, 7", 8", 9", 10", ea.	7.00--12.00
F. Open Casseroles, 1 qt., 1½ qt. 2 qt., 3 qt., ea.	7.00--10.00
G. Pie Plates, 9½", 10½"	8.00--10.00
H. Covered Bean Pot	10.00--14.00
J. Baking Sets: 4", 5", 6", ea.	8.00--12.00
K. Custard Cups	2.00-- 3.00
L. Ind. Casseroles, 5"	7.00-- 9.00
M. Glass Table Tile, 5¼"x5¼"	4.00-- 6.00
Open Roaster (not illus.) 13¾"x8½"x4"	15.00--20.00

FLAMEX COOKWARE

See next page

A. Percolater, 6 cup	15.00--20.00
B. Drip Coffee Maker, 8 cup	15.00--20.00
C. Teapot, 1¾ qt.	14.00--18.00
D. Whistling Teakettle, 1½ qt.	14.00--18.00
E. Double Boilers, 1-5/8 qt., 2-1/3 qt.	16.00--20.00
F. Covered Frying Pan, 9"	12.00--16.00
H. Open Frying Pan, 7"	8.00--10.00
J. Covered Saucepans, 1-5/8 qt., 2-1/3 qt.	10.00--14.00

MIXING BOWL, green, 7½" (Inscribed "DIAMOND CRYSTAL SHAKER SALT")	15.00--20.00
MEASURE, 2-CUP (Inscribed T & S HANDMAID)	20.00--25.00

STRAWHOLDER, green, 9½"	100.00-125.00
MISSION GRAPEFRUIT DISPENSER, 12½"	100.00-125.00
NESBITTS DISPENSER, 9"	110.00-135.00

"SIMPLETON" PLATE, 6"	2.00-- 3.00

Cook, Serve and Store Foods in Transparent Flamex Glass Ovenware

S AND R OVENWARE Reprinted from 1947 Sears catalog

FLAMEX GLASS OVENWARE

Cook and serve appetizing meals in Flamex Glass Top-of-stove Cookware

Reprinted from 1947 Sears catalog

FLAMEX TOP-OF-STOVE COOKWARE

DUCHESS SHERBET, crystal, metal holder	4.00-- 5.00
"SUNDANCE" TUMBLER, 4"	3.00-- 5.00

"DRIP DROP" is now officially CAPRI, made by Hazelware in the 60s.

Thanks to all of you who wrote me about finding pieces with original labels.

"DRIP DROP" (CAPRI) Cup and Saucer	3.00-- 4.00

KITCHEN GADGETS

Measuring Cup, 4-Cup, 7"	20.00--25.00
Ice Crusher w/Bowl	15.00--20.00
Metal Juicer w/Bowl	18.00--24.00
D & B Beater Bowl, 5½"	20.00--25.00
VIDRIO Electric Beater, 4½"	15.00--20.00
"BLOCK FROSTED" Ice Bowl, 5½"	14.00--18.00

"TRICIA" page 392

Pink, light green

Plate, 6½"	2.00-- 4.00
Plate, 8"	4.00-- 6.00
Sherbet	4.00-- 6.00

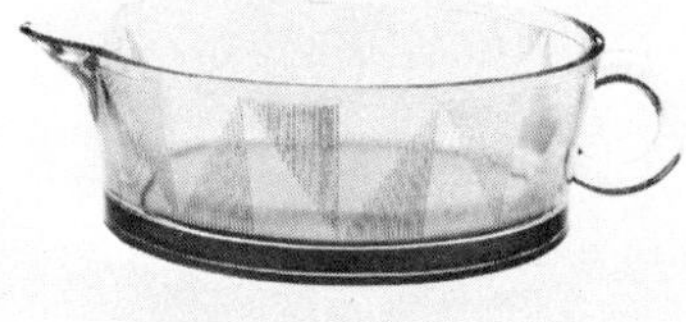

Sugar and Cover	8.00--10.00
Cream	6.00-- 8.00
Gravy Boat *(see photo)*	15.00--20.00

"HOBLIGHT" Light Fixture	12.00--15.00
"FAVE" Vase, 7"	8.00--12.00

"MY PET" Powder Jar and Cover	15.00--20.00
"ORNATE" Vase, 10¼"	25.00--30.00

"CHARADE"

Also made in topaz and green.

Plate, 8"	5.00-- 8.00
Cup and Saucer	6.00-- 8.00
Cream	7.00-- 9.00
Sugar	7.00-- 9.00
Server, sandwich, 10"	10.00--15.00

PLATES

"HUNT", 8"	4.00-- 5.00
"COLUMBUS", 8"	4.00-- 6.00
"DOILY", 8¼"	6.00-- 8.00

See in Indiana chapter

"ROSANNA", 8¾"	4.00-- 5.00
"STAR WHEEL", 8"	3.00-- 4.00
"STAR FLOWER", 9¾"	4.00-- 6.00
"CONSTELLATION", pink, green, 8"	3.00-- 4.00
"STAR WHIRL", 8-3/8"	3.00-- 5.00

"OLLIE MAY" page 393

Dresser Set	45.00--55.00
Candlestick, 6", pr.	9.00--12.00
Tray, 11½"	8.00--12.00
Ring Holder, 3-5/8"	6.00-- 9.00
Dish, 3-3/8"	4.00-- 5.00
Dish and Cover, 3-5/8"	8.00--10.00
Powder Dish and Cover, 4½"	8.00--10.00
"EBB" *(has been reported with an etching on it)* pr.	12.00--15.00
"FLO" w/o handle, pr.	12.00--15.00
"FLO" w/handle, pr.	15.00--20.00
"ZIPPER RIB" *(See in Indiana Chapter).*	
Cheese and Cracker	8.00--10.00

"ADAM'S RIB" ***console set, candy jar 8½"***

"ADAM'S RIB"

Amber, green, pink, blue. Thought to belong to Diamond Glass-Ware Co.

Tumbler, hdld., 5"	12.00--18.00
Cream and Sugar on tray 8½" x 6¾"	18.00--22.00
Plate, 8-1/8"	6.00-- 9.00
Plate, 7¼"	5.00-- 8.00
Cup and Saucer	7.00--10.00
Jug	22.00--28.00
Candy Jar and Cover, 8½"	25.00--30.00
Center Handle Server	16.00--20.00
Cheese and Cracker	20.00--25.00
Console Set *(See photo)*	50.00--65.00
"SHORT RIB" Candy Dish and Cover, 3 part	15.00--18.00
"STANDING RIB", Cocktail Shaker, 11"	15.00--20.00
Cocktail Glass, metal base, 4½"	3.50-- 5.00
"PRIME RIB" Bowl, metal base, 9"	10.00--15.00
"KRACKLE" Keg Set: Dispenser, 7¾" and 6 Tumblers	35.00--45.00
"SHIRLEY" Water Set: Jug, 8½"	20.00--25.00
Tumbler, 4¾", 8 oz.	4.00-- 6.00
Tumbler, 4½", 6 oz.	4.00-- 6.00
Tumbler, 3½", 4 oz.	4.00-- 6.00
"AUSTIN" Water Jug, 8"	12.00--16.00
Tumbler	4.00-- 6.00

"FRANCES"

See in Central Chapter. "FRANCES" has now found a home.

"COPE" Cake Stand, 6-5/8"	14.00--18.00
"MITCHELL" Vase, 9"	7.00-- 9.00
"LITTLE TY" Jug, 5½"	10.00--14.00

MISCELLANEOUS page 394, 395

"SNAPPY" server, 10"	9.00--12.00
"DROOPY ROSE" Tumbler 6-1/8"	7.00-- 9.00
"MAISY DAISY" Mug, 3½"	12.00--15.00
HUMPTY DUMPTY-TOM TOM Mug, 3½", gr.	20.00--30.00
"KIPLING" Dish, 6"	35.00--40.00'
"ADELE" Nappy, 8¼"	8.00--10.00
"AGGY" Nappy, 9"	6.00-- 8.00
"ADDY" Comport, 5¾"	6.00-- 9.00
"ABBY" Nappy, 7"	6.00-- 8.00
(Fenton)	
VARIOUS SWIRLS	
Platter, 10"	6.00-- 9.00
Jug, 8", (made by Hocking Glass Co.)	15.00--20.00
Butter Dish	20.00--25.00
Cake Plate, 10"	8.00--10.00
"SHARI" Dresser Set: 7"x 4½", *(Indiana — pink, canary)*	25.00--35.00
"FANNY BRICE" Rose Bowl, 7"	6.00-- 9.00
"FROLIC" Dresser Tray, *(Also black)* 10"x 5¾" *(Made by U.S.G.)*	10.00--12.00
"FERN" Coaster, 4-5/8" *(also found in green)*	3.00-- 5.00
"FROND" Ashtray, 4-5/8"	4.00-- 6.00
"MAGGIE BOWL", 5"	25.00--35.00
"NANCY DREW" Nappy, 5¾"	3.00-- 4.00
"STAR" Coaster, 4-3/8"	4.00-- 5.00
ODD RED PIECES	
Cup and Saucer, rnd.	6.00-- 8.00
Plate, 8¼"	4.00-- 6.00
Plate, 6"	2.00-- 3.00
Plate, 10¾"	8.00--10.00
Cream, 2¼"	5.00-- 7.00
Sugar, 2¼"	5.00-- 7.00
Tumbler, 4½", 9 oz.	6.00-- 8.00

"MILDRED"

Pink, red, green, cobalt and dark green

Cream and Sugar, 2½"	12.00--16.00
Plate, 8½"	4.00-- 6.00
Plate, 14"	9.00--14.00
Cup and Saucer	7.00-- 9.00

"COCKLESHELL" Berry Set ***(Made by Jeannette Glass Co.)***

Bowl, 8"	6.00-- 8.00
Nappy, 4½"	2.00-- 3.00

"MARYMONT" Berry Set

Pink, green

Nappy, 4½"	2.00-- 4.00
Nappy, ruffled, 4¼"	2.00-- 4.00
Nappy, 7½"	8.00--10.00

"CONCORD" Berry Set, ***Made by U.S.G.***

Green

Nappy, 7¼"	6.00-- 8.00
Nappy, 4½"	2.00-- 3.00

"LEXINGTON" Console Set

This one was made by Hocking!

Bowl, 11"	9.00--12.00
Candlestick, 6", pr.	10.00--13.00
"ANITA" Chicken Waterer, 5½"	9.00--12.00
"JOHANNA" Bird Feeder, 3¼"	4.00-- 6.00
"PARKER" Shaving Mug, 3½"	8.00--10.00
TOOTHBRUSH Holder, 6½"	8.00--10.00
"WOODPECKER" Vases, 8" *(Also in black & pink)*	10.00--15.00
"SCOTTIE" Blotter, 3½"	12.00--16.00
SPONGE Holder, 3-1/8" x 1-5/8"	3.00-- 5.00
CRACKLE BALL, 3¼"	3.00-- 5.00
"LIL FISH", 2-5/8" (Fenton)	15.00--20.00
DRAWER PULL, 4-1/8"	3.00-- 5.00
"CUTIE" Curtain tie, 6"	4.00-- 6.00
CURTAIN RING, 4", gr.	3.00-- 5.00

"DOWNEY" Curtain Holder, 4"	3.00-- 5.00
GLASS KNIVES	12.00--18.00

All those glass knives you are finding out there in original boxes by DUR-X, VITEX, and etc., were probably made by one of our known companies. Back in 1969, Jeannette Glass Co. gave me a crystal one, like the green one in the middle of the Book 2 photo, with a label on it: "Made for Popeil Bro., Chicago March 1954."

MISCELLANEOUS page 396, 397

"SWAN LAKE" Console Set, *(see Fenton reprint)*	80.00--100.00
"THRUSH" Tumbler, 6¼"	6.00-- 9.00
Comport, high, 3¼"	6.00-- 8.00
BOTTLE SET, 6"x8", tray 5½" high	25.00--30.00
"EVA" Jar and Cover, high, oval, 4"	12.00--16.00
"TOPSY" Jar and Cover, 3½" high	10.00--14.00
TROUGH, 2½"x5"	10.00--14.00
"HOLDEN" Set	12.00--16.00

POWDER JAR AND COVERS

Most come in colors other than those in Book II

"ANNETTE", 4¾"	20.00--25.00
"LOVER", 6"	20.00--25.00
"MINSTREL", 5¼"	20.00--25.00
"FLAPPERS", 4-1/8"	18.00--22.00
"MASCOT", 4½"	12.00--16.00
"HOBNAIL", 4-1/8"	10.00--12.00
"BOWSER", 5"x3¾"x3"	12.00--18.00
"BARK", 3¼"	10.00--15.00
"SPINNER," 2½"	11.00--14.00
"DIAMOND PANEL" *(No. 156 Book 1)* 4"	14.00--18.00
"FEATHER" Tumbler, 3¾", 4½"	6.00-- 8.00
"CHEERI-O" Cocktail Shaker, 10"	30.00--35.00
"JOSEPH" Cocktail Glass, 3½"	3.00-- 4.00
"RING OF RINGS" Decanter, 10"	12.00--15.00
Tumbler, 3"	3.00-- 4.00
"MICKEY" Cream and Sugar, 2½"	10.00--15.00
"CLEOPATRA" Sherbet	4.00-- 6.00
"ALTON" Set, 8½" sq. Tray, 4" sq. inserts	14.00--18.00
"VALENTI" Relish, 13"x8"	15.00--20.00
"KRAFT" Cheese Dish, 5"	12.00--15.00
"SNOWFLAKE" Cake Plate, 12¾"	15.00--20.00
"LAKE SPRINGFIELD" (U.S.G.) Console	12.00--16.00
"NIP" Nappy, 3 ftd., 6-3/8"	4.00-- 6.00
"AU GOURMET" Server, 10¼"	14.00--18.00
"BIRCH TREE" Console, 12"	15.00--20.00

OPAQUE GREEN MISCELLANEOUS

"JENNIFER" Centerpiece 8½" x 5¾" x 4½"	16.00--20.00
"CLINK" Shaker, 5½"	5.00-- 8.00
Tumbler, plain, 5½"	5.00-- 8.00
"HOWARD" Cruet, 6¾"	22.00--25.00
"MARION" Bird Bath Dish, 2-5/8"	8.00--12.00
"RICHIE" Dolphin Bowl, 6"	12.00--15.00
"CLINTON" Vase, 7"	12.00--15.00
HALL's Water Dispenser 10½" x 5" x 5"	65.00-- 85.00

BLACK GLASS MISCELLANEOUS

"BRUNO" Vase, 5", 7" *Made by L.E. Smith, (also green)*	10.00--14.00

"MOWGLI" LINE

It's easy to mistake this pattern for MODERNTONE, but it is not. Elaine Storch, Rockford MN, sent me a photo and measurements of her pieces, which was a big help. The base of the sugar and cream have concentric circles. I was told in Paden City they were Paden City, but that does not make it proof!

Plate, sherbet, 6"	2.00-- 3.00
Plate, 8½"	4.00-- 6.00
Plate, 10-5/8"	8.00--12.00
Bowl, berry, 4½"	3.50-- 4.50
Cup	4.00-- 5.00
Saucer	1.50-- 2.00
Cream	6.00-- 8.00
Sugar	6.00-- 8.00
Tumbler	6.00-- 8.00
Jug	15.00--20.00
"EBON" Soda, 5½"	6.00-- 8.00
"NADA" Cup and Saucer	5.00-- 7.00
"SIMON" Cream and Sugar, 2¾"	8.00-- 12.00
"EDAL" Manicure Set: Tray, 7" x 4½"	15.00--20.00
"SHERMAN" Candlestick, 3¾", pr.	12.00--16.00
"TRIAD" Candlestick, 2½", pr.	12.00--15.00
"SAMPSON" Candlestick, pr.	12.00--16.00

ADVERTISING ITEMS page 398

CLARKS TEABERRY GUM	
Tray, 3¼" high	25.00--35.00
LITTLE DEB Toys, 3"	3.00-- 4.00
MOBIL Ash Tray, 5"	15.00--20.00
MISSION Tumbler, 4"	4.00-- 6.00
GEORGE WASHINGTON	
Tumbler, 4½"	5.00-- 8.00
CENTENNIAL CELEBRATION	
Plate, 7½"	10.00--15.00
URBAN LIBERTY FLOUR	
Plates	
Hobnail, 8-3/8"	8.00--10.00
Swirl, 8"	8.00--10.00

ASHTRAYS

GENERAL TIRE, 3½"	5.00-- 8.00
GOODRICH SILVERTOWN	
TIRES, 4¾"	7.00--10.00
PENNSYLVANIA TIRES, 3½"	5.00-- 8.00
MACBETH EVANS	
GLASSBLOWER, 3¼"	10.00--15.00
ANCHOR HOCKING	
GLASS CORP., 4"	8.00--12.00
BAXTER CAREFUL	
LAUNDERERS, 3¼"	5.00-- 6.00

LAMPS

"CELESTIAL", 11"	40.00--50.00
(also in pink and canary)	
"SPOOL", 12½"	20.00--25.00
"OLD CAFE", 11½"	20.00--25.00
(also pink)	
"TARA GIRL", 12"	25.00--30.00
LAMP BASE, 8½"	8.00--10.00
"ZELDA", 7"	20.00--30.00

Inside to Janet Moore, Woodstock NY: Yes, "ZELDA" has nudes!

"DIAMOND", 9"	25.00--30.00
"FREDEE", 4½"	10.00--14.00
"SOUTHERN BELLE", 5"	
base, 4" shade	25.00--30.00
"BLACK BEAUTY", 7½"	25.00--30.00
"HOBNAIL, 6"	15.00--20.00
"FITZGERALD", 7½"	15.00--20.00
"SEA DOLPHIN", 7"	35.00--40.00
"BLACK ELEPHANT"	
3" base, 5" shade	25.00--30.00

In the following pages, several new "U.F.O.s" are introduced. The pattern write-ups will refer you to the correct photograph in each case.

"HUSTLE" Photo 1

pink

Tumbler, 14 oz., 6¾" 6.00-- 9.00

"VALENTINE" Lamps Photo 2

Set of boudoir lamps in pink. 2 table lamps and a headboard lamp (wire holder not in photo).

Boudoir Set: 3 pc. 65.00-- 75.00

"ROCK & ROLL" Lamp Photo 3

This is the crystal lamp collectors are reporting to be WATERFORD. It does have a Waterford design, but is heavier glass and has a ground bottom. Hocking does not claim it.

Lamp, dia., 4½" 10.00--15.00

"NEW YORK" Photo 4

The crystal butterdish w/metal cover thought to be MANHATTAN. I find no reference so far of this being made by Anchor Hocking.

Butterdish, 7"	
with chrome dome	12.00--17.00

"CHIPMUNK" Lamps Photo 4

Thin blown pink Waterford design lamps. Notice the little feet on these. I do not know who made them.

Lamp, dia. 3½", pr. 20.00-30.00

"JADE BRAID" Photo 5

Candlestick, 10", pr. 25.00-35.00

"BUSTLE" Photo 6

pink

Tumbler, 14 oz., 6¾" 6.00-- 9.00

"CHIPPERFIELD" Photo 7

Green

Dresser Set, 4 pc. 25.00--30.00

"JAY CEE" Photo 8

Jade with black base. Made by Fenton.

Plate	5.00-- 8.00
Plate, sandwich	8.00--12.00
Cup and Saucer	8.00--10.00
Cream and Sugar	18.00--24.00

Sherbet	6.00-- 8.00
Tumbler, ftd.	12.00--14.00

"HAZEL CRACKLE" Photo 9

Pink light fixture.

Light Fixture, 9", pr. 25.00--35.00

"HELEN" Photo 9

Green satin finish

Light fixture, 10½" 15.00--18.00

"NEW ORLEANS" Photo 9

Pink

Ice Bucket, 6" 12.00--15.00

"SACTO" Photo 9

Amber

Console Set, 3 pc. 15.00--20.00

"JO'S JUICER" Photo 10

Green bowl with a metal crank handle.

Reamer 30.00--35.00

"PINKY" POTTY Photo 10

Crystal, pink, green

Glass Chamber 30.00--50.00

"SAILBOAT" Photo 10

Cobalt. You will find these blotters in many colors and figures.

Blotter, 3½" 16.00--22.00

"COSMO" Photo 10

Green

Cosmetic Jar, 3" 6.00-- 9.00

WHITE KING Photo 10

Green

Soap dispenser, 1 pt. 30.00--35.00

CRYSTAL STROPPER Photo 10

Pink

Razor Sharpener, 2½" x 2½" 10.00--14.00

"SWINE SHOT" Photo 10

Pink

Tumbler, 2¾", 1 oz. 8.00--12.00

"SAN JOSE" Photo 11

green

Candle Console, 13" x 1" deep 15.00--20.00

"CHEVY" Photo 12

pink

Cheese Dish and Cover, 5¼" x 7½" 15.00--20.00

"SHIMMY" Photo 13

pink, green, crystal

Plate, 8¼" 5.00-- 6.00

"SHAKE" Photo 14

pink, green crystal

Plate, 8¼" 5.00-- 6.00

"GI GI" Photo 15

medium blue - bought in England

Dresser Set 50.00--60.00

WINDMILL Photo 16

canary

Decanter w/6 Tumblers, 14" high 60.00--80.00

"PRINCE" Photo 17

pink, green

Jug, ftd., 7½"	200.00-300.00
Tumbler, ftd., 4¾"	50.00--75.00

"WILL O' THE WISP" Photo 18

green

Fish Bowl, 7½"	20.00--25.00
Fish Bowl, 11½"	30.00--35.00

"DUMBO" & "CLONE" Photo 19

crystal

Elephant	30.00--35.00
Cup and Saucer	10.00--12.00

Photo 1
"HUSTLE" tumbler

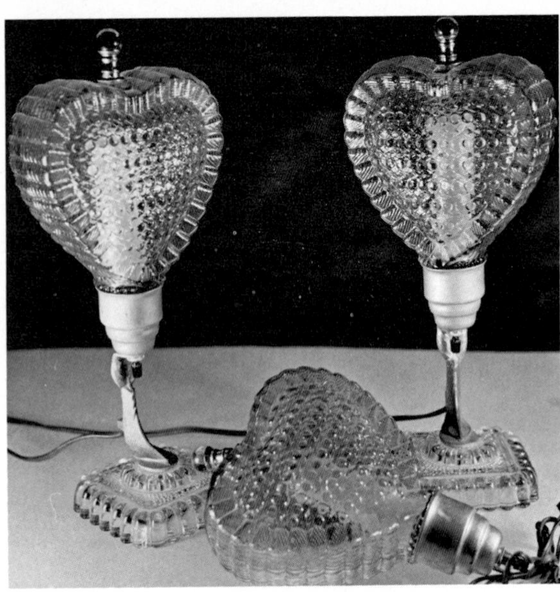

Photo 2 "VALENTINE" lamps

Photo 3 "ROCK AND ROLL" lamp

Photo 4
"NEW YORK" butterdish and "CHIPMUNK" lamps

Photo 5 "JADE BRAID" candlesticks

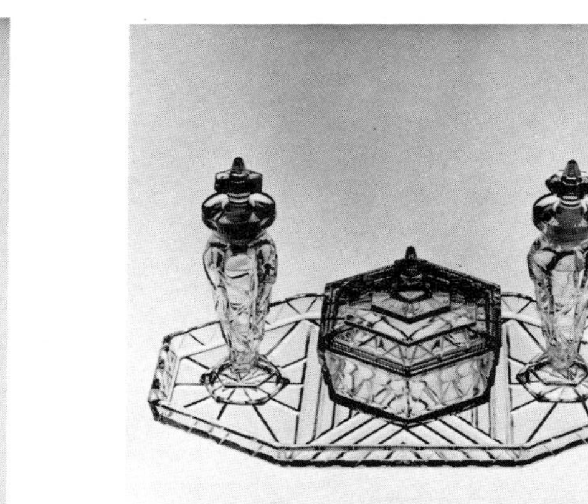

Photo 6
"BUSTLE" tumbler

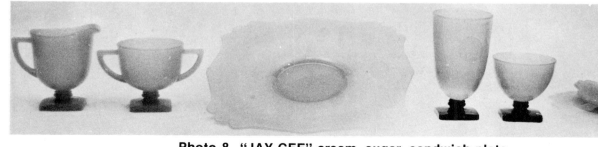

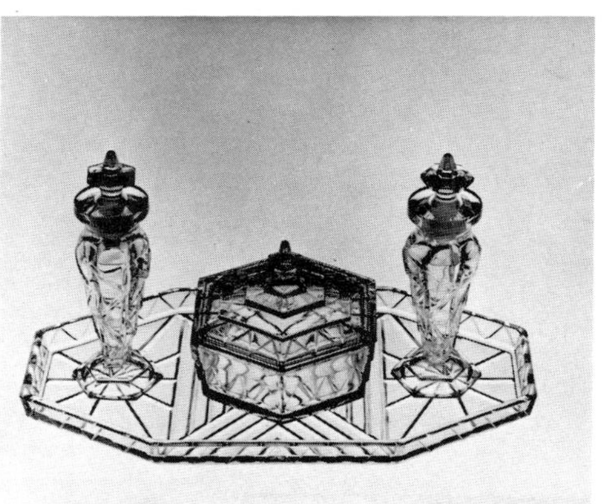

Photo 7 "CHIPPERFIELD"
dresser set

Photo 8 "JAY CEE" cream, sugar, sandwich plate, footed tumbler, sherbet, cup, saucer and plate

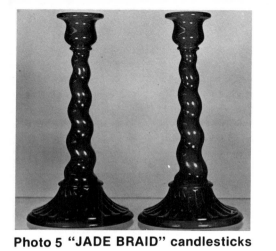

Photo 9 "HAZEL CRACKLE" light fixture, "HELEN" light fixture, "NEW ORLEANS" ice bucket and "SACTO" console set

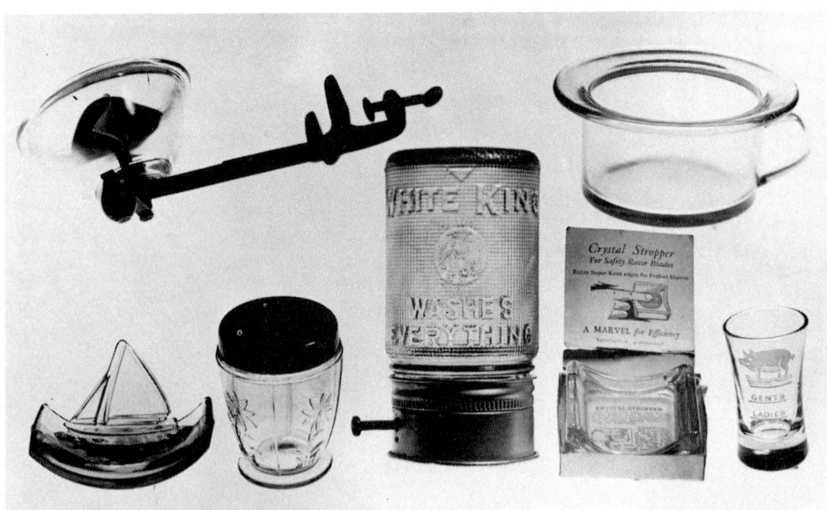

Photo 10 "JO'S JUICER", "PINKY" POTTY, "SAILBOAT" blotter, "COSMO" cosmetic jar, WHITE KING dispenser, CRYSTAL STROPPER razor sharpener and "SWINE SHOT" whiskey tumbler

Photo 11
"SAN JOSE" candle console

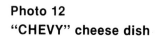

Photo 12
"CHEVY" cheese dish

Photo 13 "SHIMMY" plate

Photo 14 "SHAKE" plate

Photo 15 "GI GI" dresser set

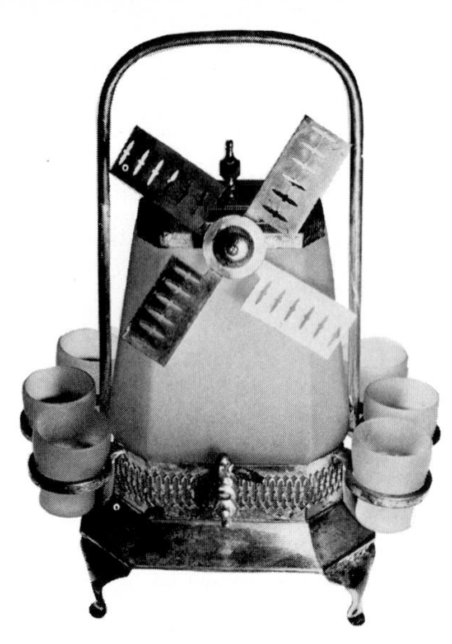

Photo 16 WINDMILL decanter

Photo 17
"PRINCE" jug and tumbler

Photo 18
"WILL O'THE WISP"
fish bowl

Photo by Thom Padick

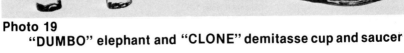

Photo 19
"DUMBO" elephant and "CLONE" demitasse cup and saucer

INDEX

INDEX

INDEX

INDEX

THE DECORATED TUMBLER 1930-1960

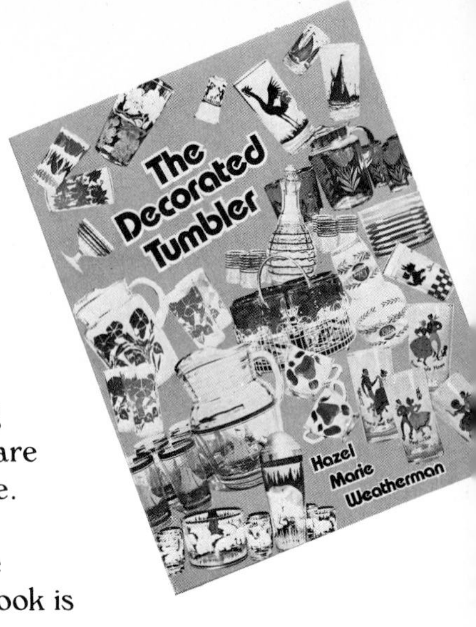

'The Tumbler Book' is Glassbooks' reply to, "What can we collect now that's new and fun?" Tumblers! Hand or machine decorated by the leading Depression era companies, they are America's newest glass collectible. Bright, beautiful, low-priced and plentiful too, they're a thrill to the young-in-heart. Our latest glassbook is 160 pages IN FULL COLOR softbound, $15.